The Millennials

AMERICANS BORN 1977 to 1994

5th EDITION

The
Millennials

AMERICANS
BORN 1977 to 1994

5th EDITION

The American
Generations Series

BY THE NEW STRATEGIST EDITORS

New Strategist Publications, Inc.
Ithaca, New York

New Strategist Publications, Inc.
P.O. Box 242, Ithaca, New York 14851
800/848-0842; 607/273-0913
www.newstrategist.com

ISBN 978-1-937737-02-3 (hardcover)
ISBN 978-1-937737-03-0 (paper)

Printed in the United States of America

Table of Contents

Chapter 4. Housing

Chapter 5. Income

Chapter 6. Labor Force

Chapter 7. Living Arrangements

Chapter 8. Population

Chapter 9. Spending

Chapter 10. Time Use

Chapter 11. Wealth

Part Two: The iGeneration

Chapter 12. Education

Chapter 13. Health

Chapter 14. Housing

Chapter 15. Income

Chapter 16. Labor Force

Chapter 17. Living Arrangements

Chapter 18. Population

Chapter 19. Spending

Chapter 20. Time Use

Tables

Part One: The Millennials

Chapter 1. Attitudes

Chapter 2. Education

Chapter 19. Spending

Chapter 20. Time Use

Illustrations

Part Two: The iGeneration

Introduction

The Millennial generation—America's young adults—was once the new kid in town. No longer. Although the youngest Millennials are not yet 20, the oldest are in their thirties. This fifth edition of *The Millennials: Americans Born 1977 to 1994* provides a demographic and socioeconomic profile of the generation that is, as of 2012, comprised entirely of adults.

Millennials ranged in age from 18 to 35 in 2012. They numbered 76 million and accounted for 24.7 percent of the total population—almost equal to the Baby Boom's 25.0 percent share. A special section in this book profiles the generation that follows Millennials—born in 1995 or later (the oldest turned 17 in 2012) and now comprising the nation's children. Today, these youngest Americans are a generation looking for a name. Although we call them the iGeneration in this book, other names are being bandied about such as the Plurals, based on research and survey findings by Magid Generational Strategies. The naming of new generations is the sport of marketers. Behind the effort, however, is a serious attempt to identify the shared characteristics of a group of people. By naming the generations, businesses and policymakers can make better sense of the chaotic jumble of more than 300 million diverse and individualistic Americans.

The Millennials

The Millennial generation's beginning marked the end of the small Generation X, once known as the Baby-Bust generation. The oldest Millennials were born in 1977, when the long anticipated echo boom of births began. In that year, the number of births ticked up to 3.3 million. This followed a 12-year lull in births that is called Generation X. By 1980, annual births were up to 3.6 million. By 1990, they topped 4 million. Altogether, 68 million babies were born between 1977 and 1994. Since then, the number of Millennials has grown to 76 million because of immigration.

As is true with Boomers, the Millennial generation is defined by its numbers. When Millennials moved through the educational system, schools were strained by rising enrollments. Colleges and universities that had been competing for scarce Gen Xers could pick and choose from among the best as applications soared. Millennials also made their mark in the housing market, with homeownership rates rising to record highs by the mid-2000s. Fortunately, few Millennials bought houses during the bubble, the majority of them avoiding the nation's overpriced real estate. In the future, these renters will be well positioned to buy at much lower prices—if they decide they want to become homeowners.

Every generation of Americans is unique, shaped not only by its numbers but also by the historical moment. Millennials are no exception. Three characteristics have emerged to define the generation. One, Millennials are racially and ethnically diverse—so diverse, in fact, that in many parts of the country the term "minority" no longer has meaning for their peer group. Two, they are fiercely independent thanks to divorce, day care, single parents, latchkey lifestyles, and the technological revolution that has made communication with family and friends instantaneous and continuous. Three, Millennials feel powerful—even in the midst of the economic downturn. Raised by indulgent parents, they have a sense of wellbeing not shared by Gen Xers. Optimistic about the future despite their trouble finding jobs and becoming independent, Millennials see opportunity where others see problems.

The Millennials: Americans Born 1977 to 1994 examines the young-adult generation as it goes to college, finds jobs, establishes households, becomes parents, and struggles to gain a foothold in the nation's increasingly fragile middle class.

The iGeneration

The section on what we call the iGeneration examines the socioeconomic status of the nation's children. The generation that follows Millennials was aged 17 or younger in 2012 (born in 1995 or later). We look at these children from the perspective of their family, exploring family incomes, time use and labor force status of parents, day care arrangements, the spending of married couples and single parents with children, and many other family characteristics. The section also includes school enrollment data, mobility statistics, and an examination of the health and wellbeing of high school students.

Soon the youngest generation will go to college, join the labor force, and begin to establish their own households. At that time, they will require a reference book entirely devoted to their unique socioeconomic characteristics. Until then, however, *The Millennials* provides a comprehensive look at young adults and children under age 18.

How to use this book

The Millennials: Americans Born 1977 to 1994 is designed for easy use. It is divided into 11 chapters, organized alphabetically: Attitudes, Education, Health, Housing, Income, Labor Force, Living Arrangements, Population, Time Use, Spending, and Wealth. The section on the iGeneration is divided into nine chapters that examine the characteristics of families with children: Education, Health, Housing, Income, Labor Force, Living Arrangements, Population, Time Use, and Spending,

The fifth edition of *The Millennials* includes the latest data on the changing demographics of homeownership, based on the Census Bureau's 2011 Housing Vacancies and Homeownership Survey. It documents the steep decline in the homeownership rate of "first-time" homebuyers—adults aged 30 to 34. The Income chapter, with 2010 income statistics, reveals the struggle of so many young Americans to find a stable job that pays a living wage as the economy climbs out of recession. The Spending chapter reveals trends in the spending of young adults and families with children through 2010, and examines how their spending changed after the Great Recession. *The Millennials* includes the latest labor force numbers showing the decline in participation among teens and young adults. The Wealth chapter presents data from the Survey of Consumer Finances revealing the impact of the Great Recession on the wealth of householders under age 35, with a look at 2007-to-2009 trends—including statistics on education loans. The Health chapter has up-to-date statistics on falling birth rates, out-of-wedlock childbearing, and health insurance coverage. The Attitudes chapter, based on New Strategist's analysis of the 2010 General Social Survey, compares and contrasts the perspectives of the generations.

Most of the tables in *The Millennials* are based on data collected by the federal government, in particular the Census Bureau, the Bureau of Labor Statistics, the National Center for Education Statistics, the National Center for Health Statistics, and the Federal Reserve Board. The federal government is the best source of up-to-date, reliable information on the changing characteristics of Americans. By having *The Millennials* on your bookshelf, you can get the answers to your questions faster than you can online. Even better, visit newstrategist.com and download the PDF version of *The Millennials* with links to each table in Excel, including all tables in the special supplement.

The chapters of *The Millennials* present the demographic and lifestyle data most important to researchers. Within each chapter, most of the tables are based on data collected by the federal government, but they are not simply reproductions of government spreadsheets—as is the case in many reference books. Instead, each table is individually compiled and created by New Strategist's editors, with calculations designed to reveal the trends. The task of extracting and processing data from the government's web sites to create a single table can require hours of effort. New Strategist has done the work for you, with each table telling a story about Millennials—a story explained by the accompanying text and chart, which analyze the data and highlight future trends. If you need more information than the tables and text provide, you can plumb the original source listed at the bottom of each table.

The book contains a comprehensive table list to help you locate the information you need. For a more detailed search, see the index at the back of the book. Also at the back of the book is the glossary, which defines commonly used terms and describes the many surveys referenced in the tables and text.

Each generation of Americans is unique and surprising in its own way. With *The Millennials: Americans Born 1977 to 1994* on your bookshelf, you will understand the nation's young adults and be ready for the generation that follows, still living at home, but soon to add its own flavor to the dynamic American culture.

1

Attitudes

■ The Millennial generation is the least trusting. Only 18 percent say most people can be trusted. In contrast, a much larger 44 percent of older Americans say others can be trusted.

■ More than one-third of Millennials are "not at all satisfied" with their financial situation. Only 36 percent of the generation calls itself "middle class."

■ Despite their financial struggles, 60 percent of Millennials think they are better off than their parents were at the same age. Nearly three out of four think their children will be better off than they themselves are today.

■ The majority of Gen Xers, Boomers, and older Americans think two children are ideal. Among Millennials, only 39 percent think two is ideal and a larger 48 percent think three, four, or more children are ideal.

■ Only 33 percent of Millennials identify themselves as Protestant compared with 59 percent of older Americans.

■ The 62 percent majority of Millennials thinks gays and lesbians should have the right to marry. Millennials are the only generation in which the majority supports gay marriage.

■ Millennials are more liberal than Gen Xers, Boomers, or older Americans. They are the only generation in which liberals outnumber conservatives (31 versus 27 percent).

■ Most Millennials and Boomers favor legalizing marijuana.

Boomers Are Most Likely to Say They Are Not Too Happy

Fewer than one in three Americans is very happy.

When asked how happy they are, only 29 percent of Americans aged 18 or older say they are very happy. The majority says it feels only pretty happy. The Millennial generation is least likely to report being very happy (25 percent), but Boomers are most likely to report being not too happy (17 percent).

The 63 percent majority of married Americans say they are very happily married. Interestingly, older Americans are least likely to report being very happily married (59 percent), while Gen Xers are most likely (66 percent).

The majority of the public thinks life is exciting (52 percent). The only generation that does not feel this way is older Americans, with only 42 percent finding life exciting and the 53 percent majority finding it pretty routine.

Few believe most people can be trusted. Only 32 percent of the public says most can be trusted. Younger generations are far less trusting than older Americans. Only 18 percent of Millennials believe most people can be trusted compared with 44 percent of people aged 65 or older.

■ Younger generations of Americans are struggling with a deteriorating economy, which reduces their happiness and increases their distrust.

Few Millennials trust others

(percent of people aged 18 or older who think most people can be trusted, by generation, 2010)

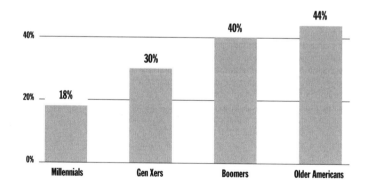

Table 1.1 General Happiness, 2010

"Taken all together, how would you say things are these days—
would you say that you are very happy, pretty happy, or not too happy?"

(percent of people aged 18 or older responding by generation, 2010)

	very happy	pretty happy	not too happy
Total people	**28.8%**	**57.0%**	**14.2%**
Millennial generation (18 to 33)	25.0	62.8	12.2
Generation X (34 to 45)	32.9	54.2	13.0
Baby Boom (46 to 64)	27.2	55.5	17.4
Older Americans (65 or older)	32.8	54.5	12.7

Source: Survey Documentation and Analysis, Computer-assisted Survey Methods Program, University of California, Berkeley, General Social Surveys, 1972–2010 Cumulative Data Files, Internet site http://sda.berkeley.edu/cgi-bin32/hsda?harcsda+gss10; calculations by New Strategist

Table 1.2 Happiness of Marriage, 2010

"Taking all things together, how would you describe your marriage?"

(percent of currently married people aged 18 or older responding by generation, 2010)

	very happy	pretty happy	not too happy
Total married people	**63.0%**	**34.3%**	**2.6%**
Millennial generation (18 to 33)	60.3	37.2	2.5
Generation X (34 to 45)	66.2	30.8	3.0
Baby Boom (46 to 64)	63.9	33.6	2.5
Older Americans (65 or older)	58.9	38.4	2.7

Source: Survey Documentation and Analysis, Computer-assisted Survey Methods Program, University of California, Berkeley, General Social Surveys, 1972–2010 Cumulative Data Files, Internet site http://sda.berkeley.edu/cgi-bin32/hsda?harcsda+gss10; calculations by New Strategist

Table 1.3 Is Life Exciting, Routine, or Dull, 2010

"In general, do you find life exciting, pretty routine, or dull?"

(percent of people aged 18 or older responding by generation, 2010)

	exciting	pretty routine	dull
Total people	**52.1%**	**43.3%**	**4.6%**
Millennial generation (18 to 33)	56.2	40.3	3.5
Generation X (34 to 45)	50.1	43.7	6.2
Baby Boom (46 to 64)	54.6	40.7	4.7
Older Americans (65 or older)	42.5	53.2	4.3

Note: Numbers do not sum to total because "don't know" is not shown.
Source: Survey Documentation and Analysis, Computer-assisted Survey Methods Program, University of California, Berkeley, General Social Surveys, 1972–2010 Cumulative Data Files, Internet site http://sda.berkeley.edu/cgi-bin32/hsda?harcsda+gss10; calculations by New Strategist

Table 1.4 Trust in Others, 2010

"Generally speaking, would you say that most people can be trusted or that you can't be too careful in life?"

(percent of people aged 18 or older responding by generation, 2010)

	can trust	cannot trust	depends
Total people	**32.2%**	**62.5%**	**5.3%**
Millennial generation (18 to 33)	17.8	76.9	5.3
Generation X (34 to 45)	30.4	64.4	5.2
Baby Boom (46 to 64)	40.2	54.8	5.1
Older Americans (65 or older)	43.7	50.6	5.7

Source: Survey Documentation and Analysis, Computer-assisted Survey Methods Program, University of California, Berkeley, General Social Surveys, 1972–2010 Cumulative Data Files, Internet site http://sda.berkeley.edu/cgi-bin32/hsda?harcsda+gss10; calculations by New Strategist

Belief in Hard Work Is Strong Across Generations

Millennials are most likely to believe hard work is they key to success.

How do people get ahead? More than two-thirds of Americans say it is by hard work. Only 10 percent believe luck alone gets people ahead. Millennials (73 percent) believe most strongly in hard work to get ahead.

Not surprisingly, Millennials are most likely to live in the same city as they did when they were 16 (48 percent), mostly because they have had less time to move than older generations. Older Americans are most likely to live in a different state (43 percent).

■ Older Americans are most likely to say (24 percent) that people get ahead through hard work and luck equally.

Many Americans live in the same city as they did when a teenager

(percent of people aged 18 or older who live in the same city/town/county as they did at age 16, by generation, 2010)

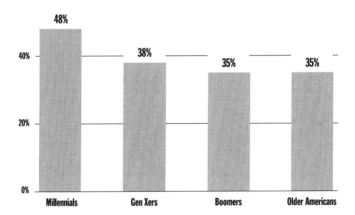

Table 1.5 How People Get Ahead, 2010

"Some people say that people get ahead by their own hard work; others say that lucky breaks or help from other people are more important. Which do you think is most important?"

(percent of people aged 18 or older responding by generation, 2010)

	hard work	both equally	luck
Total people	**69.6%**	**20.4%**	**10.0%**
Millennial generation (18 to 33)	72.7	17.4	9.9
Generation X (34 to 45)	68.4	19.8	11.8
Baby Boom (46 to 64)	69.4	21.6	9.1
Older Americans (65 or older)	67.0	24.0	9.0

Source: Survey Documentation and Analysis, Computer-assisted Survey Methods Program, University of California, Berkeley, General Social Surveys, 1972–2010 Cumulative Data Files, Internet site http://sda.berkeley.edu/cgi-bin32/hsda?harcsda+gss10; calculations by New Strategist

Table 1.6 Geographic Mobility since Age 16, 2010

"When you were 16 years old, were you living in this same (city / town / county)?"

(percent of people aged 18 or older responding by generation, 2010)

	same city	same state, different city	different state
Total people	**39.4%**	**25.7%**	**34.9%**
Millennial generation (18 to 33)	48.3	23.9	27.9
Generation X (34 to 45)	38.1	26.5	35.3
Baby Boom (46 to 64)	35.0	28.8	36.2
Older Americans (65 or older)	34.8	21.8	43.3

Source: Survey Documentation and Analysis, Computer-assisted Survey Methods Program, University of California, Berkeley, General Social Surveys, 1972–2010 Cumulative Data Files, Internet site http://sda.berkeley.edu/cgi-bin32/hsda?harcsda+gss10; calculations by New Strategist

Older Americans Are Doing Far Better than Middle-Aged or Younger Ones

People aged 65 or older are the only ones likely to say they are middle class.

The 60 percent majority of Americans aged 65 or older call themselves middle class compared with only 36 to 41 percent of younger generations, who are more likely to label themselves working class than middle class. Is the preference of younger generations for the label working class simply a matter of semantics or does it record a slippage in the standard of living among people under age 65?

Only 43 percent of Americans believe their family's income is average, down from 49 percent in 2000. Fully 36 percent say they make less than average, up from 26 percent in 2000. Older Americans are the ones least likely to say they have below average incomes and (along with Baby Boomers) most likely to say they have above average incomes.

The share of people who are satisfied with their financial situation fell to 23 percent in 2010, down from 31 percent in 2000. Satisfaction with personal finances is greatest among older Americans, only 18 percent of whom are not at all satisfied. The dissatisfied share is a much larger 32 to 35 percent among the younger generations.

When asked whether they are satisfied with the work they do—either at a job or at home, older Americans are much more likely than middle-aged or younger people to say they are very satisfied. Seventy percent of Americans aged 65 or older are very satisfied, as are the majority of Boomers and Gen Xers. Only 36 percent of Millennials are very satisfied with their work.

■ Older Americans, buoyed by the security of Medicare and Social Security, are the only ones who have managed to hold on to their middle-class status as the Great Recession swept through the economy.

Older Americans are least likely to be dissatisfied with their finances

(percent of people aged 18 or older who say they are not at all satisfied with their financial situation, by generation, 2010)

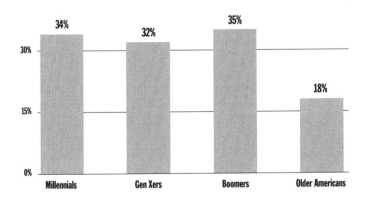

Table 1.7 **Social Class Membership, 2010**

"If you were asked to use one of four names for your social class,
which would you say you belong in: the lower class,
the working class, the middle class, or the upper class?"

(percent of people aged 18 or older responding by generation, 2010)

	lower	working	middle	upper
Total people	**8.2%**	**46.8%**	**42.4%**	**2.5%**
Millennial generation (18 to 33)	9.8	52.7	35.6	2.0
Generation X (34 to 45)	7.9	51.8	39.7	0.6
Baby Boom (46 to 64)	8.6	46.8	41.0	3.6
Older Americans (65 or older)	5.0	31.1	60.1	3.8

Source: Survey Documentation and Analysis, Computer-assisted Survey Methods Program, University of California, Berkeley, General Social Surveys, 1972–2010 Cumulative Data Files, Internet site http://sda.berkeley.edu/cgi-bin32/hsda?harcsda+gss10; calculations by New Strategist

Table 1.8 **Family Income Relative to Others, 2010**

"Compared with American families in general, would you say
your family income is far below average, below average,
average, above average, or far above average?"

(percent of people aged 18 or older responding by generation, 2010)

	far below average	below average	average	above average	far above average
Total people	**6.8%**	**28.8%**	**43.5%**	**18.4%**	**2.5%**
Millennial generation (18 to 33)	7.0	30.6	46.6	13.7	2.0
Generation X (34 to 45)	7.9	27.4	44.2	17.8	2.7
Baby Boom (46 to 64)	8.0	30.8	37.3	20.6	3.3
Older Americans (65 or older)	2.6	23.6	49.4	23.1	1.2

Source: Survey Documentation and Analysis, Computer-assisted Survey Methods Program, University of California, Berkeley, General Social Surveys, 1972–2010 Cumulative Data Files, Internet site http://sda.berkeley.edu/cgi-bin32/hsda?harcsda+gss10; calculations by New Strategist

Table 1.9 Satisfaction with Financial Situation, 2010

"So far as you and your family are concerned, would you say
that you are pretty well satisfied with your present financial
situation, more or less satisfied, or not satisfied at all?"

(percent of people aged 18 or older responding by generation, 2010)

	satisfied	more or less satisfied	not at all sarisfied
Total people	**23.3%**	**45.2%**	**31.5%**
Millennial generation (18 to 33)	20.3	45.4	34.3
Generation X (34 to 45)	19.8	47.8	32.4
Baby Boom (46 to 64)	19.9	44.8	35.3
Older Americans (65 or older)	39.9	41.9	18.1

Source: Survey Documentation and Analysis, Computer-assisted Survey Methods Program, University of California, Berkeley, General Social Surveys, 1972–2010 Cumulative Data Files, Internet site http://sda.berkeley.edu/cgi-bin32/hsda?harcsda+gss10; calculations by New Strategist

Table 1.10 Job Satisfaction, 2010

"On the whole, how satisfied are you with the work you do—would you say you
are very satisfied, moderately satisfied, a little dissatisfied, or very dissatisfied?"

(percent of people aged 18 or older responding by generation, 2010)

	very satisfied	moderately satisfied	a little dissatisfied	very dissatisfied
Total people	**49.8%**	**36.2%**	**10.3%**	**3.7%**
Millennial generation (18 to 33)	36.2	45.6	14.9	3.3
Generation X (34 to 45)	52.4	33.8	10.0	3.8
Baby Boom (46 to 64)	54.6	32.8	8.4	4.3
Older Americans (65 or older)	69.9	24.5	3.8	1.8

Note: Question refers to job or housework.
Source: Survey Documentation and Analysis, Computer-assisted Survey Methods Program, University of California, Berkeley, General Social Surveys, 1972–2010 Cumulative Data Files, Internet site http://sda.berkeley.edu/cgi-bin32/hsda?harcsda+gss10; calculations by New Strategist

The American Standard of Living Is Falling

Fewer Americans believe they are better off than their parents.

When comparing their own standard of living now with that of their parents when they were the same age, 59 percent of respondents say they are better off. The figure was 67 percent 10 years earlier. Older Americans are by far most likely to think they are better off than their parents were at the same age (73 percent). Generation Xers are least likely to feel that way (52 percent).

When asked whether they think they have a good chance of improving their standard of living, 58 percent of Americans say yes. This is down sharply from 77 percent a decade earlier. Not surprisingly, Millennials—with most of their life ahead of them—are most hopeful (65 percent). Disturbingly, Boomers are least hopeful (52 percent).

Fifty-nine percent of parents believe their children will have a better standard of living when they reach the respondent's present age. The share is 73 percent among Millennials, 60 percent among Xers, 53 percent among Boomers, and just 47 percent among older Americans. Apparently, many older Americans are aware of the declining standard of living among the younger generations. A substantial 27 percent of older Americans believe their children will be worse off in the years ahead.

■ The Americans who now have the least (Millennials) are most likely to believe things will be better in the future.

Most still believe their children will be better off

(percent of people aged 18 or older with children who think their children's standard of living will be somewhat or much better than theirs is now, by generation, 2010)

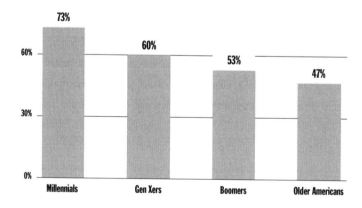

Table 1.11 Parents' Standard of Living, 2010

"Compared to your parents when they were the age you are now, do you think your own standard of living now is much better, somewhat better, about the same, somewhat worse, or much worse than theirs was?"

(percent of people aged 18 or older responding by generation, 2010)

	much better	somewhat better	about the same	somewhat worse	much worse
Total people	**29.2%**	**29.7%**	**24.8%**	**12.1%**	**4.2%**
Millennial generation (18 to 33)	27.6	32.3	25.6	10.4	4.0
Generation X (34 to 45)	25.6	26.0	29.1	16.5	2.9
Baby Boom (46 to 64)	27.8	27.7	23.7	14.9	5.9
Older Americans (65 or older)	39.2	34.0	19.6	4.6	2.6

Source: Survey Documentation and Analysis, Computer-assisted Survey Methods Program, University of California, Berkeley, General Social Surveys, 1972–2010 Cumulative Data Files, Internet site http://sda.berkeley.edu/cgi-bin32/hsda?harcsda+gss10; calculations by New Strategist

Table 1.12 Standard of Living Will Improve, 2010

"The way things are in America, people like me and my family have a good chance of improving our standard of living. Do you agree or disagree?"

(percent of people aged 18 or older responding by generation, 2010)

	strongly agree	agree	neither	disagree	strongly disagree
Total people	**13.1%**	**44.9%**	**16.2%**	**21.6%**	**4.2%**
Millennial generation (18 to 33)	15.5	49.7	16.9	15.9	2.0
Generation X (34 to 45)	18.5	38.4	16.3	22.4	4.4
Baby Boom (46 to 64)	10.7	41.6	16.4	25.0	6.2
Older Americans (65 or older)	7.4	50.8	14.1	23.5	4.2

Source: Survey Documentation and Analysis, Computer-assisted Survey Methods Program, University of California, Berkeley, General Social Surveys, 1972–2010 Cumulative Data Files, Internet site http://sda.berkeley.edu/cgi-bin32/hsda?harcsda+gss10; calculations by New Strategist

Table 1.13 Children's Standard of Living, 2010

"When your children are at the age you are now, do you think their standard of living will be much better, somewhat better, about the same, somewhat worse, or much worse than yours is now?"

(percent of people aged 18 or older with children responding by generation, 2010)

	much better	somewhat better	about the same	somewhat worse	much worse
Total people with children	**27.4%**	**32.0%**	**20.6%**	**15.0%**	**5.1%**
Millennial generation (18 to 33)	38.0	34.6	16.6	9.0	1.8
Generation X (34 to 45)	32.4	27.7	19.1	14.7	6.1
Baby Boom (46 to 64)	19.8	33.1	22.4	18.5	6.2
Older Americans (65 or older)	17.0	30.3	25.9	19.2	7.8

Source: Survey Documentation and Analysis, Computer-assisted Survey Methods Program, University of California, Berkeley, General Social Surveys, 1972–2010 Cumulative Data Files, Internet site http://sda.berkeley.edu/cgi-bin32/hsda?harcsda+gss10; calculations by New Strategist

Two Children Are Most Popular

Many Millennials think three children is the ideal number, however.

Across generations a plurality of Americans thinks two is the ideal number of children. The majority of Gen Xers, Boomers, and older Americans say two is ideal. Among Millennials, a smaller 39 percent think two is the ideal number, and a hefty 48 percent think three, four, or more is best. With a new baby bust in force because of the Great Recession, it is doubtful that Millennials will act on their larger family ideal.

Regardless of their number, most children are subject to a good, hard spanking when they misbehave. Sixty-nine percent of Americans believe children sometimes must be spanked, with little difference by generation.

As older Americans exit the stage, the preference for traditional sex roles has fallen below 50 percent even among people aged 65 or older. Only 48 percent of older Americans believe it is better for everyone involved if the man is the achiever outside the home and the woman takes care of the home and family. Among younger generations, the figure is just 31 to 35 percent. Most of the oldest generation now agrees with young and middle-aged adults that a working mother can have just as warm and secure a relationship with her children as a mother who does not work.

Support for the view that government should help people who are sick and in need is strongest among Millennials (58 percent). Ironically, those least likely to feel this way are older Americans—the only age group with government-provided health insurance. Just 35 percent believe government should help.

■ Many older Americans may not understand that Medicare is a government-provided health insurance program.

Even among older Americans, a minority thinks traditional sex roles are best

(percent of people aged 18 or older who think traditional sex roles are best, by generation, 2010)

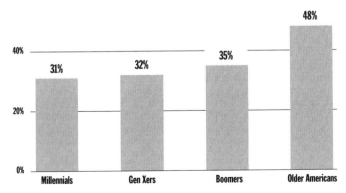

Table 1.14 Ideal Number of Children, 2010

"What do you think is the ideal number of children for a family to have?"

(percent of people aged 18 or older responding by generation, 2010)

	none	one	two	three	four or more	as many as want
Total people	**0.3%**	**2.5%**	**48.4%**	**26.3%**	**12.0%**	**10.5%**
Millennial generation (18 to 33)	0.1	2.1	39.3	32.4	15.8	10.3
Generation X (34 to 45)	0.3	1.2	54.0	23.9	11.1	9.5
Baby Boom (46 to 64)	0.5	3.4	51.7	22.1	11.3	11.0
Older Americans (65 or older)	0.2	3.0	51.7	26.3	8.0	10.8

Source: Survey Documentation and Analysis, Computer-assisted Survey Methods Program, University of California, Berkeley, General Social Surveys, 1972–2010 Cumulative Data Files, Internet site http://sda.berkeley.edu/cgi-bin32/hsda?harcsda+gss10; calculations by New Strategist

Table 1.15 Spanking Children, 2010

"Do you strongly agree, agree, disagree, or strongly disagree that it is sometimes necessary to discipline a child with a good, hard, spanking?"

(percent of people aged 18 or older responding by generation, 2010)

	strongly agree	agree	disagree	strongly disagree
Total people	**23.6%**	**45.4%**	**23.5%**	**7.5%**
Millennial generation (18 to 33)	21.3	48.1	24.0	6.7
Generation X (34 to 45)	26.6	43.9	22.6	6.8
Baby Boom (46 to 64)	22.2	45.1	23.6	9.0
Older Americans (65 or older)	25.7	43.4	23.6	7.3

Source: Survey Documentation and Analysis, Computer-assisted Survey Methods Program, University of California, Berkeley, General Social Surveys, 1972–2010 Cumulative Data Files, Internet site http://sda.berkeley.edu/cgi-bin32/hsda?harcsda+gss10; calculations by New Strategist

Table 1.16 Better for Man to Work, Woman to Tend Home, 2010

"Do you strongly agree, agree, disagree, or strongly disagree with the statement: It is much better for everyone involved if the man is the achiever outside the home and the woman takes care of the home and family?"

(percent of people aged 18 or older responding by generation, 2010)

	agree			disagree		
	total	strongly agree	agree	total	disagree	strongly disagree
Total people	**35.4%**	**6.8%**	**28.6%**	**64.7%**	**43.5%**	**21.2%**
Millennial generation (18 to 33)	31.1	5.5	25.6	68.9	42.7	26.2
Generation X (34 to 45)	31.6	5.9	25.7	68.4	42.9	25.5
Baby Boom (46 to 64)	34.8	5.5	29.3	65.2	46.5	18.7
Older Americans (65 or older)	48.5	12.8	35.7	51.5	40.0	11.5

Source: Survey Documentation and Analysis, Computer-assisted Survey Methods Program, University of California, Berkeley, General Social Surveys, 1972–2010 Cumulative Data Files, Internet site http://sda.berkeley.edu/cgi-bin32/

Table 1.17 Working Mother's Relationship with Children, 2010

"Do you strongly agree, agree, disagree, or strongly disagree with the statement: A working mother can establish just as warm and secure a relationship with her children as a mother who does not work?"

(percent of people aged 18 or older responding by generation, 2010)

	agree			disagree		
	total	strongly agree	agree	total	disagree	strongly disagree
Total people	**74.7%**	**28.8%**	**45.9%**	**25.2%**	**20.1%**	**5.1%**
Millennial generation (18 to 33)	76.0	30.2	45.8	24.0	19.5	4.5
Generation X (34 to 45)	78.4	32.6	45.8	21.6	17.0	4.6
Baby Boom (46 to 64)	74.7	28.5	46.2	25.3	19.7	5.6
Older Americans (65 or older)	68.9	22.4	46.5	31.1	25.4	5.7

Source: Survey Documentation and Analysis, Computer-assisted Survey Methods Program, University of California, Berkeley, General Social Surveys, 1972–2010 Cumulative Data Files, Internet site http://sda.berkeley.edu/cgi-bin32/ hsda?harcsda+gss10; calculations by New Strategist

Table 1.18 Should Government Help the Sick, 2010

"Some people think that it is the responsibility of the government in Washington to see to it that people have help in paying for doctors and hospital bills; they are at point 1. Others think that these matters are not the responsibility of the federal government and that people should take care of these things themselves; they are at point 5. Where would you place yourself on this scale?"

(percent of people aged 18 or older responding by generation, 2010)

	1 government should help	2	3 agree with both	4	5 people should help themselves
Total people	**30.5%**	**16.4%**	**31.9%**	**11.1%**	**10.1%**
Millennial generation (18 to 33)	35.7	21.9	27.2	9.7	5.5
Generation X (34 to 45)	27.3	12.1	37.1	15.5	8.0
Baby Boom (46 to 64)	31.6	16.6	30.3	10.0	11.6
Older Americans (65 or older)	23.3	11.7	37.1	10.1	17.7

Source: Survey Documentation and Analysis, Computer-assisted Survey Methods Program, University of California, Berkeley, General Social Surveys, 1972–2010 Cumulative Data Files, Internet site http://sda.berkeley.edu/cgi-bin32/hsda?harcsda+gss10; calculations by New Strategist

Religious Diversity Is on the Rise

Share of Protestants dwindles with each successive generation.

Asked whether science makes our way of life change too fast, the 51 percent majority of Americans disagrees with the statement. Most Millennials, Gen Xers, and Boomers disagree. But among Americans aged 65 or older, the 56 percent majority agrees that things are changing too fast.

The 56 percent majority of Americans now believes in evolution, up from an even split in 2006. The majority in every generation believes in evolution, the proportion being highest among Millennials.

Among older Americans, 59 percent are Protestants. Among Baby Boomers, the figure is 53 percent. The figure falls to 44 percent among Generation Xers and to just 33 percent among Millennials. Conversely, the share of people with no religious preference climbs from a mere 9 percent among older Americans to a substantial 27 percent among Millennials. Older Americans are twice as likely as members of younger generations to describe themselves as very religious and they are more likely to see the Bible as the word of God.

The majority of Americans disapproves of the Supreme Court decision barring local governments from requiring religious readings in public schools. While the slight majority of Millennials and nearly half the Generation Xers support the decision, only 39 percent of Baby Boomers and just 37 percent of older Americans back the Supreme Court's decision.

■ Along with the growing racial and ethnic diversity of the American population, religious preferences are also growing more diverse.

Younger generations are less likely to be Protestant

(percent of people aged 18 or older whose religious preference is Protestant, by generation, 2010)

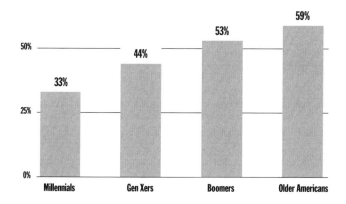

Table 1.19 Attitude toward Science, 2010

"Do you strongly agree, agree, disagree, or strongly disagree with the statement:
Science makes our way of life change too fast?"

(percent of people aged 18 or older responding by generation, 2010)

	strongly agree	agree	disagree	strongly disagree
Total people	**7.2%**	**41.5%**	**43.2%**	**8.1%**
Millennial generation (18 to 33)	8.5	40.5	45.4	5.5
Generation X (34 to 45)	8.7	39.0	47.4	5.0
Baby Boom (46 to 64)	6.3	39.4	41.1	13.2
Older Americans (65 or older)	4.7	51.4	38.7	5.2

Source: Survey Documentation and Analysis, Computer-assisted Survey Methods Program, University of California, Berkeley, General Social Surveys, 1972–2010 Cumulative Data Files, Internet site http://sda.berkeley.edu/cgi-bin32/ hsda?harcsda+gss10; calculations by New Strategist

Table 1.20 Attitude toward Evolution, 2010

"True or false: Human beings, as we know them today,
developed from earlier species of animals?"

(percent of people aged 18 or older responding by generation, 2010)

	true	false
Total people	**55.7%**	**44.3%**
Millennial generation (18 to 33)	59.5	40.5
Generation X (34 to 45)	57.7	42.3
Baby Boom (46 to 64)	52.7	47.3
Older Americans (65 or older)	52.7	47.3

Source: Survey Documentation and Analysis, Computer-assisted Survey Methods Program, University of California, Berkeley, General Social Surveys, 1972–2010 Cumulative Data Files, Internet site http://sda.berkeley.edu/cgi-bin32/ hsda?harcsda+gss10; calculations by New Strategist

Table 1.21 Religious Preference, 2010

"What is your religious preference?"

(percent of people aged 18 or older responding by generation, 2010)

	Protestant	Catholic	Jewish	none	other
Total people	**46.7%**	**25.2%**	**1.6%**	**17.8%**	**8.7%**
Millennial generation (18 to 33)	33.3	26.7	0.5	26.7	12.8
Generation X (34 to 45)	44.4	26.9	1.6	18.0	9.1
Baby Boom (46 to 64)	53.3	22.7	2.1	15.0	6.9
Older Americans (65 or older)	59.1	25.4	2.6	9.4	3.5

Source: Survey Documentation and Analysis, Computer-assisted Survey Methods Program, University of California, Berkeley, General Social Surveys, 1972–2010 Cumulative Data Files, Internet site http://sda.berkeley.edu/cgi-bin32/ hsda?harcsda+gss10; calculations by New Strategist

Table 1.22 Degree of Religiosity, 2010

"To what extent do you consider yourself a religious person?"

(percent of people aged 18 or older responding by generation, 2010)

	very religious	moderately relgious	slightly religious	not religious
Total people	**16.8%**	**41.5%**	**23.6%**	**18.1%**
Millennial generation (18 to 33)	10.8	35.8	27.8	25.6
Generation X (34 to 45)	15.0	41.0	25.9	18.1
Baby Boom (46 to 64)	20.1	42.0	22.3	15.6
Older Americans (65 or older)	22.2	51.0	16.1	10.7

Source: Survey Documentation and Analysis, Computer-assisted Survey Methods Program, University of California, Berkeley, General Social Surveys, 1972–2010 Cumulative Data Files, Internet site http://sda.berkeley.edu/cgi-bin32/ hsda?harcsda+gss10; calculations by New Strategist

Table 1.23 Belief in the Bible, 2010

"Which of these statements comes closest to describing your feelings about the Bible? 1) The Bible is the actual word of God and is to be taken literally, word for word; 2) The Bible is the inspired word of God but not everything in it should be taken literally, word for word; 3) The Bible is an ancient book of fables, legends, history, and moral precepts recorded by men."

(percent of people aged 18 or older responding by generation, 2010)

	word of God	inspired word	book of fables	other
Total people	**34.1%**	**43.6%**	**20.6%**	**1.7%**
Millennial generation (18 to 33)	30.7	44.3	23.3	1.7
Generation X (34 to 45)	31.8	45.6	21.3	1.3
Baby Boom (46 to 64)	35.3	42.7	19.9	2.1
Older Americans (65 or older)	39.9	42.0	16.5	1.6

Source: Survey Documentation and Analysis, Computer-assisted Survey Methods Program, University of California, Berkeley, General Social Surveys, 1972–2010 Cumulative Data Files, Internet site http://sda.berkeley.edu/cgi-bin32/hsda?harcsda+gss10; calculations by New Strategist

Table 1.24 Bible in the Public Schools, 2010

"The United States Supreme Court has ruled that no state or local government may require the reading of the Lord's Prayer or Bible verses in public schools. What are your views on this? Do you approve or disapprove of the court ruling?"

(percent of people aged 18 or older responding by generation, 2010)

	approve	disapprove
Total people	**44.1%**	**55.9%**
Millennial generation (18 to 33)	52.4	47.6
Generation X (34 to 45)	47.0	53.0
Baby Boom (46 to 64)	39.1	60.9
Older Americans (65 or older)	37.0	63.0

Source: Survey Documentation and Analysis, Computer-assisted Survey Methods Program, University of California, Berkeley, General Social Surveys, 1972–2010 Cumulative Data Files, Internet site http://sda.berkeley.edu/cgi-bin32/hsda?harcsda+gss10; calculations by New Strategist

Growing Tolerance of Sexual Behavior

Americans are more accepting of homosexuality.

The share of Americans who believe premarital sex is not wrong at all grew from 42 percent in 2000 to 53 percent in 2010. While the majority of Boomers and younger generations see nothing wrong with premarital sex, the share is just 37 percent among older Americans.

When it comes to sexual relations between adults of the same sex, the trend of growing tolerance is apparent as well. Each successive generation is less likely to condemn homosexuality. The 54 percent majority of Millennials sees nothing wrong with same-sex sexual relations, but support dwindles to 43 percent among Xers, 39 percent among Boomers, and a mere 30 percent among older Americans. Millennials are the only generation in which the majority (62 percent) believes gays and lesbians should have the right to marry.

■ Acceptance of gays and lesbians will grow as tolerant Millennials replace older, less tolerant generations in the population.

Most Millennials support gay marriage

(percent of people aged 18 or older who think gays and lesbians should have the right to marry, by generation, 2010)

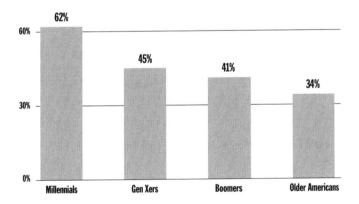

Table 1.25 Premarital Sex, 2010

"If a man and woman have sex relations before marriage,
do you think it is always wrong, almost always wrong,
wrong only sometimes, or not wrong at all?"

(percent of people aged 18 or older responding by generation, 2010)

	always wrong	almost always wrong	sometimes wrong	not wrong at all
Total people	**21.3%**	**7.8%**	**17.8%**	**53.1%**
Millennial generation (18 to 33)	15.0	5.3	20.1	59.6
Generation X (34 to 45)	16.7	8.5	17.9	56.8
Baby Boom (46 to 64)	25.0	5.3	16.4	53.4
Older Americans (65 or older)	30.9	15.7	16.5	36.9

Source: Survey Documentation and Analysis, Computer-assisted Survey Methods Program, University of California, Berkeley, General Social Surveys, 1972–2010 Cumulative Data Files, Internet site http://sda.berkeley.edu/cgi-bin32/hsda?harcsda+gss10; calculations by New Strategist

Table 1.26 Homosexual Relations, 2010

"What about sexual relations between two adults of the same sex?"

(percent of people aged 18 or older responding by generation, 2010)

	always wrong	almost always wrong	sometimes wrong	not wrong at all
Total people	**45.7%**	**3.7%**	**7.9%**	**42.7%**
Millennial generation (18 to 33)	29.6	4.6	11.5	54.3
Generation X (34 to 45)	48.1	2.5	6.1	43.3
Baby Boom (46 to 64)	50.4	3.0	7.2	39.4
Older Americans (65 or older)	58.5	5.4	6.0	30.1

Source: Survey Documentation and Analysis, Computer-assisted Survey Methods Program, University of California, Berkeley, General Social Surveys, 1972–2010 Cumulative Data Files, Internet site http://sda.berkeley.edu/cgi-bin32/hsda?harcsda+gss10; calculations by New Strategist

Table 1.27 Gay Marriage, 2010

"Do you agree or disagree: Homosexual couples should have the right to marry one another?"

(percent of people aged 18 or older responding by generation, 2010)

	agree				disagree		
	total	strongly agree	agree	neither	total	disagree	strongly disagree
Total people	**46.5%**	**21.1%**	**25.4%**	**12.8%**	**40.7%**	**15.6%**	**25.1%**
Millennial generation (18 to 33)	62.2	30.8	31.4	19.7	18.0	10.2	7.8
Generation X (34 to 45)	45.0	20.7	24.3	13.6	41.4	14.2	27.2
Baby Boom (46 to 64)	41.1	17.1	24.0	7.6	51.3	17.3	34.0
Older Americans (65 or older)	34.4	14.5	19.9	11.8	53.8	22.7	31.1

Source: Survey Documentation and Analysis, Computer-assisted Survey Methods Program, University of California, Berkeley, General Social Surveys, 1972–2010 Cumulative Data Files, Internet site http://sda.berkeley.edu/cgi-bin32/hsda?harcsda+gss10; calculations by New Strategist

Television News Is Most Important

The Internet ranks second in importance.

Nearly half of Americans get most of their news from television, 22 percent from the Internet, and 18 percent from newspapers. Together these three news outlets are the main source of news for 88 percent of the public. But there are big differences by generation. Millennials and Gen Xers are far more likely than older generations to depend on the Internet. Twenty-eight percent of Millennials and 33 percent of Gen Xers say the Internet is their most important source of news. This compares with 20 percent of Boomers and just 2 percent of older Americans. Millennials and Gen Xers are more likely to get their news from radio than newspapers.

When asked about their political leanings, the largest share of Americans likes to point to the moderate middle (38 percent). A smaller 29 percent say they are liberal, and 34 percent identify themselves as conservative. Millennials are the only generation in which liberals outnumber conservatives (31 versus 27 percent). An examination of Americans by political party identification shows that self-identified Democrats far outnumber Republicans (46 versus 33 percent). This is the case in every generation.

■ Television remains the primary source of news for every generation of Americans.

News sources differ dramatically by generation

(percent of people aged 18 or older who identify medium as their primary source for news, by generation, 2010)

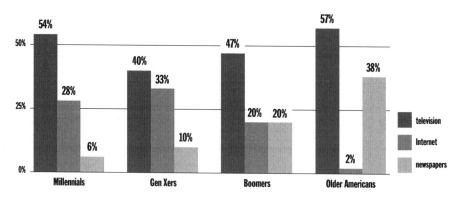

Table 1.28 Main Source of Information about Events in the News, 2010

"We are interested in how people get information about events in the news.
Where do you get most of your information about current news events?"

(percent of people aged 18 or older responding by generation, 2010)

	television	Internet	newspapers	radio	family, friends, colleagues	books, magazines, other
Total people	**49.1%**	**21.6%**	**17.7%**	**7.7%**	**2.2%**	**1.7%**
Millennial generation (18 to 33)	54.3	28.3	5.7	8.4	3.3	0.0
Generation X (34 to 45)	40.2	33.5	9.8	12.2	2.9	1.4
Baby Boom (46 to 64)	47.2	19.7	20.2	6.7	2.2	4.0
Older Americans (65 or older)	56.7	1.8	38.4	3.2	0.0	0.0

Source: Survey Documentation and Analysis, Computer-assisted Survey Methods Program, University of California, Berkeley, General Social Surveys, 1972–2010 Cumulative Data Files, Internet site http://sda.berkeley.edu/cgi-bin32/ hsda?harcsda+gss10; calculations by New Strategist

Table 1.29 Political Leanings, 2010

"We hear a lot of talk these days about liberals and conservatives.
On a seven-point scale from extremely liberal (1) to extremely
conservative (7), where would you place yourself?"

(percent of people aged 18 or older responding by generation, 2010)

	1 extremely liberal	2 liberal	3 slightly liberal	4 moderate	5 slightly conservative	6 conservative	7 extremely conservative
Total people	**3.8%**	**12.9%**	**11.9%**	**37.6%**	**12.8%**	**16.6%**	**4.4%**
Millennial generation (18 to 33)	4.0	15.7	11.1	42.0	11.5	13.2	2.6
Generation X (34 to 45)	1.4	14.6	12.7	37.1	13.8	15.0	5.5
Baby Boom (46 to 64)	4.6	10.4	11.9	37.3	12.5	18.0	5.2
Older Americans (65 or older)	4.8	10.8	12.2	31.8	14.4	21.6	4.4

Source: Survey Documentation and Analysis, Computer-assisted Survey Methods Program, University of California, Berkeley, General Social Surveys, 1972–2010 Cumulative Data Files, Internet site http://sda.berkeley.edu/cgi-bin32/ hsda?harcsda+gss10; calculations by New Strategist

Table 1.30 Political Party Affiliation, 2010

"Generally speaking, do you usually think of yourself as
a Republican, Democrat, independent, or what?"

(percent of people aged 18 or older responding by generation, 2010)

	strong Democrat	not strong Democrat	independent, near Democrat	independent	independent, near Republican	not strong Republican	strong Republican	other
Total people	**16.5%**	**15.7%**	**13.5%**	**18.8%**	**10.0%**	**13.4%**	**9.6%**	**2.6%**
Millennial generation (18 to 33)	12.1	18.2	15.3	23.9	10.3	12.1	5.1	3.1
Generation X (34 to 45)	13.1	15.9	13.6	19.5	10.0	15.1	9.4	3.3
Baby Boom (46 to 64)	17.7	13.2	14.6	16.7	10.0	13.4	12.2	2.3
Older Americans (65 or older)	25.3	16.3	8.0	13.4	9.7	13.2	12.2	1.8

Source: Survey Documentation and Analysis, Computer-assisted Survey Methods Program, University of California, Berkeley, General Social Surveys, 1972–2010 Cumulative Data Files, Internet site http://sda.berkeley.edu/cgi-bin32/ hsda?harcsda+gss10; calculations by New Strategist

Most Support Abortion if a Mother's Health Is Endangered

The majority of Millennials and Boomers favor legalizing marijuana.

Although opposition to capital punishment has grown slightly over the past decade, the great majority still supports the death penalty. In 2000, 30 percent of the public opposed the death penalty for persons convicted of murder. In 2010, the figure had increased slightly to 32 percent. The majority in every generation favors the death penalty.

Most Americans support requiring a permit for gun ownership, and there is little variation by generation. Nearly half the public supports legalizing marijuana—48 percent are for it and 52 percent are against it. More than 50 percent of Millennials and Boomers want to legalize marijuana compared with 43 percent of Gen Xers and 32 percent of older Americans.

Support for legal abortion under certain circumstances is overwhelming. Nearly 9 out of 10 Americans want abortion to be legal if a women's health is in serious danger, and three-quarters want it legal if a pregnancy is the result of rape or there is a chance of serious defect in the baby. Economic and lifestyle reasons garner substantially lower approval ratings.

The two-thirds majority of Americans favor the right of the terminally ill to die with a doctor's assistance. Support is strongest in the younger generations and weakest among Boomers and older Americans.

■ Attitudinal differences between older and younger generations have become more complex, with Gen Xers standing apart on some issues such as the legalization of marijuana.

Fewer than half of Americans in every generation favor allowing abortion for any reason

(percent of people aged 18 or older who favor legal abortion for any reason, by generation, 2010)

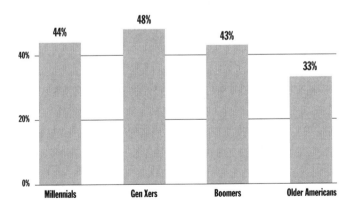

Table 1.31 Favor or Oppose Death Penalty for Murder, 2010

"Do you favor or oppose the death penalty for persons convicted of murder?"

(percent of people aged 18 or older responding by generation, 2010)

	favor	oppose
Total people	**67.8%**	**32.2%**
Millennial generation (18 to 33)	63.6	36.4
Generation X (34 to 45)	69.5	30.5
Baby Boom (46 to 64)	69.2	30.8
Older Americans (65 or older)	70.3	29.7

Source: Survey Documentation and Analysis, Computer-assisted Survey Methods Program, University of California, Berkeley, General Social Surveys, 1972–2010 Cumulative Data Files, Internet site http://sda.berkeley.edu/cgi-bin32/ hsda?harcsda+gss10; calculations by New Strategist

Table 1.32 Favor or Oppose Gun Permits, 2010

"Would you favor or oppose a law which would require a person to obtain a police permit before he or she could buy a gun?"

(percent of people aged 18 or older responding by generation, 2010)

	favor	oppose
Total people	**74.3%**	**25.7%**
Millennial generation (18 to 33)	76.4	23.6
Generation X (34 to 45)	68.8	31.2
Baby Boom (46 to 64)	73.8	26.2
Older Americans (65 or older)	79.4	20.6

Source: Survey Documentation and Analysis, Computer-assisted Survey Methods Program, University of California, Berkeley, General Social Surveys, 1972–2010 Cumulative Data Files, Internet site http://sda.berkeley.edu/cgi-bin32/ hsda?harcsda+gss10; calculations by New Strategist

Table 1.33 Legalization of Marijuana, 2010

"Do you think the use of marijuana should be made legal or not?"

(percent of people aged 18 or older responding by generation, 2010)

	made legal	not legal
Total people	**48.4%**	**51.6%**
Millennial generation (18 to 33)	55.6	44.4
Generation X (34 to 45)	43.5	56.5
Baby Boom (46 to 64)	53.9	46.1
Older Americans (65 or older)	31.9	68.1

Source: Survey Documentation and Analysis, Computer-assisted Survey Methods Program, University of California, Berkeley, General Social Surveys, 1972–2010 Cumulative Data Files, Internet site http://sda.berkeley.edu/cgi-bin32/ hsda?harcsda+gss10; calculations by New Strategist

Table 1.34 Support for Legal Abortion by Reason, 2010

"Please tell me whether or not you think it should be possible for a pregnant woman to obtain a legal abortion if..."

(percent of people aged 18 or older responding by generation, 2010)

	her health is seriously endangered	pregnancy is the result of rape	there is a serious defect in the baby	she cannot afford more children	she does not want more children	she is single and does not want to marry the man	she wants it for any reason
Total people	**86.4%**	**79.1%**	**73.9%**	**47.7%**	**44.9%**	**41.9%**	**42.9%**
Millennial generation (18 to 33)	84.7	82.3	70.9	44.2	47.3	41.2	44.4
Generation X (34 to 45)	86.4	80.9	74.1	46.2	52.1	46.6	48.2
Baby Boom (46 to 64)	87.7	75.7	74.0	46.7	50.0	44.1	42.6
Older Americans (65 or older)	86.2	78.6	78.2	39.5	36.7	31.0	33.4

Source: Survey Documentation and Analysis, Computer-assisted Survey Methods Program, University of California, Berkeley, General Social Surveys, 1972–2010 Cumulative Data Files, Internet site http://sda.berkeley.edu/cgi-bin32/ hsda?harcsda+gss10; calculations by New Strategist

Table 1.35 Doctor-Assisted Suicide, 2010

"When a person has a disease that cannot be cured, do you think
doctors should be allowed by law to end the patient's life by
some painless means if the patient and his family request it?"

(percent of people aged 18 or older responding by generation, 2010)

	yes	no
Total people	**68.4%**	**31.6%**
Millennial generation (18 to 33)	71.5	28.5
Generation X (34 to 45)	73.0	27.0
Baby Boom (46 to 64)	64.6	35.4
Older Americans (65 or older)	64.9	35.1

Source: Survey Documentation and Analysis, Computer-assisted Survey Methods Program, University of California, Berkeley, General Social Surveys, 1972–2010 Cumulative Data Files, Internet site http://sda.berkeley.edu/cgi-bin32/ hsda?harcsda+gss10; calculations by New Strategist

2

Education

■ The oldest members of the Millennial generation are well beyond their college years and embarking on a career. The youngest are still in high school. Consequently, the educational attainment of Millennials is rising rapidly.

■ Millennial women are much better educated than Millennial men. Among women aged 30 to 34, fully 38 percent have a bachelor's degree compared with a smaller 30 percent of their male counterparts.

■ Among Millennials aged 18 to 34, Asian women have the highest level of education and Hispanic men the lowest. Forty-eight percent of Asian women and only 8 percent of Hispanic men in the age group have a bachelor's degree or more education.

■ School enrollment drops sharply among people in their early twenties. The 51 percent majority of people aged 21 are in school, but the figure falls to 22 percent by age 24.

■ Fewer Americans drop out of high school. Only 7.4 percent of people aged 16 to 24 in 2010 were neither high school graduates nor currently enrolled in school. Among Hispanic men, however, the high school dropout rate was a much larger 15 percent.

■ The rate at which high school graduates enroll in college was slightly lower in 2010 than in the peak year of 2009. Sixty-eight percent enrolled in college within 12 months of high school graduation.

Many Millennials Are Still in School

Millennial women outdo their male counterparts in educational attainment.

Millennials spanned the broad age range from 16 to 33 in 2010. The older members of the generation have graduated from college and embarked on a career, but the youngest are still in school. Consequently, the educational attainment of Millennials is rising rapidly. Among 18-to-24-year-olds, just over one-half have college experience. The figure rises to 61 percent in the 25-to-34 age group. Women are further along than men. Sixty-two percent of 18-to-34-year-old women have college experience compared with only 52 percent of their male counterparts.

Among women aged 18 to 24, 11 percent have a bachelor's degree or more education. The figure is a smaller 8 percent among men in the age group. Since it takes, on average, six years to get a bachelor's degree today, it is little wonder so few in their early twenties have earned a college degree. Among 25-to-29-year-olds, 36 percent of women and 28 percent of men have at least a bachelor's degree. Among men and women in the 30-to-34 age group, the figures are 38 and 30 percent, respectively.

■ The greater educational attainment of Millennial women should help narrow the income gap between men and women in the years ahead.

Among Millennials, women are more likely to be college graduates

(percent of people aged 18 to 34 with a bachelor's degree or more education, by sex, 2010)

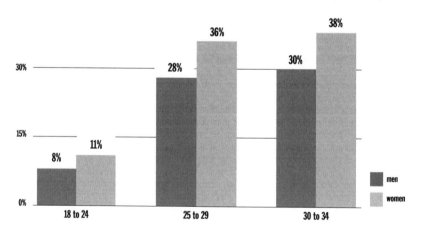

Table 2.1 Educational Attainment of Millennials, 2010

(number and percent distribution of total people aged 18 or older, and people aged 18 to 34, by highest level of education, 2010; numbers in thousands)

	total people 18 or older	aged 18 to 34			
		total	18 to 24	25 to 29	30 to 34
Total people	**229,240**	**70,398**	**29,313**	**21,453**	**19,632**
Not a high school graduate	31,436	10,490	5,726	2,408	2,356
High school graduate	71,172	19,902	8,716	5,908	5,278
Some college, no degree	44,354	18,445	10,693	4,310	3,442
Associate's degree	19,740	5,384	1,481	2,033	1,870
Bachelor's degree	41,289	12,345	2,505	5,338	4,502
Master's degree	15,357	2,929	155	1,182	1,592
Professional degree	3,097	517	23	179	315
Doctoral degree	2,793	387	14	96	277
High school graduate or more	197,802	59,909	23,587	19,046	17,276
Some college or more	126,630	40,007	14,871	13,138	11,998
Associate's degree or more	82,276	21,562	4,178	8,828	8,556
Bachelor's degree or more	62,536	16,178	2,697	6,795	6,686
Total people	**100.0%**	**100.0%**	**100.0%**	**100.0%**	**100.0%**
Not a high school graduate	13.7	14.9	19.5	11.2	12.0
High school graduate	31.0	28.3	29.7	27.5	26.9
Some college, no degree	19.3	26.2	36.5	20.1	17.5
Associate's degree	8.6	7.6	5.1	9.5	9.5
Bachelor's degree	18.0	17.5	8.5	24.9	22.9
Master's degree	6.7	4.2	0.5	5.5	8.1
Professional degree	1.4	0.7	0.1	0.8	1.6
Doctoral degree	1.2	0.5	0.0	0.4	1.4
High school graduate or more	86.3	85.1	80.5	88.8	88.0
Some college or more	55.2	56.8	50.7	61.2	61.1
Associate's degree or more	35.9	30.6	14.3	41.2	43.6
Bachelor's degree or more	27.3	23.0	9.2	31.7	34.1

Source: Bureau of the Census, Educational Attainment in the United States: 2010, detailed tables, Internet site http://www .census.gov/hhes/socdemo/education/data/cps/2010/tables.html; calculations by New Strategist

Table 2.2 Educational Attainment of Millennial Men, 2010

(number and percent distribution of total men aged 18 or older, and men aged 18 to 34, by highest level of education, 2010; numbers in thousands)

	total men 18 or older	aged 18 to 34			
		total	18 to 24	25 to 29	30 to 34
Total men	**111,162**	**35,526**	**14,837**	**10,928**	**9,761**
Not a high school graduate	16,131	5,908	3,215	1,372	1,321
High school graduate	35,449	11,225	4,767	3,451	3,007
Some college, no degree	20,967	8,921	5,059	2,154	1,708
Associate's degree	8,292	2,353	630	916	807
Bachelor's degree	19,762	5,544	1,087	2470	1,987
Master's degree	6,923	1,134	65	442	627
Professional degree	1,871	240	10	88	142
Doctoral degree	1,768	198	4	33	161
High school graduate or more	95,032	29,615	11,622	9,554	8,439
Some college or more	59,583	18,390	6,855	6,103	5,432
Associate's degree or more	38,616	9,469	1,796	3,949	3,724
Bachelor's degree or more	30,324	7,116	1,166	3,033	2,917
Total men	**100.0%**	**100.0%**	**100.0%**	**100.0%**	**100.0%**
Not a high school graduate	14.5	16.6	21.7	12.6	13.5
High school graduate	31.9	31.6	32.1	31.6	30.8
Some college, no degree	18.9	25.1	34.1	19.7	17.5
Associate's degree	7.5	6.6	4.2	8.4	8.3
Bachelor's degree	17.8	15.6	7.3	22.6	20.4
Master's degree	6.2	3.2	0.4	4.0	6.4
Professional degree	1.7	0.7	0.1	0.8	1.5
Doctoral degree	1.6	0.6	0.0	0.3	1.6
High school graduate or more	85.5	83.4	78.3	87.4	86.5
Some college or more	53.6	51.8	46.2	55.8	55.7
Associate's degree or more	34.7	26.7	12.1	36.1	38.2
Bachelor's degree or more	27.3	20.0	7.9	27.8	29.9

Source: Bureau of the Census, Educational Attainment in the United States: 2010, detailed tables, Internet site http://www.census.gov/hhes/socdemo/education/data/cps/2010/tables.html; calculations by New Strategist

Table 2.3 Educational Attainment of Millennial Women, 2010

(number and percent distribution of total women aged 18 or older, and women aged 18 to 34, by highest level of education, 2010; numbers in thousands)

	total women 18 or older	aged 18 to 34			
		total	18 to 24	25 to 29	30 to 34
Total women	**118,079**	**34,872**	**14,476**	**10,525**	**9,871**
Not a high school graduate	15,309	4,581	2,512	1,035	1,034
High school graduate	35,723	8,677	3,949	2,457	2,271
Some college, no degree	23,387	9,522	5,633	2,156	1,733
Associate's degree	11,448	3,030	851	1,117	1,062
Bachelor's degree	21,528	6,801	1,418	2868	2,515
Master's degree	8,434	1,795	90	740	965
Professional degree	1,226	277	13	90	174
Doctoral degree	1,025	188	9	63	116
High school graduate or more	102,771	30,290	11,963	9,491	8,836
Some college or more	67,048	21,613	8,014	7,034	6,565
Associate's degree or more	43,661	12,091	2,381	4,878	4,832
Bachelor's degree or more	32,213	9,061	1,530	3,761	3,770
Total women	**100.0%**	**100.0%**	**100.0%**	**100.0%**	**100.0%**
Not a high school graduate	13.0	13.1	17.4	9.8	10.5
High school graduate	30.3	24.9	27.3	23.3	23.0
Some college, no degree	19.8	27.3	38.9	20.5	17.6
Associate's degree	9.7	8.7	5.9	10.6	10.8
Bachelor's degree	18.2	19.5	9.8	27.2	25.5
Master's degree	7.1	5.1	0.6	7.0	9.8
Professional degree	1.0	0.8	0.1	0.9	1.8
Doctoral degree	0.9	0.5	0.1	0.6	1.2
High school graduate or more	87.0	86.9	82.6	90.2	89.5
Some college or more	56.8	62.0	55.4	66.8	66.5
Associate's degree or more	37.0	34.7	16.4	46.3	49.0
Bachelor's degree or more	27.3	26.0	10.6	35.7	38.2

Source: Bureau of the Census, Educational Attainment in the United States: 2010, detailed tables, Internet site http://www.census.gov/hhes/socdemo/education/data/cps/2010/tables.html; calculations by New Strategist

Asian Women Are the Best-Educated Millennials

Hispanic men are the least educated.

Among people aged 18 to 34, Asian women have the highest level of education. Already, 48 percent have a bachelor's degree or more education. Asian men rank second in educational attainment, 40 percent in the age group having a bachelor's degree or more.

Hispanics are the least educated among Millennials. Only 65 percent of Hispanic men and 72 percent of Hispanic women aged 18 to 34 are high school graduates. Just 10 percent of Hispanics in the age group have a bachelor's degree. Many Hispanics are immigrants from countries that provide little formal schooling.

■ Although the educational attainment of Millennials will rise as more of them complete high school and go to college, the gaps by race and Hispanic origin will persist.

Asians are far better educated than others

(percent of people aged 18 to 34 with college experience, by race and Hispanic origin, 2010)

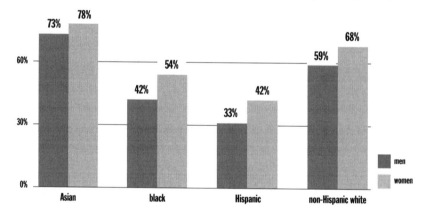

Table 2.4 Educational Attainment of Millennials by Race and Hispanic Origin, 2010

(number and percent distribution of people aged 18 to 34 by educational attainment, race, and Hispanic origin, 2010; numbers in thousands)

	total	Asian	black	Hispanic	non-Hispanic white
Total people aged 18 to 34	**70,398**	**3,907**	**10,318**	**13,557**	**42,255**
Not a high school graduate	10,490	308	1,759	4,292	4,102
High school graduate	19,902	651	3,577	4,338	11,197
Some college, no degree	18,445	916	2,823	2,784	11,829
Associate's degree	5,384	294	714	763	3,568
Bachelor's degree	12,345	1,131	1,127	1,121	8,934
Master's degree	2,929	458	238	194	2,029
Professional degree	517	76	53	48	336
Doctoral degree	387	76	31	17	261
High school graduate or more	29,615	3,602	8,563	9,265	38,154
Some college or more	18,390	2,951	4,986	4,927	26,957
Associate's degree or more	9,469	2,035	2,163	2,143	15,128
Bachelor's degree or more	7,116	1,741	1,449	1,380	11,560
Total people aged 18 to 34	**100.0%**	**100.0%**	**100.0%**	**100.0%**	**100.0%**
Not a high school graduate	14.9	7.9	17.0	31.7	9.7
High school graduate	28.3	16.7	34.7	32.0	26.5
Some college, no degree	26.2	23.4	27.4	20.5	28.0
Associate's degree	7.6	7.5	6.9	5.6	8.4
Bachelor's degree	17.5	28.9	10.9	8.3	21.1
Master's degree	4.2	11.7	2.3	1.4	4.8
Professional degree	0.7	1.9	0.5	0.4	0.8
Doctoral degree	0.5	1.9	0.3	0.1	0.6
High school graduate or more	42.1	92.2	83.0	68.3	90.3
Some college or more	26.1	75.5	48.3	36.3	63.8
Associate's degree or more	13.5	52.1	21.0	15.8	35.8
Bachelor's degree or more	10.1	44.6	14.0	10.2	27.4

Note: Asians and blacks are those who identify themselves as being of the race alone and those who identify themselves as being of the race in combination with other races. Non-Hispanic whites are those who identify themselves as being white alone and not Hispanic. Numbers do not add to total because not all races are shown and Hispanics may be of any race.
Source: Bureau of the Census, Educational Attainment in the United States: 2010, detailed tables, Internet site http://www .census.gov/hhes/socdemo/education/data/cps/2010/tables.html; calculations by New Strategist

Table 2.5 Educational Attainment of Millennial Men by Race and Hispanic Origin, 2010

(number and percent distribution of men aged 18 to 34 by educational attainment, race, and Hispanic origin, 2010; numbers in thousands)

	total	Asian	black	Hispanic	non-Hispanic white
Total men aged 18 to 34	**35,526**	**1,944**	**4,868**	**7,260**	**21,284**
Not a high school graduate	5,908	170	975	2,527	2,229
High school graduate	11,225	349	1,857	2,467	6,464
Some college, no degree	8,921	479	1,284	1,339	5,784
Associate's degree	2,353	152	248	314	1,625
Bachelor's degree	5,544	507	407	509	4,099
Master's degree	1,134	210	71	73	780
Professional degree	240	35	15	20	168
Doctoral degree	198	43	10	10	136
High school graduate or more	29,615	1,775	3,892	4,732	19,056
Some college or more	18,390	1,426	2,035	2,265	12,592
Associate's degree or more	9,469	947	751	926	6,808
Bachelor's degree or more	7,116	795	503	612	5,183
Total men aged 18 to 34	**100.0%**	**100.0%**	**100.0%**	**100.0%**	**100.0%**
Not a high school graduate	16.6	8.7	20.0	34.8	10.5
High school graduate	31.6	18.0	38.1	34.0	30.4
Some college, no degree	25.1	24.6	26.4	18.4	27.2
Associate's degree	6.6	7.8	5.1	4.3	7.6
Bachelor's degree	15.6	26.1	8.4	7.0	19.3
Master's degree	3.2	10.8	1.5	1.0	3.7
Professional degree	0.7	1.8	0.3	0.3	0.8
Doctoral degree	0.6	2.2	0.2	0.1	0.6
High school graduate or more	83.4	91.3	80.0	65.2	89.5
Some college or more	51.8	73.4	41.8	31.2	59.2
Associate's degree or more	26.7	48.7	15.4	12.8	32.0
Bachelor's degree or more	20.0	40.9	10.3	8.4	24.4

Note: Asians and blacks are those who identify themselves as being of the race alone and those who identify themselves as being of the race in combination with other races. Non-Hispanic whites are those who identify themselves as being white alone and not Hispanic. Numbers do not add to total because not all races are shown and Hispanics may be of any race.
Source: Bureau of the Census, Educational Attainment in the United States: 2010, detailed tables, Internet site http://www .census.gov/hhes/socdemo/education/data/cps/2010/tables.html; calculations by New Strategist

Table 2.6 Educational Attainment of Millennial Women by Race and Hispanic Origin, 2010

(number and percent distribution of women aged 18 to 34 by educational attainment, race, and Hispanic origin, 2010; numbers in thousands)

	total	Asian	black	Hispanic	non-Hispanic white
Total women aged 18 to 34	**34,872**	**1,964**	**5,451**	**6,297**	**20,971**
Not a high school graduate	4,581	138	790	1,765	1,872
High school graduate	8,677	302	1,718	1,870	4,733
Some college, no degree	9,522	436	1,538	1,444	6,046
Associate's degree	3,030	143	462	449	1,941
Bachelor's degree	6,801	624	719	612	4,835
Master's degree	1,795	249	167	121	1,249
Professional degree	277	41	38	28	168
Doctoral degree	188	34	21	7	125
High school graduate or more	30,290	1,829	4,663	4,531	19,097
Some college or more	21,613	1,527	2,945	2,661	14,364
Associate's degree or more	12,091	1,091	1,407	1,217	8,318
Bachelor's degree or more	9,061	948	945	768	6,377
Total women aged 18 to 34	**100.0%**	**100.0%**	**100.0%**	**100.0%**	**100.0%**
Not a high school graduate	13.1	7.0	14.5	28.0	8.9
High school graduate	24.9	15.4	31.5	29.7	22.6
Some college, no degree	27.3	22.2	28.2	22.9	28.8
Associate's degree	8.7	7.3	8.5	7.1	9.3
Bachelor's degree	19.5	31.8	13.2	9.7	23.1
Master's degree	5.1	12.7	3.1	1.9	6.0
Professional degree	0.8	2.1	0.7	0.4	0.8
Doctoral degree	0.5	1.7	0.4	0.1	0.6
High school graduate or more	86.9	93.1	85.5	72.0	91.1
Some college or more	62.0	77.7	54.0	42.3	68.5
Associate's degree or more	34.7	55.5	25.8	19.3	39.7
Bachelor's degree or more	26.0	48.3	17.3	12.2	30.4

Note: Asians and blacks are those who identify themselves as being of the race alone and those who identify themselves as being of the race in combination with other races. Non-Hispanic whites are those who identify themselves as being white alone and not Hispanic. Numbers do not add to total because not all races are shown and Hispanics may be of any race.
Source: Bureau of the Census, Educational Attainment in the United States: 2010, detailed tables, Internet site http://www.census.gov/hhes/socdemo/education/data/cps/2010/tables.html; calculations by New Strategist

Many Millennials Are Students

One-third of Millennials are still in school.

Among the nation's 79 million students in 2010, a substantial 27 million were aged 16 to 34 (Millennials were aged 16 to 33 in 2010). More than 90 percent of children aged 16 or 17 are in school. The figure falls with age, but remains above 50 percent through age 21.

■ School enrollment will remain high as the large Millennial generation has children.

School enrollment rate drops sharply among people in their early twenties

(percent of people aged 18 to 24 enrolled in school, by age, 2010)

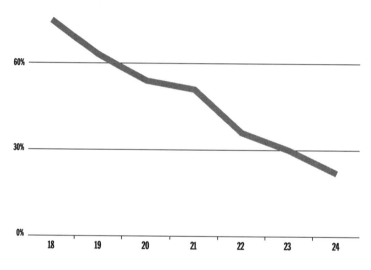

Table 2.7 School Enrollment by Sex and Age, 2010

(number of people aged 3 or older, and number and percent enrolled in school, by age, 2010; numbers in thousands)

	total	enrolled number	enrolled percent
Total people	**292,233**	**78,519**	**26.9%**
Under age 16	53,702	48,382	90.1
Aged 16 to 34	79,047	26,768	33.9
Aged 16	4,158	4,054	97.5
Aged 17	4,132	3,910	94.6
Aged 18	4,366	3,281	75.1
Aged 19	4,163	2,623	63.0
Aged 20	4,399	2,389	54.3
Aged 21	4,282	2,163	50.5
Aged 22	4,054	1,445	35.6
Aged 23	4,192	1,242	29.6
Aged 24	4,203	915	21.8
Aged 25 to 29	21,117	3,088	14.6
Aged 30 to 34	19,981	1,658	8.3
Aged 35 or older	159,483	3,371	2.1
Total females	**149,234**	**39,778**	**26.7**
Under age 16	26,247	23,734	90.4
Aged 16 to 34	39,347	13,903	35.3
Aged 16	2,066	2,031	98.3
Aged 17	1,985	1,909	96.2
Aged 18	2,172	1,646	75.8
Aged 19	2,061	1,382	67.1
Aged 20	2,069	1,230	59.4
Aged 21	2,084	1,094	52.5
Aged 22	2,137	784	36.7
Aged 23	2,163	706	32.6
Aged 24	2,087	476	22.8
Aged 25 to 29	10,494	1,653	15.8
Aged 30 to 34	10,029	992	9.9
Aged 35 or older	83,642	2,140	2.6
Total males	**142,999**	**38,741**	**27.1**
Under age 16	27,456	24,645	89.8
Aged 16 to 34	39,700	12,863	32.4
Aged 16	2,092	2,022	96.7
Aged 17	2,147	2,001	93.2
Aged 18	2,194	1,634	74.5
Aged 19	2,102	1,241	59.0
Aged 20	2,330	1,159	49.7
Aged 21	2,198	1,069	48.6
Aged 22	1,918	662	34.5
Aged 23	2,029	536	26.4
Aged 24	2,115	439	20.8
Aged 25 to 29	10,623	1,435	13.5
Aged 30 to 34	9,952	665	6.7
Aged 35 or older	75,842	1,230	1.6

Source: Bureau of the Census, School Enrollment—Social and Economic Characteristics of Students: October 2010, Internet site http://www.census.gov/hhes/school/data/cps/2010/tables.html; calculations by New Strategist

Fewer Students Are Dropping Out of High School

The dropout rate remains in the double digits among Hispanics, however.

Among people aged 16 to 24 in 2010, only 7.4 percent were neither high school graduates nor currently enrolled in school, down from 10.9 percent in 2000. Since 2000, dropout rates have fallen for both men and women and for every racial and ethnic group.

The dropout rate remains high for Hispanics. While just 5.1 percent of whites and 8.0 percent of blacks aged 16 to 24 have dropped out of high school, a much larger 15.1 percent of Hispanics are high school dropouts. Among Hispanic men, the dropout rate was 17.3 percent in 2010, down considerably from the 31.8 in 2000 but still high. Among Hispanic women aged 16 to 24, a smaller 12.8 percent were high school dropouts in 2010, down from 23.5 percent in 2000.

■ The arrival of millions of poorly educated immigrants to the United States during the past decade explains the high dropout rate among Hispanics. Some did not, in fact, drop out of an American high school, but arrived in the United States without a high school diploma.

Whites have the lowest dropout rate

(percent of people aged 16 to 24 who were neither enrolled in school nor high school graduates, by race and Hispanic origin, 2010)

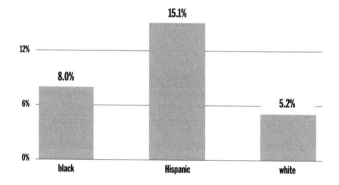

Table 2.8 High School Dropouts by Sex, Race, and Hispanic Origin, 2000 to 2010

(percentage of people aged 16 to 24 who were not enrolled in school and were not high school graduates by sex, race, and Hispanic origin, 2000 to 2010; percentage point change, 2000–2010)

	2010	2000	percentage point change 2000–10
Total people	**7.4%**	**10.9%**	**–3.5**
Black	8.0	13.1	–5.1
Hispanic	15.1	27.8	–12.7
White	5.1	6.9	–1.8
Total men	**8.5**	**12.0**	**–3.5**
Black	9.5	15.3	–5.8
Hispanic	17.3	31.8	–14.5
White	5.9	7.0	–1.1
Total women	**6.3**	**9.9**	**–3.6**
Black	6.7	11.1	–4.4
Hispanic	12.8	23.5	–10.7
White	4.2	6.9	–2.7

Source: National Center for Education Statistics, Digest of Education Statistics 2011, Internet site http://nces.ed.gov/programs/digest/2011menu_tables.asp; calculations by New Strategist

Half of College Students Have Jobs

Employment among young adults has fallen over the years.

Among 16-to-24-year-olds enrolled in college, only 51 percent are in the labor force. The figure ranges from 83 percent among part-time students to 46 percent among those attending full-time. Two-year college students are more likely to be in the labor force than four-year college students.

The summer employment of young adults has been dropping over the years. Fewer students have time for summer jobs because more are participating in extracurricular activities to boost their chances of getting into college. The Great Recession has also reduced the number of young adults in the workforce. In the summer of 2008, 65 percent of 16-to-24-year-olds were in the labor force. In 2011, the figure had fallen to 60 percent.

■ In the 16-to-24 age group, Asians are least likely to have a summer job (48 percent) and whites are most likely (62 percent).

Summer employment has declined among young adults

(percent of 16-to-24-year-olds in the labor force, July 2008 and July 2011)

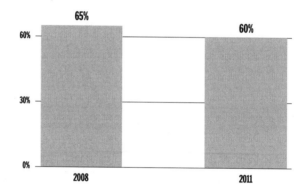

Table 2.9 Employment Status of College Students, 2010

(employment status of college students aged 16 to 24 by selected characteristics, 2010; numbers in thousands)

	civilian noninstitutional population	civilian labor force					not in labor force
		total	percent of population	employed	unemployed		
					number	percent	
Total aged 16 to 24 enrolled in college	**12,423**	**6,372**	**51.3%**	**5,556**	**815**	**12.8%**	**6,052**
Enrolled in two-year college	3,938	2,303	58.5	1,933	370	16.1	1,635
Enrolled in four-year college	8,485	4,068	47.9	3,623	445	10.9	4,417
Full-time students	10,590	4,855	45.8	4,210	645	13.3	5,735
Part-time students	1,834	1,517	82.7	1,346	171	11.3	317
Men	5,788	2,823	48.8	2,436	388	13.7	2,965
Women	6,635	3,548	53.5	3,121	428	12.1	3,087
Asian	843	305	36.2	281	24	7.9	538
Black	1,721	830	48.2	667	164	19.7	891
Hispanic	1,850	953	51.5	817	136	14.3	897
White	9,466	5,055	53.4	4,453	602	11.9	4,410

Note: Asians, blacks, and whites include Hispanics.
Source: Bureau of Labor Statistics, College Enrollment and Work Activity of 2010 High School Graduates, 2011, Internet site http://www.bls.gov/news.release/hsgec.nr0.htm

Table 2.10 Employment Status of Youth by Sex, July 2008 to July 2011

(summer employment status of people aged 16 to 24 by sex, July 2008 to July 2011; numbers in thousands)

	2011	2010	2009	2008
Total aged 16 to 24				
Civilian noninstitutional population	38,196	37,944	37,586	37,506
Civilian labor force	22,742	22,938	23,691	24,429
Participation rate	59.5%	60.5%	63.0%	65.1%
Employed	18,632	18,564	19,304	21,021
Unemployed	4,110	4,374	4,387	3,408
Unemployment rate	18.1%	19.1%	18.5%	14.0%
Not in labor force	15,454	15,006	13,895	13,076
Men aged 16 to 24				
Civilian noninstitutional population	19,425	19,126	18,935	18,919
Civilian labor force	11,930	11,997	12,298	12,882
Participation rate	61.4%	62.7%	64.9%	68.1%
Employed	9,746	9,537	9,880	10,946
Unemployed	2,184	2,460	2,418	1,935
Unemployment rate	18.3%	20.5%	19.7%	15.0%
Not in labor force	7,494	7,129	6,637	6,037
Women aged 16 to 24				
Civilian noninstitutional population	18,772	18,819	18,650	18,587
Civilian labor force	10,812	10,942	11,393	11,547
Participation rate	57.6%	58.1%	61.1%	62.1%
Employed	8,886	9,027	9,424	10,075
Unemployed	1,926	1,914	1,969	1,473
Unemployment rate	17.8%	17.5%	17.3%	12.8%
Not in labor force	7,960	7,877	7,257	7,039

Source: Bureau of Labor Statistics, Employment and Unemployment among Youth Summary, Internet site http://bls.gov/news .release/youth.nr0.htm

Table 2.11 Employment Status of Youth by Race and Hispanic Origin, July 2008 to July 2011

(summer employment status of people aged 16 to 24 by race and Hispanic origin, July 2008 to July 2011; numbers in thousands)

	2011	2010	2009	2008
Total aged 16 to 24				
Civilian noninstitutional population	38,196	37,944	37,586	37,506
Civilian labor force	22,742	22,938	23,691	24,429
Participation rate	59.5%	60.5%	63.0%	65.1%
Employed	18,632	18,564	19,304	21,021
Unemployed	4,110	4,374	4,387	3,408
Unemployment rate	18.1%	19.1%	18.5%	14.0%
Not in labor force	15,454	15,006	13,895	13,076
Asians aged 16 to 24				
Civilian noninstitutional population	1,573	1,576	1,500	1,516
Civilian labor force	753	762	740	767
Participation rate	47.9%	48.3%	49.3%	50.6%
Employed	638	597	619	703
Unemployed	40.5	37.9	41.3	46.4
Unemployment rate	15.3%	21.6%	16.3%	8.4%
Not in labor force	820	814	760	748
Blacks aged 16 to 24				
Civilian noninstitutional population	5,763	5,756	5,662	5,595
Civilian labor force	2,893	2,972	2,995	3,062
Participation rate	50.2%	51.6%	52.9%	54.7%
Employed	1,996	1,980	2,060	2,302
Unemployed	34.6	34.4	36.4	41.2
Unemployment rate	31.0%	33.4%	31.2%	24.8%
Not in labor force	2,870	2,783	2,667	2,533
Hispanics aged 16 to 24				
Civilian noninstitutional population	7,605	7,128	6,752	6,669
Civilian labor force	4,080	3,995	4,014	4,007
Participation rate	53.6%	56.1%	59.4%	60.1%
Employed	3,260	3,111	3,143	3,367
Unemployed	42.9	43.6	46.5	50.5
Unemployment rate	20.1%	22.1%	21.7%	16.0%
Not in labor force	3,525	3,133	2,738	2,662
Whites aged 16 to 24				
Civilian noninstitutional population	29,377	29,164	29,010	29,012
Civilian labor force	18,266	18,441	19,147	19,760
Participation rate	62.2%	63.2%	66.0%	68.1%
Employed	15,367	15,455	16,000	17,323
Unemployed	52.3	53	55.2	59.7
Unemployment rate	15.9%	16.2%	16.4%	12.3%
Not in labor force	11,111	10,722	9,863	9,252

Note: Asians, blacks, and whites include Hispanics.
Source: Bureau of Labor Statistics, Employment and Unemployment among Youth Summary, Internet site http://bls.gov/news .release/youth.nr0.htm

SAT Scores Vary by Income and Parent's Education

The more educated the parent, the higher the child's score.

It is well known that SAT scores vary by race and Hispanic origin. Asians and whites get higher scores than blacks or Hispanics. It is also no surprise that students with the best grades get the highest scores. Students with an A+ grade point average (97 to 100) averaged a 620 out of 800 on the math section of the SAT in 2010–11, for example. Students with a B GPA (80 to 89) scored a much lower 480 on the math section of the test.

SAT scores also vary by family income and parental education. Students with family incomes below $20,000 averaged 460 on the math portion of the SAT in 2010–11 compared with an average score of 586 among students with family incomes of $200,000 or more. Parental education also has a big impact on test scores. Among students with a parent who did not graduate from high school, the average SAT math score was 449. Among those whose parent had a graduate degree, the average math score was 574.

■ Affluent, educated parents can afford SAT prep courses for their children, which can boost test scores.

A parent's education influences a child's test score

(average SAT mathematics score by highest level of parental education, 2010–11)

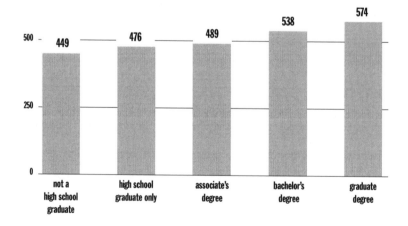

Table 2.12 SAT Scores by Selected Characteristics, 2010–11

(SAT scores by selected characteristics, 2010–11)

	critical reading	mathematics	writing
Total	**497**	**514**	**489**
Sex			
Men	500	531	482
Women	495	500	496
Race and Hispanic origin			
American Indian or Alaska Native	484	488	465
Asian or Pacific Islander	517	595	528
Black	428	427	417
Mexican American	451	466	445
Puerto Rican	452	452	442
Other Hispanic	451	462	444
White	528	535	516
High school grade point average			
A+ (97 to 100)	596	620	595
A (93 to 96)	560	583	556
A– (90 to 92)	528	548	521
B (80 to 89)	469	480	458
C (70 to 79)	416	421	401
D or F (below 70)	409	425	398
Family income			
Less than $20,000	434	460	429
$20,000 to $39,999	464	480	454
$40,000 o $59,999	487	499	475
$60,000 to $79,999	502	512	489
$80,000 to $99,999	515	527	503
$100,000 to $119,999	526	539	515
$120,000 to $139,999	530	544	520
$140,000 to $159,999	538	552	529
$160,000 to $199,999	543	557	536
$200,000 or more	568	586	567
Highest level of parental education			
Not a high school graduate	421	449	418
High school graduate	463	476	452
Associate's degree	480	489	466
Bachelor's degree	522	538	514
Graduate degree	559	574	554

Source: National Center for Education Statistics, Digest of Education Statistics 2011, Internet site http://nces.ed.gov/programs/digest/2011menu_tables.asp; calculations by New Strategist

College Enrollment Rates Are below All-Time High

The cost of college may be taking a toll on enrollment rates.

The rate at which high school graduates enroll in college was lower in 2010 than in the peak year of 2009. Among men and women aged 16 to 24 who graduated from high school in 2010, more than two-thirds (68 percent) had enrolled in college (either a two-year or a four-year school) within 12 months. Among women, the rate was 74 percent, while among men it was a lower 63 percent.

The 2010 college enrollment rate of blacks was at an all-time high, but the enrollment rate among whites was slightly below its 2005 peak. Among Hispanics, the enrollment rate was 11 percentage points higher than in 2000, but below the peak of 2008.

Children from families with high incomes are much more likely to attend college than those from low- or middle-income families. In 2010, 82 percent of high school graduates from high-income families enrolled in college within 12 months. This enrollment rate was much higher than the 67 percent for children from middle-income families and the 52 percent for children from low-income families.

■ Among men graduating from high school, 34.3 percent enroll in a four-year college within 12 months and 28.5 percent enroll in a two-year school.

The college enrollment rate is higher for women than for men

(percent of people aged 16 to 24 who graduated from high school in the previous 12 months and were enrolled in college as of October, by sex, 2010)

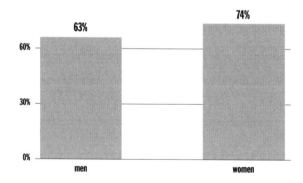

Table 2.13 College Enrollment Rates by Sex, 2000 to 2010

(percentage of people aged 16 to 24 who graduated from high school in the previous twelve months and were enrolled in college as of October, by sex, 2000 to 2010; percentage point change in enrollment rate, 2000–10)

	total	men	women
2010	68.1%	62.8%	74.0%
2009	70.1	66.0	73.8
2008	68.6	65.9	71.6
2007	67.2	66.1	68.3
2006	66.0	65.8	66.1
2005	68.6	66.5	70.4
2004	66.7	61.4	71.5
2003	63.9	61.2	66.5
2002	65.2	62.1	68.3
2001	61.7	59.7	63.6
2000	63.3	59.9	66.2

Percentage point change

| 2000 to 2010 | 4.8 | 2.9 | 7.8 |

Source: National Center for Education Statistics, Digest of Education Statistics 2011, Internet site http://nces.ed.gov/programs/ digest/2011menu_tables.asp; calculations by New Strategist

Table 2.14 College Enrollment Rates by Race and Hispanic Origin, 2000 to 2010

(percentage of people aged 16 to 24 who graduated from high school in the previous twelve months and were enrolled in college as of October, by race and Hispanic origin, 2000 to 2010; percentage point change in enrollment rate, 2000–10)

	total	non-Hispanic Asian	black	white	Hispanic
2010	68.1%	88.4%	65.6%	70.5%	59.5%
2009	70.1	88.1	62.6	71.3	61.6
2008	68.6	90.1	60.3	71.7	62.3
2007	67.2	85.8	55.7	69.5	62.0
2006	66.0	85.1	55.6	68.5	58.5
2005	68.6	80.9	58.2	73.2	57.5
2004	66.7	81.6	58.8	68.8	57.7
2003	63.9	80.0	60.0	66.2	57.7
2002	65.2	–	57.2	69.1	54.7
2001	61.8	–	56.3	64.3	52.7
2000	63.3	–	56.3	65.7	48.6

Percentage point change

| 2000 to 2010 | 4.8 | – | 9.3 | 4.8 | 10.9 |

Note: Asian, black, and Hispanic enrollment rates are three-year moving averages. "–" means data are not available.
Source: National Center for Education Statistics, The Condition of Education, Immediate Transition to College, Internet site http://nces.ed.gov/programs/coe/current_tables.asp; calculations by New Strategist

Table 2.15 College Enrollment Rate by Sex and Type of Institution, 2000 to 2010

(percentage of people aged 16 to 24 who graduated from high school in the previous 12 months and were enrolled in college as of October, by sex and type of institution, 2000 to 2010; percentage point change in enrollment rate, 2000–10)

	men			women		
	total	two-year	four-year	total	two-year	four-year
2010	62.8%	28.5%	34.3%	74.0%	24.6%	49.5%
2009	66.0	25.1	40.9	73.8	30.1	43.8
2008	65.9	24.9	41.0	71.6	30.6	40.9
2007	66.1	22.7	43.4	68.3	25.5	42.8
2006	65.8	24.9	40.9	66.1	24.5	41.7
2005	66.5	24.7	41.8	70.4	23.4	47.0
2004	61.4	21.8	39.6	71.5	23.1	48.5
2003	61.2	21.9	39.3	66.5	21.0	45.5
2002	62.1	20.5	41.7	68.3	23.0	45.3
2001	59.7	18.6	41.1	63.6	20.7	42.9
2000	59.9	23.1	36.8	66.2	20.0	46.2
Percentage point change						
2000 to 2010	2.9	5.4	–2.5	7.8	4.6	3.3

Source: National Center for Education Statistics, The Condition of Education, Immediate Transition to College (Indicator 21-2011), Internet site http://nces.ed.gov/programs/coe/indicator_trc.asp; calculations by New Strategist

Table 2.16 College Enrollment Rate by Family Income, 2000 to 2010

(percentage of people aged 16 to 24 who graduated from high school in the previous 12 months and were enrolled in college as of October, by family income level, 2000 to 2010; percentage point change in enrollment rate, 2000–10)

		family income level		
	total	low	middle	high
2010	68.1%	52.3%	66.8%	82.2%
2009	70.1	53.2	66.8	84.2
2008	68.6	56.0	65.3	81.9
2007	67.2	55.2	63.3	78.2
2006	66.0	54.5	61.4	80.7
2005	68.6	51.0	65.1	81.2
2004	66.7	51.4	63.2	80.1
2003	63.9	51.1	59.1	77.9
2002	65.2	49.2	60.7	78.2
2001	61.7	48.5	56.6	80.0
2000	63.3	47.1	59.5	76.9
Percentage point change				
2000 to 2010	4.8	5.2	7.3	5.3

Note: Low income refers to the bottom 20 percent of all family incomes, high income refers to the top 20 percent of all family incomes, and middle income refers to the 60 percent in between.
Source: National Center for Education Statistics, The Condition of Education, Immediate Transition to College (Indicator 21-2011), Internet site http://nces.ed.gov/programs/coe/indicator_trc.asp; calculations by New Strategist

More than Six Million Families Have Children in College

High-income families are most likely to have a child in college.

Among the nation's 39 million families with school-aged children (5 to 24), more than 6 million have one or more children enrolled in college—or 17 percent. Not surprisingly the likelihood that a family is sending a child to college increases with income. Families with a household income of $75,000 or more are more than twice as likely as families with incomes below $20,000 to have a child in college.

■ The economic downturn has encouraged more young adults to go to college because jobs are scarce.

College is more likely for children from the most affluent families

(percent of families with children aged 5 to 24 who have one or more children enrolled in college, by household income, 2010)

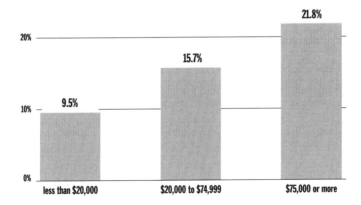

Table 2.17 Total Families with Children in College, 2010

(total number of families, number with dependent children aged 5 to 24, and number and percent with children enrolled in college by household income, 2010; numbers in thousands)

	total	families with children 5–24	with one or more children enrolled in college		
			number	percent of total families	percent of families with children 5–24
Total families	**79,647**	**38,926**	**6,619**	**8.3%**	**17.0%**
Less than $20,000	9,810	5,591	532	5.4	9.5
$20,000 to $74,999	31,614	15,185	2,384	7.5	15.7
$75,000 or more	20,789	10,610	2,314	11.1	21.8

Note: Numbers do sum to total because "not reported" is not shown.
Source: Bureau of the Census, School Enrollment—Social and Economic Characteristics of Students: October 2010, detailed tables, Internet site http://www.census.gov/hhes/school/data/cps/2010/tables.html

Millennials Populate the Nation's Campuses

Four-year schools are more popular than two-year schools.

While the oldest Millennials are beyond college and the youngest are not quite old enough to be in college yet, the broad middle of the generation populates the nation's campuses (Millennials were aged 16 to 33 in 2010). Millennial women outnumber their male counterparts in every type of college—two-year, four-year, and graduate school.

Among the nation's 20 million college students, just over half attend four-year schools. Another 29 percent are in two-year schools, and 19 percent are in graduate school.

■ Most college students attend school full-time. Even most graduate students are full-timers.

Among Millennials, women outnumber men on college campuses

(percent distribution of college students aged 15 to 19, 20 to 24, and 25 to 34 by sex, 2010)

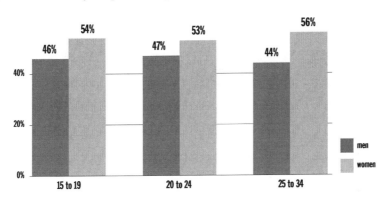

Table 2.18 College Students by Age and Sex, 2010

(number, percent, and percent distribution of people aged 15 or older enrolled in institutions of higher education, by type of institution, age, and sex, 2010; numbers in thousands)

	total	men total	men percent of total	women total	women percent of total
TOTAL COLLEGE STUDENTS					
Total students	**20,275**	**9,007**	**44.4%**	**11,268**	**55.6%**
Aged 15 to 19	4,593	2,103	45.8	2,490	54.2
Aged 20 to 24	7,849	3,689	47.0	4,160	53.0
Aged 25 to 34	4,624	2,055	44.4	2,569	55.6
Aged 35 or older	3,210	1,160	36.1	2,049	63.8
TWO-YEAR UNDERGRADUATE					
Total students	**5,904**	**2,693**	**45.6**	**3,211**	**54.4**
Aged 15 to 19	1,754	909	51.8	845	48.2
Aged 20 to 24	2,065	998	48.3	1,068	51.7
Aged 25 to 34	1,170	506	43.2	664	56.8
Aged 35 or older	915	281	30.7	634	69.3
FOUR-YEAR UNDERGRADUATE					
Total students	**10,450**	**4,607**	**44.1**	**5,844**	**55.9**
Aged 15 to 19	2,793	1,179	42.2	1,614	57.8
Aged 20 to 24	4,830	2,290	47.4	2,541	52.6
Aged 25 to 34	1,742	730	41.9	1,011	58.0
Aged 35 or older	1,086	408	37.6	678	62.4
GRADUATE SCHOOL					
Total students	**3,921**	**1,708**	**43.6**	**2,214**	**56.5**
Aged 15 to 19	47	15	31.9	32	68.1
Aged 20 to 24	954	401	42.0	552	57.9
Aged 25 to 34	1,713	819	47.8	893	52.1
Aged 35 or older	1,209	472	39.0	736	60.9

Source: Bureau of the Census, School Enrollment—Social and Economic Characteristics of Students: October 2010, detailed tables, Internet site http://www.census.gov/hhes/school/data/cps/2010/tables.html

Table 2.19 College Students by Age, Type of School, and Attendance Status, 2010

(number, percent, and percent distribution of people aged 15 or older enrolled in institutions of higher education, by age, type of school, and attendance status, 2010; numbers in thousands)

	total	two-year school number	two-year school share of total students in age group	two-year school percent distribution	four-year school number	four-year school share of total students in age group	four-year school percent distribution	graduate school number	graduate school share of total students in age group	graduate school percent distribution
TOTAL COLLEGE STUDENTS										
Total students	20,275	5,904	29.1%	100.0%	10,450	51.5%	100.0%	3,921	19.3%	100.0%
Aged 15 to 19	4,593	1,754	38.2	29.7	2,793	60.8	26.7	47	1.0	1.2
Aged 20 to 24	7,849	2,065	26.3	35.0	4,830	61.5	46.2	954	12.2	24.3
Aged 25 to 34	4,624	1,170	25.3	19.8	1,742	37.7	16.7	1,713	37.0	43.7
Aged 35 or older	3,210	915	28.5	15.5	1,086	33.8	10.4	1,209	37.7	30.8
TOTAL FULL-TIME STUDENTS										
Total students	14,600	3,870	26.5	100.0	8,485	58.1	100.0	2,246	15.4	100.0
Aged 15 to 19	4,067	1,422	35.0	36.7	2,610	64.2	30.8	34	0.8	1.5
Aged 20 to 24	6,541	1,422	21.7	36.7	4,303	65.8	50.7	817	12.5	36.4
Aged 25 to 34	2,702	653	24.2	16.9	1,021	37.8	12.0	1,027	38.0	45.7
Aged 35 or older	1,291	373	28.9	9.6	551	42.7	6.5	367	28.4	16.3
TOTAL PART-TIME STUDENTS										
Total students	5,675	2,034	35.8	100.0	1,965	34.6	100.0	1,675	29.5	100.0
Aged 15 to 19	526	332	63.1	16.3	182	34.6	9.3	11	2.1	0.7
Aged 20 to 24	1,308	644	49.2	31.7	528	40.4	26.9	137	10.5	8.2
Aged 25 to 34	1,922	517	26.9	25.4	721	37.5	36.7	686	35.7	41.0
Aged 35 or older	1,919	542	28.2	26.6	535	27.9	27.2	842	43.9	50.3

Source: Bureau of the Census, School Enrollment—Social and Economic Characteristics of Students: October 2010, detailed tables, Internet site http://www.census.gov/hhes/school/data/cps/2010/tables.html

Most Degrees Are Earned in a Few Fields

Business, social sciences, health, and law dominate the academic degrees awarded.

Nearly everyone earning a college degree these days is a member of the Millennial generation. Among the degrees Millennials are earning, a few fields dominate.

At the associate's degree level, "liberal arts and sciences, general studies, and humanities" is the most popular field. More than one-third of the associate's degrees awarded in 2009–10 were in this discipline. One in five associate's degrees was awarded in "health professions and related clinical sciences," and 16 percent were conferred in business.

At the bachelor's degree level, business was the preferred field in 2009–10, attracting 22 percent of graduates. The only other field in double digits was social sciences and history, in which 10 percent of all bachelor's degrees were awarded.

At the master's level, education was the field of choice for 26 percent, followed closely by business (also 26 percent). Together these two disciplines accounted for the 52 percent majority of all master's degrees awarded in 2009–10.

■ Almost half the students obtaining a professional degree in 2009–10 did so in the field of law.

More than one in five bachelor's degrees are in business

(percent distribution of bachelor's degrees accounted for by the six most popular fields of study, 2009–10)

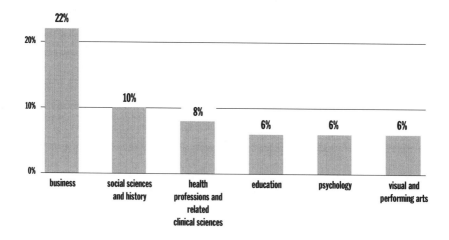

Table 2.20 Associate's Degrees Earned by Field of Study and Sex, 2009–10

(number and percent distribution of associate's degrees conferred by sex, and percent earned by women, by field of study, 2009–10)

				women	
	total	percent distribution	men	number	percent of total
Total associate's degrees	**849,452**	**100.0%**	**322,916**	**526,536**	**62.0%**
Agriculture and natural resources	5,894	0.7	3,783	2,111	35.8
Architecture and related services	552	0.1	266	286	51.8
Area, ethnic, cultural, and gender studies	199	0.0	75	124	62.3
Biological and biomedical sciences	2,664	0.3	851	1,813	68.1
Business	133,371	15.7	48,168	85,203	63.9
Communications, journalism, and related programs	2,839	0.3	1,327	1,512	53.3
Communications technologies	4,419	0.5	3,038	1,381	31.3
Computer and information sciences	32,466	3.8	24,682	7,784	24.0
Construction trades	4,617	0.5	4,350	267	5.8
Education	17,048	2.0	2,352	14,696	86.2
Engineering	2,508	0.3	2,176	332	13.2
Engineering technologies	31,850	3.7	27,562	4,288	13.5
English language and literature/letters	1,658	0.2	561	1,097	66.2
Family and consumer sciences	9,573	1.1	495	9,078	94.8
Foreign languages, literatures, and linguistics	1,683	0.2	318	1,365	81.1
Health professions and related clinical sciences	177,686	20.9	25,904	151,782	85.4
Homeland security, law enforcement, firefighting, related	37,260	4.4	19,876	17,384	46.7
Legal professions and studies	10,003	1.2	1,203	8,800	88.0
Liberal arts and sciences, general studies, and humanities	284,775	33.5	110,701	174,074	61.1
Library science	112	0.0	20	92	82.1
Mathematics and statistics	1,051	0.1	725	326	31.0
Mechanics and repair technologies	16,305	1.9	15,479	826	5.1
Military technologies	668	0.1	531	137	20.5
Multi/interdisciplinary studies	17,671	2.1	6,960	10,711	60.6
Parks, recreation, leisure, and fitness studies	2,016	0.2	1,223	793	39.3
Philosophy and religious studies	256	0.0	163	93	36.3
Physical sciences and science technologies	4,140	0.5	2,549	1,591	38.4
Precision production	2,787	0.3	2,609	178	6.4
Psychology	6,582	0.8	1,271	5,311	80.7
Public administration and social service professions	4,526	0.5	662	3,864	85.4
Social sciences and history	10,649	1.3	3,809	6,840	64.2
Theology and religious vocations	613	0.1	306	307	50.1
Transportation and materials moving	1,444	0.2	1,235	209	14.5
Visual and performing arts	19,567	2.3	7,686	11,881	60.7

Source: National Center for Education Statistics, Digest of Education Statistics 2011, Internet site http://nces.ed.gov/programs/digest/2011menu_tables.asp; calculations by New Strategist

Table 2.21 Bachelor's Degrees Earned by Field of Study and Sex, 2009–10

(number and percent distribution of bachelor's degrees conferred by sex, and percent earned by women, by field of study, 2009–10)

	total	percent distribution	men	women number	women percent of total
Total bachelor's degrees	**1,650,014**	**100.0%**	**706,633**	**943,381**	**57.2%**
Agriculture and natural resources	26,336	1.6	13,519	12,817	48.7
Architecture and related services	10,051	0.6	5,694	4,357	43.3
Area, ethnic, cultural, and gender studies	8,621	0.5	2,694	5,927	68.8
Biological and biomedical sciences	86,400	5.2	35,865	50,535	58.5
Business	358,293	21.7	183,301	174,992	48.8
Communications, journalism, and related programs	81,266	4.9	28,595	52,671	64.8
Communications technologies	4,782	0.3	3,445	1,337	28.0
Computer and information sciences	39,589	2.4	32,410	7,179	18.1
Construction trades	273	0.0	261	12	4.4
Education	101,265	6.1	20,726	80,539	79.5
Engineering	72,654	4.4	59,360	13,294	18.3
Engineering technologies	15,596	0.9	14,014	1,582	10.1
English language and literature/letters	53,231	3.2	17,050	36,181	68.0
Family and consumer sciences	21,818	1.3	2,686	19,132	87.7
Foreign languages, literatures, and linguistics	21,516	1.3	6,610	14,906	69.3
Health professions and related clinical sciences	129,634	7.9	19,306	110,328	85.1
Homeland security, law enforcement, firefighting and related	43,667	2.6	22,265	21,402	49.0
Legal professions and studies	3,886	0.2	1,096	2,790	71.8
Liberal arts and sciences, general studies, and humanities	46,953	2.8	16,619	30,334	64.6
Library science	85	0.0	11	74	87.1
Mathematics and statistics	16,030	1.0	9,087	6,943	43.3
Mechanics and repair technologies	206	0.0	198	8	3.9
Military technologies	56	0.0	54	2	3.6
Multi/interdisciplinary studies	37,648	2.3	12,129	25,519	67.8
Parks, recreation, leisure, and fitness studies	33,318	2.0	17,621	15,697	47.1
Philosophy and religious studies	12,504	0.8	7,910	4,594	36.7
Physical sciences and science technologies	23,379	1.4	13,862	9,517	40.7
Precision production	29	0.0	19	10	34.5
Psychology	97,216	5.9	22,275	74,941	77.1
Public administration and social service professions	25,414	1.5	4,578	20,836	82.0
Social sciences and history	172,780	10.5	87,406	85,374	49.4
Theology and religious vocations	8,718	0.5	5,756	2,962	34.0
Transportation and materials moving	4,998	0.3	4,443	555	11.1
Visual and performing arts	91,802	5.6	35,768	56,034	61.0

Source: National Center for Education Statistics, Digest of Education Statistics 2011, Internet site http://nces.ed.gov/programs/digest/2011menu_tables.asp; calculations by New Strategist

Table 2.22 Master's Degrees Earned by Field of Study and Sex, 2009–10

(number and percent distribution of master's degrees conferred by sex, and percent earned by women, by field of study, 2009–10)

	total	percent distribution	men	women number	percent of total
Total master's degrees	**693,025**	**100.0%**	**275,197**	**417,828**	**60.3%**
Agriculture and natural resources	5,211	0.8	2,509	2,702	51.9
Architecture and related services	7,280	1.1	4,012	3,268	44.9
Area, ethnic, cultural, and gender studies	1,775	0.3	654	1,121	63.2
Biological and biomedical sciences	10,725	1.5	4,611	6,114	57.0
Business	177,684	25.6	96,709	80,975	45.6
Communications, journalism, and related programs	7,636	1.1	2,410	5,226	68.4
Communications technologies	463	0.1	249	214	46.2
Computer and information sciences	17,953	2.6	13,017	4,936	27.5
Education	182,139	26.3	41,296	140,843	77.3
Engineering	35,088	5.1	27,281	7,807	22.2
Engineering technologies	4,258	0.6	3,240	1,018	23.9
English language and literature/letters	9,201	1.3	3,006	6,195	67.3
Family and consumer sciences	2,580	0.4	362	2,218	86.0
Foreign languages, literatures, and linguistics	3,755	0.5	1,254	2,501	66.6
Health professions and related clinical sciences	69,084	10.0	12,871	56,213	81.4
Homeland security, law enforcement, firefighting and related	6,714		3,140	3,574	53.2
Legal professions and studies	5,734	0.8	2,803	2,931	51.1
Liberal arts and sciences, general studies, and humanities	3,804	0.5	1,522	2,282	60.0
Library science	7,448	1.1	1,394	6,054	81.3
Mathematics and statistics	5,634	0.8	3,376	2,258	40.1
Multi/interdisciplinary studies	5,973	0.9	2,118	3,855	64.5
Parks, recreation, leisure, and fitness studies	5,617	0.8	3,032	2,585	46.0
Philosophy and religious studies	2,043	0.3	1,298	745	36.5
Physical sciences and science technologies	6,063	0.9	3,652	2,411	39.8
Precision production	10	0.0	5	5	50.0
Psychology	23,752	3.4	4,797	18,955	79.8
Public administration and social service professions	35,729	5.2	8,865	26,864	75.2
Social sciences and history	20,222	2.9	9,963	10,259	50.7
Theology and religious vocations	12,824	1.9	8,302	4,522	35.3
Transportation and materials moving	1,074	0.2	924	150	14.0
Visual and performing arts	15,552	2.2	6,525	9,027	58.0

Source: National Center for Education Statistics, Digest of Education Statistics 2011, Internet site http://nces.ed.gov/programs/digest/2011menu_tables.asp; calculations by New Strategist

Table 2.23 Doctoral Degrees Earned by Field of Study and Sex, 2009–10

(number and percent distribution of doctoral degrees conferred by sex, and percent earned by women, by field of study, 2009–10)

	total	percent distribution	men	women number	women percent of total
Total doctoral degrees	**158,558**	**100.0%**	**76,605**	**81,953**	**51.7%**
Agriculture and natural resources	1,147	0.7	625	522	45.5
Architecture and related services	210	0.1	116	94	44.8
Area, ethnic, cultural, and gender studies	253	0.2	107	146	57.7
Biological and biomedical sciences	7,666	4.8	3,600	4,066	53.0
Business	2,245	1.4	1,335	910	40.5
Communications, journalism, and related programs	570	0.4	224	346	60.7
Communications technologies	3	0.0	1	2	66.7
Computer and information sciences	1,599	1.0	1,250	349	21.8
Education	9,233	5.8	3,023	6,210	67.3
Engineering	7,704	4.9	5,934	1,770	23.0
Engineering technologies	67	0.0	50	17	25.4
English language and literature/letters	1,332	0.8	522	810	60.8
Family and consumer sciences	296	0.2	64	232	78.4
Foreign languages, literatures, and linguistics	1,091	0.7	446	645	59.1
Health professions and related clinical sciences	57,746	36.4	23,946	33,800	58.5
Homeland security, law enforcement, firefighting and related	106	0.1	57	49	46.2
Legal professions and studies	44,626	28.1	23,552	21,074	47.2
Liberal arts and sciences, general studies, and humanities	96	0.1	40	56	58.3
Library science	64	0.0	20	44	68.8
Mathematics and statistics	1,592	1.0	1,116	476	29.9
Multi/interdisciplinary studies	631	0.4	265	366	58.0
Parks, recreation, leisure, and fitness studies	266	0.2	140	126	47.4
Philosophy and religious studies	667	0.4	450	217	32.5
Physical sciences and science technologies	5,063	3.2	3,404	1,659	32.8
Psychology	5,540	3.5	1,478	4,062	73.3
Public administration and social service professions	838	0.5	323	515	61.5
Social sciences and history	4,238	2.7	2,292	1,946	45.9
Theology and religious vocations	2,070	1.3	1,525	545	26.3
Visual and performing arts	1,599	1.0	700	899	56.2

Source: National Center for Education Statistics, Digest of Education Statistics 2011, Internet site http://nces.ed.gov/programs/ digest/2011menu_tables.asp; calculations by New Strategist

Table 2.24 First-Professional Degrees Earned by Field of Study and Sex, 2009–10

(number and percent distribution of first-professional degrees conferred by sex, and percent earned by women, by field of study, 2009–10)

	total	percent distribution	men	women number	women percent of total
Total professional degrees	**94,103**	**100.0%**	**47,538**	**46,565**	**49.5%**
Dentistry (D.D.S. or D.M.D.)	5,062	5.4	2,745	2,317	45.8
Medicine (M.D.)	16,356	17.4	8,468	7,888	48.2
Optometry (O.D.)	1,335	1.4	457	878	65.8
Osteopathic medicine (D.O.)	3,890	4.1	1,979	1,911	49.1
Pharmacy (Pharm.D.)	11,873	12.6	4,297	7,576	63.8
Podiatry (Pod.D., D.P., or D.P.M.)	491	0.5	276	215	43.8
Veterinary medicine (D.V.M.)	2,478	2.6	555	1,923	77.6
Chiropractic (D.C. or D.C.M.)	2,601	2.8	1,610	991	38.1
Law (LL.B. or J.D.)	44,345	47.1	23,394	20,951	47.2
Theology (M.Div., M.H.L., B.D., or Ord.)	5,672	6.0	3,757	1,915	33.8

Source: National Center for Education Statistics, Digest of Education Statistics 2011, Internet site http://nces.ed.gov/programs/ digest/2011menu_tables.asp; calculations by New Strategist

Health

■ The 55 percent majority of Americans aged 18 or older are in very good or excellent health. The figure peaks at 63 percent in the 25-to-44 age group.

■ Americans have a weight problem, and young adults are no exception. The average man in his twenties weighs 188 pounds. The average woman in the age group weighs 156 pounds.

■ Among 15-to-19-year-olds, 57 percent of men and 52 percent of women are sexually experienced.

■ The Millennial generation dominates parenthood. The 52 percent majority of babies are born to women in their twenties, and another 24 percent are born to women aged 30 to 34.

■ Before the Affordable Care Act, the nation's 18-to-24-year-olds were most likely to lack health insurance. Now that dubious distinction belongs to 25-to-34-year-olds—28 percent of whom are uninsured.

■ People aged 15 to 24 visit a doctor only 1.8 times a year. This age group visits a doctor less often than others in part because many in the cohort do not have health insurance.

■ Accidents are the leading cause of death among 15-to-44-year-olds and account for 41 percent of deaths among 15-to-24-year-olds and 25 percent of deaths among 25-to-44-year-olds.

Most Young Adults Say Their Health Is Excellent or Very Good

The proportion of those who say they are in very good or excellent health declines with age.

Overall, the 55 percent majority of Americans aged 18 or older say their health is "very good" or "excellent." Not surprisingly, the percentage of those who say their health is very good or excellent is higher among young adults than among middle-aged or older people. The figure peaks at 63 percent among adults under age 35, then falls with increasing age as chronic conditions become common.

Fewer than half of people aged 65 or older report that their health is excellent or very good. Nevertheless, the proportion that says they are in poor health remains below 8 percent, regardless of age. Among people aged 65 or older, the proportion that says their health is excellent or very good (41 percent) surpasses the proportion that says their health is only fair or poor (25 percent).

■ Medical advances that allow people to manage chronic conditions should boost the proportions of people reporting excellent or very good health in the years ahead.

Nearly two-thirds of adults under age 35 say their health is excellent or very good

(percent of people aged 18 or older who say their health is excellent or very good, by age, 2010)

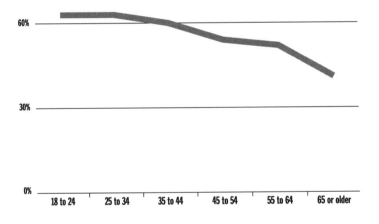

Table 3.1 Health Status by Age, 2010

(percent distribution of people aged 18 or older by self-reported health status, by age, 2010)

	total	excellent or very good			good	fair or poor		
		total	excellent	very good		total	fair	poor
Total people	**100.0%**	**54.8%**	**20.2%**	**34.6%**	**29.8%**	**14.9%**	**10.9%**	**4.0%**
Aged 18 to 24	100.0	62.6	25.0	37.6	27.5	6.7	5.6	1.1
Aged 25 to 34	100.0	62.9	25.0	37.9	28.8	9.0	7.5	1.5
Aged 35 to 44	100.0	60.2	23.0	37.2	28.6	10.6	8.2	2.4
Aged 45 to 54	100.0	54.4	20.0	34.4	29.0	15.1	10.7	4.4
Aged 55 to 64	100.0	51.7	17.6	34.1	30.3	19.0	13.2	5.8
Aged 65 or older	100.0	40.7	12.1	28.6	33.9	24.7	17.7	7.0

Source: Centers for Disease Control and Prevention, Behavioral Risk Factor Surveillance System Prevalence Data, 2010, Internet site http://apps.nccd.cdc.gov/brfss/

Weight Problems Are the Norm Even for Young Adults

Most young men and women are overweight.

Americans have a weight problem, and young adults are no exception. The average man in his twenties weighs 188 pounds. The average woman in the age group weighs 156 pounds. Fully 61 percent of men and 55 percent of women aged 20 to 34 are overweight, and more than one in four is obese.

Although many people say they exercise, only 20 percent of adults meet federal physical activity guidelines. The proportion that met both aerobic and muscle-strengthening guidelines is highest among 18-to-24-year-olds (30 percent) and falls with age to fewer than 10 percent of people aged 65 or older. The guidelines are fairly complex and demanding, however, which might explain why so few can meet them.

■ Most young adults lack the willpower to eat less or exercise more—fueling a diet and weight loss industry that never lacks for customers.

Most young adults weigh more than they should

(percent distribution of people aged 20 to 34 by weight status, by sex, 2007–10)

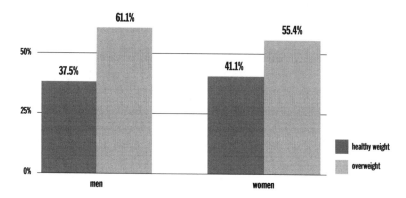

Table 3.2 Average Measured Weight by Age and Sex, 2003–06

(average weight in pounds of people aged 20 or older by age and sex, 2003–06)

	men	women
Total aged 20 or older	**194.7**	**164.7**
Aged 20 to 29	188.3	155.9
Aged 30 to 39	194.1	164.7
Aged 40 to 49	202.3	171.3
Aged 50 to 59	198.8	172.1
Aged 60 to 69	198.3	170.5
Aged 70 to 79	187.4	155.6
Aged 80 or older	168.1	142.2

Note: Data are based on measured weight of a sample of the civilian noninstitutionalized population.
Source: National Center for Health Statistics, Anthropometric Reference Data for Children and Adults: United States, 2003–2006, National Health Statistics Reports, Number 10, 2008, Internet site http://www.cdc.gov/nchs/products/pubs/pubd/nhsr/nhsr.htm; calculations by New Strategist

Table 3.3 Weight Status by Sex and Age, 2007–10

(percent distribution of people aged 20 or older by weight status, sex, and age, 2007–10)

	total	healthy weight	overweight total	overweight obese
Total people	**100.0%**	**29.6%**	**68.7%**	**34.9%**
Total men	**100.0**	**25.8**	**73.2**	**33.9**
Aged 20 to 34	100.0	37.5	61.1	27.1
Aged 35 to 44	100.0	19.8	80.2	37.2
Aged 45 to 54	100.0	21.8	76.8	36.6
Aged 55 to 64	100.0	19.4	79.8	37.3
Aged 65 to 74	100.0	21.6	77.5	41.5
Aged 75 or older	100.0	25.4	73.2	26.6
Total women	**100.0**	**33.2**	**64.5**	**35.9**
Aged 20 to 34	100.0	41.1	55.4	30.4
Aged 35 to 44	100.0	34.4	63.9	37.1
Aged 45 to 54	100.0	30.7	66.2	36.9
Aged 55 to 64	100.0	26.7	72.2	43.4
Aged 65 to 74	100.0	23.9	74.2	40.3
Aged 75 or older	100.0	35.4	63.2	28.7

Note: Data are based on measured height and weight of a sample of the civilian noninstitutionalized population. "Overweight" is defined as a body mass index of 25 or higher. "Obese" is defined as a body mass index of 30 or higher. Body mass index is calculated by dividing weight in kilograms by height in meters squared. Percentages do not add to 100 because "underweight" is not shown.
Source: National Center for Health Statistics, Health, United States, 2011, Internet site http://www.cdc.gov/nchs/hus.htm

Table 3.4 Leisure-Time Physical Activity Level by Sex and Age, 2010

(percent distribution of people aged 18 or older by leisure-time physical activity level, by sex and age, 2010)

	total	physically inactive	met at least one guideline	met aerobic and muscle-strengthening guidelines
Total people	**100.0%**	**49.5%**	**30.1%**	**20.4%**
Aged 18 to 24	100.0	39.4	31.0	29.6
Aged 25 to 44	100.0	44.4	31.3	24.3
Aged 45 to 54	100.0	48.9	31.9	19.2
Aged 55 to 64	100.0	53.7	30.4	15.9
Aged 65 or older	100.0	64.6	25.0	10.4
Total men	**100.0**	**43.8**	**31.1**	**25.1**
Aged 18 to 44	100.0	37.1	31.1	31.8
Aged 45 to 54	100.0	45.2	33.9	20.9
Aged 55 to 64	100.0	50.1	30.8	19.1
Aged 65 to 74	100.0	55.6	27.8	16.6
Aged 75 or older	100.0	62.8	28.1	9.1
Total women	**100.0**	**54.0**	**29.5**	**16.5**
Aged 18 to 44	100.0	49.0	31.4	19.6
Aged 45 to 54	100.0	52.4	30.1	17.5
Aged 55 to 64	100.0	57.0	29.9	13.1
Aged 65 to 74	100.0	63.6	25.4	11.0
Aged 75 or older	100.0	75.3	20.1	4.6

Note: The federal government recommends that adults perform at least 150 minutes (2 hours and 30 minutes) a week of moderate-intensity, or 75 minutes (1 hour and 15 minutes) a week of vigorous-intensity aerobic physical activity, or an equivalent combination. Aerobic activity should be performed in episodes of at least 10 minutes, and preferably should be spread throughout the week. It also recommends that adults perform muscle-strengthening activities that are moderate or high intensity and involve all major muscle groups on two or more days a week.
Source: National Center for Health Statistics, Health United States, 2011, Internet site http://www.cdc.gov/nchs/hus.htm

Americans Report on Their Sexual Behavior

Over half of 15-to-19-year-olds are sexually experienced.

Every few years the federal government fields the National Survey of Family Growth (NSFG), which examines the sexual behavior, contraceptive use, and childbearing patterns of Americans aged 15 to 44. Results from the 2006–08 survey are now available from the National Center for Health Statistics.

Overall, about nine of ten men and women aged 15 to 44 have had at least one opposite-sex partner in their lifetime. Among 15-to-19-year-olds, 57 percent of men and 52 percent of women are sexually experienced. By the 25-to-29 age group, the figure exceeds 90 percent. Men aged 30 to 34 have had a median of 5.7 opposite-sex partners in their lifetime, and women in the age group have had a median of 4.2 partners.

More than 93 percent of men and a smaller 83 percent of women aged 15 to 44 identify themselves as attracted only to the opposite sex. A tiny 2 percent of men and 1 percent of women identify themselves as homosexual, and another 1 percent of men and 3.5 percent of women say they are bisexual. Self-identified homosexuality is likely to be underreported. Evidence of underreporting can be found in the fact that a larger 5 percent of men and 12.5 percent of women report sexual activity with a same-sex partner in their lifetime.

■ Twenty-one percent of men and 8 percent of women report having 15 or more opposite-sex partners in their lifetime.

Sexual experience rises above 90 percent in the 25-to-29 age group

(percent of people aged 15 to 34 who have had at least one opposite-sex partner during their lifetime, by sex and age, 2006–08)

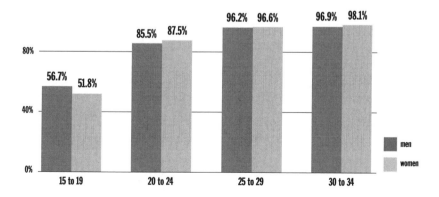

Table 3.5 Lifetime Sexual Activity of 15-to-44-Year-Olds by Sex, 2006–08

(number of people aged 15 to 44 and percent distribution by sexual experience with opposite-sex partners during lifetime, by sex and age, 2006–08; numbers in thousands)

| | total | | number of opposite-sex partners in lifetime | | | | | | | |
	number	percent	none	1 or more	1	2	3 to 6	7 to 14	15 or more	median
Total men 15–44	**62,199**	**100.0%**	**11.4%**	**88.6%**	**15.0%**	**7.6%**	**26.5%**	**18.1%**	**21.4%**	**5.1**
Aged 15 to 19	10,777	100.0	43.3	56.7	21.2	9.4	17.6	5.4	3.1	1.8
Aged 20 to 24	10,404	100.0	14.4	85.5	19.1	8.0	26.1	18.1	14.2	4.1
Aged 25 to 29	10,431	100.0	3.8	96.2	11.8	8.9	29.5	22.9	23.1	5.7
Aged 30 to 34	9,575	100.0	3.1	96.9	14.2	6.1	26.6	21.7	28.3	6.4
Aged 35 to 39	10,318	100.0	1.4	98.8	13.3	5.6	29.7	19.6	30.6	6.2
Aged 40 to 44	10,695	100.0	1.3	98.8	10.3	7.2	29.7	21.6	30.0	6.4
Total women 15–44	**61,865**	**100.0**	**11.3**	**88.8**	**22.2**	**10.7**	**31.6**	**16.0**	**8.3**	**3.2**
Aged 15 to 19	10,431	100.0	48.1	51.8	22.7	8.2	15.7	4.1	1.1	1.4
Aged 20 to 24	10,140	100.0	12.6	87.5	24.5	12.5	31.6	11.7	7.2	2.6
Aged 25 to 29	10,250	100.0	3.4	96.6	20.0	12.4	31.0	20.4	12.8	3.6
Aged 30 to 34	9,587	100.0	1.9	98.1	20.9	10.6	31.9	21.3	13.4	4.2
Aged 35 to 39	10,475	100.0	0.9	99.1	22.2	9.9	38.3	20.8	7.9	3.5
Aged 40 to 44	10,982	100.0	0.4	99.7	22.4	10.8	40.5	18.0	8.0	3.4

Source: National Center for Health Statistics, Sexual Behavior, Sexual Attraction, and Sexual Identity in the United States: Data from the 2006–2008 National Survey of Family Growth, National Health Statistics Reports, No. 36, 2011, Internet site http://www.cdc.gov/nchs/nsfg/new_nsfg.htm; calculations by New Strategist

Table 3.6 Sexual Attraction among 18-to-44-Year-Olds, 2006–08

(number of people aged 18 to 44 and percent distribution by sexual attraction, by sex and age, 2006–08; numbers in thousands)

| | total | | only opposite sex | mostly opposite sex | equally to both | mostly same sex | only same sex | not sure |
	number	percent						
Total men 18 to 44	**55,399**	**100.0%**	**93.5%**	**3.7%**	**0.5%**	**0.7%**	**1.2%**	**0.4%**
Aged 18 to 19	4,460	100.0	91.7	5.7	–	0.7	1.1	0.6
Aged 20 to 24	9,883	100.0	91.3	5.8	1.1	0.5	0.7	0.7
Aged 25 to 29	9,226	100.0	94.3	3.1	0.3	0.7	1.3	0.4
Aged 30 to 34	10,138	100.0	95.3	2.7	–	0.5	0.8	0.4
Aged 35 to 44	21,692	100.0	93.6	3.1	0.4	0.9	1.7	0.2
Total women 18 to 44	**56,032**	**100.0**	**83.3**	**11.9**	**2.8**	**0.6**	**0.8**	**0.7**
Aged 18 to 19	4,598	100.0	82.4	9.4	4.8	0.9	1.3	1.2
Aged 20 to 24	10,140	100.0	77.6	16.7	3.7	0.8	0.8	0.4
Aged 25 to 29	10,250	100.0	81.4	12.9	3.8	0.5	1.1	0.4
Aged 30 to 34	9,587	100.0	81.4	13.0	2.8	0.7	0.9	1.2
Aged 35 to 44	21,457	100.0	87.9	9.1	1.4	0.4	0.5	0.6

Note: "–" means sample is too small to make a reliable estimate.
Source: National Center for Health Statistics, Sexual Behavior, Sexual Attraction, and Sexual Identity in the United States: Data from the 2006–2008 National Survey of Family Growth, National Health Statistics Reports, No. 36, 2011, Internet site http://www.cdc.gov/nchs/nsfg/new_nsfg.htm; calculations by New Strategist

Table 3.7 Sexual Orientation of 18-to-44-Year-Olds, 2006–08

(number of people aged 18 to 44 and percent distribution by sexual orientation, by sex and age, 2006–08; numbers in thousands)

	total		heterosexual or straight	homosexual or gay	bisexual
	number	percent			
Total men 18 to 44	**55,399**	**100.0%**	**95.7%**	**1.7%**	**1.1%**
Aged 18 to 19	4,460	100.0	96.6	1.6	1.1
Aged 20 to 24	9,883	100.0	95.1	1.2	2.0
Aged 25 to 29	9,226	100.0	96.3	1.7	0.8
Aged 30 to 34	10,138	100.0	96.2	1.5	0.6
Aged 35 to 44	21,692	100.0	95.2	2.1	1.0
Total women 18 to 44	**56,032**	**100.0**	**93.7**	**1.1**	**3.5**
Aged 18 to 19	4,598	100.0	90.1	1.9	5.8
Aged 20 to 24	10,140	100.0	90.4	1.3	6.3
Aged 25 to 29	10,250	100.0	91.9	1.2	5.4
Aged 30 to 34	9,587	100.0	94.4	1.1	2.9
Aged 35 to 44	21,457	100.0	96.6	0.7	1.1

Note: Numbers do not add to 100 percent because "something else" and "not reported" are not shown.
Source: National Center for Health Statistics, Sexual Behavior, Sexual Attraction, and Sexual Identity in the United States: Data from the 2006–2008 National Survey of Family Growth, National Health Statistics Reports, No. 36, 2011, Internet site http://www.cdc.gov/nchs/nsfg/new_nsfg.htm; calculations by New Strategist

Table 3.8 Lifetime Same-Sex Sexual Activity of 15-to-44-Year-Olds, 2006–08

(percent of people aged 15 to 44 reporting any sexual activity with same-sex partners in their lifetime, by age and sex, 2006–08)

	men	women
Total aged 15 to 44	**5.2%**	**12.5%**
Aged 15 to 19	2.5	11.0
Aged 20 to 24	5.6	15.8
Aged 25 to 29	5.2	15.0
Aged 30 to 34	4.0	14.2
Aged 35 to 39	5.7	11.5
Aged 40 to 44	8.1	7.9

Source: National Center for Health Statistics, Sexual Behavior, Sexual Attraction, and Sexual Identity in the United States: Data from the 2006–2008 National Survey of Family Growth, National Health Statistics Reports, No. 36, 2011, Internet site http://www.cdc.gov/nchs/nsfg/new_nsfg.htm; calculations by New Strategist

Fertility Rates Are Falling

The Great Recession has forced many women to delay having children.

The women of the Millennial generation are in their prime childbearing years, but many are postponing having children. Fertility rates among women under age 35 had been rising in the heady days of easy money during the housing bubble. Then the bubble popped, the Great Recession hit, and fertility rates plummeted. Between 2007 and 2010, the overall fertility rate fell 8 percent, with double-digit declines among women under age 25.

Whether the current downturn in fertility is permanent or temporary remains to be seen. Studies show that economic uncertainty lowers fertility, and the Great Recession has caused much uncertainty, which continues despite the recession's end.

■ The birth rate among women aged 20 to 24 fell to an all-time low in 2010.

Birth rate peaks in the 25-to-29 age group

(births per 1,000 women in age group, 2010)

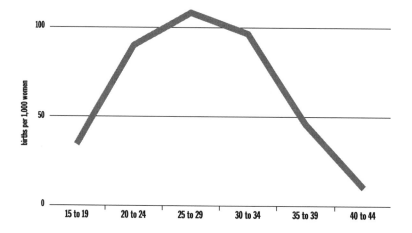

Table 3.9 **Fertility Rate by Age, 1990 to 2010**

(number of births per 1,000 women aged 15 to 44, and per 1,000 women in specified age group, 1990 to 2010; percent change for selected years)

	total	15 to 19	20 to 24	25 to 29	30 to 34	35 to 39	40 to 44	45 to 49
2010	64.1	34.3	90.0	108.3	96.6	45.9	10.2	0.7
2009	66.2	37.9	96.2	111.5	97.5	46.1	10.0	0.7
2008	68.6	41.5	103.0	115.1	99.3	46.9	9.8	0.7
2007	69.5	42.5	106.3	117.5	99.9	47.5	9.5	0.6
2006	68.5	41.9	105.9	116.7	97.7	47.3	9.4	0.6
2005	66.7	40.4	102.2	115.6	95.9	46.3	9.1	0.6
2004	66.3	41.1	101.7	115.5	95.3	45.4	8.9	0.5
2003	66.1	41.6	102.6	115.6	95.1	43.8	8.7	0.5
2002	64.8	43.0	103.6	113.6	91.5	41.4	8.3	0.5
2001	65.3	45.3	106.2	113.4	91.9	40.6	8.1	0.5
2000	65.9	47.7	109.7	113.5	91.2	39.7	8.0	0.5
1999	64.4	48.8	107.9	111.2	87.1	37.8	7.4	0.4
1998	64.3	50.3	108.4	110.2	85.2	36.9	7.4	0.4
1997	63.6	51.3	107.3	108.3	83.0	35.7	7.1	0.4
1996	64.1	53.5	107.8	108.6	82.1	34.9	6.8	0.3
1995	64.6	56.0	107.5	108.8	81.1	34.0	6.6	0.3
1994	65.9	58.2	109.2	111.0	80.4	33.4	6.4	0.3
1993	67.0	59.0	111.3	113.2	79.9	32.7	6.1	0.3
1992	68.4	60.3	113.7	115.7	79.6	32.3	5.9	0.3
1991	69.3	61.8	115.3	117.2	79.2	31.9	5.5	0.2
1990	70.9	59.9	116.5	120.2	80.8	31.7	5.5	0.2
Percent change								
2007 to 2010	−7.8%	−19.3%	−15.3%	−7.8%	−3.3%	−3.4%	7.4%	16.7%
2000 to 2010	−2.7	−28.1	−18.0	−4.6	5.9	15.6	27.5	40.0
1990 to 2010	−9.6	−42.7	−22.7	−9.9	19.6	44.8	85.5	250.0

Source: National Center for Health Statistics, Birth Data, Internet site http://www.cdc.gov/nchs/births.htm; calculations by New Strategist

Most Women Are Mothers by Age 30

Among women aged 30 to 34, the largest share has had two children.

The proportion of women who have never had a child falls from 95 percent among 15-to-19-year-olds to a much smaller (but still substantial) 19 percent among women aged 40 to 44. Overall, 53 percent of women aged 15 to 44 have had at least one child. The largest share (20 percent) has had two.

Six percent of women aged 15 to 44 had a baby in the past year, according to a 2010 survey. Women aged 25 to 29 are most likely to have had a baby in the past year, with nearly 10 percent giving birth. By race and Hispanic origin, Hispanics are most likely to have had a baby in the past year, at 7 percent. Six percent of native-born women aged 15 to 44 had a child in the past year. Among foreign-born women, the figure is a larger 8 percent.

■ The two-child family has been the norm in the United States for several decades.

Most women aged 25 or older have had at least one child

(percent of women aged 15 to 44 who have had one or more children, by age, 2010)

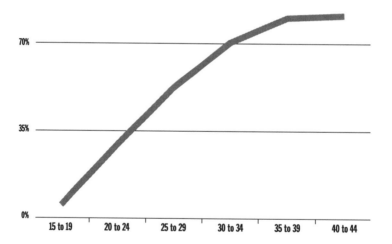

Table 3.10 Number of Children Born to Women Aged 15 to 44, 2010

(total number of women aged 15 to 44, and percent distribution by number of children ever borne, by age, 2010; numbers in thousands)

	total		number of children							
	number	percent	none	one or more	one	two	three	four	five or six	seven or more
Total aged 15 to 44	**61,481**	**100.0%**	**47.1%**	**52.9%**	**16.9%**	**20.4%**	**10.4%**	**3.4%**	**1.5%**	**0.3%**
Aged 15 to 19	10,273	100.0	94.6	5.3	4.4	0.6	0.3	0.0	0.0	0.0
Aged 20 to 24	10,493	100.0	70.5	29.5	18.1	9.0	2.0	0.3	0.1	0.0
Aged 25 to 29	10,501	100.0	47.6	52.4	22.7	18.7	7.8	2.3	0.8	0.1
Aged 30 to 34	9,923	100.0	29.7	70.4	19.2	29.2	14.3	5.2	2.1	0.4
Aged 35 to 39	9,917	100.0	19.7	80.2	18.5	32.6	19.7	5.9	3.1	0.4
Aged 40 to 44	10,374	100.0	18.8	81.2	18.5	33.3	19.1	6.8	2.7	0.8

Source: Bureau of the Census, Fertility of American Women: 2010, Detailed Tables, Internet site http://www.census.gov/hhes/fertility/data/cps/2010.html

Table 3.11 Women Giving Birth in the Past Year, 2010

(total number of women aged 15 to 44, number and percent who gave birth in the past year, and number and percent who had a first birth in past year, by age, 2010; numbers in thousands)

	total	gave birth in past year		first birth in past year	
		number	percent	number	percent
Total aged 15 to 44	**61,481**	**3,686**	**6.0%**	**1,467**	**2.4%**
Age					
Aged 15 to 19	10,273	301	2.9	229	2.2
Aged 20 to 24	10,493	916	8.7	462	4.4
Aged 25 to 29	10,501	1,014	9.7	405	3.9
Aged 30 to 34	9,923	820	8.3	225	2.3
Aged 35 to 39	9,917	503	5.1	126	1.3
Aged 40 to 44	10,374	131	1.3	20	0.2
Race and Hispanic origin					
Asian	3,616	251	6.9	102	2.8
Black	9,468	600	6.3	202	2.1
Hispanic	10,845	756	7.0	296	2.7
Non-Hispanic white	37,271	2,069	5.6	868	2.3
Nativity status					
Native born	51,981	2,952	5.7	1,221	2.3
Foreign born	9,501	734	7.7	246	2.6
Region					
Northeast	10,942	648	5.9	254	2.3
Midwest	13,124	802	6.1	308	2.3
South	22,799	1,345	5.9	545	2.4
West	14,617	891	6.1	360	2.5

Note: Numbers by race and Hispanic origin do not add to total because Asians and blacks are those who identify themselves as being of the race alone and those who identify themselves as being of the race in combination with other races, and because Hispanics may be of any race. Non-Hispanic whites are those who identify themselves as being white alone and not Hispanic. Source: Bureau of the Census, Fertility of American Women: 2010, Detailed Tables, Internet site http://www.census.gov/hhes/ fertility/data/cps/2010.html

The Millennial Generation Dominates Births

More than 85 percent of births are to women of the Millennial generation.

Despite an increase in the number of older mothers during the past few decades, the 52 percent majority of women who give birth are in their twenties. Women aged 25 to 29 account for the single largest share of births—28 percent in 2010. Interestingly, because of the sharper fertility decline among younger women, the 30-to-34 age group now accounts for a slightly larger share of births (24.1 percent) than the 20-to-24 age group (23.8 percent).

Non-Hispanic whites accounted for 54 percent of births in 2010, the figure falling below 50 percent among babies born to women under age 25. Hispanics account for nearly one in four births, blacks for 15 percent, and Asians for 6 percent. Among Asians, the largest share of babies are born to women aged 30 to 34. Many Asian women postpone childbearing until their thirties because most spend much of their twenties in college.

Among Millennials who gave birth in 2010, 43 percent were having their first child and 31 percent their second. A substantial 25 percent were having their third or higher order birth.

■ The Millennial generation has replaced Generation X as the dominant group of the nation's child-rearing parents.

Women aged 25 to 29 account for the largest share of newborns

(percent distribution of births by age of mother, 2010)

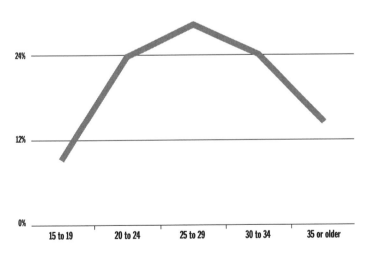

Table 3.12 Births by Age, Race, and Hispanic Origin, 2010

(number and percent distribution of births by age, race, and Hispanic origin, 2010)

	total	American Indian	Asian	non-Hispanic black	Hispanic	non-Hispanic white
Total births	**4,000,279**	**46,760**	**246,915**	**589,139**	**946,000**	**2,161,669**
Under age 15	4,500	100	50	1,572	1,811	967
Aged 15 to 34	3,416,080	42,688	187,684	524,142	823,548	1,831,581
Aged 15 to 19	367,752	7,409	6,263	88,142	121,849	143,984
Aged 20 to 24	951,900	15,746	27,738	187,754	254,868	464,645
Aged 25 to 29	1,134,008	12,223	68,379	147,549	255,236	648,473
Aged 30 to 34	962,420	7,310	85,304	100,697	191,595	574,479
Aged 35 to 39	464,943	3,212	48,095	49,693	97,652	264,044
Aged 40 to 44	107,011	722	10,315	12,752	21,793	60,572
Aged 45 to 54	7,744	38	770	980	1,196	4,504

PERCENT DISTRIBUTION BY RACE AND HISPANIC ORIGIN

	total	American Indian	Asian	non-Hispanic black	Hispanic	non-Hispanic white
Total births	**100.0%**	**1.2%**	**6.2%**	**14.7%**	**23.6%**	**54.0%**
Under age 15	100.0	2.2	1.1	34.9	40.2	21.5
Aged 15 to 34	100.0	1.2	5.5	15.3	24.1	53.6
Aged 15 to 19	100.0	2.0	1.7	24.0	33.1	39.2
Aged 20 to 24	100.0	1.7	2.9	19.7	26.8	48.8
Aged 25 to 29	100.0	1.1	6.0	13.0	22.5	57.2
Aged 30 to 34	100.0	0.8	8.9	10.5	19.9	59.7
Aged 35 to 39	100.0	0.7	10.3	10.7	21.0	56.8
Aged 40 to 44	100.0	0.7	9.6	11.9	20.4	56.6
Aged 45 to 54	100.0	0.5	9.9	12.7	15.4	58.2

PERCENT DISTRIBUTION BY AGE

	total	American Indian	Asian	non-Hispanic black	Hispanic	non-Hispanic white
Total births	**100.0%**	**100.0%**	**100.0%**	**100.0%**	**100.0%**	**100.0%**
Under age 15	0.1	0.2	0.0	0.3	0.2	0.0
Aged 15 to 34	85.4	91.3	76.0	89.0	87.1	84.7
Aged 15 to 19	9.2	15.8	2.5	15.0	12.9	6.7
Aged 20 to 24	23.8	33.7	11.2	31.9	26.9	21.5
Aged 25 to 29	28.3	26.1	27.7	25.0	27.0	30.0
Aged 30 to 34	24.1	15.6	34.5	17.1	20.3	26.6
Aged 35 to 39	11.6	6.9	19.5	8.4	10.3	12.2
Aged 40 to 44	2.7	1.5	4.2	2.2	2.3	2.8
Aged 45 to 54	0.2	0.1	0.3	0.2	0.1	0.2

Note: Births by race and Hispanic origin do not add to total because Hispanics may be of any race and "not stated" is not shown.
Source: National Center for Health Statistics, Births: Preliminary Data for 2010, National Vital Statistics Reports, Vol. 60, No. 2, 2011, Internet site http://www.cdc.gov/nchs/births.htm; calculations by New Strategist"

Table 3.13 Births by Age of Mother and Birth Order, 2010

(number and percent distribution of births by age of mother and birth order, 2010)

	total	first child	second child	third child	fourth or later child
Total births	**4,000,279**	**1,604,181**	**1,248,376**	**654,769**	**461,280**
Under age 15	4,500	4,375	74	7	2
Aged 15 to 34	3,416,080	1,468,697	1,066,934	526,979	327,278
Aged 15 to 19	367,752	298,160	57,181	8,392	1,158
Aged 20 to 24	951,900	472,391	309,206	118,836	43,964
Aged 25 to 29	1,134,008	420,183	371,861	204,848	128,631
Aged 30 to 34	962,420	277,963	328,686	194,903	153,525
Aged 35 to 39	464,943	105,097	149,453	104,573	101,547
Aged 40 to 44	107,011	23,937	29,971	21,892	30,133
Aged 45 to 54	7,744	2,075	1,945	1,317	2,319
PERCENT DISTRIBUTION BY BIRTH ORDER					
Total births	**100.0%**	**40.1%**	**31.2%**	**16.4%**	**11.5%**
Under age 15	100.0	97.2	1.6	0.2	0.0
Aged 15 to 34	100.0	43.0	31.2	15.4	9.6
Aged 15 to 19	100.0	81.1	15.5	2.3	0.3
Aged 20 to 24	100.0	49.6	32.5	12.5	4.6
Aged 25 to 29	100.0	37.1	32.8	18.1	11.3
Aged 30 to 34	100.0	28.9	34.2	20.3	16.0
Aged 35 to 39	100.0	22.6	32.1	22.5	21.8
Aged 40 to 44	100.0	22.4	28.0	20.5	28.2
Aged 45 to 54	100.0	26.8	25.1	17.0	29.9
PERCENT DISTRIBUTION BY AGE					
Total births	**100.0%**	**100.0%**	**100.0%**	**100.0%**	**100.0%**
Under age 15	0.1	0.3	0.0	0.0	0.0
Aged 15 to 34	85.4	91.6	85.5	80.5	70.9
Aged 15 to 19	9.2	18.6	4.6	1.3	0.3
Aged 20 to 24	23.8	29.4	24.8	18.1	9.5
Aged 25 to 29	28.3	26.2	29.8	31.3	27.9
Aged 30 to 34	24.1	17.3	26.3	29.8	33.3
Aged 35 to 39	11.6	6.6	12.0	16.0	22.0
Aged 40 to 44	2.7	1.5	2.4	3.3	6.5
Aged 45 to 54	0.2	0.1	0.2	0.2	0.5

Note: Numbers do not add to total because "not stated" is not shown.
Source: National Center for Health Statistics, Births: Preliminary Data for 2010, National Vital Statistics Reports, Vol. 60, No. 2, 2011, Internet site http://www.cdc.gov/nchs/births.htm; calculations by New Strategist"

Many Millennial Mothers Are Not Married

Out-of-wedlock births fall with age.

More than 40 percent of babies born in 2010 had a mother who was not married. There are sharp differences by age in the percentage of new mothers who are not married, however. The younger the woman, the more likely she is to give birth out of wedlock.

Among babies born to women under age 25 in 2010, most were born to single mothers. The figure falls to 34 percent in the 25-to-29 age group. Among babies born to women aged 30 or older, from 20 to 22 percent had a single mother.

■ Out-of-wedlock childbearing has increased enormously over the past few decades and has become common even among older mothers.

Sixty-three percent of births to women aged 20 to 24 are out of wedlock

(percent of babies born to unmarried women, by age, 2010)

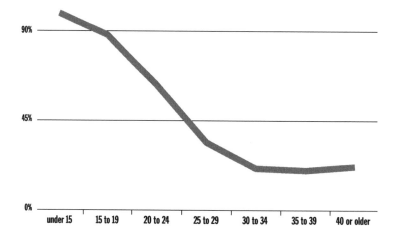

Table 3.14 Births to Unmarried Women by Age, 2010

(total number of births and number and percent to unmarried women, by age, 2010)

| | total | unmarried women | | |
		number	percent distribution	percent of total
Total births	**4,000,279**	**1,633,785**	**100.0%**	**40.8%**
Under age 15	4,500	4,467	0.3	99.3
Aged 15 to 19	367,752	323,922	19.8	88.1
Aged 20 to 24	951,900	600,971	36.8	63.1
Aged 25 to 29	1,134,008	384,955	23.6	33.9
Aged 30 to 34	962,420	203,527	12.5	21.1
Aged 35 to 39	464,943	91,085	5.6	19.6
Aged 40 or older	114,755	24,858	1.5	21.7

Source: National Center for Health Statistics, Births: Preliminary Data for 2010, National Vital Statistics Reports, Vol. 60, No. 2, 2011, Internet site http://www.cdc.gov/nchs/births.htm; calculations by New Strategist

Caesarean Deliveries Are Common among Women of All Ages

The rate is highest among older women, however.

Delayed childbearing can have an unanticipated cost. The older a woman is when she has a child, the greater the likelihood of complications that necessitate Caesarean delivery.

Among babies born in 2009, nearly 33 percent were delivered by Caesarean section. The figure ranges from only 23 percent of babies born to women under age 20 to 43 percent of babies born to women aged 35 to 39 and nearly half (49 percent) of those born to women aged 40 or older.

■ As women delay childbearing, the rate of Caesarean delivery increases. With new fertility technologies enabling more women to have children later in life, the rate is likely to rise further.

Younger mothers are least likely to require a Caesarean delivery

(percent of births delivered by Caesarean section, by age of mother, 2009)

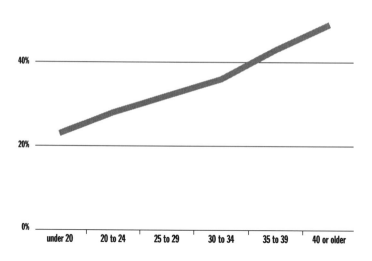

Table 3.15 Births by Age and Method of Delivery, 2009

(number and percent distribution of births by age and method of delivery, 2009)

	total births	vaginal	Caesarean
Total births	**4,130,665**	**2,764,285**	**1,353,572**
Under age 20	414,831	318,124	95,802
Aged 20 to 24	1,005,982	717,208	285,906
Aged 25 to 29	1,166,787	794,512	368,707
Aged 30 to 34	955,246	606,937	345,157
Aged 35 to 39	474,103	270,359	201,936
Aged 40 or older	113,716	57,145	56,064
PERCENT DISTRIBUTION BY METHOD OF DELIVERY			
Total births	**100.0%**	**66.9%**	**32.8%**
Under age 20	100.0	76.7	23.1
Aged 20 to 24	100.0	71.3	28.4
Aged 25 to 29	100.0	68.1	31.6
Aged 30 to 34	100.0	63.5	36.1
Aged 35 to 39	100.0	57.0	42.6
Aged 40 or older	100.0	50.3	49.3
PERCENT DISTRIBUTION BY AGE			
Total births	**100.0%**	**100.0%**	**100.0%**
Under age 20	10.0	11.5	7.1
Aged 20 to 24	24.4	25.9	21.1
Aged 25 to 29	28.2	28.7	27.2
Aged 30 to 34	23.1	22.0	25.5
Aged 35 to 39	11.5	9.8	14.9
Aged 40 or older	2.8	2.1	4.1

Note: Numbers do not add to total because "not stated" is not shown.
Source: National Center for Health Statistics, Births: Final Data for 2009, National Vital Statistics Reports, Vol. 60, No. 1, 2011, Internet site http://www.cdc.gov/nchs/births.htm; calculations by New Strategist

Cigarette Smoking Is above Average among Millennials

Many young adults have smoked cigarettes in the past month.

Cigarette smoking has been declining in the population as a whole, but among young adults it remains stubbornly high. Overall, 23 percent of people aged 12 or older smoked a cigarette in the past month, according to a 2010 survey. The proportion surpasses the national average among 18-year-olds and rises as high as 37 percent among people in their twenties.

A separate government survey shows that 20 to 24 percent of people ranging in age from 18 to 34 are current smokers. Among 18-to-24-year-olds, 73 percent say they have never smoked. The figure drops to just 58.5 percent in the 25-to-34 age group.

■ Although smoking is becoming less common, many young adults experiment with cigarettes and some will become lifelong smokers.

A large share of Millennials smoke cigarettes

(percent distribution of people age 18 to 34 by cigarette smoking status, 2010)

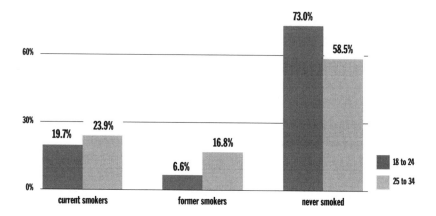

Table 3.16 Cigarette Smoking among People Aged 12 or Older, 2010

(percent of people aged 12 or older reporting any, past year, and past month use of cigarettes, 2010)

	ever smoked	smoked in past year	smoked in past month
Total people	**64.2%**	**27.0%**	**23.0%**
Aged 12 to 17	20.3	14.1	8.3
Aged 18	49.1	38.4	28.0
Aged 19	57.4	44.0	33.8
Aged 20	61.2	43.7	34.1
Aged 21	62.5	43.7	35.8
Aged 22	66.0	45.6	36.8
Aged 23	66.5	42.9	34.4
Aged 24	69.1	44.8	36.8
Aged 25	67.8	41.9	35.2
Aged 26 to 29	72.4	41.8	36.8
Aged 30 to 34	71.5	35.7	30.9
Aged 35 to 39	66.7	29.3	24.7
Aged 40 to 44	69.7	29.8	26.5
Aged 45 to 49	73.2	28.7	26.2
Aged 50 to 54	73.0	27.9	25.2
Aged 55 to 59	72.2	25.4	22.8
Aged 60 to 64	69.3	18.7	16.9
Aged 65 or older	65.8	10.4	9.1

Source: SAMHSA, Office of Applied Studies, 2010 National Survey on Drug Use and Health, Detailed Tables, Internet site http://www.samhsa.gov/data/NSDUH/2k10ResultsTables/Web/HTML/TOC.htm

Table 3.17 Cigarette Smoking Status by Age, 2010

(percent distribution of people aged 18 or older by age and cigarette smoking status, 2010)

	total	current smokers total	smoke every day	smoke some days	former smoker	never smoked
Total people	**100.0%**	**17.2%**	**12.4%**	**4.8%**	**25.1%**	**56.6%**
Aged 18 to 24	100.0	19.7	12.9	6.8	6.6	73.0
Aged 25 to 34	100.0	23.9	16.9	7.0	16.8	58.5
Aged 35 to 44	100.0	18.2	13.2	5.0	18.4	63.5
Aged 45 to 54	100.0	19.4	14.7	4.7	24.4	54.7
Aged 55 to 64	100.0	15.9	11.9	4.0	34.5	49.0
Aged 65 or older	100.0	8.5	6.3	2.2	43.6	47.9

Source: Centers for Disease Control and Prevention, Behavioral Risk Factor Surveillance System Prevalence Data, 2010, Internet site http://apps.nccd.cdc.gov/brfss/

Most Young Adults Have Had a Drink in the Past Month

Drinking peaks among 21-year-olds.

More than half of Americans aged 12 or older have had an alcoholic beverage in the past month. The figure peaks at 72 percent among 21-year-olds, perhaps in celebration of the fact that they have reached legal drinking age. Few young adults wait until their 21st birthday before they have a drink, however. The majority of 20-year-olds have had alcohol in the past month.

Many young adults take part in binge drinking, meaning they have had five or more drinks on one occasion in the past month. More than 40 percent of people ranging in age from 21 to 25 have participated in binge drinking during the past month. More than one in ten in the age group has participated in heavy drinking—meaning they have binged at least five times during the month.

In another government survey asking people aged 18 or older whether they have had a drink in the past 30 days, nearly half of 18-to-24-year-olds said yes. The figure rises to 61 percent in the 25-to-34 age group.

■ Among young adults, heavy drinking is a bigger problem than drug use.

Most young adults do not wait for legal drinking age

(percent of people aged 18 to 24 who have had an alcoholic drink in the past 30 days, by age, 2010)

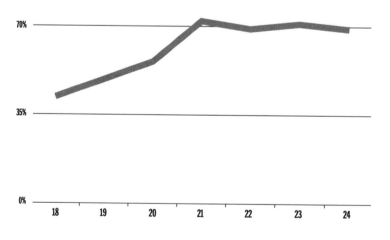

Table 3.18 Alcohol Use by People Aged 12 or Older, 2010

(percent of people aged 12 or older who drank alcoholic beverages during the past month, by level of alcohol use, 2010)

	drank at any time during past month	binge drinking during past month	heavy drinking during past month
Total people aged 12 or older	**51.8%**	**23.1%**	**6.7%**
Aged 18	41.6	28.5	8.2
Aged 19	49.4	34.3	12.2
Aged 20	55.8	37.3	13.7
Aged 21	71.6	47.9	17.7
Aged 22	68.9	45.5	16.3
Aged 23	70.9	45.7	14.5
Aged 24	68.7	44.5	13.1
Aged 25	70.0	43.8	14.0
Aged 26 to 29	65.3	38.6	11.4
Aged 30 to 34	63.9	34.6	9.3
Aged 35 to 39	60.5	28.6	7.8
Aged 40 to 44	61.1	26.5	7.5
Aged 45 to 49	58.9	25.0	7.2
Aged 50 to 54	57.6	20.6	6.0
Aged 55 to 59	52.7	16.9	5.2
Aged 60 to 64	51.6	13.8	3.3
Aged 65 or older	38.2	7.6	1.6

Note: "Binge drinking" is defined as having five or more drinks on the same occasion on at least one day in the 30 days prior to the survey. "Heavy drinking" is having five or more drinks on the same occasion on each of five or more days in 30 days prior to the survey.
Source: SAMHSA, Office of Applied Studies, 2010 National Survey on Drug Use and Health, Detailed Tables, Internet site http://www.samhsa.gov/data/NSDUH/2k10ResultsTables/Web/HTML/TOC.htm

Table 3.19 Alcohol Use by Age, 2010

(percent distribution of people aged 18 or older by whether they have had at least one drink of alcohol within the past 30 days, by age, 2010)

	total	yes	no
Total people	**100.0%**	**54.6%**	**45.4%**
Aged 18 to 24	100.0	48.3	51.7
Aged 25 to 34	100.0	61.0	39.0
Aged 35 to 44	100.0	60.2	39.8
Aged 45 to 54	100.0	57.7	42.3
Aged 55 to 64	100.0	53.6	46.4
Aged 65 or older	100.0	40.5	59.5

Source: Centers for Disease Control and Prevention, Behavioral Risk Factor Surveillance System Prevalence Data, 2010, Internet site http://apps.nccd.cdc.gov/brfss/

Drug Use Is Prevalent among Young Adults

At least one in five 18-to-23-year-olds has used an illicit drug in the past month.

Among Americans aged 12 or older, only 9 percent have used an illicit drug in the past month. Young adults are much more likely to be current drug users than the average person. The percentage of 18-to-23-year-olds who used an illicit drug in the past month ranges from 20 to 25 percent. For many, if not most, the illicit drug is marijuana.

Marijuana is widely used by young adults, and even the middle aged are likely to have used marijuana. The majority of people ranging in age from 21 to 59 (except for a slight dip below 50 percent among 35-to-39-year-olds) have used marijuana at some point in their lives. Among people aged 18 to 29, from 11 to 22 percent have used marijuana in the past month.

■ Support for legalizing marijuana is growing as Boomers and younger generations replace older people who are unfamiliar with the drug.

Many young adults use marijuana

(percent of people aged 18 to 24 who have used marijuana in the past month, by age, 2010)

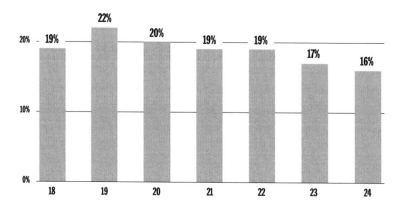

Table 3.20 Illicit Drug Use by People Aged 12 or Older, 2010

(percent of people aged 12 or older who ever used any illicit drug, who used an illicit drug in the past year, and who used an illicit drug in the past month, by age, 2010)

	ever used	used in past year	used in past month
Total people	**47.1%**	**15.3%**	**8.9%**
Aged 12 to 17	25.7	19.4	10.1
Aged 18	49.0	37.8	22.1
Aged 19	53.6	38.9	24.7
Aged 20	56.1	36.5	22.5
Aged 21	58.5	37.5	23.1
Aged 22	58.6	35.1	22.1
Aged 23	59.7	32.5	20.1
Aged 24	60.4	30.7	19.1
Aged 25	62.1	29.8	17.6
Aged 26 to 29	62.3	25.4	14.8
Aged 30 to 34	57.5	19.9	12.9
Aged 35 to 39	53.6	14.2	8.1
Aged 40 to 44	57.2	12.8	6.9
Aged 45 to 49	60.0	12.5	7.2
Aged 50 to 54	60.5	11.7	7.2
Aged 55 to 59	54.8	9.2	4.1
Aged 60 to 64	39.6	4.7	2.7
Aged 65 or older	16.0	1.7	1.1

Note: Illicit drugs include marijuana, hashish, cocaine (including crack), heroin, hallucinogens, inhalants, or any prescription-type psychotherapeutic used nonmedically.
Source: SAMHSA, Office of Applied Studies, 2010 National Survey on Drug Use and Health, Detailed Tables, Internet site http://www.samhsa.gov/data/NSDUH/2k10ResultsTables/Web/HTML/TOC.htm

Table 3.21 Marijuana Use by People Aged 12 or Older, 2010

(percent of people aged 12 or older who ever used marijuana, who used marijuana in the past year, and who used marijuana in the past month, by age, 2010)

	ever used	used in past year	used in past month
Total people	**41.9%**	**11.5%**	**6.9%**
Aged 12 to 17	17.0	14.0	7.4
Aged 18	42.6	32.9	19.3
Aged 19	47.4	33.7	21.6
Aged 20	49.6	31.7	20.0
Aged 21	53.3	31.8	19.3
Aged 22	53.1	30.1	19.3
Aged 23	55.0	27.9	17.1
Aged 24	54.3	25.5	16.4
Aged 25	55.7	23.6	14.0
Aged 26 to 29	56.6	20.0	11.4
Aged 30 to 34	51.6	15.5	9.8
Aged 35 to 39	46.9	9.8	5.8
Aged 40 to 44	51.8	8.3	4.9
Aged 45 to 49	56.2	8.4	5.0
Aged 50 to 54	56.2	7.3	4.9
Aged 55 to 59	50.2	6.5	3.1
Aged 60 to 64	36.5	3.3	1.9
Aged 65 or older	12.3	1.0	0.5

Source: SAMHSA, Office of Applied Studies, 2010 National Survey on Drug Use and Health, Detailed Tables, Internet site http://www.samhsa.gov/data/NSDUH/2k10ResultsTables/Web/HTML/TOC.htm

Millennials Are Most Likely to Lack Health Insurance

More than one in four has no insurance.

Before the Affordable Care Act allowed young adults under age 26 to remain on their parents' health insurance plan, the 18-to-24 age group was most likely to be without health insurance. Now that distinction belongs to people aged 25 to 34, 28 percent of whom were without health insurance in 2010. The figure is a smaller (27 percent) among 18-to-24-year-olds.

Most Americans obtain health insurance coverage through their employer. But among 18-to-24-year-olds, only 46 percent had employment-based coverage and just 12 percent had coverage through their own employer. In the 25-to-34 age group, the percentage with employment-based coverage increases to 56 percent, but fewer than half have coverage through their own employer.

Three out of four Millennials had a health care expense in 2009, according to the Medical Expenditure Panel Survey, with a median cost ranging between $665 and $940.

■ The Great Recession has greatly increased the number of people in their twenties and thirties without health insurance.

Many Americans do not have health insurance coverage

(percent of people aged 18 or older without health insurance, by age, 2010)

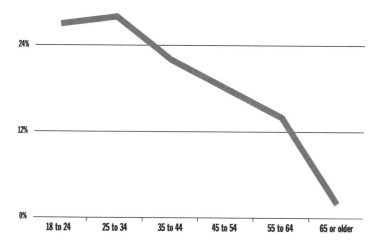

Table 3.22 Health Insurance Coverage by Age, 2010

(number and percent distribution of people by age and health insurance coverage status, 2010; numbers in thousands)

	total	with health insurance			not covered
		total	private	government	
Total people	**306,110**	**256,206**	**195,874**	**95,003**	**49,904**
Under age 65	266,931	217,819	173,206	58,374	49,112
Under age 18	74,916	67,609	44,620	28,385	7,307
Aged 18 to 24	29,651	21,573	17,407	5,579	8,078
Aged 25 to 34	41,584	29,780	25,314	5,746	11,804
Aged 35 to 44	39,842	31,149	27,426	5,046	8,692
Aged 45 to 54	43,954	36,035	31,695	6,110	7,919
Aged 55 to 64	36,984	31,672	26,743	7,509	5,312
Aged 65 or older	39,179	38,387	22,668	36,629	792

PERCENT DISTRIBUTION BY COVERAGE STATUS

	total	total	private	government	not covered
Total people	**100.0%**	**83.7%**	**64.0%**	**31.0%**	**16.3%**
Under age 65	100.0	81.6	64.9	21.9	18.4
Under age 18	100.0	90.2	59.6	37.9	9.8
Aged 18 to 24	100.0	72.8	58.7	18.8	27.2
Aged 25 to 34	100.0	71.6	60.9	13.8	28.4
Aged 35 to 44	100.0	78.2	68.8	12.7	21.8
Aged 45 to 54	100.0	82.0	72.1	13.9	18.0
Aged 55 to 64	100.0	85.6	72.3	20.3	14.4
Aged 65 or older	100.0	98.0	57.9	93.5	2.0

PERCENT DISTRIBUTION BY AGE

	total	total	private	government	not covered
Total people	**100.0%**	**100.0%**	**100.0%**	**100.0%**	**100.0%**
Under age 65	87.2	85.0	88.4	61.4	98.4
Under age 18	24.5	26.4	22.8	29.9	14.6
Aged 18 to 24	9.7	8.4	8.9	5.9	16.2
Aged 25 to 34	13.6	11.6	12.9	6.0	23.7
Aged 35 to 44	13.0	12.2	14.0	5.3	17.4
Aged 45 to 54	14.4	14.1	16.2	6.4	15.9
Aged 55 to 64	12.1	12.4	13.7	7.9	10.6
Aged 65 or older	12.8	15.0	11.6	38.6	1.6

Note: Numbers may not add to total because some people have more than one type of health insurance coverage.
Source: Bureau of the Census, Health Insurance, Internet site http://www.census.gov/hhes/www/cpstables/032011/health/toc .htm; calculations by New Strategist

Table 3.23 Private Health Insurance Coverage by Age, 2010

(number and percent distribution of people by age and private health insurance coverage status, 2010; numbers in thousands)

| | | with private health insurance | | | |
| | total | total | employment based | | direct purchase |
			total	own	
Total people	**306,110**	**195,874**	**169,264**	**87,471**	**30,147**
Under age 65	266,931	173,206	156,536	77,875	18,880
Under age 18	74,916	44,620	41,083	179	4,291
Aged 18 to 24	29,651	17,407	13,612	3,671	1,987
Aged 25 to 34	41,584	25,314	23,221	17,341	2,478
Aged 35 to 44	39,842	27,426	25,573	18,080	2,604
Aged 45 to 54	43,954	31,695	29,201	21,014	3,600
Aged 55 to 64	36,984	26,743	23,846	17,591	3,922
Aged 65 or older	39,179	22,668	12,728	9,597	11,267

PERCENT DISTRIBUTION BY COVERAGE STATUS

Total people	**100.0%**	**64.0%**	**55.3%**	**28.6%**	**9.8%**
Under age 65	100.0	64.9	58.6	29.2	7.1
Under age 18	100.0	59.6	54.8	0.2	5.7
Aged 18 to 24	100.0	58.7	45.9	12.4	6.7
Aged 25 to 34	100.0	60.9	55.8	41.7	6.0
Aged 35 to 44	100.0	68.8	64.2	45.4	6.5
Aged 45 to 54	100.0	72.1	66.4	47.8	8.2
Aged 55 to 64	100.0	72.3	64.5	47.6	10.6
Aged 65 or older	100.0	57.9	32.5	24.5	28.8

PERCENT DISTRIBUTION BY AGE

Total people	**100.0%**	**100.0%**	**100.0%**	**100.0%**	**100.0%**
Under age 65	87.2	88.4	92.5	89.0	62.6
Under age 18	24.5	22.8	24.3	0.2	14.2
Aged 18 to 24	9.7	8.9	8.0	4.2	6.6
Aged 25 to 34	13.6	12.9	13.7	19.8	8.2
Aged 35 to 44	13.0	14.0	15.1	20.7	8.6
Aged 45 to 54	14.4	16.2	17.3	24.0	11.9
Aged 55 to 64	12.1	13.7	14.1	20.1	13.0
Aged 65 or older	12.8	11.6	7.5	11.0	37.4

Note: Numbers may not add to total because some people have more than one type of health insurance coverage.
Source: Bureau of the Census, Health Insurance, Internet site http://www.census.gov/hhes/www/cpstables/032011/health/toc .htm; calculations by New Strategist

Table 3.24 Government Health Insurance Coverage by Age, 2010

(number and percent distribution of people by age and government health insurance coverage status, 2010; numbers in thousands)

	total	with government health insurance			
		total	Medicaid	Medicare	military
Total people	**306,110**	**95,003**	**48,580**	**44,327**	**12,848**
Under age 65	266,931	58,374	44,993	7,870	9,666
Under age 18	74,916	28,385	26,067	602	2,461
Aged 18 to 24	29,651	5,579	4,516	257	1,035
Aged 25 to 34	41,584	5,746	4,249	610	1,244
Aged 35 to 44	39,842	5,046	3,449	900	1,172
Aged 45 to 54	43,954	6,110	3,607	1,901	1,553
Aged 55 to 64	36,984	7,509	3,105	3,600	2,201
Aged 65 or older	39,179	36,629	3,587	36,457	3,182

PERCENT DISTRIBUTION BY COVERAGE STATUS

Total people	**100.0%**	**31.0%**	**15.9%**	**14.5%**	**4.2%**
Under age 65	100.0	21.9	16.9	2.9	3.6
Under age 18	100.0	37.9	34.8	0.8	3.3
Aged 18 to 24	100.0	18.8	15.2	0.9	3.5
Aged 25 to 34	100.0	13.8	10.2	1.5	3.0
Aged 35 to 44	100.0	12.7	8.7	2.3	2.9
Aged 45 to 54	100.0	13.9	8.2	4.3	3.5
Aged 55 to 64	100.0	20.3	8.4	9.7	6.0
Aged 65 or older	100.0	93.5	9.2	93.1	8.1

PERCENT DISTRIBUTION BY AGE

Total people	**100.0%**	**100.0%**	**100.0%**	**100.0%**	**100.0%**
Under age 65	87.2	61.4	92.6	17.8	75.2
Under age 18	24.5	29.9	53.7	1.4	19.2
Aged 18 to 24	9.7	5.9	9.3	0.6	8.1
Aged 25 to 34	13.6	6.0	8.7	1.4	9.7
Aged 35 to 44	13.0	5.3	7.1	2.0	9.1
Aged 45 to 54	14.4	6.4	7.4	4.3	12.1
Aged 55 to 64	12.1	7.9	6.4	8.1	17.1
Aged 65 or older	12.8	38.6	7.4	82.2	24.8

Note: Numbers may not add to total because some people have more than one type of health insurance coverage.
Source: Bureau of the Census, Health Insurance, Internet site http://www.census.gov/hhes/www/cpstables/032011/health/toc .htm; calculations by New Strategist

Table 3.25 Spending on Health Care by Age, 2009

(percent of people with health care expense, median expense per person, total expenses, and percent distribution of total expenses by source of payment, by age, 2009)

	total (thousands)	percent with expense	median expense per person	total expenses amount (millions)	total expenses percent distribution
Total people	**306,661**	**84.6%**	**$1,301**	**$1,259,456**	**100.0%**
Under age 18	74,836	86.5	548	143,261	11.4
Aged 18 to 24	29,787	74.0	665	54,682	4.3
Aged 25 to 34	40,861	74.3	920	96,666	7.7
Aged 35 to 44	40,495	79.7	1,174	126,885	10.1
Aged 45 to 49	21,892	83.3	1,492	90,712	7.2
Aged 50 to 54	22,699	88.8	1,958	104,769	8.3
Aged 55 to 59	19,335	91.6	2,314	123,052	9.8
Aged 60 to 64	16,417	90.9	3,129	126,709	10.1
Aged 65 or older	40,338	96.6	4,542	392,721	31.2

	percent distribution by source of payment total	out of pocket	private insurance	Medicare	Medicaid	other
Total people	**100.0%**	**14.6%**	**42.6%**	**23.8%**	**9.7%**	**9.3%**
Under age 18	100.0	12.9	57.3	1.2	21.7	6.9
Aged 18 to 24	100.0	17.6	48.5	0.7	20.2	13.0
Aged 25 to 34	100.0	16.6	55.3	2.7	14.8	10.5
Aged 35 to 44	100.0	16.1	59.5	6.3	9.2	8.8
Aged 45 to 49	100.0	15.8	55.4	9.5	8.4	10.9
Aged 50 to 54	100.0	16.6	52.3	11.7	9.9	9.5
Aged 55 to 59	100.0	15.2	56.2	10.1	8.3	10.1
Aged 60 to 64	100.0	15.1	52.5	12.6	7.8	12.0
Aged 65 or older	100.0	12.5	14.8	60.6	4.2	7.8

Note: "Other" insurance includes Department of Veterans Affairs (except Tricare), American Indian Health Service, state and local clinics, worker's compensation, homeowner's and automobile insurance, etc.
Source: Agency for Healthcare Research and Quality, Medical Expenditure Panel Survey, 2009, Internet site http://meps.ahrq
.gov/mepsweb/survey_comp/household.jsp; calculations by New Strategist

Table 3.26 Spending on Health Care by Generation, 2009

(percent of people with health care expense, median expense per person, total expenses, and percent distribution of total expenses by source of payment, by generation, 2009)

	total (thousands)	percent with expense	median expense per person	total expenses amount (millions)	total expenses percent distribution
Total people	**306,661**	**84.6%**	**$1,301**	**$1,259,456**	**100.0%**
iGeneration (under 15)	62,153	87.2	531	120,682	9.6
Millennials (15 to 32)	75,919	75.6	748	155,210	12.3
Generation X (33 to 44)	47,907	79.0	1,157	145,601	11.6
Baby Boomers (45 to 63)	77,800	88.3	2,108	426,592	33.9
Older Americans (64 or older)	42,882	96.3	4,477	411,371	32.7

	percent distribution by source of payment total	out of pocket	private insurance	Medicare	Medicaid	other
Total people	**100.0%**	**14.6%**	**42.6%**	**23.8%**	**9.7%**	**9.3%**
iGeneration (under 15)	100.0	12.0	58.3	1.3	21.9	6.5
Millennials (15 to 32)	100.0	17.3	53.1	1.3	16.7	11.6
Generation X (33 to 44)	100.0	16.1	58.3	6.2	10.8	8.6
Baby Boomers (45 to 63)	100.0	15.7	54.5	10.6	8.6	10.7
Older Americans (64 or older)	100.0	12.6	16.2	58.9	4.4	8.0

Note: "Other" insurance includes Department of Veterans Affairs (except Tricare), American Indian Health Service, state and local clinics, worker's compensation, homeowner's and automobile insurance, etc.
Source: Agency for Healthcare Research and Quality, Medical Expenditure Panel Survey, 2009, Internet site http://meps.ahrq .gov/mepsweb/survey_comp/household.jsp; calculations by New Strategist

Health Problems Are Few in the 18-to-44 Age Group

Lower back pain is by far the most common health condition in the age group.

Twenty-five percent of Americans aged 18 to 44 have experienced lower back pain for at least one full day in the past three months, making it the most common health condition in the age group. Migraines or severe headaches are second, with 20 percent having the problem. Chronic joint symptoms are third, with 17 percent reporting this problem.

The 18-to-44 age group accounts for more than half of those who have ever had asthma, and they are nearly half of those who still have asthma. They account for 60 percent of those with migraines or severe headaches.

■ As the Millennial generation ages into its thirties and forties, the percentage with health problems will rise.

Headaches are the second most common health problem among 18-to-44-year-olds

(percent of people aged 18 to 44 with health condition, 2010)

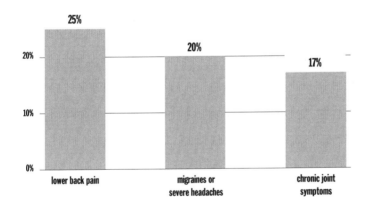

Table 3.27 Health Conditions among People Aged 18 to 44, 2010

(number of people aged 18 or older and aged 18 to 44 with selected health conditions, by type of condition, 2010; numbers in thousands)

	total	aged 18 to 44		
		total	percent with condition	share of total
Total people aged 18 or older	229,505	110,615	100.0%	48.2%
Selected circulatory diseases				
Heart disease, all types	27,066	4,897	4.4	18.1
Coronary	15,262	1,494	1.4	9.8
Hypertension	59,259	10,303	9.3	17.4
Stroke	6,226	664	0.6	10.7
Selected respiratory conditions				
Emphysema	4,314	361	0.3	8.4
Asthma, ever	29,057	15,020	13.6	51.7
Asthma, still	18,734	8,902	8.1	47.5
Hay fever	17,937	6,656	6.0	37.1
Sinusitis	29,821	11,584	10.5	38.8
Chronic bronchitis	9,882	3,265	3.0	33.0
Selected types of cancer				
Any cancer	19,441	2,427	2.2	12.5
Breast cancer	3,169	91	0.1	2.9
Cervical cancer	1,448	675	0.6	46.6
Prostate cancer	2,457	0	0.0	0.0
Other selected diseases and conditions				
Diabetes	20,974	3,022	2.8	14.4
Ulcers	14,992	4,591	4.2	30.6
Kidney disease	3,931	804	0.7	20.5
Liver disease	3,288	978	0.9	29.7
Arthritis	51,948	7,838	7.1	15.1
Chronic joint symptoms	67,024	18,794	17.0	28.0
Migraines or severe headaches	37,529	22,580	20.4	60.2
Pain in neck	36,177	14,459	13.1	40.0
Pain in lower back	66,106	27,811	25.2	42.1
Pain in face or jaw	11,460	5,460	4.9	47.6
Selected sensory problems				
Hearing	37,117	7,448	6.7	20.1
Vision	21,516	6,825	6.2	31.7
Absence of all natural teeth	17,539	2,322	2.1	13.2

Note: The conditions shown are those that have ever been diagnosed by a doctor, except as noted. Hay fever, sinusitis, and chronic bronchitis have been diagnosed in the past 12 months. Kidney and liver diseases have been diagnosed in the past 12 months and exclude kidney stones, bladder infections, and incontinence. Chronic joint symptoms are shown if respondent had pain, aching, or stiffness in or around a joint (excluding back and neck) and the condition began more than three months ago. Migraines and pain in neck, lower back, face, or jaw are shown only if pain lasted a whole day or more.
Source: National Center for Health Statistics, Summary Health Statistics for U.S. Adults: National Health Interview Survey, 2010, Vital and Health Statistics, Series 10, No. 252, 2012, Internet site http://www.cdc.gov/nchs/nhis.htm

Many Americans Turn to Alternative Medicine

More than one-third of young adults use alternative therapies.

Alternative medicine is a big business. In 2007, fully 38 percent of Americans aged 18 or older used a complementary or alternative medicine or therapy, according to a study by the National Center for Health Statistics. Alternative treatments range from popular regimens such as the South Beach Diet to chiropractic care, yoga, and acupuncture.

Middle-aged adults are most likely to use alternative medicine. Forty-four percent of people aged 50 to 59 used alternative medicine in 2007. Among Millennials (under age 30), 36 percent used alternative medicine in the past year—16 percent used biologically based therapies (which include special diets) and an even larger 21 percent used mind-body therapy (which includes meditation and yoga).

■ The use of alternative medicine falls in the older age groups as health problems become more severe.

The use of alternative medicine peaks in middle age

(percent of people aged 18 or older who have used alternative medicine in the past 12 months, by age, 2007)

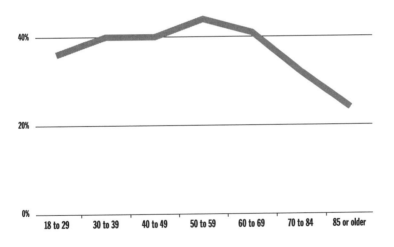

Table 3.28 Adults Who Use Complementary and Alternative Medicine by Age, 2007

(percent of people aged 18 or older who used complementary or alternative medicine in the past 12 months, by age, 2007)

	any use	biologically based therapies	mind-body therapies	alternative medical systems	manipulative and body-based therapies
Total adults	**38.3%**	**19.9%**	**19.2%**	**3.4%**	**15.2%**
Aged 18 to 29	36.3	15.9	21.3	3.2	15.1
Aged 30 to 39	39.6	19.8	19.9	3.6	17.2
Aged 40 to 49	40.1	20.4	19.7	4.6	17.4
Aged 50 to 59	44.1	24.2	22.9	4.9	17.3
Aged 60 to 69	41.0	25.4	17.3	2.8	13.8
Aged 70 to 84	32.1	19.3	11.9	1.8	9.9
Aged 85 or older	24.2	13.7	9.8	1.9	7.0

Definitions: Biologically based therapies include chelation therapy, nonvitamin, nonmineral, natural products and diet-based therapies. Mind-body therapies include biofeedback meditation, guided imagery, progressive relaxation, deep breathing exercises, hypnosis, yoga, tai chi, and qi gong. Alternative medical systems include acupuncture, ayurveda, homeopathic treatment, naturopathy, and traditional healers. Manipulative body-based therapies include chiropractic or osteopathic manipulation, massage, and movement therapies.
Source: National Center for Health Statistics, Complementary and Alternative Medicine Use Among Adults and Children: United States, 2007, National Health Statistics Report, No. 12, 2008, Internet site http://www.cdc.gov/nchs/products/nhsr.htm

More than 1 Million Americans Have Been Diagnosed with AIDS

For most, the diagnosis occurred when they were aged 30 or older.

As of 2009, more than 1 million people had been diagnosed with AIDS in the United States. Few are diagnosed younger than age 30. As of 2009, only 17 percent had been diagnosed before age 30. Nevertheless, those diagnosed with AIDS in their thirties or older often contracted the illness as young adults.

Although new drug treatments have lowered mortality rates from AIDS, the cost of treatment can be prohibitive.

■ The AIDS epidemic has boosted condom use among teens and young adults.

Few are diagnosed with AIDS before age 30

(percent distribution of cumulative number of AIDS cases by age at diagnosis, through 2009)

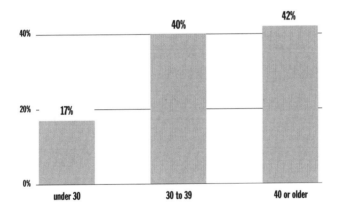

Table 3.29 Cumulative Number of AIDS Cases by Sex and Age, through 2009

(cumulative number and percent distribution of AIDS cases by sex and age at diagnosis, through 2009)

	number	percent distribution
Total cases	**1,108,611**	**100.0%**
Sex		
Males aged 13 or older	878,366	79.2
Females aged 13 or older	220,795	19.9
Age		
Under age 13	9,448	0.9
Aged 13 to 14	1,321	0.1
Aged 15 to 19	7,214	0.7
Aged 20 to 24	42,920	3.9
Aged 25 to 29	129,639	11.7
Aged 30 to 34	214,149	19.3
Aged 35 to 39	234,575	21.2
Aged 40 to 44	193,237	17.4
Aged 45 to 49	126,380	11.4
Aged 50 to 54	72,327	6.5
Aged 55 to 59	39,025	3.5
Aged 60 to 64	20,633	1.9
Aged 65 or older	17,743	1.6

Source: Centers for Disease Control and Prevention, Cases of HIV/AIDS and AIDS in the United States and Dependent Areas, 2009, Internet site http://www.cdc.gov/hiv/surveillance/resources/reports/2009report/; calculations by New Strategist

Young Adults Are Least Likely to See a Doctor

People aged 15 to 24 visit doctors fewer than two times a year, on average.

In 2009, Americans visited physicians more than 1 billion times. People aged 15 to 24 accounted for only 7 percent of physician visits. They visited a doctor only 1.8 times during the year, on average. In the broad 25-to-44 age group, doctor visits increase to an average of 3.5 times a year for women. Many of their doctor visits are due to pregnancy.

People aged 15 to 44 account for more than one-third of hospital outpatient visits. The broad age group accounts for a larger 44 percent of visits to hospital emergency departments. The 15-to-24 and 25-to-44 age groups are the ones whose emergency visits are least likely to be deemed a true emergency. Many head to the emergency room because they lack health insurance and have no other source of health care.

When people visiting a doctor or health care clinic are asked to rate the care they received, fewer than half give it the highest rating (a 9 or 10 on a scale of 0 to 10). The proportion rating their experience a 9 or 10 rises with age to a peak of 64 percent among Medicare recipients (people aged 65 or older). Only 40 percent of Millennials give the health care they received the highest rating.

■ Among adults aged 15 to 44, women visit doctors much more frequently than men because of pregnancy and childbirth.

People aged 15 to 24 see doctors less frequently than any other age group

(average number of physician visits per person per year, by age, 2009)

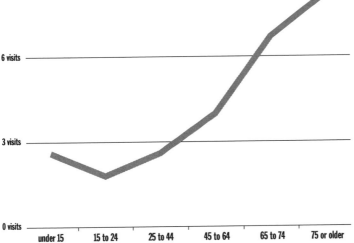

Table 3.30 Physician Office Visits by Sex and Age, 2009

(total number, percent distribution, and number of physician office visits per person per year, by sex and age, 2009; numbers in thousands)

	total	percent distribution	average visits per year
Total visits	**1,037,796**	**100.0%**	**3.4**
Under age 15	158,907	15.3	2.6
Aged 15 to 24	74,080	7.1	1.8
Aged 25 to 44	208,901	20.1	2.6
Aged 45 to 64	316,395	30.5	4.0
Aged 65 or older	279,514	26.9	7.4
Aged 65 to 74	137,452	13.2	6.7
Aged 75 or older	142,062	13.7	8.2
Visits by females	**611,064**	**58.9**	**4.0**
Under age 15	72,243	7.0	2.4
Aged 15 to 24	48,029	4.6	2.3
Aged 25 to 44	144,022	13.9	3.5
Aged 45 to 64	184,994	17.8	4.6
Aged 65 to 74	75,428	7.3	6.8
Aged 75 or older	86,348	8.3	8.2
Visits by males	**426,732**	**41.1**	**2.9**
Under age 15	86,664	8.4	2.7
Aged 15 to 24	26,052	2.5	1.2
Aged 25 to 44	64,879	6.3	1.6
Aged 45 to 64	131,400	12.7	3.4
Aged 65 to 74	62,023	6.0	6.5
Aged 75 or older	55,713	5.4	8.1

Source: National Center for Health Statistics, National Ambulatory Medical Care Survey: 2009 Summary Tables, Internet site http://www.cdc.gov/nchs/ahcd/web_tables.htm#2009

Table 3.31 Hospital Outpatient Department Visits by Age and Reason, 2008

(number and percent distribution of visits to hospital outpatient departments by age and major reason for visit, 2008; numbers in thousands)

| | total | | | | major reason for visit | | | | |
	number	percent distribution	total	new problem	chronic problem, routine	chronic problem, flare-up	pre- or post-surgery or injury follow-up	preventive care	unknown
Total visits	**109,889**	**100.0%**	**100.0%**	**38.1%**	**30.3%**	**6.1%**	**4.7%**	**19.2%**	**1.6%**
Under age 15	22,332	20.3	100.0	51.9	16.2	2.6	1.5	26.3	1.5
Aged 15 to 24	11,563	10.5	100.0	42.8	18.5	4.2	3.1	30.2	1.2
Aged 25 to 44	26,186	23.8	100.0	40.9	25.8	6.5	4.6	21.2	1.1
Aged 45 to 64	31,150	28.3	100.0	31.4	40.3	7.8	6.4	12.3	1.6
Aged 65 or older	18,658	17.0	100.0	26.1	43.8	8.3	6.7	12.5	2.5
Aged 65 to 74	10,273	9.3	100.0	26.8	42.3	8.1	7.3	13.5	2.0
Aged 75 or older	835	0.8	100.0	25.4	45.6	8.5	6.1	11.3	3.2

Source: National Center for Health Statistics, National Ambulatory Medical Care Survey: 2008 Outpatient Department Summary Tables, Internet site http://www.cdc.gov/nchs/ahcd/web_tables.htm#2009

Table 3.32 Emergency Department Visits by Age and Urgency of Problem, 2008

(number of visits to emergency rooms and percent distribution by urgency of problem, by age, 2008; numbers in thousands)

| | total | | percent distribution by urgency of problem | | | | | | |
	number	percent distribution	total	immediate	emergent	urgent	semiurgent	nonurgent	unknown
Total visits	**123,761**	**100.0%**	**100.0%**	**3.7%**	**11.9%**	**38.9%**	**21.2%**	**8.0%**	**16.3%**
Under age 15	23,157	18.7	100.0	1.9	8.3	36.0	25.1	8.8	20.0
Aged 15 to 24	19,823	16.0	100.0	2.6	9.2	37.0	24.9	9.8	16.5
Aged 25 to 44	35,185	28.4	100.0	3.1	10.1	39.0	23.0	9.1	15.7
Aged 45 to 64	26,335	21.3	100.0	5	14.0	40.2	18.4	7.1	15.3
Aged 65 or older	19,261	15.6	100.0	6.2	19.5	42.2	13.5	4.6	14.0
Aged 65 to 74	7,479	6.0	100.0	5.2	19.3	41.3	15.3	5.5	13.3
Aged 75 or older	11,781	9.5	100.0	6.9	19.7	42.8	12.4	4.0	14.4

Note: "Immediate" is a visit in which the patient should be seen immediately. "Emergent" is a visit in which the patient should be seen within 1 to 14 minutes; "urgent" is a visit in which the patient should be seen within 15 to 60 minutes; "semiurgent" is a visit in which the patient should be seen within 61 to 120 minutes; "nonurgent" is a visit in which the patient should be seen within 121 minutes to 24 hours; "unknown" is a visit with no mention of immediacy or triage or the patient was dead on arrival.
Source: National Center for Health Statistics, National Ambulatory Medical Care Survey: 2008 Emergency Department Summary Tables, Internet site http://www.cdc.gov/nchs/ahcd/web_tables.htm#2009

Table 3.33 Rating of Health Care Received from Doctor's Office or Clinic by Age, 2009

(number of people aged 18 or older visiting a doctor or health care clinic in past 12 months, and percent distribution by rating for health care received on a scale from 0 (worst) to 10 (best), by age, 2009; people in thousands)

	with health care visit		rating		
	number	percent	9 to 10	7 to 8	0 to 6
Total people	**155,909**	**100.0%**	**50.1%**	**36.5%**	**12.2%**
Aged 18 to 24	15,438	100.0	41.6	40.4	17.0
Aged 25 to 29	11,494	100.0	38.2	44.8	15.4
Aged 30 to 34	11,822	100.0	38.1	46.3	14.3
Aged 35 to 44	25,701	100.0	44.2	42.0	12.6
Aged 45 to 54	30,359	100.0	48.5	36.2	14.5
Aged 55 to 64	28,249	100.0	55.5	33.4	9.8
Aged 65 or older	32,847	100.0	64.0	26.8	7.5

Source: Agency for Healthcare Research and Quality, Medical Expenditure Panel Survey, 2009, Internet site http://meps.ahrq .gov/mepsweb/survey_comp/household.jsp; calculations by New Strategist

Table 3.34 Rating of Health Care Received from Doctor's Office or Clinic by Generation, 2009

(number of people aged 18 or older visiting a doctor or health care clinic in past 12 months, and percent distribution by rating for health care received on a scale from 0 (worst) to 10 (best), by generation, 2009; people in thousands)

	with health care visit		rating		
	number	percent	9 to 10	7 to 8	0 to 6
Total adults	**155,909**	**100.0%**	**50.1%**	**36.5%**	**12.2%**
Millennials (18 to 32)	34,072	100.0	39.9	42.8	16.1
Generation X (33 to 44)	30,382	100.0	43.1	43.0	12.6
Baby Boomers (45 to 63)	56,573	100.0	51.5	35.0	12.5
Older Americans (64 or older)	34,883	100.0	63.9	27.0	7.3

Source: Agency for Healthcare Research and Quality, Medical Expenditure Panel Survey, 2009, Internet site http://meps.ahrq .gov/mepsweb/survey_comp/household.jsp; calculations by New Strategist

Most Deaths of Young Adults Are Preventable

Accidents are the leading killers of 15-to-44-year-olds.

The deaths of young adults are often preventable. Accidents are the leading cause of death among 15-to-24-year-olds and 25-to-44-year-olds and account for 41 and 25 percent of deaths, respectively. Homicide ranks second among 15-to-24-year-olds, and suicide is third. Among 25-to-44-year-olds, suicide is fourth and homicide is fifth. HIV infection ranks seventh as a cause of death among 25-to-44-year-olds. Pregnancy and childbirth rank ninth as a cause of death among 15-to-24-year-olds.

Although more could be done to reduce deaths among young adults, some progress has been made. The life expectancy of Americans continues to rise. At birth, Americans can expect to live 78.7 years. At age 25, life expectancy is another 54.8 years.

■ As Millennials age, heart disease and cancer will become increasingly important causes of death.

Accidents are the most important cause of death among people aged 15 to 44

(percent of deaths due to accidents, homicide, and suicide among people aged 15 to 44, 2010)

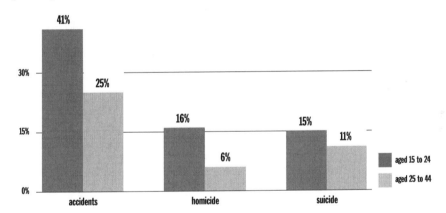

Table 3.35 Leading Causes of Death for People Aged 15 to 24, 2010

(number and percent distribution of deaths accounted for by the 10 leading causes of death for people aged 15 to 24, 2010)

			aged 15 to 24		
		total	number	percent distribution	share of total
	All causes	**2,465,932**	**29,504**	**100.0%**	**1.2%**
1.	Accidents (unintentional injuries) (5)	118,043	12,015	40.7	10.2
2.	Homicide (15)	16,065	4,651	15.8	29.0
3.	Suicide (10)	37,793	4,559	15.5	12.1
4.	Malignant neoplasms (cancer) (2)	573,855	1,594	5.4	0.3
5.	Diseases of the heart (1)	595,444	984	3.3	0.2
6.	Congenital malformations, deformations	9,587	401	1.4	4.2
7.	Cerebrovascular diseases (4)	129,180	187	0.6	0.1
8.	Influenza and pneumonia (9)	50,003	179	0.6	0.4
9.	Pregnancy and childbirth	824	162	0.5	19.7
10.	Diabetes mellitus (7)	68,905	161	0.5	0.2
	All other causes	866,233	4,611	15.6	0.5

Note: Number in parentheses shows cause of death rank for total population if cause is one of top 15.
Source: National Center for Health Statistics, Deaths: Preliminary Data for 2010, National Vital Statistics Reports, Vol. 60, No. 4, 2012, Internet site http://www.cdc.gov/nchs/deaths.htm; calculations by New Strategist

Table 3.36 Leading Causes of Death among People Aged 25 to 44, 2010

(total number of deaths, number and and percent distribution of deaths among people aged 25 to 44, and age group share of total, for the 10 leading causes of death among people aged 25 to 44, 2010)

		total	aged 25 to 44		
			number	percent distribution	share of total
	All causes	**2,465,932**	**112,177**	**100.0%**	**4.5%**
1.	Accidents (unintentional injuries) (5)	118,043	28,149	25.1	23.8
2.	Malignant neoplasms (cancer) (2)	573,855	15,389	13.7	2.7
3.	Diseases of the heart (1)	595,444	13,447	12.0	2.3
4.	Suicide (10)	37,793	12,119	10.8	32.1
5.	Homicide (15)	16,065	6,674	5.9	41.5
6.	Chronic liver disease and cirrhosis (12)	31,802	2,900	2.6	9.1
7.	Human immunodeficiency virus infection	8,352	2,638	2.4	31.6
8.	Cerebrovascular diseases (4)	129,180	2,396	2.1	1.9
9.	Diabetes mellitus (7)	68,905	2,365	2.1	3.4
10.	Influenza and pneumonia (9)	50,003	1,146	1.0	2.3
	All other causes	836,490	24,954	22.2	3.0

Note: Number in parentheses shows cause of death rank for total population if cause is one of top 15.
Source: National Center for Health Statistics, Deaths: Preliminary Data for 2010, National Vital Statistics Reports, Vol. 60, No. 4, 2012, Internet site http://www.cdc.gov/nchs/deaths.htm; calculations by New Strategist

Table 3.37 Life Expectancy by Age and Sex, 2010

(expected years of life remaining at selected ages, by sex, 2010)

	total	females	males
At birth	78.7	81.1	76.2
Aged 1	78.2	80.5	75.7
Aged 5	74.3	76.6	71.8
Aged 10	69.3	71.6	66.8
Aged 15	64.4	66.7	61.9
Aged 20	59.5	61.8	57.1
Aged 25	54.8	56.9	52.4
Aged 30	50.0	52.0	47.8
Aged 35	45.3	47.2	43.1
Aged 40	40.6	42.5	38.5
Aged 45	36.0	37.8	33.9
Aged 50	31.5	33.2	29.6
Aged 55	27.2	28.8	25.4
Aged 60	23.1	24.5	21.5
Aged 65	19.2	20.3	17.7
Aged 70	15.5	16.5	14.2
Aged 75	12.2	12.9	11.0
Aged 80	9.2	9.7	8.2
Aged 85	6.6	7.0	5.9
Aged 90	4.7	4.9	4.1
Aged 95	3.3	3.4	2.9
Aged 100	2.4	2.4	2.1

Source: National Center for Health Statistics, Deaths: Preliminary Data for 2010, National Vital Statistics Reports, Vol. 60, No. 4, 2012, Internet site http://www.cdc.gov/nchs/deaths.htm; calculations by New Strategist

4

Housing

■ The homeownership rate in the United States reached a peak of 69.0 percent in 2004. Since then, the rate has fallen by 2.9 percentage points. Among householders aged 30 to 34, the annual home-ownership rate fell below 50 percent for the first time in the history of the data series.

■ Although the Millennial generation was too young to be caught up in the worst of the housing bubble, many are too burdened by student loans to quality for a mortgage.

■ Married couples are most likely to own a home. Among the Millennial generation, the majority of married couples aged 25 to 34 are homeowners.

■ Homeownership surpasses 50 percent among non-Hispanic whites in the 25-to-34 age group. Among Asians, the majority owns a home in the 35-to-44 age group. Among blacks and Hispanics, the percentage reaches at least 50 percent in the 45-to-54 age group.

■ The majority of American households (69 percent) live in single-family homes or duplexes (one unit detached or attached). Among householders under age 35, however, only 49.6 percent live in a single-family home while 44.8 percent live in a multi-unit building.

■ Young adults are far more likely than their elders to move. Only 3 to 11 percent of people aged 35 or older moved between 2010 and 2011, but among people aged 20 to 29, the percentage was a much higher 24 percent.

Homeownership Rate Has Declined

Since 2004, rate has fallen the most among 30-to-34-year-olds.

The homeownership rate in the United States reached a peak of 69.0 percent in 2004. Since then, the rate has fallen by 2.9 percentage points, to 66.1 percent in 2011, because of the Great Recession and the collapse of the housing market. Householders aged 30 to 34 experienced the largest decline in homeownership, their rate falling by 7.6 percentage points during those years to 49.8 percent. This is the first time in the history of the data series (which dates back to 1982) that the annual homeownership rate of 30-to-34-year-olds has been below 50 percent.

The overall homeownership rate of 2011 was 1.4 percentage points below the rate of 2000. For householders under age 35, the homeownership rate was 3 percentage points lower in 2011 than in 2000. Only two age groups experienced an increase in their homeownership rate during those years: the rate among householders under age 25 climbed by 0.9 percentage points, and the rate among householders aged 65 or older increased by 0.4 percentage points.

■ The homeownership rate is falling the most among householders in their thirties because younger adults are deciding not to buy.

After peaking in 2004, homeownership rates have fallen

(percentage point change in homeownership rate for householders under age 35, by age, 2004 to 2011)

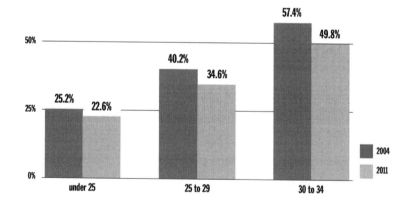

Table 4.1 Homeownership by Age of Householder, 2000 to 2011

(percentage of householders who own their home by age of householder, 2000 to 2011; percentage point change, 2004–11 and 2000–11)

	2011	2010	2004	2000	percentage point change 2004–11	2000–11
Total households	**66.1%**	**66.8%**	**69.0%**	**67.5%**	**−2.9**	**−1.4**
Under age 35	37.7	39.0	43.1	40.7	−5.4	−3.0
Under age 25	22.6	22.8	25.2	21.7	−2.6	0.9
Aged 25 to 29	34.6	36.8	40.2	38.1	−5.6	−3.5
Aged 30 to 34	49.8	51.6	57.4	54.6	−7.6	−4.8
Aged 35 to 39	59.8	61.9	66.2	65.0	−6.4	−5.2
Aged 40 to 44	66.9	67.8	71.9	70.6	−5.0	−3.7
Aged 45 to 54	72.7	73.5	77.2	76.5	−4.5	−3.8
Aged 55 to 64	78.5	79.0	81.7	80.3	−3.2	−1.8
Aged 65 or older	80.9	80.5	81.1	80.5	−0.2	0.4

Source: Bureau of the Census, Housing Vacancies and Homeownership, Internet site http://www.census.gov/hhes/www/housing/hvs/hvs.html; calculations by New Strategist

Homeownership Rises with Age

Most householders under age 35 are renters.

The Great Recession has hurt Millennials perhaps more than any other generation. Consequently, many are deciding (or being forced) to continue to rent rather than buy a home. Among householders under age 35, only 38 percent were homeowners in 2011 (Millennials were aged 17 to 34 in that year). Among householders under age 25, only 23 percent were homeowners. The homeownership rate rises to just below 50 percent among householders aged 30 to 34.

Overall, more than 60 percent of households headed by Millennials are renters. The Millennial generation accounts for only 13 percent of the nation's homeowners but 41 percent of its renters.

■ The Millennial generation has replaced the smaller Generation X in the young-adult age group, giving the rental market a boost.

Renting is the norm among Millennials

(percent distribution of householders under age 35 by homeownership status, 2011)

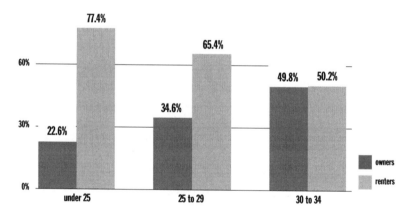

Table 4.2 Owners and Renters by Age of Householder, 2011

(number and percent distribution of householders by homeownership status, and owner and renter share of total, by age of householder, 2011; numbers in thousands)

	total	owners			renters		
		number	percent distribution	share of total	number	percent distribution	share of total
Total households	**113,534**	**75,091**	**100.0%**	**66.1%**	**38,443**	**100.0%**	**33.9%**
Under age 35	25,098	9,465	12.6	37.7	15,633	40.7	62.3
Under age 25	6,079	1,373	1.8	22.6	4,706	12.2	77.4
Aged 25 to 29	9,062	3,134	4.2	34.6	5,928	15.4	65.4
Aged 30 to 34	9,957	4,958	6.6	49.8	4,999	13.0	50.2
Aged 35 to 44	20,182	12,808	17.1	63.5	7,374	19.2	36.5
Aged 45 to 54	23,234	16,886	22.5	72.7	6,348	16.5	27.3
Aged 55 to 64	20,689	16,240	21.6	78.5	4,449	11.6	21.5
Aged 65 or older	24,330	19,693	26.2	80.9	4,637	12.1	19.1

Source: Bureau of the Census, Housing Vacancies and Homeownership, Internet site http://www.census.gov/hhes/www/housing/hvs/hvs.html; calculations by New Strategist

Married Couples Are Most Likely to Be Homeowners

Homeownership rate is highest in the Midwest.

The homeownership rate among all married couples stood at 81.5 percent in 2011, much higher than the 66.1 percent for all households. Among Millennial couples, the majority of those in the 25-to-34 age group are homeowners rather than renters. The homeownership rate is well below 50 percent for other types of households headed by Millennials.

Nationally, the homeownership rate is highest in the Midwest and lowest in the West. Among Millennials, the homeownership rate tops 50 percent only among householders aged 30 to 34 in the Midwest and South.

■ Many Millennials have a hard time qualifying for a mortgage because they are burdened by student loans.

More than 50 percent of couples aged 25 to 34 own their home

(percent of married-couple householders who own their home, by age, 2011)

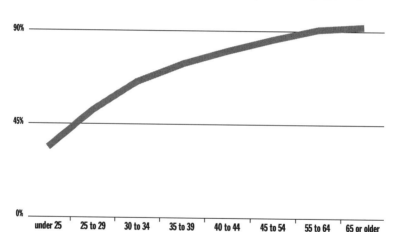

Table 4.3 Homeownership Rate by Age of Householder and Type of Household, 2011

(percent of households owning their home, by age of householder and type of household, 2011)

	total	married couples	female family householder, no spouse present	male family householder, no spouse present	people living alone	
					females	males
Total households	**66.1%**	**81.5%**	**48.1%**	**55.6%**	**58.5%**	**50.6%**
Under age 35	37.7	57.2	25.5	40.0	22.0	26.6
Under age 25	22.6	33.7	25.9	40.3	10.6	14.5
Aged 25 to 29	34.6	51.7	22.0	36.4	19.4	26.3
Aged 30 to 34	49.8	65.5	28.6	43.5	35.6	34.4
Aged 35 to 39	59.8	74.1	37.4	51.3	42.1	41.5
Aged 40 to 44	66.9	80.4	47.3	57.5	45.3	46.4
Aged 45 to 54	72.7	85.9	58.4	65.8	53.9	53.2
Aged 55 to 64	78.5	90.7	66.2	74.5	64.8	59.1
Aged 65 or older	80.9	92.1	80.5	80.4	70.9	68.9

Source: Bureau of the Census, Housing Vacancies and Homeownership, Internet site http://www.census.gov/hhes/www/housing/hvs/hvs.html; calculations by New Strategist

Table 4.4 Homeownership Rate by Age of Householder and Region, 2011

(percent of households owning their home, by age of householder and region, 2011)

	total	Northeast	Midwest	South	West
Total households	**66.1%**	**63.6%**	**70.2%**	**68.3%**	**60.5%**
Under age 35	37.7	34.5	42.7	38.9	33.2
Under age 25	22.6	21.9	23.2	23.6	20.7
Aged 25 to 29	34.6	28.9	40.3	36.8	29.4
Aged 30 to 34	49.8	45.8	58.0	50.4	44.1
Aged 35 to 39	59.8	56.8	65.4	63.2	51.2
Aged 40 to 44	66.9	65.7	72.9	69.0	58.6
Aged 45 to 54	72.7	70.2	77.5	74.4	66.9
Aged 55 to 64	78.5	75.1	81.5	81.1	74.0
Aged 65 or older	80.9	73.7	82.0	85.3	78.9

Source: Bureau of the Census, Housing Vacancies and Homeownership, Internet site http://www.census.gov/hhes/www/housing/hvs/hvs.html; calculations by New Strategist

Many Non-Hispanic White Millennials Are Homeowners

Among Millennials, Asians are more likely than blacks or Hispanics to own a home.

The homeownership rate of Asians, blacks, and Hispanics is below average. According to the 2010 census, the homeownership rate was 65.1 percent for all households in 2010. Among Asians, the rate was 58.0 percent. Among blacks it was 44.3 percent, and the Hispanic homeownership rate was 47.3 percent. In contrast, an above-average 72.2 percent of non-Hispanic whites owned their home in 2010.

Homeownership surpasses the 50 percent threshold among non-Hispanic whites in the 25-to-34 age group. Among Asians, the majority owns a home in the 35-to-44 age group. Among blacks and Hispanics, the percentage reaches at least 50 percent in the 45-to-54 age group.

■ Although Hispanics outnumber blacks in the United States, black and Hispanic homeowners are nearly equal in number.

Half of non-Hispanic whites aged 25 to 34 own their home

(homeownership rate of householders under age 25 and aged 25 to 34, by race and Hispanic origin, 2010)

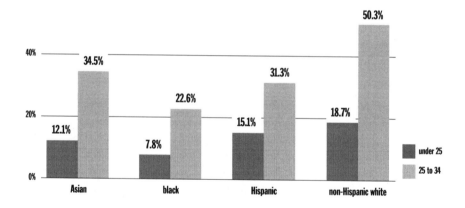

Table 4.5 Homeownership by Age, Race, and Hispanic Origin, 2010

(number and percent of households thath own their home, by age, race, and Hispanic origin of householder, 2010; numbers in thousands)

	total	Asian	black	Hispanic	non-Hispanic white
Total households	**116,716**	**4,632**	**14,130**	**13,461**	**82,333**
Under age 25	5,401	217	802	885	3,333
Aged 25 to 34	17,957	924	2,466	3,122	11,003
Aged 35 to 44	21,291	1,145	2,890	3,457	13,362
Aged 45 to 54	24,907	1,002	3,190	2,808	17,438
Aged 55 to 64	21,340	720	2,450	1,693	16,129
Aged 65 or older	25,820	624	2,331	1,496	21,069
Aged 65 to 74	13,505	371	1,374	883	10,692
Aged 75 to 84	8,716	191	722	476	7,238
Aged 85 or older	3,599	62	235	136	3,139
HOMEOWNERS					
Total households	**75,986**	**2,689**	**6,261**	**6,368**	**59,484**
Under age 25	870	26	63	133	622
Aged 25 to 34	7,547	319	557	976	5,538
Aged 35 to 44	13,256	706	1,190	1,659	9,461
Aged 45 to 54	17,804	701	1,594	1,611	13,601
Aged 55 to 64	16,503	530	1,398	1,048	13,285
Aged 65 or older	20,007	407	1,460	941	16,977
Aged 65 to 74	10,834	260	851	558	9,028
Aged 75 to 84	6,789	114	463	303	5,844
Aged 85 or older	2,384	33	146	80	2,105
HOMEOWNERSHIP RATE					
Total households	**65.1%**	**58.0%**	**44.3%**	**47.3%**	**72.2%**
Under age 25	16.1	12.1	7.8	15.1	18.7
Aged 25 to 34	42.0	34.5	22.6	31.3	50.3
Aged 35 to 44	62.3	61.7	41.2	48.0	70.8
Aged 45 to 54	71.5	69.9	50.0	57.4	78.0
Aged 55 to 64	77.3	73.6	57.0	61.9	82.4
Aged 65 or older	77.5	65.2	62.6	62.9	80.6
Aged 65 to 74	80.2	70.2	61.9	63.2	84.4
Aged 75 to 84	77.9	59.4	64.2	63.5	80.7
Aged 85 or older	66.2	52.9	62.3	59.1	67.1

Note: Asians and blacks are those who identify themselves as being of the race alone. Hispanics may be of any race. Non-Hispanic whites are those who identify themselves as being white alone and not Hispanic.
Source: Bureau of the Census, 2010 Census, American Factfinder,Internet site http://factfinder2.census.gov/faces/nav/jsf/pages/index.xhtml; calculations by New Strategist"

Only Half of Younger Adults Live in a Single-Family Home

Many younger adults live in apartment buildings.

The majority of American households (69 percent) live in single-family homes or duplexes (one unit detached or attached). Fewer than half of householders under age 35 live in this type of home, however, while a substantial 45 percent live in multi-unit buildings. Interestingly, however, adults aged 65 or older are more likely than young adults to live in a building with 50 or more units. Behind this figure is the movement of older adults into multi-unit retirement complexes and assisted living facilities.

Homeowners are much more likely than renters to live in a single-family home, and the low homeownership rate among adults under age 35 is the reason so many are in apartment buildings. Among homeowners under age 35, 85 percent are in a single-family home—about the same proportion as among older adults.

Six percent of households live in mobile homes, boats, RVs, and so on. This category is dominated by mobile homes. The proportion of householders who live in a mobile home does not vary much by age.

■ The demand for single-family homes helped to fuel the housing bubble, resulting in the Great Recession.

Younger adults are least likely to live in a single-family home

(percent of households that live in single-family homes, by age of householder, 2010)

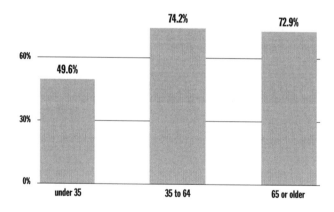

Table 4.6 Number of Units in Structure by Age of Householder and Homeownership Status, 2010

(number and percent distribution of households by age of householder, homeownership status, and number of units in structure, 2010; numbers in thousands)

	total	one detached or attached	multi-unit building total	2 to 4	5 to 19	20 to 49	50 or more	mobile home, boat, RV, etc.
Total households	**114,567**	**79,080**	**28,507**	**9,032**	**10,094**	**3,906**	**5,475**	**6,979**
Under age 35	22,695	11,267	10,160	3,060	4,214	1,424	1,462	1,267
Aged 35 to 64	66,998	49,692	13,247	4,665	4,705	1,687	2,190	4,061
Aged 65 or older	24,874	18,121	5,100	1,307	1,175	795	1,823	1,651
Owner-occupied	**74,873**	**65,779**	**3,986**	**1,590**	**1,034**	**493**	**869**	**5,108**
Under age 35	8,062	6,837	602	191	208	77	126	622
Aged 35 to 64	47,265	42,140	2,100	906	536	234	424	3,026
Aged 65 or older	19,546	16,802	1,284	493	290	182	319	1,460
Renter-occupied	**39,694**	**13,301**	**24,521**	**7,442**	**9,060**	**3,413**	**4,606**	**1,871**
Under age 35	14,633	4,430	9,558	2,869	4,006	1,347	1,336	645
Aged 35 to 64	19,733	7,552	11,147	3,759	4,169	1,453	1,766	1,035
Aged 65 or older	5,328	1,319	3,816	814	885	613	1,504	191

PERCENT DISTRIBUTION BY UNITS IN STRUCTURE

	total	one detached or attached	multi-unit building total	2 to 4	5 to 19	20 to 49	50 or more	mobile home, boat, RV, etc.
Total households	**100.0%**	**69.0%**	**24.9%**	**7.9%**	**8.8%**	**3.4%**	**4.8%**	**6.1%**
Under age 35	100.0	49.6	44.8	13.5	18.6	6.3	6.4	5.6
Aged 35 to 64	100.0	74.2	19.8	7.0	7.0	2.5	3.3	6.1
Aged 65 or older	100.0	72.9	20.5	5.3	4.7	3.2	7.3	6.6
Owner-occupied	**100.0**	**87.9**	**5.3**	**2.1**	**1.4**	**0.7**	**1.2**	**6.8**
Under age 35	100.0	84.8	7.5	2.4	2.6	1.0	1.6	7.7
Aged 35 to 64	100.0	89.2	4.4	1.9	1.1	0.5	0.9	6.4
Aged 65 or older	100.0	86.0	6.6	2.5	1.5	0.9	1.6	7.5
Renter-occupied	**100.0**	**33.5**	**61.8**	**18.7**	**22.8**	**8.6**	**11.6**	**4.7**
Under age 35	100.0	30.3	65.3	19.6	27.4	9.2	9.1	4.4
Aged 35 to 64	100.0	38.3	56.5	19.0	21.1	7.4	8.9	5.2
Aged 65 or older	100.0	24.8	71.6	15.3	16.6	11.5	28.2	3.6

Source: Bureau of the Census, 2010 American Community Survey, Internet site http://factfinder2.census.gov/faces/nav/jsf/pages/index.xhtml; calculations by New Strategist

Twentysomethings Are Most Likely to Move

About one in four moves each year.

Young adults are far more likely than their elders to move. Only 3 to 11 percent of people aged 35 or older moved between 2010 and 2011, but among people aged 20 to 29, the percentage was a much higher 24 percent.

Among all movers, most stay within the same county. Only 14 percent cross state lines. Among movers under age 30, as for all movers, housing is the primary reason for moving. Many young adults move because they are going to or coming from college.

■ Mobility has been declining in the United States for decades, and the Great Recession lowered mobility rates even further.

Mobility rate is high among people aged 20 to 29

(percent of people who moved between March 2010 and March 2011, by age)

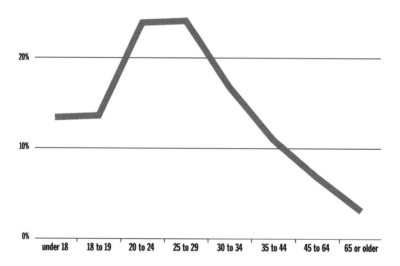

Table 4.7 Geographic Mobility by Age and Type of Move, 2010–11

(total number of people aged 1 or older, and number and percent who moved between March 2010 and March 2011, by age and type of move; numbers in thousands)

	total	total movers	same county	different county, same state	different state total	same region	different region	movers from abroad
Total, aged 1 or older	**302,005**	**35,075**	**23,325**	**5,912**	**4,779**	**2,323**	**2,456**	**1,058**
Under age 18	70,811	9,465	6,591	1,494	1,162	554	608	216
Aged 18 to 34	71,234	14,796	9,777	2,564	1,956	975	981	499
Aged 18 to 19	8,125	1,106	766	198	98	52	46	44
Aged 20 to 24	21,525	5,136	3,411	919	658	369	289	148
Aged 25 to 29	21,382	5,159	3,286	952	723	324	399	198
Aged 30 to 34	20,202	3,395	2,314	495	477	230	247	109
Aged 35 to 44	39,842	4,387	2,917	696	617	291	326	157
Aged 45 to 64	80,939	5,513	3,311	950	796	409	387	134
Aged 65 or older	39,178	1,233	729	209	246	92	154	51

PERCENT DISTRIBUTION BY MOBILITY STATUS

	total	total movers	same county	different county, same state	different state total	same region	different region	movers from abroad
Total, aged 1 or older	**100.0%**	**11.6%**	**7.7%**	**2.0%**	**1.6%**	**0.8%**	**0.8%**	**0.4%**
Under age 18	100.0	13.4	9.3	2.1	1.6	0.8	0.9	0.3
Aged 18 to 34	100.0	20.8	13.7	3.6	2.7	1.4	1.4	0.7
Aged 18 to 19	100.0	13.6	9.4	2.4	1.2	0.6	0.6	0.5
Aged 20 to 24	100.0	23.9	15.8	4.3	3.1	1.7	1.3	0.7
Aged 25 to 29	100.0	24.1	15.4	4.5	3.4	1.5	1.9	0.9
Aged 30 to 34	100.0	16.8	11.5	2.5	2.4	1.1	1.2	0.5
Aged 35 to 44	100.0	11.0	7.3	1.7	1.5	0.7	0.8	0.4
Aged 45 to 64	100.0	6.8	4.1	1.2	1.0	0.5	0.5	0.2
Aged 65 or older	100.0	3.1	1.9	0.5	0.6	0.2	0.4	0.1

PERCENT DISTRIBUTION OF MOVERS BY TYPE OF MOVE

	total	total movers	same county	different county, same state	different state total	same region	different region	movers from abroad
Total, aged 1 or older	–	**100.0%**	**66.5%**	**16.9%**	**13.6%**	**6.6%**	**7.0%**	**3.0%**
Under age 18	–	100.0	69.6	15.8	12.3	5.9	6.4	2.3
Aged 18 to 34	–	100.0	66.1	17.3	13.2	6.6	6.6	3.4
Aged 18 to 19	–	100.0	69.3	17.9	8.9	4.7	4.2	4.0
Aged 20 to 24	–	100.0	66.4	17.9	12.8	7.2	5.6	2.9
Aged 25 to 29	–	100.0	63.7	18.5	14.0	6.3	7.7	3.8
Aged 30 to 34	–	100.0	68.2	14.6	14.1	6.8	7.3	3.2
Aged 35 to 44	–	100.0	66.5	15.9	14.1	6.6	7.4	3.6
Aged 45 to 64	–	100.0	60.1	17.2	14.4	7.4	7.0	2.4
Aged 65 or older	–	100.0	59.1	17.0	20.0	7.5	12.5	4.1

Note: "–" means not applicable.
Source: Bureau of the Census, Geographic Mobility: 2010 to 2011, Detailed Tables, Internet site http://www.census.gov/hhes/migration/data/cps/cps2011.html; calculations by New Strategist

Table 4.8 Reason for Moving among People Aged 16 to 19, 2010–11

(number and percent distribution of movers aged 16 to 19 by primary reason for move and share of total movers between March 200 and March 2011, by age; numbers in thousands)

	total movers	movers aged 16 to 19		
		number	percent distribution	share of total
Total movers	**35,075**	**1,958**	**100.0%**	**5.6%**
Family reasons	**9,784**	**625**	**31.9**	**6.4**
Change in marital status	1,949	101	5.2	5.2
To establish own household	3,334	168	8.6	5.0
Other familiy reasons	4,501	356	18.2	7.9
Employment reasons	**6,481**	**240**	**12.3**	**3.7**
New job or job transfer	2,829	92	4.7	3.3
To look for work or lost job	924	40	2.0	4.3
To be closer to work/easier commute	2,081	89	4.5	4.3
Retired	108	0	0.0	0.0
Other job-related reason	539	19	1.0	3.5
Housing reasons	**15,736**	**866**	**44.2**	**5.5**
Wanted own home, not rent	1,530	61	3.1	4.0
Wanted better home/apartment	5,665	288	14.7	5.1
Wanted better neighborhood/less crime	1,360	76	3.9	5.6
Wanted cheaper housing	3,684	215	11.0	5.8
Foreclosure/eviction	412	36	1.8	8.7
Other housing reasons	3,085	190	9.7	6.2
Other reasons	**3,073**	**228**	**11.6**	**7.4**
To attend or leave college	890	121	6.2	13.6
Change of climate	149	6	0.3	4.0
Health reasons	564	21	1.1	3.7
Natural disaster	31	1	0.1	3.2
Other reasons	1,439	79	4.0	5.5

Source: Bureau of the Census, Geographic Mobility: 2010 to 2011, Detailed Tables, Internet site http://www.census.gov/hhes/migration/data/cps/cps2011.html; calculations by New Strategist

Table 4.9 Reason for Moving among People Aged 20 to 24, 2010–11

(number and percent distribution of movers aged 20 to 24 by primary reason for move and share of total movers between March 2010 and March 2011, by age; numbers in thousands)

	total movers	movers aged 20 to 24		
		number	percent distribution	share of total
Total movers	**35,075**	**5,136**	**100.0%**	**14.6%**
Family reasons	**9,784**	**1,540**	**30.0**	**15.7**
Change in marital status	1,949	265	5.2	13.6
To establish own household	3,334	793	15.4	23.8
Other familiy reasons	4,501	482	9.4	10.7
Employment reasons	**6,481**	**960**	**18.7**	**14.8**
New job or job transfer	2,829	372	7.2	13.1
To look for work or lost job	924	136	2.6	14.7
To be closer to work/easier commute	2,081	348	6.8	16.7
Retired	108	6	0.0	0.0
Other job-related reason	539	98	1.9	18.2
Housing reasons	**15,736**	**1,956**	**38.1**	**12.4**
Wanted own home, not rent	1,530	147	2.9	9.6
Wanted better home/apartment	5,665	687	13.4	12.1
Wanted better neighborhood/less crime	1,360	140	2.7	10.3
Wanted cheaper housing	3,684	529	10.3	14.4
Foreclosure/eviction	412	27	0.5	6.6
Other housing reasons	3,085	426	8.3	13.8
Other reasons	**3,073**	**680**	**13.2**	**22.1**
To attend or leave college	890	441	8.6	49.6
Change of climate	149	17	0.3	11.4
Health reasons	564	28	0.5	5.0
Natural disaster	31	1	0.0	3.2
Other reasons	1,439	193	3.8	13.4

Source: Bureau of the Census, Geographic Mobility: 2010 to 2011, Detailed Tables, Internet site http://www.census.gov/hhes/migration/data/cps/cps2011.html; calculations by New Strategist

Table 4.10 Reason for Moving among People Aged 25 to 29, 2010–11

(number and percent distribution of movers aged 25 to 29 by primary reason for move and share of total movers between March 2010 and March 2011, by age; numbers in thousands)

	total movers	movers aged 25 to 29		
		number	percent distribution	share of total
Total movers	**35,075**	**5,158**	**100.0%**	**14.7%**
Family reasons	**9,784**	**1,352**	**26.2**	**13.8**
Change in marital status	1,949	281	5.4	14.4
To establish own household	3,334	582	11.3	17.5
Other familiy reasons	4,501	489	9.5	10.9
Employment reasons	**6,481**	**1,174**	**22.8**	**18.1**
New job or job transfer	2,829	567	11.0	20.0
To look for work or lost job	924	155	3.0	16.8
To be closer to work/easier commute	2,081	370	7.2	17.8
Retired	108	0	0.0	0.0
Other job-related reason	539	82	1.6	15.2
Housing reasons	**15,736**	**2,146**	**41.6**	**13.6**
Wanted own home, not rent	1,530	228	4.4	14.9
Wanted better home/apartment	5,665	802	15.5	14.2
Wanted better neighborhood/less crime	1,360	180	3.5	13.2
Wanted cheaper housing	3,684	464	9.0	12.6
Foreclosure/eviction	412	46	0.9	11.2
Other housing reasons	3,085	426	8.3	13.8
Other reasons	**3,073**	**487**	**9.4**	**15.8**
To attend or leave college	890	182	3.5	20.4
Change of climate	149	11	0.2	7.4
Health reasons	564	65	1.3	11.5
Natural disaster	31	4	0.1	12.9
Other reasons	1,439	225	4.4	15.6

Source: Bureau of the Census, Geographic Mobility: 2010 to 2011, Detailed Tables, Internet site http://www.census.gov/hhes/ migration/data/cps/cps2011.html; calculations by New Strategist

5

Income

■ Householders under age 25 saw their median income decline by an enormous 20 percent between 2000 and 2010, after adjusting for inflation. Those aged 25 to 34 saw their median income fall 11 percent during the decade.

■ Householders under age 25 had a median income of $28,322 in 2010, well below the $49,445 overall median. Those aged 25 to 34 had a much higher median income of $50,059.

■ In most age groups married couples are the most affluent household type. Among households headed by people aged 15 to 24, male-headed families have a higher median income than married couples.

■ Between 2000 and 2010, men aged 15 to 24 saw their median income fall by an enormous 17.6 percent, after adjusting for inflation. Women of the same age experienced a 5.9 percent decline in median income during those years.

■ While 15.1 percent of Americans were poor in 2010, the poverty rate among 18-to-34-year-olds was a larger 18.0 percent.

Incomes of Millennials Have Plunged

Householders aged 25 to 34 have made some gains since 1990, however.

Nationally, median household income fell 7 percent between 2000 and 2010, after adjusting for inflation. Among householders under age 25, the decline was nearly three times as large, at 20 percent. (Millennials were aged 16 to 33 in 2010.) Householders aged 25 to 34 saw their median income fall 11 percent during the decade. For both age groups, most of the decline occurred since 2007.

Despite the Great Recession income decline, the median income of householders aged 25 to 34 was 2 percent higher in 2010 than in 1990. The same cannot be said for householders under age 25, who have seen their median household income fall 3 percent since 1990.

■ The median income of householders under age 25 is well below the national median because many are in college rather than the labor force.

Young adults have seen their incomes fall sharply since 2000

(median income of households headed by people aged 15 to 35, 2000 and 2010; in 2010 dollars)

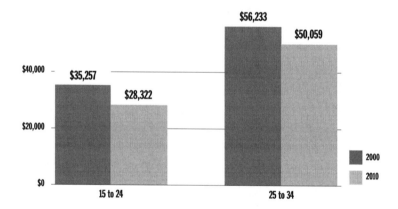

Table 5.1 Median Income of Households Headed by People under Age 35, 1990 to 2010

(median income of total households and households headed by people aged 15 to 34, and index of age group to total, 1990 to 2010; percent change for selected years; in 2010 dollars)

	total households	15 to 24	index, 15–24 to total	25 to 34	index, 25–34 to total
2010	$49,445	$28,322	57	$50,059	101
2009	50,599	31,240	62	51,028	101
2008	50,939	32,678	64	52,050	102
2007	52,823	33,429	63	53,646	102
2006	52,124	33,455	64	53,166	102
2005	51,739	32,132	62	52,915	102
2004	51,174	31,830	62	52,480	103
2003	51,353	32,071	62	53,085	103
2002	51,398	33,726	66	54,938	107
2001	52,005	34,724	67	55,518	107
2000	53,164	35,257	66	56,233	106
1999	53,252	32,907	62	55,076	103
1998	51,944	31,478	61	53,526	103
1997	50,123	30,588	61	51,706	103
1996	49,112	29,665	60	49,660	101
1995	48,408	29,802	62	49,296	102
1994	46,937	28,136	60	48,228	103
1993	46,419	28,726	62	46,479	100
1992	46,646	26,893	58	47,564	102
1991	47,032	28,590	61	48,150	102
1990	48,423	29,112	60	49,096	101
Percent change					
2007 to 2010	–6.4%	–15.3%	–	–6.7%	–
2000 to 2010	–7.0	–19.7	–	–11.0	–
1990 to 2010	2.1	–2.7	–	2.0	–

Note: The index is calculated by dividing the median income of the age group by the national median and multiplying by 100. "–" means not applicable.
Source: Bureau of the Census, Historical Income Statistics—Households, Internet site http://www.census.gov/hhes/www/income/data/historical/household/; calculations by New Strategist

Household Income Differs Sharply by Race and Hispanic Origin

Blacks and Hispanics have the lowest incomes.

Householders under age 25 had a median income of $28,322 in 2010, well below the $49,445 overall median. Black householders in the age group have a median income of just $19,531, in part because of above-average unemployment rates. Asian householders in the age group have the highest median income—more than $37,000 in 2010. The non-Hispanic white median was $32,093, and the Hispanic median was $28,246.

Household income rises substantially in the 25-to-34 age group as young men and women marry and more households have two earners. At $50,059, the median income of householders aged 25 to 34 is just above the overall median. Asians have the highest median income within the 25-to-34 age group, a comfortable $62,432.

■ Differences in household income among young adults by race and Hispanic origin are due to differences in household composition, educational attainment, and unemployment rates.

Asians and non-Hispanic whites have the highest incomes

(median income of householders aged 15 to 34, by race and Hispanic origin, 2010)

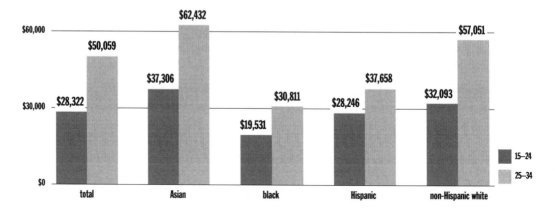

Table 5.2 Income of Households Headed by People under Age 35, 2010: Total Households

(number and percent distribution of total households and households headed by people under age 35, by household income, 2010; households in thousands as of 2011)

	total	15 to 24	aged 25 to 34 total	25 to 29	30 to 34
Total households	**118,682**	**6,140**	**19,572**	**9,331**	**10,241**
Under $10,000	9,231	1,138	1,471	790	681
$10,000 to $19,999	14,321	1,062	1,810	943	868
$20,000 to $29,999	13,667	998	2,275	1,252	1,024
$30,000 to $39,999	12,055	756	2,134	1,088	1,046
$40,000 to $49,999	10,557	571	2,080	979	1,101
$50,000 to $59,999	9,291	410	1,816	915	901
$60,000 to $69,999	7,991	361	1,521	741	781
$70,000 to $79,999	6,887	202	1,325	603	722
$80,000 to $89,999	5,823	168	1,154	500	654
$90,000 to $99,999	4,626	79	813	340	473
$100,000 or more	24,234	396	3,174	1,179	1,995
$100,000 to $124,999	9,008	178	1,452	595	858
$125,000 to $149,999	5,294	86	765	302	462
$150,000 to $174,999	3,386	40	337	91	245
$175,000 to $199,999	1,919	30	216	52	165
$200,000 or more	4,627	62	404	139	265
Median income	$49,445	$28,322	$50,059	$45,413	$53,711
Total households	**100.0%**	**100.0%**	**100.0%**	**100.0%**	**100.0%**
Under $10,000	7.8	18.5	7.5	8.5	6.6
$10,000 to $19,999	12.1	17.3	9.2	10.1	8.5
$20,000 to $29,999	11.5	16.3	11.6	13.4	10.0
$30,000 to $39,999	10.2	12.3	10.9	11.7	10.2
$40,000 to $49,999	8.9	9.3	10.6	10.5	10.8
$50,000 to $59,999	7.8	6.7	9.3	9.8	8.8
$60,000 to $69,999	6.7	5.9	7.8	7.9	7.6
$70,000 to $79,999	5.8	3.3	6.8	6.5	7.1
$80,000 to $89,999	4.9	2.7	5.9	5.4	6.4
$90,000 to $99,999	3.9	1.3	4.2	3.6	4.6
$100,000 or more	20.4	6.4	16.2	12.6	19.5
$100,000 to $124,999	7.6	2.9	7.4	6.4	8.4
$125,000 to $149,999	4.5	1.4	3.9	3.2	4.5
$150,000 to $174,999	2.9	0.7	1.7	1.0	2.4
$175,000 to $199,999	1.6	0.5	1.1	0.6	1.6
$200,000 or more	3.9	1.0	2.1	1.5	2.6

Source: Bureau of the Census, 2011 Current Population Survey, Internet site http://www.census.gov/hhes/www/cpstables/032011/hhinc/toc.htm; calculations by New Strategist

Table 5.3 Income of Households Headed by People under Age 35, 2010: Asian Households

(number and percent distribution of total Asian households and Asian households headed by people under age 35, by income, 2010; households in thousands as of 2011)

	total	15 to 24	aged 25 to 34 total	25 to 29	30 to 34
Total Asian households	**5,040**	**295**	**1,070**	**495**	**576**
Under $10,000	353	56	44	28	16
$10,000 to $19,999	406	24	75	42	34
$20,000 to $29,999	460	41	107	62	44
$30,000 to $39,999	358	33	80	48	32
$40,000 to $49,999	382	36	102	48	54
$50,000 to $59,999	376	18	91	45	46
$60,000 to $69,999	387	19	91	39	52
$70,000 to $79,999	265	18	60	27	33
$80,000 to $89,999	243	9	67	26	41
$90,000 to $99,999	213	6	47	15	31
$100,000 or more	1,594	38	305	114	192
$100,000 to $124,999	508	13	122	54	69
$125,000 to $149,999	335	8	68	33	35
$150,000 to $174,999	258	6	41	9	32
$175,000 to $199,999	135	5	27	5	22
$200,000 or more	358	6	47	13	34
Median income	$63,726	$37,306	$62,432	$53,988	$71,523
Total Asian households	**100.0%**	**100.0%**	**100.0%**	**100.0%**	**100.0%**
Under $10,000	7.0	19.0	4.1	5.7	2.8
$10,000 to $19,999	8.1	8.1	7.0	8.5	5.9
$20,000 to $29,999	9.1	13.9	10.0	12.5	7.6
$30,000 to $39,999	7.1	11.2	7.5	9.7	5.6
$40,000 to $49,999	7.6	12.2	9.5	9.7	9.4
$50,000 to $59,999	7.5	6.1	8.5	9.1	8.0
$60,000 to $69,999	7.7	6.4	8.5	7.9	9.0
$70,000 to $79,999	5.3	6.1	5.6	5.5	5.7
$80,000 to $89,999	4.8	3.1	6.3	5.3	7.1
$90,000 to $99,999	4.2	2.0	4.4	3.0	5.4
$100,000 or more	31.6	12.9	28.5	23.0	33.3
$100,000 to $124,999	10.1	4.4	11.4	10.9	12.0
$125,000 to $149,999	6.6	2.7	6.4	6.7	6.1
$150,000 to $174,999	5.1	2.0	3.8	1.8	5.6
$175,000 to $199,999	2.7	1.7	2.5	1.0	3.8
$200,000 or more	7.1	2.0	4.4	2.6	5.9

Note: Asians are those who identify themselves as being of the race alone and those who identify themselves as being of the race in combination with other races.
Source: Bureau of the Census, 2011 Current Population Survey, Internet site http://www.census.gov/hhes/www/ cpstables/032011/hhinc/toc.htm; calculations by New Strategist

Table 5.4 Income of Households Headed by People under Age 35, 2010: Black Households

(number and percent distribution of total black households and black households headed by people under age 35, by income, 2010; households in thousands as of 2011)

| | | | aged 25 to 34 | | |
	total	15 to 24	total	25 to 29	30 to 34
Total black households	**15,613**	**1,201**	**2,997**	**1,471**	**1,526**
Under $10,000	2,564	359	523	272	251
$10,000 to $19,999	2,573	250	465	222	244
$20,000 to $29,999	2,208	200	481	250	231
$30,000 to $39,999	1,770	112	343	173	170
$40,000 to $49,999	1,454	104	327	137	191
$50,000 to $59,999	1,063	53	213	107	107
$60,000 to $69,999	836	43	161	75	87
$70,000 to $79,999	777	30	148	88	60
$80,000 to $89,999	507	10	88	54	34
$90,000 to $99,999	354	11	49	19	31
$100,000 or more	1,509	29	197	74	120
$100,000 to $124,999	675	8	81	30	50
$125,000 to $149,999	345	6	46	20	24
$150,000 to $174,999	213	6	34	11	23
$175,000 to $199,999	84	1	15	6	9
$200,000 or more	192	8	21	7	14
Median income	$32,106	$19,531	$30,811	$29,549	$31,910
Total black households	**100.0%**	**100.0%**	**100.0%**	**100.0%**	**100.0%**
Under $10,000	16.4	29.9	17.5	18.5	16.4
$10,000 to $19,999	16.5	20.8	15.5	15.1	16.0
$20,000 to $29,999	14.1	16.7	16.0	17.0	15.1
$30,000 to $39,999	11.3	9.3	11.4	11.8	11.1
$40,000 to $49,999	9.3	8.7	10.9	9.3	12.5
$50,000 to $59,999	6.8	4.4	7.1	7.3	7.0
$60,000 to $69,999	5.4	3.6	5.4	5.1	5.7
$70,000 to $79,999	5.0	2.5	4.9	6.0	3.9
$80,000 to $89,999	3.2	0.8	2.9	3.7	2.2
$90,000 to $99,999	2.3	0.9	1.6	1.3	2.0
$100,000 or more	9.7	2.4	6.6	5.0	7.9
$100,000 to $124,999	4.3	0.7	2.7	2.0	3.3
$125,000 to $149,999	2.2	0.5	1.5	1.4	1.6
$150,000 to $174,999	1.4	0.5	1.1	0.7	1.5
$175,000 to $199,999	0.5	0.1	0.5	0.4	0.6
$200,000 or more	1.2	0.7	0.7	0.5	0.9

Note: Blacks are those who identify themselves as being of the race alone and those who identify themselves as being of the race in combination with other races.
Source: Bureau of the Census, 2011 Current Population Survey, Internet site http://www.census.gov/hhes/www/ cpstables/032011/hhinc/toc.htm; calculations by New Strategist

Table 5.5 Income of Households Headed by People under Age 35, 2010: Hispanic Households

(number and percent distribution of total Hispanic households and Hispanic households headed by people under age 35, by income, 2010; households in thousands as of 2011)

	total	15 to 24	aged 25 to 34 total	25 to 29	30 to 34
Total Hispanic households	**13,665**	**1,135**	**3,212**	**1,476**	**1,737**
Under $10,000	1,363	183	295	149	145
$10,000 to $19,999	1,967	197	441	209	231
$20,000 to $29,999	2,100	219	530	259	271
$30,000 to $39,999	1,678	134	427	195	231
$40,000 to $49,999	1,329	120	324	141	183
$50,000 to $59,999	1,132	81	268	137	132
$60,000 to $69,999	895	60	228	93	135
$70,000 to $79,999	679	33	164	69	95
$80,000 to $89,999	564	30	142	52	90
$90,000 to $99,999	391	17	106	49	56
$100,000 or more	1,563	62	289	121	170
$100,000 to $124,999	665	35	151	65	87
$125,000 to $149,999	390	11	88	40	50
$150,000 to $174,999	211	4	33	13	20
$175,000 to $199,999	97	2	11	2	9
$200,000 or more	200	10	6	1	4
Median income	$37,759	$28,246	$37,658	$36,063	$39,508
Total Hispanic households	**100.0%**	**100.0%**	**100.0%**	**100.0%**	**100.0%**
Under $10,000	10.0	16.1	9.2	10.1	8.3
$10,000 to $19,999	14.4	17.4	13.7	14.2	13.3
$20,000 to $29,999	15.4	19.3	16.5	17.5	15.6
$30,000 to $39,999	12.3	11.8	13.3	13.2	13.3
$40,000 to $49,999	9.7	10.6	10.1	9.6	10.5
$50,000 to $59,999	8.3	7.1	8.3	9.3	7.6
$60,000 to $69,999	6.5	5.3	7.1	6.3	7.8
$70,000 to $79,999	5.0	2.9	5.1	4.7	5.5
$80,000 to $89,999	4.1	2.6	4.4	3.5	5.2
$90,000 to $99,999	2.9	1.5	3.3	3.3	3.2
$100,000 or more	11.4	5.5	9.0	8.2	9.8
$100,000 to $124,999	4.9	3.1	4.7	4.4	5.0
$125,000 to $149,999	2.9	1.0	2.7	2.7	2.9
$150,000 to $174,999	1.5	0.4	1.0	0.9	1.2
$175,000 to $199,999	0.7	0.2	0.3	0.1	0.5
$200,000 or more	1.5	0.9	0.2	0.1	0.2

Source: Bureau of the Census, 2011 Current Population Survey, Internet site http://www.census.gov/hhes/www/ cpstables/032011/hhinc/toc.htm; calculations by New Strategist

Table 5.6 Income of Households Headed by People under Age 35, 2010: Non-Hispanic White Households

(number and percent distribution of total non-Hispanic white households and non-Hispanic white households headed by people under age 35, by income, 2010; households in thousands as of 2011)

	total	15 to 24	aged 25 to 34 total	25 to 29	30 to 34
Total non-Hispanic white households	**83,471**	**3,481**	**12,188**	**5,845**	**6,344**
Under $10,000	4,859	527	603	325	278
$10,000 to $19,999	9,247	569	809	457	352
$20,000 to $29,999	8,796	542	1,153	681	472
$30,000 to $39,999	8,157	480	1,265	664	602
$40,000 to $49,999	7,312	318	1,308	653	657
$50,000 to $59,999	6,650	250	1,241	623	617
$60,000 to $69,999	5,813	234	1,039	537	503
$70,000 to $79,999	5,116	127	943	415	527
$80,000 to $89,999	4,455	119	848	362	486
$90,000 to $99,999	3,641	47	614	260	354
$100,000 or more	19,425	267	2,365	869	1,497
$100,000 to $124,999	7,093	122	1,094	448	648
$125,000 to $149,999	4,187	59	554	205	347
$150,000 to $174,999	2,686	27	227	59	169
$175,000 to $199,999	1,596	22	164	41	123
$200,000 or more	3,863	37	326	116	210
Median income	$54,620	$32,093	$57,051	$51,493	$63,268
Total non-Hispanic white households	**100.0%**	**100.0%**	**100.0%**	**100.0%**	**100.0%**
Under $10,000	5.8	15.1	4.9	5.6	4.4
$10,000 to $19,999	11.1	16.3	6.6	7.8	5.5
$20,000 to $29,999	10.5	15.6	9.5	11.7	7.4
$30,000 to $39,999	9.8	13.8	10.4	11.4	9.5
$40,000 to $49,999	8.8	9.1	10.7	11.2	10.4
$50,000 to $59,999	8.0	7.2	10.2	10.7	9.7
$60,000 to $69,999	7.0	6.7	8.5	9.2	7.9
$70,000 to $79,999	6.1	3.6	7.7	7.1	8.3
$80,000 to $89,999	5.3	3.4	7.0	6.2	7.7
$90,000 to $99,999	4.4	1.4	5.0	4.4	5.6
$100,000 or more	23.3	7.7	19.4	14.9	23.6
$100,000 to $124,999	8.5	3.5	9.0	7.7	10.2
$125,000 to $149,999	5.0	1.7	4.5	3.5	5.5
$150,000 to $174,999	3.2	0.8	1.9	1.0	2.7
$175,000 to $199,999	1.9	0.6	1.3	0.7	1.9
$200,000 or more	4.6	1.1	2.7	2.0	3.3

Note: Non-Hispanic whites are those who identify themselves as being white alone and not Hispanic.
Source: Bureau of the Census, 2011 Current Population Survey, Internet site http://www.census.gov/hhes/www/ cpstables/032011/hhinc/toc.htm; calculations by New Strategist

Married Couples Have Above-Average Incomes

Among householders under age 25, the median income of male-headed families is slightly higher than that of married couples, however.

In most age groups married couples are the most affluent household type. Among households headed by people aged 15 to 24, however, the $41,003 median income of male-headed families is higher than the $38,301 median of married couples. Female-headed family households in the age group had a median income of just $21,627, while women who live alone had the lowest incomes, a median of just $16,415.

Male-headed families often have more than one working adult in the household, which boosts income. While most married couples also have more than one earner in the household, among young couples a relatively large proportion has a stay-at-home wife. Many of these couples have young children, and the wife is taking care of the kids rather than working outside the home—lowering household income.

In the 25-to-34 age group, the incomes of married couples soar as dual earners become more common. The median income of married couples aged 25 to 34 stood at $66,584 in 2010, well above that of any other household type. Among men and women in the age group who live alone, women's median income is almost identical to men's—$35,097 versus $35,628.

■ Households headed by people under age 25 are diverse, many having at best one earner, which limits their incomes.

Women who live alone have the lowest incomes

(median income of householders aged 25 to 34 by household type, 2010)

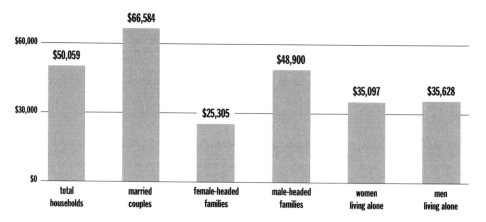

Table 5.7 Income of Households by Household Type, 2010: Aged 15 to 24

(number and percent distribution of households headed by people aged 15 to 24, by household income and household type, 2010; households in thousands as of 2011)

	total	family households			nonfamily households			
					female householder		male householder	
		married couples	female householder, no spouse present	male householder, no spouse present	total	living alone	total	living alone
Total households headed by 15-to-24-year-olds	**6,140**	**1,077**	**1,414**	**825**	**1,355**	**711**	**1,469**	**734**
Under $10,000	1,138	97	346	69	326	250	300	233
$10,000 to $19,999	1,062	148	301	118	235	154	261	166
$20,000 to $29,999	998	154	260	118	218	116	247	140
$30,000 to $39,999	756	165	155	98	163	69	176	79
$40,000 to $49,999	571	138	107	84	124	52	119	36
$50,000 to $59,999	410	107	68	63	84	35	87	31
$60,000 to $69,999	361	93	44	67	52	15	104	17
$70,000 to $79,999	202	52	27	32	39	6	50	9
$80,000 to $89,999	168	45	28	31	34	4	31	8
$90,000 to $99,999	79	19	8	27	15	0	13	4
$100,000 or more	396	60	72	118	66	11	79	12
$100,000 to $124,999	178	43	24	47	21	6	42	4
$125,000 to $149,999	86	5	24	29	16	0	11	6
$150,000 to $174,999	40	3	5	11	12	0	9	2
$175,000 to $199,999	30	1	4	7	7	0	11	0
$200,000 or more	62	8	15	24	10	5	6	0
Median income	$28,322	$38,301	$21,627	$41,003	$25,263	$16,415	$26,030	$17,118
Total households headed by 15-to-24-year-olds	**100.0%**	**100.0%**	**100.0%**	**100.0%**	**100.0%**	**100.0%**	**100.0%**	**100.0%**
Under $10,000	18.5	9.0	24.5	8.4	24.1	35.2	20.4	31.7
$10,000 to $19,999	17.3	13.7	21.3	14.3	17.3	21.7	17.8	22.6
$20,000 to $29,999	16.3	14.3	18.4	14.3	16.1	16.3	16.8	19.1
$30,000 to $39,999	12.3	15.3	11.0	11.9	12.0	9.7	12.0	10.8
$40,000 to $49,999	9.3	12.8	7.6	10.2	9.2	7.3	8.1	4.9
$50,000 to $59,999	6.7	9.9	4.8	7.6	6.2	4.9	5.9	4.2
$60,000 to $69,999	5.9	8.6	3.1	8.1	3.8	2.1	7.1	2.3
$70,000 to $79,999	3.3	4.8	1.9	3.9	2.9	0.8	3.4	1.2
$80,000 to $89,999	2.7	4.2	2.0	3.8	2.5	0.6	2.1	1.1
$90,000 to $99,999	1.3	1.8	0.6	3.3	1.1	0.0	0.9	0.5
$100,000 or more	6.4	5.6	5.1	14.3	4.9	1.5	5.4	1.6
$100,000 to $124,999	2.9	4.0	1.7	5.7	1.5	0.8	2.9	0.5
$125,000 to $149,999	1.4	0.5	1.7	3.5	1.2	0.0	0.7	0.8
$150,000 to $174,999	0.7	0.3	0.4	1.3	0.9	0.0	0.6	0.3
$175,000 to $199,999	0.5	0.1	0.3	0.8	0.5	0.0	0.7	0.0
$200,000 or more	1.0	0.7	1.1	2.9	0.7	0.7	0.4	0.0

Source: Bureau of the Census, 2011 Current Population Survey, Internet site http://www.census.gov/hhes/www/cpstables/032011/hhinc/toc.htm; calculations by New Strategist

Table 5.8 Income of Households by Household Type, 2010: Aged 25 to 34

(number and percent distribution of households headed by people aged 25 to 34, by income and household type, 2010; households in thousands as of 2011)

| | | family households | | | nonfamily households | | | |
| | | | female householder, no spouse present | male householder, no spouse present | female householder | | male householder | |
	total	married couples			total	living alone	total	living alone
Total households headed by 25-to-34-year-olds	**19,572**	**8,551**	**3,281**	**1,234**	**2,696**	**1,839**	**3,811**	**2,318**
Under $10,000	1,471	198	676	65	236	211	297	270
$10,000 to $19,999	1,810	448	613	103	266	230	380	316
$20,000 to $29,999	2,275	648	628	157	374	318	468	370
$30,000 to $39,999	2,134	717	380	157	393	320	486	359
$40,000 to $49,999	2,080	810	362	147	325	252	437	287
$50,000 to $59,999	1,816	899	187	108	258	176	364	215
$60,000 to $69,999	1,521	792	118	100	191	99	319	152
$70,000 to $79,999	1,325	744	86	87	158	84	250	122
$80,000 to $89,999	1,154	702	47	53	121	45	233	88
$90,000 to $99,999	813	524	53	51	81	22	104	27
$100,000 or more	3,174	2,068	128	201	294	81	470	114
$100,000 to $124,999	1,452	965	68	86	125	36	204	62
$125,000 to $149,999	765	487	37	44	65	17	129	19
$150,000 to $174,999	337	218	10	13	45	15	47	9
$175,000 to $199,999	216	141	1	23	19	5	31	0
$200,000 or more	404	257	12	35	40	8	59	24
Median income	$50,059	$66,584	$25,305	$48,900	$42,012	$35,097	$45,662	$35,628
Total households headed by 25-to-34-year-olds	**100.0%**	**100.0%**	**100.0%**	**100.0%**	**100.0%**	**100.0%**	**100.0%**	**100.0%**
Under $10,000	7.5	2.3	20.6	5.3	8.8	11.5	7.8	11.6
$10,000 to $19,999	9.2	5.2	18.7	8.3	9.9	12.5	10.0	13.6
$20,000 to $29,999	11.6	7.6	19.1	12.7	13.9	17.3	12.3	16.0
$30,000 to $39,999	10.9	8.4	11.6	12.7	14.6	17.4	12.8	15.5
$40,000 to $49,999	10.6	9.5	11.0	11.9	12.1	13.7	11.5	12.4
$50,000 to $59,999	9.3	10.5	5.7	8.8	9.6	9.6	9.6	9.3
$60,000 to $69,999	7.8	9.3	3.6	8.1	7.1	5.4	8.4	6.6
$70,000 to $79,999	6.8	8.7	2.6	7.1	5.9	4.6	6.6	5.3
$80,000 to $89,999	5.9	8.2	1.4	4.3	4.5	2.4	6.1	3.8
$90,000 to $99,999	4.2	6.1	1.6	4.1	3.0	1.2	2.7	1.2
$100,000 or more	16.2	24.2	3.9	16.3	10.9	4.4	12.3	4.9
$100,000 to $124,999	7.4	11.3	2.1	7.0	4.6	2.0	5.4	2.7
$125,000 to $149,999	3.9	5.7	1.1	3.6	2.4	0.9	3.4	0.8
$150,000 to $174,999	1.7	2.5	0.3	1.1	1.7	0.8	1.2	0.4
$175,000 to $199,999	1.1	1.6	0.0	1.9	0.7	0.3	0.8	0.0
$200,000 or more	2.1	3.0	0.4	2.8	1.5	0.4	1.5	1.0

Source: Bureau of the Census, 2011 Current Population Survey, Internet site http://www.census.gov/hhes/www/ cpstables/032011/hhinc/toc.htm; calculations by New Strategist

Table 5.9 Income of Households by Household Type, 2010: Aged 25 to 29

(number and percent distribution of households headed by people aged 25 to 29, by income and household type, 2010; households in thousands as of 2011)

| | | family households | | | nonfamily households | | | |
| | | | | | female householder | | male householder | |
	total	married couples	female householder, no spouse present	male householder, no spouse present	total	living alone	total	living alone
Total households headed by 25-to-29-year-olds	**9,331**	**3,348**	**1,585**	**623**	**1,670**	**1,058**	**2,104**	**1,186**
Under $10,000	790	83	376	32	152	128	148	133
$10,000 to $19,999	943	216	308	48	170	139	202	159
$20,000 to $29,999	1,252	298	320	85	270	228	279	220
$30,000 to $39,999	1,088	341	172	84	228	175	263	202
$40,000 to $49,999	979	352	149	70	180	123	227	119
$50,000 to $59,999	915	410	76	53	163	106	213	107
$60,000 to $69,999	741	338	50	49	118	54	187	78
$70,000 to $79,999	603	290	36	52	100	43	124	56
$80,000 to $89,999	500	244	20	23	78	21	135	46
$90,000 to $99,999	340	191	19	23	47	5	59	10
$100,000 or more	1,179	583	60	104	164	35	266	56
$100,000 to $124,999	595	311	35	41	80	16	128	37
$125,000 to $149,999	302	145	20	23	40	12	74	11
$150,000 to $174,999	91	38	2	5	19	4	26	0
$175,000 to $199,999	52	26	1	12	4	0	9	0
$200,000 or more	139	63	2	23	21	3	29	8
Median income	$45,413	$59,056	$23,108	$48,566	$40,855	$31,517	$46,703	$33,255
Total households headed by 25-to-29-year-olds	**100.0%**	**100.0%**	**100.0%**	**100.0%**	**100.0%**	**100.0%**	**100.0%**	**100.0%**
Under $10,000	8.5	2.5	23.7	5.1	9.1	12.1	7.0	11.2
$10,000 to $19,999	10.1	6.5	19.4	7.7	10.2	13.1	9.6	13.4
$20,000 to $29,999	13.4	8.9	20.2	13.6	16.2	21.6	13.3	18.5
$30,000 to $39,999	11.7	10.2	10.9	13.5	13.7	16.5	12.5	17.0
$40,000 to $49,999	10.5	10.5	9.4	11.2	10.8	11.6	10.8	10.0
$50,000 to $59,999	9.8	12.2	4.8	8.5	9.8	10.0	10.1	9.0
$60,000 to $69,999	7.9	10.1	3.2	7.9	7.1	5.1	8.9	6.6
$70,000 to $79,999	6.5	8.7	2.3	8.3	6.0	4.1	5.9	4.7
$80,000 to $89,999	5.4	7.3	1.3	3.7	4.7	2.0	6.4	3.9
$90,000 to $99,999	3.6	5.7	1.2	3.7	2.8	0.5	2.8	0.8
$100,000 or more	12.6	17.4	3.8	16.7	9.8	3.3	12.6	4.7
$100,000 to $124,999	6.4	9.3	2.2	6.6	4.8	1.5	6.1	3.1
$125,000 to $149,999	3.2	4.3	1.3	3.7	2.4	1.1	3.5	0.9
$150,000 to $174,999	1.0	1.1	0.1	0.8	1.1	0.4	1.2	0.0
$175,000 to $199,999	0.6	0.8	0.1	1.9	0.2	0.0	0.4	0.0
$200,000 or more	1.5	1.9	0.1	3.7	1.3	0.3	1.4	0.7

Source: Bureau of the Census, 2011 Current Population Survey, Internet site http://www.census.gov/hhes/www/cpstables/032011/hhinc/toc.htm; calculations by New Strategist

Table 5.10 Income of Households by Household Type, 2010: Aged 30 to 34

(number and percent distribution of households headed by people aged 30 to 34, by income and household type, 2010; households in thousands as of 2011)

| | | family households | | | nonfamily households | | | |
| | | | female householder, no spouse present | male householder, no spouse present | female householder | | male householder | |
	total	married couples			total	living alone	total	living alone
Total households headed by 30-to-34-year-olds	**10,241**	**5,203**	**1,696**	**610**	**1,025**	**781**	**1,707**	**1,132**
Under $10,000	681	115	300	33	84	83	149	137
$10,000 to $19,999	868	231	306	56	96	92	178	157
$20,000 to $29,999	1,024	350	309	72	103	89	190	150
$30,000 to $39,999	1,046	376	208	73	165	145	223	157
$40,000 to $49,999	1,101	457	213	77	143	127	210	168
$50,000 to $59,999	901	489	111	56	95	70	152	108
$60,000 to $69,999	781	454	68	52	74	44	133	74
$70,000 to $79,999	722	453	50	35	58	40	126	66
$80,000 to $89,999	654	458	26	30	43	24	96	41
$90,000 to $99,999	473	333	33	27	34	17	45	16
$100,000 or more	1,995	1,488	70	98	129	49	205	60
$100,000 to $124,999	858	654	34	45	46	21	78	26
$125,000 to $149,999	462	343	18	20	25	7	54	8
$150,000 to $174,999	245	182	8	9	25	11	21	9
$175,000 to $199,999	165	115	0	12	14	5	22	0
$200,000 or more	265	194	10	12	19	5	30	17
Median income	$53,711	$71,831	$27,152	$49,188	$43,212	$38,745	$44,124	$37,856
Total households headed by 30-to-34-year-olds	**100.0%**	**100.0%**	**100.0%**	**100.0%**	**100.0%**	**100.0%**	**100.0%**	**100.0%**
Under $10,000	6.6	2.2	17.7	5.4	8.2	10.6	8.7	12.1
$10,000 to $19,999	8.5	4.4	18.0	9.2	9.4	11.8	10.4	13.9
$20,000 to $29,999	10.0	6.7	18.2	11.8	10.0	11.4	11.1	13.3
$30,000 to $39,999	10.2	7.2	12.3	12.0	16.1	18.6	13.1	13.9
$40,000 to $49,999	10.8	8.8	12.6	12.6	14.0	16.3	12.3	14.8
$50,000 to $59,999	8.8	9.4	6.5	9.2	9.3	9.0	8.9	9.5
$60,000 to $69,999	7.6	8.7	4.0	8.5	7.2	5.6	7.8	6.5
$70,000 to $79,999	7.1	8.7	2.9	5.7	5.7	5.1	7.4	5.8
$80,000 to $89,999	6.4	8.8	1.5	4.9	4.2	3.1	5.6	3.6
$90,000 to $99,999	4.6	6.4	1.9	4.4	3.3	2.2	2.6	1.4
$100,000 or more	19.5	28.6	4.1	16.1	12.6	6.3	12.0	5.3
$100,000 to $124,999	8.4	12.6	2.0	7.4	4.5	2.7	4.6	2.3
$125,000 to $149,999	4.5	6.6	1.1	3.3	2.4	0.9	3.2	0.7
$150,000 to $174,999	2.4	3.5	0.5	1.5	2.4	1.4	1.2	0.8
$175,000 to $199,999	1.6	2.2	0.0	2.0	1.4	0.6	1.3	0.0
$200,000 or more	2.6	3.7	0.6	2.0	1.9	0.6	1.8	1.5

Source: Bureau of the Census, 2011 Current Population Survey, Internet site http://www.census.gov/hhes/www/cpstables/032011/hhinc/toc.htm; calculations by New Strategist

Men and Women under Age 35 Have Lost Ground

Men's incomes in 2010 were lower than in 1990.

Between 2000 and 2010, men aged 15 to 24 saw their median income fall by an enormous 17.6 percent, after adjusting for inflation. Women of the same age experienced a 5.9 percent decline in median income during those years.

The story was similar among men aged 25 to 34, who saw their median income decline by 17 percent between 2000 and 2010, after adjusting for inflation. Women aged 25 to 34 saw their median income decline by a smaller 3.7 percent. Men under age 35 had a lower median income in 2010 than in 1990. Women made considerable gains during the two-decade time period.

■ Many young adults have student loans to pay off even as their incomes are declining.

Incomes of men and women aged 15 to 24 are low because many work part-time

(median income of people aged 15 to 34, by age and sex, 2010)

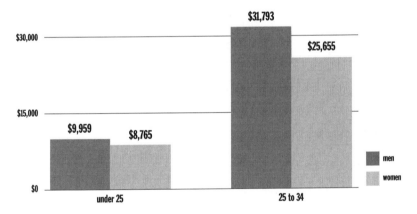

Table 5.11 Median Income of Men under Age 35, 1990 to 2010

(median income of men aged 15 or older and under age 35, and index of age group to total, 1990 to 2010; percent change for selected years; in 2010 dollars)

	total men	15 to 24	index, 15–24 to total	25 to 34	index, 25–34 to total
2010	$32,137	$9,959	31	$31,793	99
2009	32,715	10,202	31	32,441	99
2008	33,580	10,914	33	33,838	101
2007	34,908	11,787	34	34,570	99
2006	34,891	11,856	34	34,746	100
2005	34,929	11,692	33	34,802	100
2004	35,224	11,638	33	35,774	102
2003	35,483	11,809	33	36,231	102
2002	35,435	11,686	33	37,179	105
2001	35,839	11,455	32	37,574	105
2000	35,885	12,086	34	38,305	107
1999	35,714	10,926	31	38,441	108
1998	35,389	10,941	31	37,560	106
1997	34,149	10,115	30	35,211	103
1996	32,980	9,631	29	34,841	106
1995	32,051	9,821	31	33,539	105
1994	31,598	10,253	32	32,887	104
1993	31,354	9,553	30	32,580	104
1992	31,145	9,588	31	32,731	105
1991	31,956	9,806	31	33,714	106
1990	32,817	10,219	31	34,596	105
Percent change					
2000 to 2010	−10.4%	−17.6%	–	−17.0%	–
1990 to 2010	−2.1	−2.5	–	−8.1	–

Note: The index is calculated by dividing the median income of the age group by the national median and multiplying by 100. "–" means not applicable.
Source: Bureau of the Census, Historical Income Statistics—People, Internet site http://www.census.gov/hhes/www/income/data/historical/people/; calculations by New Strategist

Table 5.12 Median Income of Women under Age 35, 1990 to 2010

(median income of women aged 15 or older and under age 35, and index of age group to total, 1990 to 2010; percent change for selected years; in 2010 dollars)

	total women	15 to 24	index, 15–24 to total	25 to 34	index, 25–34 to total
2010	$20,831	$8,765	42	$25,655	123
2009	21,303	9,098	43	25,653	120
2008	21,131	9,014	43	25,876	122
2007	22,001	9,421	43	27,219	124
2006	21,643	9,357	43	26,147	121
2005	20,747	9,180	44	25,481	123
2004	20,393	8,891	44	25,472	125
2003	20,460	8,814	43	26,071	127
2002	20,375	9,189	45	26,238	129
2001	20,461	9,196	45	26,445	129
2000	20,338	9,319	46	26,650	131
1999	20,026	8,738	44	25,265	126
1998	19,276	8,728	45	24,388	127
1997	18,560	8,590	46	23,903	129
1996	17,733	8,138	46	22,671	128
1995	17,232	7,543	44	22,100	128
1994	16,681	8,013	48	21,653	130
1993	16,413	7,951	48	20,784	127
1992	16,313	7,872	48	20,754	127
1991	16,355	8,114	50	20,239	124
1990	16,285	7,927	49	20,359	125
Percent change					
2000 to 2010	2.4%	–5.9%	–	–3.7%	–
1990 to 2010	27.9	10.6	–	26.0	–

Note: The index is calculated by dividing the median income of the age group by the national median and multiplying by 100. "–" means not applicable.
Source: Bureau of the Census, Historical Income Statistics—People, Internet site http://www.census.gov/hhes/www/income/data/historical/people/; calculations by New Strategist

By Age 30 to 34, Men's Incomes Are above Average

The incomes of men under age 25 are low because few work full-time.

The median income of men aged 15 to 24 was a meager $9,959 in 2010. Among men aged 25 to 34, median income was a much larger $31,793. (Millennials were aged 17 to 33 in 2010.) Behind the low figure for the younger age group lies the fact that few men under age 25 work full-time—only 16 percent in 2010. In the 25-to-34 age group, 62 percent of men work full-time, hence their higher incomes.

Among men under age 25, Hispanics have the highest median income ($11,912) because they are most likely to work full-time. Among the 19 percent with full-time jobs, median income was $21,974 in 2010. In the 25-to-34 age group, things change. Among full-time workers, the median income of Hispanic men is lower than that of Asians, blacks, or non-Hispanic whites because they are the least educated. Among men aged 25 to 34 who work full-time, median income ranges from a low of $30,606 for Hispanics to a high of $48,457 for Asians.

■ Men's incomes rise steeply as they enter their thirties and embark on a career.

Among men aged 25 to 34, Hispanics have the lowest median income

(median income of men aged 25 to 34 who work full-time, by race and Hispanic origin, 2010)

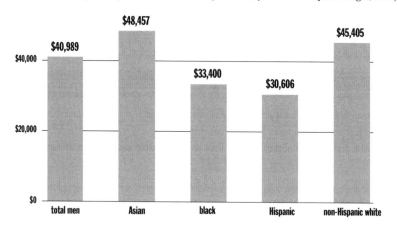

Table 5.13 Income of Men under Age 35, 2010: Total Men

(number and percent distribution of men aged 15 or older and men under age 35 by income and age, 2010; median income of men with income and of men working full-time, year-round; percent working full-time, year-round; men in thousands as of 2011)

| | | | aged 25 to 34 | | |
	total	15 to 24	total	25 to 29	30 to 34
Total men	**118,871**	**21,651**	**20,985**	**10,917**	**10,067**
Without income	13,520	8,613	1,550	925	624
With income	105,351	13,038	19,435	9,992	9,443
Under $5,000	7,350	3,986	951	597	354
$5,000 to $9,999	7,741	2,551	1,339	858	481
$10,000 to $14,999	8,933	1,667	1,515	820	695
$15,000 to $19,999	8,914	1,419	1,683	922	761
$20,000 to $24,999	8,525	1,015	1,870	1,078	792
$25,000 to $29,999	7,133	687	1,510	853	657
$30,000 to $34,999	6,846	491	1,620	918	702
$35,000 to $39,999	5,840	300	1,412	725	686
$40,000 to $44,999	5,714	259	1,357	662	695
$45,000 to $49,999	4,325	154	974	445	529
$50,000 to $54,999	4,978	111	1,082	509	572
$55,000 to $59,999	3,091	63	561	235	326
$60,000 to $64,999	3,416	73	666	322	343
$65,000 to $69,999	2,335	51	459	203	257
$70,000 to $74,999	2,371	45	424	165	258
$75,000 to $79,999	2,040	15	355	139	216
$80,000 to $84,999	1,979	17	289	116	172
$85,000 to $89,999	1,211	18	187	74	113
$90,000 to $94,999	1,362	20	145	39	106
$95,000 to $99,999	860	14	90	31	60
$100,000 or more	10,386	84	948	281	667
Median income					
Men with income	$32,137	$9,959	$31,793	$28,894	$36,581
Working full-time	50,063	24,695	40,989	37,101	45,035
Percent full-time	47.5%	16.3%	61.7%	57.9%	65.9%
PERCENT DISTRIBUTION					
Total men	**100.0%**	**100.0%**	**100.0%**	**100.0%**	**100.0%**
Without income	11.4	39.8	7.4	8.5	6.2
With income	88.6	60.2	92.6	91.5	93.8
Under $15,000	20.2	37.9	18.1	20.8	15.2
$15,000 to $24,999	14.7	11.2	16.9	18.3	15.4
$25,000 to $34,999	11.8	5.4	14.9	16.2	13.5
$35,000 to $49,999	13.4	3.3	17.8	16.8	19.0
$50,000 to $74,999	13.6	1.6	15.2	13.1	17.4
$75,000 or more	15.0	0.8	9.6	6.2	13.3

Source: Bureau of the Census, 2011 Current Population Survey Annual Social and Economic Supplement, Internet site http://www.census.gov/hhes/www/cpstables/032011/perinc/toc.htm; calculations by New Strategist

Table 5.14 Income of Men under Age 35, 2010: Asian Men

(number and percent distribution of Asian men aged 15 or older and under age 35 by income and age, 2010; median income of men with income and of men working full-time, year-round; percent working full-time, year-round; men in thousands as of 2011)

			aged 25 to 34		
	total	15 to 24	total	25 to 29	30 to 34
Asian men	**5,787**	**1,059**	**1,209**	**601**	**608**
Without income	865	490	100	63	37
With income	4,922	569	1,109	538	571
Under $5,000	356	173	72	50	23
$5,000 to $9,999	304	86	37	27	11
$10,000 to $14,999	401	90	75	36	41
$15,000 to $19,999	334	57	98	66	32
$20,000 to $24,999	395	57	86	40	46
$25,000 to $29,999	318	31	73	33	40
$30,000 to $34,999	314	21	87	57	31
$35,000 to $39,999	227	15	67	43	25
$40,000 to $44,999	210	4	58	32	26
$45,000 to $49,999	186	10	53	23	30
$50,000 to $54,999	202	4	44	11	33
$55,000 to $59,999	111	2	28	16	12
$60,000 to $64,999	195	4	63	32	31
$65,000 to $69,999	100	0	38	13	25
$70,000 to $74,999	135	3	38	15	24
$75,000 to $79,999	108	4	29	13	16
$80,000 to $84,999	100	2	14	6	9
$85,000 to $89,999	91	0	25	8	16
$90,000 to $94,999	78	0	16	4	12
$95,000 to $99,999	40	0	3	1	3
$100,000 or more	716	5	101	16	85
Median income					
Men with income	$35,622	$10,946	$36,232	$31,100	$46,543
Working full-time	52,444	25,349	48,457	40,452	56,887
Percent full-time	53.0%	12.4%	63.2%	54.2%	72.0%
PERCENT DISTRIBUTION					
Asian men	**100.0%**	**100.0%**	**100.0%**	**100.0%**	**100.0%**
Without income	14.9	46.3	8.3	10.5	6.1
With income	85.1	53.7	91.7	89.5	93.9
Under $15,000	18.3	33.0	15.2	18.8	12.3
$15,000 to $24,999	12.6	10.8	15.2	17.6	12.8
$25,000 to $34,999	10.9	4.9	13.2	15.0	11.7
$35,000 to $49,999	10.8	2.7	14.7	16.3	13.3
$50,000 to $74,999	12.8	1.2	17.5	14.5	20.6
$75,000 or more	19.6	1.0	15.6	8.0	23.2

Note: Asians are those who identify themselves as being of the race alone and those who identify themselves as being of the race in combination with other races.
Source: Bureau of the Census, 2011 Current Population Survey Annual Social and Economic Supplement, Internet site http://www.census.gov/hhes/www/cpstables/032011/perinc/toc.htm; calculations by New Strategist

Table 5.15 Income of Men under Age 35, 2010: Black Men

(number and percent distribution of black men aged 15 or older and under age 35 by income and age, 2010; median income of men with income and of men working full-time, year-round; percent working full-time, year-round; men in thousands as of 2011)

			aged 25 to 34		
	total	15 to 24	total	25 to 29	30 to 34
Black men	**14,101**	**3,341**	**2,779**	**1,486**	**1,293**
Without income	2,843	1,648	445	252	192
With income	11,258	1,693	2,334	1,234	1,101
Under $5,000	1,052	493	202	140	61
$5,000 to $9,999	1,471	433	261	134	128
$10,000 to $14,999	1,270	242	232	109	123
$15,000 to $19,999	1,035	183	213	110	104
$20,000 to $24,999	1,067	108	306	171	135
$25,000 to $29,999	831	83	196	110	86
$30,000 to $34,999	795	54	178	103	75
$35,000 to $39,999	617	36	152	70	82
$40,000 to $44,999	568	28	143	75	68
$45,000 to $49,999	432	7	96	58	36
$50,000 to $54,999	367	4	89	52	37
$55,000 to $59,999	252	2	31	7	23
$60,000 to $64,999	244	5	53	18	35
$65,000 to $69,999	195	8	36	17	19
$70,000 to $74,999	217	0	36	16	20
$75,000 to $79,999	122	2	23	11	13
$80,000 to $84,999	132	0	22	13	8
$85,000 to $89,999	55	0	0	0	0
$90,000 to $94,999	66	0	7	0	7
$95,000 to $99,999	51	0	3	0	3
$100,000 or more	418	7	56	16	40
Median income					
Men with income	$23,061	$9,068	$23,462	$22,566	$25,006
Working full-time	37,805	22,969	33,400	31,654	36,260
Percent full-time	38.0%	11.9%	49.4%	48.3%	50.7%
PERCENT DISTRIBUTION					
Black men	**100.0%**	**100.0%**	**100.0%**	**100.0%**	**100.0%**
Without income	20.2	49.3	16.0	17.0	14.8
With income	79.8	50.7	84.0	83.0	85.2
Under $15,000	26.9	35.0	25.0	25.8	24.1
$15,000 to $24,999	14.9	8.7	18.7	18.9	18.5
$25,000 to $34,999	11.5	4.1	13.5	14.3	12.5
$35,000 to $49,999	11.5	2.1	14.1	13.7	14.4
$50,000 to $74,999	9.0	0.6	8.8	7.4	10.4
$75,000 or more	6.0	0.3	4.0	2.7	5.5

Note: Blacks are those who identify themselves as being of the race alone and those who identify themselves as being of the race in combination with other races.
Source: Bureau of the Census, 2011 Current Population Survey Annual Social and Economic Supplement, Internet site http://www.census.gov/hhes/www/cpstables/032011/perinc/toc.htm; calculations by New Strategist

Table 5.16 Income of Men under Age 35, 2010: Hispanic Men

(number and percent distribution of Hispanic men aged 15 or older and under age 35 by income and age, 2010; median income of men with income and of men working full-time, year-round; percent working full-time, year-round; men in thousands as of 2011)

			aged 25 to 34		
	total	15 to 24	total	25 to 29	30 to 34
Hispanic men	**18,105**	**4,506**	**4,414**	**2,321**	**2,093**
Without income	3,140	2,106	358	235	123
With income	14,965	2,400	4,056	2,086	1,970
Under $5,000	1,094	561	186	96	90
$5,000 to $9,999	1,573	464	337	226	111
$10,000 to $14,999	1,918	335	536	284	252
$15,000 to $19,999	1,902	335	602	314	289
$20,000 to $24,999	1,669	245	522	272	250
$25,000 to $29,999	1,305	167	352	180	172
$30,000 to $34,999	1,041	92	341	185	155
$35,000 to $39,999	780	48	245	106	139
$40,000 to $44,999	711	42	226	109	116
$45,000 to $49,999	503	33	152	69	83
$50,000 to $54,999	516	16	150	70	80
$55,000 to $59,999	275	8	69	29	40
$60,000 to $64,999	328	18	70	25	45
$65,000 to $69,999	171	5	41	21	20
$70,000 to $74,999	168	12	38	14	24
$75,000 to $79,999	149	0	32	13	20
$80,000 to $84,999	147	1	46	23	23
$85,000 to $89,999	91	4	19	12	7
$90,000 to $94,999	71	2	12	3	9
$95,000 to $99,999	42	2	10	5	5
$100,000 or more	511	10	67	29	39
Median income					
Men with income	$22,233	$11,912	$22,499	$21,604	$24,734
Working full-time	31,671	21,974	30,606	29,464	31,533
Percent full-time	46.3%	19.4%	58.5%	55.9%	61.5%
PERCENT DISTRIBUTION					
Hispanic men	**100.0%**	**100.0%**	**100.0%**	**100.0%**	**100.0%**
Without income	17.3	46.7	8.1	10.1	5.9
With income	82.7	53.3	91.9	89.9	94.1
Under $15,000	25.3	30.2	24.0	26.1	21.6
$15,000 to $24,999	19.7	12.9	25.5	25.2	25.8
$25,000 to $34,999	13.0	5.7	15.7	15.7	15.6
$35,000 to $49,999	11.0	2.7	14.1	12.2	16.1
$50,000 to $74,999	8.1	1.3	8.3	6.9	10.0
$75,000 or more	5.6	0.4	4.2	3.7	4.9

Source: Bureau of the Census, 2011 Current Population Survey Annual Social and Economic Supplement, Internet site http:// www.census.gov/hhes/www/cpstables/032011/perinc/toc.htm; calculations by New Strategist

Table 5.17 Income of Men under Age 35, 2010: Non-Hispanic White Men

(number and percent distribution of non-Hispanic white men aged 15 or older and under age 35 by income and age, 2010; median income of men with income and of men working full-time, year-round; percent working full-time, year-round; men in thousands as of 2011)

	total	15 to 24	aged 25 to 34 total	25 to 29	30 to 34
Non-Hispanic white men	**80,108**	**12,688**	**12,524**	**6,479**	**6,045**
Without income	6,617	4,360	646	381	265
With income	73,491	8,328	11,878	6,098	5,780
Under $5,000	4,754	2,705	485	308	177
$5,000 to $9,999	4,356	1,580	706	465	241
$10,000 to $14,999	5,318	1,013	676	391	284
$15,000 to $19,999	5,542	837	730	422	308
$20,000 to $24,999	5,388	613	988	608	379
$25,000 to $29,999	4,633	399	879	522	357
$30,000 to $34,999	4,634	316	994	556	437
$35,000 to $39,999	4,169	198	945	505	440
$40,000 to $44,999	4,193	184	931	449	484
$45,000 to $49,999	3,165	102	673	296	377
$50,000 to $54,999	3,860	83	796	376	421
$55,000 to $59,999	2,412	51	432	182	249
$60,000 to $64,999	2,615	46	475	244	231
$65,000 to $69,999	1,868	41	341	153	189
$70,000 to $74,999	1,840	29	308	118	189
$75,000 to $79,999	1,650	10	268	103	165
$80,000 to $84,999	1,586	14	206	75	132
$85,000 to $89,999	968	14	141	51	90
$90,000 to $94,999	1,133	18	109	32	78
$95,000 to $99,999	718	11	73	25	49
$100,000 or more	8,691	62	722	218	504
Median income					
Men with income	$37,037	$9,531	$36,946	$32,095	$41,801
Working full-time	54,192	25,849	45,405	41,088	50,143
Percent full-time	49.1%	16.7%	65.6%	61.5%	69.9%
PERCENT DISTRIBUTION					
Non-Hispanic white men	**100.0%**	**100.0%**	**100.0%**	**100.0%**	**100.0%**
Without income	8.3	34.4	5.2	5.9	4.4
With income	91.7	65.6	94.8	94.1	95.6
Under $15,000	18.0	41.8	14.9	18.0	11.6
$15,000 to $24,999	13.6	11.4	13.7	15.9	11.4
$25,000 to $34,999	11.6	5.6	15.0	16.6	13.1
$35,000 to $49,999	14.4	3.8	20.4	19.3	21.5
$50,000 to $74,999	15.7	2.0	18.8	16.6	21.2
$75,000 or more	18.4	1.0	12.1	7.8	16.8

Note: Non-Hispanic whites are those who identify themselves as being white alone and not Hispanic.
Source: Bureau of the Census, 2011 Current Population Survey Annual Social and Economic Supplement, Internet site http://www.census.gov/hhes/www/cpstables/032011/perinc/toc.htm; calculations by New Strategist

By Age 25 to 29, Women's Incomes Are above Average

The incomes of women under age 25 are low because few work full-time.

The median income of women aged 15 to 24 was just $8,765 in 2010. Among women aged 25 to 34, median income was a larger $25,655. (Millennials were aged 17 to 33 in 2010.) Behind the low figure for the younger age group lies the fact that few women under age 25 work full-time—only 13 percent in 2010. In the 25-to-34 age group, 47 percent of women work full-time, hence their higher incomes.

Among full-time workers in the 25-to-34 age group, the median income of Hispanic women is lower than that of Asians, blacks, or non-Hispanic whites because they are the least educated. Among women aged 25 to 34 who work full-time, median income ranges from a low of $29,401 for Hispanics to a high of $42,555 for Asians.

■ Women's incomes rise as they enter their late twenties and thirties and embark on a career.

Among women aged 25 to 34, Hispanics have the lowest median income

(median income of women aged 25 to 34 who work full-time, by race and Hispanic origin, 2010)

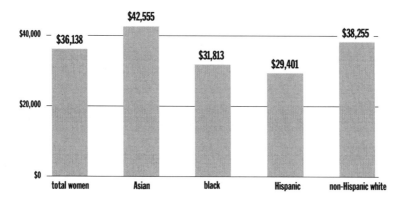

Table 5.18 Income of Women under Age 35, 2010: Total Women

(number and percent distribution of women aged 15 or older and women under age 35 by income and age, 2010; median income of women with income and of women working full-time, year-round; percent working full-time, year-round; women in thousands as of 2011)

	total	15 to 24	aged 25 to 34 total	25 to 29	30 to 34
Total women	**125,084**	**20,761**	**20,599**	**10,464**	**10,135**
Without income	18,942	8,385	2,954	1,495	1,459
With income	106,142	12,376	17,645	8,969	8,676
Under $5,000	12,538	4,089	1,916	932	984
$5,000 to $9,999	14,061	2,685	1,695	942	754
$10,000 to $14,999	13,672	1,848	1,662	912	751
$15,000 to $19,999	10,971	1,268	1,681	957	723
$20,000 to $24,999	8,842	832	1,640	893	745
$25,000 to $29,999	7,228	489	1,398	757	640
$30,000 to $34,999	6,582	349	1,518	813	706
$35,000 to $39,999	5,443	276	1,267	611	657
$40,000 to $44,999	4,778	155	1,110	510	600
$45,000 to $49,999	3,701	116	792	369	423
$50,000 to $54,999	3,527	85	683	356	327
$55,000 to $59,999	2,239	47	392	148	244
$60,000 to $64,999	2,276	34	402	194	208
$65,000 to $69,999	1,464	20	305	136	168
$70,000 to $74,999	1,492	19	260	97	163
$75,000 to $79,999	1,060	7	182	85	98
$80,000 to $84,999	971	18	159	63	96
$85,000 to $89,999	669	3	100	48	52
$90,000 to $94,999	619	0	77	16	61
$95,000 to $99,999	425	0	38	14	25
$100,000 or more	3,584	38	369	120	249
Median income					
Women with income	$20,831	$8,765	$25,655	$23,875	$27,312
Working full-time	38,531	22,024	36,138	34,144	38,156
Percent full-time	34.2%	12.7%	46.6%	46.3%	47.0%
PERCENT DISTRIBUTION					
Total women	**100.0%**	**100.0%**	**100.0%**	**100.0%**	**100.0%**
Without income	15.1	40.4	14.3	14.3	14.4
With income	84.9	59.6	85.7	85.7	85.6
Under $15,000	32.2	41.5	25.6	26.6	24.6
$15,000 to $24,999	15.8	10.1	16.1	17.7	14.5
$25,000 to $34,999	11.0	4.0	14.2	15.0	13.3
$35,000 to $49,999	11.1	2.6	15.4	14.2	16.6
$50,000 to $74,999	8.8	1.0	9.9	8.9	11.0
$75,000 or more	5.9	0.3	4.5	3.3	5.7

Source: Bureau of the Census, 2011 Current Population Survey Annual Social and Economic Supplement, Internet site http://www.census.gov/hhes/www/cpstables/032011/perinc/toc.htm; calculations by New Strategist

Table 5.19 Income of Women under Age 35, 2010: Asian Women

(number and percent distribution of Asian women aged 15 or older and under age 35 by income and age, 2010; median income of women with income and of women working full-time, year-round; percent working full-time, year-round; women in thousands as of 2011)

	total	15 to 24	aged 25 to 34 total	25 to 29	30 to 34
Asian women	**6,460**	**1,011**	**1,300**	**635**	**665**
Without income	1,413	483	296	147	148
With income	5,047	528	1,004	488	517
Under $5,000	694	184	111	48	62
$5,000 to $9,999	617	118	92	57	34
$10,000 to $14,999	518	68	69	41	28
$15,000 to $19,999	397	35	59	44	16
$20,000 to $24,999	380	33	82	48	34
$25,000 to $29,999	293	27	62	23	38
$30,000 to $34,999	333	21	84	31	53
$35,000 to $39,999	229	16	62	31	31
$40,000 to $44,999	250	7	65	31	34
$45,000 to $49,999	144	3	50	22	28
$50,000 to $54,999	188	10	43	24	20
$55,000 to $59,999	113	6	19	6	14
$60,000 to $64,999	146	1	47	27	21
$65,000 to $69,999	89	0	17	12	4
$70,000 to $74,999	92	0	24	5	20
$75,000 to $79,999	68	0	18	9	9
$80,000 to $84,999	76	0	19	9	11
$85,000 to $89,999	42	0	10	4	7
$90,000 to $94,999	58	0	18	2	16
$95,000 to $99,999	20	0	6	2	4
$100,000 or more	297	1	48	12	36
Median income					
Women with income	$23,664	$7,491	$31,461	$25,929	$34,301
Working full-time	41,821	25,676	42,555	41,484	44,785
Percent full-time	36.6%	9.2%	44.9%	40.9%	48.7%
PERCENT DISTRIBUTION					
Asian women	**100.0%**	**100.0%**	**100.0%**	**100.0%**	**100.0%**
Without income	21.9	47.8	22.8	23.1	22.3
With income	78.1	52.2	77.2	76.9	77.7
Under $15,000	28.3	36.6	20.9	23.0	18.6
$15,000 to $24,999	12.0	6.7	10.8	14.5	7.5
$25,000 to $34,999	9.7	4.7	11.2	8.5	13.7
$35,000 to $49,999	9.6	2.6	13.6	13.2	14.0
$50,000 to $74,999	9.7	1.7	11.5	11.7	11.9
$75,000 or more	8.7	0.1	9.2	6.0	12.5

Note: Asians are those who identify themselves as being of the race alone and those who identify themselves as being of the race in combination with other races.
Source: Bureau of the Census, 2011 Current Population Survey Annual Social and Economic Supplement, Internet site http://www.census.gov/hhes/www/cpstables/032011/perinc/toc.htm; calculations by New Strategist

Table 5.20 Income of Women under Age 35, 2010: Black Women

(number and percent distribution of black women aged 15 or older and under age 35 by income and age, 2010; median income of women with income and of women working full-time, year-round; percent working full-time, year-round; women in thousands as of 2011)

	total	15 to 24	aged 25 to 34 total	25 to 29	30 to 34
Black women	**16,879**	**3,511**	**3,134**	**1,610**	**1,524**
Without income	2,948	1,641	336	162	174
With income	13,931	1,870	2,798	1,448	1,350
Under $5,000	1,507	610	287	146	141
$5,000 to $9,999	2,173	448	346	201	144
$10,000 to $14,999	1,965	276	314	162	152
$15,000 to $19,999	1,402	155	305	172	133
$20,000 to $24,999	1,274	108	343	171	171
$25,000 to $29,999	1,086	110	243	140	103
$30,000 to $34,999	925	49	199	112	87
$35,000 to $39,999	730	30	206	95	111
$40,000 to $44,999	612	21	169	65	103
$45,000 to $49,999	452	20	89	34	55
$50,000 to $54,999	416	12	87	47	40
$55,000 to $59,999	242	12	43	22	21
$60,000 to $64,999	248	3	19	9	10
$65,000 to $69,999	128	4	19	6	13
$70,000 to $74,999	144	3	26	11	16
$75,000 to $79,999	108	0	24	14	10
$80,000 to $84,999	111	0	16	11	5
$85,000 to $89,999	60	2	11	10	2
$90,000 to $94,999	65	0	16	5	11
$95,000 to $99,999	36	0	9	2	8
$100,000 or more	247	5	27	11	15
Median income					
Women with income	$19,634	$8,602	$21,718	$20,991	$22,454
Working full-time	33,918	22,278	31,813	30,653	34,469
Percent full-time	35.7%	12.8%	45.4%	44.2%	46.8%
PERCENT DISTRIBUTION					
Black women	**100.0%**	**100.0%**	**100.0%**	**100.0%**	**100.0%**
Without income	17.5	46.7	10.7	10.1	11.4
With income	82.5	53.3	89.3	89.9	88.6
Under $15,000	33.4	38.0	30.2	31.6	28.7
$15,000 to $24,999	15.9	7.5	20.7	21.3	19.9
$25,000 to $34,999	11.9	4.5	14.1	15.7	12.5
$35,000 to $49,999	10.6	2.0	14.8	12.0	17.7
$50,000 to $74,999	7.0	1.0	6.2	5.9	6.6
$75,000 or more	3.7	0.2	3.3	3.3	3.3

Note: Blacks are those who identify themselves as being of the race alone and those who identify themselves as being of the race in combination with other races.
Source: Bureau of the Census, 2011 Current Population Survey Annual Social and Economic Supplement, Internet site http://www.census.gov/hhes/www/cpstables/032011/perinc/toc.htm; calculations by New Strategist

Table 5.21 Income of Women under Age 35, 2010: Hispanic Women

(number and percent distribution of Hispanic women aged 15 or older and under age 35 by income and age, 2010; median income of women with income and of women working full-time, year-round; percent working full-time, year-round; women in thousands as of 2011)

	total	15 to 24	aged 25 to 34 total	25 to 29	30 to 34
Hispanic women	**16,964**	**3,892**	**3,716**	**1,862**	**1,854**
Without income	4,842	1,968	977	475	502
With income	12,122	1,924	2,739	1,387	1,352
Under $5,000	1,654	600	322	165	157
$5,000 to $9,999	2,058	433	309	171	138
$10,000 to $14,999	1,901	328	375	208	169
$15,000 to $19,999	1,442	204	351	195	156
$20,000 to $24,999	1,165	154	315	167	147
$25,000 to $29,999	829	62	228	113	115
$30,000 to $34,999	713	52	221	93	128
$35,000 to $39,999	570	41	177	87	91
$40,000 to $44,999	410	23	112	50	61
$45,000 to $49,999	257	8	89	41	48
$50,000 to $54,999	270	10	68	36	33
$55,000 to $59,999	133	3	28	11	17
$60,000 to $64,999	154	0	36	14	22
$65,000 to $69,999	100	1	35	9	24
$70,000 to $74,999	68	0	10	5	4
$75,000 to $79,999	56	0	12	4	9
$80,000 to $84,999	59	0	12	9	3
$85,000 to $89,999	45	2	10	5	6
$90,000 to $94,999	33	0	6	0	6
$95,000 to $99,999	16	0	2	0	1
$100,000 or more	187	2	22	4	18
Median income					
Women with income	$16,269	$9,071	$20,140	$18,287	$21,501
Working full-time	28,944	20,922	29,401	27,109	30,867
Percent full-time	30.5%	11.0%	38.3%	37.1%	39.6%
PERCENT DISTRIBUTION					
Hispanic women	**100.0%**	**100.0%**	**100.0%**	**100.0%**	**100.0%**
Without income	28.5	50.6	26.3	25.5	27.1
With income	71.5	49.4	73.7	74.5	72.9
Under $15,000	33.1	35.0	27.1	29.2	25.0
$15,000 to $24,999	15.4	9.2	17.9	19.4	16.3
$25,000 to $34,999	9.1	2.9	12.1	11.1	13.1
$35,000 to $49,999	7.3	1.8	10.2	9.6	10.8
$50,000 to $74,999	4.3	0.4	4.8	4.0	5.4
$75,000 or more	2.3	0.1	1.7	1.2	2.3

Source: Bureau of the Census, 2011 Current Population Survey Annual Social and Economic Supplement, Internet site http://www.census.gov/hhes/www/cpstables/032011/perinc/toc.htm; calculations by New Strategist

Table 5.22 Income of Women under Age 35, 2010: Non-Hispanic White Women

(number and percent distribution of non-Hispanic white women aged 15 or older and under age 35 by income and age, 2010; median income of women with income and of women working full-time, year-round; percent working full-time, year-round; women in thousands as of 2011)

	total	15 to 24	aged 25 to 34 total	25 to 29	30 to 34
Non-Hispanic white women	**84,028**	**12,302**	**12,336**	**6,303**	**6,033**
Without income	9,663	4,263	1,337	685	652
With income	74,365	8,039	10,999	5,618	5,381
Under $5,000	8,605	2,693	1,186	562	624
$5,000 to $9,999	9,108	1,681	945	514	432
$10,000 to $14,999	9,217	1,163	903	506	397
$15,000 to $19,999	7,665	881	954	547	408
$20,000 to $24,999	5,946	531	885	506	380
$25,000 to $29,999	4,964	292	853	473	381
$30,000 to $34,999	4,551	221	1,002	569	432
$35,000 to $39,999	3,868	191	806	393	414
$40,000 to $44,999	3,505	106	759	362	396
$45,000 to $49,999	2,820	88	554	273	282
$50,000 to $54,999	2,638	51	483	248	234
$55,000 to $59,999	1,738	27	300	110	188
$60,000 to $64,999	1,728	30	306	147	158
$65,000 to $69,999	1,129	12	231	107	124
$70,000 to $74,999	1,172	16	199	75	124
$75,000 to $79,999	826	7	127	58	69
$80,000 to $84,999	717	18	111	33	79
$85,000 to $89,999	518	1	67	29	38
$90,000 to $94,999	462	0	35	8	27
$95,000 to $99,999	344	0	20	8	11
$100,000 or more	2,844	30	274	93	181
Median income					
Women with income	$21,754	$8,794	$28,377	$26,586	$30,604
Working full-time	41,307	22,263	38,255	35,962	41,178
Percent full-time	34.6%	13.6%	49.6%	50.2%	49.0%
PERCENT DISTRIBUTION					
Non-Hispanic white women	**100.0%**	**100.0%**	**100.0%**	**100.0%**	**100.0%**
Without income	11.5	34.7	10.8	10.9	10.8
With income	88.5	65.3	89.2	89.1	89.2
Under $15,000	32.0	45.0	24.6	25.1	24.1
$15,000 to $24,999	16.2	11.5	14.9	16.7	13.1
$25,000 to $34,999	11.3	4.2	15.0	16.5	13.5
$35,000 to $49,999	12.1	3.1	17.2	16.3	18.1
$50,000 to $74,999	10.0	1.1	12.3	10.9	13.7
$75,000 or more	6.8	0.5	5.1	3.6	6.7

Note: Non-Hispanic whites are those who identify themselves as being white alone and not Hispanic.
Source: Bureau of the Census, 2011 Current Population Survey Annual Social and Economic Supplement, Internet site http://www.census.gov/hhes/www/cpstables/032011/perinc/toc.htm; calculations by New Strategist

Earnings Rise with Education

The highest earners are men and women with graduate degrees.

For many years, a college degree has been well worth the cost. Even among young adults, the higher the education the greater the earnings. Among people aged 25 to 34 who work full-time, men with a professional degree and men and women with a doctoral degree earned a median of more than $66,000 in 2010.

Among men aged 25 to 34 who went no further than high school, full-time workers earned only $33,262 in 2010. For their counterparts with a bachelor's degree, median earnings were $51,141. The pattern is the same for women. Among women aged 25 to 34 who went no further than high school, full-time workers earned only $25,433 in 2010. Among women in the age group with a bachelor's degree, median earnings were above $41,623.

■ Steeply rising tuition costs may reduce the financial return of a college degree.

College bonus still exists for Millennials

(median earnings of men aged 25 to 34 with earnings, by education, 2010)

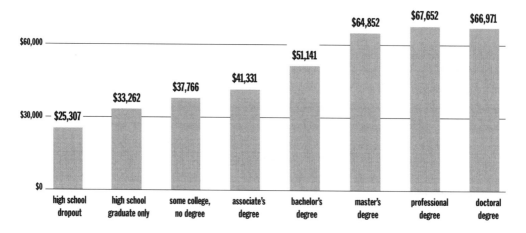

Table 5.23 Earnings of Men by Education, 2010: Aged 25 to 34

(number and percent distribution of men aged 25 to 34 who work full-time, year-round, by earnings and educational attainment, 2010; median earnings of men with earnings; men in thousands as of 2011)

	total	less than 9th grade	9th to 12th grade, no degree	high school graduate	some college	associate's degree	bachelor's degree or more				
							total	bachelor's degree	master's degree	professional degree	doctoral degree
Men aged 25 to 34 who work full-time	**12,951**	**378**	**728**	**3,689**	**2,253**	**1,282**	**4,620**	**3,517**	**766**	**182**	**155**
Under $5,000	49	2	3	22	12	0	11	11	0	0	0
$5,000 to $9,999	133	10	18	58	23	9	15	10	6	0	0
$10,000 to $14,999	422	47	66	137	91	32	48	46	2	0	0
$15,000 to $19,999	783	98	115	303	137	50	78	66	8	3	3
$20,000 to $24,999	1,148	72	151	466	209	91	159	136	19	4	0
$25,000 to $29,999	1,133	44	113	451	209	115	201	183	13	0	5
$30,000 to $34,999	1,379	32	75	482	272	156	360	301	45	5	9
$35,000 to $39,999	1,161	27	47	349	256	125	356	298	45	11	1
$40,000 to $44,999	1,176	13	34	390	230	138	372	312	37	17	4
$45,000 to $49,999	874	16	26	218	188	104	322	255	51	10	6
$50,000 to $54,999	996	4	33	255	137	122	445	360	37	26	22
$55,000 to $59,999	514	4	10	128	70	50	252	175	58	7	12
$60,000 to $64,999	616	0	10	105	101	67	332	263	62	1	5
$65,000 to $69,999	404	4	2	53	56	54	236	173	42	8	12
$70,000 to $74,999	382	0	3	62	81	37	198	138	50	8	2
$75,000 to $79,999	310	3	2	53	37	28	186	129	46	4	7
$80,000 to $84,999	267	0	3	31	28	21	184	127	50	4	4
$85,000 to $89,999	157	0	2	22	8	16	110	83	13	7	8
$90,000 to $94,999	128	0	5	19	9	14	82	55	25	1	0
$95,000 to $99,999	80	0	0	6	6	4	63	30	25	8	0
$100,000 or more	844	2	9	79	95	50	610	366	131	58	55
Median earnings	$40,716	$21,741	$25,307	$33,262	$37,766	$41,331	$52,596	$51,141	$64,852	$67,652	$66,971

PERCENT DISTRIBUTION

	total	less than 9th grade	9th to 12th grade, no degree	high school graduate	some college	associate's degree	bachelor's degree or more				
							total	bachelor's degree	master's degree	professional degree	doctoral degree
Men aged 25 to 34 who work full-time	100.0%	100.0%	100.0%	100.0%	100.0%	100.0%	100.0%	100.0%	100.0%	100.0%	100.0%
Under $15,000	4.7	15.6	12.0	5.9	5.6	3.2	1.6	1.9	1.0	0.0	0.0
$15,000 to $24,999	14.9	45.0	36.5	20.8	15.4	11.0	5.1	5.7	3.5	3.8	1.9
$25,000 to $34,999	19.4	20.1	25.8	25.3	21.3	21.1	12.1	13.8	7.6	2.7	9.0
$35,000 to $49,999	24.8	14.8	14.7	25.9	29.9	28.6	22.7	24.6	17.4	20.9	7.1
$50,000 to $74,999	22.5	3.2	8.0	16.3	19.8	25.7	31.7	31.5	32.5	27.5	34.2
$75,000 to $99,999	7.3	0.8	1.6	3.6	3.9	6.5	13.5	12.1	20.8	13.2	12.3
$100,000 or more	6.5	0.5	1.2	2.1	4.2	3.9	13.2	10.4	17.1	31.9	35.5

Note: Earnings include wages and salary only.
Source: Bureau of the Census, 2011 Current Population Survey Annual Social and Economic Supplement, Internet site http://www.census.gov/hhes/www/cpstables/032011/perinc/toc.htm; calculations by New Strategist

Table 5.24 Earnings of Women by Education, 2010: Aged 25 to 34

(number and percent distribution of women aged 25 to 34 who work full-time, year-round, by earnings and edu-cational attainment, 2010; median earnings of women with earnings; women in thousands as of 2011)

| | total | less than 9th grade | 9th to 12th grade, no degree | high school graduate | some college | associate's degree | bachelor's degree or more | | | |
							total	bachelor's degree	master's degree	professional degree	doctoral degree
Women aged 25 to 34 who work full-time	**9,609**	**126**	**277**	**1,847**	**1,688**	**1,187**	**4,484**	**3,059**	**1,096**	**167**	**161**
Under $5,000	34	2	6	12	6	3	5	3	2	0	0
$5,000 to $9,999	122	8	12	51	23	6	22	16	7	0	0
$10,000 to $14,999	431	28	59	155	95	35	58	54	5	0	0
$15,000 to $19,999	830	36	77	276	182	79	180	146	24	10	0
$20,000 to $24,999	1,064	25	60	402	278	116	183	158	22	3	0
$25,000 to $29,999	974	9	16	231	275	168	275	244	25	2	3
$30,000 to $34,999	1,190	10	21	256	258	184	461	361	97	4	0
$35,000 to $39,999	1,043	1	13	160	199	137	534	371	142	14	7
$40,000 to $44,999	867	0	1	111	105	111	538	356	161	8	13
$45,000 to $49,999	644	0	6	71	82	95	390	264	85	21	19
$50,000 to $54,999	561	1	0	30	83	73	373	224	125	15	10
$55,000 to $59,999	281	3	0	15	20	38	205	133	56	10	6
$60,000 to $64,999	321	0	0	25	14	34	248	170	58	6	13
$65,000 to $69,999	239	0	3	7	14	30	183	137	30	5	11
$70,000 to $74,999	227	0	0	14	18	44	152	97	37	14	3
$75,000 to $79,999	150	0	0	9	14	7	122	62	42	5	12
$80,000 to $84,999	148	1	0	15	7	12	113	57	41	6	9
$85,000 to $89,999	79	0	0	4	4	8	63	42	20	0	2
$90,000 to $94,999	60	0	0	3	0	1	56	29	18	3	7
$95,000 to $99,999	36	0	0	0	4	0	31	18	10	4	1
$100,000 or more	307	0	2	1	6	7	290	120	89	36	46
Median earnings	$35,504	$17,645	$18,304	$25,433	$29,644	$35,060	$44,727	$41,623	$48,078	$58,367	$69,013

PERCENT DISTRIBUTION

Women aged 25 to 34 who work full-time	100.0%	100.0%	100.0%	100.0%	100.0%	100.0%	100.0%	100.0%	100.0%	100.0%	100.0%
Under $15,000	6.1	30.2	27.8	11.8	7.3	3.7	1.9	2.4	1.3	0.0	0.0
$15,000 to $24,999	19.7	48.4	49.5	36.7	27.3	16.4	8.1	9.9	4.2	7.8	0.0
$25,000 to $34,999	22.5	15.1	13.4	26.4	31.6	29.7	16.4	19.8	11.1	3.6	1.9
$35,000 to $49,999	26.6	0.8	7.2	18.5	22.9	28.9	32.6	32.4	35.4	25.7	24.2
$50,000 to $74,999	17.0	3.2	1.1	4.9	8.8	18.4	25.9	24.9	27.9	29.9	26.7
$75,000 to $99,999	4.9	0.8	0.0	1.7	1.7	2.4	8.6	6.8	12.0	10.8	19.3
$100,000 or more	3.2	0.0	0.7	0.1	0.4	0.6	6.5	3.9	8.1	21.6	28.6

Note: Earnings include wages and salary only.
Source: Bureau of the Census, 2011 Current Population Survey Annual Social and Economic Supplement, Internet site http://www.census.gov/hhes/www/cpstables/032011/perinc/toc.htm; calculations by New Strategist

Many Young Adults Are Poor

The Millennial generation accounts for 28 percent of people living in poverty.

Children and young adults are much more likely to be poor than middle-aged or older adults. While 15.1 percent of Americans were poor in 2010, the poverty rate among 18-to-34-year-olds (the Millennial generation was aged 16 to 33 in 2010) was a larger 18.0 percent.

There is variation in the poverty rate among Millennials by race and Hispanic origin. The figure ranges from a low of 14 percent among Asians and non-Hispanic whites to a high of 25 to 28 percent among Hispanics and blacks. Non-Hispanic whites account for a 45 percent minority of the Millennial poor, while Hispanics are 27 percent and blacks 23 percent.

■ Poverty rates for Millennials are above average because many live in female-headed families—the poorest household type.

Among Millennials, Asians and non-Hispanic whites have the lowest poverty rate

(percent of people aged 18 to 34 who live below the poverty level, by race and Hispanic origin, 2010)

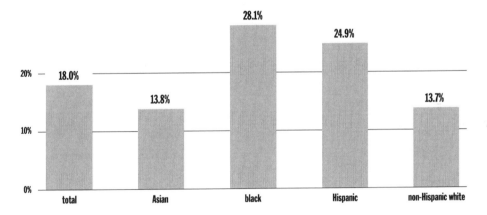

Table 5.25 People below Poverty Level by Age, Race, and Hispanic Origin, 2010

(number, percent, and percent distribution of people below poverty level by age, race, and Hispanic origin, 2010; people in thousands as of 2011)

	total	Asian	black	Hispanic	non-Hispanic white
NUMBER IN POVERTY					
Total people	**46,180**	**1,859**	**11,361**	**13,243**	**19,599**
Under age 18	16,401	547	4,817	6,110	5,002
Aged 18 to 34	12,840	551	2,999	3,464	5,814
Aged 18 to 24	6,507	296	1,514	1,547	3,132
Aged 25 to 34	6,333	255	1,485	1,917	2,682
Aged 35 to 44	5,028	223	1,032	1,618	2,129
Aged 45 to 54	4,662	181	1,039	968	2,421
Aged 55 to 59	1,972	89	445	308	1,095
Aged 60 to 64	1,755	56	393	261	1,024
Aged 65 or older	3,520	213	636	514	2,116
PERCENT IN POVERTY					
Total people	**15.1%**	**11.9%**	**27.4%**	**26.6%**	**9.9%**
Under age 18	22.0	13.6	38.2	35.0	12.4
Aged 18 to 34	18.0	13.8	28.1	24.9	13.7
Aged 18 to 24	21.9	19.8	31.9	26.8	17.8
Aged 25 to 34	15.2	10.2	25.1	23.6	10.8
Aged 35 to 44	12.6	8.8	19.8	22.9	8.6
Aged 45 to 54	10.6	8.7	19.0	18.1	7.9
Aged 55 to 59	10.1	10.2	20.5	17.1	7.6
Aged 60 to 64	10.1	8.0	21.2	18.0	7.7
Aged 65 or older	9.0	14.4	18.2	18.0	6.8
PERCENT DISTRIBUTION OF POOR BY AGE					
Total people	**100.0%**	**100.0%**	**100.0%**	**100.0%**	**100.0%**
Under age 18	35.5	29.4	42.4	46.1	25.5
Aged 18 to 34	27.8	29.6	26.4	26.2	29.7
Aged 18 to 24	14.1	15.9	13.3	11.7	16.0
Aged 25 to 34	13.7	13.7	13.1	14.5	13.7
Aged 35 to 44	10.9	12.0	9.1	12.2	10.9
Aged 45 to 54	10.1	9.7	9.1	7.3	12.4
Aged 55 to 59	4.3	4.8	3.9	2.3	5.6
Aged 60 to 64	3.8	3.0	3.5	2.0	5.2
Aged 65 or older	7.6	11.5	5.6	3.9	10.8

	total	Asian	black	Hispanic	non-Hispanic white
PERCENT DISTRIBUTION OF POOR BY RACE AND HISPANIC ORIGIN					
Total people	**100.0%**	**4.0%**	**24.6%**	**28.7%**	**42.4%**
Under age 18	100.0	3.3	29.4	37.3	30.5
Aged 18 to 34	100.0	4.3	23.4	27.0	45.3
Aged 18 to 24	100.0	4.5	23.3	23.8	48.1
Aged 25 to 34	100.0	4.0	23.4	30.3	42.3
Aged 35 to 44	100.0	4.4	20.5	32.2	42.3
Aged 45 to 54	100.0	3.9	22.3	20.8	51.9
Aged 55 to 59	100.0	4.5	22.6	15.6	55.5
Aged 60 to 64	100.0	3.2	22.4	14.9	58.3
Aged 65 or older	100.0	6.1	18.1	14.6	60.1

Note: Numbers do not add to total because Asians and blacks are those who identify themselves as being of the race alone and those who identify themselves as being of the race in combination with other races, because Hispanics may be of any race, and because not all races are shown. Non-Hispanic whites are those who identify themselves as being white alone and not Hispanic. Source: Bureau of the Census, 2011 Current Population Survey Annual Social and Economic Supplement, Internet site http://www.census.gov/hhes/www/cpstables/032011/pov/toc.htm; calculations by New Strategist

6

Labor Force

■ The percentage of men and women under age 35 (Millennials were aged 17 to 34 in 2011) who are in the labor force fell sharply between 2000 and 2011. The decline was particularly steep among teenagers.

■ Workers under age 35 constitute a large share of the nation's unemployed. Among the 13.7 million unemployed workers in 2011, nearly 7 million (50 percent) were under age 35.

■ Nearly one-fourth of black men under age 35 were unemployed in 2011. In contrast, only 8 percent of Asian men in the age group were unemployed.

■ Workers under age 35 account for 75 percent of waiters and waitresses, 65 percent of cashiers, 63 percent of food preparation workers, 49 percent of retail salespersons, and 47 percent of customer service representatives.

■ Among the nation's 74 million workers who were paid hourly rates in 2011, only 3.8 million made minimum wage or less. Of those workers, more than 70 percent are under age 35.

■ Between 2010 and 2020, the Millennial generation will age into its late thirties and early forties. The number of workers aged 25 to 44 will expand by nearly 5 million.

Fewer Teenagers Have Jobs

Labor force participation rate has fallen sharply among 16-to-19-year-olds.

Teenage labor force participation has plummeted over the past decade. The labor force participation of boys aged 16 to 17 fell 20.5 percentage points between 2000 and 2011. Among girls in the age group, labor force participation fell 18.2 percentage points. Teens aged 18 to 19 also experienced a steep decline in labor force participation, their rate falling by 16.7 and 13.9 percent points, respectively, among boys and girls. Labor force participation rates are also down among men and women in their twenties and early thirites.

The weak economy is one factor behind declining labor force participation rates among teens and young adults. Another factor is high school students' greater focus on academics and extracurricular activities as they position themselves for college.

■ With college costs rising, many teens are polishing their academic resumes and hoping for scholarships.

A shrinking share of teenagers is in the labor force

(percent of people aged 16 to 19 in the labor force, by sex, 2000 and 2011)

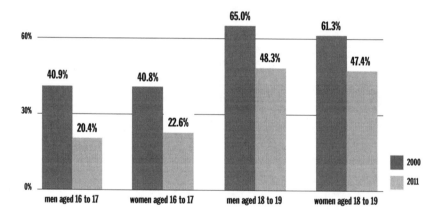

Table 6.1 Labor Force Participation Rate by Sex and Age, 2000 to 2011

(civilian labor force participation rate of people aged 16 or older, by sex and age, 2000 to 2011; percentage point change, 2000–11)

	2011	2010	2000	percentage point change 2000–11
Men aged 16 or older	**70.5%**	**71.2%**	**74.8%**	**–4.3**
Aged 16 to 17	20.4	21.8	40.9	–20.5
Aged 18 to 19	48.3	49.6	65.0	–16.7
Aged 20 to 24	74.7	74.5	82.6	–7.9
Aged 25 to 29	87.8	88.4	92.5	–4.7
Aged 30 to 34	90.6	91.1	94.2	–3.6
Aged 35 to 39	91.5	92.2	93.2	–1.7
Aged 40 to 44	90.4	90.7	92.1	–1.7
Aged 45 to 49	88.1	88.5	90.2	–2.1
Aged 50 to 54	84.2	85.1	86.8	–2.6
Aged 55 to 59	78.2	78.5	77.0	1.2
Aged 60 to 64	59.1	60.0	54.9	4.2
Aged 65 or older	22.8	22.1	17.7	5.1
Women aged 16 or older	**58.1**	**58.6**	**59.9**	**–1.8**
Aged 16 to 17	22.6	23.0	40.8	–18.2
Aged 18 to 19	47.4	48.6	61.3	–13.9
Aged 20 to 24	67.8	68.3	73.1	–5.3
Aged 25 to 29	74.4	75.6	76.7	–2.3
Aged 30 to 34	73.4	73.8	75.5	–2.1
Aged 35 to 39	73.7	74.1	75.7	–2.0
Aged 40 to 44	75.6	76.2	78.7	–3.1
Aged 45 to 49	76.5	76.8	79.1	–2.6
Aged 50 to 54	74.3	74.6	74.1	0.2
Aged 55 to 59	67.7	68.4	61.4	6.3
Aged 60 to 64	50.3	50.7	40.2	10.1
Aged 65 or older	14.0	13.8	9.4	4.6

Source: Bureau of Labor Statistics, Labor Force Statistics from the Current Population Survey, Internet site http://www.bls.gov/cps/tables.htm#empstat; calculations by New Strategist

Most Young Adults Are in the Labor Force

More than 70 percent of 20-to-24-year-olds are working or looking for work.

Young men join the labor force at a slower rate than they once did. Among men aged 18 to 19, only 48 percent have jobs because most are in college. The labor force participation rate of young men increases to 75 percent in the 20-to-24 age group, then rises to 91 percent among men aged 25 to 29.

The labor force participation rate of women under age 25 is almost identical to that of men. Among 18-to-19-year old women, 47 percent are in the labor force. The proportion increases to 68 percent among women aged 20 to 24. A substantial gap in the participation rate emerges in the 25-to-29 age group. While 88 percent of men aged 25 to 29 are in the labor force, the figure is a smaller 74 percent among women.

Workers under age 35 account for a large share of the nation's unemployed. Among the 13.7 million unemployed workers in 2011, nearly 7 million (50 percent) were under age 35. The unemployment rate in the under-35 age group was 12.5 percent in 2011—much higher than the 8.9 percent national rate. Unemployment was highest among 16-to-17-year-olds at 28 percent.

■ Young adults are much more likely than older workers to be unemployed because many are in entry-level positions and are the first to be let go during economic downturns.

Unemployment falls with increasing age

(unemployment rate of people aged 20 to 34, by sex and age, 2011)

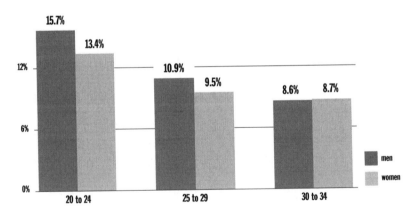

Table 6.2 Employment Status by Sex and Age, 2011

(number and percent of people aged 16 or older in the civilian labor force by sex and age, 2011; numbers in thousands)

	civilian noninstitutional population	civilian labor force			unemployed	
		total	percent of population	employed	number	percent of labor force
Total, aged 16 or older	**239,618**	**153,617**	**64.1%**	**139,869**	**13,747**	**8.9%**
Aged 16 to 34	79,562	54,721	68.8	47,901	6,821	12.5
Aged 16 to 17	8,727	1,873	21.5	1,355	519	27.7
Aged 18 to 19	8,048	3,853	47.9	2,972	881	22.9
Aged 20 to 24	21,423	15,270	71.3	13,036	2,234	14.6
Aged 25 to 29	21,119	17,137	81.1	15,380	1,757	10.3
Aged 30 to 34	20,245	16,588	81.9	15,158	1,430	8.6
Aged 35 to 44	39,499	32,660	82.7	30,270	2,389	7.3
Aged 45 to 54	43,842	35,360	80.7	32,867	2,493	7.1
Aged 55 to 64	36,987	23,765	64.3	22,186	1,579	6.6
Aged 65 or older	39,729	7,112	17.9	6,647	465	6.5
Men, aged 16 or older	**116,317**	**81,975**	**70.5**	**74,290**	**7,684**	**9.4**
Aged 16 to 34	40,136	29,465	73.4	25,609	3,858	13.1
Aged 16 to 17	4,486	917	20.4	650	267	29.1
Aged 18 to 19	4,095	1,978	48.3	1,459	520	26.3
Aged 20 to 24	10,844	8,101	74.7	6,826	1,275	15.7
Aged 25 to 29	10,666	9,364	87.8	8,347	1,017	10.9
Aged 30 to 34	10,045	9,105	90.6	8,327	779	8.6
Aged 35 to 44	19,446	17,686	90.9	16,370	1,316	7.4
Aged 45 to 54	21,451	18,483	86.2	17,113	1,370	7.4
Aged 55 to 64	17,810	12,350	69.3	11,469	882	7.1
Aged 65 or older	17,474	3,990	22.8	3,730	261	6.5
Women, aged 16 or older	**123,300**	**71,642**	**58.1**	**65,579**	**6,063**	**8.5**
Aged 16 to 34	39,425	25,256	64.1	22,291	2,966	11.7
Aged 16 to 17	4,241	957	22.6	705	252	26.3
Aged 18 to 19	3,952	1,875	47.4	1,514	362	19.3
Aged 20 to 24	10,579	7,169	67.8	6,209	960	13.4
Aged 25 to 29	10,453	7,773	74.4	7,032	741	9.5
Aged 30 to 34	10,200	7,482	73.4	6,831	651	8.7
Aged 35 to 44	20,053	14,973	74.7	13,900	1,073	7.2
Aged 45 to 54	22,391	16,876	75.4	15,753	1,123	6.7
Aged 55 to 64	19,177	11,414	59.5	10,717	697	6.1
Aged 65 or older	22,255	3,121	14.0	2,917	204	6.5

Source: Bureau of Labor Statistics, Labor Force Statistics from the Current Population Survey, Internet site http://www.bls.gov/cps/tables.htm#empstat; calculations by New Strategist

Among Young Adults, Labor Force Participation Varies by Race and Hispanic Origin

Young black men are most likely to be unemployed.

Among teenagers, the labor force participation rate is higher for Hispanics than for Asians or blacks. While 48 percent of Hispanic men aged 18 to 19 are in the labor force, the figure is just 38 percent among blacks and 32 percent among Asians. The pattern is the same for women in the age group, with Hispanics being more likely to work than Asians or blacks. There are striking differences in the 20-to-24 age group as well. Among Asian men aged 20 to 24, only 57 percent are in the labor force. Among blacks, the figure is a larger 67 percent. The labor force participation rate of Hispanic men aged 20 to 24 is a much higher 79 percent. Behind the lower labor force participation rate of Asian men is their greater college attendance.

Teenagers and young adults have relatively high unemployment rates regardless of race or Hispanic origin, but young black men have a much higher unemployment rate than anyone else. Among black men under age 35, fully 24 percent were unemployed in 2011. This compares with an unemployment rate of 13 percent for Hispanics and 8 percent for Asians.

■ Black men have so much difficulty finding a job that some drop out of the labor force entirely.

Nearly one-fourth of young black men are unemployed

(unemployment rate among men under age 35, by race and Hispanic origin, 2011)

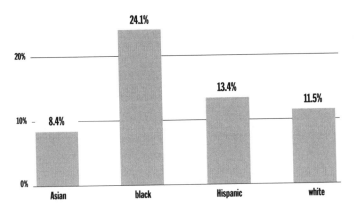

Table 6.3 Employment Status of Men by Race, Hispanic Origin, and Age, 2011

(number and percent of men aged 16 or older in the civilian labor force by race, Hispanic origin, and age, 2011; numbers in thousands)

| | civilian noninstitutional population | civilian labor force | | | unemployed | |
		total	percent of population	employed	number	percent of labor force
ASIAN MEN						
Total aged 16 or older	**5,429**	**3,972**	**73.2%**	**3,703**	**269**	**6.8%**
Aged 16 to 34	1,916	1,305	68.1	1,197	110	8.4
Aged 16 to 17	162	12	7.7	8	5	–
Aged 18 to 19	169	54	32.0	38	16	28.8
Aged 20 to 24	472	269	57.1	238	32	11.7
Aged 25 to 29	543	450	82.9	417	33	7.4
Aged 30 to 34	570	520	91.2	496	24	4.6
Aged 35 to 44	1,186	1,092	92.1	1,045	47	4.3
Aged 45 to 54	956	874	91.4	810	63	7.2
Aged 55 to 64	707	531	75.0	492	39	7.3
Aged 65 or older	663	169	25.5	158	11	6.4
BLACK MEN						
Total aged 16 or older	**13,164**	**8,454**	**64.2**	**6,953**	**1,502**	**17.8**
Aged 16 to 34	5,404	3,501	64.8	2,654	845	24.1
Aged 16 to 17	642	89	13.8	49	39	44.5
Aged 18 to 19	640	241	37.6	138	102	42.5
Aged 20 to 24	1,510	1,012	67.0	734	278	27.4
Aged 25 to 29	1,379	1,126	81.7	889	237	21.0
Aged 30 to 34	1,233	1,033	83.7	844	189	18.3
Aged 35 to 44	2,222	1,860	83.7	1,583	277	14.9
Aged 45 to 54	2,435	1,854	76.1	1,621	233	12.5
Aged 55 to 64	1,759	983	55.9	858	125	12.7
Aged 65 or older	1,344	257	19.1	236	21	8.2
HISPANIC MEN						
Total aged 16 or older	**17,753**	**13,576**	**76.5**	**12,049**	**1,527**	**11.2**
Aged 16 to 34	8,469	6,366	75.2	5,513	854	13.4
Aged 16 to 17	951	129	13.6	76	53	40.7
Aged 18 to 19	861	416	48.4	287	129	31.0
Aged 20 to 24	2,278	1,811	79.5	1,535	277	15.3
Aged 25 to 29	2,214	2,008	90.7	1,798	210	10.5
Aged 30 to 34	2,165	2,002	92.5	1,817	185	9.2
Aged 35 to 44	3,702	3,421	92.4	3,124	297	8.7
Aged 45 to 54	2,717	2,372	87.3	2,141	231	9.8
Aged 55 to 64	1,604	1,122	69.9	1,006	116	10.4
Aged 65 or older	1,260	293	23.3	266	28	9.5

	civilian noninstitutional population	civilian labor force				
		total	percent of population	employed	unemployed	
					number	percent of labor force
WHITE MEN						
Total aged 16 or older	**94,801**	**67,551**	**71.3%**	**61,920**	**5,631**	**8.3%**
Aged 16 to 34	31,428	23,711	75.4	20,980	2,730	11.5
Aged 16 to 17	3,496	780	22.3	573	208	26.6
Aged 18 to 19	3,114	1,606	51.6	1,229	377	23.5
Aged 20 to 24	8,485	6,539	77.1	5,630	909	13.9
Aged 25 to 29	8,412	7,506	89.2	6,804	701	9.3
Aged 30 to 34	7,921	7,280	91.9	6,744	535	7.4
Aged 35 to 44	15,540	14,317	92.1	13,366	951	6.6
Aged 45 to 54	17,602	15,400	87.5	14,370	1,030	6.7
Aged 55 to 64	15,018	10,629	70.8	9,932	697	6.6
Aged 65 or older	15,213	3,494	23.0	3,271	223	6.4

Note: People who selected more than one race are not included. Hispanics may be of any race. "–" means sample is too small to make a reliable estimate.
Source: Bureau of Labor Statistics, Labor Force Statistics from the Current Population Survey, Internet site http://www.bls.gov/cps/tables.htm#empstat; calculations by New Strategist

Table 6.4 Employment Status of Women by Race, Hispanic Origin, and Age, 2011

(number and percent of women aged 16 or older in the civilian labor force by race, Hispanic origin, and age, 2011; numbers in thousands)

	civilian noninstitutional population	civilian labor force			unemployed	
		total	percent of population	employed	number	percent of labor force
ASIAN WOMEN						
Total aged 16 or older	**6,011**	**3,414**	**56.8%**	**3,165**	**250**	**7.3%**
Aged 16 to 34	1,985	1,102	55.5	1,002	99	9.0
Aged 16 to 17	160	22	13.8	18	4	–
Aged 18 to 19	161	53	32.8	41	11	21.6
Aged 20 to 24	467	249	53.2	223	25	10.1
Aged 25 to 29	570	368	64.7	339	29	7.9
Aged 30 to 34	627	410	65.4	381	30	7.2
Aged 35 to 44	1,279	917	71.7	859	58	6.4
Aged 45 to 54	1,058	797	75.3	750	47	5.9
Aged 55 to 64	848	501	59.1	461	40	7.9
Aged 65 or older	841	97	11.6	92	5	5.3
BLACK WOMEN						
Total aged 16 or older	**15,950**	**9,427**	**59.1**	**8,098**	**1,329**	**14.1**
Aged 16 to 34	5,963	3,686	61.8	2,931	754	20.5
Aged 16 to 17	712	99	13.9	50	49	49.5
Aged 18 to 19	600	219	36.4	142	76	34.8
Aged 20 to 24	1,657	1,093	65.9	840	253	23.1
Aged 25 to 29	1,522	1,143	75.1	932	211	18.4
Aged 30 to 34	1,472	1,132	76.9	967	165	14.6
Aged 35 to 44	2,773	2,168	78.2	1,916	252	11.6
Aged 45 to 54	2,922	2,104	72.0	1,892	211	10.0
Aged 55 to 64	2,196	1,172	53.4	1,086	86	7.4
Aged 65 or older	2,096	298	14.2	272	25	8.5
HISPANIC WOMEN						
Total aged 16 or older	**16,685**	**9,322**	**55.9**	**8,220**	**1,102**	**11.8**
Aged 16 to 34	7,238	4,031	55.7	3,444	588	14.6
Aged 16 to 17	857	122	14.3	79	44	35.7
Aged 18 to 19	738	297	40.3	223	74	25.0
Aged 20 to 24	1,915	1,206	63.0	1,010	196	16.3
Aged 25 to 29	1,863	1,218	65.4	1,077	141	11.5
Aged 30 to 34	1,865	1,188	63.7	1,055	133	11.2
Aged 35 to 44	3,401	2,282	67.1	2,055	227	9.9
Aged 45 to 54	2,696	1,899	70.4	1,707	192	10.1
Aged 55 to 64	1,707	893	52.3	814	78	8.8
Aged 65 or older	1,643	217	13.2	200	17	8.0

	civilian noninstitutional population	civilian labor force				
		total	percent of population	employed	unemployed	
					number	percent of labor force
WHITE WOMEN						
Total aged 16 or older	**98,276**	**57,028**	**58.0%**	**52,770**	**4,257**	**7.5%**
Aged 16 to 34	30,088	19,636	65.3	17,660	1,974	10.1
Aged 16 to 17	3,177	800	25.2	617	184	22.9
Aged 18 to 19	3,031	1,528	50.4	1,272	255	16.7
Aged 20 to 24	8,077	5,581	69.1	4,943	637	11.4
Aged 25 to 29	8,025	6,027	75.1	5,558	468	7.8
Aged 30 to 34	7,778	5,700	73.3	5,270	430	7.5
Aged 35 to 44	15,490	11,517	74.4	10,789	728	6.3
Aged 45 to 54	17,925	13,636	76.1	12,806	829	6.1
Aged 55 to 64	15,781	9,559	60.6	9,005	554	5.8
Aged 65 or older	18,992	2,681	14.1	2,509	171	6.4

Note: People who selected more than one race are not included. Hispanics may be of any race. "–" means sample is too small to make a reliable estimate.
Source: Bureau of Labor Statistics, Labor Force Statistics from the Current Population Survey, Internet site http://www.bls .gov/cps/tables.htm#empstat; calculations by New Strategist

Most Couples under Age 35 Are Dual Earners

The husband is the sole support of only 22 percent of young couples.

Dual incomes are by far the norm among married couples. Both husband and wife are in the labor force in 53 percent of the nation's couples. In another 22 percent, the husband is the only worker. Not far behind are the 17 percent of couples in which neither spouse is in the labor force. The wife is the sole worker among 7 percent of couples.

Sixty-three percent of couples under age 35 are dual earners. The proportion is just 54 percent among couples under age 25, but is a larger 63 percent among those aged 25 to 29 and rises to 66 percent among couples aged 30 to 34. The dual-earner share falls to just 50 percent among couples aged 55 to 64 because many are retired.

■ The proportion of couples in which the husband is the sole earner is highest among the youngest adults because many wives are at home with newborns.

Dual earners dominate married couples under age 55

(percent of married couples in which both husband and wife are in the labor force, by age, 2011)

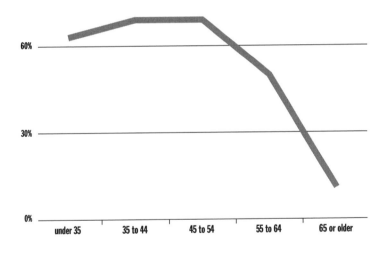

Table 6.5 Labor Force Status of Married-Couple Family Groups by Age, 2011

(number and percent distribution of married-couple family groups by age of reference person and labor force status of husband and wife, 2011; numbers in thousands)

	total	husband and wife in labor force	husband only in labor force	wife only in labor force	neither husband nor wife in labor force
Total married-couple family groups	**60,155**	**31,994**	**13,241**	**4,455**	**10,464**
Under age 35	10,252	6,495	3,170	359	229
Under age 25	1,304	706	489	57	53
Aged 25 to 29	3,550	2,240	1,071	151	89
Aged 30 to 34	5,398	3,549	1,610	151	87
Aged 35 to 44	12,478	8,609	3,098	494	277
Aged 45 to 54	14,017	9,609	2,963	869	577
Aged 55 to 64	12,158	6,035	2,601	1,615	1,906
Aged 65 or older	11,248	1,247	1,409	1,118	7,475

PERCENT DISTRIBUTION BY LABOR FORCE STATUS

	total	husband and wife in labor force	husband only in labor force	wife only in labor force	neither husband nor wife in labor force
Total married-couple family groups	**100.0%**	**53.2%**	**22.0%**	**7.4%**	**17.4%**
Under age 35	100.0	63.4	30.9	3.5	2.2
Under age 25	100.0	54.1	37.5	4.4	4.1
Aged 25 to 29	100.0	63.1	30.2	4.3	2.5
Aged 30 to 34	100.0	65.7	29.8	2.8	1.6
Aged 35 to 44	100.0	69.0	24.8	4.0	2.2
Aged 45 to 54	100.0	68.6	21.1	6.2	4.1
Aged 55 to 64	100.0	49.6	21.4	13.3	15.7
Aged 65 or older	100.0	11.1	12.5	9.9	66.5

PERCENT DISTRIBUTION BY AGE

	total	husband and wife in labor force	husband only in labor force	wife only in labor force	neither husband nor wife in labor force
Total married-couple family groups	**100.0%**	**100.0%**	**100.0%**	**100.0%**	**100.0%**
Under age 35	17.0	20.3	23.9	8.1	2.2
Under age 25	2.2	2.2	3.7	1.3	0.5
Aged 25 to 29	5.9	7.0	8.1	3.4	0.9
Aged 30 to 34	9.0	11.1	12.2	3.4	0.8
Aged 35 to 44	20.7	26.9	23.4	11.1	2.6
Aged 45 to 54	23.3	30.0	22.4	19.5	5.5
Aged 55 to 64	20.2	18.9	19.6	36.3	18.2
Aged 65 or older	18.7	3.9	10.6	25.1	71.4

Source: Bureau of the Census, America's Families and Living Arrangements: 2011, Internet site http://www.census.gov/population/www/socdemo/hh-fam/cps2011.html; calculations by New Strategist

The Youngest Workers Dominate Many Entry-Level Positions

They account for 63 percent of food preparation workers.

Among the 140 million employed Americans in 2011, 48 million were under age 35—or 34 percent. In some occupations, however, workers under age 35 account for a disproportionate share. While workers under age 35 are only 20 percent of the nation's managers, they are 75 percent of waiters and waitresses.

More than one in four employed 16-to-19-year-olds works in a food preparation and serving occupation. The figure declines with age to 6 percent among workers aged 25 to 34. Another 23 percent of workers aged 16 to 19 are in sales occupations, a figure that falls to 10 percent among workers aged 25 to 34. Workers under age 35 account for 65 percent of cashiers, 46 percent of grounds maintenance workers, 49 percent of retail salespersons, and 47 percent of customer service representatives. Most young adults will move out of these entry-level positions as they earn educational credentials and gain job experience.

■ Young adults account for a large share of workers in occupations with a great deal of public contact.

Many occupations are dominated by young adults

(percent of workers under age 35 by occupation, 2011)

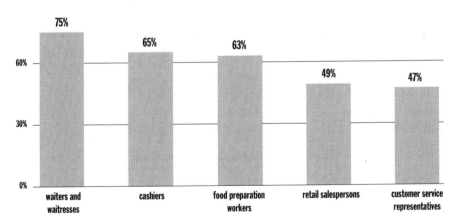

Table 6.6 Occupations of Workers under Age 35, 2011

(number of employed workers aged 16 or older, median age of workers, and number of workers under age 35, by occupation, 2011; numbers in thousands)

	total	median age	under age 35			
			total	16 to 19	20 to 24	25 to 34
TOTAL WORKERS	**139,869**	**42.1**	**47,900**	**4,327**	**13,036**	**30,537**
Management and professional occupations	**52,547**	**44.2**	**14,544**	**290**	**2,611**	**11,643**
Management, business and financial operations	21,589	45.7	4,925	57	777	4,091
Management	15,250	46.7	3,067	42	451	2,574
Business and financial operations	6,339	43.3	1,857	15	326	1,516
Professional and related occupations	30,957	43.1	9,620	234	1,834	7,552
Computer and mathematical	3,608	40.5	1,248	14	198	1,036
Architecture and engineering	2,785	43.9	797	8	139	650
Life, physical, and social sciences	1,303	42.3	456	5	85	366
Community and social services	2,352	44.8	674	15	123	536
Legal	1,770	46.1	431	3	41	387
Education, training, and library	8,619	43.6	2,628	92	579	1,957
Arts, design, entertainment, sports, and media	2,779	40.9	1,052	68	273	711
Health care practitioner and technician	7,740	43.3	2,332	29	395	1,908
Service occupations	**24,787**	**37.6**	**11,132**	**1,829**	**3,788**	**5,515**
Health care support	3,359	38.8	1,424	81	478	865
Protective service	3,210	40.4	1,178	90	267	821
Food preparation and serving	7,747	29.3	4,843	1,189	1,846	1,808
Building and grounds cleaning and maintenance	5,492	43.8	1,669	174	473	1,022
Personal care and service	4,979	39.5	2,019	296	724	999
Sales and office occupations	**33,066**	**41.5**	**12,256**	**1,482**	**3,972**	**6,802**
Sales and related occupations	15,330	39.9	6,269	993	2,124	3,152
Office and administrative support	17,736	42.7	5,987	489	1,848	3,650
Natural resources, construction, and maintenance occupations	**13,009**	**41.0**	**4,661**	**278**	**1,146**	**3,237**
Farming, fishing, and forestry	1,001	37.0	466	100	138	228
Construction and extraction	7,125	40.4	2,645	118	598	1,929
Installation, maintenance, and repair	4,883	42.6	1,551	60	411	1,080
Production, transportation, and material-moving occupations	**16,461**	**42.8**	**5,307**	**447**	**1,519**	**3,341**
Production	8,142	43.1	2,539	142	712	1,685
Transportation and material moving	8,318	42.6	2,767	305	807	1,655

Source: Bureau of Labor Statistics, unpublished data from the 2011 Current Population Survey; calculations by New Strategist

Table 6.7 Share of Workers under Age 35 by Occupation, 2011

(percent distribution of total employed people aged 16 or older by occupation and age, 2011)

	total	under age 35			
		total	16 to 19	20 to 24	25 to 34
TOTAL WORKERS	**100.0%**	**34.2%**	**3.1%**	**9.3%**	**21.8%**
Management and professional occupations	**100.0**	**27.7**	**0.6**	**5.0**	**22.2**
Management, business and financial operations	100.0	22.8	0.3	3.6	18.9
Management	100.0	20.1	0.3	3.0	16.9
Business and financial operations	100.0	29.3	0.2	5.1	23.9
Professional and related occupations	100.0	31.1	0.8	5.9	24.4
Computer and mathematical	100.0	34.6	0.4	5.5	28.7
Architecture and engineering	100.0	28.6	0.3	5.0	23.3
Life, physical, and social sciences	100.0	35.0	0.4	6.5	28.1
Community and social services	100.0	28.7	0.6	5.2	22.8
Legal	100.0	24.4	0.2	2.3	21.9
Education, training, and library	100.0	30.5	1.1	6.7	22.7
Arts, design, entertainment, sports, and media	100.0	37.9	2.4	9.8	25.6
Health care practitioner and technician	100.0	30.1	0.4	5.1	24.7
Service occupations	**100.0**	**44.9**	**7.4**	**15.3**	**22.2**
Health care support	100.0	42.4	2.4	14.2	25.8
Protective service	100.0	36.7	2.8	8.3	25.6
Food preparation and serving	100.0	62.5	15.3	23.8	23.3
Building and grounds cleaning and maintenance	100.0	30.4	3.2	8.6	18.6
Personal care and service	100.0	40.6	5.9	14.5	20.1
Sales and office occupations	**100.0**	**37.1**	**4.5**	**12.0**	**20.6**
Sales and related occupations	100.0	40.9	6.5	13.9	20.6
Office and administrative support	100.0	33.8	2.8	10.4	20.6
Natural resources, construction, maintenance occupations	**100.0**	**35.8**	**2.1**	**8.8**	**24.9**
Farming, fishing, and forestry	100.0	46.6	10.0	13.8	22.8
Construction and extraction	100.0	37.1	1.7	8.4	27.1
Installation, maintenance, and repair	100.0	31.8	1.2	8.4	22.1
Production, transportation, and material-moving occupations	**100.0**	**32.2**	**2.7**	**9.2**	**20.3**
Production	100.0	31.2	1.7	8.7	20.7
Transportation and material moving	100.0	33.3	3.7	9.7	19.9

Source: Bureau of Labor Statistics, unpublished data from the 2011 Current Population Survey; calculations by New Strategist

Table 6.8 Distribution of Workers under Age 35 by Occupation, 2011

(percent distribution of employed people aged 16 or older and under age 35 by occupation, 2011)

	total	under age 35 total	16 to 19	20 to 24	25 to 34
TOTAL WORKERS	100.0%	100.0%	100.0%	100.0%	100.0%
Management and professional occupations	**37.6**	**30.4**	**6.7**	**20.0**	**38.1**
Management, business and financial operations	15.4	10.3	1.3	6.0	13.4
Management	10.9	6.4	1.0	3.5	8.4
Business and financial operations	4.5	3.9	0.3	2.5	5.0
Professional and related occupations	22.1	20.1	5.4	14.1	24.7
Computer and mathematical	2.6	2.6	0.3	1.5	3.4
Architecture and engineering	2.0	1.7	0.2	1.1	2.1
Life, physical, and social sciences	0.9	1.0	0.1	0.7	1.2
Community and social services	1.7	1.4	0.3	0.9	1.8
Legal	1.3	0.9	0.1	0.3	1.3
Education, training, and library	6.2	5.5	2.1	4.4	6.4
Arts, design, entertainment, sports, and media	2.0	2.2	1.6	2.1	2.3
Health care practitioner and technician	5.5	4.9	0.7	3.0	6.2
Service occupations	**17.7**	**23.2**	**42.3**	**29.1**	**18.1**
Health care support	2.4	3.0	1.9	3.7	2.8
Protective service	2.3	2.5	2.1	2.0	2.7
Food preparation and serving	5.5	10.1	27.5	14.2	5.9
Building and grounds cleaning and maintenance	3.9	3.5	4.0	3.6	3.3
Personal care and service	3.6	4.2	6.8	5.6	3.3
Sales and office occupations	**23.6**	**25.6**	**34.3**	**30.5**	**22.3**
Sales and related occupations	11.0	13.1	22.9	16.3	10.3
Office and administrative support	12.7	12.5	11.3	14.2	12.0
Natural resources, construction, maintenance occupations	**9.3**	**9.7**	**6.4**	**8.8**	**10.6**
Farming, fishing, and forestry	0.7	1.0	2.3	1.1	0.7
Construction and extraction	5.1	5.5	2.7	4.6	6.3
Installation, maintenance, and repair	3.5	3.2	1.4	3.2	3.5
Production, transportation, and material-moving occupations	**11.8**	**11.1**	**10.3**	**11.7**	**10.9**
Production	5.8	5.3	3.3	5.5	5.5
Transportation and material moving	5.9	5.8	7.0	6.2	5.4

Source: Bureau of Labor Statistics, unpublished data from the 2011 Current Population Survey; calculations by New Strategist

Table 6.9 Workers under Age 35 by Detailed Occupation, 2011

(number of employed workers aged 16 or older, median age, and number and percent under age 35, for detailed occupations with at least 100,000 workers, 2011; numbers in thousands)

	total workers	median age	total under 35		aged 16 to 19		aged 20 to 24		aged 25 to 34	
			number	percent of total	number	percent of total	number	percent of total	number	percent of total
TOTAL WORKERS	**139,869**	**42.1**	**47,900**	**34.2%**	**4,327**	**3.1%**	**13,036**	**9.3%**	**30,537**	**21.87%**
Chief executives	1,515	52.0	124	8.2	1	–	8	0.5	116	7.7
General and operations managers	978	45.4	194	19.8	1	–	19	1.9	175	17.9
Marketing and sales managers	1,009	42.1	298	29.5	4	0.4	36	3.6	258	25.6
Administrative services managers	128	48.9	22	17.2	2	1.6	3	2.3	17	13.3
Computer and information systems managers	553	43.1	–	–	–	–	10	1.8	103	18.6
Financial managers	1,107	43.6	286	25.8	1	0.1	43	3.9	242	21.9
Human resources managers	243	45.1	–	–	–	–	7	2.9	39	16.0
Industrial production managers	259	46.3	43	16.6	1	0.4	4	1.5	38	14.7
Purchasing managers	204	48.7	36	17.6	0	0.0	2	1.0	34	16.7
Transportation, storage, and distribution managers	254	43.8	65	25.6	0	0.0	13	5.1	52	20.5
Farmers, ranchers, and other agricultural managers	978	55.9	125	12.8	5	0.5	28	2.9	92	9.4
Construction managers	926	46.9	–	–	–	–	18	1.9	157	17.0
Education administrators	853	46.9	162	19.0	0	0.0	16	1.9	146	17.1
Architectural and engineering managers	106	47.6	–	–	–	–	1	0.9	10	9.4
Food service managers	1,051	39.7	407	38.7	15	1.4	118	11.2	274	26.1
Lodging managers	148	46.7	36	24.3	1	0.7	7	4.7	28	18.9
Medical and health services managers	529	49.6	77	14.6	1	0.2	3	0.6	73	13.8
Property, real estate, community association managers	587	49.5	109	18.6	1	0.2	13	2.2	95	16.2
Social and community service managers	329	48.2	66	20.1	1	0.3	11	3.3	54	16.4
Managers, all other	3,173	46.6	593	18.7	8	–	84	2.6	509	16.0
Wholesale and retail buyers, except farm products	170	40.7	63	37.1	2	–	16	9.4	47	27.6
Purchasing agents, except wholesale, retail, and farm products	259	43.5	65	25.1	2	–	11	4.2	54	20.8
Claims adjusters, appraisers, examiners, and investigators	296	42.6	87	29.4	–	–	16	5.4	71	24.0
Compliance officers	198	45.9	–	–	–	–	3	1.5	31	15.7
Cost estimators	119	44.7	–	–	–	–	7	5.9	29	24.4
Human resources workers	595	42.4	174	29.2	0	0.0	30	5.0	144	24.2
Training, development specialists	130	45.0	30	23.1	1	0.8	4	3.1	25	19.2
Management analysts	707	46.6	169	23.9	2	0.3	19	2.7	148	20.9
Meeting, convention, event planners	109	37.4	55	50.5	1	0.9	17	15.6	37	33.9
Market research analysts and marketing specialists	205	36.4	102	49.8	1	0.5	18	8.8	83	40.5
Business operations specialists, all other	281	43.6	77	27.4	1	0.4	18	6.4	58	20.6
Accountants and auditors	1,653	43.1	489	29.6	1	0.1	93	5.6	395	23.9
Personal financial advisors	371	43.9	111	29.9	0	0.0	14	3.8	97	26.1
Insurance underwriters	117	44.0	–	–	–	–	0	0.0	31	26.5
Credit counselors and loan officers	326	42.0	–	–	–	–	16	4.9	84	25.8
Tax preparers	110	50.2	–	–	–	–	4	3.6	22	20.0
Computer systems analysts	447	43.1	122	27.3	1	0.2	12	2.7	109	24.4

	total workers	median age	total under 35		aged 16 to 19		aged 20 to 24		aged 25 to 34	
			number	percent of total	number	percent of total	number	percent of total	number	percent of total
Computer programmers	459	41.8	144	31.4%	4	0.9%	30	6.5%	110	24.0%
Software developers, applications and systems software	1,044	39.4	376	36.0	1	0.1	44	4.2	331	31.7
Web developers	182	37.0	81	44.5	1	–	20	11.0	61	33.5
Computer support specialists	461	39.1	189	41.0	3	0.7	40	8.7	146	31.7
Database administrators	134	42.5	–	–	–	–	5	3.7	34	25.4
Network and computer systems administrators	233	40.6	78	33.5	0	0.0	9	3.9	69	29.6
Computer occupations, all other	306	40.8	106	34.6	4	1.3	21	6.9	81	26.5
Operations research analysts	116	41.3	–	–	–	–	6	5.2	33	28.4
Architects, except naval	181	46.7	–	–	–	–	4	2.2	41	22.7
Aerospace engineers	144	43.9	–	–	–	–	6	4.2	36	25.0
Civil engineers	383	42.5	–	–	–	–	20	5.2	100	26.1
Electrical and electronics engineers	309	45.0	87	28.2	0	0.0	14	4.5	73	23.6
Industrial engineers, including health and safety	174	43.4	46	26.4	0	0.0	7	4.0	39	22.4
Mechanical engineers	322	42.5	–	–	–	–	12	3.7	83	25.8
Engineers, all other	337	43.3	–	–	–	–	14	4.2	92	27.3
Drafters	147	44.0	42	28.6	1	0.7	10	6.8	31	21.1
Engineering technicians, except drafters	376	46.5	87	23.1	4	1.1	28	7.4	55	14.6
Biological scientists	114	42.6	42	36.8	0	0.0	5	4.4	37	32.5
Medical scientists	156	39.5	58	37.2	0	0.0	9	5.8	49	31.4
Physical scientists, all other	152	40.4	–	–	–	–	6	3.9	52	34.2
Psychologists	197	48.3	42	21.3	0	0.0	2	1.0	40	20.3
Counselors	732	43.0	253	34.6	8	1.1	45	6.1	200	27.3
Social workers	769	42.6	234	30.4	1	0.1	28	3.6	205	26.7
Social and human service assistants	131	44.1	46	35.1	3	2.3	14	10.7	29	22.1
Clergy	414	52.5	50	12.1	1	0.2	10	2.4	39	9.4
Lawyers	1,085	47.2	226	20.8	0	0.0	2	0.2	224	20.6
Paralegals and legal assistants	404	42.8	141	34.9	3	0.7	26	6.4	112	27.7
Misc. legal support workers	209	44.8	–	–	–	–	12	5.7	39	18.7
Postsecondary teachers	1,355	45.7	390	28.8	5	0.4	86	6.3	299	22.1
Preschool, kindergarten teachers	707	39.2	282	39.9	6	0.8	92	13.0	184	26.0
Elementary and middle school teachers	2,848	43.0	832	29.2	7	0.2	124	4.4	701	24.6
Secondary school teachers	1,136	43.2	338	29.8	5	0.4	44	3.9	289	25.4
Special education teachers	388	43.3	114	29.4	1	0.3	11	2.8	102	26.3
Other teachers and instructors	812	43.7	289	35.6	37	4.6	95	11.7	157	19.3
Librarians	198	52.0	38	19.2	1	0.5	10	5.1	27	13.6
Teacher assistants	950	44.9	285	30.0	23	2.4	99	10.4	163	17.2
Other education, training, and library workers	140	46.3	34	24.3	2	1.4	9	6.4	23	16.4
Artists and related workers	180	45.3	45	25.0	1	0.6	10	5.6	34	18.9
Designers	766	41.8	263	34.3	5	0.7	51	6.7	207	27.0
Producers and directors	149	40.3	63	42.3	2	1.3	15	10.1	46	30.9
Athletes, coaches, umpires, and related workers	272	30.8	157	57.7	39	14.3	59	21.7	59	21.7
Musicians, singers, and related workers	191	43.2	65	34.0	3	1.6	22	11.5	40	20.9
Public relations specialists	158	39.2	62	39.2	1	0.6	14	8.9	47	29.7
Editors	166	41.4	66	39.8	1	0.6	16	9.6	49	29.5
Writers and authors	218	46.1	64	29.4	1	0.5	14	6.4	49	22.5
Broadcast and sound engineering technicians and radio operators	106	39.7	44	41.5	2	1.9	13	12.3	29	27.4

	total workers	median age	total under 35		aged 16 to 19		aged 20 to 24		aged 25 to 34	
			number	percent of total	number	percent of total	number	percent of total	number	percent of total
Photographers	148	40.6	55	37.2%	2	1.4%	12	8.1%	41	27.7%
Dentists	181	51.0	–	–	–	–	–	–	24	13.3
Dietitians and nutritionists	102	47.7	27	26.5	2	2.0	5	4.9	20	19.6
Pharmacists	274	41.1	94	34.3	1	0.4	13	4.7	80	29.2
Physicians and surgeons	822	46.3	173	21.0	1	0.1	4	0.5	168	20.4
Occupational therapists	112	41.7	–	–	–	–	1	0.9	30	26.8
Physical therapists	222	40.5	71	32.0	0	0.0	11	5.0	60	27.0
Respiratory therapists	134	44.5	33	24.6	0	0.0	6	4.5	27	20.1
Speech-language pathologists	125	40.5	–	–	–	–	6	4.8	41	32.8
Therapists, all other	138	40.7	53	38.4	0	0.0	7	5.1	46	33.3
Registered nurses	2,706	44.7	741	27.4	3	0.1	110	4.1	628	23.2
Nurse practitioners	100	46.9	–	–	–	–	1	1.0	13	13.0
Clinical laboratory technologists and technicians	321	43.2	106	33.0	1	0.3	25	7.8	80	24.9
Dental hygienists	148	42.2	–	–	–	–	5	3.4	41	27.7
Diagnostic related technologists and technicians	342	42.1	–		–	–	21	6.1	87	25.4
Emergency medical technicians and paramedics	185	31.8	113	61.1	2	1.1	30	16.2	81	43.8
Health practitioner support technologists and technicians	511	34.8	266	52.1	13	2.5	86	16.8	167	32.7
Licensed practical and licensed vocational nurses	560	43.2	166	29.6	4	0.7	30	5.4	132	23.6
Medical records and health information technicians	116	42.7	41	35.3	1	0.9	8	6.9	32	27.6
Nursing, psychiatric, and home health aides	1,981	40.3	767	38.7	47	2.4	275	13.9	445	22.5
Massage therapists	146	40.5	59	40.4	1	0.7	14	9.6	44	30.1
Dental assistants	307	36.3	141	45.9	3	1.0	46	15.0	92	30.0
Medical assistants	395	34.6	213	53.9	5	1.3	56	14.2	152	38.5
Phlebotomists	119	38.3	49	41.2	2	1.7	16	13.4	31	26.1
First-line supervisors of police and detectives	107	46.0	–	–	–	–	–	–	9	8.4
First-line supervisors of protective service workers, all other	111	47.2	–	–	–	–	4	3.6	21	18.9
Firefighters	305	37.3	141	46.2	2	0.7	21	6.9	118	38.7
Bailiffs, correctional officers, and jailers	446	39.7	161	36.1	3	0.7	29	6.5	129	28.9
Detectives, criminal investigators	151	42.3	–	–	–	–	3	2.0	32	21.2
Police and sheriff's patrol officers	668	39.3	240	35.9	2	0.3	20	3.0	218	32.6
Security guards and gaming surveillance officers	963	41.9	383	39.8	17	1.8	137	14.2	229	23.8
Lifeguards, other recreational, all other protective service workers	146	21.8	115	78.8	64	43.8	39	26.7	12	8.2
Chefs and head cooks	347	38.8	144	41.5	11	3.2	33	9.5	100	28.8
First-line supervisors of food preparation and serving workers	505	36.8	237	46.9	16	3.2	90	17.8	131	25.9
Cooks	1,990	33.8	1,042	52.4	207	10.4	355	17.8	480	24.1
Food preparation workers	784	28.0	494	63.0	153	19.5	187	23.9	154	19.6
Bartenders	392	31.8	232	59.2	4	1.0	71	18.1	157	40.1
Combined food preparation, serving workers, including fast food	326	28.1	208	63.8	58	17.8	85	26.1	65	19.9
Counter attendants, cafeteria, food concession, and coffee shop	255	21.4	217	85.1	122	47.8	72	28.2	23	9.0
Waiters and waitresses	2,059	26.1	1,537	74.6	309	15.0	681	33.1	547	26.6
Food servers, nonrestaurant	181	32.3	96	53.0	28	15.5	39	21.5	29	16.0

	total workers	median age	total under 35		aged 16 to 19		aged 20 to 24		aged 25 to 34	
			number	percent of total	number	percent of total	number	percent of total	number	percent of total
Diningroom, cafeteria attendants and bartender helpers	347	25.4	220	63.4%	87	25.1%	84	24.2%	49	14.1%
Dishwashers	273	28.3	169	61.9	64	23.4	55	20.1	50	18.3
Hosts and hostesses, restaurant, lounge, and coffee shop	286	21.4	243	85.0	128	44.8	92	32.2	23	8.0
First-line supervisors of housekeeping, janitorial workers	292	48.9	38	13.0	0	0.0	3	1.0	35	12.0
First-line supervisors of landscaping, lawn service, groundskeeping workers	274	43.5	70	25.5	1	0.4	10	3.6	59	21.5
Janitors and building cleaners	2,186	46.4	585	26.8	78	3.6	189	8.6	318	14.5
Maids and housekeeping cleaners	1,419	45.2	376	26.5	29	2.0	94	6.6	253	17.8
Grounds maintenance workers	1,247	37.1	577	46.3	65	5.2	171	13.7	341	27.3
First-line supervisors of gaming workers	120	40.6	44	36.7	2	1.7	14	11.7	28	23.3
First-line supervisors of personal service workers	192	43.1	47	24.5	0	0.0	16	8.3	31	16.1
Nonfarm animal caretakers	179	37.2	81	45.3	15	8.4	39	21.8	27	15.1
Gaming services workers	113	40.5	42	37.2	3	2.7	8	7.1	31	27.4
Misc. entertainment attendants and related workers	182	26.4	117	64.3	41	22.5	46	25.3	30	16.5
Hairdressers, hairstylists, and cosmetologists	758	39.8	297	39.2	7	0.9	94	12.4	196	25.9
Misc. personal appearance workers	251	40.8	80	31.9	5	2.0	13	5.2	62	24.7
Childcare workers	1,231	37.2	560	45.5	126	10.2	219	17.8	215	17.5
Personal care aides	1,057	43.9	344	32.5	21	2.0	129	12.2	194	18.4
Recreation and fitness workers	390	36.6	182	46.7	38	9.7	62	15.9	82	21.0
Personal care and service workers, all other	105	33.2	55	52.4	14	13.3	21	20.0	20	19.0
First-line supervisors of retail sales workers	3,217	42.6	1,072	33.3	17	0.5	271	8.4	784	24.4
First-line supervisors of nonretail sales workers	1,088	46.3	223	20.5	2	0.2	34	3.1	187	17.2
Cashiers	3,158	27.2	2,043	64.7	635	20.1	843	26.7	565	17.9
Counter and rental clerks	139	38.2	64	46.0	11	7.9	29	20.9	24	17.3
Parts salespersons	131	40.9	49	37.4	2	1.5	16	12.2	31	23.7
Retail salespersons	3,224	35.9	1,575	48.9	273	8.5	663	20.6	639	19.8
Advertising sales agents	254	39.6	104	40.9	0	0.0	22	8.7	82	32.3
Insurance sales agents	531	45.8	138	26.0	4	0.8	26	4.9	108	20.3
Securities, commodities, and financial services sales agents	267	41.7	–	–	–	–	13	4.9	81	30.3
Sales representatives, services, all other	503	40.7	175	34.8	5	1.0	41	8.2	129	25.6
Sales representatives, wholesale and manufacturing	1,297	44.6	339	26.1	13	1.0	60	4.6	266	20.5
Real estate brokers, sales agents	811	50.3	147	18.1	1	0.1	24	3.0	122	15.0
Telemarketers	108	30.5	69	63.9	9	8.3	28	25.9	32	29.6
Door-to-door sales workers, news, street vendors, related workers	201	43.8	66	32.8	8	4.0	19	9.5	39	19.4
Sales and related workers, all other	226	44.2	61	27.0	4	1.8	16	7.1	41	18.1
First-line supervisors of office and administrative support workers	1,423	45.7	322	22.6	4	0.3	49	3.4	269	18.9
Bill and account collectors	211	38.9	93	44.1	1	0.5	27	12.8	65	30.8
Billing and posting clerks	471	42.2	155	32.9	3	0.6	35	7.4	117	24.8
Bookkeeping, accounting, and auditing clerks	1,300	48.5	260	20.0	4	0.3	64	4.9	192	14.8
Payroll and timekeeping clerks	168	46.1	25	14.9	1	0.6	4	2.4	20	11.9

	total workers	median age	total under 35		aged 16 to 19		aged 20 to 24		aged 25 to 34	
			number	percent of total	number	percent of total	number	percent of total	number	percent of total
Tellers	413	31.8	234	56.7%	17	4.1%	106	25.7%	111	26.9%
Customer service representatives	1,916	37.0	891	46.5	90	4.7	305	15.9	496	25.9
File Clerks	334	40.8	126	37.7	23	6.9	48	14.4	55	16.5
Hotel, motel, and resort desk clerks	135	30.1	83	61.5	5	3.7	38	28.1	40	29.6
Interviewers, except eligibility, loan	153	40.8	60	39.2	6	3.9	15	9.8	39	25.5
Library assistants, clerical	113	44.8	44	38.9	7	6.2	26	23.0	11	9.7
Loan interviewers and clerks	117	40.4	41	35.0	1	0.9	6	5.1	34	29.1
Order clerks	113	41.7	40	35.4	4	3.5	15	13.3	21	18.6
Receptionists, information clerks	1,259	38.3	556	44.2	66	5.2	232	18.4	258	20.5
Information, record clerks, all other	118	45.7	37	31.4	3	2.5	7	5.9	27	22.9
Couriers and messengers	249	46.5	55	22.1	3	1.2	11	4.4	41	16.5
Dispatchers	239	41.5	84	35.1	5	2.1	13	5.4	66	27.6
Postal service clerks	146	53.1	9	6.2	0	0.0	1	0.7	8	5.5
Postal service mail carriers	348	49.9	45	12.9	0	0.0	9	2.6	36	10.3
Production, planning, expediting clerks	236	44.1	61	25.8	0	0.0	13	5.5	48	20.3
Shipping, receiving, traffic clerks	559	40.0	211	37.7	15	2.7	64	11.4	132	23.6
Stock clerks and order fillers	1,503	34.2	783	52.1	126	8.4	306	20.4	351	23.4
Secretaries, admin. assistants	2,871	47.9	649	22.6	32	1.1	150	5.2	467	16.3
Computer operators	126	48.9	33	26.2	2	1.6	9	7.1	22	17.5
Data entry keyers	334	40.0	128	38.3	6	1.8	31	9.3	91	27.2
Word processors and typists	136	46.5	33	24.3	2	1.5	9	6.6	22	16.2
Insurance claims and policy processing clerks	246	41.7	87	35.4	2	0.8	19	7.7	66	26.8
Office clerks, general	1,061	42.2	381	35.9	46	4.3	124	11.7	211	19.9
Office and administrative support workers, all other	513	42.4	169	32.9	4	0.8	41	8.0	124	24.2
Miscellaneous agricultural workers	708	33.8	376	53.1	91	12.9	112	15.8	173	24.4
First-line supervisors of construction trades and extraction workers	634	45.2	146	23.0	1	0.2	15	2.4	130	20.5
Brickmasons, blockmasons, and stonemasons	146	41.8	53	36.3	2	1.4	12	8.2	39	26.7
Carpenters	1,330	41.4	442	33.2	16	1.2	94	7.1	332	25.0
Carpet, floor, and tile installers and finishers	189	37.0	89	47.1	7	3.7	21	11.1	61	32.3
Construction laborers	1,253	36.9	572	45.7	39	3.1	154	12.3	379	30.2
Operating engineers and other construction equipment operators	369	43.0	114	30.9	4	1.1	22	6.0	88	23.8
Drywall installers, ceiling tile installers, and tapers	150	37.6	63	42.0	1	0.7	12	8.0	50	33.3
Electricians	682	41.5	240	35.2	6	0.9	50	7.3	184	27.0
Painters, construction, maintenance	528	40.9	185	35.0	12	2.3	40	7.6	133	25.2
Pipelayers, plumbers, pipefitters, and steamfitters	519	41.4	174	33.5	5	1.0	30	5.8	139	26.8
Roofers	222	34.2	121	54.5	4	1.8	31	14.0	86	38.7
Sheet metal workers	126	40.0	53	42.1	5	4.0	16	12.7	32	25.4
Highway maintenance workers	105	45.3	26	24.8	1	1.0	8	7.6	17	16.2
First-line supervisors of mechanics, installers, and repairers	313	49.7	57	18.2	0	0.0	8	2.6	49	15.7
Computer, automated teller, and office machine repairers	305	40.6	113	37.0	3	1.0	38	12.5	72	23.6
Radio and telecommunications equipment installers, repairers	150	41.9	44	29.3	1	0.7	9	6.0	34	22.7
Aircraft mechanics and service technicians	164	44.0	–	–	–	–	7	4.3	36	22.0
Automotive body, related repairers	140	41.1	45	32.1	1	0.7	17	12.1	27	19.3

	total workers	median age	total under 35		aged 16 to 19		aged 20 to 24		aged 25 to 34	
			number	percent of total	number	percent of total	number	percent of total	number	percent of total
Automotive service technicians and mechanics	855	39.1	338	39.5%	12	1.4%	120	14.0%	206	24.1%
Bus and truck mechanics and diesel engine specialists	312	42.4	106	34.0	3	1.0	28	9.0	75	24.0
Heavy vehicle and mobile equip. service technicians, mechanics	199	43.4	62	31.2	1	0.5	12	6.0	49	24.6
Heating, air conditioning, refrigeration mechanics, installers	338	39.4	128	37.9	5	1.5	24	7.1	99	29.3
Industrial and refractory machinery mechanics	433	45.7	96	22.2	2	0.5	11	2.5	83	19.2
Maintenance and repair workers, general	422	48.4	84	19.9	3	0.7	20	4.7	61	14.5
Electrical power-line installers and repairers	124	40.6	50	40.3	1	0.8	10	8.1	39	31.5
Telecommunications line installers and repairers	201	39.8	68	33.8	2	1.0	14	7.0	52	25.9
Other installation, maintenance, and repair workers	215	41.8	72	33.5	2	0.9	27	12.6	43	20.0
First-line supervisors of production and operating workers	727	47.1	139	19.1	1	0.1	20	2.8	118	16.2
Electrical, electronics, and electromechanical assemblers	156	45.9	40	25.6	2	1.3	17	10.9	21	13.5
Misc. assemblers and fabricators	860	41.5	296	34.4	19	2.2	87	10.1	190	22.1
Bakers	207	40.3	81	39.1	8	3.9	33	15.9	40	19.3
Butchers and other meat, poultry, and fish processing workers	342	39.0	148	43.3	11	3.2	46	13.5	91	26.6
Food processing workers, all other	115	41.0	42	36.5	1	0.9	12	10.4	29	25.2
Cutting, punching, press machine setters, operators, tenders, metal and plastic	100	40.0	34	34.0	1	1.0	11	11.0	22	22.0
Machinists	419	45.6	106	25.3	4	1.0	29	6.9	73	17.4
Welding, soldering, brazing workers	505	40.9	186	36.8	6	1.2	53	10.5	127	25.1
Metal workers and plastic workers, all other	368	41.7	121	32.9	5	1.4	33	9.0	83	22.6
Printing press operators	217	43.6	65	30.0	4	1.8	20	9.2	41	18.9
Laundry and dry-cleaning workers	174	44.6	54	31.0	5	2.9	19	10.9	30	17.2
Sewing machine operators	169	48.0	33	19.5	0	0.0	4	2.4	29	17.2
Inspectors, testers, sorters, samplers, and weighers	647	43.6	195	30.1	6	0.9	54	8.3	135	20.9
Packaging and filling machine operators and tenders	288	39.1	115	39.9	10	3.5	36	12.5	69	24.0
Painting workers	120	40.8	40	33.3	2	1.7	9	7.5	29	24.2
Production workers, all other	777	42.2	252	32.4	16	2.1	70	9.0	166	21.4
Supervisors of transportation and material-moving workers	228	44.3	58	25.4	0	0.0	15	6.6	43	18.9
Aircraft pilots and flight engineers	121	49.0	19	15.7	0	0.0	3	2.5	16	13.2
Bus drivers	573	52.6	54	9.4	3	0.5	5	0.9	46	8.0
Driver/sales workers, truck drivers	3,059	45.4	760	24.8	43	1.4	167	5.5	550	18.0
Taxi drivers and chauffeurs	342	48.8	79	23.1	0	0.0	15	4.4	64	18.7
Industrial truck, tractor operators	528	39.8	206	39.0	9	1.7	55	10.4	142	26.9
Cleaners of vehicles and equipment	331	32.7	180	54.4	43	13.0	62	18.7	75	22.7
Laborers and freight, stock, and material movers, hand	1,787	35.0	907	50.8	161	9.0	323	18.1	423	23.7
Packers and packagers, hand	393	37.9	177	45.0	16	4.1	63	16.0	98	24.9

Note: "–" means sample is too small to make a reliable estimate.
Source: Bureau of Labor Statistics, unpublished tables from the 2011 Current Population Survey; calculations by New Strategist

The Youngest Workers Are Part-Timers

Among employed 20-to-24-year-olds, however, most work full-time.

Among people aged 16 or older in the civilian labor force, 20 percent of men and 33 percent of women work part-time. Among teenagers, however, part-time work predominates—73 percent of male and 83 percent of female workers aged 16 to 19 have part-time jobs. Many are high school students with after-school jobs or college students trying to earn tuition money.

Among 20-to-24-year-olds in the labor force, most work full-time. Women in the age group are more likely than their male counterparts to work part-time—48 percent of women and 37 percent of men have part-time jobs. Among workers in the broad 25-to-54 age group, the great majority of both men and women have full-time jobs.

Most workers with part-time jobs prefer to work part-time. But a substantial portion would like a full-time job. Among 16-to-19-year-olds with part-time jobs, from 13 to 15 percent would prefer full-time. Among 20-to-24-year-olds with part-time jobs, the figure is a higher 25 to 33 percent. Among men aged 25 to 54 with part-time jobs, 39 percent would prefer full-time work.

■ With college costs rising and family savings disappearing, part-time work will probably become more important in the educational plans of young adults.

Most working teens have part-time jobs

(percent of employed workers aged 16 to 24 who work part-time, by sex, 2011)

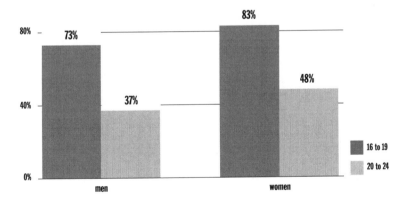

Table 6.10 Full-Time and Part-Time Workers by Age and Sex, 2011

(number and percent distribution of people aged 16 or older at work in nonagricultural industries by age, employment status, and sex, 2011; numbers in thousands)

	total			men			women		
	total	full-time	part-time	total	full-time	part-time	total	full-time	part-time
Total at work	**132,717**	**98,446**	**34,271**	**70,440**	**56,598**	**13,841**	**62,278**	**41,848**	**20,430**
Aged 16 to 19	4,065	888	3,178	1,951	534	1,417	2,114	353	1,761
Aged 20 to 24	12,515	7,226	5,289	6,543	4,097	2,446	5,972	3,129	2,843
Aged 25 to 54	89,430	71,366	18,064	47,964	41,213	6,751	41,466	30,153	11,313
Aged 55 or older	26,707	18,967	7,741	13,982	10,754	3,228	12,726	8,213	4,513

PERCENT DISTRIBUTION BY EMPLOYMENT STATUS

	total			men			women		
Total at work	**100.0%**	**74.2%**	**25.8%**	**100.0%**	**80.3%**	**19.6%**	**100.0%**	**67.2%**	**32.8%**
Aged 16 to 19	100.0	21.8	78.2	100.0	27.4	72.6	100.0	16.7	83.3
Aged 20 to 24	100.0	57.7	42.3	100.0	62.6	37.4	100.0	52.4	47.6
Aged 25 to 54	100.0	79.8	20.2	100.0	85.9	14.1	100.0	72.7	27.3
Aged 55 or older	100.0	71.0	29.0	100.0	76.9	23.1	100.0	64.5	35.5

PERCENT DISTRIBUTION BY AGE

	total			men			women		
Total at work	**100.0%**	**100.0%**	**100.0%**	**100.0%**	**100.0%**	**100.0%**	**100.0%**	**100.0%**	**100.0%**
Aged 16 to 19	3.1	0.9	9.3	2.8	0.9	10.2	3.4	0.8	8.6
Aged 20 to 24	9.4	7.3	15.4	9.3	7.2	17.7	9.6	7.5	13.9
Aged 25 to 54	67.4	72.5	52.7	68.1	72.8	48.8	66.6	72.1	55.4
Aged 55 or older	20.1	19.3	22.6	19.8	19.0	23.3	20.4	19.6	22.1

Note: "Part-time" work is less than 35 hours per week. Part-time workers exclude those who worked less than 35 hours in the previous week because of vacation, holidays, child care problems, weather issues, and other temporary, noneconomic reasons. Source: Bureau of Labor Statistics, Labor Force Statistics from the Current Population Survey, Internet site http://www.bls.gov/cps/tables.htm#empstat; calculations by New Strategist

Table 6.11 Part-Time Workers by Sex, Age, and Reason, 2011

(total number of people aged 16 or older who work in nonagricultural industries part-time, and number and percent working part-time for economic reasons, by sex and age, 2011; numbers in thousands)

| | total | working part-time for economic reasons | |
		number	share of total
Men working part-time	**13,841**	**4,285**	**31.0%**
Aged 16 to 19	1,417	217	15.3
Aged 20 to 24	2,446	816	33.4
Aged 25 to 54	6,751	2,627	38.9
Aged 55 or older	3,228	625	19.4
Women working part-time	**20,430**	**4,138**	**20.3**
Aged 16 to 19	1,761	226	12.8
Aged 20 to 24	2,843	703	24.7
Aged 25 to 54	11,313	2,556	22.6
Aged 55 or older	4,513	653	14.5

Note: "Part-time" work is less than 35 hours per week. Part-time workers exclude those who worked less than 35 hours in the previous week because of vacation, holidays, child care problems, weather issues, and other temporary, noneconomic reasons. "Economic reasons" means a worker's hours have been reduced or workers cannot find full-time employment.
Source: Bureau of Labor Statistics, Labor Force Statistics from the Current Population Survey, Internet site http://www.bls .gov/cps/tables.htm#empstat; calculations by New Strategist

Few Millennials Are Self-Employed

Self-employment rises with age and experience.

Although many teens and young adults may dream of being their own boss, few are able to do so. Among the nation's 140 million employed workers, only 6.8 percent are self-employed. Among workers under age 35, the figure is only 2 to 4 percent.

As people age, self-employment increases, peaking at 18 percent among workers aged 65 or older. Self-employment increases with age because it takes years of experience to gain marketable skills.

■ Self-employment is relatively uncommon in the United States because the cost of buying private health insurance is prohibitive.

Self-employment rises with age

(percent of workers who are self-employed, by age, 2011)

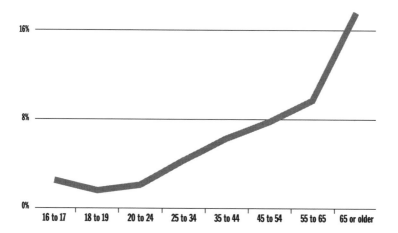

Table 6.12 Self-Employed Workers by Sex and Age, 2011

(number of employed workers aged 16 or older, number and percent who are self-employed, and percent distribution of self-employed, by age, 2011; numbers in thousands)

	total	self-employed number	percent	percent distribution of self-employed by age
Total workers aged 16 or older	**139,869**	**9,449**	**6.8%**	**100.0%**
Aged 16 to 17	1,355	34	2.5	0.4
Aged 18 to 19	2,972	47	1.6	0.5
Aged 20 to 24	13,036	273	2.1	2.9
Aged 25 to 34	30,538	1,312	4.3	13.9
Aged 35 to 44	30,271	1,906	6.3	20.2
Aged 45 to 54	32,867	2,567	7.8	27.2
Aged 55 to 64	22,186	2,141	9.7	22.7
Aged 65 or older	6,647	1,168	17.6	12.4
Total men 16 or older	**74,290**	**5,894**	**7.9**	**100.0**
Aged 16 to 17	649	26	4.0	0.4
Aged 18 to 19	1,459	28	1.9	0.5
Aged 20 to 24	6,826	171	2.5	2.9
Aged 25 to 34	16,674	820	4.9	13.9
Aged 35 to 44	16,370	1,158	7.1	19.6
Aged 45 to 54	17,113	1,588	9.3	26.9
Aged 55 to 64	11,469	1,337	11.7	22.7
Aged 65 or older	3,729	764	20.5	13.0
Total women 16 or older	**65,579**	**3,555**	**5.4**	**100.0**
Aged 16 to 17	705	8	1.1	0.2
Aged 18 to 19	1,513	19	1.3	0.5
Aged 20 to 24	6,209	102	1.6	2.9
Aged 25 to 34	13,864	492	3.5	13.8
Aged 35 to 44	13,901	748	5.4	21.0
Aged 45 to 54	15,753	980	6.2	27.6
Aged 55 to 64	10,717	803	7.5	22.6
Aged 65 or older	2,917	404	13.8	11.4

Source: Bureau of Labor Statistics, Labor Force Statistics from the Current Population Survey, Internet site http://www.bls .gov/cps/tables.htm#empstat; calculations by New Strategist

Most Minimum-Wage Workers Are Teens and Young Adults

More than 70 percent are under age 35.

Among the nation's 74 million workers who were paid hourly rates in 2011, only 3.8 million (5 percent) made minimum wage or less, according to the Bureau of Labor Statistics. Of those workers, half are under age 25.

Twenty-three percent of minimum wage workers are aged 16 to 19, and another 26 percent are aged 20 to 24. Among workers paid hourly rates in the 16-to-19 age group, 23 percent earn minimum wage or less. In the 20-to-24 age group, 9 percent earn minimum wage or less.

■ Younger workers are most likely to earn minimum wage or less because many are in entry-level jobs.

Teens and young adults account for the majority of minimum wage workers

(percent distribution of worker who make minimum wage or less, by age, 2011)

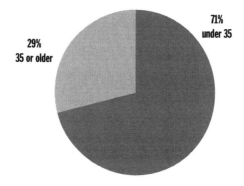

29%
35 or older

71%
under 35

Table 6.13 Workers Earning Minimum Wage by Age, 2011

(number, percent, and percent distribution of workers paid hourly rates at or below minimum wage, by age, 2011; numbers in thousands)

	total paid hourly rates	at or below minimum wage		
		number	share of total	percent distribution
Total aged 16 or older	**73,926**	**3,829**	**5.2%**	**100.0%**
Aged 16 to 24	14,437	1,896	13.1	49.5
Aged 16 to 19	3,936	899	22.8	23.5
Aged 20 to 24	10,501	997	9.5	26.0
Aged 25 to 34	17,155	808	4.7	21.1
Aged 25 to 29	9,229	460	5.0	12.0
Aged 30 to 34	7,926	348	4.4	9.1
Aged 35 to 44	14,168	399	2.8	10.4
Aged 45 to 54	15,331	382	2.5	10.0
Aged 55 to 64	10,046	221	2.2	5.8
Aged 65 or older	2,790	123	4.4	3.2

Source: Bureau of Labor Statistics, Characteristics of Minimum Wage Workers, 2011, Internet site http://www.bls.gov/cps/ minwage2011.htm; calculations by New Strategist

Few Millennials Are Represented by a Union

Men and women are almost equally likely to be represented by a union.

Union representation has fallen sharply over the past few decades. In 2011, only 13 percent of employed wage and salary workers were represented by a union.

The percentage of workers represented by a union peaks in the 55-to-64 age group at 17 percent. Among workers under age 25, only 5 percent are represented by a union. Among workers aged 25 to 34, the figure is 11 percent.

■ Union representation may rise along with workers' concerns about job security and the cost of health care coverage.

Few workers are represented by a union

(percent of employed wage and salary workers who are represented by unions, by age, 2011)

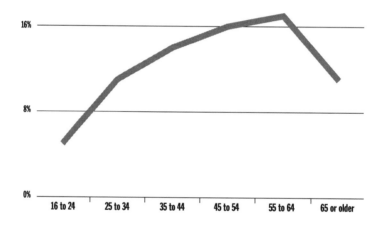

Table 6.14 Union Representation by Sex and Age, 2011

(number and percent of employed wage and salary workers aged 16 or older by union representation status, sex, and age, 2011; numbers in thousands)

	total employed	represented by unions number	represented by unions percent
Total aged 16 or older	**125,187**	**16,290**	**13.0%**
Aged 16 to 24	16,910	845	5.0
Aged 25 to 34	28,682	3,155	11.0
Aged 35 to 44	27,231	3,804	14.0
Aged 45 to 54	28,693	4,707	16.4
Aged 55 to 64	18,751	3,219	17.2
Aged 65 or older	4,920	559	11.4
Men aged 16 or older	**64,686**	**8,731**	**13.5**
Aged 16 to 24	8,636	486	5.6
Aged 25 to 34	15,465	1,706	11.0
Aged 35 to 44	14,412	2,114	14.7
Aged 45 to 54	14,415	2,513	17.4
Aged 55 to 64	9,212	1,623	17.6
Aged 65 or older	2,547	290	11.4
Women aged 16 or older	**60,502**	**7,558**	**12.5**
Aged 16 to 24	8,274	360	4.8
Aged 25 to 34	13,218	1,449	11.0
Aged 35 to 44	12,819	1,690	13.2
Aged 45 to 54	14,278	2,195	15.4
Aged 55 to 64	9,540	1,596	16.7
Aged 65 or older	2,373	269	10.7

Note: Workers represented by unions are either members of a labor union or similar employee association or workers who report no union affiliation but whose jobs are covered by a union or an employee association contract.
Source: Bureau of Labor Statistics, Labor Force Statistics from the Current Population Survey, Internet site http://www.bls.gov/cps/tables.htm#empstat; calculations by New Strategist

Millennial Generation Will Expand Labor Force

The number of workers aged 25 to 34 will increase during the coming decade.

Between 2010 and 2020, the Millennial generation will age into its late thirties and early forties (the oldest Millennials turn 43 in 2020). The number of workers aged 25 to 34 will expand by 8 percent between 2010 and 2020, a gain of nearly 3 million, according to the Bureau of Labor Statistics. At the same time, the number of workers aged 35 to 44 will increase by nearly 2 million for a gain of 5 percent.

The number of older workers is projected to soar during the coming decade as Boomers age into their late sixties and early seventies. Between 2010 and 2020, the Bureau of Labor Statistics projects a 73 percent increase in the number of male workers and an even larger 90 percent increase in the number of female workers aged 65 or older.

■ As Boomers remain in the labor force well into old age, they may slow the movement of younger workers up the career ladder

Number of workers aged 25 to 44 will increase

(change in number of workers by age, 2010–20)

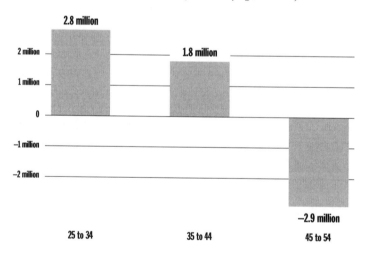

Table 6.15 Projections of the Labor Force by Sex and Age, 2010 and 2020

(number of people aged 16 or older in the civilian labor force by sex and age, 2010 and 2020; percent change, 2010–20; numbers in thousands)

	2010	2020	percent change
Total labor force	**153,889**	**164,360**	**6.8%**
Aged 16 to 19	5,906	4,548	−23.0
Aged 20 to 24	15,028	13,783	−8.3
Aged 25 to 34	33,615	36,421	8.4
Aged 35 to 44	33,366	35,147	5.3
Aged 45 to 54	35,960	33,050	−8.1
Aged 55 to 64	23,297	29,299	25.8
Aged 65 or older	6,717	12,112	80.3
Total men in labor force	**81,985**	**87,128**	**6.3**
Aged 16 to 19	2,991	2,413	−19.3
Aged 20 to 24	7,864	7,276	−7.5
Aged 25 to 34	18,352	19,667	7.2
Aged 35 to 44	18,119	19,303	6.5
Aged 45 to 54	18,856	17,415	−7.6
Aged 55 to 64	12,103	14,662	21.1
Aged 65 or older	3,700	6,391	72.7
Total women in labor force	**71,904**	**77,232**	**7.4**
Aged 16 to 19	2,914	2,134	−26.8
Aged 20 to 24	7,164	6,506	−9.2
Aged 25 to 34	15,263	16,754	9.8
Aged 35 to 44	15,247	15,844	3.9
Aged 45 to 54	17,104	15,635	−8.6
Aged 55 to 64	11,194	14,637	30.8
Aged 65 or older	3,017	5,721	89.6

Source: Bureau of Labor Statistics, Employment Projections, Internet site http://www.bls.gov/emp/; calculations by New Strategist

Table 6.16 Projections of Labor Force Participation by Sex and Age, 2010 and 2020

(percent of people aged 16 or older in the civilian labor force by sex and age, 2010 and 2020; percentage point change, 2010–20)

	2010	2020	percentage point change
Total labor force participation rate	**64.7%**	**62.5%**	**−2.2**
Men in labor force	**71.2**	**68.2**	**−3.0**
Aged 16 to 19	34.9	27.9	−7.0
Aged 20 to 24	74.5	69.4	−5.1
Aged 25 to 34	90.3	86.9	−3.4
Aged 35 to 44	91.5	91.3	−0.2
Aged 45 to 54	86.8	86.0	−0.8
Aged 55 to 64	70.0	71.1	1.1
Aged 65 or older	22.1	26.7	4.6
Women in labor force	**58.6**	**57.1**	**−1.5**
Aged 16 to 19	35.0	25.2	−9.8
Aged 20 to 24	68.3	62.3	−6.0
Aged 25 to 34	74.7	74.2	−0.5
Aged 35 to 44	75.2	74.0	−1.2
Aged 45 to 54	75.7	75.7	0.0
Aged 55 to 64	60.2	66.6	6.4
Aged 65 or older	13.8	19.2	5.4

Source: Bureau of Labor Statistics, Employment Projections, Internet site http://www.bls.gov/emp/; calculations by New Strategist

CHAPTER
7

Living Arrangements

■ People younger than age 35 headed 22 percent of the nation's 119 million households in 2011 (Millennials were aged 17 to 34 in that year).

■ The living arrangements of young adults depend greatly on their race and Hispanic origin. Married couples account for 41 percent of households headed by Hispanics under age 35 but for only 17 percent of black households in the age group.

■ Only 28 percent of households headed by people under age 25 include children. The figure rises to 42 percent among householders aged 25 to 29, then reaches 58 percent among householders aged 30 to 34.

■ The Millennial generation now heads the majority of households with preschoolers (59 percent) and infants (72 percent).

■ Among people under age 35, a substantial 44 percent of men and 36 percent of women live with their parents.

■ The majority of men and women under age 35 have never married. Among men under age 35, fully 73 percent have never married. The figure is 64 percent for their female counterparts.

Millennial Generation Heads More than One in Five Households

Millennials account for only 17 percent of married couples, however.

People under age 35 accounted for 22 percent of the nation's 119 million householders in 2011 (Millennials were aged 17 to 34 in that year). Young adults have been slow to establish their own households because high unemployment rates and student loans are forcing many to live with their parents.

Households headed by Millennials are extremely diverse. Married couples account for the 37 percent plurality of Millennial households, but this figure ranges from a low of 18 percent among householders under age 25 to a high of 51 percent among those aged 30 to 34. Nearly 22 percent of Millennial householders are men and women living alone, while another 18 percent are female-headed families. Fourteen percent of householders under age 35 are nonrelatives living together, some being roommates and others being romantic partners. Eight percent of householders under age 35 represent male-headed families, including 13 percent of households headed by people under age 25.

■ The diversity of Millennial living arrangements makes it difficult for marketers, politicians, and community organizations to reach them.

Married couples become the majority of households in the 30-to-34 age group

(percent of households headed by married couples, by age of householder, 2011)

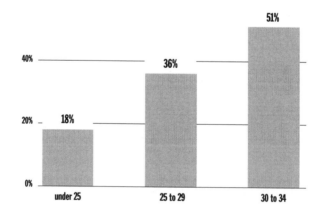

Table 7.1 Households Headed by People under Age 35 by Household Type, 2011: Total Households

(number and percent distribution of total households and households headed by people under age 35, by household type, 2011; numbers in thousands)

| | | aged 15 to 34 | | | aged 25 to 34 | |
	total	total	15 to 24	total	25 to 29	30 to 34
TOTAL HOUSEHOLDS	118,682	25,712	6,140	19,572	9,331	10,241
Family households	78,613	16,381	3,315	13,066	5,557	7,509
Married couples	58,036	9,628	1,077	8,551	3,348	5,203
Female householder, no spouse present	15,019	4,695	1,414	3,281	1,585	1,696
Male householder, no spouse present	5,559	2,058	825	1,233	623	610
Nonfamily households	40,069	9,330	2,824	6,506	3,774	2,732
Female householder	21,234	4,050	1,355	2,695	1,670	1,025
Living alone	18,184	2,550	711	1,839	1,058	781
Male householder	18,835	5,279	1,468	3,811	2,104	1,707
Living alone	14,539	3,052	734	2,318	1,186	1,132
Percent distribution by type						
TOTAL HOUSEHOLDS	100.0%	100.0%	100.0%	100.0%	100.0%	100.0%
Family households	66.2	63.7	54.0	66.8	59.6	73.3
Married couples	48.9	37.4	17.5	43.7	35.9	50.8
Female householder, no spouse present	12.7	18.3	23.0	16.8	17.0	16.6
Male householder, no spouse present	4.7	8.0	13.4	6.3	6.7	6.0
Nonfamily households	33.8	36.3	46.0	33.2	40.4	26.7
Female householder	17.9	15.8	22.1	13.8	17.9	10.0
Living alone	15.3	9.9	11.6	9.4	11.3	7.6
Male householder	15.9	20.5	23.9	19.5	22.5	16.7
Living alone	12.3	11.9	12.0	11.8	12.7	11.1
Percent distribution by age						
TOTAL HOUSEHOLDS	100.0%	21.7%	5.2%	16.5%	7.9%	8.6%
Family households	100.0	20.8	4.2	16.6	7.1	9.6
Married couples	100.0	16.6	1.9	14.7	5.8	9.0
Female householder, no spouse present	100.0	31.3	9.4	21.8	10.6	11.3
Male householder, no spouse present	100.0	37.0	14.8	22.2	11.2	11.0
Nonfamily households	100.0	23.3	7.0	16.2	9.4	6.8
Female householder	100.0	19.1	6.4	12.7	7.9	4.8
Living alone	100.0	14.0	3.9	10.1	5.8	4.3
Male householder	100.0	28.0	7.8	20.2	11.2	9.1
Living alone	100.0	21.0	5.0	15.9	8.2	7.8

Source: Bureau of the Census, America's Families and Living Arrangements: 2011, Internet site http://www.census.gov/population/www/socdemo/hh-fam/cps2011.html; calculations by New Strategist

Millennial Households Differ by Race and Hispanic Origin

A large share of the nation's young families are Hispanic.

Non-Hispanic whites account for the 61 percent majority of householders under age 35 (Millennials were aged 17 to 34 in 2011). But the figure varies greatly by type of household. Non-Hispanic whites account for 68 percent of nonfamily householders under age 35, but for only 39 percent of female-headed families in the age group. Among married couples under age 30, Hispanics head 19 percent.

Female-headed families account for the 39 percent plurality of black households headed by Millennials. In contrast, among non-Hispanic white and Asian households headed by Millennials, a much smaller 12 percent are female-headed families. Married couples account for the 41 percent plurality of households headed by Hispanic Millennials, but for only 17 percent of black households headed by people under age 35.

■ Young adults have different wants and needs depending on their living arrangements.

Hispanic young adults are least likely to live alone

(percent of householders under age 35 who live alone, by race and Hispanic origin, 2011)

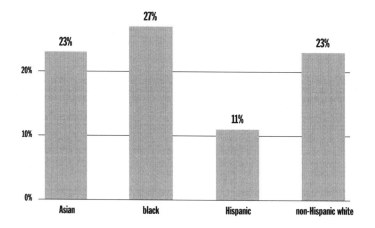

Table 7.2 Households Headed by People under Age 35 by Household Type, Race, and Hispanic Origin, 2011

(number and percent distribution of households headed by people under age 35, by household type, race, and Hispanic origin, 2011; numbers in thousands)

	total	Asian	black	Hispanic	non-Hispanic white
TOTAL HOUSEHOLDERS UNDER AGE 35	25,712	1,366	4,198	4,348	15,670
Family households	16,381	841	2,741	3,439	9,310
Married couples	9,628	532	724	1,795	6,541
Female householder, no spouse present	4,695	162	1,633	1,055	1,844
Male householder, no spouse present	2,058	147	382	588	924
Nonfamily households	9,330	523	1,457	909	6,360
Female householder	4,050	249	746	356	2,661
Living alone	2,550	157	606	215	1,551
Male householder	5,279	274	711	553	3,698
Living alone	3,052	161	508	273	2,085
Percent distribution by race and Hispanic origin					
TOTAL HOUSEHOLDERS UNDER AGE 35	100.0%	5.3%	16.3%	16.9%	60.9%
Family households	100.0	5.1	16.7	21.0	56.8
Married couples	100.0	5.5	7.5	18.6	67.9
Female householder, no spouse present	100.0	3.5	34.8	22.5	39.3
Male householder, no spouse present	100.0	7.1	18.6	28.6	44.9
Nonfamily households	100.0	5.6	15.6	9.7	68.2
Female householder	100.0	6.1	18.4	8.8	65.7
Living alone	100.0	6.2	23.8	8.4	60.8
Male householder	100.0	5.2	13.5	10.5	70.1
Living alone	100.0	5.3	16.6	8.9	68.3

Note: Numbers do not add to total because Asians and blacks are those who identify themselves as being of the race alone and those who identify themselves as being of the race in combination with other races. Hispanics may be of any race. Non-Hispanic whites are who those identify themselves as being white alone and not Hispanic.
Source: Bureau of the Census, America's Families and Living Arrangements: 2011, Internet site http://www.census.gov/ population/www/socdemo/hh-fam/cps2011.html; calculations by New Strategist

Table 7.3 Households Headed by People under Age 35 by Household Type, 2011: Asian Households

(number and percent distribution of total households headed by Asians and households headed by Asians under age 35, by household type, 2011; numbers in thousands)

| | | | aged 15 to 34 | | | |
| | | | | | aged 25 to 34 | |
	total	total	15 to 24	total	25 to 29	30 to 34
TOTAL ASIAN HOUSEHOLDS	**5,040**	**1,366**	**295**	**1,071**	**495**	**576**
Family households	**3,722**	**841**	**144**	**697**	**261**	**436**
Married couples	2,939	532	27	505	162	343
Female householder, no spouse present	492	162	50	112	57	55
Male householder, no spouse present	291	147	67	80	42	38
Nonfamily households	**1,318**	**523**	**150**	**373**	**233**	**140**
Female householder	702	249	70	179	116	63
Living alone	558	157	28	129	82	47
Male householder	616	274	80	194	117	77
Living alone	437	161	34	127	68	59

Percent distribution by type

TOTAL ASIAN HOUSEHOLDS	**100.0%**	**100.0%**	**100.0%**	**100.0%**	**100.0%**	**100.0%**
Family households	**73.8**	**61.6**	**48.8**	**65.1**	**52.7**	**75.7**
Married couples	58.3	38.9	9.2	47.2	32.7	59.5
Female householder, no spouse present	9.8	11.9	16.9	10.5	11.5	9.5
Male householder, no spouse present	5.8	10.8	22.7	7.5	8.5	6.6
Nonfamily households	**26.2**	**38.3**	**50.8**	**34.8**	**47.1**	**24.3**
Female householder	13.9	18.2	23.7	16.7	23.4	10.9
Living alone	11.1	11.5	9.5	12.0	16.6	8.2
Male householder	12.2	20.1	27.1	18.1	23.6	13.4
Living alone	8.7	11.8	11.5	11.9	13.7	10.2

Percent distribution by age

Total Asian households	**100.0%**	**27.1%**	**5.9%**	**21.3%**	**9.8%**	**11.4%**
Family households	**100.0**	**22.6**	**3.9**	**18.7**	**7.0**	**11.7**
Married couples	100.0	18.1	0.9	17.2	5.5	11.7
Female householder, no spouse present	100.0	32.9	10.2	22.8	11.6	11.2
Male householder, no spouse present	100.0	50.5	23.0	27.5	14.4	13.1
Nonfamily households	**100.0**	**39.7**	**11.4**	**28.3**	**17.7**	**10.6**
Female householder	100.0	35.5	10.0	25.5	16.5	9.0
Living alone	100.0	28.1	5.0	23.1	14.7	8.4
Male householder	100.0	44.5	13.0	31.5	19.0	12.5
Living alone	100.0	36.8	7.8	29.1	15.6	13.5

Note: Asians are those who identify themselves as being of the race alone and those who identify themselves as being of the race in combination with other races.
Source: Bureau of the Census, America's Families and Living Arrangements: 2011, Internet site http://www.census.gov/ population/www/socdemo/hh-fam/cps2011.html; calculations by New Strategist

Table 7.4 Households Headed by People under Age 35 by Household Type, 2011: Black Households

(number and percent distribution of total households headed by blacks and households headed by blacks under age 35, by household type, 2011; numbers in thousands)

| | total | aged 15 to 34 | | | | |
| | | total | 15 to 24 | aged 25 to 34 | | |
				total	25 to 29	30 to 34
TOTAL BLACK HOUSEHOLDS	15,613	4,198	1,201	2,997	1,471	1,526
Family households	9,766	2,741	693	2,048	970	1,078
Married couples	4,353	724	82	642	270	372
Female householder, no spouse present	4,459	1,633	460	1,173	559	614
Male householder, no spouse present	954	382	150	232	141	91
Nonfamily households	5,847	1,457	508	949	501	448
Female householder	3,238	746	270	476	274	202
Living alone	2,933	606	212	394	219	175
Male householder	2,609	711	238	473	226	247
Living alone	2,189	508	149	359	156	203
Percent distribution by type						
TOTAL BLACK HOUSEHOLDS	100.0%	100.0%	100.0%	100.0%	100.0%	100.0%
Family households	62.6	65.3	57.7	68.3	65.9	70.6
Married couples	27.9	17.2	6.8	21.4	18.4	24.4
Female householder, no spouse present	28.6	38.9	38.3	39.1	38.0	40.2
Male householder, no spouse present	6.1	9.1	12.5	7.7	9.6	6.0
Nonfamily households	37.4	34.7	42.3	31.7	34.1	29.4
Female householder	20.7	17.8	22.5	15.9	18.6	13.2
Living alone	18.8	14.4	17.7	13.1	14.9	11.5
Male householder	16.7	16.9	19.8	15.8	15.4	16.2
Living alone	14.0	12.1	12.4	12.0	10.6	13.3
Percent distribution by age						
TOTAL BLACK HOUSEHOLDS	100.0%	26.9%	7.7%	19.2%	9.4%	9.8%
Family households	100.0	28.1	7.1	21.0	9.9	11.0
Married couples	100.0	16.6	1.9	14.7	6.2	8.5
Female householder, no spouse present	100.0	36.6	10.3	26.3	12.5	13.8
Male householder, no spouse present	100.0	40.0	15.7	24.3	14.8	9.5
Nonfamily households	100.0	24.9	8.7	16.2	8.6	7.7
Female householder	100.0	23.0	8.3	14.7	8.5	6.2
Living alone	100.0	20.7	7.2	13.4	7.5	6.0
Male householder	100.0	27.3	9.1	18.1	8.7	9.5
Living alone	100.0	23.2	6.8	16.4	7.1	9.3

Note: Blacks are those who identify themselves as being of the race alone and those who identify themselves as being of the race in combination with other races.
Source: Bureau of the Census, America's Families and Living Arrangements: 2011, Internet site http://www.census.gov/population/www/socdemo/hh-fam/cps2011.html; calculations by New Strategist

Table 7.5 Households Headed by People under Age 35 by Household Type, 2011: Hispanic Households

(number and percent distribution of total households headed by Hispanics and households headed by Hispanics under age 35, by household type, 2011; numbers in thousands)

| | | aged 15 to 34 | | | | |
| | | | | aged 25 to 34 | | |
	total	total	15 to 24	total	25 to 29	30 to 34
TOTAL HISPANIC HOUSEHOLDS	**13,665**	**4,348**	**1,135**	**3,213**	**1,476**	**1,737**
Family households	**10,659**	**3,439**	**872**	**2,567**	**1,139**	**1,428**
Married couples	6,725	1,795	269	1,526	600	926
Female householder, no spouse present	2,754	1,055	335	720	370	350
Male householder, no spouse present	1,180	588	266	322	169	153
Nonfamily households	**3,006**	**909**	**263**	**646**	**337**	**309**
Female householder	1,371	356	134	222	129	93
Living alone	1,098	215	64	151	86	65
Male householder	1,635	553	130	423	207	216
Living alone	1,100	273	62	211	88	123
Percent distribution by type						
TOTAL HISPANIC HOUSEHOLDS	**100.0%**	**100.0%**	**100.0%**	**100.0%**	**100.0%**	**100.0%**
Family households	**78.0**	**79.1**	**76.8**	**79.9**	**77.2**	**82.2**
Married couples	49.2	41.3	23.7	47.5	40.7	53.3
Female householder, no spouse present	20.2	24.3	29.5	22.4	25.1	20.1
Male householder, no spouse present	8.6	13.5	23.4	10.0	11.4	8.8
Nonfamily households	**22.0**	**20.9**	**23.2**	**20.1**	**22.8**	**17.8**
Female householder	10.0	8.2	11.8	6.9	8.7	5.4
Living alone	8.0	4.9	5.6	4.7	5.8	3.7
Male householder	12.0	12.7	11.5	13.2	14.0	12.4
Living alone	8.0	6.3	5.5	6.6	6.0	7.1
Percent distribution by age						
TOTAL HISPANIC HOUSEHOLDS	**100.0%**	**31.8%**	**8.3%**	**23.5%**	**10.8%**	**12.7%**
Family households	**100.0**	**32.3**	**8.2**	**24.1**	**10.7**	**13.4**
Married couples	100.0	26.7	4.0	22.7	8.9	13.8
Female householder, no spouse present	100.0	38.3	12.2	26.1	13.4	12.7
Male householder, no spouse present	100.0	49.8	22.5	27.3	14.3	13.0
Nonfamily households	**100.0**	**30.2**	**8.7**	**21.5**	**11.2**	**10.3**
Female householder	100.0	26.0	9.8	16.2	9.4	6.8
Living alone	100.0	19.6	5.8	13.8	7.8	5.9
Male householder	100.0	33.8	8.0	25.9	12.7	13.2
Living alone	100.0	24.8	5.6	19.2	8.0	11.2

Source: Bureau of the Census, America's Families and Living Arrangements: 2011, Internet site http://www.census.gov/ population/www/socdemo/hh-fam/cps2011.html; calculations by New Strategist

Table 7.6 Households Headed by People under Age 35 by Household Type, 2011: Non-Hispanic White Households

(number and percent distribution of total households headed by non-Hispanic whites and households headed by non-Hispanic whites under age 35, by household type, 2011; numbers in thousands)

| | | aged 15 to 34 | | | | |
| | | | | aged 25 to 34 | | |
	total	total	15 to 24	total	25 to 29	30 to 34
TOTAL NON-HISPANIC WHITE HOUSEHOLDS	**83,471**	**15,670**	**3,481**	**12,189**	**5,845**	**6,344**
Family households	**53,859**	**9,310**	**1,607**	**7,703**	**3,176**	**4,527**
Married couples	43,554	6,541	694	5,847	2,303	3,544
Female householder, no spouse present	7,277	1,844	574	1,270	604	666
Male householder, no spouse present	3,078	924	338	586	269	317
Nonfamily households	**29,562**	**6,360**	**1,874**	**4,486**	**2,669**	**1,817**
Female householder	15,749	2,661	862	1,799	1,137	662
Living alone	13,456	1,551	397	1,154	665	489
Male householder	13,813	3,698	1,012	2,686	1,532	1,154
Living alone	10,675	2,085	485	1,600	856	744

Percent distribution by type

	total	total	15 to 24	total	25 to 29	30 to 34
TOTAL NON-HISPANIC WHITE HOUSEHOLDS	**100.0%**	**100.0%**	**100.0%**	**100.0%**	**100.0%**	**100.0%**
Family households	**64.5**	**59.4**	**46.2**	**63.2**	**54.3**	**71.4**
Married couples	52.2	41.7	19.9	48.0	39.4	55.9
Female householder, no spouse present	8.7	11.8	16.5	10.4	10.3	10.5
Male householder, no spouse present	3.7	5.9	9.7	4.8	4.6	5.0
Nonfamily households	**35.4**	**40.6**	**53.8**	**36.8**	**45.7**	**28.6**
Female householder	18.9	17.0	24.8	14.8	19.5	10.4
Living alone	16.1	9.9	11.4	9.5	11.4	7.7
Male householder	16.5	23.6	29.1	22.0	26.2	18.2
Living alone	12.8	13.3	13.9	13.1	14.6	11.7

Percent distribution by age

	total	total	15 to 24	total	25 to 29	30 to 34
TOTAL NON-HISPANIC WHITE HOUSEHOLDS	**100.0%**	**18.8%**	**4.2%**	**14.6%**	**7.0%**	**7.6%**
Family households	**100.0**	**17.3**	**3.0**	**14.3**	**5.9**	**8.4**
Married couples	100.0	15.0	1.6	13.4	5.3	8.1
Female householder, no spouse present	100.0	25.3	7.9	17.5	8.3	9.2
Male householder, no spouse present	100.0	30.0	11.0	19.0	8.7	10.3
Nonfamily households	**100.0**	**21.5**	**6.3**	**15.2**	**9.0**	**6.1**
Female householder	100.0	16.9	5.5	11.4	7.2	4.2
Living alone	100.0	11.5	3.0	8.6	4.9	3.6
Male householder	100.0	26.8	7.3	19.4	11.1	8.4
Living alone	100.0	19.5	4.5	15.0	8.0	7.0

Note: Non-Hispanic whites are those who identify themselves as being white alone and not Hispanic.
Source: Bureau of the Census, America's Families and Living Arrangements: 2011, Internet site http://www.census.gov/ population/www/socdemo/hh-fam/cps2011.html; calculations by New Strategist

Households of Young Adults Are about Average in Size

Household size creeps above average for householders aged 30 to 34.

Households headed by people under age 35 (the Millennial generation was aged 17 to 34 in 2011) vary in size. At one extreme are the 3.21 people who live in households headed by the youngest adults (under age 20). At the other extreme are the 2.51 people in households headed by 20-to-24-year-olds.

Overall, household size grows as householders age through their thirties. It peaks among householders aged 35 to 39—at 3.36 people—because this age group is most likely to be raising children. As householders age into their forties and fifties, the nest empties and household size shrinks.

■ As young adults marry and have children, the nest will become increasingly crowded.

Among householders in their twenties, average household size is less than three

(average household size by age of householder, 2011)

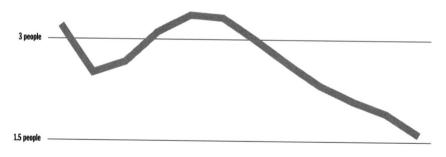

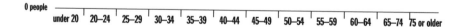

Table 7.7 Average Size of Household by Age of Householder, 2011

(number of households, average number of people per household, and average number of people under age 18 per household, by age of householder, 2011; number of households in thousands)

	number	average number of people	average number of people under age 18
Total households	**118,682**	**2.58**	**0.63**
Under age 20	771	3.21	1.01
Aged 20 to 24	5,369	2.51	0.54
Aged 25 to 29	9,331	2.67	0.83
Aged 30 to 34	10,241	3.11	1.28
Aged 35 to 39	10,334	3.36	1.45
Aged 40 to 44	10,917	3.32	1.27
Aged 45 to 49	12,220	3.00	0.83
Aged 50 to 54	12,310	2.65	0.45
Aged 55 to 59	11,445	2.32	0.22
Aged 60 to 64	10,383	2.09	0.15
Aged 65 to 74	13,348	1.91	0.09
Aged 75 or older	12,015	1.60	0.04

Source: Bureau of the Census, America's Families and Living Arrangements: 2011, Internet site http://www.census.gov/population/www/socdemo/hh-fam/cps2011.html; calculations by New Strategist

Most Householders Aged 30 to 34 Are Raising Children

Among Hispanics, most are raising children beginning in the 25-to-29 age group.

Only 28 percent of households headed by people under age 25 include children. The figure rises to 42 percent among householders aged 25 to 29, then reaches 58 percent among householders aged 30 to 34. Most married couples and female-headed families with a householder under age 35 are raising children.

The percentage of households with children under age 18 varies greatly by race and Hispanic origin. Fifty-nine percent of Hispanic householders aged 25 to 29 have children under age 18, as do 53 percent of their black counterparts. This compares with a smaller 36 percent of non-Hispanic white and 23 percent of Asian households in the age group.

■ The lifestyles of young adults are diverse, ranging from students with class schedules to parents with family and work schedules.

Few households headed by Asians under age 30 include children

(percent of householders aged 25 to 34 with children under age 18, by race and Hispanic origin, 2011)

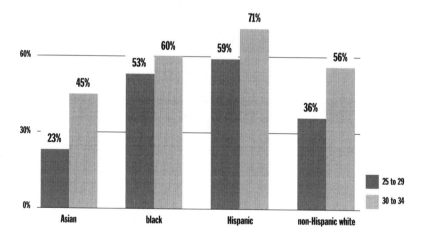

Table 7.8 Households by Type, Age of Householder, and Presence of Children, 2011: Total Households

(total number of households and number and percent with own children under age 18 or of any age at home, by household type and age of householder, 2011; numbers in thousands)

	total	with own children under 18		with own children, any age	
		number	percent	number	percent
TOTAL HOUSEHOLDS	**118,682**	**34,760**	**29.3%**	**47,150**	**39.7%**
Under age 25	6,140	1,738	28.3	1,779	29.0
Aged 25 to 29	9,331	3,883	41.6	3,902	41.8
Aged 30 to 34	10,241	5,971	58.3	6,033	58.9
Aged 35 to 39	10,334	6,824	66.0	6,997	67.7
Aged 40 to 44	10,917	6,576	60.2	7,251	66.4
Aged 45 to 49	12,220	5,251	43.0	7,070	57.9
Aged 50 to 54	12,310	2,957	24.0	5,483	44.5
Aged 55 to 64	21,828	1,371	6.3	5,442	24.9
Aged 65 to 74	13,348	127	1.0	1,830	13.7
Aged 75 or older	12,015	62	0.5	1,361	11.3
MARRIED COUPLES	**58,036**	**23,938**	**41.2**	**30,928**	**53.3**
Under age 25	1,077	580	53.9	587	54.5
Aged 25 to 29	3,348	2,207	65.9	2,219	66.3
Aged 30 to 34	5,203	4,070	78.2	4,106	78.9
Aged 35 to 39	5,820	4,811	82.7	4,887	84.0
Aged 40 to 44	6,267	4,901	78.2	5,245	83.7
Aged 45 to 49	6,721	3,927	58.4	5,054	75.2
Aged 50 to 54	6,785	2,226	32.8	3,888	57.3
Aged 55 to 64	11,851	1,087	9.2	3,663	30.9
Aged 65 to 74	6,871	91	1.3	926	13.5
Aged 75 or older	4,092	38	0.9	354	8.7
FEMALE-HEADED FAMILIES	**15,019**	**8,597**	**57.2**	**12,794**	**85.2**
Under age 25	1,414	962	68.0	975	69.0
Aged 25 to 29	1,585	1,359	85.7	1,365	86.1
Aged 30 to 34	1,696	1,547	91.2	1,570	92.6
Aged 35 to 39	1,780	1,614	90.7	1,697	95.3
Aged 40 to 44	1,700	1,313	77.2	1,577	92.8
Aged 45 to 49	1,741	1,046	60.1	1,602	92.0
Aged 50 to 54	1,393	536	38.5	1,209	86.8
Aged 55 to 64	1,745	177	10.1	1,301	74.6
Aged 65 to 74	976	19	1.9	680	69.7
Aged 75 or older	988	24	2.4	818	82.8
MALE-HEADED FAMILIES	**5,559**	**2,225**	**40.0**	**3,428**	**61.7**
Under age 25	825	196	23.8	217	26.3
Aged 25 to 29	623	316	50.7	317	50.9
Aged 30 to 34	610	354	58.0	357	58.5
Aged 35 to 39	572	399	69.8	414	72.4
Aged 40 to 44	569	362	63.6	430	75.6
Aged 45 to 49	585	277	47.4	414	70.8
Aged 50 to 54	565	195	34.5	386	68.3
Aged 55 to 64	672	108	16.1	478	71.1
Aged 65 to 74	300	18	6.0	225	75.0
Aged 75 or older	237	0	0.0	189	79.7

Source: Bureau of the Census, America's Families and Living Arrangements: 2011, Internet site http://www.census.gov/ population/www/socdemo/hh-fam/cps2011.html; calculations by New Strategist

Table 7.9 Households by Type, Age of Householder, and Presence of Children, 2011: Asian Households

(total number of Asian households and number and percent with own children under age 18 or of any age at home, by household type and age of householder, 2011; numbers in thousands)

	total	with own children under 18		with own children, any age	
		number	percent	number	percent
TOTAL ASIAN HOUSEHOLDS	**5,040**	**1,774**	**35.2%**	**2,417**	**48.0%**
Under age 25	295	37	12.5	38	12.9
Aged 25 to 29	495	113	22.8	113	22.8
Aged 30 to 34	576	260	45.1	263	45.7
Aged 35 to 39	649	417	64.3	426	65.6
Aged 40 to 44	513	358	69.8	367	71.5
Aged 45 to 49	581	344	59.2	415	71.4
Aged 50 to 54	470	160	34.0	304	64.7
Aged 55 to 64	763	77	10.1	323	42.3
Aged 65 to 74	428	6	1.4	122	28.5
Aged 75 or older	270	3	1.1	46	17.0
MARRIED COUPLES	**2,939**	**1,513**	**51.5**	**1,993**	**67.8**
Under age 25	27	18	66.7	18	66.7
Aged 25 to 29	162	79	48.8	79	48.8
Aged 30 to 34	343	224	65.3	226	65.9
Aged 35 to 39	439	365	83.1	369	84.1
Aged 40 to 44	357	301	84.3	310	86.8
Aged 45 to 49	407	309	75.9	360	88.5
Aged 50 to 54	332	140	42.2	256	77.1
Aged 55 to 64	502	68	13.5	258	51.4
Aged 65 to 74	256	5	2.0	96	37.5
Aged 75 or older	115	3	2.6	20	17.4
FEMALE-HEADED FAMILIES	**492**	**214**	**43.5**	**343**	**69.7**
Under age 25	50	18	36.0	18	36.0
Aged 25 to 29	57	27	47.4	27	47.4
Aged 30 to 34	55	34	61.8	34	61.8
Aged 35 to 39	52	45	86.5	48	92.3
Aged 40 to 44	49	43	87.8	44	89.8
Aged 45 to 49	52	24	46.2	43	82.7
Aged 50 to 54	57	16	28.1	41	71.9
Aged 55 to 64	64	6	9.4	47	73.4
Aged 65 to 74	33	0	0.0	23	69.7
Aged 75 or older	24	0	0.0	18	75.0
MALE-HEADED FAMILIES	**291**	**47**	**16.2**	**81**	**27.8**
Under age 25	67	1	1.5	2	3.0
Aged 25 to 29	42	6	14.3	6	14.3
Aged 30 to 34	38	2	5.3	2	5.3
Aged 35 to 39	30	6	20.0	9	30.0
Aged 40 to 44	27	14	51.9	14	51.9
Aged 45 to 49	29	10	34.5	12	41.4
Aged 50 to 54	15	4	26.7	7	46.7
Aged 55 to 64	26	3	11.5	18	69.2
Aged 65 to 74	7	0	0.0	3	42.9
Aged 75 or older	10	0	0.0	8	80.0

Note: Asians are those who identify themselves as being of the race alone and those who identify themselves as being of the race in combination with other races.
Source: Bureau of the Census, America's Families and Living Arrangements: 2011, Internet site http://www.census.gov/ population/www/socdemo/hh-fam/cps2011.html; calculations by New Strategist.

Table 7.10 Households by Type, Age of Householder, and Presence of Children, 2011: Black Households

(total number of black households and number and percent with own children under age 18 or of any age at home, by household type and age of householder, 2011; numbers in thousands)

	total	with own children under 18		with own children, any age	
		number	percent	number	percent
TOTAL BLACK HOUSEHOLDS	**15,613**	**4,966**	**31.8%**	**6,916**	**44.3%**
Under age 25	1,201	410	34.1	416	34.6
Aged 25 to 29	1,471	786	53.4	793	53.9
Aged 30 to 34	1,526	919	60.2	936	61.3
Aged 35 to 39	1,514	980	64.7	1,035	68.4
Aged 40 to 44	1,494	808	54.1	940	62.9
Aged 45 to 49	1,650	553	33.5	843	51.1
Aged 50 to 54	1,661	307	18.5	670	40.3
Aged 55 to 64	2,682	161	6.0	761	28.4
Aged 65 to 74	1,423	28	2.0	299	21.0
Aged 75 or older	990	13	1.3	222	22.4
MARRIED COUPLES	**4,353**	**1,898**	**43.6**	**2,578**	**59.2**
Under age 25	82	60	73.2	60	73.2
Aged 25 to 29	270	211	78.1	217	80.4
Aged 30 to 34	372	299	80.4	307	82.5
Aged 35 to 39	480	401	83.5	413	86.0
Aged 40 to 44	508	389	76.6	423	83.3
Aged 45 to 49	532	270	50.8	374	70.3
Aged 50 to 54	556	154	27.7	288	51.8
Aged 55 to 64	892	94	10.5	358	40.1
Aged 65 to 74	462	16	3.5	100	21.6
Aged 75 or older	200	4	2.0	36	18.0
FEMALE-HEADED FAMILIES	**4,459**	**2,673**	**59.9**	**3,782**	**84.8**
Under age 25	460	319	69.3	325	70.7
Aged 25 to 29	559	496	88.7	497	88.9
Aged 30 to 34	614	563	91.7	572	93.2
Aged 35 to 39	560	503	89.8	543	97.0
Aged 40 to 44	479	362	75.6	445	92.9
Aged 45 to 49	451	239	53.0	412	91.4
Aged 50 to 54	406	130	32.0	341	84.0
Aged 55 to 64	475	45	9.5	321	67.6
Aged 65 to 74	239	6	2.5	166	69.5
Aged 75 or older	216	9	4.2	160	74.1
MALE-HEADED FAMILIES	**954**	**396**	**41.5**	**556**	**58.3**
Under age 25	150	30	20.0	31	20.7
Aged 25 to 29	141	79	56.0	79	56.0
Aged 30 to 34	91	58	63.7	58	63.7
Aged 35 to 39	103	77	74.8	79	76.7
Aged 40 to 44	96	57	59.4	72	75.0
Aged 45 to 49	89	45	50.6	57	64.0
Aged 50 to 54	83	23	27.7	41	49.4
Aged 55 to 64	114	22	19.3	82	71.9
Aged 65 to 74	55	6	10.9	33	60.0
Aged 75 or older	32	0	0.0	25	78.1

Note: Blacks are those who identify themselves as being of the race alone and those who identify themselves as being of the race in combination with other races.
Source: Bureau of the Census, America's Families and Living Arrangements: 2011, Internet site http://www.census.gov/population/www/socdemo/hh-fam/cps2011.html; calculations by New Strategist

Table 7.11 Households by Type, Age of Householder, and Presence of Children, 2011: Hispanic Households

(total number of Hispanic households and number and percent with own children under age 18 or of any age at home, by household type and age of householder, 2011; numbers in thousands)

	total	with own children under 18		with own children, any age	
		number	percent	number	percent
TOTAL HISPANIC HOUSEHOLDS	**13,665**	**6,373**	**46.6%**	**7,992**	**58.5%**
Under age 25	1,135	468	41.2	471	41.5
Aged 25 to 29	1,476	874	59.2	877	59.4
Aged 30 to 34	1,737	1,231	70.9	1,237	71.2
Aged 35 to 39	1,739	1,276	73.4	1,307	75.2
Aged 40 to 44	1,628	1,124	69.0	1,227	75.4
Aged 45 to 49	1,484	775	52.2	1,036	69.8
Aged 50 to 54	1,245	404	32.4	748	60.1
Aged 55 to 64	1,729	177	10.2	735	42.5
Aged 65 to 74	917	33	3.6	236	25.7
Aged 75 or older	574	11	1.9	118	20.6
MARRIED COUPLES	**6,725**	**4,106**	**61.1**	**5,034**	**74.9**
Under age 25	269	187	69.5	187	69.5
Aged 25 to 29	600	473	78.8	473	78.8
Aged 30 to 34	926	829	89.5	830	89.6
Aged 35 to 39	981	840	85.6	854	87.1
Aged 40 to 44	938	794	84.6	840	89.6
Aged 45 to 49	843	547	64.9	707	83.9
Aged 50 to 54	677	268	39.6	493	72.8
Aged 55 to 64	878	135	15.4	477	54.3
Aged 65 to 74	416	25	6.0	122	29.3
Aged 75 or older	196	8	4.1	51	26.0
FEMALE-HEADED FAMILIES	**2,754**	**1,803**	**65.5**	**2,345**	**85.1**
Under age 25	335	221	66.0	223	66.6
Aged 25 to 29	370	318	85.9	319	86.2
Aged 30 to 34	350	324	92.6	328	93.7
Aged 35 to 39	372	345	92.7	357	96.0
Aged 40 to 44	338	278	82.2	319	94.4
Aged 45 to 49	281	179	63.7	255	90.7
Aged 50 to 54	235	110	46.8	199	84.7
Aged 55 to 64	266	22	8.3	200	75.2
Aged 65 to 74	135	5	3.7	91	67.4
Aged 75 or older	73	3	4.1	55	75.3
MALE-HEADED FAMILIES	**1,180**	**465**	**39.4**	**613**	**51.9**
Under age 25	266	61	22.9	62	23.3
Aged 25 to 29	169	84	49.7	85	50.3
Aged 30 to 34	153	79	51.6	79	51.6
Aged 35 to 39	150	91	60.7	95	63.3
Aged 40 to 44	113	52	46.0	68	60.2
Aged 45 to 49	101	49	48.5	74	73.3
Aged 50 to 54	90	26	28.9	57	63.3
Aged 55 to 64	89	20	22.5	58	65.2
Aged 65 to 74	28	3	10.7	24	85.7
Aged 75 or older	19	0	0.0	12	63.2

Source: Bureau of the Census, America's Families and Living Arrangements: 2011, Internet site http://www.census.gov/population/www/socdemo/hh-fam/cps2011.html; calculations by New Strategist

Table 7.12 Households by Type, Age of Householder, and Presence of Children, 2011: Non-Hispanic White Households

(total number of non-Hispanic white households and number and percent with own children under age 18 or of any age at home, by household type and age of householder, 2011; numbers in thousands)

	total	with own children under 18		with own children, any age	
		number	percent	number	percent
TOTAL NON-HISPANIC WHITE HOUSEHOLDS	**83,471**	**21,457**	**25.7%**	**29,529**	**35.4%**
Under age 25	3,481	830	23.8	859	24.7
Aged 25 to 29	5,845	2,103	36.0	2,113	36.2
Aged 30 to 34	6,344	3,531	55.7	3,568	56.2
Aged 35 to 39	6,340	4,085	64.4	4,162	65.6
Aged 40 to 44	7,220	4,262	59.0	4,684	64.9
Aged 45 to 49	8,394	3,532	42.1	4,732	56.4
Aged 50 to 54	8,842	2,068	23.4	3,731	42.2
Aged 55 to 64	16,439	949	5.8	3,573	21.7
Aged 65 to 74	10,473	62	0.6	1,145	10.9
Aged 75 or older	10,093	33	0.3	961	9.5
MARRIED COUPLES	**43,554**	**16,267**	**37.3**	**21,110**	**48.5**
Under age 25	694	323	46.5	332	47.8
Aged 25 to 29	2,303	1,436	62.4	1,443	62.7
Aged 30 to 34	3,544	2,709	76.4	2,732	77.1
Aged 35 to 39	3,845	3,139	81.6	3,181	82.7
Aged 40 to 44	4,424	3,391	76.7	3,642	82.3
Aged 45 to 49	4,878	2,763	56.6	3,569	73.2
Aged 50 to 54	5,171	1,654	32.0	2,830	54.7
Aged 55 to 64	9,467	785	8.3	2,541	26.8
Aged 65 to 74	5,672	45	0.8	595	10.5
Aged 75 or older	3,557	23	0.6	246	6.9
FEMALE-HEADED FAMILIES	**7,277**	**3,903**	**53.6**	**6,292**	**86.5**
Under age 25	574	406	70.7	412	71.8
Aged 25 to 29	604	524	86.8	527	87.3
Aged 30 to 34	666	614	92.2	624	93.7
Aged 35 to 39	803	727	90.5	757	94.3
Aged 40 to 44	838	639	76.3	774	92.4
Aged 45 to 49	952	593	62.3	887	93.2
Aged 50 to 54	701	280	39.9	629	89.7
Aged 55 to 64	917	104	11.3	717	78.2
Aged 65 to 74	556	8	1.4	388	69.8
Aged 75 or older	665	10	1.5	576	86.6
MALE-HEADED FAMILIES	**3,078**	**1,286**	**41.8**	**2,127**	**69.1**
Under age 25	338	101	29.9	116	34.3
Aged 25 to 29	269	144	53.5	144	53.5
Aged 30 to 34	317	209	65.9	212	66.9
Aged 35 to 39	283	220	77.7	224	79.2
Aged 40 to 44	323	233	72.1	268	83.0
Aged 45 to 49	368	176	47.8	276	75.0
Aged 50 to 54	366	135	36.9	271	74.0
Aged 55 to 64	435	60	13.8	315	72.4
Aged 65 to 74	206	9	4.4	162	78.6
Aged 75 or older	172	0	0.0	139	80.8

Note: Non-Hispanic whites are those who identify themselves as being white alone and not Hispanic.
Source: Bureau of the Census, America's Families and Living Arrangements: 2011, Internet site http://www.census.gov/population/www/socdemo/hh-fam/cps2011.html; calculations by New Strategist

More than One-third of Millennial Households Include Preschoolers

The proportion with infants is also well above average.

Most young adults go to college after high school, postponing marriage and family until their late twenties or early thirties. Consequently, the proportion of households headed by young adults that include children rises from a low of 28 percent among householders under age 25 to the 58 percent majority among householders aged 30 to 34.

While 13 percent of all households include children under age 6, the proportion is a much larger 35 percent among householders under age 35. Similarly, while only 2 percent of all households include infants under age 1, the figure is 8 percent among householders under age 35. The Millennial generation now heads the majority of households with preschoolers (59 percent) and infants (72 percent).

■ While most young adults postpone childbearing, others establish independent households because they have children.

Millennials are the majority of parents with preschoolers

(percent of households with children that are headed by people under age 35, by age of child, 2011)

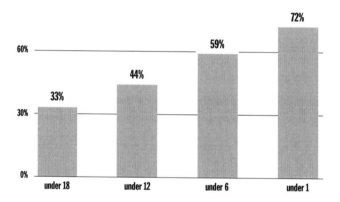

Table 7.13 Households by Presence and Age of Children and Age of Householder, 2011

(number and percent distribution of households by presence of own children at home, by age of children and age of householder, 2011; numbers in thousands)

| | total | under age 35 | | | | 35 to 44 | 45 to 54 | 55 to 64 | 65 or older |
		total	under 25	25 to 29	30 to 34				
TOTAL HOUSEHOLDS	118,682	25,712	6,140	9,331	10,241	21,251	46,358	21,828	25,363
With children of any age	47,150	11,714	1,779	3,902	6,033	14,248	17,995	5,442	3,191
Under age 25	41,108	11,683	1,773	3,896	6,014	14,204	14,836	3,184	385
Under age 18	34,760	11,592	1,738	3,883	5,971	13,400	9,579	1,371	189
Under age 12	25,392	11,172	1,714	3,833	5,625	10,242	3,880	415	98
Under age 6	15,314	9,044	1,666	3,310	4,068	5,213	1,009	106	49
Under age 1	2,942	2,124	509	757	858	726	82	4	10
Aged 12 to 17	16,247	1,796	35	187	1,574	6,945	7,395	1,101	111

Percemt distribution by age of child

	total	total	under 25	25 to 29	30 to 34	35 to 44	45 to 54	55 to 64	65 or older
TOTAL HOUSEHOLDS	100.0%	100.0%	100.0%	100.0%	100.0%	100.0%	100.0%	100.0%	100.0%
With children of any age	39.7	45.6	29.0	41.8	58.9	67.0	38.8	24.9	12.6
Under age 25	34.6	45.4	28.9	41.8	58.7	66.8	32.0	14.6	1.5
Under age 18	29.3	45.1	28.3	41.6	58.3	63.1	20.7	6.3	0.7
Under age 12	21.4	43.5	27.9	41.1	54.9	48.2	8.4	1.9	0.4
Under age 6	12.9	35.2	27.1	35.5	39.7	24.5	2.2	0.5	0.2
Under age 1	2.5	8.3	8.3	8.1	8.4	3.4	0.2	0.0	0.0
Aged 12 to 17	13.7	7.0	0.6	2.0	15.4	32.7	16.0	5.0	0.4

Percemt distribution by age of householder

	total	total	under 25	25 to 29	30 to 34	35 to 44	45 to 54	55 to 64	65 or older
TOTAL HOUSEHOLDS	100.0%	21.7%	5.2%	7.9%	8.6%	17.9%	39.1%	18.4%	21.4%
With children of any age	100.0	24.8	3.8	8.3	12.8	30.2	38.2	11.5	6.8
Under age 25	100.0	28.4	4.3	9.5	14.6	34.6	36.1	7.7	0.9
Under age 18	100.0	33.3	5.0	11.2	17.2	38.6	27.6	3.9	0.5
Under age 12	100.0	44.0	6.8	15.1	22.2	40.3	15.3	1.6	0.4
Under age 6	100.0	59.1	10.9	21.6	26.6	34.0	6.6	0.7	0.3
Under age 1	100.0	72.2	17.3	25.7	29.2	24.7	2.8	0.1	0.3
Aged 12 to 17	100.0	11.1	0.2	1.2	9.7	42.7	45.5	6.8	0.7

Source: Bureau of the Census, America's Families and Living Arrangements: 2011, Internet site http://www.census.gov/ population/www/socdemo/hh-fam/cps2011.html; calculations by New Strategist

Millennial Parents Typically Have One or Two Children

Nearly one in four couples have three or more, however.

Among married couples under age 35 with children, 38 percent have only one child (most will eventually have more) and 39 percent have two. Although small families are most common, a substantial 23 percent of married-couple parents under age 35 are raising three or more children.

Among female-headed families headed by people under age 35, a larger 44 percent have only one child. Their male counterparts are even more likely to have only one child (60 percent).

■ The percentage of married parents who are raising three or more children reaches 27 percent in the 30-to-34 age group.

Among married-couple parents under age 35, most have one or two children

(percent of married couples under age 35 with children under age 18, by number of children, 2011)

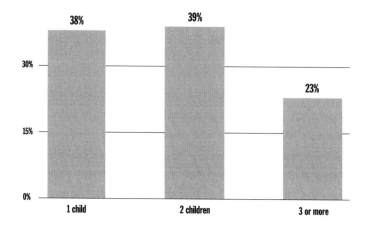

Table 7.14 Married Couples with Children by Number of Children and Age of Householder, 2011

(number and percent distribution of married couples with own children under age 18 at home, by number of children and age of householder, 2011; numbers in thousands)

	total	under age 35 total	under 25	25 to 29	30 to 34	35 to 44	45 or older
Married couples with children under age 18	23,938	6,857	580	2,207	4,070	9,712	7,369
One	9,300	2,626	326	985	1,315	2,793	3,881
Two	9,527	2,659	199	817	1,643	4,360	2,508
Three	3,618	1,069	41	283	745	1,802	746
Four or more	1,493	501	13	121	367	757	234

PERCENT DISTRIBUTION BY NUMBER OF CHILDREN

Married couples with children under age 18	100.0%	100.0%	100.0%	100.0%	100.0%	100.0%	100.0%
One	38.9	38.3	56.2	44.6	32.3	28.8	52.7
Two	39.8	38.8	34.3	37.0	40.4	44.9	34.0
Three	15.1	15.6	7.1	12.8	18.3	18.6	10.1
Four or more	6.2	7.3	2.2	5.5	9.0	7.8	3.2

PERCENT DISTRIBUTION BY AGE OF HOUSEHOLDER

Married couples with children under age 18	100.0%	28.6%	2.4%	9.2%	17.0%	40.6%	30.8%
One	100.0	28.2	3.5	10.6	14.1	30.0	41.7
Two	100.0	27.9	2.1	8.6	17.2	45.8	26.3
Three	100.0	29.5	1.1	7.8	20.6	49.8	20.6
Four or more	100.0	33.6	0.9	8.1	24.6	50.7	15.7

Source: Bureau of the Census, America's Families and Living Arrangements: 2011, Internet site http://www.census.gov/population/www/socdemo/hh-fam/cps2011.html; calculations by New Strategist

Table 7.15 Female-headed Families with Children by Number of Children and Age of Householder, 2011

(number and percent distribution of female-headed families with own children under age 18 at home, by number of children and age of householder, 2011; numbers in thousands)

	total	under age 35 total	under 25	25 to 29	30 to 34	35 to 44	45 or older
Female-headed families with children under 18	8,597	3,868	962	1,359	1,547	2,927	1,802
One	4,375	1,720	619	575	526	1,385	1,270
Two	2,681	1,295	251	473	571	995	391
Three	1,100	556	73	221	262	421	122
Four or more	441	297	20	90	187	125	19

PERCENT DISTRIBUTION BY NUMBER OF CHILDREN

	total	under age 35 total	under 25	25 to 29	30 to 34	35 to 44	45 or older
Female-headed families with children under 18	100.0%	100.0%	100.0%	100.0%	100.0%	100.0%	100.0%
One	50.9	44.5	64.3	42.3	34.0	47.3	70.5
Two	31.2	33.5	26.1	34.8	36.9	34.0	21.7
Three	12.8	14.4	7.6	16.3	16.9	14.4	6.8
Four or more	5.1	7.7	2.1	6.6	12.1	4.3	1.1

PERCENT DISTRIBUTION BY AGE OF HOUSEHOLDER

	total	under age 35 total	under 25	25 to 29	30 to 34	35 to 44	45 or older
Female-headed families with children under 18	100.0%	45.0%	11.2%	15.8%	18.0%	34.0%	21.0%
One	100.0	39.3	14.1	13.1	12.0	31.7	29.0
Two	100.0	48.3	9.4	17.6	21.3	37.1	14.6
Three	100.0	50.5	6.6	20.1	23.8	38.3	11.1
Four or more	100.0	67.3	4.5	20.4	42.4	28.3	4.3

Source: Bureau of the Census, America's Families and Living Arrangements: 2011, Internet site http://www.census.gov/ population/www/socdemo/hh-fam/cps2011.html; calculations by New Strategist

Table 7.16 Male-headed Families with Children by Number of Children and Age of Householder, 2011

(number and percent distribution of male-headed families with own children under age 18 at home, by number of children and age of householder, 2011; numbers in thousands)

| | total | under age 35 | | | | 35 to 44 | 45 or older |
		total	under 25	25 to 29	30 to 34		
Male-headed families with children under 18	**2,225**	**866**	**196**	**316**	**354**	**761**	**598**
One	1,337	520	136	166	218	385	432
Two	627	256	47	120	89	254	117
Three	199	70	14	24	32	93	37
Four or more	63	20	0	5	15	31	11

PERCENT DISTRIBUTION BY NUMBER OF CHILDREN

	total	total	under 25	25 to 29	30 to 34	35 to 44	45 or older
Male-headed families with children under 18	**100.0%**	**100.0%**	**100.0%**	**100.0%**	**100.0%**	**100.0%**	**100.0%**
One	60.1	60.0	69.4	52.5	61.6	50.6	72.2
Two	28.2	29.6	24.0	38.0	25.1	33.4	19.6
Three	8.9	8.1	7.1	7.6	9.0	12.2	6.2
Four or more	2.8	2.3	0.0	1.6	4.2	4.1	1.8

PERCENT DISTRIBUTION BY AGE OF HOUSEHOLDER

	total	total	under 25	25 to 29	30 to 34	35 to 44	45 or older
Male-headed families with children under 18	**100.0%**	**38.9%**	**8.8%**	**14.2%**	**15.9%**	**34.2%**	**26.9%**
One	100.0	38.9	10.2	12.4	16.3	28.8	32.3
Two	100.0	40.8	7.5	19.1	14.2	40.5	18.7
Three	100.0	35.2	7.0	12.1	16.1	46.7	18.6
Four or more	100.0	31.7	0.0	7.9	23.8	49.2	17.5

Source: Bureau of the Census, America's Families and Living Arrangements: 2011, Internet site http://www.census.gov/population/www/socdemo/hh-fam/cps2011.html; calculations by New Strategist

Many Young Men Live with Their Parents

Few live by themselves.

Among people under age 35, a substantial 44 percent of men and 36 percent of women live with their parents. These figures include college students in dormitories because they are considered dependents. Not surprisingly, the proportion of young adults who live with their parents falls with age—more slowly for men than for women. Among men aged 20 to 24, the 51 percent majority still lives with parents, a figure that drops to a still substantial 24 percent in the 25-to-29 age group. Among women aged 20 to 24, a smaller 40 percent live with their parents, as do 13 percent of those aged 25 to 29.

Few young adults live by themselves. In 2011, only 6 to 7 percent of men and women under age 35 lived by themselves. The figure exceeds 10 percent among men aged 25 to 34, however.

■ With more young adults going to college and job hunting in the midst of the struggling economy, the dependency of childhood has stretched well into the twenties.

Many young adults live with parents

(percent of people aged 15 to 34 who live with their parents, by sex and age, 2011)

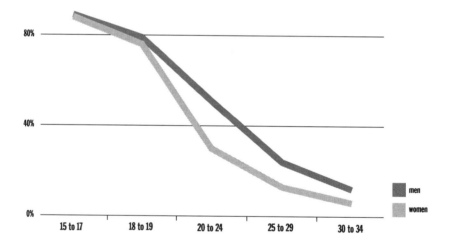

Table 7.17 People under Age 35 Living with Their Parents, 2011

(number and percent of people aged 15 to 34 who are children of the householder, by sex and age, 2011; numbers in thousands)

	total	child of householder	
		number	percent
Total men under age 35	**42,621**	**18,596**	**43.6%**
Aged 15 to 17	6,570	5,822	88.6
Aged 18 to 19	4,120	3,244	78.7
Aged 20 to 24	10,953	5,630	51.4
Aged 25 to 29	10,913	2,656	24.3
Aged 30 to 34	10,065	1,244	12.4
Total women under age 35	**41,352**	**14,732**	**35.6**
Aged 15 to 17	6,190	5,419	87.5
Aged 18 to 19	4,004	3,042	76.0
Aged 20 to 24	10,564	4,272	40.4
Aged 25 to 29	10,460	1,378	13.2
Aged 30 to 34	10,134	621	6.1

Source: Bureau of the Census, America's Families and Living Arrangements: 2011, Internet site http://www.census.gov/population/www/socdemo/hh-fam/cps2011.html; calculations by New Strategist

Table 7.18 People Who Live Alone by Age, 2011

(number of people aged 15 or older and number, percent, and percent distribution of people who live alone by sex and age, 2011; numbers in thousands)

| | total | living alone | | |
		number	percent	percent distribution
Total people	**243,955**	**32,723**	**13.4%**	**100.0%**
Under age 35	83,996	5,602	6.7	17.1
Under age 25	42,412	1,445	3.4	4.4
Aged 25 to 29	21,381	2,244	10.5	6.9
Aged 30 to 34	20,202	1,913	9.5	5.8
Aged 35 to 44	39,842	3,552	8.9	10.9
Aged 45 to 64	80,938	12,266	15.2	37.5
Aged 65 or older	39,179	11,304	28.9	34.5
Total men	**118,871**	**14,539**	**12.2**	**100.0**
Under age 35	42,636	3,052	7.2	21.0
Under age 25	21,651	734	3.4	5.0
Aged 25 to 29	10,917	1,186	10.9	8.2
Aged 30 to 34	10,067	1,132	11.2	7.8
Aged 35 to 44	19,714	2,162	11.0	14.9
Aged 45 to 64	39,441	6,115	15.5	42.1
Aged 65 or older	17,081	3,210	18.8	22.1
Total women	**125,084**	**18,184**	**14.5**	**100.0**
Under age 35	41,360	2,550	6.2	14.0
Under age 25	20,761	711	3.4	3.9
Aged 25 to 29	10,464	1,058	10.1	5.8
Aged 30 to 34	10,135	781	7.7	4.3
Aged 35 to 44	20,128	1,390	6.9	7.6
Aged 45 to 64	41,497	6,151	14.8	33.8
Aged 65 or older	22,098	8,094	36.6	44.5

Source: Bureau of the Census, 2011 Current Population Survey, Internet site http://www.census.gov/hhes/www/income/data/ incpovhlth/2010/dtables.html; calculations by New Strategist

Among Young Adults, the Married Are a Minority

Most men are single until their early thirties.

The majority of men and women under age 35 have never married. Among men under age 35, fully 73 percent have never married. The figure is 64 percent for their female counterparts. The percentage of women who have never married drops sharply in the 25-to-29 age group, to just 50 percent. But the 64 percent majority of men aged 25 to 29 are still single. For men, the proportion that has married surpasses 50 percent in the 30-to-34 age group.

Marital patterns vary somewhat by race and Hispanic origin. Among Asians and non-Hispanic whites, most men and women aged 30 to 34 are married. Among Hispanics, the same pattern is true, although a relatively large share of Hispanic men is married but living apart from their spouse. Among blacks, men aged 55 or older are the only ones likely to be currently married and living with their spouse.

■ The great diversity in the living arrangements of young adults is the consequence of postponed marriages.

Men and women are marrying later

(percent of people who are married and living with their spouse, by sex and age, 2011)

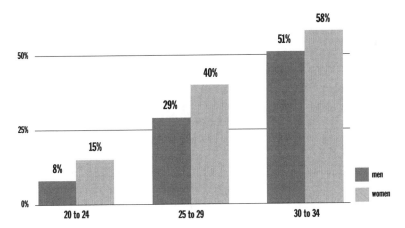

Table 7.19 Marital Status by Sex and Age, 2011: Total People

(number and percent distribution of people aged 15 or older by sex, age, and current marital status, 2011; numbers in thousands)

	total	never married	married spouse present	married spouse absent	separated	divorced	widowed
Total men	**118,828**	**38,685**	**60,129**	**1,944**	**2,144**	**9,782**	**2,916**
Under age 35	42,621	31,112	9,225	551	643	1,056	36
Aged 15 to 17	6,570	6,457	12	24	59	19	0
Aged 18 to 19	4,120	4,016	38	20	42	4	0
Aged 20 to 24	10,953	9,763	875	93	128	92	3
Aged 25 to 29	10,913	6,980	3,188	228	206	300	12
Aged 30 to 34	10,065	3,896	5,112	186	208	641	21
Aged 35 to 44	19,709	4,266	12,341	361	623	2,023	95
Aged 45 to 54	21,486	3,105	14,070	379	556	3,150	227
Aged 55 to 64	17,937	1,605	12,476	267	363	2,804	422
Aged 65 or older	17,076	760	12,044	258	228	1,637	2,149
Total women	**125,030**	**34,963**	**60,155**	**1,754**	**3,091**	**13,762**	**11,306**
Under age 35	41,352	26,521	11,747	573	934	1,467	109
Aged 15 to 17	6,190	6,072	8	33	64	9	5
Aged 18 to 19	4,004	3,818	93	29	49	14	0
Aged 20 to 24	10,564	8,526	1,578	107	167	169	17
Aged 25 to 29	10,460	5,243	4,215	212	306	440	43
Aged 30 to 34	10,134	2,862	5,853	192	348	835	44
Aged 35 to 44	20,122	3,356	12,811	302	772	2,669	212
Aged 45 to 54	22,450	2,594	14,188	360	761	3,733	815
Aged 55 to 64	19,032	1,544	11,760	286	413	3,384	1,645
Aged 65 or older	22,075	948	9,648	235	212	2,508	8,526
PERCENT DISTRIBUTION							
Total men	**100.0%**	**32.6%**	**50.6%**	**1.6%**	**1.8%**	**8.2%**	**2.5%**
Under age 35	100.0	73.0	21.6	1.3	1.5	2.5	0.1
Aged 15 to 17	100.0	98.3	0.2	0.4	0.9	0.3	0.0
Aged 18 to 19	100.0	97.5	0.9	0.5	1.0	0.1	0.0
Aged 20 to 24	100.0	89.1	8.0	0.8	1.2	0.8	0.0
Aged 25 to 29	100.0	64.0	29.2	2.1	1.9	2.7	0.1
Aged 30 to 34	100.0	38.7	50.8	1.8	2.1	6.4	0.2
Aged 35 to 44	100.0	21.6	62.6	1.8	3.2	10.3	0.5
Aged 45 to 54	100.0	14.5	65.5	1.8	2.6	14.7	1.1
Aged 55 to 64	100.0	8.9	69.6	1.5	2.0	15.6	2.4
Aged 65 or older	100.0	4.5	70.5	1.5	1.3	9.6	12.6
Total women	**100.0**	**28.0**	**48.1**	**1.4**	**2.5**	**11.0**	**9.0**
Under age 35	100.0	64.1	28.4	1.4	2.3	3.5	0.3
Aged 15 to 17	100.0	98.1	0.1	0.5	1.0	0.1	0.1
Aged 18 to 19	100.0	95.4	2.3	0.7	1.2	0.3	0.0
Aged 20 to 24	100.0	80.7	14.9	1.0	1.6	1.6	0.2
Aged 25 to 29	100.0	50.1	40.3	2.0	2.9	4.2	0.4
Aged 30 to 34	100.0	28.2	57.8	1.9	3.4	8.2	0.4
Aged 35 to 44	100.0	16.7	63.7	1.5	3.8	13.3	1.1
Aged 45 to 54	100.0	11.6	63.2	1.6	3.4	16.6	3.6
Aged 55 to 64	100.0	8.1	61.8	1.5	2.2	17.8	8.6
Aged 65 or older	100.0	4.3	43.7	1.1	1.0	11.4	38.6

Source: Bureau of the Census, America's Families and Living Arrangements: 2011, Internet site http://www.census.gov/ population/www/socdemo/hh-fam/cps2011.html; calculations by New Strategist

Table 7.20 Marital Status by Sex and Age, 2011: Asians

(number and percent distribution of Asians aged 15 or older by sex, age, and current marital status, 2011; numbers in thousands)

	total	never married	married spouse present	married spouse absent	separated	divorced	widowed
Total Asian men	**5,786**	**2,031**	**3,234**	**168**	**55**	**208**	**89**
Under age 35	2,267	1,654	528	45	16	23	2
Aged 15 to 17	277	273	0	2	2	0	0
Aged 18 to 19	201	198	0	1	2	0	0
Aged 20 to 24	580	540	32	3	5	0	0
Aged 25 to 29	601	433	130	27	4	6	1
Aged 30 to 34	608	210	366	12	3	17	1
Aged 35 to 44	1,191	215	845	41	20	71	0
Aged 45 to 54	988	93	797	38	8	41	9
Aged 55 to 64	708	47	567	25	8	48	13
Aged 65 or older	632	23	498	19	4	25	64
Total Asian women	**6,460**	**1,742**	**3,600**	**177**	**112**	**365**	**464**
Under age 35	2,311	1,367	815	47	28	51	6
Aged 15 to 17	297	291	0	1	5	0	0
Aged 18 to 19	181	167	7	0	5	2	0
Aged 20 to 24	533	456	67	7	2	2	0
Aged 25 to 29	635	301	288	21	7	14	5
Aged 30 to 34	665	152	453	18	9	33	1
Aged 35 to 44	1,336	174	995	34	34	90	9
Aged 45 to 54	1,099	113	786	41	19	105	35
Aged 55 to 64	862	56	589	33	15	75	94
Aged 65 or older	850	33	416	23	16	43	319
PERCENT DISTRIBUTION							
Total Asian men	**100.0%**	**35.1%**	**55.9%**	**2.9%**	**1.0%**	**3.6%**	**1.5%**
Under age 35	100.0	73.0	23.3	2.0	0.7	1.0	0.1
Aged 15 to 17	100.0	98.6	0.0	0.7	0.7	0.0	0.0
Aged 18 to 19	100.0	98.5	0.0	0.5	1.0	0.0	0.0
Aged 20 to 24	100.0	93.1	5.5	0.5	0.9	0.0	0.0
Aged 25 to 29	100.0	72.0	21.6	4.5	0.7	1.0	0.2
Aged 30 to 34	100.0	34.5	60.2	2.0	0.5	2.8	0.2
Aged 35 to 44	100.0	18.1	70.9	3.4	1.7	6.0	0.0
Aged 45 to 54	100.0	9.4	80.7	3.8	0.8	4.1	0.9
Aged 55 to 64	100.0	6.6	80.1	3.5	1.1	6.8	1.8
Aged 65 or older	100.0	3.6	78.8	3.0	0.6	4.0	10.1
Total Asian women	**100.0**	**27.0**	**55.7**	**2.7**	**1.7**	**5.7**	**7.2**
Under age 35	100.0	59.2	35.3	2.0	1.2	2.2	0.3
Aged 15 to 17	100.0	98.0	0.0	0.3	1.7	0.0	0.0
Aged 18 to 19	100.0	92.3	3.9	0.0	2.8	1.1	0.0
Aged 20 to 24	100.0	85.6	12.6	1.3	0.4	0.4	0.0
Aged 25 to 29	100.0	47.4	45.4	3.3	1.1	2.2	0.8
Aged 30 to 34	100.0	22.9	68.1	2.7	1.4	5.0	0.2
Aged 35 to 44	100.0	13.0	74.5	2.5	2.5	6.7	0.7
Aged 45 to 54	100.0	10.3	71.5	3.7	1.7	9.6	3.2
Aged 55 to 64	100.0	6.5	68.3	3.8	1.7	8.7	10.9
Aged 65 or older	100.0	3.9	48.9	2.7	1.9	5.1	37.5

Note: Asians are those who identify themselves as being of the race alone and those who identify themselves as being of the race in combination with other races.
Source: Bureau of the Census, America's Families and Living Arrangements: 2011, Internet site http://www.census.gov/population/www/socdemo/hh-fam/cps2011.html; calculations by New Strategist

Table 7.21 Marital Status by Sex and Age, 2011: Blacks

(number and percent distribution of blacks aged 15 or older by sex, age, and current marital status, 2011; numbers in thousands)

	total	never married	married spouse present	married spouse absent	separated	divorced	widowed
Total black men	**14,096**	**6,970**	**4,627**	**273**	**540**	**1,352**	**334**
Under age 35	6,121	5,046	724	77	142	124	8
Aged 15 to 17	1,047	1,031	2	3	6	5	0
Aged 18 to 19	706	698	1	0	4	2	0
Aged 20 to 24	1,589	1,461	78	8	27	15	0
Aged 25 to 29	1,486	1,098	262	31	53	37	6
Aged 30 to 34	1,293	758	381	35	52	65	2
Aged 35 to 44	2,334	828	1,040	53	132	272	10
Aged 45 to 54	2,459	666	1,161	65	114	422	29
Aged 55 to 64	1,812	340	918	43	91	337	82
Aged 65 or older	1,369	89	784	35	60	196	205
Total black women	**16,875**	**7,803**	**4,383**	**375**	**802**	**2,105**	**1,406**
Under age 35	6,645	5,249	873	104	177	208	32
Aged 15 to 17	1,063	1,049	0	0	10	2	2
Aged 18 to 19	697	682	6	2	5	3	0
Aged 20 to 24	1,751	1,579	100	13	32	20	5
Aged 25 to 29	1,610	1,113	328	50	52	59	8
Aged 30 to 34	1,524	826	439	39	78	124	17
Aged 35 to 44	2,883	1,082	1,043	78	192	447	40
Aged 45 to 54	3,001	861	1,093	89	251	568	137
Aged 55 to 64	2,218	431	829	71	117	541	229
Aged 65 or older	2,128	180	544	33	64	340	967
PERCENT DISTRIBUTION							
Total black men	**100.0%**	**49.4%**	**32.8%**	**1.9%**	**3.8%**	**9.6%**	**2.4%**
Under age 35	100.0	82.4	11.8	1.3	2.3	2.0	0.1
Aged 15 to 17	100.0	98.5	0.2	0.3	0.6	0.5	0.0
Aged 18 to 19	100.0	98.9	0.1	0.0	0.6	0.3	0.0
Aged 20 to 24	100.0	91.9	4.9	0.5	1.7	0.9	0.0
Aged 25 to 29	100.0	73.9	17.6	2.1	3.6	2.5	0.4
Aged 30 to 34	100.0	58.6	29.5	2.7	4.0	5.0	0.2
Aged 35 to 44	100.0	35.5	44.6	2.3	5.7	11.7	0.4
Aged 45 to 54	100.0	27.1	47.2	2.6	4.6	17.2	1.2
Aged 55 to 64	100.0	18.8	50.7	2.4	5.0	18.6	4.5
Aged 65 or older	100.0	6.5	57.3	2.6	4.4	14.3	15.0
Total black women	**100.0**	**46.2**	**26.0**	**2.2**	**4.8**	**12.5**	**8.3**
Under age 35	100.0	79.0	13.1	1.6	2.7	3.1	0.5
Aged 15 to 17	100.0	98.7	0.0	0.0	0.9	0.2	0.2
Aged 18 to 19	100.0	97.8	0.9	0.3	0.7	0.4	0.0
Aged 20 to 24	100.0	90.2	5.7	0.7	1.8	1.1	0.3
Aged 25 to 29	100.0	69.1	20.4	3.1	3.2	3.7	0.5
Aged 30 to 34	100.0	54.2	28.8	2.6	5.1	8.1	1.1
Aged 35 to 44	100.0	37.5	36.2	2.7	6.7	15.5	1.4
Aged 45 to 54	100.0	28.7	36.4	3.0	8.4	18.9	4.6
Aged 55 to 64	100.0	19.4	37.4	3.2	5.3	24.4	10.3
Aged 65 or older	100.0	8.5	25.6	1.6	3.0	16.0	45.4

Note: Blacks are those who identify themselves as being of the race alone and those who identify themselves as being of the race in combination with other races.
Source: Bureau of the Census, America's Families and Living Arrangements: 2011, Internet site http://www.census.gov/ population/www/socdemo/hh-fam/cps2011.html; calculations by New Strategist

Table 7.22 Marital Status by Sex and Age, 2011: Hispanics

(number and percent distribution of Hispanics aged 15 or older by sex, age, and current marital status, 2011; numbers in thousands)

	total	never married	married spouse present	married spouse absent	separated	divorced	widowed
Total Hispanic men	**18,097**	**8,118**	**7,382**	**652**	**1,090**	**553**	**302**
Under age 35	8,916	6,474	1,859	230	151	187	12
Aged 15 to 17	1,386	1,362	5	7	2	10	0
Aged 18 to 19	846	819	8	6	0	12	0
Aged 20 to 24	2,274	1,946	225	38	22	42	0
Aged 25 to 29	2,317	1,447	662	91	55	60	1
Aged 30 to 34	2,093	900	959	88	72	63	11
Aged 35 to 44	3,686	941	2,078	164	308	174	22
Aged 45 to 54	2,693	436	1,691	157	288	96	27
Aged 55 to 64	1,572	154	1,020	55	241	57	44
Aged 65 or older	1,230	114	735	46	103	39	195
Total Hispanic women	**16,954**	**5,909**	**7,491**	**374**	**1,495**	**742**	**942**
Under age 35	7,605	4,655	2,290	156	238	241	25
Aged 15 to 17	1,249	1,218	5	12	0	14	0
Aged 18 to 19	743	685	39	12	4	3	0
Aged 20 to 24	1,899	1,411	372	26	37	48	5
Aged 25 to 29	1,860	857	790	53	67	82	11
Aged 30 to 34	1,854	484	1,084	53	130	94	9
Aged 35 to 44	3,377	608	2,080	73	373	209	35
Aged 45 to 54	2,668	353	1,585	64	398	164	106
Aged 55 to 64	1,679	166	917	47	279	85	185
Aged 65 or older	1,624	126	621	34	208	44	591
PERCENT DISTRIBUTION							
Total Hispanic men	**100.0%**	**44.9%**	**40.8%**	**3.6%**	**6.0%**	**3.1%**	**1.7%**
Under age 35	100.0	72.6	20.9	2.6	1.7	2.1	0.1
Aged 15 to 17	100.0	98.3	0.4	0.5	0.1	0.7	0.0
Aged 18 to 19	100.0	96.8	0.9	0.7	0.0	1.4	0.0
Aged 20 to 24	100.0	85.6	9.9	1.7	1.0	1.8	0.0
Aged 25 to 29	100.0	62.5	28.6	3.9	2.4	2.6	0.0
Aged 30 to 34	100.0	43.0	45.8	4.2	3.4	3.0	0.5
Aged 35 to 44	100.0	25.5	56.4	4.4	8.4	4.7	0.6
Aged 45 to 54	100.0	16.2	62.8	5.8	10.7	3.6	1.0
Aged 55 to 64	100.0	9.8	64.9	3.5	15.3	3.6	2.8
Aged 65 or older	100.0	9.3	59.8	3.7	8.4	3.2	15.9
Total Hispanic women	**100.0**	**34.9**	**44.2**	**2.2**	**8.8**	**4.4**	**5.6**
Under age 35	100.0	61.2	30.1	2.1	3.1	3.2	0.3
Aged 15 to 17	100.0	97.5	0.4	1.0	0.0	1.1	0.0
Aged 18 to 19	100.0	92.2	5.2	1.6	0.5	0.4	0.0
Aged 20 to 24	100.0	74.3	19.6	1.4	1.9	2.5	0.3
Aged 25 to 29	100.0	46.1	42.5	2.8	3.6	4.4	0.6
Aged 30 to 34	100.0	26.1	58.5	2.9	7.0	5.1	0.5
Aged 35 to 44	100.0	18.0	61.6	2.2	11.0	6.2	1.0
Aged 45 to 54	100.0	13.2	59.4	2.4	14.9	6.1	4.0
Aged 55 to 64	100.0	9.9	54.6	2.8	16.6	5.1	11.0
Aged 65 or older	100.0	7.8	38.2	2.1	12.8	2.7	36.4

Source: Bureau of the Census, America's Families and Living Arrangements: 2011, Internet site http://www.census.gov/ population/www/socdemo/hh-fam/cps2011.html; calculations by New Strategist

Table 7.23 Marital Status by Sex and Age, 2011: Non-Hispanic Whites

(number and percent distribution of non-Hispanic whites (NHW) aged 15 or older by sex, age, and current marital status, 2011; numbers in thousands)

	total	never married	married spouse present	married spouse absent	separated	divorced	widowed
Total NHW men	**80,079**	**23,589**	**44,413**	**731**	**1,266**	**7,921**	**2,160**
Under age 35	25,202	17,844	6,092	201	299	755	12
Aged 15 to 17	3,845	3,778	5	12	38	12	0
Aged 18 to 19	2,367	2,305	25	12	24	2	0
Aged 20 to 24	6,470	5,789	529	43	50	55	3
Aged 25 to 29	6,478	3,970	2,130	80	93	202	3
Aged 30 to 34	6,042	2,002	3,403	54	94	484	6
Aged 35 to 44	12,352	2,267	8,252	106	309	1,364	53
Aged 45 to 54	15,158	1,880	10,308	125	333	2,357	154
Aged 55 to 64	13,659	1,063	9,841	140	203	2,139	273
Aged 65 or older	13,708	534	9,919	158	124	1,305	1,668
Total NHW women	**83,992**	**19,435**	**44,265**	**812**	**1,429**	**9,662**	**8,389**
Under age 35	24,635	15,175	7,731	256	473	951	45
Aged 15 to 17	3,582	3,518	3	16	35	5	3
Aged 18 to 19	2,367	2,266	41	17	38	6	0
Aged 20 to 24	6,352	5,050	1,041	56	86	112	6
Aged 25 to 29	6,302	2,947	2,793	85	157	300	19
Aged 30 to 34	6,032	1,394	3,853	82	157	528	17
Aged 35 to 44	12,432	1,508	8,599	117	347	1,735	125
Aged 45 to 54	15,520	1,257	10,608	165	335	2,623	531
Aged 55 to 64	14,083	881	9,316	134	187	2,451	1,113
Aged 65 or older	17,322	611	8,009	139	87	1,902	6,574

PERCENT DISTRIBUTION

	total	never married	married spouse present	married spouse absent	separated	divorced	widowed
Total NHW men	**100.0%**	**29.5%**	**55.5%**	**0.9%**	**1.6%**	**9.9%**	**2.7%**
Under age 35	100.0	70.8	24.2	0.8	1.2	3.0	0.0
Aged 15 to 17	100.0	98.3	0.1	0.3	1.0	0.3	0.0
Aged 18 to 19	100.0	97.4	1.1	0.5	1.0	0.1	0.0
Aged 20 to 24	100.0	89.5	8.2	0.7	0.8	0.9	0.0
Aged 25 to 29	100.0	61.3	32.9	1.2	1.4	3.1	0.0
Aged 30 to 34	100.0	33.1	56.3	0.9	1.6	8.0	0.1
Aged 35 to 44	100.0	18.4	66.8	0.9	2.5	11.0	0.4
Aged 45 to 54	100.0	12.4	68.0	0.8	2.2	15.5	1.0
Aged 55 to 64	100.0	7.8	72.0	1.0	1.5	15.7	2.0
Aged 65 or older	100.0	3.9	72.4	1.2	0.9	9.5	12.2
Total NHW women	**100.0**	**23.1**	**52.7**	**1.0**	**1.7**	**11.5**	**10.0**
Under age 35	100.0	61.6	31.4	1.0	1.9	3.9	0.2
Aged 15 to 17	100.0	98.2	0.1	0.4	1.0	0.1	0.1
Aged 18 to 19	100.0	95.7	1.7	0.7	1.6	0.3	0.0
Aged 20 to 24	100.0	79.5	16.4	0.9	1.4	1.8	0.1
Aged 25 to 29	100.0	46.8	44.3	1.3	2.5	4.8	0.3
Aged 30 to 34	100.0	23.1	63.9	1.4	2.6	8.8	0.3
Aged 35 to 44	100.0	12.1	69.2	0.9	2.8	14.0	1.0
Aged 45 to 54	100.0	8.1	68.4	1.1	2.2	16.9	3.4
Aged 55 to 64	100.0	6.3	66.2	1.0	1.3	17.4	7.9
Aged 65 or older	100.0	3.5	46.2	0.8	0.5	11.0	38.0

Note: Non-Hispanic whites are those who identify themselves as being white alone and not Hispanic.
Source: Bureau of the Census, America's Families and Living Arrangements: 2011, Internet site http://www.census.gov/population/www/socdemo/hh-fam/cps2011.html; calculations by New Strategist

Divorce Is Highest among Men and Women in Their Fifties

Few Millennials have experienced divorce since many have yet to marry.

The experience of divorce is most common among men aged 50 to 69 and women aged 50 to 59. Among men in their fifties and sixties, about 36 percent have ever divorced, according to a Census Bureau study of marriage and divorce. Among women in their fifties, 37 percent have experienced divorce.

Among all Americans aged 15 or older, 40.6 percent of women and 42.5 percent of men had married once and were still married. The figure tops 50 percent for men aged 30 or older and for women aged 30 to 49.

■ Government studies have suggested that the Vietnam War and women's changing roles were factors in the higher divorce rate of Boomers.

More than one in five adults have experienced divorce

(percent of people aged 15 or older by selected marital history and sex, 2009)

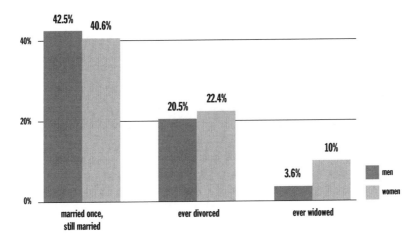

Table 7.24 Marital History of Men by Age, 2009

(number of men aged 15 or older and percent distribution by marital history and age, 2009; numbers in thousands)

	total	15–19	20–24	25–29	30–34	35–39	40–49	50–59	60–69	70+
TOTAL MEN, NUMBER	115,797	10,870	10,152	10,567	9,518	9,995	21,504	19,568	12,774	10,849
TOTAL MEN, PERCENT	100.0%	100.0%	100.0%	100.0%	100.0%	100.0%	100.0%	100.0%	100.0%	100.0%
Never married	33.0	98.0	87.5	59.7	35.6	23.5	16.4	10.8	4.6	3.4
Ever married	67.0	2.0	12.5	40.3	64.4	76.5	83.6	89.2	95.4	96.6
Married once	52.3	1.9	12.5	38.8	59.4	66.9	65.8	63.4	64.8	72.3
Still married	42.5	1.3	11.2	34.2	52.2	56.1	52.2	50.4	53.5	54.0
Married twice	11.6	0.1	0.0	1.5	4.8	8.7	14.8	20.0	22.1	18.9
Still married	9.0	0.1	0.0	1.3	4.0	7.4	11.3	15.5	17.5	13.2
Married three or more times	3.1	0.0	0.0	0.1	0.2	1.0	3.0	5.8	8.5	5.4
Still married	2.3	0.0	0.0	0.1	0.2	0.8	2.2	4.3	6.5	3.8
Ever divorced	20.5	0.3	0.8	5.0	10.5	17.9	28.5	35.7	36.5	23.4
Currently divorced	9.1	0.2	0.7	3.7	6.2	9.5	14.2	15.5	12.4	7.2
Ever widowed	3.6	0.4	0.1	0.3	0.2	0.5	1.3	2.5	6.4	22.6
Currently widowed	2.6	0.3	0.1	0.3	0.1	0.3	0.9	1.6	3.9	17.4

Source: Bureau of the Census, Number, Timing, and Duration of Marriages and Divorces: 2009, Current Population Reports P70-125, 2011, Internet site http://www.census.gov/hhes/socdemo/marriage/data/sipp/index.html; calculations by New Strategist

Table 7.25 Marital History of Women by Age, 2009

(number of women aged 15 or older and percent distribution by marital history and age, 2009; numbers in thousands)

	total	15–19	20–24	25–29	30–34	35–39	40–49	50–59	60–69	70+
TOTAL WOMEN, NUMBER	123,272	10,478	10,158	10,408	9,645	10,267	22,119	20,702	14,288	15,207
TOTAL WOMEN, PERCENT	100.0%	100.0%	100.0%	100.0%	100.0%	100.0%	100.0%	100.0%	100.0%	100.0%
Never married	27.2	97.5	77.3	46.8	26.7	17.3	13.0	9.1	6.0	4.3
Ever married	72.8	2.5	22.7	53.2	73.3	82.7	87.0	90.9	94.0	95.7
Married once	57.5	2.5	22.4	50.8	64.5	69.3	67.4	65.5	67.7	76.1
Still married	40.6	1.9	19.7	43.2	54.5	55.8	51.6	47.5	45.7	30.1
Married twice	12.1	0.1	0.3	2.3	8.0	11.6	15.8	19.5	20.1	15.2
Still married	7.9	0.6	0.2	2.0	6.9	9.1	11.3	13.4	13.2	5.2
Married three or more times	3.2	0.0	0.0	0.0	0.8	1.9	3.8	5.9	6.2	4.4
Still married	1.9	0.0	0.0	0.0	0.7	1.4	2.5	4.1	3.6	1.4
Ever divorced	22.4	0.2	1.8	7.3	15.6	22.7	31.0	37.3	34.5	21.4
Currently divorced	11.3	0.1	1.5	5.3	8.1	11.8	16.4	18.6	16.0	9.9
Ever widowed	10.0	0.3	0.1	0.2	0.6	1.4	2.6	6.5	17.0	51.2
Currently widowed	8.9	0.3	0.1	0.1	0.4	0.8	1.8	4.9	13.9	48.3

Source: Bureau of the Census, Number, Timing, and Duration of Marriages and Divorces: 2009, Current Population Reports P70-125, 2011, Internet site http://www.census.gov/hhes/socdemo/marriage/data/sipp/index.html; calculations by New Strategist

8

Population

■ The Millennial generation numbers 76 million, a figure that includes everyone born between 1977 and 1994 (aged 16 to 33 in 2010). Millennials account for 25 percent of the total population—just slightly smaller than the Boomer share.

■ Millennials are much more diverse than middle-aged or older people. Non-Hispanic whites account for 72 percent of Boomers, for example, but for only 58 percent of Millennials.

■ Millennials account for a large share of immigrants. Forty-three percent of immigrants admitted to the United States in 2011 were aged 15 to 34.

■ In many states, the Millennial and younger generations are quite diverse. In Mississippi, for example, from 40 to 46 percent of the population under age 35 is black. In California, from 43 to 53 percent of the under-age-35 population is Hispanic.

Millennials Are the Second-Largest Generation

They reinvigorated the youth market.

The Millennial generation numbers 76 million, a figure that includes everyone born between 1977 and 1994 (aged 16 to 33 in 2010). Millennials account for just under 25 percent of the total population, which makes them the second-largest generation. Boomers, who are the parents of many Millennials, are in first place. They numbered 77 million in 2010 and accounted for 25 percent of the population.

Between 2000 and 2010, Millennials entirely filled the 20-to-29 age group. The number of people aged 20 to 24 grew 13 percent during those years. Consequently, the competition to get into college heated up. Now Millennials are battling one another for jobs. Competitive positioning is the defining characteristic of large generations, and it continues throughout life.

■ Millennials brought renewed attention to the youth market because of their numbers and the devotion of their Boomer parents.

The Millennial generation is almost as big as the Baby-Boom generation

(number of people by generation, 2010)

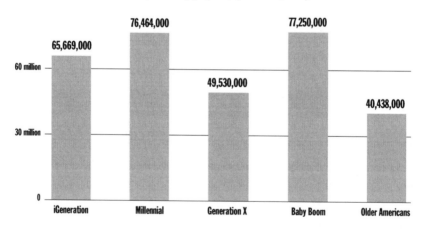

Table 8.1 Population by Age and Generation, 2010

(number and percent distribution of people by age and generation, 2010; numbers in thousands)

	number	percent distribution
Total people	**309,350**	**100.0%**
Under age 5	20,201	6.5
Aged 5 to 9	20,382	6.6
Aged 10 to 14	20,694	6.7
Aged 15 to 34	84,874	27.4
Aged 15 to 19	21,959	7.1
Aged 20 to 24	21,668	7.0
Aged 25 to 29	21,153	6.8
Aged 30 to 34	20,094	6.5
Aged 35 to 39	20,082	6.5
Aged 40 to 44	20,899	6.8
Aged 45 to 49	22,648	7.3
Aged 50 to 54	22,365	7.2
Aged 55 to 59	19,779	6.4
Aged 60 to 64	16,987	5.5
Aged 65 to 69	12,515	4.0
Aged 70 to 74	9,326	3.0
Aged 75 to 79	7,313	2.4
Aged 80 to 84	5,750	1.9
Aged 85 or older	5,533	1.8
Total people	**309,350**	**100.0**
iGeneration (under 16)	65,669	21.2
Millennial (16 to 33)	76,464	24.7
Generation X (34 to 45)	49,530	16.0
Baby Boom (46 to 64)	77,250	25.0
Older Americans (65 or older)	40,438	13.1

Source: Bureau of the Census, Population Estimates, http://www.census.gov/popest/data/intercensal/national/nat2010.html; calculations by New Strategist

Table 8.2 Population by Age and Sex, 2010

(number of people by age and sex, and sex ratio by age, 2010; numbers in thousands)

	total	female	male	sex ratio
Total people	**309,350**	**157,242**	**152,108**	**97**
Under age 5	20,201	9,883	10,318	104
Aged 5 to 9	20,382	9,975	10,407	104
Aged 10 to 14	20,694	10,107	10,587	105
Aged 15 to 34	84,874	41,816	43,058	103
Aged 15 to 19	21,959	10,696	11,263	105
Aged 20 to 24	21,668	10,612	11,056	104
Aged 25 to 29	21,153	10,477	10,676	102
Aged 30 to 34	20,094	10,030	10,063	100
Aged 35 to 39	20,082	10,086	9,997	99
Aged 40 to 44	20,899	10,500	10,399	99
Aged 45 to 49	22,648	11,465	11,183	98
Aged 50 to 54	22,365	11,399	10,966	96
Aged 55 to 59	19,779	10,199	9,580	94
Aged 60 to 64	16,987	8,829	8,159	92
Aged 65 to 69	12,515	6,623	5,892	89
Aged 70 to 74	9,326	5,057	4,269	84
Aged 75 to 79	7,313	4,130	3,184	77
Aged 80 to 84	5,750	3,448	2,302	67
Aged 85 or older	5,533	3,726	1,807	49

Note: The sex ratio is the number of males per 100 females.
Source: Bureau of the Census, Population Estimates, http://www.census.gov/popest/data/intercensal/national/nat2010.html; calculations by New Strategist

Table 8.3 Population by Age, 2000 and 2010

(number of people by age, 2000 and 2010; percent change, 2000–10; numbers in thousands)

	2010	2000	percent change 2000–10
Total people	**309,350**	**282,162**	**9.6%**
Under age 5	20,201	19,178	5.3
Aged 5 to 9	20,382	20,464	–0.4
Aged 10 to 14	20,694	20,638	0.3
Aged 15 to 19	21,959	20,295	8.2
Aged 20 to 24	21,668	19,117	13.3
Aged 25 to 29	21,153	19,280	9.7
Aged 30 to 34	20,094	20,524	–2.1
Aged 35 to 39	20,082	22,651	–11.3
Aged 40 to 44	20,899	22,518	–7.2
Aged 45 to 49	22,648	20,220	12.0
Aged 50 to 54	22,365	17,779	25.8
Aged 55 to 59	19,779	13,566	45.8
Aged 60 to 64	16,987	10,863	56.4
Aged 65 to 69	12,515	9,524	31.4
Aged 70 to 74	9,326	8,860	5.3
Aged 75 to 79	7,313	7,439	–1.7
Aged 80 to 84	5,750	4,985	15.4
Aged 85 or older	5,533	4,262	29.8
Aged 18 to 24	30,708	27,315	12.4
Aged 18 or older	235,154	209,786	12.1
Aged 65 or older	40,438	35,070	15.3

Source: Bureau of the Census, Population Estimates, http://www.census.gov/popest/data/intercensal/national/nat2010.html; calculations by New Strategist

The Nation's Children and Young Adults Are Diverse

Hispanics outnumber blacks among Millennials.

America's children and young adults are much more diverse than middle-aged or older people. While non-Hispanic whites account for 64 percent of all Americans, their share is a smaller 58 percent among Millennials, aged 16 to 33 in 2010. Among the iGeneration (children under age 16), non-Hispanic whites account for only 54 percent of the population.

Among the 7 million multiracial U.S. residents counted by the 2010 census, more than 5 million are children and adults under age 35. When the multiracials are included in the count of Asians and blacks, those populations expand considerably.

Hispanics account for a larger share of the Millennial generation than blacks—20 percent are Hispanic and 15 percent are black. In the iGeneration, Hispanics outnumber blacks by an even larger margin—23 to 17 percent. Among Asians, Hispanics, and blacks, Millennials are the largest generation, outnumbering Boomers. Among non-Hispanic whites, Boomers outnumber Millennials.

■ Racial and ethnic differences between young and old may divide the nation in the years ahead as older non-Hispanic whites push their agenda, which is often at odds with the wants and needs of younger, more diverse generations.

Minorities account for a large share of children and young adults

(minority share of population by generation, 2010)

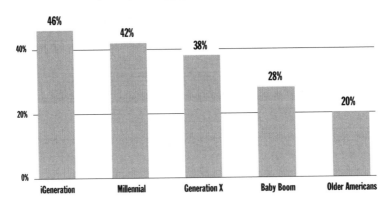

Table 8.4 Number of People by Age, Race Alone, and Hispanic Origin, 2010

(number of people by age, race alone, and Hispanic origin, 2010; numbers in thousands)

	total	Asian	black	Hispanic	non-Hispanic white	two or more races
Total people	**308,746**	**15,160**	**40,251**	**50,478**	**197,319**	**7,026**
Under age 5	20,201	948	3,055	5,114	10,307	1,123
Aged 5 to 9	20,349	972	3,013	4,791	10,885	948
Aged 10 to 14	20,677	922	3,154	4,525	11,449	836
Aged 15 to 34	84,690	4,710	12,467	17,289	48,655	2,213
Aged 15 to 19	22,040	999	3,573	4,532	12,387	726
Aged 20 to 24	21,586	1,149	3,240	4,322	12,467	571
Aged 25 to 29	21,102	1,279	2,911	4,310	12,268	491
Aged 30 to 34	19,962	1,284	2,743	4,124	11,534	424
Aged 35 to 39	20,180	1,334	2,706	3,856	12,018	357
Aged 40 to 44	20,891	1,188	2,752	3,442	13,250	315
Aged 45 to 49	22,709	1,105	2,901	3,022	15,387	302
Aged 50 to 54	22,298	1,004	2,753	2,441	15,813	269
Aged 55 to 59	19,665	863	2,246	1,841	14,476	209
Aged 60 to 64	16,818	703	1,715	1,372	12,839	157
Aged 65 to 69	12,435	483	1,181	949	9,693	106
Aged 70 to 74	9,278	361	865	700	7,265	73
Aged 75 to 79	7,318	255	625	511	5,867	51
Aged 80 to 84	5,743	171	430	351	4,751	35
Aged 85 or older	5,493	140	386	271	4,664	30
PERCENT DISTRIBUTION						
Total people	**100.0%**	**4.9%**	**13.0%**	**16.3%**	**63.9%**	**2.3%**
Under age 5	100.0	4.7	15.1	25.3	51.0	5.6
Aged 5 to 9	100.0	4.8	14.8	23.5	53.5	4.7
Aged 10 to 14	100.0	4.5	15.3	21.9	55.4	4.0
Aged 15 to 34	100.0	5.6	14.7	20.4	57.5	2.6
Aged 15 to 19	100.0	4.5	16.2	20.6	56.2	3.3
Aged 20 to 24	100.0	5.3	15.0	20.0	57.8	2.6
Aged 25 to 29	100.0	6.1	13.8	20.4	58.1	2.3
Aged 30 to 34	100.0	6.4	13.7	20.7	57.8	2.1
Aged 35 to 39	100.0	6.6	13.4	19.1	59.6	1.8
Aged 40 to 44	100.0	5.7	13.2	16.5	63.4	1.5
Aged 45 to 49	100.0	4.9	12.8	13.3	67.8	1.3
Aged 50 to 54	100.0	4.5	12.3	10.9	70.9	1.2
Aged 55 to 59	100.0	4.4	11.4	9.4	73.6	1.1
Aged 60 to 64	100.0	4.2	10.2	8.2	76.3	0.9
Aged 65 to 69	100.0	3.9	9.5	7.6	78.0	0.9
Aged 70 to 74	100.0	3.9	9.3	7.5	78.3	0.8
Aged 75 to 79	100.0	3.5	8.5	7.0	80.2	0.7
Aged 80 to 84	100.0	3.0	7.5	6.1	82.7	0.6
Aged 85 or older	100.0	2.5	7.0	4.9	84.9	0.6

Note: Asians and blacks are those who identify themselves as being of the race alone. Numbers do not add to total because not all races are shown and Hispanics may be of any race. Non-Hispanic whites are those who identify themselves as being white alone and not Hispanic.
Source: Bureau of the Census, 2010 Census, American Factfinder, Internet site Population Estimates, http:// factfinder2.census.gov/faces/nav/jsf/pages/index.xhtml; calculations by New Strategist

Table 8.5 Number of People by Age, Race Alone or in Combination, and Hispanic Origin, 2010

(number of people by age, race alone or in combination, and Hispanic origin, 2010; numbers in thousands)

	total	Asian	black	Hispanic	non-Hispanic white
Total people	**308,746**	**17,321**	**42,021**	**50,478**	**197,319**
Under age 5	20,201	1,317	3,538	5,114	10,307
Aged 5 to 9	20,349	1,285	3,389	4,791	10,885
Aged 10 to 14	20,677	1,184	3,468	4,525	11,449
Aged 15 to 34	84,690	5,407	12,897	17,289	48,655
Aged 15 to 19	22,040	1,229	3,796	4,532	12,387
Aged 20 to 24	21,586	1,333	3,350	4,322	12,467
Aged 25 to 29	21,102	1,433	2,971	4,310	12,268
Aged 30 to 34	19,962	1,412	2,780	4,124	11,534
Aged 35 to 39	20,180	1,445	2,738	3,856	12,018
Aged 40 to 44	20,891	1,279	2,773	3,442	13,250
Aged 45 to 49	22,709	1,188	2,922	3,022	15,387
Aged 50 to 54	22,298	1,076	2,775	2,441	15,813
Aged 55 to 59	19,665	916	2,267	1,841	14,476
Aged 60 to 64	16,818	740	1,732	1,372	12,839
Aged 65 to 69	12,435	508	1,192	949	9,693
Aged 70 to 74	9,278	379	873	700	7,265
Aged 75 to 79	7,318	269	631	511	5,867
Aged 80 to 84	5,743	180	435	351	4,751
Aged 85 or older	5,493	147	392	271	4,664
PERCENT DISTRIBUTION					
Total people	**100.0%**	**5.6%**	**13.6%**	**16.3%**	**63.9%**
Under age 5	100.0	6.5	17.5	25.3	51.0
Aged 5 to 9	100.0	6.3	16.7	23.5	53.5
Aged 10 to 14	100.0	5.7	16.8	21.9	55.4
Aged 15 to 34	100.0	6.4	15.2	20.4	57.5
Aged 15 to 19	100.0	5.6	17.2	20.6	56.2
Aged 20 to 24	100.0	6.2	15.5	20.0	57.8
Aged 25 to 29	100.0	6.8	14.1	20.4	58.1
Aged 30 to 34	100.0	7.1	13.9	20.7	57.8
Aged 35 to 39	100.0	7.2	13.6	19.1	59.6
Aged 40 to 44	100.0	6.1	13.3	16.5	63.4
Aged 45 to 49	100.0	5.2	12.9	13.3	67.8
Aged 50 to 54	100.0	4.8	12.4	10.9	70.9
Aged 55 to 59	100.0	4.7	11.5	9.4	73.6
Aged 60 to 64	100.0	4.4	10.3	8.2	76.3
Aged 65 to 69	100.0	4.1	9.6	7.6	78.0
Aged 70 to 74	100.0	4.1	9.4	7.5	78.3
Aged 75 to 79	100.0	3.7	8.6	7.0	80.2
Aged 80 to 84	100.0	3.1	7.6	6.1	82.7
Aged 85 or older	100.0	2.7	7.1	4.9	84.9

Note: Asians and blacks are those who identify themselves as being of the race alone and those who identify themselves as being of the race in combination with other races. Numbers do not add to total because not all races are shown, some mix-race individuals are counted more than once, and Hispanics may be of any race. Non-Hispanic whites are those who identify themselves as being white alone and not Hispanic.
Source: Bureau of the Census, 2010 Census, American Factfinder, Internet site Population Estimates, http:// factfinder2.census.gov/faces/nav/jsf/pages/index.xhtml; calculations by New Strategist

Table 8.6 Population by Generation, Race Alone or in Combination, and Hispanic Origin, 2010

(number and percent distribution of people by generation, race alone or in combination, and Hispanic origin, 2010; numbers in thousands)

	total	Asian	black	Hispanic	non-Hispanic white
Total people	**308,746**	**17,321**	**42,021**	**50,478**	**197,319**
iGeneration (under age 16)	65,635	4,031	11,154	15,337	35,119
Millennial (16 to 33)	76,290	4,879	11,582	15,558	43,871
Generation X (34 to 45)	49,605	3,244	6,651	8,728	30,651
Baby Boom (46 to 64)	76,948	3,683	9,111	8,073	55,437
Older Americans (65 or older)	40,268	1,483	3,522	2,782	32,241

PERCENT DISTRIBUTION BY RACE AND HISPANIC ORIGIN

	total	Asian	black	Hispanic	non-Hispanic white
Total people	**100.0%**	**5.6%**	**13.6%**	**16.3%**	**63.9%**
iGeneration (under age 16)	100.0	6.1	17.0	23.4	53.5
Millennial (16 to 33)	100.0	6.4	15.2	20.4	57.5
Generation X (34 to 45)	100.0	6.5	13.4	17.6	61.8
Baby Boom (46 to 64)	100.0	4.8	11.8	10.5	72.0
Older Americans (65 or older)	100.0	3.7	8.7	6.9	80.1

PERCENT DISTRIBUTION BY GENERATION

	total	Asian	black	Hispanic	non-Hispanic white
Total people	**100.0%**	**100.0%**	**100.0%**	**100.0%**	**100.0%**
iGeneration (under age 16)	21.3	23.3	26.5	30.4	17.8
Millennial (16 to 33)	24.7	28.2	27.6	30.8	22.2
Generation X (34 to 45)	16.1	18.7	15.8	17.3	15.5
Baby Boom (46 to 64)	24.9	21.3	21.7	16.0	28.1
Older Americans (65 or older)	13.0	8.6	8.4	5.5	16.3

Note: Asians and blacks are those who identify themselves as being of the race alone and those who identify themselves as being of the race in combination with other races. Numbers do not add to total because not all races are shown, some mixed-race individuals are counted more than once, and Hispanics may be of any race. Non-Hispanic whites are those who identify themselves as being white alone and not Hispanic.
Source: Bureau of the Census, 2010 Census, American Factfinder, Internet site Population Estimates, http://factfinder2.census.gov/faces/nav/jsf/pages/index.xhtml; calculations by New Strategist

Most Millennials Live in Their State of Birth

Among 18-to-34-year-olds, one in six is foreign-born.

According to the 2010 American Community Survey, 58 percent of people aged 18 to 34 (Millennials were aged 16 to 33 in that year) were born in the state of their current residence—a greater percentage than among older Americans because Millennials have not had time yet to move around. Twenty-five percent of Millennials were born in the United States, but in a different state. Sixteen percent were born in another country—a greater share than the 13 percent of all U.S. residents who are foreign-born.

Among the nation's foreign-born, the broad 18-to-24 age group accounts for 50 percent of the total. The figure is largest among the foreign-born from Mexico, 61 percent of whom are aged 18 to 44. The figure is smallest among the foreign-born from Europe, only 33 percent of whom are young adults.

■ The foreign-born population adds to the multicultural mix, which is now a significant factor in American business and politics.

Among the foreign-born, those from Mexico are the youngest

(median age of the foreign-born by world region of birth, 2010)

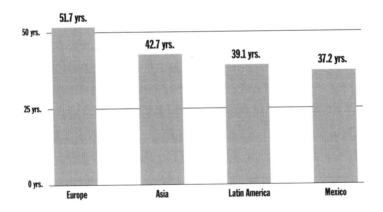

Table 8.7 Population by Age and Place of Birth, 2010

(number and percent distribution of people by age and place of birth, 2010; numbers in thousands)

	total	born in the United States — in state of current residence	outside state of current residence	citizen born outside U.S.	foreign-born
Total people	**309,350**	**181,748**	**83,418**	**4,228**	**39,956**
Under age 5	20,134	17,981	1,768	121	263
Aged 5 to 17	54,031	42,287	8,580	597	2,568
Aged 18 to 34	71,867	41,326	18,018	1,130	11,393
Aged 18 to 24	30,895	19,665	7,263	468	3,499
Aged 25 to 34	40,972	21,661	10,755	662	7,894
Aged 35 to 44	41,192	19,842	11,949	701	8,701
Aged 45 to 54	44,929	22,521	14,474	738	7,196
Aged 55 to 59	19,683	9,944	6,803	270	2,666
Aged 60 to 61	7,222	3,583	2,595	94	951
Aged 62 to 64	9,857	4,752	3,714	135	1,256
Aged 65 to 74	21,854	10,324	8,430	255	2,845
Aged 75 or older	18,579	9,187	7,087	188	2,118

PERCENT DISTRIBUTION BY PLACE OF BIRTH

	total	in state	outside state	citizen born outside U.S.	foreign-born
Total people	**100.0%**	**58.8%**	**27.0%**	**1.4%**	**12.9%**
Under age 5	100.0	89.3	8.8	0.6	1.3
Aged 5 to 17	100.0	78.3	15.9	1.1	4.8
Aged 18 to 34	100.0	57.5	25.1	1.6	15.9
Aged 18 to 24	100.0	63.7	23.5	1.5	11.3
Aged 25 to 34	100.0	52.9	26.2	1.6	19.3
Aged 35 to 44	100.0	48.2	29.0	1.7	21.1
Aged 45 to 54	100.0	50.1	32.2	1.6	16.0
Aged 55 to 59	100.0	50.5	34.6	1.4	13.5
Aged 60 to 61	100.0	49.6	35.9	1.3	13.2
Aged 62 to 64	100.0	48.2	37.7	1.4	12.7
Aged 65 to 74	100.0	47.2	38.6	1.2	13.0
Aged 75 or older	100.0	49.4	38.1	1.0	11.4

PERCENT DISTRIBUTION BY AGE

	total	in state	outside state	citizen born outside U.S.	foreign-born
Total people	**100.0%**	**100.0%**	**100.0%**	**100.0%**	**100.0%**
Under age 5	6.5	9.9	2.1	2.9	0.7
Aged 5 to 17	17.5	23.3	10.3	14.1	6.4
Aged 18 to 34	23.2	22.7	21.6	26.7	28.5
Aged 18 to 24	10.0	10.8	8.7	11.1	8.8
Aged 25 to 34	13.2	11.9	12.9	15.7	19.8
Aged 35 to 44	13.3	10.9	14.3	16.6	21.8
Aged 45 to 54	14.5	12.4	17.4	17.5	18.0
Aged 55 to 59	6.4	5.5	8.2	6.4	6.7
Aged 60 to 61	2.3	2.0	3.1	2.2	2.4
Aged 62 to 64	3.2	2.6	4.5	3.2	3.1
Aged 65 to 74	7.1	5.7	10.1	6.0	7.1
Aged 75 or older	6.0	5.1	8.5	4.5	5.3

Source: Bureau of the Census, 2010 American Community Survey, http://factfinder2.census.gov/faces/nav/jsf/pages/index.xhtml; calculations by New Strategist

Table 8.8 Foreign-Born Population by Age and World Region of Birth, 2010

(number and percent distribution of foreign-born by age and world region of birth, 2010; numbers in thousands)

	total	Asian	Europe	Latin America total	Mexico
Total foreign-born, number	39,956	11,284	4,817	21,224	11,711
Total foreign-born, percent	100.0%	100.0%	100.0%	100.0%	100.0%
Under age 5	0.7	0.9	0.5	0.5	0.5
Aged 5 to 17	6.4	6.0	5.1	6.7	7.4
Aged 18 to 24	8.8	7.7	5.5	10.1	11.1
Aged 25 to 44	41.5	39.9	27.4	46.0	50.1
Aged 45 to 54	18.0	18.7	16.7	17.9	16.2
Aged 55 to 64	12.2	14.1	16.3	10.2	8.4
Aged 65 to 74	7.1	7.8	13.8	5.3	0.4
Aged 75 to 84	3.9	3.7	10.0	2.6	1.7
Aged 85 or older	1.4	1.1	4.6	0.8	0.6
Median age	41.4	42.7	51.7	39.1	37.2

Note: Number of foreign-born by region do not add to total because "other region" is not shown.
Source: Bureau of the Census, 2010 American Community Survey, http://factfinder2.census.gov/faces/nav/jsf/pages/index.xhtml; calculations by New Strategist

Millennials Are a Large Share of Immigrants

More than 40 percent of 2011 immigrants were Millennials

In 2010, more than 1 million legal immigrants were admitted to the United States, and 452,000 of them were aged 15 to 34 (Millennials were aged 16 to 33 in that year). Many immigrants to the United States are young adults looking for job opportunities.

The 15-to-34 age group accounted for 43 percent of total immigrants admitted to the United States in 2011. By five-year age group, 30-to-34-year-olds account for the largest share of immigrants—12 percent in 2011.

■ Immigrants are adding to the diversity of the young adult population.

Many 2011 immigrants were young adults

(percent distribution of 2011 immigrants by age)

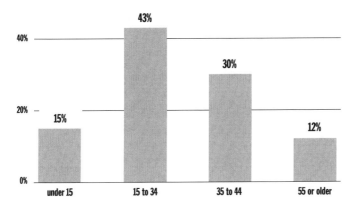

Table 8.9 Immigrants by Age, 2011

(number and percent distribution of immigrants by age, 2011)

	number	percent distribution
Total immigrants	**1,062,040**	**100.0%**
Under age 1	4,361	0.4
Aged 1 to 4	34,017	3.2
Aged 5 to 9	52,828	5.0
Aged 10 to 14	70,295	6.6
Aged 15 to 34	452,031	42.6
Aged 15 to 19	88,970	8.4
Aged 20 to 24	110,144	10.4
Aged 25 to 29	122,128	11.5
Aged 30 to 34	130,789	12.3
Aged 35 to 39	112,983	10.6
Aged 40 to 44	84,394	7.9
Aged 45 to 49	68,174	6.4
Aged 50 to 54	52,623	5.0
Aged 55 to 59	42,941	4.0
Aged 60 to 64	34,257	3.2
Aged 65 to 74	39,386	3.7
Aged 75 or older	13,740	1.3

Note: Immigrants are those granted legal permanent residence in the United States. They either arrive in the United States with immigrant visas issued abroad or adjust their status in the United States from temporary to permanent residence. Numbers may not sum to total because "age not stated" is not shown.
Source: Department of Homeland Security, 2011 Yearbook of Immigration Statistics, http://www.dhs.gov/files/statistics/publications/yearbook.shtm

Many Working-Age Adults Do Not Speak English at Home

Most are Spanish speakers, and half have trouble speaking English.

Sixty million residents of the United States speak a language other than English at home, according to the Census Bureau's 2010 American Community Survey—21 percent of the population aged 5 or older. The 62 percent majority of those who do not speak English at home are Spanish speakers.

Among working-age adults (aged 18 to 64), 22 percent do not speak English at home, and 62 percent of those who do not speak English at home are Spanish speakers. Among the Spanish speakers, 50 percent say they speak English less than "very well."

■ The language barrier is a problem for many working-age adults.

Half of adults who speak Spanish at home cannot speak English very well

(percent of people aged 18 to 64 who speak a language other than English at home who speak English less than "very well," by language spoken at home, 2010)

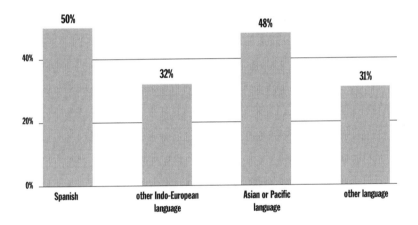

Table 8.10 Language Spoken at Home by People Aged 18 to 64, 2010

(number and percent distribution of people aged 5 or older and aged 18 to 64 who speak a language other than English at home by language spoken at home and ability to speak English very well, 2010; numbers in thousands)

	total		aged 18 to 64	
	number	percent distribution	number	percent distribution
Total, aged 5 or older	**289,216**	**100.0%**	**194,751**	**100.0%**
Speak only English at home	229,673	79.4	152,732	78.4
Speak a language other than English at home	59,542	20.6	42,018	21.6
Speak English less than very well	21,853	7.6	19,149	9.8
Total who speak a language other than English at home	**59,542**	**100.0**	**42,018**	**100.0**
Speak Spanish at home	36,996	62.1	25,934	61.7
Speak other Indo-European language at home	10,666	17.9	7,268	17.3
Speak Asian or Pacific Island language at home	9,340	15.7	6,943	16.5
Speak other language at home	2,540	4.3	1,873	4.5
Speak Spanish at home	36,996	100.0	25,934	100.0
Speak English less than very well	16,523	44.7	12,882	49.7
Speak other Indo-European language at home	10,666	100.0	7,268	100.0
Speak English less than very well	3,440	32.3	2,333	32.1
Speak Asian or Pacific Island language at home	9,340	100.0	6,943	100.0
Speak English less than very well	4,471	47.9	3,348	48.2
Speak other language at home	2,540	100.0	1,873	100.0
Speak English less than very well	786	30.9	586	31.3

Source: Bureau of the Census, 2010 American Community Survey, http://factfinder2.census.gov/faces/nav/jsf/pages/index.xhtml; calculations by New Strategist

Largest Share of Millennials Lives in the South

Millennials account for 29 percent of Utah's population.

The South is home to the largest share of the population, and consequently to the largest share of Millennials. Thirty-seven percent of Millennials live in the South, according to Census Bureau estimates for 2010. There, they account for 25 percent of the population.

Millennials range from a low of 21 percent of the population of Maine to a high of 29 percent of the population of Utah. Boomers outnumber Millennials in most states, but in some states—including Texas and California—Millennials outnumber Boomers.

In many states, the Millennial and iGenerations are quite diverse. In Mississippi, for example, from 40 to 46 percent of the population under age 35 is black. In California, from 43 to 53 percent of the under-age-35 population is Hispanic.

■ Millennials will outnumber Boomers in a growing number of states as the Boomer population ages.

The Northeast is home to just 17 percent of Millennials

(percent distribution of the Millennial generation, by region, 2010)

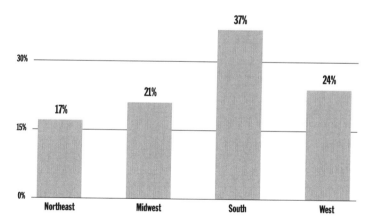

Table 8.11 Population by Age and Region, 2010

(number of people by age and region, 2010; numbers in thousands)

	total	Northeast	Midwest	South	West
Total people	**309,350**	**55,361**	**66,976**	**114,866**	**72,147**
Under age 5	20,201	3,219	4,329	7,680	4,973
Aged 5 to 9	20,382	3,339	4,432	7,691	4,921
Aged 10 to 14	20,694	3,498	4,520	7,711	4,965
Aged 15 to 34	84,874	14,758	18,006	31,467	20,643
Aged 15 to 19	21,959	3,873	4,781	8,062	5,243
Aged 20 to 24	21,668	3,830	4,595	8,038	5,205
Aged 25 to 29	21,153	3,623	4,427	7,861	5,243
Aged 30 to 34	20,094	3,433	4,203	7,506	4,952
Aged 35 to 39	20,082	3,487	4,159	7,596	4,840
Aged 40 to 44	20,899	3,888	4,387	7,751	4,872
Aged 45 to 49	22,648	4,261	4,931	8,359	5,096
Aged 50 to 54	22,365	4,225	5,013	8,122	5,005
Aged 55 to 59	19,779	3,691	4,449	7,186	4,453
Aged 60 to 64	16,987	3,165	3,702	6,335	3,785
Aged 65 to 69	12,515	2,298	2,702	4,789	2,726
Aged 70 to 74	9,326	1,718	2,046	3,571	1,992
Aged 75 to 79	7,313	1,416	1,638	2,730	1,530
Aged 80 to 84	5,750	1,191	1,335	2,039	1,184
Aged 85 or older	5,533	1,206	1,328	1,836	1,162

Source: Bureau of the Census, State Population Estimates, http://www.census.gov/popest/data/intercensal/state/state2010.html; calculations by New Strategist

Table 8.12 Regional Distribution of Population by Age, 2010

(regional distribution of people by age, 2010)

	total	Northeast	Midwest	South	West
Total people	**100.0%**	**17.9%**	**21.7%**	**37.1%**	**23.3%**
Under age 5	100.0	15.9	21.4	38.0	24.6
Aged 5 to 9	100.0	16.4	21.7	37.7	24.1
Aged 10 to 14	100.0	16.9	21.8	37.3	24.0
Aged 15 to 34	100.0	17.4	21.2	37.1	24.3
Aged 15 to 19	100.0	17.6	21.8	36.7	23.9
Aged 20 to 24	100.0	17.7	21.2	37.1	24.0
Aged 25 to 29	100.0	17.1	20.9	37.2	24.8
Aged 30 to 34	100.0	17.1	20.9	37.4	24.6
Aged 35 to 39	100.0	17.4	20.7	37.8	24.1
Aged 40 to 44	100.0	18.6	21.0	37.1	23.3
Aged 45 to 49	100.0	18.8	21.8	36.9	22.5
Aged 50 to 54	100.0	18.9	22.4	36.3	22.4
Aged 55 to 59	100.0	18.7	22.5	36.3	22.5
Aged 60 to 64	100.0	18.6	21.8	37.3	22.3
Aged 65 to 69	100.0	18.4	21.6	38.3	21.8
Aged 70 to 74	100.0	18.4	21.9	38.3	21.4
Aged 75 to 79	100.0	19.4	22.4	37.3	20.9
Aged 80 to 84	100.0	20.7	23.2	35.5	20.6
Aged 85 or older	100.0	21.8	24.0	33.2	21.0

Source: Bureau of the Census, State Population Estimates, http://www.census.gov/popest/data/intercensal/state/state2010.html; calculations by New Strategist

Table 8.13 Age Distribution of Population by Region, 2010

(age distribution of people by region, 2010)

	total	Northeast	Midwest	South	West
Total people	**100.0%**	**100.0%**	**100.0%**	**100.0%**	**100.0%**
Under age 5	6.5	5.8	6.5	6.7	6.9
Aged 5 to 9	6.6	6.0	6.6	6.7	6.8
Aged 10 to 14	6.7	6.3	6.7	6.7	6.9
Aged 15 to 34	27.4	26.7	26.9	27.4	28.6
Aged 15 to 19	7.1	7.0	7.1	7.0	7.3
Aged 20 to 24	7.0	6.9	6.9	7.0	7.2
Aged 25 to 29	6.8	6.5	6.6	6.8	7.3
Aged 30 to 34	6.5	6.2	6.3	6.5	6.9
Aged 35 to 39	6.5	6.3	6.2	6.6	6.7
Aged 40 to 44	6.8	7.0	6.6	6.7	6.8
Aged 45 to 49	7.3	7.7	7.4	7.3	7.1
Aged 50 to 54	7.2	7.6	7.5	7.1	6.9
Aged 55 to 59	6.4	6.7	6.6	6.3	6.2
Aged 60 to 64	5.5	5.7	5.5	5.5	5.2
Aged 65 to 69	4.0	4.2	4.0	4.2	3.8
Aged 70 to 74	3.0	3.1	3.1	3.1	2.8
Aged 75 to 79	2.4	2.6	2.4	2.4	2.1
Aged 80 to 84	1.9	2.2	2.0	1.8	1.6
Aged 85 or older	1.8	2.2	2.0	1.6	1.6

Source: Bureau of the Census, State Population Estimates, http://www.census.gov/popest/data/intercensal/state/state2010.html; calculations by New Strategist

Table 8.14 Population by Generation and Region, 2010

(number and percent distribution of people by generation and region, 2010; numbers in thousands)

	total	Northeast	Midwest	South	West
Total people	**309,350**	**55,361**	**66,976**	**114,866**	**72,147**
iGeneration (under 16)	65,669	10,831	14,236	24,695	15,907
Millennial (16 to 33)	76,464	13,297	16,209	28,353	18,604
Generation X (34 to 45)	49,530	8,914	10,373	18,521	11,722
Baby Boom (46 to 64)	77,250	14,489	17,109	28,332	17,320
Older Americans (65 or older)	40,438	7,829	9,049	14,965	8,595
PERCENT DISTRIBUTION BY GENERATION					
Total people	**100.0%**	**100.0%**	**100.0%**	**100.0%**	**100.0%**
iGeneration (under 16)	21.2	19.6	21.3	21.5	22.0
Millennial (16 to 33)	24.7	24.0	24.2	24.7	25.8
Generation X (34 to 45)	16.0	16.1	15.5	16.1	16.2
Baby Boom (46 to 64)	25.0	26.2	25.5	24.7	24.0
Older Americans (65 or older)	13.1	14.1	13.5	13.0	11.9
PERCENT DISTRIBUTION BY REGION					
Total people	**100.0%**	**17.9%**	**21.7%**	**37.1%**	**23.3%**
iGeneration (under 16)	100.0	16.5	21.7	37.6	24.2
Millennial (16 to 33)	100.0	17.4	21.2	37.1	24.3
Generation X (34 to 45)	100.0	18.0	20.9	37.4	23.7
Baby Boom (46 to 64)	100.0	18.8	22.1	36.7	22.4
Older Americans (65 or older)	100.0	19.4	22.4	37.0	21.3

Source: Bureau of the Census, State Population Estimates, http://www.census.gov/popest/data/intercensal/state/state2010.html; calculations by New Strategist

Table 8.15 State Populations by Age, 2010

(total number of people and number aged 15 to 34 by state, 2010; numbers in thousands)

	total population	aged 15 to 34				
		total	15 to 19	20 to 24	25 to 29	30 to 34
United States	**309,350**	**84,874**	**21,959**	**21,668**	**21,153**	**20,094**
Alabama	4,785	1,290	342	337	312	300
Alaska	714	211	52	55	56	48
Arizona	6,414	1,766	461	445	441	420
Arkansas	2,922	781	203	200	193	185
California	37,349	10,926	2,819	2,777	2,746	2,584
Colorado	5,049	1,420	339	350	374	357
Connecticut	3,577	900	250	229	215	207
Delaware	900	240	64	63	58	54
District of Columbia	604	230	40	64	70	56
Florida	18,843	4,756	1,224	1,234	1,182	1,117
Georgia	9,713	2,734	707	684	676	667
Hawaii	1,364	367	86	96	97	88
Idaho	1,571	434	115	109	107	103
Illinois	12,843	3,582	918	882	912	871
Indiana	6,491	1,758	473	453	421	411
Iowa	3,050	815	216	214	199	186
Kansas	2,859	788	203	205	199	181
Kentucky	4,346	1,156	295	291	286	283
Louisiana	4,544	1,298	325	340	334	298
Maine	1,328	313	88	80	73	72
Maryland	5,786	1,566	404	395	395	371
Massachusetts	6,557	1,787	461	477	443	406
Michigan	9,878	2,573	734	670	590	578
Minnesota	5,311	1,442	366	357	374	345
Mississippi	2,970	824	223	212	200	190
Missouri	5,996	1,616	422	415	405	375
Montana	991	258	66	67	64	59
Nebraska	1,830	505	129	130	130	117
Nevada	2,705	748	182	178	197	192
New Hampshire	1,317	323	93	85	73	72
New Jersey	8,802	2,251	595	543	554	559
New Mexico	2,066	561	150	143	140	128
New York	19,392	5,440	1,360	1,414	1,381	1,285
North Carolina	9,562	2,576	657	665	629	625
North Dakota	674	198	47	59	50	41
Ohio	11,536	2,999	819	765	720	696
Oklahoma	3,762	1,044	263	270	267	243
Oregon	3,839	1,034	254	254	266	261
Pennsylvania	12,710	3,294	900	876	783	734
Rhode Island	1,053	290	80	82	66	62
South Carolina	4,636	1,257	328	334	306	290

	total population	aged 15 to 34				
		total	15 to 19	20 to 24	25 to 29	30 to 34
South Dakota	816	222	58	58	56	50
Tennessee	6,357	1,692	435	428	419	410
Texas	25,257	7,343	1,882	1,829	1,859	1,773
Utah	2,776	898	221	228	231	218
Vermont	626	160	46	44	36	34
Virginia	8,025	2,221	549	575	567	530
Washington	6,744	1,863	461	463	482	457
West Virginia	1,854	459	119	118	109	113
Wisconsin	5,691	1,510	397	388	373	352
Wyoming	564	157	38	41	42	37

Source: Bureau of the Census, State Population Estimates, http://www.census.gov/popest/data/intercensal/state/state2010.html; calculations by New Strategist

Table 8.16 Distribution of State Populations by Age, 2010

(percent distribution of people by state and age, 2010)

	total population	aged 15 to 34				
		total	15 to 19	20 to 24	25 to 29	30 to 34
United States	**100.0%**	**27.4%**	**7.1%**	**7.0%**	**6.8%**	**6.5%**
Alabama	100.0	27.0	7.1	7.0	6.5	6.3
Alaska	100.0	29.6	7.3	7.7	7.8	6.8
Arizona	100.0	27.5	7.2	6.9	6.9	6.5
Arkansas	100.0	26.7	6.9	6.9	6.6	6.3
California	100.0	29.3	7.5	7.4	7.4	6.9
Colorado	100.0	28.1	6.7	6.9	7.4	7.1
Connecticut	100.0	25.2	7.0	6.4	6.0	5.8
Delaware	100.0	26.6	7.2	7.0	6.4	6.0
District of Columbia	100.0	38.1	6.6	10.7	11.6	9.2
Florida	100.0	25.2	6.5	6.5	6.3	5.9
Georgia	100.0	28.2	7.3	7.0	7.0	6.9
Hawaii	100.0	26.9	6.3	7.0	7.1	6.5
Idaho	100.0	27.6	7.3	6.9	6.8	6.6
Illinois	100.0	27.9	7.1	6.9	7.1	6.8
Indiana	100.0	27.1	7.3	7.0	6.5	6.3
Iowa	100.0	26.7	7.1	7.0	6.5	6.1
Kansas	100.0	27.6	7.1	7.2	6.9	6.3
Kentucky	100.0	26.6	6.8	6.7	6.6	6.5
Louisiana	100.0	28.6	7.2	7.5	7.4	6.6
Maine	100.0	23.6	6.6	6.0	5.5	5.5
Maryland	100.0	27.1	7.0	6.8	6.8	6.4
Massachusetts	100.0	27.3	7.0	7.3	6.8	6.2
Michigan	100.0	26.0	7.4	6.8	6.0	5.8
Minnesota	100.0	27.2	6.9	6.7	7.0	6.5
Mississippi	100.0	27.8	7.5	7.1	6.7	6.4
Missouri	100.0	26.9	7.0	6.9	6.7	6.3
Montana	100.0	26.0	6.7	6.8	6.5	6.0
Nebraska	100.0	27.6	7.0	7.1	7.1	6.4
Nevada	100.0	27.7	6.7	6.6	7.3	7.1
New Hampshire	100.0	24.5	7.1	6.4	5.6	5.5
New Jersey	100.0	25.6	6.8	6.2	6.3	6.4
New Mexico	100.0	27.1	7.2	6.9	6.8	6.2
New York	100.0	28.1	7.0	7.3	7.1	6.6
North Carolina	100.0	26.9	6.9	7.0	6.6	6.5
North Dakota	100.0	29.3	7.0	8.8	7.4	6.1
Ohio	100.0	26.0	7.1	6.6	6.2	6.0
Oklahoma	100.0	27.7	7.0	7.2	7.1	6.5
Oregon	100.0	26.9	6.6	6.6	6.9	6.8
Pennsylvania	100.0	25.9	7.1	6.9	6.2	5.8
Rhode Island	100.0	27.5	7.6	7.8	6.3	5.8
South Carolina	100.0	27.1	7.1	7.2	6.6	6.3

	total population	aged 15 to 34				
		total	15 to 19	20 to 24	25 to 29	30 to 34
South Dakota	100.0%	27.2%	7.0%	7.1%	6.9%	6.2%
Tennessee	100.0	26.6	6.8	6.7	6.6	6.4
Texas	100.0	29.1	7.5	7.2	7.4	7.0
Utah	100.0	32.3	8.0	8.2	8.3	7.9
Vermont	100.0	25.5	7.3	7.0	5.7	5.5
Virginia	100.0	27.7	6.8	7.2	7.1	6.6
Washington	100.0	27.6	6.8	6.9	7.1	6.8
West Virginia	100.0	24.8	6.4	6.3	5.9	6.1
Wisconsin	100.0	26.5	7.0	6.8	6.6	6.2
Wyoming	100.0	27.8	6.7	7.2	7.4	6.5

Source: Bureau of the Census, State Population Estimates, http://www.census.gov/popest/data/intercensal/state/state2010.html; calculations by New Strategist

Table 8.17 State Populations by Generation, 2010

(number of people by state and generation, 2010; numbers in thousands)

	total population	iGeneration (under 16)	Millennial (16 to 33)	Generation X (34 to 45)	Baby Boom (46 to 64)	Older Americans (65 or older)
United States	**309,350**	**65,669**	**76,464**	**49,530**	**77,250**	**40,438**
Alabama	4,785	1,001	1,162	746	1,217	660
Alaska	714	167	191	114	187	55
Arizona	6,414	1,454	1,590	991	1,491	887
Arkansas	2,922	633	704	443	720	421
California	37,349	8,208	9,845	6,236	8,790	4,270
Colorado	5,049	1,096	1,281	845	1,273	553
Connecticut	3,577	715	809	582	963	508
Delaware	900	182	216	140	232	130
District of Columbia	604	92	211	100	133	69
Florida	18,843	3,531	4,288	2,930	4,820	3,274
Georgia	9,713	2,216	2,459	1,673	2,327	1,037
Hawaii	1,364	269	332	213	352	198
Idaho	1,571	383	390	233	370	195
Illinois	12,843	2,757	3,224	2,082	3,165	1,615
Indiana	6,491	1,425	1,581	1,014	1,626	844
Iowa	3,050	647	734	444	771	454
Kansas	2,859	648	711	422	700	377
Kentucky	4,346	908	1,040	696	1,121	580
Louisiana	4,544	993	1,173	688	1,130	560
Maine	1,328	240	281	206	389	211
Maryland	5,786	1,192	1,411	960	1,512	711
Massachusetts	6,557	1,251	1,614	1,069	1,719	906
Michigan	9,878	2,052	2,310	1,535	2,617	1,364
Minnesota	5,311	1,136	1,300	829	1,360	685
Mississippi	2,970	669	742	453	725	381
Missouri	5,996	1,261	1,456	909	1,528	841
Montana	991	198	232	138	275	147
Nebraska	1,830	410	456	269	448	248
Nevada	2,705	590	674	459	656	326
New Hampshire	1,317	251	290	215	382	179
New Jersey	8,802	1,812	2,020	1,487	2,292	1,190
New Mexico	2,066	461	505	303	523	274
New York	19,392	3,801	4,911	3,149	4,904	2,627
North Carolina	9,562	2,033	2,320	1,589	2,379	1,240
North Dakota	674	134	180	92	170	98
Ohio	11,536	2,403	2,696	1,781	3,030	1,626
Oklahoma	3,762	831	942	561	918	509
Oregon	3,839	769	932	603	1,000	536
Pennsylvania	12,710	2,452	2,967	1,946	3,380	1,965
Rhode Island	1,053	198	261	165	277	152
South Carolina	4,636	962	1,134	724	1,182	635

	total population	iGeneration (under 16)	Millennial (16 to 33)	Generation X (34 to 45)	Baby Boom (46 to 64)	Older Americans (65 or older)
South Dakota	816	181	200	114	204	117
Tennessee	6,357	1,326	1,523	1,026	1,625	857
Texas	25,257	6,138	6,612	4,169	5,718	2,620
Utah	2,776	788	810	407	520	251
Vermont	626	113	144	95	183	91
Virginia	8,025	1,645	2,005	1,337	2,055	982
Washington	6,744	1,402	1,680	1,097	1,733	833
West Virginia	1,854	343	412	285	515	298
Wisconsin	5,691	1,182	1,360	880	1,490	779
Wyoming	564	121	142	82	149	70

Source: Bureau of the Census, State Population Estimates, http://www.census.gov/popest/data/intercensal/state/state2010.html; calculations by New Strategist

Table 8.18 Distribution of State Populations by Generation, 2010

(percent distribution of people by state and generation, 2010)

	total population	iGeneration (under 16)	Millennial (16 to 33)	Generation X (34 to 45)	Baby Boom (46 to 64)	Older Americans (65 or older)
United States	**100.0%**	**21.2%**	**24.7%**	**16.0%**	**25.0%**	**13.1%**
Alabama	100.0	20.9	24.3	15.6	25.4	13.8
Alaska	100.0	23.4	26.7	15.9	26.2	7.7
Arizona	100.0	22.7	24.8	15.5	23.3	13.8
Arkansas	100.0	21.7	24.1	15.2	24.6	14.4
California	100.0	22.0	26.4	16.7	23.5	11.4
Colorado	100.0	21.7	25.4	16.7	25.2	11.0
Connecticut	100.0	20.0	22.6	16.3	26.9	14.2
Delaware	100.0	20.3	24.0	15.6	25.7	14.4
District of Columbia	100.0	15.3	34.9	16.5	21.9	11.4
Florida	100.0	18.7	22.8	15.5	25.6	17.4
Georgia	100.0	22.8	25.3	17.2	24.0	10.7
Hawaii	100.0	19.7	24.3	15.6	25.8	14.5
Idaho	100.0	24.4	24.8	14.8	23.5	12.4
Illinois	100.0	21.5	25.1	16.2	24.6	12.6
Indiana	100.0	22.0	24.4	15.6	25.1	13.0
Iowa	100.0	21.2	24.1	14.5	25.3	14.9
Kansas	100.0	22.7	24.9	14.8	24.5	13.2
Kentucky	100.0	20.9	23.9	16.0	25.8	13.4
Louisiana	100.0	21.9	25.8	15.1	24.9	12.3
Maine	100.0	18.1	21.2	15.5	29.3	15.9
Maryland	100.0	20.6	24.4	16.6	26.1	12.3
Massachusetts	100.0	19.1	24.6	16.3	26.2	13.8
Michigan	100.0	20.8	23.4	15.5	26.5	13.8
Minnesota	100.0	21.4	24.5	15.6	25.6	12.9
Mississippi	100.0	22.5	25.0	15.3	24.4	12.8
Missouri	100.0	21.0	24.3	15.2	25.5	14.0
Montana	100.0	19.9	23.5	14.0	27.8	14.9
Nebraska	100.0	22.4	24.9	14.7	24.5	13.5
Nevada	100.0	21.8	24.9	17.0	24.2	12.1
New Hampshire	100.0	19.0	22.0	16.4	29.0	13.6
New Jersey	100.0	20.6	23.0	16.9	26.0	13.5
New Mexico	100.0	22.3	24.5	14.7	25.3	13.2
New York	100.0	19.6	25.3	16.2	25.3	13.5
North Carolina	100.0	21.3	24.3	16.6	24.9	13.0
North Dakota	100.0	19.9	26.7	13.7	25.2	14.5
Ohio	100.0	20.8	23.4	15.4	26.3	14.1
Oklahoma	100.0	22.1	25.1	14.9	24.4	13.5
Oregon	100.0	20.0	24.3	15.7	26.1	14.0
Pennsylvania	100.0	19.3	23.3	15.3	26.6	15.5
Rhode Island	100.0	18.8	24.8	15.7	26.3	14.4
South Carolina	100.0	20.7	24.5	15.6	25.5	13.7

	total population	iGeneration (under 16)	Millennial (16 to 33)	Generation X (34 to 45)	Baby Boom (46 to 64)	Older Americans (65 or older)
South Dakota	100.0%	22.2%	24.5%	14.0%	25.0%	14.3%
Tennessee	100.0	20.9	24.0	16.1	25.6	13.5
Texas	100.0	24.3	26.2	16.5	22.6	10.4
Utah	100.0	28.4	29.2	14.7	18.7	9.0
Vermont	100.0	18.1	23.0	15.1	29.2	14.6
Virginia	100.0	20.5	25.0	16.7	25.6	12.2
Washington	100.0	20.8	24.9	16.3	25.7	12.3
West Virginia	100.0	18.5	22.2	15.4	27.8	16.1
Wisconsin	100.0	20.8	23.9	15.5	26.2	13.7
Wyoming	100.0	21.5	25.1	14.5	26.5	12.4

Source: Bureau of the Census, State Population Estimates, http://www.census.gov/popest/data/intercensal/state/state2010.html; calculations by New Strategist

Table 8.19 State Populations by Age, Race Alone or in Combination, and Hispanic Origin, 2010

(total number of people and percent distribution by age, race alone or in combination, and Hispanic origin, by state, 2010; numbers in thousands)

	total number	total percent	Asian	black	Hispanic	non-Hispanic white
Total population	**308,746**	**100.0%**	**5.6%**	**13.6%**	**16.3%**	**63.9%**
Under age 5	20,201	100.0	6.5	17.5	25.3	51.0
Aged 5 to 9	20,349	100.0	6.3	16.7	23.5	53.5
Aged 10 to 14	20,677	100.0	5.7	16.8	21.9	55.4
Aged 15 to 19	22,040	100.0	5.6	17.2	20.6	56.2
Aged 20 to 24	21,586	100.0	6.2	15.5	20.0	57.8
Aged 25 to 29	21,102	100.0	6.8	14.1	20.4	58.1
Aged 30 to 34	19,962	100.0	7.1	13.9	20.7	57.8
Aged 35 to 39	20,180	100.0	7.2	13.6	19.1	59.6
Aged 40 to 44	20,891	100.0	6.1	13.3	16.5	63.4
Aged 45 to 49	22,709	100.0	5.2	12.9	13.3	67.8
Aged 50 to 54	22,298	100.0	4.8	12.4	10.9	70.9
Aged 55 to 59	19,665	100.0	4.7	11.5	9.4	73.6
Aged 60 to 64	16,818	100.0	4.4	10.3	8.2	76.3
Aged 65 to 69	12,435	100.0	4.1	9.6	7.6	78.0
Aged 70 to 74	9,278	100.0	4.1	9.4	7.5	78.3
Aged 75 to 79	7,318	100.0	3.7	8.6	7.0	80.2
Aged 80 to 84	5,743	100.0	3.1	7.6	6.1	82.7
Aged 85 or older	5,493	100.0	2.7	7.1	4.9	84.9
Alabama	**4,780**	**100.0**	**1.4**	**26.8**	**3.9**	**67.0**
Under age 5	305	100.0	1.9	32.4	8.2	56.9
Aged 5 to 9	308	100.0	1.8	31.3	6.3	59.8
Aged 10 to 14	320	100.0	1.6	32.0	4.6	60.9
Aged 15 to 19	343	100.0	1.4	33.1	4.2	60.4
Aged 20 to 24	335	100.0	1.7	31.0	6.1	60.5
Aged 25 to 29	311	100.0	2.0	29.0	7.0	61.2
Aged 30 to 34	298	100.0	2.0	28.5	6.3	62.4
Aged 35 to 39	308	100.0	1.9	26.6	4.7	65.9
Aged 40 to 44	311	100.0	1.6	25.5	3.4	68.5
Aged 45 to 49	346	100.0	1.3	25.3	2.3	70.0
Aged 50 to 54	347	100.0	1.1	25.7	1.7	70.3
Aged 55 to 59	312	100.0	1.0	24.7	1.3	72.0
Aged 60 to 64	276	100.0	0.9	20.9	1.0	76.3
Aged 65 to 69	210	100.0	0.7	18.3	0.9	79.2
Aged 70 to 74	161	100.0	0.6	18.0	0.8	79.9
Aged 75 to 79	123	100.0	0.5	17.2	0.7	80.9
Aged 80 to 84	89	100.0	0.4	17.0	0.7	81.4
Aged 85 or older	76	100.0	0.3	18.6	0.6	80.1

	total		Asian	black	Hispanic	non-Hispanic white
	number	percent				
Alaska	**710**	**100.0%**	**7.1%**	**4.7%**	**5.5%**	**64.1%**
Under age 5	54	100.0	8.6	7.5	8.7	51.0
Aged 5 to 9	51	100.0	9.0	7.1	8.1	51.8
Aged 10 to 14	51	100.0	8.8	6.6	7.5	53.1
Aged 15 to 19	52	100.0	8.3	5.8	6.9	54.6
Aged 20 to 24	54	100.0	7.2	5.6	7.1	58.5
Aged 25 to 29	55	100.0	6.7	5.1	6.4	63.4
Aged 30 to 34	48	100.0	6.8	4.7	6.0	65.2
Aged 35 to 39	46	100.0	7.4	4.4	5.6	66.3
Aged 40 to 44	47	100.0	7.1	3.8	5.1	67.5
Aged 45 to 49	55	100.0	6.3	3.5	4.2	69.8
Aged 50 to 54	56	100.0	5.8	3.1	3.5	73.6
Aged 55 to 59	50	100.0	5.5	2.9	2.9	75.5
Aged 60 to 64	36	100.0	5.7	2.3	2.6	76.5
Aged 65 to 69	22	100.0	5.5	2.1	2.4	75.6
Aged 70 to 74	13	100.0	6.3	2.6	2.4	73.0
Aged 75 to 79	9	100.0	6.2	2.2	2.1	71.9
Aged 80 to 84	6	100.0	6.2	2.1	1.6	73.3
Aged 85 or older	5	100.0	4.9	2.1	1.7	77.8
Arizona	**6,392**	**100.0**	**3.6**	**5.0**	**29.6**	**57.8**
Under age 5	456	100.0	4.5	7.3	44.9	39.6
Aged 5 to 9	454	100.0	4.3	6.8	43.9	41.1
Aged 10 to 14	449	100.0	3.9	6.8	42.2	42.8
Aged 15 to 19	462	100.0	3.7	6.7	39.8	44.8
Aged 20 to 24	443	100.0	4.0	6.1	35.9	48.9
Aged 25 to 29	440	100.0	4.5	5.6	34.2	51.1
Aged 30 to 34	417	100.0	4.8	5.3	35.0	50.5
Aged 35 to 39	416	100.0	5.0	5.1	33.0	52.9
Aged 40 to 44	407	100.0	4.2	4.9	29.7	57.2
Aged 45 to 49	427	100.0	3.5	4.6	24.9	62.9
Aged 50 to 54	416	100.0	3.0	4.2	20.9	68.0
Aged 55 to 59	375	100.0	2.8	3.5	17.6	72.6
Aged 60 to 64	351	100.0	2.4	2.8	14.1	77.7
Aged 65 to 69	283	100.0	2.0	2.4	12.1	80.7
Aged 70 to 74	215	100.0	2.0	2.2	11.4	81.7
Aged 75 to 79	162	100.0	1.8	2.0	10.7	83.2
Aged 80 to 84	118	100.0	1.3	1.6	9.9	85.1
Aged 85 or older	103	100.0	1.1	1.5	8.2	87.3

	total		Asian	black	Hispanic	non-Hispanic white
	number	percent				
Arkansas	**2,916**	**100.0%**	**1.5%**	**16.1%**	**6.4%**	**74.5%**
Under age 5	198	100.0	2.1	21.4	12.5	62.7
Aged 5 to 9	197	100.0	2.0	20.2	11.1	65.1
Aged 10 to 14	198	100.0	1.7	20.6	9.3	66.9
Aged 15 to 19	204	100.0	1.7	20.6	8.2	67.8
Aged 20 to 24	200	100.0	2.1	18.9	8.4	69.0
Aged 25 to 29	192	100.0	2.3	17.6	9.2	69.4
Aged 30 to 34	184	100.0	2.2	17.2	9.1	69.9
Aged 35 to 39	184	100.0	2.0	15.5	7.9	73.1
Aged 40 to 44	183	100.0	1.7	15.1	6.3	75.4
Aged 45 to 49	206	100.0	1.3	15.0	4.3	77.8
Aged 50 to 54	202	100.0	1.2	15.2	3.3	78.7
Aged 55 to 59	184	100.0	1.1	14.4	2.4	80.7
Aged 60 to 64	167	100.0	0.9	11.4	1.8	84.6
Aged 65 to 69	133	100.0	0.7	9.2	1.3	87.5
Aged 70 to 74	101	100.0	0.6	8.9	1.2	88.3
Aged 75 to 79	78	100.0	0.5	8.5	0.9	89.1
Aged 80 to 84	56	100.0	0.4	8.8	0.8	89.1
Aged 85 or older	51	100.0	0.3	9.8	0.6	88.6
California	**37,254**	**100.0**	**14.9**	**7.2**	**37.6**	**40.1**
Under age 5	2,531	100.0	14.7	8.5	53.3	25.5
Aged 5 to 9	2,506	100.0	14.6	8.2	51.6	27.0
Aged 10 to 14	2,591	100.0	13.9	8.5	50.3	28.3
Aged 15 to 19	2,824	100.0	13.9	8.7	47.9	30.0
Aged 20 to 24	2,766	100.0	14.7	7.9	44.0	33.4
Aged 25 to 29	2,744	100.0	15.4	6.9	42.6	34.8
Aged 30 to 34	2,573	100.0	16.1	6.7	42.9	33.9
Aged 35 to 39	2,574	100.0	17.1	6.5	41.3	34.7
Aged 40 to 44	2,609	100.0	15.7	6.9	37.6	39.2
Aged 45 to 49	2,690	100.0	14.9	7.2	31.6	45.3
Aged 50 to 54	2,563	100.0	14.8	7.1	27.1	49.9
Aged 55 to 59	2,204	100.0	15.0	6.6	23.5	53.9
Aged 60 to 64	1,832	100.0	14.6	6.1	20.3	57.9
Aged 65 to 69	1,304	100.0	14.1	6.0	19.4	59.5
Aged 70 to 74	972	100.0	15.1	6.2	19.0	58.9
Aged 75 to 79	767	100.0	14.6	5.5	18.0	61.2
Aged 80 to 84	603	100.0	13.1	4.6	16.1	65.4
Aged 85 or older	601	100.0	11.2	4.5	12.6	71.2

	total		Asian	black	Hispanic	non-Hispanic white
	number	percent				
Colorado	**5,029**	**100.0%**	**3.7%**	**5.0%**	**20.7%**	**70.0%**
Under age 5	344	100.0	4.9	7.4	32.8	55.5
Aged 5 to 9	349	100.0	4.9	6.8	31.3	57.1
Aged 10 to 14	333	100.0	4.5	6.7	29.3	59.4
Aged 15 to 19	339	100.0	4.0	6.6	26.8	62.0
Aged 20 to 24	349	100.0	4.1	5.7	24.1	65.2
Aged 25 to 29	372	100.0	4.2	5.0	23.3	66.5
Aged 30 to 34	354	100.0	4.3	4.9	23.9	66.1
Aged 35 to 39	354	100.0	4.6	4.7	22.2	67.6
Aged 40 to 44	346	100.0	3.9	4.6	19.3	71.1
Aged 45 to 49	372	100.0	3.2	4.5	15.9	75.3
Aged 50 to 54	371	100.0	2.7	4.1	13.1	79.0
Aged 55 to 59	328	100.0	2.4	3.6	11.4	81.5
Aged 60 to 64	269	100.0	2.3	3.0	10.6	83.2
Aged 65 to 69	182	100.0	2.3	3.0	10.3	83.5
Aged 70 to 74	127	100.0	2.3	3.1	10.9	82.8
Aged 75 to 79	97	100.0	2.3	3.0	10.1	83.9
Aged 80 to 84	73	100.0	2.0	2.4	8.9	86.2
Aged 85 or older	70	100.0	1.6	1.9	7.1	89.0
Connecticut	**3,574**	**100.0**	**4.4**	**11.3**	**13.4**	**71.2**
Under age 5	202	100.0	7.1	16.5	23.2	55.5
Aged 5 to 9	223	100.0	6.1	14.9	19.7	60.9
Aged 10 to 14	240	100.0	4.7	14.7	18.1	63.7
Aged 15 to 19	251	100.0	4.1	15.2	17.6	64.1
Aged 20 to 24	228	100.0	4.9	14.4	18.3	63.0
Aged 25 to 29	214	100.0	6.9	13.3	19.4	60.8
Aged 30 to 34	206	100.0	7.3	13.1	19.7	60.1
Aged 35 to 39	222	100.0	6.6	12.0	16.5	65.0
Aged 40 to 44	262	100.0	4.7	11.1	13.3	70.9
Aged 45 to 49	291	100.0	3.6	10.0	10.4	75.8
Aged 50 to 54	284	100.0	3.0	9.0	8.3	79.5
Aged 55 to 59	240	100.0	2.8	8.0	7.0	82.1
Aged 60 to 64	203	100.0	2.5	7.7	6.2	83.4
Aged 65 to 69	149	100.0	2.3	7.5	5.6	84.5
Aged 70 to 74	106	100.0	2.2	7.6	5.4	84.6
Aged 75 to 79	89	100.0	1.7	6.2	4.2	87.8
Aged 80 to 84	77	100.0	1.1	4.8	3.1	90.9
Aged 85 or older	85	100.0	0.6	3.9	2.2	93.1

| | total | | | | | non-Hispanic |
	number	percent	Asian	black	Hispanic	white
Delaware	**898**	**100.0%**	**3.8%**	**22.9%**	**8.2%**	**65.3%**
Under age 5	56	100.0	5.2	31.1	16.2	49.3
Aged 5 to 9	56	100.0	4.9	30.4	14.0	52.0
Aged 10 to 14	57	100.0	3.9	30.6	11.4	55.1
Aged 15 to 19	65	100.0	3.7	29.3	10.0	57.7
Aged 20 to 24	63	100.0	3.9	25.1	11.2	60.1
Aged 25 to 29	58	100.0	5.6	23.4	12.8	58.5
Aged 30 to 34	54	100.0	6.0	23.9	12.3	58.0
Aged 35 to 39	55	100.0	5.5	23.9	10.3	60.3
Aged 40 to 44	61	100.0	4.1	24.1	7.8	64.0
Aged 45 to 49	68	100.0	3.3	22.2	5.4	68.8
Aged 50 to 54	66	100.0	2.7	20.6	4.0	72.3
Aged 55 to 59	58	100.0	2.5	18.7	3.3	75.2
Aged 60 to 64	53	100.0	2.3	16.4	2.6	78.3
Aged 65 to 69	42	100.0	2.3	14.5	2.1	80.7
Aged 70 to 74	31	100.0	2.3	14.0	2.1	81.2
Aged 75 to 79	24	100.0	1.6	12.6	1.7	83.7
Aged 80 to 84	17	100.0	1.2	10.7	1.7	86.0
Aged 85 or older	16	100.0	1.0	10.8	1.4	86.5
District of Columbia	**602**	**100.0**	**4.5**	**52.2**	**9.1**	**34.8**
Under age 5	33	100.0	4.5	59.6	13.8	23.8
Aged 5 to 9	26	100.0	3.2	67.5	12.6	18.3
Aged 10 to 14	25	100.0	2.4	75.5	10.4	12.9
Aged 15 to 19	40	100.0	4.0	63.0	9.0	25.2
Aged 20 to 24	64	100.0	6.3	38.7	9.5	46.1
Aged 25 to 29	70	100.0	6.7	31.4	10.3	51.9
Aged 30 to 34	55	100.0	7.2	35.5	11.5	46.4
Aged 35 to 39	43	100.0	6.2	43.0	11.7	39.7
Aged 40 to 44	38	100.0	4.1	51.5	10.2	34.7
Aged 45 to 49	39	100.0	3.0	60.5	8.5	28.4
Aged 50 to 54	37	100.0	2.7	64.1	7.2	26.5
Aged 55 to 59	34	100.0	2.6	62.2	5.8	29.6
Aged 60 to 64	30	100.0	2.7	58.0	5.3	34.2
Aged 65 to 69	21	100.0	2.3	57.7	4.8	35.3
Aged 70 to 74	15	100.0	2.5	64.1	4.7	29.0
Aged 75 to 79	12	100.0	2.2	67.6	3.6	26.6
Aged 80 to 84	10	100.0	1.8	67.9	3.5	27.0
Aged 85 or older	10	100.0	1.9	63.4	2.5	32.2

	total		Asian	black	Hispanic	non-Hispanic white
	number	percent				
Florida	**18,801**	**100.0%**	**3.0%**	**17.0%**	**22.5%**	**57.9%**
Under age 5	1,074	100.0	4.0	25.4	29.1	43.2
Aged 5 to 9	1,080	100.0	4.0	24.1	27.7	45.4
Aged 10 to 14	1,131	100.0	3.5	23.4	26.9	47.0
Aged 15 to 19	1,228	100.0	3.3	23.7	26.1	47.7
Aged 20 to 24	1,229	100.0	3.5	21.8	26.4	48.9
Aged 25 to 29	1,179	100.0	3.8	20.3	27.0	49.5
Aged 30 to 34	1,110	100.0	4.1	19.3	28.8	48.3
Aged 35 to 39	1,178	100.0	4.1	17.9	28.3	50.1
Aged 40 to 44	1,253	100.0	3.6	16.6	25.8	54.3
Aged 45 to 49	1,401	100.0	2.9	15.6	22.8	58.9
Aged 50 to 54	1,340	100.0	2.7	15.2	18.6	63.4
Aged 55 to 59	1,202	100.0	2.6	13.6	16.6	67.1
Aged 60 to 64	1,135	100.0	2.2	10.9	14.3	72.5
Aged 65 to 69	959	100.0	1.9	9.3	13.7	75.2
Aged 70 to 74	769	100.0	1.7	8.9	14.4	75.1
Aged 75 to 79	616	100.0	1.3	7.7	13.8	77.3
Aged 80 to 84	482	100.0	0.9	6.5	12.6	80.1
Aged 85 or older	434	100.0	0.7	6.0	11.2	82.2
Georgia	**9,688**	**100.0**	**3.8**	**31.5**	**8.8**	**55.9**
Under age 5	687	100.0	4.4	36.5	15.5	44.3
Aged 5 to 9	695	100.0	4.4	35.6	13.4	47.1
Aged 10 to 14	690	100.0	3.9	36.8	10.8	48.7
Aged 15 to 19	710	100.0	3.7	38.3	9.7	48.4
Aged 20 to 24	680	100.0	4.0	34.7	11.6	49.9
Aged 25 to 29	674	100.0	4.6	32.6	13.4	49.7
Aged 30 to 34	662	100.0	4.8	32.7	13.2	49.4
Aged 35 to 39	698	100.0	5.1	31.8	10.6	52.6
Aged 40 to 44	699	100.0	4.2	31.3	8.2	56.1
Aged 45 to 49	723	100.0	3.5	30.7	5.9	59.6
Aged 50 to 54	669	100.0	3.2	29.6	4.4	62.4
Aged 55 to 59	574	100.0	2.9	28.1	3.3	65.3
Aged 60 to 64	496	100.0	2.6	24.5	2.5	70.0
Aged 65 to 69	356	100.0	2.5	22.2	2.2	72.7
Aged 70 to 74	250	100.0	2.3	21.5	2.1	73.7
Aged 75 to 79	183	100.0	1.9	19.9	1.8	76.1
Aged 80 to 84	129	100.0	1.4	18.7	1.7	77.9
Aged 85 or older	114	100.0	1.0	19.3	1.4	78.1

	total					non-Hispanic
	number	percent	Asian	black	Hispanic	white
Hawaii	**1,360**	**100.0%**	**57.4%**	**2.9%**	**8.9%**	**22.7%**
Under age 5	87	100.0	58.4	5.4	16.9	14.7
Aged 5 to 9	83	100.0	61.4	4.9	15.3	13.0
Aged 10 to 14	82	100.0	63.0	4.4	13.6	12.4
Aged 15 to 19	86	100.0	61.9	3.8	12.6	13.7
Aged 20 to 24	96	100.0	49.0	4.3	11.5	25.7
Aged 25 to 29	97	100.0	49.3	4.0	10.7	26.5
Aged 30 to 34	88	100.0	52.2	3.6	10.2	24.3
Aged 35 to 39	87	100.0	55.8	3.1	9.0	22.5
Aged 40 to 44	90	100.0	57.4	2.6	7.7	22.9
Aged 45 to 49	96	100.0	57.1	2.0	6.8	24.2
Aged 50 to 54	98	100.0	56.6	1.7	5.8	26.7
Aged 55 to 59	93	100.0	55.3	1.4	4.7	30.2
Aged 60 to 64	82	100.0	54.7	1.1	3.9	32.3
Aged 65 to 69	59	100.0	57.4	0.9	3.9	29.7
Aged 70 to 74	41	100.0	62.5	0.7	3.7	25.5
Aged 75 to 79	35	100.0	67.6	0.6	3.3	21.8
Aged 80 to 84	30	100.0	71.8	0.5	2.5	20.1
Aged 85 or older	30	100.0	73.4	0.4	2.1	20.6
Idaho	**1,568**	**100.0**	**1.9**	**1.0**	**11.2**	**84.0**
Under age 5	122	100.0	2.4	2.0	18.8	75.1
Aged 5 to 9	121	100.0	2.4	1.8	17.1	76.7
Aged 10 to 14	117	100.0	2.3	1.7	16.1	77.9
Aged 15 to 19	115	100.0	2.2	1.6	15.2	78.7
Aged 20 to 24	108	100.0	2.3	1.4	14.2	79.9
Aged 25 to 29	107	100.0	2.4	1.1	14.1	80.4
Aged 30 to 34	102	100.0	2.3	1.0	13.2	81.6
Aged 35 to 39	97	100.0	2.4	0.9	12.6	82.1
Aged 40 to 44	95	100.0	2.0	0.8	10.8	84.4
Aged 45 to 49	104	100.0	1.7	0.6	8.5	87.2
Aged 50 to 54	105	100.0	1.4	0.5	6.4	89.6
Aged 55 to 59	97	100.0	1.3	0.4	5.0	91.4
Aged 60 to 64	83	100.0	1.1	0.3	4.0	92.9
Aged 65 to 69	63	100.0	1.0	0.2	3.5	93.7
Aged 70 to 74	46	100.0	0.8	0.2	3.1	94.4
Aged 75 to 79	34	100.0	0.9	0.1	2.8	94.9
Aged 80 to 84	26	100.0	0.9	0.2	2.1	95.8
Aged 85 or older	25	100.0	0.9	0.2	1.7	96.5

	total		Asian	black	Hispanic	non-Hispanic white
	number	percent				
Illinois	**12,831**	**100.0%**	**5.2%**	**15.4%**	**15.8%**	**63.7%**
Under age 5	836	100.0	6.3	18.7	25.5	50.4
Aged 5 to 9	859	100.0	5.9	18.2	24.1	52.4
Aged 10 to 14	879	100.0	5.0	19.2	21.9	54.4
Aged 15 to 19	922	100.0	4.6	20.3	19.7	55.7
Aged 20 to 24	879	100.0	5.8	17.1	19.2	58.1
Aged 25 to 29	910	100.0	6.7	14.6	19.6	59.1
Aged 30 to 34	866	100.0	7.0	14.5	20.7	57.8
Aged 35 to 39	856	100.0	6.9	14.9	19.5	58.7
Aged 40 to 44	870	100.0	5.6	14.4	16.0	63.9
Aged 45 to 49	940	100.0	4.4	14.3	11.9	69.1
Aged 50 to 54	931	100.0	4.1	14.3	9.8	71.6
Aged 55 to 59	808	100.0	4.4	13.4	8.3	73.6
Aged 60 to 64	665	100.0	4.5	12.6	7.1	75.5
Aged 65 to 69	485	100.0	4.4	12.5	6.3	76.6
Aged 70 to 74	364	100.0	3.9	12.7	5.8	77.4
Aged 75 to 79	289	100.0	3.0	11.7	5.2	79.9
Aged 80 to 84	235	100.0	2.3	9.8	4.0	83.6
Aged 85 or older	235	100.0	1.8	8.5	2.8	86.8
Indiana	**6,484**	**100.0**	**2.0**	**10.1**	**6.0**	**81.5**
Under age 5	434	100.0	2.7	15.0	11.6	70.6
Aged 5 to 9	445	100.0	2.5	13.8	10.2	73.3
Aged 10 to 14	452	100.0	2.1	13.4	8.3	75.8
Aged 15 to 19	476	100.0	2.2	12.8	7.2	77.4
Aged 20 to 24	452	100.0	3.1	11.0	7.3	78.2
Aged 25 to 29	420	100.0	2.9	10.8	8.4	77.6
Aged 30 to 34	408	100.0	2.7	10.7	8.7	77.6
Aged 35 to 39	417	100.0	2.6	10.0	7.2	79.7
Aged 40 to 44	424	100.0	2.1	9.2	5.5	82.7
Aged 45 to 49	474	100.0	1.5	8.6	3.9	85.3
Aged 50 to 54	473	100.0	1.2	8.5	3.2	86.5
Aged 55 to 59	419	100.0	1.1	7.7	2.5	88.0
Aged 60 to 64	351	100.0	1.1	6.7	2.1	89.6
Aged 65 to 69	259	100.0	0.9	6.5	1.7	90.3
Aged 70 to 74	193	100.0	0.8	6.2	1.6	91.0
Aged 75 to 79	152	100.0	0.7	6.0	1.6	91.3
Aged 80 to 84	122	100.0	0.5	5.2	1.4	92.5
Aged 85 or older	115	100.0	0.3	4.8	1.0	93.5

	total		Asian	black	Hispanic	non-Hispanic white
	number	percent				
Iowa	**3,046**	**100.0%**	**2.1%**	**3.7%**	**5.0%**	**88.7%**
Under age 5	202	100.0	2.9	7.6	10.3	78.8
Aged 5 to 9	201	100.0	2.9	6.8	9.1	80.8
Aged 10 to 14	201	100.0	2.5	6.1	7.8	83.0
Aged 15 to 19	217	100.0	2.6	5.6	6.8	84.4
Aged 20 to 24	213	100.0	3.7	4.8	6.6	84.3
Aged 25 to 29	198	100.0	3.3	4.2	6.7	85.2
Aged 30 to 34	185	100.0	3.0	4.0	6.6	85.7
Aged 35 to 39	177	100.0	3.0	3.7	6.1	86.6
Aged 40 to 44	187	100.0	2.3	3.0	4.9	89.2
Aged 45 to 49	216	100.0	1.6	2.6	3.3	92.0
Aged 50 to 54	223	100.0	1.2	2.2	2.4	93.7
Aged 55 to 59	204	100.0	1.1	1.8	1.8	94.8
Aged 60 to 64	168	100.0	1.0	1.5	1.5	95.6
Aged 65 to 69	124	100.0	0.9	1.3	1.2	96.2
Aged 70 to 74	100	100.0	0.8	1.2	1.0	96.7
Aged 75 to 79	83	100.0	0.6	1.0	0.8	97.3
Aged 80 to 84	70	100.0	0.4	0.9	0.7	97.8
Aged 85 or older	75	100.0	0.2	0.7	0.6	98.4
Kansas	**2,853**	**100.0**	**2.9**	**7.1**	**10.5**	**78.2**
Under age 5	205	100.0	4.0	11.1	19.1	65.3
Aged 5 to 9	202	100.0	3.9	9.9	17.5	67.9
Aged 10 to 14	199	100.0	3.3	9.5	15.4	70.5
Aged 15 to 19	204	100.0	3.1	9.4	13.6	72.4
Aged 20 to 24	204	100.0	3.9	8.4	12.7	73.5
Aged 25 to 29	198	100.0	3.9	7.6	13.2	73.9
Aged 30 to 34	180	100.0	3.9	7.2	13.7	73.8
Aged 35 to 39	172	100.0	4.2	6.6	12.7	74.9
Aged 40 to 44	174	100.0	3.3	6.3	10.5	78.2
Aged 45 to 49	202	100.0	2.3	6.2	7.3	82.7
Aged 50 to 54	204	100.0	2.0	5.9	5.6	85.1
Aged 55 to 59	183	100.0	1.9	4.9	4.4	87.4
Aged 60 to 64	149	100.0	1.8	4.5	3.7	88.7
Aged 65 to 69	108	100.0	1.7	4.2	3.3	89.7
Aged 70 to 74	83	100.0	1.4	4.2	3.0	90.3
Aged 75 to 79	69	100.0	1.0	3.6	2.7	91.8
Aged 80 to 84	57	100.0	0.7	3.1	2.4	93.1
Aged 85 or older	59	100.0	0.5	2.6	1.7	94.6

	total		Asian	black	Hispanic	non-Hispanic white
	number	percent				
Kentucky	**4,339**	**100.0%**	**1.4%**	**8.7%**	**3.1%**	**86.3%**
Under age 5	282	100.0	2.2	13.0	6.6	78.0
Aged 5 to 9	283	100.0	2.2	11.8	5.2	80.4
Aged 10 to 14	284	100.0	1.7	11.3	3.8	82.7
Aged 15 to 19	297	100.0	1.4	11.5	3.5	83.1
Aged 20 to 24	290	100.0	1.7	10.5	4.5	82.8
Aged 25 to 29	285	100.0	2.0	9.2	5.0	83.3
Aged 30 to 34	281	100.0	2.1	9.1	4.5	83.9
Aged 35 to 39	285	100.0	2.0	8.2	3.8	85.5
Aged 40 to 44	291	100.0	1.6	7.8	2.7	87.4
Aged 45 to 49	324	100.0	1.1	7.6	2.0	88.6
Aged 50 to 54	319	100.0	0.9	7.6	1.3	89.4
Aged 55 to 59	288	100.0	0.8	6.9	1.0	90.7
Aged 60 to 64	251	100.0	0.8	5.7	0.8	92.1
Aged 65 to 69	186	100.0	0.7	5.0	0.8	92.9
Aged 70 to 74	140	100.0	0.6	4.9	0.7	93.2
Aged 75 to 79	105	100.0	0.5	4.9	0.7	93.4
Aged 80 to 84	78	100.0	0.4	4.8	0.6	93.7
Aged 85 or older	69	100.0	0.3	5.1	0.5	93.7
Louisiana	**4,533**	**100.0**	**1.9**	**32.8**	**4.2**	**60.3**
Under age 5	314	100.0	2.1	40.4	6.2	50.8
Aged 5 to 9	306	100.0	2.1	39.8	4.8	52.6
Aged 10 to 14	307	100.0	1.8	39.2	4.1	53.9
Aged 15 to 19	327	100.0	1.8	40.3	4.2	52.8
Aged 20 to 24	338	100.0	2.3	36.6	5.7	54.7
Aged 25 to 29	333	100.0	2.5	33.8	6.3	56.8
Aged 30 to 34	296	100.0	2.4	33.4	6.1	57.4
Aged 35 to 39	276	100.0	2.5	30.9	5.4	60.4
Aged 40 to 44	288	100.0	2.0	31.0	4.3	61.7
Aged 45 to 49	325	100.0	1.6	30.6	3.5	63.3
Aged 50 to 54	329	100.0	1.6	30.3	2.9	64.4
Aged 55 to 59	293	100.0	1.6	29.3	2.6	65.8
Aged 60 to 64	243	100.0	1.4	26.5	2.3	69.0
Aged 65 to 69	178	100.0	1.2	24.4	2.2	71.5
Aged 70 to 74	134	100.0	1.1	23.7	2.3	72.3
Aged 75 to 79	103	100.0	0.9	21.9	2.1	74.4
Aged 80 to 84	77	100.0	0.7	20.0	2.0	76.7
Aged 85 or older	66	100.0	0.6	20.9	1.8	76.2

	total					non-Hispanic
	number	percent	Asian	black	Hispanic	white
Maine	**1,328**	**100.0%**	**1.4%**	**1.6%**	**1.3%**	**94.4%**
Under age 5	70	100.0	2.4	5.0	2.9	88.1
Aged 5 to 9	74	100.0	2.3	3.8	2.4	89.9
Aged 10 to 14	79	100.0	2.1	3.3	2.0	91.1
Aged 15 to 19	88	100.0	2.3	2.9	2.1	91.1
Aged 20 to 24	80	100.0	1.9	2.5	2.0	92.0
Aged 25 to 29	73	100.0	1.9	1.9	1.8	92.8
Aged 30 to 34	72	100.0	1.8	1.7	1.7	93.4
Aged 35 to 39	80	100.0	1.8	1.6	1.2	94.1
Aged 40 to 44	91	100.0	1.4	1.2	1.1	94.9
Aged 45 to 49	108	100.0	1.0	0.9	0.9	95.9
Aged 50 to 54	111	100.0	0.9	0.7	0.7	96.4
Aged 55 to 59	102	100.0	0.8	0.6	0.6	96.9
Aged 60 to 64	90	100.0	0.6	0.4	0.5	97.4
Aged 65 to 69	65	100.0	0.5	0.4	0.4	97.7
Aged 70 to 74	48	100.0	0.6	0.4	0.4	97.8
Aged 75 to 79	39	100.0	0.4	0.3	0.4	98.3
Aged 80 to 84	30	100.0	0.3	0.2	0.3	98.6
Aged 85 or older	29	100.0	0.2	0.3	0.3	98.8
Maryland	**5,774**	**100.0**	**6.4**	**30.9**	**8.2**	**54.7**
Under age 5	364	100.0	8.0	36.6	13.8	42.8
Aged 5 to 9	367	100.0	7.6	35.7	11.2	46.3
Aged 10 to 14	379	100.0	6.6	36.1	9.5	48.4
Aged 15 to 19	406	100.0	6.1	36.5	8.9	48.9
Aged 20 to 24	394	100.0	6.4	33.5	11.1	49.3
Aged 25 to 29	394	100.0	7.3	31.3	12.8	48.8
Aged 30 to 34	368	100.0	8.4	31.8	13.2	46.8
Aged 35 to 39	377	100.0	8.5	32.1	10.8	48.7
Aged 40 to 44	418	100.0	6.9	31.9	8.2	53.0
Aged 45 to 49	462	100.0	5.8	30.4	6.0	57.5
Aged 50 to 54	441	100.0	5.5	28.9	4.7	60.7
Aged 55 to 59	378	100.0	5.2	27.3	3.8	63.5
Aged 60 to 64	318	100.0	5.1	25.8	3.0	65.7
Aged 65 to 69	227	100.0	5.0	24.3	2.7	67.7
Aged 70 to 74	160	100.0	5.3	24.0	2.6	67.9
Aged 75 to 79	125	100.0	4.3	21.9	2.4	71.2
Aged 80 to 84	99	100.0	3.2	18.2	2.0	76.4
Aged 85 or older	98	100.0	2.3	16.3	1.5	79.7

	total					non-Hispanic
	number	percent	Asian	black	Hispanic	white
Massachusetts	**6,548**	**100.0%**	**6.0%**	**7.8%**	**9.6%**	**76.1%**
Under age 5	367	100.0	8.5	11.8	17.2	62.6
Aged 5 to 9	386	100.0	7.8	10.7	14.7	67.2
Aged 10 to 14	406	100.0	6.2	10.3	13.7	69.9
Aged 15 to 19	463	100.0	6.5	10.6	13.6	69.3
Aged 20 to 24	476	100.0	7.9	9.5	12.8	69.4
Aged 25 to 29	442	100.0	8.8	8.5	12.6	69.0
Aged 30 to 34	404	100.0	8.9	8.7	13.0	68.2
Aged 35 to 39	418	100.0	8.5	8.1	11.0	71.5
Aged 40 to 44	469	100.0	6.1	7.4	9.1	76.5
Aged 45 to 49	515	100.0	4.9	6.7	7.3	80.3
Aged 50 to 54	497	100.0	4.2	6.3	5.9	82.9
Aged 55 to 59	433	100.0	3.9	5.6	5.0	85.0
Aged 60 to 64	371	100.0	3.4	5.0	4.3	86.8
Aged 65 to 69	264	100.0	3.3	4.9	3.9	87.5
Aged 70 to 74	192	100.0	3.6	4.8	3.7	87.5
Aged 75 to 79	163	100.0	2.9	4.1	2.9	89.5
Aged 80 to 84	138	100.0	2.1	3.3	2.1	92.0
Aged 85 or older	145	100.0	1.5	2.9	1.5	93.7
Michigan	**9,884**	**100.0**	**2.9**	**15.2**	**4.4**	**76.6**
Under age 5	596	100.0	4.2	20.8	8.8	65.8
Aged 5 to 9	638	100.0	4.1	18.9	7.8	68.6
Aged 10 to 14	675	100.0	3.4	18.9	6.6	70.2
Aged 15 to 19	740	100.0	3.1	20.1	5.7	70.3
Aged 20 to 24	669	100.0	3.8	17.5	5.4	72.4
Aged 25 to 29	590	100.0	4.0	15.8	5.8	73.5
Aged 30 to 34	575	100.0	4.3	16.0	5.9	72.9
Aged 35 to 39	612	100.0	4.1	16.5	5.1	73.3
Aged 40 to 44	665	100.0	3.2	14.6	3.9	77.3
Aged 45 to 49	745	100.0	2.4	12.9	3.0	80.6
Aged 50 to 54	765	100.0	1.9	13.0	2.4	81.8
Aged 55 to 59	683	100.0	1.7	12.5	2.1	82.8
Aged 60 to 64	569	100.0	1.8	12.0	1.9	83.5
Aged 65 to 69	419	100.0	1.7	10.7	1.6	85.2
Aged 70 to 74	306	100.0	1.6	10.1	1.5	86.1
Aged 75 to 79	244	100.0	1.2	10.2	1.5	86.6
Aged 80 to 84	201	100.0	0.9	9.2	1.3	88.2
Aged 85 or older	192	100.0	0.6	8.8	1.0	89.1

	total					non-Hispanic
	number	percent	Asian	black	Hispanic	white
Minnesota	**5,304**	**100.0%**	**4.7%**	**6.2%**	**4.7%**	**83.1%**
Under age 5	356	100.0	7.5	12.0	9.5	69.3
Aged 5 to 9	356	100.0	7.0	10.5	8.4	72.5
Aged 10 to 14	352	100.0	6.2	9.2	6.9	75.9
Aged 15 to 19	368	100.0	6.3	8.7	6.1	77.1
Aged 20 to 24	356	100.0	6.7	7.9	6.1	77.5
Aged 25 to 29	373	100.0	6.5	7.3	6.5	78.2
Aged 30 to 34	343	100.0	6.1	6.9	6.9	78.7
Aged 35 to 39	328	100.0	6.1	6.8	6.0	79.8
Aged 40 to 44	353	100.0	4.4	5.7	4.3	84.2
Aged 45 to 49	406	100.0	3.0	4.3	2.9	88.4
Aged 50 to 54	402	100.0	2.4	3.8	2.1	90.4
Aged 55 to 59	350	100.0	2.2	3.1	1.7	91.9
Aged 60 to 64	280	100.0	2.1	2.5	1.3	92.9
Aged 65 to 69	203	100.0	2.0	2.2	1.1	93.8
Aged 70 to 74	152	100.0	1.8	1.9	1.0	94.5
Aged 75 to 79	122	100.0	1.5	1.6	0.9	95.4
Aged 80 to 84	100	100.0	1.2	1.2	0.6	96.6
Aged 85 or older	107	100.0	0.9	0.9	0.5	97.4
Mississippi	**2,967**	**100.0**	**1.1**	**37.6**	**2.7**	**58.0**
Under age 5	211	100.0	1.2	45.8	4.7	47.8
Aged 5 to 9	206	100.0	1.3	44.3	3.6	50.2
Aged 10 to 14	208	100.0	1.1	44.9	2.8	50.7
Aged 15 to 19	225	100.0	1.1	45.8	2.8	49.8
Aged 20 to 24	211	100.0	1.3	41.9	4.2	52.1
Aged 25 to 29	199	100.0	1.5	40.5	4.8	52.8
Aged 30 to 34	188	100.0	1.4	40.0	4.4	53.6
Aged 35 to 39	187	100.0	1.5	37.4	3.5	57.1
Aged 40 to 44	188	100.0	1.3	36.3	2.7	59.2
Aged 45 to 49	208	100.0	1.0	35.3	2.0	61.1
Aged 50 to 54	209	100.0	0.9	35.5	1.5	61.4
Aged 55 to 59	187	100.0	0.9	33.7	1.1	63.8
Aged 60 to 64	161	100.0	0.7	28.6	0.9	69.3
Aged 65 to 69	121	100.0	0.6	25.5	0.9	72.6
Aged 70 to 74	94	100.0	0.5	24.8	0.7	73.5
Aged 75 to 79	70	100.0	0.5	22.9	0.7	75.6
Aged 80 to 84	52	100.0	0.4	22.5	0.6	76.1
Aged 85 or older	44	100.0	0.3	25.1	0.5	73.8

	total		Asian	black	Hispanic	non-Hispanic white
	number	percent				
Missouri	**5,989**	**100.0%**	**2.1%**	**12.5%**	**3.5%**	**81.0%**
Under age 5	390	100.0	2.8	17.2	6.9	72.4
Aged 5 to 9	390	100.0	2.7	16.2	6.0	74.4
Aged 10 to 14	397	100.0	2.3	16.0	4.9	75.9
Aged 15 to 19	424	100.0	2.2	16.8	4.5	75.4
Aged 20 to 24	413	100.0	2.9	14.5	4.8	76.9
Aged 25 to 29	403	100.0	2.9	13.0	4.8	78.4
Aged 30 to 34	372	100.0	3.0	12.9	4.8	78.5
Aged 35 to 39	368	100.0	2.9	12.8	4.2	79.1
Aged 40 to 44	381	100.0	2.3	12.1	3.3	81.3
Aged 45 to 49	445	100.0	1.6	11.2	2.4	83.7
Aged 50 to 54	444	100.0	1.3	11.0	1.9	84.6
Aged 55 to 59	390	100.0	1.3	10.0	1.6	86.1
Aged 60 to 64	333	100.0	1.2	8.8	1.3	87.7
Aged 65 to 69	257	100.0	1.1	8.1	1.1	88.8
Aged 70 to 74	193	100.0	1.0	7.8	1.1	89.3
Aged 75 to 79	155	100.0	0.8	7.4	1.0	90.2
Aged 80 to 84	119	100.0	0.6	6.7	0.9	91.3
Aged 85 or older	114	100.0	0.4	6.1	0.8	92.2
Montana	**989**	**100.0**	**1.1**	**0.8**	**2.9**	**87.8**
Under age 5	62	100.0	1.6	2.0	5.5	78.2
Aged 5 to 9	61	100.0	1.5	1.8	5.1	79.7
Aged 10 to 14	61	100.0	1.5	1.5	4.7	81.8
Aged 15 to 19	67	100.0	1.6	1.4	4.4	82.4
Aged 20 to 24	67	100.0	1.7	1.3	4.1	83.7
Aged 25 to 29	64	100.0	1.3	0.9	3.5	85.9
Aged 30 to 34	59	100.0	1.3	0.8	3.2	86.8
Aged 35 to 39	56	100.0	1.2	0.6	3.0	87.5
Aged 40 to 44	57	100.0	1.1	0.5	2.6	88.7
Aged 45 to 49	71	100.0	0.8	0.4	2.2	89.9
Aged 50 to 54	79	100.0	0.7	0.4	1.7	91.2
Aged 55 to 59	76	100.0	0.6	0.3	1.5	92.8
Aged 60 to 64	63	100.0	0.6	0.2	1.3	93.6
Aged 65 to 69	47	100.0	0.4	0.2	1.1	94.3
Aged 70 to 74	34	100.0	0.4	0.2	1.1	94.2
Aged 75 to 79	26	100.0	0.4	0.2	1.0	95.0
Aged 80 to 84	20	100.0	0.3	0.1	0.8	96.5
Aged 85 or older	20	100.0	0.3	0.1	0.7	97.3

	total					non-Hispanic
	number	percent	Asian	black	Hispanic	white
Nebraska	**1,826**	**100.0%**	**2.2%**	**5.4%**	**9.2%**	**82.1%**
Under age 5	132	100.0	3.1	9.2	17.2	69.2
Aged 5 to 9	129	100.0	3.0	8.2	15.6	71.8
Aged 10 to 14	123	100.0	2.6	7.7	13.9	74.4
Aged 15 to 19	129	100.0	2.5	7.3	12.1	76.7
Aged 20 to 24	129	100.0	3.2	6.4	11.3	77.9
Aged 25 to 29	129	100.0	3.2	6.0	11.6	78.1
Aged 30 to 34	116	100.0	3.0	5.7	12.0	78.1
Aged 35 to 39	110	100.0	3.1	5.4	11.2	79.3
Aged 40 to 44	110	100.0	2.5	4.9	9.3	82.1
Aged 45 to 49	128	100.0	1.6	4.5	6.1	86.7
Aged 50 to 54	130	100.0	1.3	4.0	4.7	89.0
Aged 55 to 59	118	100.0	1.2	3.4	3.6	90.8
Aged 60 to 64	95	100.0	1.2	3.0	3.0	92.0
Aged 65 to 69	69	100.0	1.1	2.7	2.5	93.0
Aged 70 to 74	54	100.0	0.9	2.6	2.1	93.7
Aged 75 to 79	46	100.0	0.6	2.3	1.8	94.8
Aged 80 to 84	38	100.0	0.5	1.8	1.4	96.0
Aged 85 or older	39	100.0	0.3	1.3	1.0	97.0
Nevada	**2,701**	**100.0**	**9.0**	**9.4**	**26.5**	**54.1**
Under age 5	187	100.0	9.2	12.6	41.5	37.8
Aged 5 to 9	183	100.0	9.3	12.0	40.3	38.9
Aged 10 to 14	183	100.0	9.3	11.8	38.4	40.4
Aged 15 to 19	183	100.0	9.0	12.5	35.7	42.3
Aged 20 to 24	178	100.0	9.4	10.9	33.0	45.7
Aged 25 to 29	197	100.0	9.4	9.7	31.3	48.4
Aged 30 to 34	191	100.0	9.7	9.4	31.8	48.0
Aged 35 to 39	192	100.0	10.2	9.2	30.4	49.2
Aged 40 to 44	191	100.0	9.5	9.0	26.6	53.6
Aged 45 to 49	194	100.0	8.9	8.8	21.3	59.4
Aged 50 to 54	183	100.0	8.8	8.1	17.0	64.5
Aged 55 to 59	165	100.0	8.8	7.3	13.8	68.5
Aged 60 to 64	151	100.0	8.4	6.5	10.7	72.9
Aged 65 to 69	116	100.0	7.9	6.4	9.7	74.5
Aged 70 to 74	82	100.0	7.9	6.7	9.2	74.9
Aged 75 to 79	58	100.0	7.3	6.0	8.6	77.0
Aged 80 to 84	39	100.0	5.8	5.1	7.6	80.4
Aged 85 or older	30	100.0	4.1	4.8	6.5	83.6

	total					non-Hispanic
	number	percent	Asian	black	Hispanic	white
New Hampshire	**1,316**	**100.0%**	**2.6%**	**1.7%**	**2.8%**	**92.3%**
Under age 5	70	100.0	4.9	3.9	6.0	84.8
Aged 5 to 9	78	100.0	4.2	3.3	5.0	87.0
Aged 10 to 14	85	100.0	3.2	2.8	4.1	89.2
Aged 15 to 19	94	100.0	2.7	2.4	4.0	90.2
Aged 20 to 24	85	100.0	3.1	2.4	3.8	90.0
Aged 25 to 29	73	100.0	3.9	2.0	4.1	89.4
Aged 30 to 34	71	100.0	4.5	2.0	3.9	88.8
Aged 35 to 39	82	100.0	4.1	1.7	3.2	90.3
Aged 40 to 44	97	100.0	2.7	1.4	2.6	92.6
Aged 45 to 49	114	100.0	1.9	1.2	2.0	94.2
Aged 50 to 54	112	100.0	1.5	0.9	1.5	95.4
Aged 55 to 59	96	100.0	1.5	0.7	1.2	96.0
Aged 60 to 64	82	100.0	1.3	0.6	1.0	96.6
Aged 65 to 69	57	100.0	1.2	0.6	0.9	96.9
Aged 70 to 74	40	100.0	0.9	0.5	0.9	97.3
Aged 75 to 79	32	100.0	0.9	0.4	0.8	97.5
Aged 80 to 84	25	100.0	0.6	0.4	0.6	98.0
Aged 85 or older	25	100.0	0.4	0.2	0.5	98.5
New Jersey	**8,792**	**100.0**	**9.0**	**14.8**	**17.7**	**59.3**
Under age 5	541	100.0	11.5	18.0	25.6	47.1
Aged 5 to 9	565	100.0	10.7	17.3	22.5	51.4
Aged 10 to 14	587	100.0	9.3	17.6	20.5	54.1
Aged 15 to 19	598	100.0	8.1	18.8	21.1	53.3
Aged 20 to 24	541	100.0	8.5	17.9	24.1	50.7
Aged 25 to 29	553	100.0	11.6	15.8	24.6	49.0
Aged 30 to 34	557	100.0	13.2	15.5	24.1	48.1
Aged 35 to 39	588	100.0	12.6	15.2	21.3	51.7
Aged 40 to 44	650	100.0	9.9	14.8	18.1	57.8
Aged 45 to 49	705	100.0	8.4	14.1	15.2	62.8
Aged 50 to 54	675	100.0	7.8	13.2	12.8	66.6
Aged 55 to 59	566	100.0	7.4	12.2	11.3	69.4
Aged 60 to 64	481	100.0	7.1	11.6	10.0	71.4
Aged 65 to 69	351	100.0	6.8	11.6	9.5	72.3
Aged 70 to 74	260	100.0	6.4	11.8	9.4	72.6
Aged 75 to 79	216	100.0	4.6	10.2	7.9	77.5
Aged 80 to 84	179	100.0	3.1	8.1	6.1	82.7
Aged 85 or older	180	100.0	2.2	6.8	4.5	86.4

	total					non-Hispanic
	number	percent	Asian	black	Hispanic	white
New Mexico	**2,059**	**100.0%**	**2.0%**	**2.8%**	**46.3%**	**40.5%**
Under age 5	145	100.0	2.4	4.3	59.6	24.8
Aged 5 to 9	143	100.0	2.3	3.8	58.9	25.6
Aged 10 to 14	142	100.0	2.2	3.7	57.8	26.9
Aged 15 to 19	150	100.0	2.0	3.6	55.0	28.6
Aged 20 to 24	142	100.0	2.2	3.5	51.4	32.2
Aged 25 to 29	140	100.0	2.4	3.1	50.5	34.3
Aged 30 to 34	128	100.0	2.6	2.8	50.1	35.0
Aged 35 to 39	123	100.0	2.5	2.7	49.4	36.3
Aged 40 to 44	125	100.0	2.3	2.5	47.1	39.3
Aged 45 to 49	145	100.0	1.9	2.4	43.3	43.9
Aged 50 to 54	147	100.0	1.7	2.2	39.0	49.5
Aged 55 to 59	137	100.0	1.5	2.0	34.3	55.3
Aged 60 to 64	120	100.0	1.4	1.6	32.3	58.6
Aged 65 to 69	88	100.0	1.2	1.5	31.1	60.2
Aged 70 to 74	66	100.0	1.1	1.5	32.8	58.6
Aged 75 to 79	50	100.0	1.0	1.5	31.9	60.1
Aged 80 to 84	36	100.0	1.0	1.4	30.9	62.0
Aged 85 or older	32	100.0	0.7	1.3	27.1	66.4
New York	**19,378**	**100.0**	**8.2**	**17.2**	**17.6**	**58.3**
Under age 5	1,156	100.0	8.7	20.7	24.6	48.8
Aged 5 to 9	1,164	100.0	8.4	20.2	22.5	51.1
Aged 10 to 14	1,211	100.0	7.8	20.5	21.2	52.4
Aged 15 to 19	1,366	100.0	7.7	21.0	21.3	51.8
Aged 20 to 24	1,411	100.0	9.3	19.1	21.3	52.0
Aged 25 to 29	1,380	100.0	10.4	17.3	21.5	52.3
Aged 30 to 34	1,279	100.0	10.7	17.3	22.0	51.4
Aged 35 to 39	1,254	100.0	10.2	17.0	20.6	53.4
Aged 40 to 44	1,356	100.0	8.7	17.2	18.2	56.9
Aged 45 to 49	1,459	100.0	8.0	17.0	15.5	60.4
Aged 50 to 54	1,420	100.0	7.7	16.1	13.4	63.6
Aged 55 to 59	1,237	100.0	7.3	14.9	12.2	66.4
Aged 60 to 64	1,066	100.0	6.8	14.1	11.3	68.5
Aged 65 to 69	773	100.0	6.2	14.6	11.0	68.9
Aged 70 to 74	587	100.0	6.2	14.3	11.0	69.3
Aged 75 to 79	475	100.0	5.2	12.3	9.6	73.5
Aged 80 to 84	392	100.0	3.9	10.6	7.7	78.2
Aged 85 or older	391	100.0	3.1	9.8	6.2	81.3

	total		Asian	black	Hispanic	non-Hispanic white
	number	percent				
North Carolina	**9,535**	**100.0%**	**2.6%**	**22.6%**	**8.4%**	**65.3%**
Under age 5	632	100.0	3.7	26.8	16.9	51.9
Aged 5 to 9	636	100.0	3.6	25.9	14.4	55.3
Aged 10 to 14	631	100.0	3.1	27.1	11.4	57.1
Aged 15 to 19	660	100.0	2.8	28.6	9.7	57.6
Aged 20 to 24	662	100.0	3.1	25.1	11.2	59.6
Aged 25 to 29	627	100.0	3.7	22.4	13.3	59.6
Aged 30 to 34	620	100.0	3.7	22.4	13.4	59.4
Aged 35 to 39	660	100.0	3.5	21.9	10.4	62.9
Aged 40 to 44	667	100.0	2.9	22.1	7.6	66.2
Aged 45 to 49	699	100.0	2.2	22.0	5.3	69.2
Aged 50 to 54	670	100.0	1.9	21.9	3.8	71.1
Aged 55 to 59	601	100.0	1.7	21.0	2.6	73.4
Aged 60 to 64	538	100.0	1.4	18.3	1.9	77.1
Aged 65 to 69	403	100.0	1.3	16.5	1.7	79.4
Aged 70 to 74	295	100.0	1.2	16.2	1.5	80.0
Aged 75 to 79	224	100.0	1.0	15.4	1.3	81.4
Aged 80 to 84	165	100.0	0.7	14.7	1.1	82.8
Aged 85 or older	147	100.0	0.5	15.2	0.9	82.8
North Dakota	**673**	**100.0**	**1.4**	**1.6**	**2.0**	**88.9**
Under age 5	45	100.0	1.8	4.2	4.5	79.0
Aged 5 to 9	40	100.0	1.7	3.2	3.8	80.9
Aged 10 to 14	40	100.0	1.4	2.7	3.1	83.4
Aged 15 to 19	47	100.0	1.6	2.3	2.9	84.8
Aged 20 to 24	59	100.0	2.9	2.8	2.8	85.1
Aged 25 to 29	50	100.0	2.2	2.3	2.7	86.4
Aged 30 to 34	41	100.0	1.9	2.0	2.5	86.8
Aged 35 to 39	37	100.0	1.9	1.5	2.0	88.1
Aged 40 to 44	38	100.0	1.4	1.1	1.6	89.6
Aged 45 to 49	46	100.0	0.9	0.7	1.2	91.7
Aged 50 to 54	50	100.0	0.6	0.6	1.0	93.4
Aged 55 to 59	46	100.0	0.5	0.5	0.7	94.7
Aged 60 to 64	36	100.0	0.7	0.4	0.6	95.0
Aged 65 to 69	26	100.0	0.6	0.3	0.5	95.5
Aged 70 to 74	21	100.0	0.4	0.2	0.4	96.3
Aged 75 to 79	18	100.0	0.3	0.1	0.4	97.0
Aged 80 to 84	16	100.0	0.3	0.1	0.3	97.9
Aged 85 or older	17	100.0	0.1	0.1	0.3	98.7

	total					non-Hispanic
	number	percent	Asian	black	Hispanic	white
Ohio	**11,537**	**100.0%**	**2.1%**	**13.4%**	**3.1%**	**81.1%**
Under age 5	721	100.0	3.0	19.7	6.2	71.3
Aged 5 to 9	748	100.0	2.8	17.7	5.2	74.2
Aged 10 to 14	775	100.0	2.2	17.1	4.3	76.1
Aged 15 to 19	824	100.0	2.1	17.4	3.9	76.2
Aged 20 to 24	763	100.0	2.7	15.4	4.1	77.5
Aged 25 to 29	719	100.0	3.1	14.1	4.3	78.2
Aged 30 to 34	691	100.0	3.1	13.7	4.1	78.7
Aged 35 to 39	718	100.0	2.9	13.2	3.4	80.0
Aged 40 to 44	761	100.0	2.2	12.1	2.7	82.4
Aged 45 to 49	855	100.0	1.7	11.7	2.1	83.9
Aged 50 to 54	887	100.0	1.3	11.5	1.7	84.8
Aged 55 to 59	787	100.0	1.3	10.7	1.4	86.1
Aged 60 to 64	665	100.0	1.2	9.6	1.3	87.4
Aged 65 to 69	479	100.0	1.2	9.1	1.1	88.1
Aged 70 to 74	371	100.0	1.1	9.2	1.0	88.3
Aged 75 to 79	298	100.0	0.8	9.0	1.0	88.8
Aged 80 to 84	244	100.0	0.6	8.0	0.8	90.2
Aged 85 or older	230	100.0	0.4	7.2	0.7	91.5
Oklahoma	**3,751**	**100.0**	**2.2**	**8.7**	**8.9**	**68.7**
Under age 5	264	100.0	2.9	12.8	16.8	53.0
Aged 5 to 9	259	100.0	2.7	11.9	15.0	55.3
Aged 10 to 14	254	100.0	2.5	11.6	12.6	57.6
Aged 15 to 19	264	100.0	2.6	11.5	11.3	59.8
Aged 20 to 24	269	100.0	3.0	10.3	11.8	62.9
Aged 25 to 29	266	100.0	3.0	9.2	12.0	64.0
Aged 30 to 34	241	100.0	2.8	9.0	11.8	64.6
Aged 35 to 39	233	100.0	2.9	8.4	10.2	66.9
Aged 40 to 44	228	100.0	2.5	8.0	8.5	70.0
Aged 45 to 49	261	100.0	1.9	7.7	6.2	73.5
Aged 50 to 54	264	100.0	1.7	7.6	4.6	76.1
Aged 55 to 59	236	100.0	1.6	6.8	3.6	78.6
Aged 60 to 64	205	100.0	1.4	5.8	2.8	81.1
Aged 65 to 69	159	100.0	1.2	5.1	2.3	83.0
Aged 70 to 74	121	100.0	1.1	4.7	2.0	84.4
Aged 75 to 79	95	100.0	0.9	4.4	1.7	86.1
Aged 80 to 84	69	100.0	0.7	4.0	1.5	88.0
Aged 85 or older	62	100.0	0.5	4.0	1.3	89.1

	total					non-Hispanic
	number	percent	Asian	black	Hispanic	white
Oregon	**3,831**	**100.0%**	**4.9%**	**2.6%**	**11.7%**	**78.5%**
Under age 5	238	100.0	6.6	4.7	23.3	63.2
Aged 5 to 9	237	100.0	6.6	4.2	21.8	65.0
Aged 10 to 14	243	100.0	6.0	4.1	19.5	67.7
Aged 15 to 19	255	100.0	5.9	3.8	16.9	70.4
Aged 20 to 24	253	100.0	6.0	3.2	15.1	72.8
Aged 25 to 29	265	100.0	5.5	2.8	15.0	74.1
Aged 30 to 34	259	100.0	5.8	2.7	15.3	73.8
Aged 35 to 39	251	100.0	6.4	2.5	14.3	74.4
Aged 40 to 44	248	100.0	5.4	2.3	11.5	78.2
Aged 45 to 49	263	100.0	4.6	2.1	8.3	82.4
Aged 50 to 54	276	100.0	3.8	1.9	5.9	85.9
Aged 55 to 59	273	100.0	3.2	1.5	4.3	88.8
Aged 60 to 64	236	100.0	2.8	1.3	3.4	90.4
Aged 65 to 69	170	100.0	2.6	1.1	2.9	91.5
Aged 70 to 74	120	100.0	2.7	1.1	2.7	91.8
Aged 75 to 79	92	100.0	2.5	0.9	2.2	92.9
Aged 80 to 84	74	100.0	2.3	0.8	1.9	94.0
Aged 85 or older	78	100.0	1.7	0.7	1.5	95.3
Pennsylvania	**12,702**	**100.0**	**3.2**	**11.9**	**5.7**	**79.5**
Under age 5	730	100.0	4.5	17.9	10.9	67.9
Aged 5 to 9	754	100.0	4.2	16.3	9.6	70.8
Aged 10 to 14	791	100.0	3.5	15.8	8.5	72.8
Aged 15 to 19	905	100.0	3.4	16.1	7.9	73.1
Aged 20 to 24	874	100.0	4.3	14.5	7.7	73.9
Aged 25 to 29	782	100.0	4.8	12.9	7.8	74.7
Aged 30 to 34	730	100.0	4.8	12.9	7.9	74.7
Aged 35 to 39	764	100.0	4.5	12.0	6.7	76.9
Aged 40 to 44	851	100.0	3.4	11.4	5.6	79.7
Aged 45 to 49	956	100.0	2.7	10.6	4.3	82.3
Aged 50 to 54	985	100.0	2.2	9.9	3.3	84.4
Aged 55 to 59	879	100.0	2.1	9.0	2.7	86.0
Aged 60 to 64	743	100.0	2.0	8.2	2.4	87.3
Aged 65 to 69	553	100.0	1.8	7.7	2.1	88.2
Aged 70 to 74	427	100.0	1.7	7.5	1.8	88.9
Aged 75 to 79	362	100.0	1.3	7.0	1.4	90.1
Aged 80 to 84	312	100.0	0.8	5.9	1.1	92.0
Aged 85 or older	306	100.0	0.6	5.6	0.8	92.9

	total					non-Hispanic
	number	percent	Asian	black	Hispanic	white
Rhode Island	**1,053**	**100.0%**	**3.5%**	**7.4%**	**12.4%**	**76.4%**
Under age 5	57	100.0	5.2	13.4	23.2	59.2
Aged 5 to 9	60	100.0	4.6	11.7	20.7	63.4
Aged 10 to 14	64	100.0	3.9	10.8	19.1	66.3
Aged 15 to 19	80	100.0	4.6	10.3	17.3	67.8
Aged 20 to 24	82	100.0	5.6	9.1	15.3	69.7
Aged 25 to 29	66	100.0	5.7	8.7	16.9	68.3
Aged 30 to 34	61	100.0	4.9	8.5	16.7	69.3
Aged 35 to 39	64	100.0	4.0	7.7	14.7	73.1
Aged 40 to 44	73	100.0	3.1	6.7	12.3	77.2
Aged 45 to 49	81	100.0	2.6	5.9	9.4	81.4
Aged 50 to 54	81	100.0	2.3	5.6	7.5	83.9
Aged 55 to 59	71	100.0	2.1	4.8	6.2	86.3
Aged 60 to 64	60	100.0	1.9	3.8	5.2	88.5
Aged 65 to 69	43	100.0	1.7	3.4	4.8	89.4
Aged 70 to 74	31	100.0	1.8	3.7	4.4	89.3
Aged 75 to 79	27	100.0	1.2	3.3	3.4	91.3
Aged 80 to 84	25	100.0	0.9	2.6	2.3	93.5
Aged 85 or older	27	100.0	0.6	1.8	1.6	95.2
South Carolina	**4,625**	**100.0**	**1.6**	**28.8**	**5.1**	**64.1**
Under age 5	302	100.0	2.2	35.7	9.9	52.2
Aged 5 to 9	296	100.0	2.2	34.0	8.0	55.7
Aged 10 to 14	297	100.0	1.9	34.4	6.0	57.4
Aged 15 to 19	329	100.0	1.7	35.6	5.6	56.7
Aged 20 to 24	332	100.0	1.8	32.2	7.5	58.2
Aged 25 to 29	304	100.0	2.2	29.8	9.0	58.7
Aged 30 to 34	288	100.0	2.2	29.2	8.4	59.8
Aged 35 to 39	297	100.0	2.2	27.5	6.5	63.3
Aged 40 to 44	305	100.0	1.8	27.8	4.9	64.9
Aged 45 to 49	333	100.0	1.5	27.8	3.3	66.7
Aged 50 to 54	327	100.0	1.3	27.9	2.5	67.6
Aged 55 to 59	303	100.0	1.2	26.8	1.8	69.6
Aged 60 to 64	281	100.0	1.0	23.1	1.4	74.0
Aged 65 to 69	216	100.0	0.9	20.6	1.2	76.8
Aged 70 to 74	153	100.0	0.9	20.3	1.1	77.4
Aged 75 to 79	113	100.0	0.7	19.4	1.0	78.6
Aged 80 to 84	79	100.0	0.5	18.9	0.9	79.4
Aged 85 or older	71	100.0	0.4	20.0	0.8	78.6

	total					non-Hispanic
	number	percent	Asian	black	Hispanic	white
South Dakota	**814**	**100.0%**	**1.3%**	**1.8%**	**2.7%**	**84.7%**
Under age 5	60	100.0	1.8	4.2	5.4	72.7
Aged 5 to 9	56	100.0	1.7	3.5	4.7	74.5
Aged 10 to 14	54	100.0	1.7	2.9	4.0	76.8
Aged 15 to 19	58	100.0	1.6	2.4	3.6	78.6
Aged 20 to 24	58	100.0	2.1	2.4	3.7	80.3
Aged 25 to 29	56	100.0	1.7	2.5	3.7	81.4
Aged 30 to 34	50	100.0	1.7	2.0	3.7	82.7
Aged 35 to 39	46	100.0	1.7	1.9	3.0	83.8
Aged 40 to 44	47	100.0	1.3	1.5	2.6	85.4
Aged 45 to 49	58	100.0	1.0	1.1	1.9	88.4
Aged 50 to 54	59	100.0	0.8	0.8	1.3	90.6
Aged 55 to 59	54	100.0	0.6	0.6	0.9	92.3
Aged 60 to 64	44	100.0	0.6	0.4	0.8	92.9
Aged 65 to 69	32	100.0	0.4	0.3	0.7	93.9
Aged 70 to 74	26	100.0	0.4	0.3	0.6	94.4
Aged 75 to 79	22	100.0	0.3	0.2	0.5	95.8
Aged 80 to 84	18	100.0	0.2	0.2	0.4	96.8
Aged 85 or older	19	100.0	0.1	0.2	0.5	97.6
Tennessee	**6,346**	**100.0**	**1.8**	**17.4**	**4.6**	**75.6**
Under age 5	408	100.0	2.5	23.1	9.6	64.6
Aged 5 to 9	412	100.0	2.5	21.7	7.7	67.8
Aged 10 to 14	419	100.0	2.0	22.2	5.8	69.5
Aged 15 to 19	437	100.0	1.9	23.0	5.2	69.4
Aged 20 to 24	426	100.0	2.0	21.0	6.8	69.7
Aged 25 to 29	418	100.0	2.4	18.9	7.8	70.4
Aged 30 to 34	406	100.0	2.5	18.2	7.3	71.5
Aged 35 to 39	424	100.0	2.4	17.2	5.5	74.3
Aged 40 to 44	431	100.0	2.0	16.6	4.0	76.7
Aged 45 to 49	467	100.0	1.5	16.2	2.8	78.7
Aged 50 to 54	459	100.0	1.3	16.2	2.1	79.7
Aged 55 to 59	415	100.0	1.2	15.1	1.5	81.4
Aged 60 to 64	371	100.0	1.0	12.2	1.2	84.8
Aged 65 to 69	281	100.0	0.9	10.3	1.0	87.1
Aged 70 to 74	207	100.0	0.8	10.1	0.9	87.7
Aged 75 to 79	155	100.0	0.7	9.9	0.8	88.1
Aged 80 to 84	112	100.0	0.5	9.4	0.7	88.9
Aged 85 or older	100	100.0	0.3	9.6	0.6	89.1

| | total | | | | | non-Hispanic |
	number	percent	Asian	black	Hispanic	white
Texas	**25,146**	**100.0%**	**4.4%**	**12.6%**	**37.6%**	**45.3%**
Under age 5	1,928	100.0	4.7	14.2	50.6	31.7
Aged 5 to 9	1,928	100.0	4.7	13.8	49.1	33.2
Aged 10 to 14	1,882	100.0	4.2	14.1	46.9	35.2
Aged 15 to 19	1,883	100.0	4.0	14.6	44.9	36.7
Aged 20 to 24	1,817	100.0	4.5	13.5	42.8	39.2
Aged 25 to 29	1,853	100.0	5.1	12.7	41.8	40.3
Aged 30 to 34	1,760	100.0	5.5	12.8	42.1	39.6
Aged 35 to 39	1,764	100.0	5.9	12.6	40.1	41.2
Aged 40 to 44	1,695	100.0	5.2	12.7	36.7	45.0
Aged 45 to 49	1,760	100.0	4.3	12.7	31.7	50.7
Aged 50 to 54	1,675	100.0	3.9	12.4	27.8	55.3
Aged 55 to 59	1,423	100.0	3.9	11.6	25.2	58.7
Aged 60 to 64	1,175	100.0	3.6	10.2	23.2	62.3
Aged 65 to 69	853	100.0	3.3	9.2	21.6	65.2
Aged 70 to 74	619	100.0	3.1	8.8	21.5	66.0
Aged 75 to 79	477	100.0	2.5	8.5	20.5	68.1
Aged 80 to 84	347	100.0	2.0	7.7	19.4	70.4
Aged 85 or older	305	100.0	1.5	7.8	16.4	73.9
Utah	**2,764**	**100.0**	**2.8**	**1.6**	**13.0**	**80.4**
Under age 5	264	100.0	2.9	2.5	17.2	74.9
Aged 5 to 9	250	100.0	2.9	2.4	16.6	75.6
Aged 10 to 14	228	100.0	2.9	2.3	16.1	76.0
Aged 15 to 19	221	100.0	3.1	2.1	15.3	76.5
Aged 20 to 24	227	100.0	3.4	1.8	14.1	78.1
Aged 25 to 29	230	100.0	3.2	1.4	13.7	79.2
Aged 30 to 34	216	100.0	2.9	1.3	14.3	79.4
Aged 35 to 39	178	100.0	3.2	1.3	15.4	77.9
Aged 40 to 44	154	100.0	3.2	1.3	14.3	79.0
Aged 45 to 49	155	100.0	2.8	1.2	11.2	82.6
Aged 50 to 54	152	100.0	2.4	1.0	8.7	85.9
Aged 55 to 59	133	100.0	2.3	0.8	7.0	88.1
Aged 60 to 64	107	100.0	2.2	0.7	6.0	89.6
Aged 65 to 69	79	100.0	1.8	0.5	5.2	91.0
Aged 70 to 74	59	100.0	1.7	0.5	4.8	91.8
Aged 75 to 79	46	100.0	1.6	0.4	4.2	92.9
Aged 80 to 84	34	100.0	1.6	0.4	3.6	93.6
Aged 85 or older	31	100.0	1.6	0.5	2.9	94.2

	total					non-Hispanic
	number	percent	Asian	black	Hispanic	white
Vermont	**626**	**100.0%**	**1.7%**	**1.5%**	**1.5%**	**94.3%**
Under age 5	32	100.0	2.7	3.9	2.5	89.9
Aged 5 to 9	35	100.0	2.7	3.3	2.3	90.7
Aged 10 to 14	38	100.0	2.4	2.8	2.0	91.6
Aged 15 to 19	46	100.0	2.7	2.6	2.6	91.2
Aged 20 to 24	44	100.0	2.6	2.2	2.6	91.6
Aged 25 to 29	35	100.0	2.4	2.0	2.0	92.5
Aged 30 to 34	34	100.0	2.3	1.7	1.8	93.1
Aged 35 to 39	36	100.0	2.4	1.3	1.5	93.7
Aged 40 to 44	42	100.0	1.7	1.0	1.2	95.0
Aged 45 to 49	50	100.0	1.2	0.8	1.1	95.7
Aged 50 to 54	52	100.0	0.9	0.7	0.8	96.3
Aged 55 to 59	49	100.0	0.8	0.6	0.7	96.7
Aged 60 to 64	41	100.0	0.7	0.4	0.7	97.1
Aged 65 to 69	29	100.0	0.5	0.4	0.6	97.5
Aged 70 to 74	20	100.0	0.6	0.3	0.5	97.9
Aged 75 to 79	16	100.0	0.5	0.3	0.7	97.8
Aged 80 to 84	13	100.0	0.4	0.2	0.6	98.1
Aged 85 or older	13	100.0	0.3	0.3	0.7	98.4
Virginia	**8,001**	**100.0**	**6.5**	**20.7**	**7.9**	**64.8**
Under age 5	510	100.0	8.6	24.9	13.4	53.9
Aged 5 to 9	512	100.0	8.3	24.4	11.3	56.6
Aged 10 to 14	511	100.0	7.1	24.7	9.8	58.7
Aged 15 to 19	551	100.0	6.3	25.8	9.0	59.0
Aged 20 to 24	572	100.0	6.5	22.9	10.5	60.1
Aged 25 to 29	564	100.0	7.8	20.8	11.7	59.7
Aged 30 to 34	526	100.0	8.8	20.2	12.1	58.8
Aged 35 to 39	540	100.0	9.1	19.5	10.1	61.2
Aged 40 to 44	569	100.0	7.3	20.1	8.0	64.3
Aged 45 to 49	621	100.0	5.9	20.2	6.0	67.5
Aged 50 to 54	593	100.0	5.2	19.8	4.7	69.8
Aged 55 to 59	513	100.0	4.8	18.6	3.6	72.5
Aged 60 to 64	442	100.0	4.5	16.1	2.8	76.1
Aged 65 to 69	320	100.0	4.3	15.4	2.4	77.4
Aged 70 to 74	230	100.0	4.2	15.9	2.2	77.4
Aged 75 to 79	174	100.0	3.5	15.5	1.9	78.8
Aged 80 to 84	131	100.0	2.6	14.3	1.6	81.2
Aged 85 or older	122	100.0	1.8	14.2	1.4	82.3

	total					non-Hispanic
	number	percent	Asian	black	Hispanic	white
Washington	**6,725**	**100.0%**	**9.0%**	**4.8%**	**11.2%**	**72.5%**
Under age 5	440	100.0	11.3	8.2	21.7	57.0
Aged 5 to 9	430	100.0	10.9	7.5	19.6	59.8
Aged 10 to 14	438	100.0	9.8	7.1	17.4	62.9
Aged 15 to 19	462	100.0	10.0	6.5	15.5	65.0
Aged 20 to 24	462	100.0	10.2	5.8	14.9	66.3
Aged 25 to 29	480	100.0	10.5	5.3	14.5	67.0
Aged 30 to 34	453	100.0	10.9	5.0	14.4	67.0
Aged 35 to 39	449	100.0	11.2	4.7	12.9	68.6
Aged 40 to 44	460	100.0	9.5	4.5	10.2	73.3
Aged 45 to 49	493	100.0	8.1	4.1	7.4	77.7
Aged 50 to 54	495	100.0	7.3	3.8	5.7	80.7
Aged 55 to 59	453	100.0	6.8	3.1	4.3	83.4
Aged 60 to 64	382	100.0	6.3	2.6	3.6	85.5
Aged 65 to 69	270	100.0	6.0	2.2	3.2	86.7
Aged 70 to 74	187	100.0	6.5	2.1	2.9	86.6
Aged 75 to 79	142	100.0	6.1	1.9	2.5	87.9
Aged 80 to 84	111	100.0	5.2	1.7	2.1	89.9
Aged 85 or older	117	100.0	4.0	1.5	1.5	92.3
West Virginia	**1,853**	**100.0**	**0.9**	**4.2**	**1.2**	**93.2**
Under age 5	104	100.0	1.3	7.2	2.4	88.8
Aged 5 to 9	106	100.0	1.2	6.2	2.0	90.2
Aged 10 to 14	109	100.0	1.0	5.8	1.7	90.9
Aged 15 to 19	120	100.0	1.0	5.9	1.7	90.8
Aged 20 to 24	117	100.0	1.4	5.6	1.8	90.7
Aged 25 to 29	108	100.0	1.4	4.7	1.7	91.5
Aged 30 to 34	112	100.0	1.2	4.5	1.6	92.2
Aged 35 to 39	117	100.0	1.1	3.8	1.3	93.2
Aged 40 to 44	120	100.0	0.9	3.5	1.1	93.9
Aged 45 to 49	133	100.0	0.7	3.5	0.9	94.1
Aged 50 to 54	143	100.0	0.6	3.5	0.7	94.4
Aged 55 to 59	139	100.0	0.6	3.2	0.6	94.9
Aged 60 to 64	125	100.0	0.6	2.6	0.5	95.6
Aged 65 to 69	92	100.0	0.6	2.2	0.5	95.9
Aged 70 to 74	72	100.0	0.5	2.1	0.5	96.3
Aged 75 to 79	55	100.0	0.4	2.1	0.4	96.6
Aged 80 to 84	43	100.0	0.2	2.4	0.4	96.4
Aged 85 or older	36	100.0	0.2	2.5	0.4	96.4

	total		Asian	black	Hispanic	non-Hispanic white
	number	percent				
Wisconsin	**5,687**	**100.0%**	**2.7%**	**7.1%**	**5.9%**	**83.3%**
Under age 5	358	100.0	4.6	12.5	12.3	69.9
Aged 5 to 9	369	100.0	4.1	11.1	10.9	72.9
Aged 10 to 14	376	100.0	3.7	10.8	9.0	75.5
Aged 15 to 19	399	100.0	3.8	10.3	7.6	77.0
Aged 20 to 24	387	100.0	4.2	8.6	7.5	78.5
Aged 25 to 29	372	100.0	4.1	8.0	8.4	78.4
Aged 30 to 34	349	100.0	3.5	7.8	8.6	79.1
Aged 35 to 39	345	100.0	3.1	7.5	7.4	80.9
Aged 40 to 44	380	100.0	2.3	6.3	5.3	84.9
Aged 45 to 49	438	100.0	1.7	5.4	3.6	88.2
Aged 50 to 54	436	100.0	1.3	5.0	2.8	89.8
Aged 55 to 59	386	100.0	1.2	4.5	2.2	91.2
Aged 60 to 64	314	100.0	1.1	3.9	1.9	92.3
Aged 65 to 69	227	100.0	1.0	3.4	1.6	93.2
Aged 70 to 74	173	100.0	1.0	3.2	1.4	93.7
Aged 75 to 79	141	100.0	0.8	2.8	1.2	94.6
Aged 80 to 84	117	100.0	0.6	2.2	1.0	95.9
Aged 85 or older	119	100.0	0.5	1.6	0.7	96.8
Wyoming	**564**	**100.0**	**1.2**	**1.3**	**8.9**	**85.9**
Under age 5	40	100.0	1.5	2.5	14.8	77.5
Aged 5 to 9	37	100.0	1.5	2.0	13.9	78.8
Aged 10 to 14	36	100.0	1.5	2.0	12.7	80.1
Aged 15 to 19	38	100.0	1.4	2.0	11.1	81.9
Aged 20 to 24	40	100.0	2.1	2.2	11.0	81.8
Aged 25 to 29	41	100.0	1.6	1.3	11.0	83.3
Aged 30 to 34	36	100.0	1.4	1.2	10.7	84.0
Aged 35 to 39	34	100.0	1.5	1.1	9.9	84.6
Aged 40 to 44	33	100.0	1.2	1.0	8.4	86.4
Aged 45 to 49	39	100.0	0.9	0.9	6.9	88.7
Aged 50 to 54	44	100.0	0.8	0.8	5.6	90.6
Aged 55 to 59	41	100.0	0.8	0.6	4.7	91.9
Aged 60 to 64	33	100.0	0.6	0.5	4.4	92.4
Aged 65 to 69	23	100.0	0.5	0.4	4.0	93.2
Aged 70 to 74	17	100.0	0.5	0.5	4.3	92.9
Aged 75 to 79	12	100.0	0.5	0.6	4.2	93.1
Aged 80 to 84	9	100.0	0.4	0.5	3.7	94.3
Aged 85 or older	9	100.0	0.4	0.6	3.0	95.1

Note: Asians and blacks are those who identify themselves as being of the race alone and those who identify themselves as being of the race in combination with other races. Numbers do not add to total because not all races are shown, some mixed-race individuals are counted more than once, and Hispanics may be of any race. Non-Hispanic whites are those who identify themselves as being white alone and not Hispanic.
Source: Bureau of the Census, 2010 Census, American Factfinder, Population Estimates, http://factfinder2.census.gov/faces/nav/jsf/pages/index.xhtml; calculations by New Strategist

9

Spending

■ The Great Recession has been devastating to young adults. Households headed by people under age 25 cut their spending by 10 percent between 2006 and 2010, after adjusting for inflation.

■ Households headed by people aged 25 to 34 cut their spending by 9 percent between 2006 and 2010, after adjusting for inflation. Their spending in 2010 was 5 percent below the level of 2000.

■ Many members of the Millennial generation are adults living at home with their parents. Couples with adult children at home spent $67,057 in 2010, nearly 12 percent less than in 2006, after adjusting for inflation.

Spending Has Dropped among Young Adults

Their spending on new cars has plunged.

Households headed by people under age 25 cut their spending by 10 percent between 2006 and 2010, after adjusting for inflation. The Great Recession has been so devastating to young adults that households headed by people under age 25 spent 4 percent less in 2010 than they did in 2000.

Householders under age 25 reduced their spending on many discretionary items between 2006 and 2010. Their spending on food away from home fell 12 percent, after adjusting for inflation. Their spending on alcoholic beverages was down an even larger 21 percent. Spending on new cars and trucks fell by a stunning 61 percent. Spending on mortgage interest, which had doubled between 2000 and 2006, fell 30 percent between 2006 and 2010 as young adults entering the age group decided against buying a home.

Many householders under age 25 are in college, and their spending on education climbed 40 percent between 2006 and 2010 despite the Great Recession. At the same time, these householders cut their spending on entertainment by 16 percent.

■ The Great Recession has been a major setback for young adults. Because many are in debt, it will take years for them to regain economic stability.

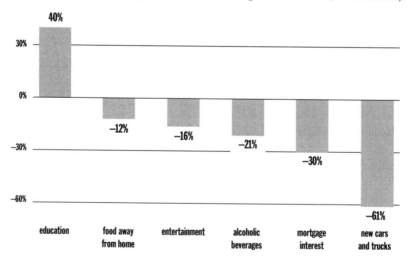

Young adults are spending much less on many items

(percent change in spending by householders under age 30, 2006 to 2010; in 2010 dollars)

Table 9.1 Average Household Spending, 2000 to 2010

(average annual spending of consumer units on products and services, 2000 to 2010; percent change for selected years; in 2010 dollars)

	average spending			percent change		
	2010	2006	2000	2006–10	2000–06	2000–10
Number of consumer units (in 000s)	121,107	118,843	109,367	1.9%	8.7%	10.7%
Average annual spending of consumer units	$48,109	$52,349	$48,176	–8.1	8.7	–0.1
FOOD	6,129	6,610	6,532	–7.3	1.2	–6.2
Food at home	3,624	3,696	3,825	–1.9	–3.4	–5.3
Cereals and bakery products	502	482	574	4.1	–15.9	–12.5
Cereals and cereal products	165	155	198	6.7	–21.7	–16.5
Bakery products	337	329	376	2.5	–12.6	–10.4
Meats, poultry, fish, and eggs	784	862	1,007	–9.1	–14.4	–22.1
Beef	217	255	301	–15.0	–15.3	–28.0
Pork	149	170	211	–12.3	–19.7	–29.5
Other meats	117	114	128	3.0	–11.2	–8.5
Poultry	138	153	184	–9.5	–16.9	–24.8
Fish and seafood	117	132	139	–11.3	–5.3	–16.0
Eggs	46	40	43	14.9	–7.0	6.8
Dairy products	380	398	412	–4.5	–3.3	–7.7
Fresh milk and cream	141	151	166	–6.9	–8.7	–15.0
Other dairy products	240	247	244	–2.7	0.9	–1.8
Fruits and vegetables	679	640	660	6.0	–2.9	2.9
Fresh fruits	232	211	206	10.0	2.2	12.4
Fresh vegetables	210	209	201	0.6	3.7	4.3
Processed fruits	113	118	146	–4.2	–19.0	–22.4
Processed vegetables	124	103	106	20.7	–3.4	16.6
Other food at home	1,278	1,311	1,174	–2.5	11.7	8.9
Sugar and other sweets	132	135	148	–2.4	–8.7	–10.9
Fats and oils	103	93	105	10.7	–11.5	–2.0
Miscellaneous foods	667	678	553	–1.6	22.6	20.5
Nonalcoholic beverages	333	359	317	–7.3	13.4	5.2
Food prepared by consumer unit on trips	43	47	51	–7.5	–8.2	–15.1
Food away from home	2,505	2,914	2,706	–14.0	7.7	–7.4
ALCOHOLIC BEVERAGES	412	538	471	–23.4	14.1	–12.5
HOUSING	16,557	17,702	15,599	–6.5	13.5	6.1
Shelter	9,812	10,463	9,008	–6.2	16.1	8.9
Owned dwellings	6,277	7,048	5,827	–10.9	20.9	7.7
Mortgage interest and charges	3,351	4,059	3,342	–17.4	21.5	0.3
Property taxes	1,814	1,784	1,442	1.7	23.7	25.8
Maintenance, repair, insurance, other expenses	1,112	1,206	1,045	–7.8	15.4	6.4
Rented dwellings	2,900	2,801	2,576	3.5	8.8	12.6
Other lodging	635	613	605	3.5	1.3	4.9
Utilities, fuels, and public services	3,660	3,674	3,152	–0.4	16.6	16.1
Natural gas	440	551	389	–20.1	41.6	13.2
Electricity	1,413	1,369	1,154	3.2	18.7	22.5
Fuel oil and other fuels	140	149	123	–6.2	21.5	14.0

	average spending			percent change		
	2010	2006	2000	2006–10	2000–06	2000–10
Telephone	$1,178	$1,176	$1,111	0.2%	5.9%	6.1%
Water and other public services	489	429	375	13.9	14.6	30.5
Household services	**1,007**	**1,025**	**866**	**−1.8**	**18.4**	**16.3**
Personal services	340	425	413	−20.0	3.0	−17.6
Other household services	667	600	453	11.1	32.4	47.1
Housekeeping supplies	**612**	**692**	**610**	**−11.6**	**13.4**	**0.3**
Laundry and cleaning supplies	150	163	166	−8.2	−1.5	−9.6
Other household products	329	357	286	−7.8	24.7	15.0
Postage and stationery	132	172	160	−23.2	7.8	−17.3
Household furnishings and equipment	**1,467**	**1,847**	**1,961**	**−20.6**	**−5.8**	**−25.2**
Household textiles	102	167	134	−38.8	24.1	−24.0
Furniture	355	501	495	−29.1	1.1	−28.3
Floor coverings	36	52	56	−30.7	−6.8	−35.4
Major appliances	209	261	239	−19.8	8.9	−12.7
Small appliances and miscellaneous housewares	107	118	110	−9.2	7.0	−2.9
Miscellaneous household equipment	657	750	926	−12.3	−19.0	−29.0
APPAREL AND RELATED SERVICES	**1,700**	**2,027**	**2,350**	**−16.1**	**−13.8**	**−27.7**
Men and boys	**382**	**480**	**557**	**−20.5**	**−13.8**	**−31.4**
Men, aged 16 or older	304	382	436	−20.4	−12.3	−30.2
Boys, aged 2 to 15	78	98	122	−20.8	−19.0	−35.8
Women and girls	**663**	**812**	**918**	**−18.4**	**−11.5**	**−27.8**
Women, aged 16 or older	562	680	769	−17.4	−11.5	−26.9
Girls, aged 2 to 15	101	132	149	−23.5	−11.7	−32.4
Children under age 2	**91**	**104**	**104**	**−12.4**	**0.0**	**−12.4**
Footwear	**303**	**329**	**434**	**−7.9**	**−24.3**	**−30.2**
Other apparel products and services	**261**	**303**	**337**	**−13.8**	**−10.1**	**−22.5**
TRANSPORTATION	**7,677**	**9,202**	**9,392**	**−16.6**	**−2.0**	**−18.3**
Vehicle purchases	**2,588**	**3,700**	**4,328**	**−30.1**	**−14.5**	**−40.2**
Cars and trucks, new	1,219	1,945	2,032	−37.3	−4.3	−40.0
Cars and trucks, used	1,318	1,696	2,241	−22.3	−24.3	−41.2
Gasoline and motor oil	**2,132**	**2,409**	**1,635**	**−11.5**	**47.3**	**30.4**
Other vehicle expenses	**2,464**	**2,547**	**2,888**	**−3.3**	**−11.8**	**−14.7**
Vehicle finance charges	243	322	415	−24.6	−22.4	−41.5
Maintenance and repairs	787	744	790	5.8	−5.8	−0.4
Vehicle insurance	1,010	958	985	5.4	−2.7	2.5
Vehicle rentals, leases, licenses, other charges	423	521	698	−18.9	−25.3	−39.4
Public transportation	**493**	**546**	**541**	**−9.7**	**1.0**	**−8.8**
HEALTH CARE	**3,157**	**2,992**	**2,616**	**5.5**	**14.4**	**20.7**
Health insurance	1,831	1,585	1,245	15.6	27.3	47.1
Medical services	722	725	719	−0.4	0.8	0.4
Drugs	485	556	527	−12.8	5.5	−7.9
Medical supplies	119	127	125	−6.0	0.9	−5.1
ENTERTAINMENT	**2,504**	**2,570**	**2,359**	**−2.6**	**8.9**	**6.1**
Fees and admissions	581	655	652	−11.4	0.5	−10.9
Television, radio, and sound equipment	954	980	788	−2.6	24.4	21.1
Pets, toys, and playground equipment	606	446	423	36.0	5.4	43.3
Other entertainment products and services	364	488	498	−25.4	−2.0	−26.9

	average spending			percent change		
	2010	2006	2000	2006–10	2000–06	2000–10
PERSONAL CARE PRODUCTS AND SERVICES	$582	$633	$714	–8.0%	–11.4%	–18.5%
READING	100	127	185	–21.0	–31.5	–45.9
EDUCATION	1,074	960	800	11.8	20.0	34.2
TOBACCO PRODUCTS AND SMOKING SUPPLIES	362	354	404	2.3	–12.4	–10.4
MISCELLANEOUS	849	915	983	–7.2	–6.9	–13.6
CASH CONTRIBUTIONS	1,633	2,022	1,509	–19.2	33.9	8.2
PERSONAL INSURANCE AND PENSIONS	5,373	5,700	4,261	–5.7	33.8	26.1
Life and other personal insurance	318	348	505	–8.7	–31.1	–37.1
Pensions and Social Security*	5,054	5,352	–	–5.6	–	–
PERSONAL TAXES	1,769	2,631	3,947	–32.8	–33.4	–55.2
Federal income taxes	1,136	1,851	3,051	–38.6	–39.3	–62.8
State and local income taxes	482	561	712	–14.1	–21.1	–32.3
Other taxes	151	218	185	–30.9	18.2	–18.3
GIFTS FOR PEOPLE IN OTHER HOUSEHOLDS	1,029	1,248	1,371	–17.6	–9.0	–25.0

Because of changes in methodology, the 2006 and 2010 data on pensions and Social Security are not comparable with earlier years.

Note: The Bureau of Labor Statistics uses consumer unit rather than household as the sampling unit in the Consumer Expenditure Survey. For the definition of consumer unit, see the glossary. Spending on gifts is also included in the preceding product and service categories.

Source: Bureau of Labor Statistics, 2000, 2006, and 2010 Consumer Expenditure Surveys, Internet site http://www.bls.gov/cex/; calculations by New Strategist

Table 9.2 Average Spending by Householders under Age 25, 2000 to 2010

(average annual spending of consumer units headed by people under age 25 on products and services, 2000 to 2010; percent change for selected years; in 2010 dollars)

	average spending			percent change		
	2010	2006	2000	2006–10	2000–06	2000–10
Number of consumer units under 25 (in 000s)	8,034	8,167	8,306	–1.6%	–1.7%	–3.3%
Average annual spending of consumer units	$27,483	$30,481	$28,546	–9.8	6.8	–3.7
FOOD	**4,073**	**4,239**	**4,069**	**–3.9**	**4.2**	**0.1**
Food at home	**2,197**	**2,105**	**2,081**	**4.4**	**1.2**	**5.6**
Cereals and bakery products	312	260	301	20.2	–13.9	3.5
Cereals and cereal products	103	102	114	1.3	–10.8	–9.6
Bakery products	209	158	187	32.3	–15.7	11.5
Meats, poultry, fish, and eggs	447	469	553	–4.8	–15.2	–19.2
Beef	136	140	171	–2.5	–18.4	–20.4
Pork	83	96	113	–13.8	–14.6	–26.4
Other meats	69	64	70	8.1	–8.4	–0.9
Poultry	84	87	109	–2.9	–20.5	–22.9
Fish and seafood	45	57	66	–21.5	–12.9	–31.7
Eggs	31	25	27	24.6	–6.4	16.6
Dairy products	218	237	222	–8.0	6.9	–1.6
Fresh milk and cream	88	100	92	–11.6	7.6	–4.8
Other dairy products	130	137	128	–5.4	7.4	1.6
Fruits and vegetables	395	345	320	14.5	7.7	23.3
Fresh fruits	119	107	98	11.1	9.8	22.0
Fresh vegetables	131	107	94	22.3	14.3	39.8
Processed fruits	68	74	79	–7.5	–6.3	–13.4
Processed vegetables	77	57	52	34.3	10.4	48.3
Other food at home	826	794	685	4.0	15.9	20.6
Sugar and other sweets	63	75	76	–15.6	–1.8	–17.1
Fats and oils	64	51	53	25.9	–4.4	20.3
Miscellaneous foods	463	434	343	6.7	26.4	34.9
Nonalcoholic beverages	223	216	186	3.1	16.2	19.8
Food prepared by consumer unit on trips	13	17	24	–24.9	–28.1	–46.0
Food away from home	**1,876**	**2,134**	**1,987**	**–12.1**	**7.4**	**–5.6**
ALCOHOLIC BEVERAGES	**406**	**512**	**496**	**–20.6**	**3.1**	**–18.2**
HOUSING	**9,553**	**10,119**	**9,002**	**–5.6**	**12.4**	**6.1**
Shelter	**6,166**	**6,406**	**5,792**	**–3.8**	**10.6**	**6.5**
Owned dwellings	1,123	1,520	803	–26.1	89.3	39.9
Mortgage interest and charges	686	984	489	–30.3	101.4	40.3
Property taxes	252	387	223	–34.9	73.7	13.1
Maintenance, repair, insurance, other expenses	185	148	91	24.8	62.5	102.9
Rented dwellings	4,813	4,667	4,581	3.1	1.9	5.1
Other lodging	231	220	408	5.2	–46.2	–43.3
Utilities, fuels, and public services	**1,818**	**1,926**	**1,580**	**–5.6**	**21.9**	**15.0**
Natural gas	186	201	129	–7.5	55.8	44.0
Electricity	716	750	562	–4.5	33.3	27.3
Fuel oil and other fuels	20	32	27	–38.4	22.0	–24.8

	average spending			percent change		
	2010	2006	2000	2006–10	2000–06	2000–10
Telephone	$713	$781	$746	–8.7%	4.7%	–4.4%
Water and other public services	184	162	115	13.4	40.8	59.7
Household services	**416**	**405**	**286**	**2.8**	**41.4**	**45.4**
Personal services	154	230	195	–33.2	18.1	–21.0
Other household services	261	174	91	49.9	91.0	186.3
Housekeeping supplies	**279**	**319**	**246**	**–12.6**	**29.9**	**13.6**
Laundry and cleaning supplies	90	90	70	0.3	28.9	29.2
Other household products	155	161	113	–3.8	43.0	37.5
Postage and stationery	34	69	63	–50.9	9.3	–46.3
Household furnishings and equipment	**874**	**1,062**	**1,098**	**–17.7**	**–3.3**	**–20.4**
Household textiles	53	61	44	–12.5	36.7	19.6
Furniture	268	379	342	–29.2	10.7	–21.6
Floor coverings	8	26	8	–69.2	241.7	5.3
Major appliances	92	112	98	–18.2	15.4	–5.6
Small appliances and miscellaneous housewares	45	56	63	–20.0	–11.2	–28.9
Miscellaneous household equipment	409	428	543	–4.5	–21.2	–24.7
APPAREL AND RELATED SERVICES	**1,559**	**1,584**	**1,798**	**–1.5**	**–11.9**	**–13.3**
Men and boys	**260**	**318**	**405**	**–18.2**	**–21.5**	**–35.8**
Men, aged 16 or older	219	295	372	–25.8	–20.7	–41.2
Boys, aged 2 to 15	41	23	33	80.5	–31.0	24.5
Women and girls	**670**	**599**	**551**	**11.8**	**8.8**	**21.6**
Women, aged 16 or older	628	562	513	11.7	9.7	22.5
Girls, aged 2 to 15	42	36	39	17.7	–9.1	7.0
Children under age 2	**146**	**141**	**128**	**3.8**	**9.9**	**14.2**
Footwear	**305**	**271**	**460**	**12.3**	**–40.9**	**–33.6**
Other apparel products and services	**177**	**253**	**255**	**–30.1**	**–0.6**	**–30.5**
TRANSPORTATION	**4,692**	**6,130**	**6,571**	**–23.5**	**–6.7**	**–28.6**
Vehicle purchases	**1,591**	**2,592**	**3,328**	**–38.6**	**–22.1**	**–52.2**
Cars and trucks, new	393	1,020	1,344	–61.5	–24.1	–70.7
Cars and trucks, used	1,107	1,521	1,959	–27.2	–22.4	–43.5
Gasoline and motor oil	**1,493**	**1,771**	**1,199**	**–15.7**	**47.7**	**24.5**
Other vehicle expenses	**1,333**	**1,528**	**1,769**	**–12.8**	**–13.6**	**–24.6**
Vehicle finance charges	137	215	289	–36.4	–25.4	–52.5
Maintenance and repairs	480	433	560	10.9	–22.7	–14.2
Vehicle insurance	498	593	569	–16.0	4.3	–12.4
Vehicle rentals, leases, licenses, other charges	217	288	352	–24.6	–18.3	–38.4
Public transportation	**275**	**239**	**274**	**15.0**	**–12.6**	**0.5**
HEALTH CARE	**775**	**764**	**638**	**1.5**	**19.7**	**21.4**
Health insurance	405	397	267	2.0	48.6	51.6
Medical services	236	209	225	13.1	–7.4	4.7
Drugs	102	105	103	–2.8	2.3	–0.6
Medical supplies	32	53	43	–39.6	23.1	–25.7
ENTERTAINMENT	**1,221**	**1,458**	**1,382**	**–16.3**	**5.5**	**–11.6**
Fees and admissions	235	303	343	–22.4	–11.7	–31.5
Audio and visual equipment and services	595	727	599	–18.1	21.4	–0.7
Pets, toys, hobbies, and playground equipment	232	226	219	2.6	3.2	5.9
Other entertainment products and services	158	202	222	–21.9	–8.7	–28.7

	average spending			percent change		
	2010	**2006**	**2000**	**2006–10**	**2000–06**	**2000–10**
PERSONAL CARE PRODUCTS AND SERVICES	$347	$376	$437	−7.8%	−13.8%	−20.6%
READING	39	50	72	−21.6	−31.1	−46.0
EDUCATION	1,906	1,362	1,592	40.0	−14.4	19.7
TOBACCO PRODUCTS AND SMOKING SUPPLIES	283	309	300	−8.5	3.1	−5.7
MISCELLANEOUS	277	420	408	−34.0	2.9	−32.1
CASH CONTRIBUTIONS	314	684	239	−54.1	185.6	31.2
PERSONAL INSURANCE AND PENSIONS	2,036	2,478	1,540	−17.8	60.9	32.2
Life and other personal insurance	22	45	68	−51.6	−33.6	−67.8
Pensions and Social Security*	2,013	2,433	–	−17.2	–	–
PERSONAL TAXES	104	565	1,179	−81.6	−52.1	−91.2
Federal income taxes	−47	359	881	−113.1	−59.3	−105.3
State and local income taxes	145	178	286	−18.8	−37.6	−49.3
Other taxes	6	27	11	−77.8	137.3	−47.4
GIFTS FOR PEOPLE IN OTHER HOUSEHOLDS	$423	$425	$756	−0.5	−43.8	−44.0

* Because of changes in methodology, the 2006 and 2010 data on pensions and Social Security are not comparable with earlier years.
Note: The Bureau of Labor Statistics uses consumer unit rather than household as the sampling unit in the Consumer Expenditure Survey. For the definition of consumer unit, see the glossary. Spending on gifts is also included in the preceding product and service categories.
Source: Bureau of Labor Statistics, 2000, 2006, and 2010 Consumer Expenditure Surveys, Internet site http://www.bls.gov/cex/; calculations by New Strategist

Millennial Household Spending Has Dropped Sharply

Householders aged 25 to 34 spent less in 2010 than they did in 2000.

Households headed by people aged 25 to 34 (the oldest Millennials turned 33 in 2010) cut their spending by 9 percent between 2006 and 2010, after adjusting for inflation. Their spending in 2010 was 5 percent below the level of 2000.

Householders aged 25 to 34 reduced their spending on many discretionary items in the 2006-to-2010 time period, after adjusting for inflation. Their spending on food away from home fell 13 percent, and spending on alcoholic beverages decreased by an even larger 33 percent. Average household spending on new cars and trucks fell 30 percent. Mortgage interest spending was down 26 percent as some in the age group lost their homes and others entering the age group during the time period decided not to buy. The age group's spending on entertainment fell 7 percent between 2006 and 2010.

Many householders in the 25-to-34 age group have education expenses, including student loans. Their average spending on education climbed 9 percent between 2006 and 2010, after adjusting for inflation.

■ The widespread unemployment of the Great Recession has been a setback for householders aged 25 to 34.

The 25-to-34 age group has cut its spending on many items, but education spending has grown

(percent change in spending by householders aged 25 to 34, 2006 to 2010; in 2010 dollars)

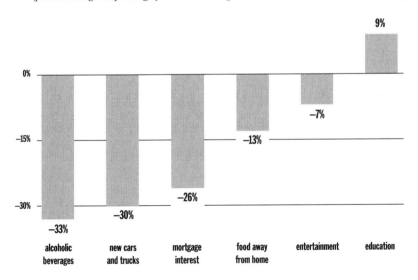

Table 9.3 Average Spending by Householders Aged 25 to 34, 2000 to 2010

(average annual spending of consumer units headed by people aged 25 to 34, 2000 to 2010; percent change for selected years; in 2010 dollars)

	average spending			percent change		
	2010	2006	2000	2006–10	2000–06	2000–10
Number of consumer units aged 25 to 34 (in 000s)	20,166	20,071	18,887	0.5%	6.3%	6.8%
Average annual spending of consumer units	$46,617	$51,466	$49,316	–9.4	4.4	–5.5
FOOD	6,091	6,602	6,661	–7.7	–0.9	–8.6
Food at home	3,338	3,446	3,737	–3.1	–7.8	–10.7
Cereals and bakery products	441	439	543	0.4	–19.2	–18.8
Cereals and cereal products	153	155	211	–1.1	–26.9	–27.6
Bakery products	288	284	333	1.2	–14.6	–13.5
Meats, poultry, fish, and eggs	713	807	975	–11.6	–17.2	–26.9
Beef	182	248	303	–26.5	–18.2	–39.9
Pork	124	153	196	–18.7	–22.3	–36.8
Other meats	105	100	124	5.5	–19.8	–15.4
Poultry	152	155	184	–1.7	–15.8	–17.2
Fish and seafood	104	117	129	–11.0	–9.6	–19.5
Eggs	46	37	38	25.1	–3.2	21.1
Dairy products	353	381	401	–7.3	–5.2	–12.1
Fresh milk and cream	135	154	170	–12.1	–9.5	–20.4
Other dairy products	218	227	232	–4.0	–2.0	–5.9
Fruits and vegetables	614	581	618	5.7	–6.0	–0.6
Fresh fruits	210	178	185	17.7	–3.5	13.6
Fresh vegetables	190	193	187	–1.3	2.7	1.4
Processed fruits	102	118	143	–13.5	–17.6	–28.7
Processed vegetables	113	93	104	21.5	–10.4	8.8
Other food at home	1,217	1,237	1,198	–1.6	3.3	1.6
Sugar and other sweets	111	103	133	8.0	–22.7	–16.5
Fats and oils	86	82	98	4.6	–15.7	–11.8
Miscellaneous foods	684	674	614	1.5	9.7	11.4
Nonalcoholic beverages	311	341	313	–8.7	8.9	–0.6
Food prepared by consumer unit on trips	25	38	39	–34.0	–3.6	–36.3
Food away from home	2,753	3,156	2,924	–12.8	7.9	–5.8
ALCOHOLIC BEVERAGES	473	711	546	–33.4	30.2	–13.3
HOUSING	16,845	18,538	16,525	–9.1	12.2	1.9
Shelter	10,451	11,600	10,010	–9.9	15.9	4.4
Owned dwellings	5,126	6,633	5,245	–22.7	26.5	–2.3
Mortgage interest and charges	3,415	4,632	3,657	–26.3	26.6	–6.6
Property taxes	1,108	1,288	956	–14.0	34.7	15.9
Maintenance, repair, insurance, other expenses	602	714	632	–15.7	13.0	–4.7
Rented dwellings	4,989	4,636	4,450	7.6	4.2	12.1
Other lodging	336	332	314	1.2	5.7	7.0
Utilities, fuels, and public services	3,228	3,345	2,964	–3.5	12.9	8.9
Natural gas	355	455	346	–22.0	31.7	2.7
Electricity	1,253	1,225	1,046	2.2	17.2	19.8
Fuel oil and other fuels	70	79	73	–11.3	7.5	–4.7

	average spending			percent change		
	2010	**2006**	**2000**	**2006–10**	**2000–06**	**2000–10**
Telephone	$1,160	$1,221	$1,203	–5.0%	1.5%	–3.6%
Water and other public services	390	365	296	7.0	23.0	31.6
Household services	**1,244**	**1,222**	**1,103**	**1.8**	**10.8**	**12.8**
Personal services	757	764	812	–0.9	–5.9	–6.7
Other household services	487	459	291	6.2	57.5	67.2
Housekeeping supplies	**465**	**574**	**553**	**–19.0**	**3.8**	**–16.0**
Laundry and cleaning supplies	126	168	158	–24.8	5.9	–20.4
Other household products	245	288	255	–14.8	13.0	–3.7
Postage and stationery	93	120	142	–22.5	–15.3	–34.4
Household furnishings and equipment	**1,458**	**1,796**	**1,893**	**–18.8**	**–5.2**	**–23.0**
Household textiles	79	134	152	–41.1	–11.7	–48.0
Furniture	429	552	579	–22.2	–4.7	–25.9
Floor coverings	44	38	53	16.2	–28.8	–17.3
Major appliances	160	210	229	–23.7	–8.4	–30.2
Small appliances and miscellaneous housewares	97	118	99	–17.7	19.4	–1.8
Miscellaneous household equipment	650	743	781	–12.5	–4.9	–16.8
APPAREL AND RELATED SERVICES	**2,087**	**2,328**	**2,607**	**–10.3**	**–10.7**	**–20.0**
Men and boys	**429**	**588**	**647**	**–27.1**	**–9.1**	**–33.7**
Men, aged 16 or older	325	442	466	–26.5	–5.1	–30.3
Boys, aged 2 to 15	104	146	181	–28.8	–19.4	–42.6
Women and girls	**675**	**797**	**891**	**–15.3**	**–10.6**	**–24.3**
Women, aged 16 or older	550	626	710	–12.2	–11.8	–22.6
Girls, aged 2 to 15	125	171	182	–26.9	–6.3	–31.4
Children under age 2	**195**	**202**	**209**	**–3.6**	**–3.2**	**–6.7**
Footwear	**313**	**401**	**499**	**–22.0**	**–19.6**	**–37.3**
Other apparel products and services	**475**	**339**	**361**	**40.3**	**–6.2**	**31.6**
TRANSPORTATION	**8,231**	**9,785**	**10,582**	**–15.9**	**–7.5**	**–22.2**
Vehicle purchases	**3,415**	**4,231**	**5,241**	**–19.3**	**–19.3**	**–34.8**
Cars and trucks, new	1,483	2,120	2,336	–30.0	–9.3	–36.5
Cars and trucks, used	1,894	2,035	2,807	–6.9	–27.5	–32.5
Gasoline and motor oil	**2,208**	**2,537**	**1,698**	**–13.0**	**49.4**	**30.0**
Other vehicle expenses	**2,174**	**2,533**	**3,143**	**–14.2**	**–19.4**	**–30.8**
Vehicle finance charges	303	434	552	–30.1	–21.4	–45.1
Maintenance and repairs	705	675	722	4.5	–6.5	–2.3
Vehicle insurance	741	889	980	–16.7	–9.3	–24.4
Vehicle rentals, leases, licenses, other charges	424	535	888	–20.8	–39.7	–52.2
Public transportation	**434**	**485**	**500**	**–10.4**	**–3.1**	**–13.2**
HEALTH CARE	**1,800**	**1,787**	**1,590**	**0.7**	**12.3**	**13.2**
Health insurance	1,086	955	810	13.7	17.8	34.0
Medical services	443	507	465	–12.7	9.2	–4.7
Drugs	200	263	229	–23.9	14.7	–12.7
Medical supplies	71	63	87	13.2	–28.2	–18.7
ENTERTAINMENT	**2,251**	**2,420**	**2,376**	**–7.0**	**1.9**	**–5.2**
Fees and admissions	460	514	582	–10.5	–11.8	–21.0
Audio and visual equipment and services	965	1,048	861	–7.9	21.7	12.1
Pets, toys, hobbies, and playground equipment	480	441	444	8.8	–0.7	8.0
Other entertainment products and services	346	416	488	–16.9	–14.6	–29.0

	average spending			percent change		
	2010	2006	2000	2006–10	2000–06	2000–10
PERSONAL CARE PRODUCTS AND SERVICES	$517	$592	$729	−12.6%	−18.9%	−29.1%
READING	61	89	149	−31.2	−40.6	−59.2
EDUCATION	839	768	741	9.3	3.7	13.3
TOBACCO PRODUCTS AND SMOKING SUPPLIES	362	344	393	5.2	−12.4	−7.8
MISCELLANEOUS	668	665	1,018	0.4	−34.7	−34.4
CASH CONTRIBUTIONS	1,074	1,157	821	−7.2	41.0	30.9
PERSONAL INSURANCE AND PENSIONS	5,318	5,681	4,576	−6.4	24.1	16.2
Life and other personal insurance	167	186	306	−10.2	−39.3	−45.5
Pensions and Social Security*	5,151	5,494	–	−6.2	–	–
PERSONAL TAXES	1,055	1,657	3,587	−36.3	−53.8	−70.6
Federal income taxes	521	1,071	2,792	−51.3	−61.6	−81.3
State and local income taxes	463	479	722	−3.4	−33.6	−35.9
Other taxes	71	107	73	−33.7	45.8	−3.3
GIFTS FOR PEOPLE IN OTHER HOUSEHOLDS	541	1,005	907	−46.2	10.8	−40.3

* Because of changes in methodology, the 2006 and 2010 data on pensions and Social Security are not comparable with earlier years.

The Bureau of Labor Statistics uses consumer unit rather than household as the sampling unit in the Consumer Expenditure Survey. For the definition of consumer unit, see the glossary. Spending on gifts is also included in the preceding product and service categories.

Source: Bureau of Labor Statistics, 2000, 2006, and 2010 Consumer Expenditure Surveys, Internet site http://www.bls.gov/cex/; calculations by New Strategist

Young Adults Spend Less than Average

Householders aged 25 to 34 spend close to the average on most things.

The incomes of householders under age 25 are well below average, and so is their spending. On some things, however, this age group spends more. Not surprisingly, householders in the age group spend 66 percent more than average on rent. Because many young adults are parents, they spend 60 percent more than the average household on clothes for children under age 2. Householders under age 25 spend 77 percent more than average on education. Many are students paying for college at least partly out of their own pocket.

Householders aged 25 to 34 spend close to what the average household spends on most things. Their spending is above average on some items such as food away from home (with an index of 110), alcoholic beverages (115), and new cars and trucks (122). Not surprisingly, they spend more than twice the average on household personal services (mostly day care), and clothes for infants. They spend 72 percent more than average on rent.

■ Although the Great Recession hit the Millennial generation hard, spending patterns by age remain intact.

The youngest householders are big spenders on alcohol, rent, and education

(indexed spending by householders under age 25 on selected items, 2010)

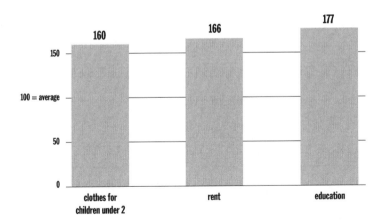

Table 9.4 Average, Indexed, and Market Share of Spending by Householders under Age 25, 2010

(average annual spending of total consumer units and average annual, indexed, and market share of spending by consumer units headed by people under age 25, 2010)

	total consumer units	consumer units headed by people under age 25		
		average spending	indexed spending	market share
Number of consumer units (in 000s)	121,107	8,034	–	6.6%
Average annual spending	$48,109	$27,483	57	3.8
FOOD	6,129	4,073	66	4.4
Food at home	3,624	2,197	61	4.0
Cereals and bakery products	502	312	62	4.1
Cereals and cereal products	165	103	62	4.1
Bakery products	337	209	62	4.1
Meats, poultry, fish, and eggs	784	447	57	3.8
Beef	217	136	63	4.2
Pork	149	83	56	3.7
Other meats	117	69	59	3.9
Poultry	138	84	61	4.0
Fish and seafood	117	45	38	2.6
Eggs	46	31	67	4.5
Dairy products	380	218	57	3.8
Fresh milk and cream	141	88	62	4.1
Other dairy products	240	130	54	3.6
Fruits and vegetables	679	395	58	3.9
Fresh fruits	232	119	51	3.4
Fresh vegetables	210	131	62	4.1
Processed fruits	113	68	60	4.0
Processed vegetables	124	77	62	4.1
Other food at home	1,278	826	65	4.3
Sugar and other sweets	132	63	48	3.2
Fats and oils	103	64	62	4.1
Miscellaneous foods	667	463	69	4.6
Nonalcoholic beverages	333	223	67	4.4
Food prepared by consumer unit on trips	43	13	30	2.0
Food away from home	2,505	1,876	75	5.0
ALCOHOLIC BEVERAGES	412	406	99	6.5
HOUSING	16,557	9,553	58	3.8
Shelter	9,812	6,166	63	4.2
Owned dwellings	6,277	1,123	18	1.2
Mortgage interest and charges	3,351	686	20	1.4
Property taxes	1,814	252	14	0.9
Maintenance, repair, insurance, other expenses	1,112	185	17	1.1
Rented dwellings	2,900	4,813	166	11.0
Other lodging	635	231	36	2.4
Utilities, fuels, and public services	3,660	1,818	50	3.3
Natural gas	440	186	42	2.8
Electricity	1,413	716	51	3.4
Fuel oil and other fuels	140	20	14	0.9

	total consumer units	consumer units headed by people under age 25		
		average spending	indexed spending	market share
Telephone	$1,178	$713	61	4.0%
Water and other public services	489	184	38	2.5
Household services	**1,007**	**416**	**41**	**2.7**
Personal services	340	154	45	3.0
Other household services	667	261	39	2.6
Housekeeping supplies	**612**	**279**	**46**	**3.0**
Laundry and cleaning supplies	150	90	60	4.0
Other household products	329	155	47	3.1
Postage and stationery	132	34	26	1.7
Household furnishings and equipment	**1,467**	**874**	**60**	**4.0**
Household textiles	102	53	52	3.4
Furniture	355	268	75	5.0
Floor coverings	36	8	22	1.5
Major appliances	209	92	44	2.9
Small appliances and miscellaneous housewares	107	45	42	2.8
Miscellaneous household equipment	657	409	62	4.1
APPAREL AND RELATED SERVICES	**1,700**	**1,559**	**92**	**6.1**
Men and boys	**382**	**260**	**68**	**4.5**
Men, aged 16 or older	304	219	72	4.8
Boys, aged 2 to 15	78	41	53	3.5
Women and girls	**663**	**670**	**101**	**6.7**
Women, aged 16 or older	562	628	112	7.4
Girls, aged 2 to 15	101	42	42	2.8
Children under age 2	**91**	**146**	**160**	**10.6**
Footwear	**303**	**305**	**101**	**6.7**
Other apparel products and services	**261**	**177**	**68**	**4.5**
TRANSPORTATION	**7,677**	**4,692**	**61**	**4.1**
Vehicle purchases	**2,588**	**1,591**	**61**	**4.1**
Cars and trucks, new	1,219	393	32	2.1
Cars and trucks, used	1,318	1,107	84	5.6
Gasoline and motor oil	**2,132**	**1,493**	**70**	**4.6**
Other vehicle expenses	**2,464**	**1,333**	**54**	**3.6**
Vehicle finance charges	243	137	56	3.7
Maintenance and repairs	787	480	61	4.0
Vehicle insurance	1,010	498	49	3.3
Vehicle rentals, leases, licenses, other charges	423	217	51	3.4
Public transportation	**493**	**275**	**56**	**3.7**
HEALTH CARE	**3,157**	**775**	**25**	**1.6**
Health insurance	1,831	405	22	1.5
Medical services	722	236	33	2.2
Drugs	485	102	21	1.4
Medical supplies	119	32	27	1.8
ENTERTAINMENT	**2,504**	**1,221**	**49**	**3.2**
Fees and admissions	581	235	40	2.7
Audio and visual equipment and services	954	595	62	4.1
Pets, toys, hobbies, and playground equipment	606	232	38	2.5
Other entertainment products and services	364	158	43	2.9

	total consumer units	consumer units headed by people under age 25		
		average spending	indexed spending	market share
PERSONAL CARE PRODUCTS AND SERVICES	$582	$347	60	4.0%
READING	100	39	39	2.6
EDUCATION	1,074	1,906	177	11.8
TOBACCO PRODUCTS AND SMOKING SUPPLIES	362	283	78	5.2
MISCELLANEOUS	849	277	33	2.2
CASH CONTRIBUTIONS	1,633	314	19	1.3
PERSONAL INSURANCE AND PENSIONS	5,373	2,036	38	2.5
Life and other personal insurance	318	22	7	0.5
Pensions and Social Security	5,054	2,013	40	2.6
PERSONAL TAXES	1,769	104	6	0.4
Federal income taxes	1,136	−47	−4	−0.3
State and local income taxes	482	145	30	2.0
Other taxes	151	6	4	0.3
GIFTS FOR PEOPLE IN OTHER HOUSEHOLDS	1,029	423	41	2.7

Note: The Bureau of Labor Statistics uses consumer unit rather than household as the sampling unit in the Consumer Expenditure Survey. For the definition of consumer unit, see the glossary. Spending on gifts is also included in the preceding product and service categories. "−" means not applicable.
Source: Bureau of Labor Statistics, 2010 Consumer Expenditure Survey, Internet site http://www.bls.gov/cex/; calculations by New Strategist

Table 9.5 Average, Indexed, and Market Share of Spending by Householders Aged 25 to 34, 2010

(average annual spending of total consumer units and average annual, indexed, and market share of spending by consumer units headed by people aged 25 to 34, 2010)

	total consumer units	average spending	indexed spending	market share
		consumer units headed by people aged 25 to 34		
Number of consumer units (in 000s)	121,107	20,166	–	16.7%
Average annual spending	$48,109	$46,617	97	16.1
FOOD	6,129	6,091	99	16.5
Food at home	3,624	3,338	92	15.3
Cereals and bakery products	502	441	88	14.6
Cereals and cereal products	165	153	93	15.4
Bakery products	337	288	85	14.2
Meats, poultry, fish, and eggs	784	713	91	15.1
Beef	217	182	84	14.0
Pork	149	124	83	13.9
Other meats	117	105	90	14.9
Poultry	138	152	110	18.3
Fish and seafood	117	104	89	14.8
Eggs	46	46	100	16.7
Dairy products	380	353	93	15.5
Fresh milk and cream	141	135	96	15.9
Other dairy products	240	218	91	15.1
Fruits and vegetables	679	614	90	15.1
Fresh fruits	232	210	91	15.1
Fresh vegetables	210	190	90	15.1
Processed fruits	113	102	90	15.0
Processed vegetables	124	113	91	15.2
Other food at home	1,278	1,217	95	15.9
Sugar and other sweets	132	111	84	14.0
Fats and oils	103	86	83	13.9
Miscellaneous foods	667	684	103	17.1
Nonalcoholic beverages	333	311	93	15.6
Food prepared by consumer unit on trips	43	25	58	9.7
Food away from home	2,505	2,753	110	18.3
ALCOHOLIC BEVERAGES	412	473	115	19.1
HOUSING	16,557	16,845	102	16.9
Shelter	9,812	10,451	107	17.7
Owned dwellings	6,277	5,126	82	13.6
Mortgage interest and charges	3,351	3,415	102	17.0
Property taxes	1,814	1,108	61	10.2
Maintenance, repair, insurance, other expenses	1,112	602	54	9.0
Rented dwellings	2,900	4,989	172	28.6
Other lodging	635	336	53	8.8
Utilities, fuels, and public services	3,660	3,228	88	14.7
Natural gas	440	355	81	13.4
Electricity	1,413	1,253	89	14.8
Fuel oil and other fuels	140	70	50	8.3

	total consumer units	consumer units headed by people aged 25 to 34		
		average spending	indexed spending	market share
Telephone	$1,178	$1,160	98	16.4%
Water and other public services	489	390	80	13.3
Household services	**1,007**	**1,244**	**124**	**20.6**
Personal services	340	757	223	37.1
Other household services	667	487	73	12.2
Housekeeping supplies	**612**	**465**	**76**	**12.7**
Laundry and cleaning supplies	150	126	84	14.0
Other household products	329	245	74	12.4
Postage and stationery	132	93	70	11.7
Household furnishings and equipment	**1,467**	**1,458**	**99**	**16.5**
Household textiles	102	79	77	12.9
Furniture	355	429	121	20.1
Floor coverings	36	44	122	20.4
Major appliances	209	160	77	12.7
Small appliances and miscellaneous housewares	107	97	91	15.1
Miscellaneous household equipment	657	650	99	16.5
APPAREL AND RELATED SERVICES	**1,700**	**2,087**	**123**	**20.4**
Men and boys	**382**	**429**	**112**	**18.7**
Men, aged 16 or older	304	325	107	17.8
Boys, aged 2 to 15	78	104	133	22.2
Women and girls	**663**	**675**	**102**	**17.0**
Women, aged 16 or older	562	550	98	16.3
Girls, aged 2 to 15	101	125	124	20.6
Children under age 2	**91**	**195**	**214**	**35.7**
Footwear	**303**	**313**	**103**	**17.2**
Other apparel products and services	**261**	**475**	**182**	**30.3**
TRANSPORTATION	**7,677**	**8,231**	**107**	**17.9**
Vehicle purchases	**2,588**	**3,415**	**132**	**22.0**
Cars and trucks, new	1,219	1,483	122	20.3
Cars and trucks, used	1,318	1,894	144	23.9
Gasoline and motor oil	**2,132**	**2,208**	**104**	**17.2**
Other vehicle expenses	**2,464**	**2,174**	**88**	**14.7**
Vehicle finance charges	243	303	125	20.8
Maintenance and repairs	787	705	90	14.9
Vehicle insurance	1,010	741	73	12.2
Vehicle rentals, leases, licenses, other charges	423	424	100	16.7
Public transportation	**493**	**434**	**88**	**14.7**
HEALTH CARE	**3,157**	**1,800**	**57**	**9.5**
Health insurance	1,831	1,086	59	9.9
Medical services	722	443	61	10.2
Drugs	485	200	41	6.9
Medical supplies	119	71	60	9.9
ENTERTAINMENT	**2,504**	**2,251**	**90**	**15.0**
Fees and admissions	581	460	79	13.2
Audio and visual equipment and services	954	965	101	16.8
Pets, toys, hobbies, and playground equipment	606	480	79	13.2
Other entertainment products and services	364	346	95	15.8

	total consumer units	consumer units headed by people aged 25 to 34		
		average spending	indexed spending	market share
PERSONAL CARE PRODUCTS AND SERVICES	**$582**	**$517**	**89**	**14.8%**
READING	**100**	**61**	**61**	**10.2**
EDUCATION	**1,074**	**839**	**78**	**13.0**
TOBACCO PRODUCTS AND SMOKING SUPPLIES	**362**	**362**	**100**	**16.7**
MISCELLANEOUS	**849**	**668**	**79**	**13.1**
CASH CONTRIBUTIONS	**1,633**	**1,074**	**66**	**11.0**
PERSONAL INSURANCE AND PENSIONS	**5,373**	**5,318**	**99**	**16.5**
Life and other personal insurance	318	167	53	8.7
Pensions and Social Security	5,054	5,151	102	17.0
PERSONAL TAXES	**1,769**	**1,055**	**60**	**9.9**
Federal income taxes	1,136	521	46	7.6
State and local income taxes	482	463	96	16.0
Other taxes	151	71	47	7.8
GIFTS FOR PEOPLE IN OTHER HOUSEHOLDS	**1,029**	**541**	**53**	**8.8**

Note: The Bureau of Labor Statistics uses consumer unit rather than household as the sampling unit in the Consumer Expenditure Survey. For the definition of consumer unit, see the glossary. Spending on gifts is also included in the preceding product and service categories. "–" means not applicable.
Source: Bureau of Labor Statistics, 2010 Consumer Expenditure Survey, Internet site http://www.bls.gov/cex/; calculations by New Strategist

Couples with Adult Children at Home Are Spending Less

Education and health insurance are among the few items on which these households are spending more.

Many members of the Millennial generation are adults living at home with their parents. Married couples with grown children (aged 18 or older) at home rank among the most affluent households because they have more earners—2.4 versus 1.6 earners in the average household. Couples with adult children at home cut their spending sharply between 2006 and 2010. In 2010, they spent $67,057 on average, nearly 12 percent less than in 2006, after adjusting for inflation, and 3 percent less than they spent in 2000.

Married couples with adult children at home are spending less on many items. They cut their spending on food away from home by 15 percent between 2006 and 2010, and their spending on alcoholic beverages fell 23 percent after adjusting for inflation. Spending on mortgage interest fell 17 percent as some lost their homes during the Great Recession. Spending on furniture fell by an even larger 26 percent. Spending on entertainment declined by 4 percent.

Many couples with adult children at home have children in college. That explains why the spending of these households on education rose slightly between 2006 and 2010, a remarkable gain considering the spending reduction in most other areas.

■ Many couples with adult children at home are cutting corners on discretionary items as they pay for their children's college education.

Couples with adult children at home are spending much more for health insurance

(percent change in spending by married couples with children aged 18 or older at home, 2006 and 2010; in 2010 dollars)

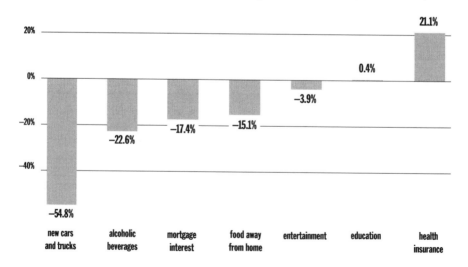

Table 9.6 Average Spending of Married Couples with Oldest Child Aged 18 or Older, 2000 to 2010

(average annual spending of married-couple consumer units with oldest child aged 18 or older at home, 2000 to 2010; percent change for selected years; in 2010 dollars)

	average spending			percent change		
	2010	2006	2000	2006–10	2000–06	2000–10
Number of consumer units (in 000s)	8,745	8,452	8,090	3.5%	4.5%	8.1%
Average annual spending of consumer units	$67,057	$75,967	$69,076	–11.7	10.0	–2.9
FOOD	9,054	10,120	9,951	–10.5	1.7	–9.0
Food at home	5,587	6,033	5,982	–7.4	0.9	–6.6
Cereals and bakery products	781	773	948	1.0	–18.5	–17.7
Cereals and cereal products	255	254	318	0.3	–20.0	–19.8
Bakery products	527	519	629	1.5	–17.5	–16.3
Meats, poultry, fish, and eggs	1,247	1,515	1,609	–17.7	–5.8	–22.5
Beef	372	450	495	–17.3	–9.1	–24.9
Pork	229	301	339	–23.8	–11.4	–32.5
Other meats	184	208	215	–11.4	–3.5	–14.5
Poultry	211	270	291	–22.0	–7.2	–27.6
Fish and seafood	184	228	198	–19.4	15.5	–6.9
Eggs	66	58	71	13.0	–17.6	–6.9
Dairy products	590	593	639	–0.5	–7.3	–7.7
Fresh milk and cream	219	215	261	1.7	–17.5	–16.0
Other dairy products	371	377	379	–1.7	–0.3	–2.0
Fruits and vegetables	1,027	1,035	976	–0.8	6.0	5.2
Fresh fruits	342	337	305	1.3	10.6	12.1
Fresh vegetables	313	372	290	–15.9	28.3	7.9
Processed fruits	172	177	206	–3.0	–14.1	–16.7
Processed vegetables	200	148	175	35.0	–15.2	14.5
Other food at home	1,941	2,117	1,808	–8.3	17.1	7.3
Sugar and other sweets	204	216	256	–5.7	–15.4	–20.2
Fats and oils	164	159	171	3.1	–7.0	–4.1
Miscellaneous foods	1,006	1,094	795	–8.0	37.5	26.5
Nonalcoholic beverages	509	580	523	–12.2	10.9	–2.7
Food prepared by consumer unit on trips	59	68	63	–13.4	7.6	–6.8
Food away from home	3,467	4,085	3,969	–15.1	2.9	–12.6
ALCOHOLIC BEVERAGES	420	543	604	–22.6	–10.1	–30.5
HOUSING	20,460	22,197	19,674	–7.8	12.8	4.0
Shelter	11,526	12,137	10,866	–5.0	11.7	6.1
Owned dwellings	8,963	9,673	8,539	–7.3	13.3	5.0
Mortgage interest and charges	4,725	5,719	4,987	–17.4	14.7	–5.2
Property taxes	2,798	2,398	2,177	16.7	10.2	28.5
Maintenance, repair, insurance, other expenses	1,441	1,555	1,375	–7.4	13.1	4.8
Rented dwellings	1,618	1,386	1,257	16.8	10.2	28.7
Other lodging	944	1,078	1,070	–12.5	0.8	–11.8
Utilities, fuels, and public services	5,136	5,204	4,307	–1.3	20.8	19.3
Natural gas	616	746	529	–17.5	41.0	16.4
Electricity	1,924	1,898	1,617	1.4	17.4	19.0
Fuel oil and other fuels	197	194	165	1.8	17.6	19.7

	average spending			percent change		
	2010	2006	2000	2006–10	2000–06	2000–10
Telephone	$1,737	$1,760	$1,435	−1.3%	22.7%	21.1%
Water and other public services	663	605	561	9.7	7.8	18.2
Household services	**903**	**1,096**	**676**	**−17.6**	**62.0**	**33.5**
Personal services	121	443	135	−72.7	227.3	−10.7
Other household services	782	652	541	19.9	20.6	44.6
Housekeeping supplies	**839**	**1,094**	**924**	**−23.3**	**18.3**	**−9.2**
Laundry and cleaning supplies	213	274	253	−22.2	8.1	−15.9
Other household products	436	592	447	−26.3	32.4	−2.5
Postage and stationery	190	227	224	−16.4	1.3	−15.2
Household furnishings and equipment	**2,057**	**2,667**	**2,901**	**−22.9**	**−8.1**	**−29.1**
Household textiles	154	301	206	−48.8	45.7	−25.4
Furniture	422	572	613	−26.2	−6.6	−31.1
Floor coverings	29	69	137	−58.1	−49.4	−78.8
Major appliances	315	471	433	−33.1	8.6	−27.3
Small appliances and miscellaneous housewares	190	199	157	−4.5	26.7	21.0
Miscellaneous household equipment	947	1,056	1,356	−10.3	−22.2	−30.2
APPAREL AND RELATED SERVICES	**2,214**	**3,059**	**3,416**	**−27.6**	**−10.5**	**−35.2**
Men and boys	**614**	**817**	**921**	**−24.8**	**−11.3**	**−33.3**
Men, aged 16 or older	525	732	785	−28.3	−6.7	−33.1
Boys, aged 2 to 15	89	84	135	5.5	−37.7	−34.3
Women and girls	**858**	**1,322**	**1,507**	**−35.1**	**−12.3**	**−43.1**
Women, aged 16 or older	761	1,166	1,366	−34.7	−14.7	−44.3
Girls, aged 2 to 15	97	156	141	−37.7	10.8	−31.0
Children under age 2	**68**	**77**	**80**	**−11.5**	**−3.7**	**−14.8**
Footwear	**416**	**511**	**490**	**−18.5**	**4.2**	**−15.1**
Other apparel products and services	**258**	**334**	**419**	**−22.8**	**−20.3**	**−38.4**
TRANSPORTATION	**11,569**	**15,044**	**15,396**	**−23.1**	**−2.3**	**−24.9**
Vehicle purchases	**3,658**	**6,192**	**7,238**	**−40.9**	**−14.4**	**−49.5**
Cars and trucks, new	1,340	2,961	3,240	−54.8	−8.6	−58.6
Cars and trucks, used	2,217	3,111	3,950	−28.7	−21.2	−43.9
Gasoline and motor oil	**3,381**	**3,980**	**2,649**	**−15.1**	**50.3**	**27.6**
Other vehicle expenses	**3,905**	**4,110**	**4,803**	**−5.0**	**−14.4**	**−18.7**
Vehicle finance charges	377	526	704	−28.3	−25.3	−46.5
Maintenance and repairs	1,228	1,192	1,251	3.0	−4.7	−1.8
Vehicle insurance	1,621	1,737	1,783	−6.7	−2.6	−9.1
Vehicle rentals, leases, licenses, other charges	679	654	1,065	3.8	−38.6	−36.2
Public transportation	**624**	**763**	**707**	**−18.2**	**7.9**	**−11.7**
HEALTH CARE	**4,289**	**3,875**	**3,395**	**10.7**	**14.2**	**26.3**
Health insurance	2,408	1,989	1,650	21.1	20.6	45.9
Medical services	1,017	967	927	5.2	4.3	9.7
Drugs	682	734	645	−7.1	13.9	5.8
Medical supplies	182	185	175	−1.6	5.8	4.1
ENTERTAINMENT	**3,186**	**3,314**	**3,275**	**−3.9**	**1.2**	**−2.7**
Fees and admissions	814	862	897	−5.6	−3.8	−9.2
Audio and visual equipment and services	1,151	1,283	1,045	−10.3	22.8	10.2
Pets, toys, hobbies, and playground equipment	808	596	536	35.6	11.3	50.8
Other entertainment products and services	414	574	796	−27.9	−27.9	−48.0

	average spending			percent change		
	2010	2006	2000	2006–10	2000–06	2000–10
PERSONAL CARE PRODUCTS AND SERVICES	$840	$996	$1,070	−15.7%	−6.9%	−21.5%
READING	123	158	229	−22.1	−31.1	−46.3
EDUCATION	3,068	3,057	2,240	0.4	36.5	37.0
TOBACCO PRODUCTS AND SMOKING SUPPLIES	429	390	576	9.9	−32.2	−25.5
MISCELLANEOUS	1,025	1,110	1,151	−7.6	−3.6	−11.0
CASH CONTRIBUTIONS	1,958	2,731	1,735	−28.3	57.4	12.9
PERSONAL INSURANCE AND PENSIONS	8,422	9,373	6,366	−10.1	47.2	32.3
Life and other personal insurance	577	602	889	−4.2	−32.2	−35.1
Pensions and Social Security*	7,844	8,771	–	−10.6	–	–
PERSONAL TAXES	2,696	3,964	5,217	−32.0	−24.0	−48.3
Federal income taxes	1,615	2,724	4,129	−40.7	−34.0	−60.9
State and local income taxes	741	928	859	−20.2	8.1	−13.7
Other taxes	341	313	229	9.1	36.4	48.8
GIFTS FOR PEOPLE IN OTHER HOUSEHOLDS	1,182	1,392	2,188	−15.1	−36.4	−46.0

* Because of changes in methodology, the 2006 and 2010 data on pensions and Social Security are not comparable with earlier years.
The Bureau of Labor Statistics uses consumer unit rather than household as the sampling unit in the Consumer Expenditure Survey. For the definition of consumer unit, see the glossary. Spending on gifts is also included in the preceding product and service categories.
Source: Bureau of Labor Statistics, 2000, 2006, and 2010 Consumer Expenditure Surveys, Internet site http://www.bls.gov/cex/; calculations by New Strategist

Table 9.7 Average, Indexed, and Market Share of Spending by Married Couples with Oldest Child Aged 18 or Older, 2010

(average annual spending of total consumer units, and average annual, indexed, and market share of spending by married-couple consumer units with children aged 18 or older at home, 2010)

	total consumer units	consumer units headed by married couples with children aged 18 or older at home		
		average spending	indexed spending	market share
Number of consumer units (in 000s)	121,107	8,745	–	7.2%
Average annual spending	$48,109	$67,057	139	10.1
FOOD	6,129	9,054	148	10.7
Food at home	3,624	5,587	154	11.1
Cereals and bakery products	502	781	156	11.2
Cereals and cereal products	165	255	155	11.2
Bakery products	337	527	156	11.3
Meats, poultry, fish, and eggs	784	1,247	159	11.5
Beef	217	372	171	12.4
Pork	149	229	154	11.1
Other meats	117	184	157	11.4
Poultry	138	211	153	11.0
Fish and seafood	117	184	157	11.4
Eggs	46	66	143	10.4
Dairy products	380	590	155	11.2
Fresh milk and cream	141	219	155	11.2
Other dairy products	240	371	155	11.2
Fruits and vegetables	679	1,027	151	10.9
Fresh fruits	232	342	147	10.6
Fresh vegetables	210	313	149	10.8
Processed fruits	113	172	152	11.0
Processed vegetables	124	200	161	11.6
Other food at home	1,278	1,941	152	11.0
Sugar and other sweets	132	204	155	11.2
Fats and oils	103	164	159	11.5
Miscellaneous foods	667	1,006	151	10.9
Nonalcoholic beverages	333	509	153	11.0
Food prepared by consumer unit on trips	43	59	137	9.9
Food away from home	2,505	3,467	138	10.0
ALCOHOLIC BEVERAGES	412	420	102	7.4
HOUSING	16,557	20,460	124	8.9
Shelter	9,812	11,526	117	8.5
Owned dwellings	6,277	8,963	143	10.3
Mortgage interest and charges	3,351	4,725	141	10.2
Property taxes	1,814	2,798	154	11.1
Maintenance, repair, insurance, other expenses	1,112	1,441	130	9.4
Rented dwellings	2,900	1,618	56	4.0
Other lodging	635	944	149	10.7
Utilities, fuels, and public services	3,660	5,136	140	10.1
Natural gas	440	616	140	10.1
Electricity	1,413	1,924	136	9.8
Fuel oil and other fuels	$140	197	141	10.2

	total consumer units	consumer units headed by married couples with children aged 18 or older at home		
		average spending	indexed spending	market share
Telephone	$1,178	$1,737	147	10.6%
Water and other public services	489	663	136	9.8
Household services	**1,007**	**903**	**90**	**6.5**
Personal services	340	121	36	2.6
Other household services	667	782	117	8.5
Housekeeping supplies	**612**	**839**	**137**	**9.9**
Laundry and cleaning supplies	150	213	142	10.3
Other household products	329	436	133	9.6
Postage and stationery	132	190	144	10.4
Household furnishings and equipment	**1,467**	**2,057**	**140**	**10.1**
Household textiles	102	154	151	10.9
Furniture	355	422	119	8.6
Floor coverings	36	29	81	5.8
Major appliances	209	315	151	10.9
Small appliances and miscellaneous housewares	107	190	178	12.8
Miscellaneous household equipment	657	947	144	10.4
APPAREL AND RELATED SERVICES	**1,700**	**2,214**	**130**	**9.4**
Men and boys	**382**	**614**	**161**	**11.6**
Men, aged 16 or older	304	525	173	12.5
Boys, aged 2 to 15	78	89	114	8.2
Women and girls	**663**	**858**	**129**	**9.3**
Women, aged 16 or older	562	761	135	9.8
Girls, aged 2 to 15	101	97	96	6.9
Children under age 2	**91**	**68**	**75**	**5.4**
Footwear	**303**	**416**	**137**	**9.9**
Other apparel products and services	**261**	**258**	**99**	**7.1**
TRANSPORTATION	**7,677**	**11,569**	**151**	**10.9**
Vehicle purchases	**2,588**	**3,658**	**141**	**10.2**
Cars and trucks, new	1,219	1,340	110	7.9
Cars and trucks, used	1,318	2,217	168	12.1
Gasoline and motor oil	**2,132**	**3,381**	**159**	**11.5**
Other vehicle expenses	**2,464**	**3,905**	**158**	**11.4**
Vehicle finance charges	243	377	155	11.2
Maintenance and repairs	787	1,228	156	11.3
Vehicle insurance	1,010	1,621	160	11.6
Vehicle rentals, leases, licenses, other charges	423	679	161	11.6
Public transportation	**493**	**624**	**127**	**9.1**
HEALTH CARE	**3,157**	**4,289**	**136**	**9.8**
Health insurance	1,831	2,408	132	9.5
Medical services	722	1,017	141	10.2
Drugs	485	682	141	10.2
Medical supplies	119	182	153	11.0
ENTERTAINMENT	**2,504**	**3,186**	**127**	**9.2**
Fees and admissions	581	814	140	10.1
Audio and visual equipment and services	954	1,151	121	8.7
Pets, toys, hobbies, and playground equipment	606	808	133	9.6
Other entertainment products and services	364	414	114	8.2

| | total consumer units | consumer units headed by married couples with children aged 18 or older at home | | |
		average spending	indexed spending	market share
PERSONAL CARE PRODUCTS AND SERVICES	$582	$840	144	10.4%
READING	100	123	123	8.9
EDUCATION	1,074	3,068	286	20.6
TOBACCO PRODUCTS AND SMOKING SUPPLIES	362	429	119	8.6
MISCELLANEOUS	849	1,025	121	8.7
CASH CONTRIBUTIONS	1,633	1,958	120	8.7
PERSONAL INSURANCE AND PENSIONS	5,373	8,422	157	11.3
Life and other personal insurance	318	577	181	13.1
Pensions and Social Security	5,054	7,844	155	11.2
PERSONAL TAXES	1,769	2,696	152	11.0
Federal income taxes	1,136	1,615	142	10.3
State and local income taxes	482	741	154	11.1
Other taxes	151	341	226	16.3
GIFTS FOR PEOPLE IN OTHER HOUSEHOLDS	1,029	1,182	115	8.3

Note: The Bureau of Labor Statistics uses consumer unit rather than household as the sampling unit in the Consumer Expenditure Survey. For the definition of consumer unit, see the glossary. Spending on gifts is also included in the preceding product and service categories. "–" means not applicable.
Source: Bureau of Labor Statistics, 2010 Consumer Expenditure Survey, Internet site http://www.bls.gov/cex/; calculations by New Strategist

CHAPTER
10

Time Use

■ People aged 15 to 19 have on average 4.58 hours of leisure time per day. This increases to 4.73 hours of leisure a day for 20-to-24-year-olds. Then reality hits.

■ People aged 25 to 34 spend more time working (4.25 hours) on an average day than they do at leisure (3.84), a situation that will continue until they reach the 55-to-64-age group.

■ Women aged 25 to 34 spend more than twice as much time as the average woman caring for household children.

■ Men aged 25 to 34 spend only 0.23 hours per day doing housework, much less than the 0.74 hours per day the average woman in the age group spends doing housework.

Adults Aged 25 to 34 Spend More Time at Work than at Play

Teenagers and younger adults have more leisure time.

Time use varies sharply by age, with teenagers aged 15 to 19 having more leisure time than adults in their late twenties and early thirties. People aged 15 to 19 have 4.58 hours of leisure time per day. On an average day, teenagers spend much more time in leisure activities than they do working (0.84 hours) or in school (3.21 hours).

In the 20-to-24 age group, average time spent working expands to 3.05 hours per day, and as school pressures are easing leisure time expands to 4.73 hours. Then reality sets in. People aged 25 to 34 spend more time working (4.25 hours) on an average day than they do at leisure (3.84), a situation that will continue for many years—until they reach the 55-to-64-age group.

■ Women aged 25 to 34 spend more than twice as much time as the average woman caring for household children.

Leisure time falls when people are raising children

(average number of hours per day spent in socializing, relaxing, and leisure, by age, 2010)

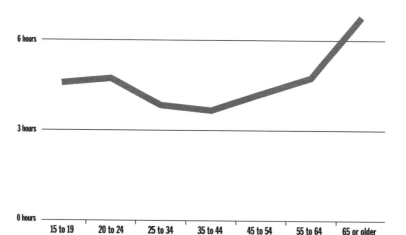

Table 10.1 Detailed Time Use of People Aged 15 to 19, 2010

(hours per day spent in primary activities by total people aged 15 or older and people aged 15 to 19, index of age group to total, and number and percent of people aged 15 to 19 participating in activity on an average day, 2010)

	average hours per day for total people	average hours per day for people aged 15 to 19	index, 15 to 19 to total	people aged 15 to 19 participating in activity number (in 000s)	percent
Total, all activities	**24.00**	**24.00**	**100**	**20,980**	**100.0%**
Personal care activities	9.45	10.31	109	20,980	100.0
Sleeping	8.67	9.47	109	20,980	100.0
Grooming	0.69	0.79	114	18,251	87.0
Health-related self-care	0.09	–	–	402	1.9
Household activities	1.82	0.79	43	12,190	58.1
Housework	0.57	0.25	44	4,907	23.4
Food preparation and cleanup	0.56	0.17	30	5,238	25.0
Lawn, garden, and houseplants	0.21	0.07	33	894	4.3
Animals and pets	0.10	0.07	70	1,871	8.9
Vehicles	0.04	0.03	75	584	2.8
Household management	0.19	0.13	68	4,235	20.2
Financial management	0.03	0.00	0	168	0.8
Household and personal organization and planning	0.09	0.07	78	3,091	14.7
Household and personal mail and messages (except email)	0.02	–	–	208	1.0
Household and personal email and messages	0.05	0.05	100	1,146	5.5
Caring for and helping household members	0.43	0.11	26	2,591	12.3
Caring for and helping household children	0.36	0.10	28	2,126	10.1
Caring for household adults	0.01	0.00	0	137	0.7
Helping household adults	0.01	0.01	100	411	2.0
Caring for and helping people in other households	0.15	0.10	67	3,740	17.8
Caring for and helping children in other households	0.07	0.05	71	1,905	9.1
Caring for adults in other households	0.01	0.00	0	22	0.1
Helping adults in other households	0.07	0.05	71	2,016	9.6
Working and work-related activities	3.22	0.93	29	4,083	19.5
Working	3.14	0.84	27	3,089	14.7
Job search and interviewing	0.05	–	–	336	1.6
Educational activities	0.45	3.21	713	11,043	52.6
Taking class	0.28	2.39	854	8,512	40.6
Homework and research	0.16	0.75	469	7,345	35.0
Consumer purchases	0.37	0.28	76	6,497	31.0
Grocery shopping	0.10	0.03	30	1,005	4.8
Shopping (except groceries, food, and gas)	0.24	0.22	92	3,617	17.2
Professional and personal care services	0.08	0.03	38	762	3.6
Medical and care services	0.05	0.02	40	432	2.1
Eating and drinking	1.13	0.89	79	19,813	94.4
Socializing, relaxing, and leisure	4.63	4.58	99	20,053	95.6
Socializing and communicating	0.63	0.79	125	10,160	48.4
Attending or hosting social events	0.08	0.06	75	509	2.4

	average hours per day for total people	average hours per day for people aged 15 to 19	index, 15 to 19 to total	people aged 15 to 19 participating in activity	
				number (in 000s)	percent
Relaxing and leisure	3.84	3.67	96	19,049	90.8%
Television and movies	2.73	2.31	85	16,062	76.6
Playing games	0.21	0.58	276	4,693	22.4
Computer use for leisure (except games)	0.20	0.34	170	4,386	20.9
Reading for personal interest	0.30	0.12	40	2,152	10.3
Arts and entertainment (other than sports)	0.08	0.07	88	573	2.7
Attending movies	0.03	0.05	167	489	2.3
Sports, exercise, and recreation	0.33	0.78	236	7,337	35.0
Participating in sports, exercise, and recreation	0.31	0.70	226	7,007	33.4
Attending sporting or recreational events	0.03	0.07	233	636	3.0
Religious and spiritual activities	0.16	0.10	63	1,033	4.9
Volunteer activities	0.15	0.13	87	1,468	7.0
Telephone calls	0.10	0.22	220	3,715	17.7
Traveling	1.19	1.15	97	18,736	89.3

Note: Primary activities are those respondents identified as their main activity. Other activities done simultaneously are not included. Travel related to activities is reported separately. Numbers do not sum to total because not all activities are shown. The index is calculated by dividing time spent by age group by time spent by the average person and multiplying by 100. "–" means sample is too small to make a reliable estimate.
Source: Bureau of Labor Statistics, unpublished tables from the 2010 American Time Use Survey, Internet site http://www.bls .gov/tus/home.htm; calculations by New Strategist

Table 10.2 Detailed Time Use of People Aged 20 to 24, 2010

(hours per day spent in primary activities by total people aged 15 or older and people aged 20 to 24, index of age group to total, and number and percent of people aged 20 to 24 participating in activity on an average day, 2010)

	average hours per day for total people	average hours per day for people aged 20 to 24	index, 20 to 24 to total	people aged 20 to 24 participating in activity	
				number (in 000s)	percent
Total, all activities	**24.00**	**24.00**	**100**	**21,048**	**100.0%**
Personal care activities	9.45	9.78	103	21,020	99.9
Sleeping	8.67	9.02	104	21,020	99.9
Grooming	0.69	0.74	107	17,371	82.5
Health-related self-care	0.09	–	–	581	2.8
Household activities	1.82	1.24	68	12,940	61.5
Housework	0.57	0.44	77	5,164	24.5
Food preparation and cleanup	0.56	0.39	70	8,460	40.2
Lawn, garden, and houseplants	0.21	0.03	14	333	1.6
Animals and pets	0.10	–	–	1,831	8.7
Vehicles	0.04	–	–	597	2.8
Household management	0.19	0.13	68	4,597	21.8
Financial management	0.03	–	–	302	1.4
Household and personal organization and planning	0.09	0.08	89	3,107	14.8
Household and personal mail and messages (except email)	0.02	–	–	305	1.4
Household and personal email and messages	0.05	0.03	60	1,236	5.9
Caring for and helping household members	0.43	0.49	114	4,827	22.9
Caring for and helping household children	0.36	0.44	122	3,850	18.3
Caring for household adults	0.01	0.00	0	244	1.2
Helping household adults	0.01	–	–	1,278	6.1
Caring for and helping people in other households	0.15	0.12	80	2,967	14.1
Caring for and helping children in other households	0.07	0.04	57	586	2.8
Caring for adults in other households	0.01	0.00	0	111	0.5
Helping adults in other households	0.07	–	–	2,353	11.2
Working and work-related activities	3.22	3.13	97	9,481	45.0
Working	3.14	3.05	97	8,767	41.7
Job search and interviewing	0.05	0.07	140	690	3.3
Educational activities	0.45	0.90	200	3,859	18.3
Taking class	0.28	0.42	150	2,541	12.1
Homework and research	0.16	0.48	300	2,921	13.9
Consumer purchases	0.37	0.33	89	8,484	40.3
Grocery shopping	0.10	0.07	70	2,214	10.5
Shopping (except groceries, food, and gas)	0.24	0.22	92	4,412	21.0
Professional and personal care services	0.08	0.06	75	1,248	5.9
Medical and care services	0.05	–	–	343	1.6
Eating and drinking	1.13	1.04	92	19,875	94.4
Socializing, relaxing, and leisure	4.63	4.73	102	20,123	95.6
Socializing and communicating	0.63	0.85	135	7,991	38.0
Attending or hosting social events	0.08	0.08	100	659	3.1

	average hours per day for total people	average hours per day for people aged 20 to 24	index, 20 to 24 to total	people aged 20 to 24 participating in activity	
				number (in 000s)	percent
Relaxing and leisure	3.84	3.61	94	18,779	89.2%
Television and movies	2.73	2.31	85	16,532	78.5
Playing games	0.21	0.44	210	3,528	16.8
Computer use for leisure (except games)	0.20	0.28	140	2,599	12.3
Reading for personal interest	0.30	–	–	1,628	7.7
Arts and entertainment (other than sports)	0.08	0.18	225	995	4.7
Attending movies	0.03	0.05	167	456	2.2
Sports, exercise, and recreation	0.33	0.31	94	3,478	16.5
Participating in sports, exercise, and recreation	0.31	0.28	90	3,358	16.0
Attending sporting or recreational events	0.03	–	–	224	1.1
Religious and spiritual activities	0.16	0.11	69	1,349	6.4
Volunteer activities	0.15	0.07	47	1,058	5.0
Telephone calls	0.10	0.09	90	2,392	11.4
Traveling	1.19	1.23	103	18,650	88.6

Note: Primary activities are those respondents identified as their main activity. Other activities done simultaneously are not included. Travel related to activities is reported separately. Numbers do not sum to total because not all activities are shown. The index is calculated by dividing time spent by age group by time spent by the average person and multiplying by 100. "–" means sample is too small to make a reliable estimate.
Source: Bureau of Labor Statistics, unpublished tables from the 2010 American Time Use Survey, Internet site http://www.bls .gov/tus/home.htm; calculations by New Strategist

Table 10.3 Detailed Time Use of People Aged 25 to 34, 2010

(hours per day spent in primary activities by total people aged 15 or older and people aged 25 to 34, index of age group to total, and number and percent of people aged 25 to 34 participating in activity on an average day, 2010)

	average hours per day for total people	average hours per day for people aged 25 to 34	index, 25 to 34 to total	people aged 25 to 34 participating in activity number (in 000s)	percent
Total, all activities	**24.00**	**24.00**	**100**	**40,904**	**100.0%**
Personal care activities	9.45	9.37	99	40,904	100.0
Sleeping	8.67	8.58	99	40,887	100.0
Grooming	0.69	0.72	104	33,773	82.6
Health-related self-care	0.09	–	–	794	1.9
Household activities	1.82	1.45	80	30,281	74.0
Housework	0.57	0.48	84	12,919	31.6
Food preparation and cleanup	0.56	0.52	93	22,150	54.2
Lawn, garden, and houseplants	0.21	0.09	43	1,978	4.8
Animals and pets	0.10	0.07	70	4,298	10.5
Vehicles	0.04	0.04	100	1,204	2.9
Household management	0.19	0.14	74	9,226	22.6
Financial management	0.03	0.01	33	965	2.4
Household and personal organization and planning	0.09	0.08	89	5,349	13.1
Household and personal mail and messages (except email)	0.02	0.00	0	848	2.1
Household and personal email and messages	0.05	0.04	80	3,311	8.1
Caring for and helping household members	0.43	0.90	209	16,943	41.4
Caring for and helping household children	0.36	0.82	228	16,085	39.3
Caring for household adults	0.01	0.00	0	459	1.1
Helping household adults	0.01	–	–	1,304	3.2
Caring for and helping people in other households	0.15	0.12	80	4,350	10.6
Caring for and helping children in other households	0.07	0.04	57	1,097	2.7
Caring for adults in other households	0.01	0.00	0	211	0.5
Helping adults in other households	0.07	0.08	114	3,320	8.1
Working and work-related activities	3.22	4.31	134	23,810	58.2
Working	3.14	4.25	135	22,907	56.0
Job search and interviewing	0.05	0.04	80	946	2.3
Educational activities	0.45	0.24	53	2,407	5.9
Taking class	0.28	0.11	39	1,274	3.1
Homework and research	0.16	0.13	81	1,898	4.6
Consumer purchases	0.37	0.37	100	17,955	43.9
Grocery shopping	0.10	0.10	100	5,296	12.9
Shopping (except groceries, food, and gas)	0.24	0.23	96	9,392	23.0
Professional and personal care services	0.08	0.05	63	2,674	6.5
Medical and care services	0.05	0.03	60	828	2.0
Eating and drinking	1.13	1.11	98	38,639	94.5
Socializing, relaxing, and leisure	4.63	3.84	83	38,171	93.3
Socializing and communicating	0.63	0.68	108	14,464	35.4
Attending or hosting social events	0.08	0.11	138	1,206	2.9

	average hours per day for total people	average hours per day for people aged 25 to 34	index, 25 to 34 to total	people aged 25 to 34 participating in activity	
				number (in 000s)	percent
Relaxing and leisure	3.84	2.96	77	35,633	87.1%
Television and movies	2.73	2.18	80	30,683	75.0
Playing games	0.21	0.17	81	3,166	7.7
Computer use for leisure (except games)	0.20	0.22	110	5,682	13.9
Reading for personal interest	0.30	0.14	47	4,751	11.6
Arts and entertainment (other than sports)	0.08	0.09	113	1,299	3.2
Attending movies	0.03	0.04	133	664	1.6
Sports, exercise, and recreation	0.33	0.31	94	7,389	18.1
Participating in sports, exercise, and recreation	0.31	0.29	94	7,090	17.3
Attending sporting or recreational events	0.03	0.01	33	319	0.8
Religious and spiritual activities	0.16	0.11	69	2,560	6.3
Volunteer activities	0.15	0.12	80	1,664	4.1
Telephone calls	0.10	0.08	80	4,928	12.0
Traveling	1.19	1.32	111	37,820	92.5

Note: Primary activities are those respondents identified as their main activity. Other activities done simultaneously are not included. Travel related to activities is reported separately. Numbers do not sum to total because not all activities are shown. The index is calculated by dividing time spent by age group by time spent by the average person and multiplying by 100. "–" means sample is too small to make a reliable estimate.

Source: Bureau of Labor Statistics, unpublished tables from the 2010 American Time Use Survey, Internet site http://www.bls .gov/tus/home.htm; calculations by New Strategist

Table 10.4 Detailed Time Use of Men Aged 15 to 19, 2010

(hours per day spent in primary activities by total men aged 15 or older and men aged 15 to 19, index of age group to total, and number and percent of men aged 15 to 19 participating in activity on an average day, 2010)

	average hours per day for total men	average hours per day for men aged 15 to 19	index, 15 to 19 to total	men aged 15 to 19 participating in activity number (in 000s)	percent
Total, all activities	**24.00**	**24.00**	**100**	**10,615**	**100.0%**
Personal care activities	9.24	10.22	111	10,615	100.0
Sleeping	8.56	9.47	111	10,615	100.0
Grooming	0.58	0.66	114	8,907	83.9
Health-related self-care	0.08	–	–	221	2.1
Household activities	1.44	0.72	50	5,523	52.0
Housework	0.26	0.20	77	2,071	19.5
Food preparation and cleanup	0.32	0.11	34	1,950	18.4
Lawn, garden, and houseplants	0.31	0.12	39	656	6.2
Animals and pets	0.08	0.03	38	687	6.5
Vehicles	0.08	0.05	63	471	4.4
Household management	0.16	0.11	69	1,779	16.8
Financial management	0.02	0.00	0	108	1.0
Household and personal organization and planning	0.07	0.04	57	1,216	11.5
Household and personal mail and messages (except email)	0.01	0.00	0	61	0.6
Household and personal email and messages	0.05	–	–	563	5.3
Caring for and helping household members	0.28	0.04	14	871	8.2
Caring for and helping household children	0.23	0.03	13	654	6.2
Caring for household adults	0.01	0.00	0	63	0.6
Helping household adults	0.01	0.00	0	217	2.0
Caring for and helping people in other households	0.14	0.08	57	1,888	17.8
Caring for and helping children in other households	0.05	–	–	800	7.5
Caring for adults in other households	–	0.00	–	0	0.0
Helping adults in other households	0.08	0.06	75	1,120	10.6
Working and work-related activities	3.75	0.91	24	2,084	19.6
Working	3.65	0.81	22	1,463	13.8
Job search and interviewing	0.06	–	–	248	2.3
Educational activities	0.44	2.97	675	5,008	47.2
Taking class	0.30	2.38	793	4,152	39.1
Homework and research	0.13	0.56	431	3,130	29.5
Consumer purchases	0.30	0.24	80	3,164	29.8
Grocery shopping	0.08	0.03	38	492	4.6
Shopping (except groceries, food, and gas)	0.19	0.18	95	1,699	16.0
Professional and personal care services	0.06	0.02	33	320	3.0
Medical and care services	0.04	0.00	0	136	1.3
Eating and drinking	1.17	0.83	71	9,939	93.6
Socializing, relaxing, and leisure	4.88	4.86	100	10,260	96.7
Socializing and communicating	0.61	0.81	133	5,166	48.7
Attending or hosting social events	0.07	–	–	145	1.4

	average hours per day for total men	average hours per day for men aged 15 to 19	index, 15 to 19 to total	men aged 15 to 19 participating in activity	
				number (in 000s)	percent
Relaxing and leisure	4.11	3.94	96	9,858	92.9%
Television and movies	2.94	2.29	78	8,234	77.6
Playing games	0.27	0.95	352	3,537	33.3
Computer use for leisure (except games)	0.20	0.33	165	2,011	18.9
Reading for personal interest	0.25	0.06	24	738	7.0
Arts and entertainment (other than sports)	0.09	0.08	89	318	3.0
Attending movies	0.03	0.06	200	274	2.6
Sports, exercise, and recreation	0.45	1.05	233	4,553	42.9
Participating in sports, exercise, and recreation	0.42	1.00	238	4,443	41.9
Attending sporting or recreational events	0.03	0.05	167	285	2.7
Religious and spiritual activities	0.13	0.10	77	435	4.1
Volunteer activities	0.12	0.13	108	662	6.2
Telephone calls	0.07	0.22	314	1,616	15.2
Traveling	1.22	1.16	95	9,617	90.6

Note: Primary activities are those respondents identified as their main activity. Other activities done simultaneously are not included. Travel related to activities is reported separately. Numbers will do sum to total because not all activities are shown. The index is calculated by dividing time spent by age group by time spent by the average man and multiplying by 100. "–" means sample is too small to make a reliable estimate.
Source: Bureau of Labor Statistics, unpublished tables from the 2010 American Time Use Survey, Internet site http://www.bls .gov/tus/home.htm; calculations by New Strategist

Table 10.5 Detailed Time Use of Men Aged 20 to 24, 2010

(hours per day spent in primary activities by total men aged 15 or older and men aged 20 to 24, index of age group to total, and number and percent of men aged 20 to 24 participating in activity on an average day, 2010)

	average hours per day for total men	average hours per day for men aged 20 to 24	index, 20 to 24 to total	men aged 20 to 24 participating in activity	
				number (in 000s)	percent
Total, all activities	**24.00**	**24.00**	**100**	**10,551**	**100.0%**
Personal care activities	9.24	9.62	104	10,551	100.0
Sleeping	8.56	8.95	105	10,551	100.0
Grooming	0.58	0.63	109	8,783	83.2
Health-related self-care	0.08	–	–	151	1.4
Household activities	1.44	0.97	67	5,387	51.1
Housework	0.26	0.27	104	1,657	15.7
Food preparation and cleanup	0.32	0.18	56	2,734	25.9
Lawn, garden, and houseplants	0.31	–	–	238	2.3
Animals and pets	0.08	0.03	38	659	6.2
Vehicles	0.08	–	–	422	4.0
Household management	0.16	0.13	81	1,888	17.9
Financial management	0.02	–	–	159	1.5
Household and personal organization and planning	0.07	0.07	100	1,358	12.9
Household and personal mail and messages (except email)	0.01	–	–	214	2.0
Household and personal email and messages	0.05	–	–	405	3.8
Caring for and helping household members	0.28	0.08	29	1,026	9.7
Caring for and helping household children	0.23	0.06	26	553	5.2
Caring for household adults	0.01	0.00	0	54	0.5
Helping household adults	0.01	–	–	494	4.7
Caring for and helping people in other households	0.14	0.12	86	1,733	16.4
Caring for and helping children in other households	0.05	0.06	120	426	4.0
Caring for adults in other households	–	–	–	111	1.1
Helping adults in other households	0.08	–	–	1,237	11.7
Working and work-related activities	3.75	3.25	87	4,779	45.3
Working	3.65	3.18	87	4,400	41.7
Job search and interviewing	0.06	–	–	364	3.4
Educational activities	0.44	1.14	259	2,166	20.5
Taking class	0.30	0.58	193	1,550	14.7
Homework and research	0.13	0.56	431	1,652	15.7
Consumer purchases	0.30	0.27	90	3,864	36.6
Grocery shopping	0.08	0.05	63	722	6.8
Shopping (except groceries, food, and gas)	0.19	0.19	100	1,914	18.1
Professional and personal care services	0.06	–	–	539	5.1
Medical and care services	0.04	–	–	92	0.9
Eating and drinking	1.17	1.08	92	9,911	93.9
Socializing, relaxing, and leisure	4.88	5.15	106	10,084	95.6
Socializing and communicating	0.61	0.95	156	3,858	36.6
Attending or hosting social events	0.07	–	–	170	1.6

	average hours per day for total men	average hours per day for men aged 20 to 24	index, 20 to 24 to total	men aged 20 to 24 participating in activity	
				number (in 000s)	percent
Relaxing and leisure	4.11	3.95	96	9,561	90.6%
Television and movies	2.94	2.30	78	8,042	76.2
Playing games	0.27	0.68	252	2,627	24.9
Computer use for leisure (except games)	0.20	0.32	160	1,385	13.1
Reading for personal interest	0.25	0.11	44	773	7.3
Arts and entertainment (other than sports)	0.09	0.19	211	576	5.5
Attending movies	0.03	–	–	243	2.3
Sports, exercise, and recreation	0.45	0.45	100	2,458	23.3
Participating in sports, exercise, and recreation	0.42	0.41	98	2,395	22.7
Attending sporting or recreational events	0.03	–	–	167	1.6
Religious and spiritual activities	0.13	0.09	69	497	4.7
Volunteer activities	0.12	–	–	410	3.9
Telephone calls	0.07	–	–	884	8.4
Traveling	1.22	1.25	102	9,772	92.6

Note: Primary activities are those respondents identified as their main activity. Other activities done simultaneously are not included. Travel related to activities is reported separately. Numbers do not sum to total because not all activities are shown. The index is calculated by dividing time spent by age group by time spent by the average man and multiplying by 100. "–" means sample is too small to make a reliable estimate.

Source: Bureau of Labor Statistics, unpublished tables from the 2010 American Time Use Survey, Internet site http://www.bls .gov/tus/home.htm; calculations by New Strategist

Table 10.6 Detailed Time Use of Men Aged 25 to 34, 2010

(hours per day spent in primary activities by total men aged 15 or older and men aged 25 to 34, index of age group to total, and number and percent of men aged 25 to 34 participating in activity on an average day, 2010)

	average hours per day for total men	average hours per day for men aged 25 to 34	index, 25 to 34 to total	men aged 25 to 34 participating in activity number (in 000s)	percent
Total, all activities	**24.00**	**24.00**	**100**	**20,466**	**100.0%**
Personal care activities	9.24	8.96	97	20,466	100.0
Sleeping	8.56	8.28	97	20,449	99.9
Grooming	0.58	0.64	110	16,583	81.0
Health-related self-care	0.08	–	–	410	2.0
Household activities	1.44	1.09	76	13,376	65.4
Housework	0.26	0.23	88	3,722	18.2
Food preparation and cleanup	0.32	0.30	94	8,898	43.5
Lawn, garden, and houseplants	0.31	0.14	45	1,389	6.8
Animals and pets	0.08	0.07	88	2,112	10.3
Vehicles	0.08	0.07	88	946	4.6
Household management	0.16	0.12	75	4,196	20.5
Financial management	0.02	0.01	50	334	1.6
Household and personal organization and planning	0.07	0.07	100	2,134	10.4
Household and personal mail and messages (except email)	0.01	0.00	0	468	2.3
Household and personal email and messages	0.05	0.04	80	1,620	7.9
Caring for and helping household members	0.28	0.52	186	6,032	29.5
Caring for and helping household children	0.23	0.48	209	5,632	27.5
Caring for household adults	0.01	0.00	0	190	0.9
Helping household adults	0.01	–	–	637	3.1
Caring for and helping people in other households	0.14	0.13	93	2,324	11.4
Caring for and helping children in other households	0.05	–	–	544	2.7
Caring for adults in other households	–	0.00	–	33	0.2
Helping adults in other households	0.08	0.09	113	1,801	8.8
Working and work-related activities	3.75	5.07	135	13,565	66.3
Working	3.65	5.00	137	13,050	63.8
Job search and interviewing	0.06	0.05	83	563	2.8
Educational activities	0.44	0.24	55	1,053	5.1
Taking class	0.30	0.14	47	692	3.4
Homework and research	0.13	0.10	77	809	4.0
Consumer purchases	0.30	0.30	100	8,565	41.8
Grocery shopping	0.08	0.08	100	2,030	9.9
Shopping (except groceries, food, and gas)	0.19	0.19	100	4,325	21.1
Professional and personal care services	0.06	–	–	987	4.8
Medical and care services	0.04	–	–	221	1.1
Eating and drinking	1.17	1.15	98	19,336	94.5
Socializing, relaxing, and leisure	4.88	4.14	85	19,234	94.0
Socializing and communicating	0.61	0.66	108	6,789	33.2
Attending or hosting social events	0.07	0.11	157	484	2.4

	average hours per day for total men	average hours per day for men aged 25 to 34	index, 25 to 34 to total	men aged 25 to 34 participating in activity	
				number (in 000s)	percent
Relaxing and leisure	4.11	3.27	80	18,073	88.3%
Television and movies	2.94	2.40	82	15,560	76.0
Playing games	0.27	0.26	96	2,176	10.6
Computer use for leisure (except games)	0.20	0.18	90	2,682	13.1
Reading for personal interest	0.25	0.12	48	2,006	9.8
Arts and entertainment (other than sports)	0.09	0.11	122	762	3.7
Attending movies	0.03	0.05	167	450	2.2
Sports, exercise, and recreation	0.45	0.39	87	4,089	20.0
Participating in sports, exercise, and recreation	0.42	0.37	88	3,929	19.2
Attending sporting or recreational events	0.03	0.00	0	178	0.9
Religious and spiritual activities	0.13	0.12	92	1,166	5.7
Volunteer activities	0.12	0.09	75	751	3.7
Telephone calls	0.07	0.08	114	2,143	10.5
Traveling	1.22	1.41	116	19,450	95.0

Note: Primary activities are those respondents identified as their main activity. Other activities done simultaneously are not included. Travel related to activities is reported separately. Numbers do not sum to total because not all activities are shown. The index is calculated by dividing time spent by age group by time spent by the average man and multiplying by 100. "–" means sample is too small to make a reliable estimate.
Source: Bureau of Labor Statistics, unpublished tables from the 2010 American Time Use Survey, Internet site http://www.bls.gov/tus/home.htm; calculations by New Strategist

Table 10.7 Detailed Time Use of Women Aged 15 to 19, 2010

(hours per day spent in primary activities by total women aged 15 or older and women aged 15 to 19, index of age group to total, and number and percent of women aged 15 to 19 participating in activity on an average day, 2010)

	average hours per day for total women	average hours per day for women aged 15 to 19	index, 15 to 19 to total	women aged 15 to 19 participating in activity	
				number (in 000s)	percent
Total, all activities	**24.00**	**24.00**	**100**	**10,364**	**100.0%**
Personal care activities	9.66	10.40	108	10,364	100.0
Sleeping	8.76	9.47	108	10,364	100.0
Grooming	0.79	0.93	118	9,344	90.2
Health-related self-care	0.10	0.00	0	181	1.7
Household activities	2.18	0.87	40	6,667	64.3
Housework	0.87	0.30	34	2,835	27.4
Food preparation and cleanup	0.79	0.23	29	3,288	31.7
Lawn, garden, and houseplants	0.12	0.03	25	238	2.3
Animals and pets	0.11	0.12	109	1,184	11.4
Vehicles	0.01	0.00	0	113	1.1
Household management	0.22	0.15	68	2,455	23.7
Financial management	0.04	0.00	0	60	0.6
Household and personal organization and planning	0.11	–	–	1,875	18.1
Household and personal mail and messages (except email)	0.03	0.00	0	148	1.4
Household and personal email and messages	0.05	0.03	60	583	5.6
Caring for and helping household members	0.58	0.18	31	1,719	16.6
Caring for and helping household children	0.48	0.17	35	1,472	14.2
Caring for household adults	0.02	0.00	0	74	0.7
Helping household adults	0.01	–	–	194	1.9
Caring for and helping people in other households	0.16	0.11	69	1,852	17.9
Caring for and helping children in other households	0.08	0.07	88	1,105	10.7
Caring for adults in other households	0.02	0.00	0	22	0.2
Helping adults in other households	0.06	0.04	67	896	8.6
Working and work-related activities	2.73	0.94	34	2,000	19.3
Working	2.66	0.86	32	1,626	15.7
Job search and interviewing	0.03	0.00	0	88	0.8
Educational activities	0.45	3.46	769	6,035	58.2
Taking class	0.26	2.40	923	4,360	42.1
Homework and research	0.18	0.96	533	4,215	40.7
Consumer purchases	0.44	0.33	75	3,333	32.2
Grocery shopping	0.13	0.04	31	514	5.0
Shopping (except groceries, food, and gas)	0.28	0.26	93	1,917	18.5
Professional and personal care services	0.10	0.04	40	442	4.3
Medical and care services	0.06	–	–	295	2.8
Eating and drinking	1.09	0.95	87	9,875	95.3
Socializing, relaxing, and leisure	4.39	4.28	97	9,794	94.5
Socializing and communicating	0.65	0.76	117	4,994	48.2
Attending or hosting social events	0.08	0.07	88	364	3.5

	average hours per day for total women	average hours per day for women aged 15 to 19	index, 15 to 19 to total	women aged 15 to 19 participating in activity	
				number (in 000s)	percent
Relaxing and leisure	3.59	3.39	94	9,190	88.7%
Television and movies	2.52	2.33	92	7,828	75.5
Playing games	0.15	0.20	133	1,156	11.2
Computer use for leisure (except games)	0.19	0.36	189	2,375	22.9
Reading for personal interest	0.35	0.17	49	1,414	13.6
Arts and entertainment (other than sports)	0.08	0.05	63	255	2.5
Attending movies	0.03	0.04	133	215	2.1
Sports, exercise, and recreation	0.23	0.50	217	2,784	26.9
Participating in sports, exercise, and recreation	0.20	0.40	200	2,564	24.7
Attending sporting or recreational events	0.03	0.10	333	351	3.4
Religious and spiritual activities	0.18	0.10	56	597	5.8
Volunteer activities	0.18	0.13	72	806	7.8
Telephone calls	0.13	0.22	169	2,099	20.3
Traveling	1.16	1.14	98	9,119	88.0

Note: Primary activities are those respondents identified as their main activity. Other activities done simultaneously are not included. Travel related to activities is reported separately. Numbers do not sum to total because not all activities are shown. The index is calculated by dividing time spent by age group by time spent by the average woman and multiplying by 100. "–" means sample is too small to make a reliable estimate.

Source: Bureau of Labor Statistics, unpublished tables from the 2010 American Time Use Survey, Internet site http://www.bls .gov/tus/home.htm; calculations by New Strategist

Table 10.8 Detailed Time Use of Women Aged 20 to 24, 2010

(hours per day spent in primary activities by total women aged 15 or older and women aged 20 to 24, index of age group to total, and number and percent of women aged 20 to 24 participating in activity on an average day, 2010)

	average hours per day for total women	average hours per day for women aged 20 to 24	index, 20 to 24 to total	women aged 20 to 24 participating in activity	
				number (in 000s)	percent
Total, all activities	**24.00**	**24.00**	**100**	**10,497**	**100.0%**
Personal care activities	9.66	9.94	103	10,469	99.7
Sleeping	8.76	9.09	104	10,469	99.7
Grooming	0.79	0.85	108	8,588	81.8
Health-related self-care	0.10	0.00	0	430	4.1
Household activities	2.18	1.52	70	7,552	71.9
Housework	0.87	0.62	71	3,507	33.4
Food preparation and cleanup	0.79	0.60	76	5,726	54.5
Lawn, garden, and houseplants	0.12	–	–	95	0.9
Animals and pets	0.11	–	–	1,173	11.2
Vehicles	0.01	–	–	174	1.7
Household management	0.22	0.12	55	2,710	25.8
Financial management	0.04	0.00	0	142	1.4
Household and personal organization and planning	0.11	0.08	73	1,749	16.7
Household and personal mail and messages (except email)	0.03	0.00	0	91	0.9
Household and personal email and messages	0.05	0.03	60	831	7.9
Caring for and helping household members	0.58	0.89	153	3,801	36.2
Caring for and helping household children	0.48	0.82	171	3,297	31.4
Caring for household adults	0.02	0.00	0	191	1.8
Helping household adults	0.01	0.02	200	783	7.5
Caring for and helping people in other households	0.16	–	–	1,234	11.8
Caring for and helping children in other households	0.08	–	–	160	1.5
Caring for adults in other households	0.02	0.00	0	0	0.0
Helping adults in other households	0.06	–	–	1,116	10.6
Working and work-related activities	2.73	3.02	111	4,702	44.8
Working	2.66	2.93	110	4,367	41.6
Job search and interviewing	0.03	–	–	326	3.1
Educational activities	0.45	0.65	144	1,693	16.1
Taking class	0.26	0.25	96	991	9.4
Homework and research	0.18	0.40	222	1,269	12.1
Consumer purchases	0.44	0.38	86	4,619	44.0
Grocery shopping	0.13	0.10	77	1,492	14.2
Shopping (except groceries, food, and gas)	0.28	0.25	89	2,498	23.8
Professional and personal care services	0.10	0.06	60	709	6.8
Medical and care services	0.06	–	–	252	2.4
Eating and drinking	1.09	1.00	92	9,964	94.9
Socializing, relaxing, and leisure	4.39	4.30	98	10,039	95.6
Socializing and communicating	0.65	0.75	115	4,134	39.4
Attending or hosting social events	0.08	0.12	150	489	4.7

	average hours per day for total women	average hours per day for women aged 20 to 24	index, 20 to 24 to total	women aged 20 to 24 participating in activity	
				number (in 000s)	percent
Relaxing and leisure	3.59	3.27	91	9,219	87.8%
Television and movies	2.52	2.33	92	8,490	80.9
Playing games	0.15	0.21	140	901	8.6
Computer use for leisure (except games)	0.19	–	–	1,213	11.6
Reading for personal interest	0.35	–	–	855	8.1
Arts and entertainment (other than sports)	0.08	0.17	213	419	4.0
Attending movies	0.03	–	–	213	2.0
Sports, exercise, and recreation	0.23	0.18	78	1,020	9.7
Participating in sports, exercise, and recreation	0.20	0.16	80	963	9.2
Attending sporting or recreational events	0.03	–	–	57	0.5
Religious and spiritual activities	0.18	0.13	72	852	8.1
Volunteer activities	0.18	0.11	61	649	6.2
Telephone calls	0.13	0.11	85	1,508	14.4
Traveling	1.16	1.20	103	8,879	84.6

Note: Primary activities are those respondents identified as their main activity. Other activities done simultaneously are not included. Travel related to activities is reported separately. Numbers do not sum to total because not all activities are shown. The index is calculated by dividing time spent by age group by time spent by the average woman and multiplying by 100. "–" means sample is too small to make a reliable estimate.
Source: Bureau of Labor Statistics, unpublished tables from the 2010 American Time Use Survey, Internet site http://www.bls .gov/tus/home.htm; calculations by New Strategist

Table 10.9 Detailed Time Use of Women Aged 25 to 34, 2010

(hours per day spent in primary activities by total women aged 15 or older and women aged 25 to 34, index of age group to total, and number and percent of women aged 25 to 34 participating in activity on an average day, 2010)

	average hours per day for total women	average hours per day for women aged 25 to 34	index, 25 to 34 to total	women aged 25 to 34 participating in activity	
				number (in 000s)	percent
Total, all activities	**24.00**	**24.00**	**100**	**20,438**	**100.0%**
Personal care activities	9.66	9.77	101	20,438	100.0
Sleeping	8.76	8.89	101	20,438	100.0
Grooming	0.79	0.80	101	17,190	84.1
Health-related self-care	0.10	–	–	384	1.9
Household activities	2.18	1.80	83	16,905	82.7
Housework	0.87	0.74	85	9,197	45.0
Food preparation and cleanup	0.79	0.75	95	13,252	64.8
Lawn, garden, and houseplants	0.12	0.04	33	589	2.9
Animals and pets	0.11	0.07	64	2,185	10.7
Vehicles	0.01	0.01	100	259	1.3
Household management	0.22	0.15	68	5,031	24.6
Financial management	0.04	0.02	50	631	3.1
Household and personal organization and planning	0.11	0.08	73	3,215	15.7
Household and personal mail and messages (except email)	0.03	0.00	0	380	1.9
Household and personal email and messages	0.05	0.05	100	1,691	8.3
Caring for and helping household members	0.58	1.28	221	10,911	53.4
Caring for and helping household children	0.48	1.15	240	10,453	51.1
Caring for household adults	0.02	0.00	0	269	1.3
Helping household adults	0.01	–	–	667	3.3
Caring for and helping people in other households	0.16	0.12	75	2,026	9.9
Caring for and helping children in other households	0.08	–	–	553	2.7
Caring for adults in other households	0.02	0.01	50	179	0.9
Helping adults in other households	0.06	0.07	117	1,519	7.4
Working and work-related activities	2.73	3.55	130	10,245	50.1
Working	2.66	3.50	132	9,857	48.2
Job search and interviewing	0.03	–	–	383	1.9
Educational activities	0.45	0.25	56	1,354	6.6
Taking class	0.26	0.08	31	582	2.8
Homework and research	0.18	0.17	94	1,089	5.3
Consumer purchases	0.44	0.43	98	9,391	45.9
Grocery shopping	0.13	0.13	100	3,266	16.0
Shopping (except groceries, food, and gas)	0.28	0.27	96	5,067	24.8
Professional and personal care services	0.10	0.07	70	1,687	8.3
Medical and care services	0.06	0.04	67	607	3.0
Eating and drinking	1.09	1.07	98	19,303	94.4
Socializing, relaxing, and leisure	4.39	3.55	81	18,938	92.7
Socializing and communicating	0.65	0.70	108	7,675	37.6
Attending or hosting social events	0.08	0.12	150	722	3.5

	average hours per day for total women	average hours per day for women aged 25 to 34	index, 25 to 34 to total	women aged 25 to 34 participating in activity	
				number (in 000s)	percent
Relaxing and leisure	3.59	2.66	74	17,561	85.9%
Television and movies	2.52	1.97	78	15,123	74.0
Playing games	0.15	0.07	47	991	4.8
Computer use for leisure (except games)	0.19	0.25	132	2,999	14.7
Reading for personal interest	0.35	0.15	43	2,745	13.4
Arts and entertainment (other than sports)	0.08	0.07	88	538	2.6
Attending movies	0.03	0.02	67	214	1.0
Sports, exercise, and recreation	0.23	0.23	100	3,301	16.2
Participating in sports, exercise, and recreation	0.20	0.22	110	3,160	15.5
Attending sporting or recreational events	0.03	0.01	33	140	0.7
Religious and spiritual activities	0.18	0.11	61	1,393	6.8
Volunteer activities	0.18	0.15	83	913	4.5
Telephone calls	0.13	0.09	69	2,785	13.6
Traveling	1.16	1.23	106	18,370	89.9

Note: Primary activities are those respondents identified as their main activity. Other activities done simultaneously are not included. Travel related to activities is reported separately. Numbers do not sum to total because not all activities are shown. The index is calculated by dividing time spent by age group by time spent by the average woman and multiplying by 100. "–" means sample is too small to make a reliable estimate.
Source: Bureau of Labor Statistics, unpublished tables from the 2010 American Time Use Survey, Internet site http://www.bls.gov/tus/home.htm; calculations by New Strategist

11

Wealth

■ No generation has been hurt more by the Great Recession than Millennials. The net worth of householders under age 35 fell by 37 percent between 2007 and 2009—to just $9,000. This was the biggest decline among age groups.

■ The median financial assets of householders under age 35 held steady between 2007 and 2009, after adjusting for inflation. But this age group has only $7,400 in financial assets.

■ Householders under age 35 were the only ones to see their nonfinancial assets grow in value between 2007 and 2009, after adjusting for inflation. Behind the growth was the increase in their homeownership rate.

■ The debt of householders under age 35 soared between 2007 and 2009, rising by 35 percent after adjusting for inflation. Members of this age group owe more for their primary residence ($144,600) than any other age group because many bought homes during the housing bubble. The increase in debt explains why their net worth plunged.

■ A substantial 37 percent of householders under age 35 have education loans, owing a median of $15,000. This is more than households in the age group owe on credit cards ($3,000) or for their vehicles ($12,200).

Net Worth Fell Sharply during the Great Recession

Every age group lost ground during the economic downturn.

Net worth is what remains when a household's debts are subtracted from its assets. During the Great Recession, which officially lasted from December 2007 until June 2009, the value of houses, stocks, and retirement accounts fell sharply. At the same time, debt increased. Consequently, net worth fell 23 percent between 2007 and 2009, after adjusting for inflation. These data come from a unique follow-up to the 2007 Survey of Consumer Finances. The survey is taken only every three years. Because of the severity of the Great Recession, however, the Federal Reserve Board arranged for the 2007 respondents to be re-interviewed in 2009 to determine the impact of the Great Recession on household assets, debt, and net worth.

The impact was severe. Net worth fell in every age group. It declined the most—by 37 percent—among householders under age 35, many of them recent homebuyers who bought at the peak. It fell by the smallest percentage, 12 percent, among householders aged 65 to 74, many of whom bought their house decades ago.

■ Net worth typically rises with age as people pay off their debts. That pattern has not changed. In 2009, median household net worth peaked in the 55-to-64 age group at $222,300.

Net worth peaks among householders aged 55 to 64

(median household net worth by age of householder, 2009)

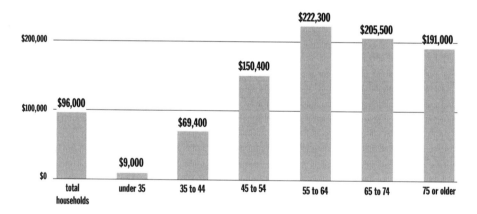

Table 11.1 Net Worth of Households, 2007 and 2009

(median net worth of households by age of householder, 2007 and 2009; percent change, 2007–09; in 2009 dollars)

	2009	2007	percent change
Total households	**$96,000**	**$125,400**	**–23.4%**
Under age 35	9,000	14,200	–36.6
Aged 35 to 44	69,400	97,100	–28.5
Aged 45 to 54	150,400	203,000	–25.9
Aged 55 to 64	222,300	257,700	–13.7
Aged 65 to 74	205,500	232,700	–11.7
Aged 75 or older	191,000	228,900	–16.6

Source: Federal Reserve Board, 2007-09 Panel Survey of Consumer Finances, Internet site http://www.federalreserve.gov/econresdata/scf/scf_2009p.htm; calculations by New Strategist

Financial Asset Value Declined in Most Age Groups

Householders aged 35 to 44 gained ground, however.

Most households own financial assets, which range from transaction accounts (checking and saving) to stocks, mutual funds, retirement accounts, and life insurance. The median value of the financial assets owned by the average household stood at $29,600 in 2009, down by a relatively modest 5 percent since 2007 after adjusting for inflation. Householders aged 35 to 44 were the only ones to make gains in the value of their financial assets between 2007 and 2009.

Transaction accounts, the most commonly owned financial asset, are held by 92 percent of households. Their median value was just $4,000 in 2009—slightly lower than the $4,100 of 2007. Retirement accounts are the second most commonly owned financial asset, with 56 percent of households having one. Most retirement accounts are not large, however, with an overall median value of just $48,000 in 2009. This figure is 5 percent lower than the $50,600 of 2007, after adjusting for inflation.

Only 18.5 percent of households owned stock directly in 2009 (outside of a retirement account). The median value of stock owned by stockholding households was just $12,000 in 2009, 35 percent less than the value in 2007 after adjusting for inflation.

■ The median value of household financial assets peaks in the 55-to-64 age group, at $72,500.

Median value of retirement accounts is modest, even in the older age groups

(median value of retirement accounts owned by households, by age of householder, 2009)

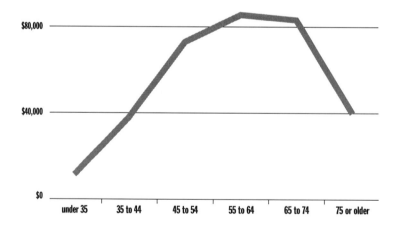

Table 11.2 Ownership and Value of Financial Assets, 2007 and 2009

(percentage of households owning any financial asset and median value of financial assets for owners, by age of householder, 2007 and 2009; percentage point change in ownership and percent change in value, 2007–09; in 2009 dollars)

	2009	2007	percentage point change
PERCENT OWNING			
Total households	**94.6%**	**94.3%**	**0.3**
Under age 35	91.4	90.2	1.2
Aged 35 to 44	92.3	93.5	–1.2
Aged 45 to-54	96.0	94.1	1.9
Aged 55 to 64	97.0	97.9	–0.9
Aged 65 to 74	97.8	96.1	1.7
Aged 75 or older	95.8	98.1	–2.3

	2009	2007	percent change
MEDIAN VALUE			
Total households	**$29,600**	**$31,300**	**–5.4%**
Under age 35	7,400	7,400	0.0
Aged 35 to 44	27,500	25,500	7.8
Aged 45 to 54	58,500	64,300	–9.0
Aged 55 to 64	72,500	78,200	–7.3
Aged 65 to 74	48,000	63,900	–24.9
Aged 75 or older	39,000	41,400	–5.8

Source: Federal Reserve Board, 2007-09 Panel Survey of Consumer Finances, Internet site http://www.federalreserve.gov/econresdata/scf/scf_2009p.htm; calculations by New Strategist

Table 11.3 Households Owning Transaction Accounts, Life Insurance, and CDs, 2007 and 2009

(percentage of households owning transaction accounts, cash value life insurance, and certificates of deposit, and median value for owners, by age of householder, 2007 and 2009; percentage point change in ownership and percent change in value, 2007–09; in 2009 dollars)

	transaction accounts			cash value life insurance			certificates of deposit		
	2009	2007	percentage point change	2009	2007	percentage point change	2009	2007	percentage point change
PERCENT OWNING									
Total households	**92.3%**	**92.6%**	**−0.3**	**24.3%**	**23.2%**	**1.1**	**15.9%**	**15.4%**	**0.5**
Under age 35	88.5	88.0	0.5	13.1	12.4	0.7	7.9	6.5	1.4
Aged 35 to 44	89.8	91.8	−2.0	16.8	17.1	−0.3	9.4	8.9	0.5
Aged 45 to 54	94.1	92.8	1.3	25.3	22.0	3.3	13.9	14.5	−0.6
Aged 55 to 64	95.3	96.5	−1.2	33.4	35.7	−2.3	20.2	19.5	0.7
Aged 65 to 74	95.0	95.0	0.0	36.3	34.6	1.7	24.8	23.0	1.8
Aged 75 or older	94.2	95.1	−0.9	34.2	29.2	5.0	35.2	36.8	−1.6

	transaction accounts			cash value life insurance			certificates of deposit		
	2009	2007	percent change	2009	2007	percent change	2009	2007	percent change
MEDIAN VALUE									
Total households	**$4,000**	**$4,100**	**−2.4%**	**$7,300**	**$8,300**	**−12.0%**	**$20,000**	**$20,700**	**−3.4%**
Under age 35	2,300	2,600	−11.5	2,500	3,600	−30.6	9,000	4,900	83.7
Aged 35 to 44	3,000	3,500	−14.3	7,000	8,300	−15.7	10,000	5,200	92.3
Aged 45 to 54	5,000	4,800	4.2	8,000	10,400	−23.1	18,000	18,600	−3.2
Aged 55 to 64	5,500	5,600	−1.8	10,000	10,400	−3.8	25,000	20,700	20.8
Aged 65 to 74	5,500	7,000	−21.4	10,000	10,600	−5.7	27,700	22,800	21.5
Aged 75 or older	7,000	6,200	12.9	8,000	5,200	53.8	31,400	31,100	1.0

Source: Federal Reserve Board, 2007-09 Panel Survey of Consumer Finances, Internet site http://www.federalreserve.gov/econresdata/scf/scf_2009p.htm; calculations by New Strategist

Table 11.4 Households Owning Retirement Accounts and Stocks, 2007 and 2009

(percentage of households owning retirement accounts and stocks, and median value for owners, by age of householder, 2007 and 2009; percentage point change in ownership and percent change in value, 2007–09; in 2009 dollars)

	retirement accounts			stocks		
	2009	2007	percentage point change	2009	2007	percentage point change
PERCENT OWNING						
Total households	**56.2%**	**55.6%**	**0.6**	**18.5%**	**18.4%**	**0.1**
Under age 35	48.4	44.9	3.5	12.6	14.6	–2.0
Aged 35 to 44	61.2	59.4	1.8	18.9	17.0	1.9
Aged 45 to 54	68.2	68.0	0.2	20.3	18.4	1.9
Aged 55 to 64	62.7	64.3	–1.6	21.3	21.2	0.1
Aged 65 to 74	51.8	53.3	–1.5	21.9	21.0	0.9
Aged 75 or older	29.5	31.3	–1.8	18.6	22.8	–4.2

	retirement accounts			stocks		
	2009	2007	percent change	2009	2007	percent change
MEDIAN VALUE						
Total households	**$48,000**	**$50,600**	**–5.1%**	**$12,000**	**$18,500**	**–35.1%**
Under age 35	11,400	10,400	9.6	3,000	3,100	–3.2
Aged 35 to 44	38,000	38,300	–0.8	12,000	15,500	–22.6
Aged 45 to 54	73,000	81,400	–10.3	11,700	19,700	–40.6
Aged 55 to 64	85,600	103,600	–17.4	16,000	24,900	–35.7
Aged 65 to 74	83,200	79,700	4.4	25,000	36,200	–30.9
Aged 75 or older	40,000	36,200	10.5	35,000	101,500	–65.5

Note: Stock ownership is direct ownership outside of a retirement account or mutual fund.
Source: Federal Reserve Board, 2007-09 Panel Survey of Consumer Finances, Internet site http://www.federalreserve.gov/econresdata/scf/scf_2009p.htm; calculations by New Strategist

Table 11.5 Households Owning Pooled Investment Funds and Bonds, 2007 and 2009

(percentage of households owning pooled investment funds and bonds, and median value for owners, by age of householder, 2007 and 2009; percentage point change in ownership and percent change in value, 2007–09; in 2009 dollars)

	pooled investment funds			bonds		
	2009	2007	percentage point change	2009	2007	percentage point change
PERCENT OWNING						
Total households	**10.8%**	**11.5%**	**–0.7**	**2.6%**	**1.7%**	**0.9**
Under age 35	5.4	5.8	–0.4	0.5	0.2	0.3
Aged 35 to 44	10.0	11.7	–1.7	1.3	0.7	0.6
Aged 45 to 54	13.2	12.6	0.6	2.4	1.1	1.3
Aged 55 to 64	14.5	14.1	0.4	3.3	2.4	0.9
Aged 65 to 74	11.5	13.8	–2.3	6.2	4.5	1.7
Aged 75 or older	12.6	15.1	–2.5	5.5	3.9	1.6

	pooled investment funds			bonds		
	2009	2007	percent change	2009	2007	percent change
MEDIAN VALUE						
Total households	**$47,000**	**$58,700**	**–19.9%**	**$50,000**	**$62,100**	**–19.5%**
Under age 35	10,000	15,000	–33.3	–	–	–
Aged 35 to 44	35,000	27,300	28.2	5,000	103,600	–95.2
Aged 45 to 54	35,000	51,800	–32.4	27,000	127,600	–78.8
Aged 55 to 64	70,400	115,000	–38.8	65,000	82,800	–21.5
Aged 65 to 74	100,000	155,300	–35.6	86,000	51,600	66.7
Aged 75 or older	70,000	77,700	–9.9	37,400	96,500	–61.2

Note: "Pooled investment funds" exclude money market funds and indirectly held mutual funds. They include open-end and closed-end mutual funds, real estate investment trusts, and hedge funds. "–" means sample is too small to make a reliable estimate.
Source: Federal Reserve Board, 2007-09 Panel Survey of Consumer Finances, Internet site http://www.federalreserve.gov/econresdata/scf/scf_2009p.htm; calculations by New Strategist

Nonfinancial Assets Are the Basis of Household Wealth

The average household saw the value of its nonfinancial assets fall during the Great Recession.

The median value of the nonfinancial assets owned by the average American household stood at $204,000 in 2009, far surpassing the $29,600 median in financial assets. Between 2007 and 2009, the value of the nonfinancial assets owned by the average household fell 13 percent, after adjusting for inflation. Nearly every age group saw its nonfinancial assets fall in value, primarily because of the decline in housing values. Householders under age 35 were the only ones who made gains.

Eighty-seven percent of households own a vehicle, the most commonly held nonfinancial asset. The value of the vehicles owned by the average household fell steeply (down 26 percent) between 2007 and 2009, after adjusting for inflation. Behind the decline was the reluctance of households to buy new vehicles during the Great Recession.

The second most commonly owned nonfinancial asset is a home, owned by 70 percent. Homes are by far the most valuable asset owned by Americans, and they account for the largest share of net worth. In 2009, the median value of the average owned home was $176,000, 15 percent below the median of $207,100 in 2007 (in 2009 dollars). Housing prices have continued to decline, driving median home values even lower than the numbers shown here.

■ The continuing decline in housing values may have reduced average household net worth below the 2009 figure.

Median housing value peaks in the 45-to-54 age group

(median value of the primary residence among homeowners, by age of householder, 2009)

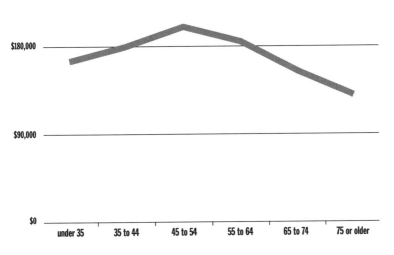

Table 11.6 Ownership and Value of Nonfinancial Assets, 2007 and 2009

(percentage of households owning any nonfinancial asset and median value of nonfinancial assets for owners, by age of householder, 2007 and 2009; percentage point change in ownership and percent change in value, 2007–09; in 2009 dollars)

	2009	2007	percentage point change
PERCENT OWNING			
Total households	**92.6%**	**92.7%**	**−0.1**
Under age 35	89.5	88.1	1.4
Aged 35 to 44	92.3	91.8	0.5
Aged 45 to 54	95.0	95.2	−0.2
Aged 55 to 64	95.5	96.1	−0.6
Aged 65 to 74	96.0	95.3	0.7
Aged 75 or older	86.2	90.4	−4.2

	2009	2007	percent change
MEDIAN VALUE			
Total households	**$204,000**	**$234,800**	**−13.1%**
Under age 35	52,800	44,400	18.9
Aged 35 to 44	196,500	232,000	−15.3
Aged 45 to 54	289,500	326,600	−11.4
Aged 55 to 64	308,000	361,900	−14.9
Aged 65 to 74	253,000	306,200	−17.4
Aged 75 or older	193,100	238,900	−19.2

Source: Federal Reserve Board, 2007-09 Panel Survey of Consumer Finances, Internet site http://www.federalreserve.gov/econresdata/scf/scf_2009p.htm; calculations by New Strategist

Table 11.7 **Households Owning Primary Residence, Other Residential Property, and Nonresidential Property, 2007 and 2009**

(percentage of households owning primary residence, other residential property, and nonresidential property, and median value for owners, by age of householder, 2007 and 2009; percentage point change in ownership and percent change in value, 2007–09; in 2009 dollars)

	primary residence			other residential property			nonresidential property		
	2009	2007	percentage point change	2009	2007	percentage point change	2009	2007	percentage point change
PERCENT OWNING									
Total households	70.3%	68.9%	1.4	13.0%	13.9%	–0.9	7.6%	8.3%	–0.7
Under age 35	44.6	40.5	4.1	7.1	5.3	1.8	3.1	3.1	0.0
Aged 35 to 44	68.9	66.6	2.3	11.4	12.5	–1.1	7.0	7.9	–0.9
Aged 45 to 54	78.1	77.3	0.8	14.4	15.5	–1.1	9.5	10.0	–0.5
Aged 55 to 64	81.9	82.2	–0.3	18.6	21.0	–2.4	10.9	11.5	–0.6
Aged 65 to 74	86.8	85.5	1.3	17.9	19.2	–1.3	11.1	10.9	0.2
Aged 75 or older	77.2	79.2	–2.0	11.2	14.3	–3.1	5.7	9.0	–3.3

	primary residence			other residential property			nonresidential property		
	2009	2007	percent change	2009	2007	percent change	2009	2007	percent change
MEDIAN VALUE									
Total households	$176,000	$207,100	–15.0%	$150,000	$141,700	5.9%	$69,000	$78,800	–12.4%
Under age 35	165,000	186,400	–11.5	100,000	62,100	61.0	30,000	51,800	–42.1
Aged 35 to 44	180,000	212,300	–15.2	155,700	155,300	0.3	28,600	59,000	–51.5
Aged 45 to 54	200,000	238,200	–16.0	176,000	163,800	7.4	90,000	79,000	13.9
Aged 55 to 64	185,000	207,100	–10.7	150,000	155,300	–3.4	100,000	103,600	–3.5
Aged 65 to 74	155,000	191,600	–19.1	149,500	139,800	6.9	100,000	103,600	–3.5
Aged 75 or older	130,000	155,300	–16.3	160,000	103,600	54.4	60,000	103,600	–42.1

Source: Federal Reserve Board, 2007-09 Panel Survey of Consumer Finances, Internet site http://www.federalreserve.gov/econresdata/scf/scf_2009p.htm; calculations by New Strategist

Table 11.8 Households Owning Vehicles and Business Equity, 2007 and 2009

(percentage of households owning vehicles and business equity, and median value for owners, by age of householder, 2007 and 2009; percentage point change in ownership and percent change in value, 2007–09; in 2009 dollars)

	vehicles			business equity		
	2009	**2007**	**percentage point change**	**2009**	**2007**	**percentage point change**
PERCENT OWNING						
Total households	**86.8%**	**87.9%**	**−1.1**	**11.9%**	**12.4%**	**−0.5**
Under age 35	87.2	85.8	1.4	7.7	7.1	0.6
Aged 35 to 44	87.6	87.9	−0.3	15.4	15.8	−0.4
Aged 45 to 54	90.6	91.1	−0.5	15.0	15.1	−0.1
Aged 55 to 64	90.5	92.5	−2.0	15.9	17.2	−1.3
Aged 65 to 74	88.3	90.8	−2.5	9.1	10.1	−1.0
Aged 75 or older	67.6	74.3	−6.7	3.8	5.4	−1.6

	vehicles			business equity		
	2009	**2007**	**percent change**	**2009**	**2007**	**percent change**
MEDIAN VALUE						
Total households	**$12,000**	**$16,200**	**−25.9%**	**$94,500**	**$103,600**	**−8.8%**
Under age 35	10,500	14,500	−27.6	41,300	46,600	−11.4
Aged 35 to 44	15,000	18,100	−17.1	70,000	98,700	−29.1
Aged 45 to 54	15,000	18,600	−19.4	80,000	103,600	−22.8
Aged 55 to 64	15,000	17,800	−15.7	150,000	152,500	−1.6
Aged 65 to 74	12,000	15,200	−21.1	500,000	517,800	−3.4
Aged 75 or older	7,900	9,700	−18.6	250,000	258,900	−3.4

Source: Federal Reserve Board, 2007-09 Panel Survey of Consumer Finances, Internet site http://www.federalreserve.gov/econresdata/scf/scf_2009p.htm; calculations by New Strategist

Most Households Are in Debt

Among households with debt, the amount owed increased between 2007 and 2009.

Seventy-eight percent of households have debt, owing a median of $75,600 in 2009. The median amount of debt owed by the average debtor household increased by 7.5 percent between 2007 and 2009, after adjusting for inflation. The percentage of households in debt fell slightly, however.

Householders aged 35 to 54 are most likely to be in debt, with 87 to 88 percent owing money. Debt declines with age, falling to a low of 35 percent among householders aged 75 or older.

Four types of debt are most common—debt secured by the primary residence (mortgages), which is held by 47 percent of households; credit card debt (43 percent); vehicle loans (34 percent); and education loans (18 percent). Mortgages account for the largest share of debt. The median amount owed by the average homeowner for the primary residence stood at $113,500 in 2009. Education loans are second in size, the average household with this type of debt owing a median of $15,000—more than the $12,400 owed by (the more numerous) households with vehicle loans. Credit card debt is tiny by comparison, the average household with a credit card balance owing only $3,300.

■ Americans are attempting to pay down their debts, reducing consumer demand.

Education loans are common among young and middle-aged householders

(percent of households with education loans, by age of householder, 2009)

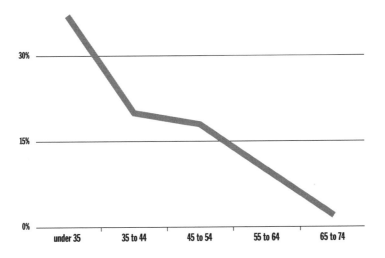

Table 11.9 Debt of Households, 2007 and 2009

(percentage of households with debt and median amount of debt for debtors, by age of householder, 2007 and 2009; percentage point change in households with debt and percent change in amount of debt, 2007–09; in 2009 dollars)

	2009	2007	percentage point change
PERCENT WITH DEBT			
Total households	**77.5%**	**79.7%**	**−2.2**
Under age 35	84.6	85.4	−0.8
Aged 35 to 44	87.7	87.3	0.4
Aged 45 to 54	86.6	88.1	−1.5
Aged 55 to 64	77.7	83.4	−5.7
Aged 65 to 74	62.1	68.5	−6.4
Aged 75 or older	35.0	36.2	−1.2

	2009	2007	percent change
MEDIAN AMOUNT OWED			
Total households	**$75,600**	**$70,300**	**7.5%**
Under age 35	51,000	37,800	34.9
Aged 35 to 44	109,500	113,700	−3.7
Aged 45 to 54	100,200	103,500	−3.2
Aged 55 to 64	62,000	64,300	−3.6
Aged 65 to 74	48,100	41,800	15.1
Aged 75 or older	8,200	20,000	−59.0

Source: Federal Reserve Board, 2007-09 Panel Survey of Consumer Finances, Internet site http://www.federalreserve.gov/'econresdata/scf/scf_2009p.htm; calculations by New Strategist

Table 11.10 Households with Residential Debt, 2007 and 2009

(percentage of households with residential debt, and median amount of debt for debtors, by age of householder, 2007 and 2009; percentage point change in households with debt and percent change in amount of debt, 2007–09; in 2009 dollars)

	secured by residential property								
	secured by primary residence			home equity line of credit			other residential debt		
	2009	2007	percentage point change	2009	2007	percentage point change	2009	2007	percentage point change
PERCENT WITH DEBT									
Total households	**46.6%**	**47.8%**	**−1.2**	**10.5%**	**8.7%**	**1.8**	**5.1%**	**5.7%**	**−0.6**
Under age 35	39.8	37.4	2.4	4.3	3.7	0.6	3.3	3.2	0.1
Aged 35 to 44	60.0	60.0	0.0	10.2	8.5	1.7	6.0	7.0	−1.0
Aged 45 to 54	62.2	64.3	−2.1	14.0	12.3	1.7	6.7	7.7	−1.0
Aged 55 to 64	46.8	51.9	−5.1	17.1	12.8	4.3	6.6	8.3	−1.7
Aged 65 to 74	34.9	37.4	−2.5	11.9	10.3	1.6	4.7	4.3	0.4
Aged 75 or older	11.5	13.4	−1.9	4.3	3.8	0.5	0.9	0.6	0.3

	secured by residential property								
	secured by primary residence			home equity line of credit			other residential debt		
	2009	2007	percent change	2009	2007	percent change	2009	2007	percent change
MEDIAN AMOUNT OWED									
Total households	**$113,500**	**$113,900**	**−0.4%**	**$21,500**	**$22,800**	**−5.7%**	**$130,000**	**$98,400**	**32.1%**
Under age 35	144,600	140,100	3.2	20,000	20,300	−1.5	118,000	80,800	46.0
Aged 35 to 44	127,800	128,300	−0.4	20,000	24,900	−19.7	150,000	110,600	35.6
Aged 45 to 54	111,600	113,900	−2.0	30,000	25,900	15.8	115,000	86,000	33.7
Aged 55 to 64	95,000	93,200	1.9	20,000	21,900	−8.7	155,000	110,900	39.8
Aged 65 to 74	80,000	81,800	−2.2	28,000	15,500	80.6	115,000	116,000	−0.9
Aged 75 or older	49,000	33,900	44.5	13,000	25,900	−49.8	23,000	51,800	−55.6

Source: Federal Reserve Board, 2007-09 Panel Survey of Consumer Finances, Internet site http://www.federalreserve.gov/econresdata/scf/scf_2009p.htm; calculations by New Strategist

Table 11.11 Households with Credit Card Debt, Vehicle Loans, and Education Loans, 2007 and 2009

(percentage of households with credit card, vehicle, and education debt, and median amount of debt for debtors, by age of householder, 2007 and 2009; percentage point change in households with debt and percent change in amount of debt, 2007–09; in 2009 dollars)

	credit card balances			vehicle loans			education loans		
	2009	2007	percentage point change	2009	2007	percentage point change	2009	2007	percentage point change
PERCENT WITH DEBT									
Total households	**43.2%**	**47.8%**	**–4.6**	**33.9%**	**36.0%**	**–2.1**	**17.7%**	**16.3%**	**1.4**
Under age 35	42.8	50.6	–7.8	43.1	46.0	–2.9	36.8	35.7	1.1
Aged 35 to 44	49.6	52.6	–3.0	44.7	44.1	0.6	19.7	15.7	4.0
Aged 45 to 54	50.5	54.1	–3.6	35.5	38.3	–2.8	18.0	14.8	3.2
Aged 55 to 64	44.6	50.4	–5.8	30.8	35.5	–4.7	9.9	11.3	–1.4
Aged 65 to 74	35.0	38.7	–3.7	21.3	21.9	–0.6	1.9	1.9	0.0
Aged 75 or older	20.2	21.8	–1.6	5.5	7.2	–1.7	0.0	0.5	–0.5

	credit card balances			vehicle loans			education loans		
	2009	2007	percent change	2009	2007	percent change	2009	2007	percent change
MEDIAN AMOUNT OWED									
Total households	**$3,300**	**$3,100**	**6.5%**	**$12,400**	**$11,200**	**10.7%**	**$15,000**	**$12,400**	**21.0%**
Under age 35	3,000	1,900	57.9	12,200	11,300	8.0	15,000	14,500	3.4
Aged 35 to 44	3,000	3,600	–16.7	13,000	12,300	5.7	16,000	12,400	29.0
Aged 45 to 54	4,000	3,700	8.1	13,000	10,900	19.3	15,000	10,700	40.2
Aged 55 to 64	4,500	4,100	9.8	12,000	9,600	25.0	12,000	7,300	64.4
Aged 65 to 74	2,900	3,200	–9.4	10,000	12,500	–20.0	–	–	–
Aged 75 or older	2,000	800	150.0	9,500	7,600	25.0	–	–	–

Note: "–" means sample is too small to make a reliable estimate.
Source: Federal Reserve Board, 2007-09 Panel Survey of Consumer Finances, Internet site http://www.federalreserve.gov/econresdata/scf/scf_2009p.htm; calculations by New Strategist

Retirement Worries Are Growing

Few workers are very confident in having enough money for a comfortable retirement.

Only 14 percent of workers are "very confident" in their ability to afford a comfortable retirement, according to the 2012 Retirement Confidence Survey. The 14 percent figure is well below the 23 percent who felt very confident in 2002. There is little variation in retirement confidence by age.

Reality may be dawning on many workers. Since 2002, the expected age of retirement has climbed. The percentage of all workers expecting to retire at age 65 or older (including those who say they will never retire) increased from 52 to 70 percent between 2002 and 2012. Among workers aged 55 or older, fully 74 percent expect to retire at age 65 or older.

One reason so many are putting off retirement is that they have little in the way of retirement savings. Among workers approaching retirement—those aged 55 or older—the 60 percent majority has saved less than $100,000 for retirement (not counting the value of their home).

■ Nearly one-third of workers aged 55 or older have saved less than $10,000 for retirement.

Most workers are not planning on an early retirement

(percent of workers aged 25 or older who expect to retire at age 65 or older, by age, 2012)

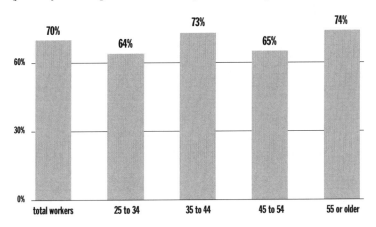

Table 11.12 Retirement Confidence, 2002 and 2012

(percentage of workers aged 25 or older who are "very confident" in financial aspects of retirement, by age, 2002 and 2012; percentage point change, 2002–12)

	total workers	25 to 34	35 to 44	45 to 54	55 or older
You will have enough money to live comfortably throughout your retirement years					
2012	14%	13%	16%	12%	16%
2002	23	26	20	21	25
You will have enough money to take care of basic expenses during retirement					
2012	26	26	27	25	27
2002	38	40	38	39	32
You are doing a good job of preparing financially for retirement					
2012	19	22	21	14	18
2002	23	26	23	21	24
You will have enough money to take care of medical expenses during retirement					
2012	13	14	15	11	14
2002	20	19	17	19	26
You will have enough money to pay for long-term care during retirement					
2012	9	10	11	8	8
2002	13	15	14	10	14
The Social Security system will continue to provide benefits of at least equal value to the benefits received by retirees today					
2012	6	4	4	4	12
2002	6	1	4	7	16
The Medicare system will continue to provide benefits of at least equal value to the benefits received by retirees today					
2012	4	2	3	6	7
2002	5	3	4	5	15

Source: Employee Benefit Research Institute, Retirement Confidence Surveys, Internet site http://www.ebri.org/surveys/rcs/2012/

Table 11.13 Expected Age of Retirement, 2002 and 2012

(expected age of retirement among workers aged 25 or older, by age, 2002 and 2012; percentage point change, 2002–12)

	2012	2002	percentage point change
ALL WORKERS			
Before age 60	8%	17%	–9
Aged 60 to 64	16	22	–6
Age 65	26	29	–3
Aged 66 or older	37	18	19
Never retire	7	5	2
Don't know/refused	5	9	–4
AGED 25 TO 34			
Before age 60	15	21	–6
Aged 60 to 64	16	20	–4
Age 65	27	33	–6
Aged 66 or older	34	17	17
Never retire	3	4	–1
Don't know/refused	4	5	–1
AGED 35 TO 44			
Before age 60	5	16	–11
Aged 60 to 64	15	27	–12
Age 65	29	30	–1
Aged 66 or older	35	14	21
Never retire	9	6	3
Don't know/refused	6	8	–2
AGED 45 TO 54			
Before age 60	10	21	–11
Aged 60 to 64	18	17	1
Age 65	22	28	–6
Aged 66 or older	34	21	13
Never retire	9	7	2
Don't know/refused	6	6	0
AGED 55 OR OLDER			
Before age 60	1	6	–5
Aged 60 to 64	15	25	–10
Age 65	23	23	0
Aged 66 or older	44	26	18
Never retire	7	2	5
Don't know/refused	8	18	–10

Source: Employee Benefit Research Institute, Retirement Confidence Surveys, Internet site http://www.ebri.org/surveys/rcs/2012/

Table 11.14 Retirement Savings by Age, 2012

(percent distribution of workers aged 25 or older by savings and investments, not including value of primary residence, by age, 2012)

	total	25 to 34	35 to 44	45 to 54	55 or older
Total workers	**100%**	**100%**	**100%**	**100%**	**100%**
Less than $10,000	48	57	51	46	31
$10,000 to $24,999	12	19	10	8	9
$25,000 to $49,999	10	12	11	9	8
$50,000 to $99,999	10	6	14	9	12
$100,000 or more	20	6	15	29	40
$100,000 to $249,999	10	5	12	12	18
$250,000 or more	10	1	3	17	22

Source: Employee Benefit Research Institute, 2012 Retirement Confidence Survey, Internet site http://www.ebri.org/surveys/rcs/2012/

The iGeneration

Americans Born 1995 to the Present

12

Education

■ Most young children today are in school. The percentage of 3-to-4-year-olds enrolled in nursery school or kindergarten has grown substantially over the decades, from 37 percent in 1980 to 53 percent in 2010.

■ Over the past decade, enrollment in the nation's public schools has grown, while private school enrollment has declined—largely because of the Great Recession. Fewer than one in 10 children aged 6 to 17 is enrolled in private school.

■ Only 27 percent of students in the nation's private schools are minority compared with 45 percent of students in public schools.

■ Children's participation in extracurricular activities is heavily dependent on the socioeconomic status of their parents. Among children aged 12 to 17 whose parents have the highest family incomes, 38 percent take lessons. In contrast, only 16 percent of children from the lowest income group take lessons.

■ Most of today's parents are actively involved in their children's education. The parents of 89 percent of the nation's elementary and secondary school children say they attended a PTA or general school meeting during the past year.

■ Complaints about the nation's schools are commonplace, but in fact the parents of most children in kindergarten through 12th grade are very satisfied with various aspects of their child's school.

Most Young Children Attend School

The percentage of 3- and 4-year-olds enrolled in school rises with mother's education.

Most young children today are in school. The percentage of 3-to-4-year-olds enrolled in nursery school or kindergarten has grown substantially over the decades, from 38 percent in 1987 to the 53 percent majority in 2010. The 2010 figure is down from a peak of 56 percent in 2006 because of the widespread unemployment caused by the Great Recession.

A mother's labor force status has a surprisingly small effect on nursery school or kindergarten enrollment. Among 3-to-4-year-olds whose mother works full-time, 59 percent were enrolled in school in 2010. Among those whose mother is not in the labor force, 47 percent were in school. A mother's educational attainment is a more important factor in the school enrollment of young children. Among 3-to-4-year-olds whose mother has a bachelor's degree, two-thirds are in nursery school or kindergarten compared with a much smaller 41 percent of children whose mother did not graduate from high school.

■ Enrolling children in preschool has become the norm, especially for working women and college graduates.

The school enrollment of young children has grown substantially

(percent of 3-to-4-year-olds enrolled in nursery school or kindergarten, 1980 and 2010)

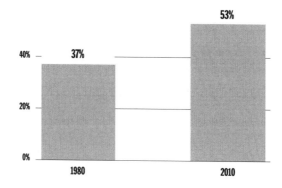

Table 12.1 Three- and Four-Year-Olds Enrolled in School, 1980 to 2010

(percentage of three- and four-year-olds enrolled in nursery school or kindergarten, 1980 to 2010)

2010	53.2%
2009	52.4
2008	52.8
2007	54.5
2006	55.7
2005	53.6
2004	54.0
2003	55.1
2002	54.5
2001	52.2
2000	52.1
1999	54.2
1998	52.1
1997	52.6
1996	48.3
1995	48.7
1994	47.3
1993	40.1
1992	39.7
1991	40.5
1990	44.4
1989	39.1
1988	38.2
1987	38.3
1986	39.0
1985	38.9
1984	36.3
1983	37.6
1982	36.4
1981	36.0
1980	36.7

Source: Bureau of the Census, School Enrollment, Historical Tables, Internet site http://www.census.gov/hhes/school/data/cps/historical/index.html

Table 12.2 School Enrollment Status of Children Aged 3 to 6 by Labor Force Status of Mother, 2010

(number and percent distribution of children aged 3 to 6 by labor force status of mother and school enrollment status, by age of child, 2010; numbers in thousands)

	total	not enrolled	enrolled nursery school	kindergarten	elementary school
Aged 3 to 4	**8,850**	**4,144**	**4,245**	**462**	**0**
Mother employed full-time	3,191	1,320	1,713	158	0
Mother employed part-time	1,349	524	757	69	0
Mother unemployed	594	301	268	25	0
Mother not in the labor force	2,991	1,588	1,219	183	0
Aged 5	**4,099**	**312**	**552**	**2,987**	**247**
Mother employed full-time	1,526	86	222	1,120	98
Mother employed part-time	667	51	88	499	29
Mother unemployed	299	30	46	207	16
Mother not in the labor force	1,282	121	160	906	95
Aged 6	**4,320**	**152**	**38**	**653**	**3,478**
Mother employed full-time	1,586	42	4	243	1,297
Mother employed part-time	786	18	15	142	611
Mother unemployed	240	3	0	40	197
Mother not in the labor force	1,383	79	17	163	1,124

PERCENT DISTRIBUTION BY SCHOOL ENROLLMENT STATUS

	total	not enrolled	enrolled nursery school	kindergarten	elementary school
Aged 3 to 4	**100.0%**	**46.8%**	**48.0%**	**5.2%**	**0.0%**
Mother employed full-time	100.0	41.4	53.7	5.0	0.0
Mother employed part-time	100.0	38.8	56.1	5.1	0.0
Mother unemployed	100.0	50.7	45.1	4.2	0.0
Mother not in the labor force	100.0	53.1	40.8	6.1	0.0
Aged 5	**100.0**	**7.6**	**13.5**	**72.9**	**6.0**
Mother employed full-time	100.0	5.6	14.5	73.4	6.4
Mother employed part-time	100.0	7.6	13.2	74.8	4.3
Mother unemployed	100.0	10.0	15.4	69.2	5.4
Mother not in the labor force	100.0	9.4	12.5	70.7	7.4
Aged 6	**100.0**	**3.5**	**0.9**	**15.1**	**80.5**
Mother employed full-time	100.0	2.6	0.3	15.3	81.8
Mother employed part-time	100.0	2.3	1.9	18.1	77.7
Mother unemployed	100.0	1.3	0.0	16.7	82.1
Mother not in the labor force	100.0	5.7	1.2	11.8	81.3

Note: Numbers do not add to age totals because children not living with mother are not shown.
Source: Bureau of the Census, School Enrollment—Social and Economic Characteristics of Students: October 2010, Internet site http://www.census.gov/hhes/school/data/cps/2010/tables.html; calculations by New Strategist

Table 12.3 School Enrollment Status of Children Aged 3 to 6 by Education of Mother, 2010

(number and percent distribution of children aged 3 to 6 by educational attainment of mother and school enroll-ment status, by age of child, 2010; numbers in thousands)

			enrolled		
	total	not enrolled	nursery school	kindergarten	elementary school
Aged 3 to 4	**8,850**	**4,144**	**4,245**	**462**	**0**
Not a high school graduate	1,242	743	451	48	0
High school graduate	1,948	1,037	770	141	0
Some college or associate's degree	2,424	1,124	1,182	118	0
Bachelor's degree or more	2,511	830	1,554	127	0
Aged 5	**4,099**	**312**	**552**	**2,987**	**247**
Not a high school graduate	525	59	56	376	33
High school graduate	973	90	118	696	69
Some college or associate's degree	1,094	76	159	766	93
Bachelor's degree or more	1,181	64	183	892	42
Aged 6	**4,320**	**152**	**38**	**653**	**3,478**
Not a high school graduate	529	37	5	95	391
High school graduate	976	20	13	148	796
Some college or associate's degree	1,190	40	7	131	1,012
Bachelor's degree or more	1,299	44	12	213	1,030

PERCENT DISTRIBUTION BY SCHOOL ENROLLMENT STATUS

Aged 3 to 4	**100.0%**	**46.8%**	**48.0%**	**5.2%**	**0.0%**
Not a high school graduate	100.0	59.8	36.3	3.9	0.0
High school graduate	100.0	53.2	39.5	7.2	0.0
Some college or associate's degree	100.0	46.4	48.8	4.9	0.0
Bachelor's degree or more	100.0	33.1	61.9	5.1	0.0
Aged 5	**100.0**	**7.6**	**13.5**	**72.9**	**6.0**
Not a high school graduate	100.0	11.2	10.7	71.6	6.3
High school graduate	100.0	9.2	12.1	71.5	7.1
Some college or associate's degree	100.0	6.9	14.5	70.0	8.5
Bachelor's degree or more	100.0	5.4	15.5	75.5	3.6
Aged 6	**100.0**	**3.5**	**0.9**	**15.1**	**80.5**
Not a high school graduate	100.0	7.0	0.9	18.0	73.9
High school graduate	100.0	2.0	1.3	15.2	81.6
Some college or associate's degree	100.0	3.4	0.6	11.0	85.0
Bachelor's degree or more	100.0	3.4	0.9	16.4	79.3

Note: Numbers do not add to age totals because children not living with mother are not shown.
Source: Bureau of the Census, School Enrollment—Social and Economic Characteristics of Students: October 2010, Internet site http://www.census.gov/hhes/school/data/cps/2010/tables.html; calculations by New Strategist

Diversity in Public Schools Is on the Rise

In 11 states minority students are the majority.

School attendance has become common even among preschoolers. Among children aged 5, fully 92 percent attended school in 2010. The figure was 69 percent among children aged 4 and a substantial 38 percent among 3-year-olds.

Over the past decade, enrollment in the nation's public schools has grown, while private school enrollment has declined—largely because of the Great Recession. Fewer than one in 10 children aged 6 to 17 is enrolled in private school. Not surprisingly, the figure is highest among children whose parents have at least a bachelor's degree and in families with the highest incomes. Twenty-seven percent of private school students are minorities. Among public school students, minorities account for a much larger 45 percent.

■ The minority share of public school students varies considerably by state, ranging from a low of 8.7 percent in Vermont to a high of more than 70 percent in California, Hawaii, New Mexico, and the District of Columbia.

Minorities account for a relatively small share of private school students

(percent of students who are minorities, by control of school, 2009–10)

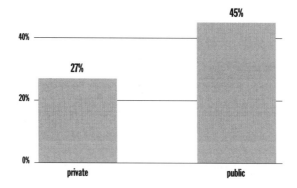

Table 12.4 School Enrollment by Age, 2010

(total people, number aged 3 to 16, and number and percent enrolled in school, by age, 2010; numbers in thousands)

	total	enrolled	
		number	percent
Total people	**292,233**	**78,519**	**26.9%**
Aged 3 to 15	53,702	48,382	90.1
Aged 3	4,492	1,718	38.2
Aged 4	4,358	2,988	68.6
Aged 5	4,099	3,787	92.4
Aged 6	4,320	4,169	96.5
Aged 7	4,183	4,089	97.8
Aged 8	4,114	4,016	97.6
Aged 9	4,135	4,047	97.9
Aged 10	4,067	3,985	98.0
Aged 11	3,988	3,901	97.8
Aged 12	4,141	4,073	98.4
Aged 13	3,922	3,872	98.7
Aged 14	3,900	3,811	97.7
Aged 15	3,983	3,926	98.6
Aged 16 or older	238,531	30,137	12.6

Source: Bureau of the Census, School Enrollment—Social and Economic Characteristics of Students: October 2010, Internet site http://www.census.gov/hhes/school/data/cps/2010/tables.html; calculations by New Strategist

Table 12.5 Enrollment in Nursery School through High School, 2010

(number and percent distribution of people attending nursery school through high school, fall 2010; numbers in thousands)

	number	percent distribution
Total, nursery school–12th grade	**58,243**	**100.0%**
Nursery school	**4,835**	**8.3**
Kindergarten	**4,172**	**7.2**
Elementary and middle	**32,662**	**56.1**
1st grade	4,100	7.0
2nd grade	4,335	7.4
3rd grade	4,139	7.1
4th grade	4,066	7.0
5th grade	4,233	7.3
6th grade	4,085	7.0
7th grade	3,861	6.6
8th grade	3,843	6.6
High school	**16,574**	**28.5**
9th grade	3,974	6.8
10th grade	4,245	7.3
11th grade	4,036	6.9
12th grade	4,319	7.4

Source: Bureau of the Census, School Enrollment—Social and Economic Characteristics of Students: October 2010, Internet site http://www.census.gov/hhes/school/data/cps/2010/tables.html; calculations by New Strategist

Table 12.6 Enrollment in Elementary and High School by Control of School, 2000 to 2010

(number of students enrolled in elementary, middle, and high school by control of school, and private school share of total, fall 2000 to fall 2010; percent and percentage point change, 2000–10; numbers in thousands)

	total	public	private number	private percent
Elementary and middle school				
2010	32,663	29,841	2,822	8.6%
2009	32,238	29,365	2,874	8.9
2008	32,344	29,162	3,182	9.8
2007	32,169	29,052	3,117	9.7
2006	32,089	28,975	3,113	9.7
2005	32,438	29,072	3,366	10.4
2004	32,556	29,166	3,389	10.4
2003	32,565	29,204	3,361	10.3
2002	33,132	29,658	3,474	10.5
2001	33,166	29,800	3,366	10.1
2000	32,898	29,378	3,520	10.7
	percent change			percentage point change
2000 to 2010	−0.7%	1.6%	−19.8%	−2.1

	total	public	private number	private percent
High school				
2010	16,574	15,338	1,236	7.5%
2009	16,445	15,269	1,177	7.2
2008	16,715	15,397	1,319	7.9
2007	17,082	15,804	1,278	7.5
2006	17,149	15,617	1,532	8.9
2005	17,354	15,934	1,420	8.2
2004	16,791	15,498	1,293	7.7
2003	17,062	15,785	1,276	7.5
2002	16,374	15,064	1,310	8.0
2001	16,059	14,830	1,230	7.7
2000	15,770	14,431	1,339	8.5
	percent change			percentage point change
2000 to 2010	5.1%	6.3%	−7.7%	−1.0

Source: Bureau of the Census, School Enrollment, Historical Tables, Internet site http://www.census.gov/hhes/school/data/cps/historical/index.html

Table 12.7 Children Enrolled in Private School, 2009

(percent of children aged 6 to 17 enrolled in private school by type of school and selected characteristics of child and parent, 2009)

| | percent enrolled in private school | | |
	total	religious	nonreligious
Total children	**7.7%**	**5.2%**	**2.5%**
Race/Hispanic origin of child			
Asian	7.2	4.9	2.3
Black	4.6	3.1	1.6
Hispanic	3.8	2.0	1.8
Non-Hispanic white	10.1	7.1	3.0
Marital status of parent			
Married	8.9	6.2	2.7
Separated, divorced, widowed	5.7	3.5	2.3
Never married	3.8	2.4	1.4
Educational attainment of parent			
Not a high school graduate	4.2	2.5	1.7
High school graduate only	4.3	3.0	1.2
Some college	6.3	4.2	2.1
Associate's degree	6.9	4.5	2.5
Bachelor's degree	13.6	9.9	3.7
Graduate degree	14.6	9.3	5.3
Employment status of parent			
Worked full-time last month	7.5	5.2	2.4
Worked part-time last month	9.1	6.3	2.8
Did not work last month	7.1	4.7	2.4
Monthly family income			
Under $1,500	3.7	2.3	1.3
$1,500 to $2,999	4.3	2.9	1.4
$3,000 to $4,499	7.2	5.3	1.9
$4,500 to $5,999	7.9	5.1	2.9
$6,000 or more	11.2	7.6	3.6

Note: Asians and blacks are those who identify themselves as being of the race alone.
Source: Census Bureau, A Child's Day: 2009, Internet site http://www.census.gov/hhes/socdemo/children/data/sipp/well2009/tables.html

Table 12.8 Enrollment in Private Elementary and Secondary Schools by Race and Hispanic Origin, 2009–10

(total number and percent distribution of students enrolled in private elementary and secondary schools by race and Hispanic origin, by school affiliation and region, 2009–10; numbers in thousands)

	number	total	non-Hispanic white	minority total	Asian	black	Hispanic
Total students	**5,488**	**100.0%**	**72.6%**	**27.4%**	**5.7%**	**9.2%**	**9.4%**
Affiliation							
Roman Catholic	2,160	100.0	70.8	29.2	5.1	7.5	13.3
Other religions	2,076	100.0	76.3	23.7	4.9	10.3	6.2
Nonsectarian	1,252	100.0	69.2	30.8	8.5	10.6	7.3
Region							
Northeast	1,310	100.0	74.3	25.7	5.1	10.5	7.7
Midwest	1,296	100.0	80.9	19.1	3.1	7.9	5.6
South	1,842	100.0	73.1	26.9	3.9	11.2	9.4
West	1,041	100.0	58.5	41.5	13.0	5.4	16.6

Note: Race categories exclude persons of Hispanic ethnicity. Numbers by race and Hispanic origin do not sum to total minority because not all minorities are shown.
Source: National Center for Education Statistics, The Condition of Education, Private School Enrollment, Internet site http://nces.ed.gov/programs/coe/indicator_pri.asp

Table 12.9 **Enrollment in Public Elementary and Secondary School by State, Race, and Hispanic Origin, 2010**

(percent distribution of students enrolled in public elementary and secondary school by state, race, and Hispanc origin, 2010)

	total	minority students						non-Hispanic white
		total	American Indian	Asian	black	Hispanic	two or more races	
Total public school children	**100.0%**	**48.3%**	**0.8%**	**4.2%**	**15.3%**	**24.0%**	**3.5%**	**51.7%**
Alabama	100.0	43.2	0.6	0.9	34.3	5.2	2.0	56.8
Alaska	100.0	50.1	20.1	5.2	3.4	8.3	11.9	49.9
Arizona	100.0	58.8	5.3	2.1	4.6	43.5	2.8	41.2
Arkansas	100.0	36.5	0.6	1.2	21.5	10.2	2.6	63.5
California	100.0	74.7	0.3	10.4	5.9	53.7	3.8	25.3
Colorado	100.0	43.5	0.4	2.4	4.2	32.0	4.3	56.5
Connecticut	100.0	40.0	–	3.4	12.0	20.8	3.3	60.0
Delaware	100.0	52.6	–	2.6	30.7	15.1	4.2	47.4
District of Columbia	100.0	94.1	–	1.2	76.9	14.1	1.8	5.9
Florida	100.0	56.3	0.2	2.3	22.8	27.7	2.8	43.7
Georgia	100.0	55.8	0.1	3.2	37.6	12.1	2.6	44.2
Hawaii	100.0	88.5	–	26.0	1.9	15.5	30.2	11.5
Idaho	100.0	22.7	1.1	1.5	0.5	16.7	2.8	77.3
Illinois	100.0	48.5	0.1	3.9	17.9	23.7	2.8	51.5
Indiana	100.0	26.5	0.1	1.6	11.8	9.3	3.5	73.5
Iowa	100.0	18.9	0.2	1.9	4.8	8.4	3.5	81.1
Kansas	100.0	31.9	1.0	2.4	6.5	17.5	4.4	68.1
Kentucky	100.0	19.1	0.2	1.0	10.0	4.9	2.9	80.9
Louisiana	100.0	52.6	0.8	1.1	44.2	4.2	2.0	47.4
Maine	100.0	10.2	0.8	1.9	2.7	1.6	3.2	89.8
Maryland	100.0	56.2	0.1	5.3	34.9	11.2	4.4	43.8
Massachusetts	100.0	33.4	0.1	5.5	8.9	15.3	3.0	66.6
Michigan	100.0	32.4	0.6	2.7	17.6	7.0	4.2	67.6
Minnesota	100.0	27.1	1.2	5.3	7.3	8.0	5.2	72.9
Mississippi	100.0	56.1	0.4	0.7	50.6	2.7	1.5	43.9
Missouri	100.0	26.1	0.2	1.3	16.0	5.3	3.1	73.9
Montana	100.0	19.9	10.2	0.5	0.8	5.0	3.6	80.1
Nebraska	100.0	28.1	1.0	1.4	6.2	15.6	3.7	71.9
Nevada	100.0	61.2	1.0	5.7	9.6	39.3	4.8	38.8
New Hampshire	100.0	11.0	–	2.5	1.1	4.3	2.4	89.0
New Jersey	100.0	50.3	0.2	7.9	15.6	23.4	2.7	49.7
New Mexico	100.0	74.4	11.0	0.8	1.1	59.0	2.3	25.6
New York	100.0	52.2	0.2	7.0	17.6	24.1	2.8	47.8
North Carolina	100.0	46.4	1.1	2.4	25.7	13.0	3.7	53.6
North Dakota	100.0	16.6	6.6	1.5	1.4	3.0	4.1	83.4
Ohio	100.0	25.7	0.1	1.6	15.2	4.5	4.1	74.3
Oklahoma	100.0	44.4	9.1	1.4	8.5	13.4	11.7	55.6
Oregon	100.0	34.2	1.6	3.7	2.5	20.7	5.0	65.8
Pennsylvania	100.0	30.1	0.1	2.8	14.2	9.4	3.3	69.9

	total	minority students						non-Hispanic white
		total	American Indian	Asian	black	Hispanic	two or more races	
Rhode Island	100.0%	36.8%	–	3.0%	7.1%	21.1%	4.8%	63.2%
South Carolina	100.0	47.9	0.1%	0.9	36.3	7.1	3.3	52.1
South Dakota	100.0	26.3	14.5	0.9	1.6	4.6	4.4	73.7
Tennessee	100.0	33.9	0.1	1.6	22.8	6.7	2.6	66.1
Texas	100.0	68.2	0.2	3.2	12.7	49.9	1.9	31.8
Utah	100.0	25.2	1.1	1.4	1.3	17.2	2.9	74.8
Vermont	100.0	8.7	–	1.4	3.3	1.9	2.1	91.3
Virginia	100.0	44.7	0.1	5.0	23.6	10.7	4.7	55.3
Washington	100.0	39.5	1.6	6.7	3.9	19.2	7.2	60.5
West Virginia	100.0	9.4	–	0.6	2.8	2.0	3.9	90.6
Wisconsin	100.0	26.1	0.9	3.1	9.0	9.8	3.1	73.9
Wyoming	100.0	20.4	3.7	1.3	–	13.4	1.6	79.6

Note: Minority students by race/Hispanic origin will not sum to total because some races are not shown. "–" means sample is too small to make a reliable estimate or not available.
Source: National Center for Education Statistics, The Condition of Education, Internet site http://nces.ed.gov/programs/coe/current_tables.asp; calculations by New Strategist

Many Children Are in Gifted Classes

Children of affluent, educated parents are most likely to be in gifted classes and take part in a variety of extracurricular activities.

Among teenagers aged 12 to 17, a substantial 27 percent are in gifted classes at school. The percentage of children in gifted classes rises directly with the educational level of the parent and the family's income. Among teens whose parents graduated from college, nearly four of 10 are in gifted classes. In contrast, children with the least educated parents or in families with the lowest incomes are most likely to have repeated a grade or been suspended.

Children's participation in extracurricular activities is heavily dependent on the socioeconomic status of their parents. Among children aged 12 to 17 whose parents have the highest family incomes, more than half take part in sports, 42 percent take part in clubs, and 38 percent take lessons. In contrast, children from the lowest income group are about 20 percentage points less likely to participate in these activities.

■ Because extracurricular activities are an important part of college admissions, children with less educated parents or from poor families are at a disadvantage in the college application process.

Socioeconomic status greatly affects participation in extracurricular activities

(percent of children aged 12 to 17 who participate in extracurricular activities, by type of activity and family income, 2009)

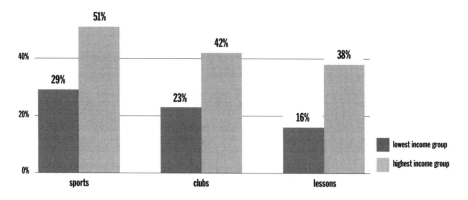

Table 12.10 Academic Performance and Experiences of Children, 2009

(percent of children aged 6 to 17 in gifted classes, who changed schools, ever repeated a grade, or were ever suspended, by selected characteristics of child and parent, 2009)

	gifted classes		change of schools		ever repeated grade		ever suspended,
	6 to 11	12 to 17	6 to 11	12 to 17	6 to 11	12 to 17	12 to 17
Total children	**13.6%**	**26.8%**	**23.6%**	**40.3%**	**4.9%**	**9.4%**	**10.6%**
Race/Hispanic origin of child							
Asian	19.7	31.3	22.2	42.8	1.9	4.1	7.7
Black	13.4	20.5	30.2	44.7	5.8	13.5	19.2
Hispanic	9.6	18.4	23.5	40.4	5.9	12.9	10.4
Non-Hispanic white	15.0	30.8	21.9	38.1	4.4	7.7	8.1
Marital status of parent							
Married	14.6	29.0	21.5	38.1	3.7	8.0	8.5
Separated, divorced, widowed	12.6	24.4	28.8	44.3	7.2	11.9	13.4
Never married	9.9	17.8	28.1	46.1	7.8	13.1	18.5
Educational attainment of parent							
Not a high school graduate	6.4	14.0	21.3	38.3	7.9	17.4	14.1
High school graduate only	9.6	20.1	25.0	39.6	6.7	9.0	11.3
Some college	12.7	26.8	28.8	46.3	4.6	9.7	11.0
Associate's degree	15.1	27.4	26.2	42.7	4.5	9.8	11.7
Bachelor's degree	20.5	38.7	18.0	35.1	2.2	4.8	7.4
Graduate degree	18.5	39.9	20.5	38.8	2.5	5.6	5.5
Employment status of parent							
Worked full-time last month	14.0	28.6	21.6	38.5	4.3	7.9	10.2
Worked part-time last month	13.4	27.5	23.2	36.7	4.9	8.0	8.0
Did not work last month	13.3	23.7	26.2	45.4	5.5	12.6	12.9
Monthly family income							
Under $1,500	10.5	17.7	29.9	48.7	7.5	14.4	14.6
$1,500 to $2,999	10.9	17.2	26.2	41.7	6.3	13.3	13.4
$3,000 to $4,499	10.9	22.7	24.3	39.4	5.9	10.3	11.7
$4,500 to $5,999	17.0	27.1	22.9	39.5	3.8	8.5	10.3
$6,000 or more	16.7	36.0	19.1	37.3	2.8	5.9	7.1

Note: Asians and blacks are those who identify themselves as being of the race alone. Percent who changed schools does not include normal progression from elementary and middle schools.
Source: Census Bureau, A Child's Day: 2009, Internet site http://www.census.gov/hhes/socdemo/children/data/sipp/well2009/tables.html

Table 12.11 Extracurricular Activities of Children, 2009

(percent of children aged 6 to 17 participating in specified extracurricular activities, by selected characteristics of child and parent, 2009)

| | percent participating in specified extracurricular activity | | | | | | percent in all three types of activities | |
| | sports | | clubs | | lessons | | | |
	6 to 11	12 to 17	6 to 11	12 to 17	6 to 11	12 to 17	6 to 11	12 to 17
Total children	**31.7%**	**40.6%**	**29.7%**	**32.3%**	**31.7%**	**28.8%**	**8.5%**	**9.1%**
Race/Hispanic origin of child								
Asian	22.5	36.9	32.7	36.4	39.9	40.7	7.3	9.2
Black	20.9	35.9	26.3	26.7	24.0	19.5	5.4	5.6
Hispanic	20.7	30.2	18.3	18.1	23.7	20.5	3.9	4.9
Non-Hispanic white	39.3	45.2	35.0	37.9	36.1	32.6	11.1	11.4
Marital status of parent								
Married	34.8	43.3	32.5	35.7	35.4	32.1	9.9	10.2
Separated, divorced, widowed	28.5	36.6	26.6	27.8	26.1	24.0	6.9	8.0
Never married	19.5	31.1	19.7	19.2	19.6	17.0	3.6	4.1
Educational attainment of parent								
Not a high school graduate	15.6	25.6	15.1	15.9	16.2	13.3	2.2	1.7
High school graduate only	25.1	33.6	22.2	25.2	21.3	21.7	4.4	5.7
Some college	31.3	42.4	28.5	34.1	30.8	28.8	7.6	7.7
Associate's degree	31.0	40.9	32.5	34.5	32.7	30.9	7.9	9.8
Bachelor's degree	47.0	54.2	41.7	43.8	46.5	40.7	15.3	16.2
Graduate degree	43.0	52.5	41.2	46.4	50.0	44.0	17.6	16.7
Employment status of parent								
Worked full-time last month	35.6	43.4	30.2	33.3	32.2	29.6	9.2	9.5
Worked part-time last month	36.1	44.1	33.2	36.8	34.6	32.3	9.9	11.3
Did not work last month	24.8	33.6	27.4	28.2	29.1	25.2	7.2	7.2
Monthly family income								
Under $1,500	18.2	28.6	18.8	22.8	20.2	16.3	4.5	4.3
$1,500 to $2,999	23.9	31.7	24.1	22.2	23.1	20.7	4.4	4.6
$3,000 to $4,499	30.7	36.4	27.9	27.2	26.4	25.7	6.7	7.2
$4,500 to $5,999	32.8	40.2	31.5	33.4	33.4	29.4	7.4	8.7
$6,000 or more	42.8	51.0	38.3	42.1	43.2	38.4	14.0	13.9

Note: Asians and blacks are those who identify themselves as being of the race alone.
Source: Census Bureau, A Child's Day: 2009, Internet site http://www.census.gov/hhes/socdemo/children/data/sipp/well2009/tables.html

Parents Are Involved in Their Children's Education

During a given year, most attend a school meeting, a parent-teacher conference, and a school or class event

Most of today's parents are actively involved in their children's education. The parents of 89 percent of the nation's elementary and secondary school children say they attended a PTA or general school meeting during the past year, according to a 2006–07 survey by the National Center for Education Statistics. Seventy-eight percent attended a parent–teacher conference, 74 percent attended a class event, and 46 percent volunteered.

Participation in a child's education typically rises with the educational attainment of the parent. The percentage of children whose parents attended a class event, for example, climbs from 48 percent among parents who did not graduate from high school to more than 80 percent among parents with at least a bachelor's degree. Surprisingly, however, the most educated parents are least likely to check their children's homework. Among students with homework, only 81 percent of parents with a graduate degree check to make sure their child has done his homework compared with 94 percent of parents without a high school diploma.

■ Poor parents are more likely than the nonpoor to make sure their child has done her homework.

Educated parents are most likely to attend their children's class events

(percent of children whose parents attended a class event in the past year, by educational attainment of parent, 2006–07)

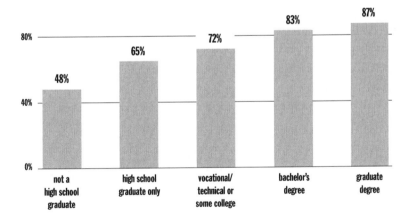

Table 12.12 Parental Involvement in School Activities, 2006–07

(total number and percent of elementary and secondary school children whose parents reported participation in school activities, by selected characteristics of child and parent, 2006–07)

	total		parent attended a PTA or general school meeting	parent attended a parent–teacher conference	parent attended a school or class event	parent volunteered at school	parent participated in school fundraising
	number	percent					
Total children	**51,600**	**100%**	**89%**	**78%**	**74%**	**46%**	**65%**
Race and Hispanic origin of child							
Asian, non-Hispanic	1,566	100	90	80	72	46	62
Black, non-Hispanic	7,837	100	87	77	65	35	58
Hispanic	9,767	100	87	80	65	32	51
White, non-Hispanic	29,832	100	91	78	80	54	72
Educational attainment of parent							
Not a high school graduate	3,504	100	75	70	48	20	34
High school graduate	11,070	100	84	74	65	33	55
Vocational/technical or some college	14,844	100	89	77	72	42	67
Bachelor's degree	11,353	100	94	81	83	56	72
Graduate degree	10,829	100	95	82	87	64	77
School type							
Public, assigned	37,168	100	89	76	72	42	63
Public, chosen	7,951	100	88	81	74	45	62
Private, religious	4,560	100	96	96	86	73	85
Private, nonreligious	1,438	100	97	90	86	68	72
Student's grade level							
Kindergarten through 2nd grade	11,516	100	93	90	78	63	72
3rd through 5th grade	11,519	100	94	92	83	57	71
6th through 8th grade	12,058	100	91	76	72	38	63
9th through 12th grade	16,503	100	83	61	68	34	57
Poverty status							
Poor	10,012	100	81	77	56	26	45
Not poor	41,587	100	91	78	79	51	70

Source: National Center for Education Statistics, National Household Education Survey, Internet site http://nces.ed.gov/nhes/

Table 12.13 Parental Involvement in Child's Homework, 2006–07

(total number and percent of elementary and secondary school children whose parents reported involvement with child's homework, by selected characteristics of child and parent, 2006–07)

| | total | | student does homework outside of school | | |
	number	percent	total	place in home set aside for homework	adult in household checks that homework is done
Total children	**51,600**	**100%**	**94%**	**89%**	**85%**
Race and Hispanic origin of child					
Asian, non-Hispanic	1,566	100	96	93	83
Black, non-Hispanic	7,837	100	94	94	94
Hispanic	9,767	100	94	84	91
White, non-Hispanic	29,832	100	95	89	82
Educational attainment of parent					
Not a high school graduate	3,504	100	90	83	94
High school graduate	11,070	100	93	89	89
Vocational/technical or some college	14,844	100	94	90	86
Bachelor's degree	11,353	100	96	87	83
Graduate degree	10,829	100	96	90	81
School type					
Public, assigned	37,168	100	94	89	86
Public, chosen	7,951	100	95	90	88
Private, religious	4,560	100	97	86	79
Private, nonreligious	1,438	100	90	85	84
Student's grade level					
Kindergarten through 2nd grade	11,516	100	93	84	100
3rd through 5th grade	11,519	100	97	89	97
6th through 8th grade	12,058	100	95	91	88
9th through 12th grade	16,503	100	93	91	65
Poverty status					
Poor	10,012	100	93	87	93
Not poor	41,587	100	95	89	84

Source: National Center for Education Statistics, National Household Education Survey, Internet site http://nces.ed.gov/nhes/

Most Parents Are Satisfied with Their Child's School

Most are also satisfied with their child's teachers and the amount of homework.

Complaints about the nation's schools are commonplace, but in fact the parents of most children in kindergarten through 12th grade are very satisfied with various aspects of their child's school. Fifty-nine percent of school children have parents who claim to be very satisfied with their child's school. The percentage of parents who are very satisfied with the teachers is an even higher 64 percent. Similar proportions are very satisfied with their school's academic standards and discipline. Seventy-five percent say the amount of homework assigned to their child is about right.

The biggest difference in satisfaction levels is by type of school and grade level. Typically, private school parents are happier than public school parents, and the parents of younger children are happier than the parents of children in middle or high school. Nevertheless, the majority of parents, regardless of type of school or grade level, say they are very satisfied with their child's school.

■ Although most parents are very satisfied with their child's school, a substantial minority is not. Unhappy parents are one factor driving the push for school reform.

Blacks are least likely to be very satisfied with their child's school

(percent of children in kindergarten through 12th grade whose parents are "very satisfied" with their child's school, by race and Hispanic origin, 2006–07)

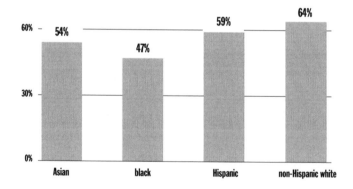

Table 12.14 Parental Satisfaction with School, 2006–07

(total number, percent distribution, and percent of elementary and secondary school children whose parents report satisfaction with school characteristics and amount of homework, by selected characteristics of child and parent, 2006–07)

	total		parent reports being "very satisfied"					
	number	percent	with the school	with teachers student had this year	with academic standards of the school	with order, discipline at the school	with the way school staff interacts with parents	amount of homework assigned is about right
Total children	51,600	100%	59%	64%	63%	62%	55%	75%
Race and Hispanic origin of child								
Asian, non-Hispanic	1,566	100	54	59	56	57	50	67
Black, non-Hispanic	7,837	100	47	57	55	54	49	66
Hispanic	9,767	100	59	65	60	63	59	78
White, non-Hispanic	29,832	100	64	66	66	65	57	77
Educational attainment of parent								
Not a high school graduate	3,504	100	54	62	56	60	55	79
High school graduate	11,070	100	54	59	56	58	51	74
Vocational/technical or some college	14,844	100	55	61	59	57	53	73
Bachelor's degree	11,353	100	64	67	67	65	57	76
Graduate degree	10,829	100	68	70	71	70	62	76
School type								
Public, assigned	37,168	100	55	61	58	58	51	74
Public, chosen	7,951	100	63	68	67	63	59	72
Private, religious	4,560	100	81	79	84	83	77	80
Private, nonreligious	1,438	100	82	78	84	83	76	88
Student's grade level								
Kindergarten through 2nd grade	11,516	100	69	78	69	72	67	80
3rd through 5th grade	11,519	100	65	69	67	66	63	79
6th through 8th grade	12,058	100	55	58	60	59	51	71
9th through 12th grade	16,503	100	52	54	57	54	46	72
Poverty status								
Poor	10,012	100	56	64	59	57	56	73
Not poor	41,587	100	60	64	63	63	55	75

Source: National Center for Education Statistics, National Household Education Survey, Internet site http://nces.ed.gov/nhes/

CHAPTER 13

Health

■ The 55 percent majority of children under age 18 are in excellent health, according to their parents. Only about 2 percent of parents rate their child's health as only fair or poor.

■ A government study of high school students found 16 percent of girls to be overweight. A larger 33 percent of girls thought they were overweight, and 59 percent were trying to lose weight.

■ Among boys, 53 percent are sexually experienced by 11th grade. The figure rises to 60 percent in 12th grade. The statistics are similar for girls.

■ In a government survey of high school students, 42 percent say they used alcohol in the past month, a figure that climbs above 50 percent among 12th graders.

■ Among all Americans, 16 percent lacked health insurance in 2010. The figure was a smaller 10 percent among children.

■ Ten million children (13.5 percent) have taken prescription medications regularly for at least three months during the past year.

■ Among children aged 1 to 14, accidents are by far the leading cause of death.

Most Children Are in Excellent Health

Fewer than one in five is overweight.

The 55 percent majority of children under age 18 are in excellent health, according to their parents. Only about 2 percent of parents rate their child's health as only fair or poor.

In a study that measured the prevalence of obesity among children based on physical examinations, the federal government found a substantial 11 percent of 2-to-5-year-olds to be obese and found obesity to be a problem among an even larger 18 to 19 percent of older children. In a separate study of high school students, 16 percent of girls and boys were found to be overweight. A larger 33 percent of girls and 23 percent of boys thought they were overweight, however. An even larger proportion was trying to lose weight.

Weight problems lie ahead for today's children, in part because fewer are taking part in physical activities. The percentage of children who participate in a variety of sports has fallen over the past decade, according to the National Sporting Goods Association. The percentage of 7-to-11-year-olds who rode a bicycle more than once in the past year fell from 48 to 39 percent between 2001 and 2010. Only 37 percent of high school students are physically active for at least one hour a day on five or more days per week. Among 12th graders, fewer than half are in physical education classes.

■ Although most teenage girls are weight conscious, those concerns are unlikely to prevent them from becoming overweight as young adults.

Many girls think they are overweight

(percent of girls in 9th to 12th grade who are overweight, percent who think they are overweight, and percent trying to lose weight, 2009)

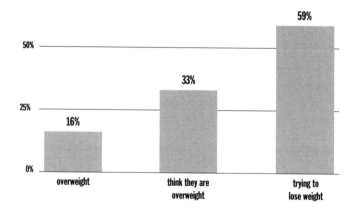

Table 13.1 Health Status of Children under Age 18, 2010

(parent-reported health status of people under age 18, by age, 2010)

	total	excellent	very good	good	fair/poor
Total children	**100.0%**	**55.1%**	**27.0%**	**15.8%**	**2.0%**
Under age 5	100.0	57.5	26.6	14.3	1.6
Aged 5 to 11	100.0	54.4	27.7	15.8	2.1
Aged 12 to 17	100.0	53.8	26.7	17.3	2.2

Source: National Center for Health Statistics, Summary Health Statistics for U.S. Children: National Health Interview Survey, 2010, Series 10, No. 250, 2011, Internet site http://www.cdc.gov/nchs/nhis.htm

Table 13.2 Obesity among Children, 2007–10

(percent of children aged 2 to 19 who are overweight, by sex, race, Hispanic origin, and age, 2007–10)

	2 to 5	6 to 11	12 to 19
Total children	**11.1%**	**18.8%**	**18.2%**
Total boys	**11.9**	**20.7**	**19.4**
Black, non-Hispanic	15.7	23.3	21.2
Mexican	19.1	24.3	27.9
White, non-Hispanic	8.8	18.6	17.1
Total girls	**10.2**	**16.9**	**16.9**
Black, non-Hispanic	14.2	24.5	27.1
Mexican	9.9	22.4	18.0
White, non-Hispanic	9.2	14.0	14.6

Note: Data are based on physical examinations. Obesity is defined as a body mass index at or above the sex- and age-specific 95th percentile BMI cutoff points from the 2000 CDC growth charts.
Source: National Center for Health Statistics, Health United States, 2011, Internet site http://www.cdc.gov/nchs/hus.htm

Table 13.3 Weight Problems and Dieting Behavior of 9th to 12th Graders by Sex, 2009

(percent of 9th to 12th graders by weight status and dieting behavior, by sex and grade, 2009)

	total	9th grade	10th grade	11th grade	12th grade
BOYS					
Overweight*	15.7%	16.7%	16.9%	14.4%	14.4%
Described themselves as overweight	22.7	22.7	21.2	21.8	25.5
Were trying to lose weight	30.5	31.8	29.5	28.0	32.8
Ate less food, fewer calories, or foods low in fat to lose weight or to avoid gaining weight in past 30 days	28.4	27.5	26.7	27.8	32.4
Exercised to lose weight or to avoid gaining weight in past 30 days	55.7	57.6	53.6	53.6	58.0
Went without eating for at least 24 hours to lose weight or to avoid gaining weight in past 30 days	6.9	6.7	6.5	7.2	7.3
Took diet pills, powders, or liquids without a doctor's advice to lose weight or avoid gaining weight in past 30 days	3.8	3.7	3.0	4.0	4.6
Vomited or took a laxative to lose weight or to avoid gaining weight in past 30 days	2.6	2.8	2.2	2.7	2.6
GIRLS					
Overweight*	15.9	17.9	16.9	13.5	15.1
Described themselves as overweight	33.1	32.2	31.1	33.5	36.0
Were trying to lose weight	59.3	57.0	59.4	60.8	60.3
Ate less food, fewer calories, or foods low in fat to lose weight or to avoid gaining weight in past 30 days	51.6	49.1	52.6	52.7	52.0
Exercised to lose weight or to avoid gaining weight in past 30 days	67.9	67.4	69.6	67.5	66.7
Went without eating for at least 24 hours to lose weight or to avoid gaining weight in past 30 days	14.5	15.7	14.5	14.8	12.6
Took diet pills, powders, or liquids without a doctor's advice to lose weight or avoid gaining weight in past 30 days	6.3	4.7	6.0	8.1	6.6
Vomited or took a laxative to lose weight or to avoid gaining weight in past 30 days	5.4	5.6	5.3	6.3	4.2

* Students who were overweight were at or above the 85th percentile for body mass index, by age and sex, based on reference data.
Source: Centers for Disease Control and Prevention, Youth Risk Behavior Surveillance—United States, 2009, Internet site http://www.cdc.gov/HealthyYouth/yrbs/index.htm

Table 13.4 Sports Participation of Children Aged 7 to 17, 2001 and 2010

(number and percent of people aged 7 to 17 having participated in selected sports at least once during past year, by age, 2001 and 2010; percent change in number and percentage point change in participation rate; numbers in thousands)

	2010		2001		percent change in number	percentage point change in participation rate
	number	percent	number	percent		
AGED 7 TO 11						
Total children	**20,554**	**100.0%**	**20,262**	**100.0%**	**1.4%**	–
Baseball	3,383	16.5	4,654	23.0	–27.3	–6.5
Basketball	5,533	26.9	6,356	31.4	–12.9	–4.4
Bicycle riding	8,041	39.1	9,753	48.1	–17.6	–9.0
Bowling	5,282	25.7	5,330	26.3	–0.9	–0.6
Fishing	3,354	16.3	5,124	25.3	–34.5	–9.0
Football (tackle)	1,888	9.2	1,460	7.2	29.3	2.0
Golf	1,297	6.3	1,011	5.0	28.3	1.3
Ice hockey	513	2.5	384	1.9	33.6	0.6
Mountain biking (off road)	706	3.4	530	2.6	33.2	0.8
Rollerskating (in-line)	1,868	9.1	7,108	35.1	–73.7	–26.0
Scooter riding	3,570	17.4	7,427	36.7	–51.9	–19.3
Skateboarding	2,302	11.2	4,512	22.3	–49.0	–11.1
Skiing (alpine)	1,227	6.0	614	3.0	99.8	2.9
Snowboarding	775	3.8	–	–	–	–
Soccer	4,439	21.6	5,867	29.0	–24.3	–7.4
Softball	1,577	7.7	2,486	12.3	–36.6	–4.6
Tennis	1,474	7.2	728	3.6	102.5	3.6
AGED 12 TO 17						
Total children	**24,645**	**100.0**	**23,782**	**100.0**	**3.6**	–
Baseball	2,882	11.7	4,095	17.2	–29.6	–5.5
Basketball	6,424	26.1	7,818	32.9	–17.8	–6.8
Bicycle riding	6,546	26.6	7,255	30.5	–9.8	–3.9
Bowling	4,911	19.9	5,893	24.8	–16.7	–4.9
Fishing	3,506	14.2	4,480	18.8	–21.7	–4.6
Football (tackle)	2,904	11.8	3,593	15.1	–19.2	–3.3
Golf	1,388	5.6	2,264	9.5	–38.7	–3.9
Ice hockey	607	2.5	441	1.9	37.6	0.6
Mountain biking (off road)	994	4.0	1,195	5.0	–16.8	–1.0
Rollerskating (in-line)	1,590	6.5	5,059	21.3	–68.6	–14.8
Scooter riding	1,406	5.7	3,425	14.4	–58.9	–8.7
Skateboarding	2,687	10.9	3,961	16.7	–32.2	–5.8
Skiing (alpine)	1,085	4.4	1,453	6.1	–25.3	–1.7
Snowboarding	1,210	4.9	–	–	–	–
Soccer	3,362	13.6	3,831	16.1	–12.2	–2.5
Softball	2,060	8.4	2,286	9.6	–9.9	–1.3
Tennis	1,859	7.5	1,963	8.3	–5.3	–0.7

Note: "–" means not applicable or data not available.
Source: National Sporting Goods Association, Internet site http://www.nsga.org

Table 13.5 **Participation of High School Students in Physical Education Classes, Team Sports, and Physical Activity, 2009**

(percent of 9th through 12th graders who attended a physical education class at least one day a week, participated in at least one sports team, and who were physically active at least 60 minutes a day five or more days a week, by sex and grade, 2009)

	attended physical education class	played on sports team in past year	physically active at least 1 hour/day five days/week
Total high school students	**56.4%**	**58.3%**	**37.0%**
Boys	**57.7**	**63.8**	**45.6**
9th grade	70.7	65.9	47.5
10th grade	58.6	66.8	47.4
11th grade	50.9	63.4	46.2
12th grade	46.9	57.9	40.4
Girls	**55.0**	**52.3**	**27.7**
9th grade	74.3	56.6	30.8
10th grade	56.4	56.4	30.5
11th grade	45.3	51.3	26.0
12th grade	40.7	44.1	22.4

Source: Centers for Disease Control and Prevention, Youth Risk Behavior Surveillance—United States, 2009, Internet site http://www.cdc.gov/HealthyYouth/yrbs/index.htm

The Majority of 11th and 12th Graders Have Had Sex

Most sexually active teens use birth control.

Among boys, the 53 percent majority of 11th graders have had sexual intercourse. The figure rises to 60 percent among boys in 12th grade. The statistics are similar for girls—nearly 53 percent of 11th graders and 65 percent of 12th graders have had sexual intercourse. A smaller share of teens is currently sexually active—meaning they have had sexual intercourse in the past three months.

Among sexually active teens, most used birth control the last time they had sex. Among sexually active boys, 69 percent say they used a condom and 16.5 percent say their partner was on the pill. Among sexually active girls, 54 percent say their partner used a condom and 23 percent say they were taking the pill.

■ With teenagers being sexually active, preventing pregnancy and sexually transmitted diseases is of prime concern to parents and schools.

Girls and boys are almost equally sexually active

(percent of 9th to 12th graders who have had sexual intercourse, by sex, 2009)

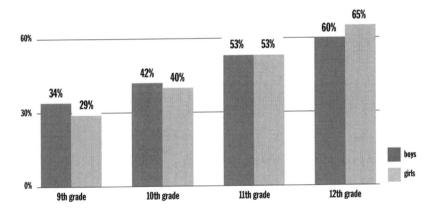

Table 13.6 Sexual Behavior of 9th to 12th Graders by Sex, 2009

(percent of 9th to 12th graders engaging in selected sexual activities, by sex and grade, 2009)

	total	9th grade	10th grade	11th grade	12th grade
Boys					
Ever had sexual intercourse	46.1%	33.6%	41.9%	53.4%	59.6%
Currently sexually active*	32.6	21.2	28.8	39.1	45.1
Four or more sex partners during lifetime	16.2	11.1	15.3	17.5	22.7
Condom use during last sexual intercourse	68.6	69.9	71.9	68.9	65.0
Birth control pill use before last sexual intercourse	16.5	10.7	14.0	18.9	19.6
Girls					
Ever had sexual intercourse	45.7	29.3	39.6	52.5	65.0
Currently sexually active*	35.6	21.6	29.3	41.5	53.1
Four or more sex partners during lifetime	11.2	6.3	7.6	12.9	19.1
Condom use during last sexual intercourse	53.9	57.7	63.5	54.0	46.3
Birth control pill use before last sexual intercourse	23.0	9.7	15.6	22.5	34.4

* Sexual intercourse during the three months preceding the survey.
Source: Centers for Disease Control and Prevention, Youth Risk Behavior Surveillance—United States, 2009, Internet site http://www.cdc.gov/HealthyYouth/yrbs/index.htm

Many Teens Smoke Cigarettes

Eight percent of 12-to-17-year-olds have smoked a cigarette in the past month.

Cigarette smoking has been declining in the population as a whole, but among teenagers it remains stubbornly high. Overall, 23 percent of people aged 12 or older smoked a cigarette in the past month, according to a 2009 survey. The proportion of teenagers who have ever smoked rises steadily with age to 38 percent among 17-year-olds.

In another government survey of high school students, about 20 percent report having smoked a cigarette in the past month. The figure peaks at 28 percent among boys in 12th grade.

■ Most teens have tried a cigarette by 11th grade and some will make smoking a lifelong habit.

Cigarette smoking doubles between ages 15 and 17

(percent of people aged 12 to 17 who have smoked a cigarette in the past month, by age, 2010)

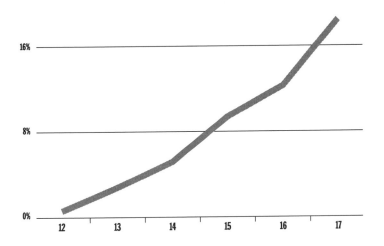

Table 13.7 Cigarette Smoking among People Aged 12 to 17, 2010

(percent of people aged 12 or older and people aged 12 to 17 reporting any, past year, and past month use of cigarettes, 2010)

	ever smoked	smoked in past year	smoked in past month
Total people aged 12 or older	**64.2%**	**27.0%**	**23.0%**
Total people aged 12 to 17	**20.3**	**14.1**	**8.3**
Aged 12	3.9	1.7	0.6
Aged 13	9.0	6.0	2.8
Aged 14	14.7	10.2	5.2
Aged 15	24.1	16.5	9.4
Aged 16	29.5	21.2	12.3
Aged 17	38.3	27.4	18.5

Source: SAMHSA, Office of Applied Studies, 2010 National Survey on Drug Use and Health, Detailed Tables, Internet site http://www.samhsa.gov/data/NSDUH/2k10ResultsTables/Web/HTML/TOC.htm

Table 13.8 Cigarette Use by 9th to 12th Graders, 2009

(percent of 9th to 12th graders who have ever tried cigarette smoking or who have smoked cigarettes in the past 30 days, by sex, 2009)

	lifetime cigarette use	past month cigarette use
Total high school students	**46.3%**	**19.5%**
Boys	46.3	19.8
9th grade	37.9	12.1
10th grade	44.0	17.8
11th grade	50.0	23.9
12th grade	56.1	28.1
Girls	46.1	19.1
9th grade	37.4	15.2
10th grade	44.0	18.7
11th grade	50.0	20.6
12th grade	54.8	22.4

Source: Centers for Disease Control and Prevention, Youth Risk Behavior Surveillance—United States, 2009, Internet site http://www.cdc.gov/HealthyYouth/yrbs/index.htm

Most Teens Don't Wait for Legal Drinking Age

The majority of 20-year-olds have had an alcoholic beverage in the past month.

More than half of Americans aged 12 or older have had an alcoholic beverage in the past month. The figure climbs above 50 percent among 20-year-olds although the legal drinking age is 21.

Many teens and young adults take part in binge drinking, meaning they have had five or more drinks on one occasion in the past month. Among people aged 19 and 20, more than one in ten participated in heavy drinking during the past month—meaning they binged at least five times during the past month.

In another survey of high school students, 42 percent say they used alcohol in the past month. The figure rises with grade level to the majority of boys and girls in 12th grade.

■ Heavy drinking is a bigger problem than drug use among teenagers.

Many teens drink alcohol

(percent of people aged 16 to 20 who have consumed alcoholic beverages in the past month, by age, 2010)

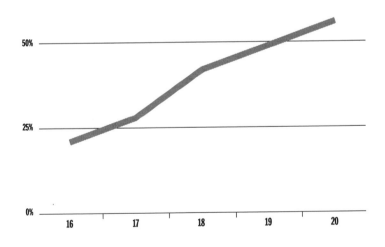

Table 13.9 Alcohol Use by People Aged 12 to 20, 2010

(percent of people aged 12 or older and people aged 12 to 20 who drank alcoholic beverages during the past month, by level of alcohol use, 2010)

	drank at any time during past month	binge drinking during past month	heavy drinking during past month
Total people aged 12 or older	**51.8%**	**23.1%**	**6.7%**
Aged 12	1.6	0.4	0.0
Aged 13	4.6	1.6	0.2
Aged 14	9.0	4.1	0.6
Aged 15	15.5	9.2	1.7
Aged 16	21.1	12.4	2.7
Aged 17	28.0	18.2	4.5
Aged 18	41.6	28.5	8.2
Aged 19	49.4	34.3	12.2
Aged 20	55.8	37.3	13.7

Note: "Binge drinking" is defined as having five or more drinks on the same occasion on at least one day in the 30 days prior to the survey. "Heavy drinking" is having five or more drinks on the same occasion on each of five or more days in 30 days prior to the survey.

Source: SAMHSA, Office of Applied Studies, 2010 National Survey on Drug Use and Health, Detailed Tables, Internet site http://www.samhsa.gov/data/NSDUH/2k10ResultsTables/Web/HTML/TOC.htm

Table 13.10 Alcohol Use by 9th to 12th Graders, 2009

(percent of 9th to 12th graders who have ever drunk alcohol or who have drunk alcohol in the past 30 days, by sex, 2009)

	lifetime alcohol use	past month alcohol use
Total high school students	**72.5%**	**41.8%**
Boys	**70.8**	**40.8**
9th grade	60.8	28.4
10th grade	69.9	40.1
11th grade	76.5	45.7
12th grade	79.0	52.6
Girls	**74.2**	**42.9**
9th grade	66.4	35.3
10th grade	72.5	41.2
11th grade	79.0	45.6
12th grade	80.3	50.7

Source: Centers for Disease Control and Prevention, Youth Risk Behavior Surveillance—United States, 2009, Internet site http://www.cdc.gov/HealthyYouth/yrbs/index.htm

Drug Use Is Prevalent among Teens

More than one in four 12-to-17-year-olds has ever used an illicit drug.

Among Americans aged 12 or older, only 9 percent have used an illicit drug in the past month. Teens and young adults are much more likely to be current drug users than the average person. Among 17-year-olds, 18 percent have used an illicit drug in the past month.

Marijuana is the most commonly used illicit drug. Among all 12-to-17-year olds, 7 percent have used marijuana in the past month. The figure rises to more than 10 percent among 16- and 17-year-olds.

In a survey of high school students, 37 percent say they have used marijuana in their lifetime and 21 percent have used it in the past month. The proportion that has used marijuana in the past month rises with grade level to 30 percent of senior boys and 19 percent of junior and senior girls.

■ Drinking is a bigger problem among teens than drug use.

More than 10 percent of 15-to-17-year-olds have used an illicit drug in the past month

(percent of people aged 12 to 17 who have used an illicit drug in the past month, by age, 2010)

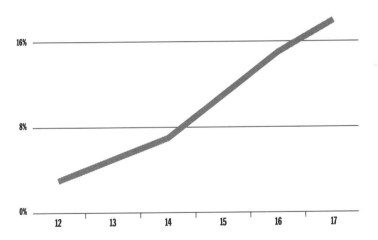

Table 13.11 Illicit Drug Use by People Aged 12 to 17, 2010

(percent of people aged 12 to 17 who ever used any illicit drug, who used an illicit drug in the past year, and who used an illicit drug in the past month, 2010)

	ever used	used in past year	used in past month
Total people aged 12 or older	**47.1%**	**15.3%**	**8.9%**
Total people aged 12 to 17	**25.7**	**19.4**	**10.1**
Aged 12	10.0	6.6	3.2
Aged 13	15.5	10.5	4.8
Aged 14	20.1	14.7	7.2
Aged 15	30.2	22.9	11.3
Aged 16	34.3	26.7	14.9
Aged 17	41.9	33.4	18.4

Note: Illicit drugs include marijuana, hashish, cocaine (including crack), heroin, hallucinogens, inhalants, or any prescription-type psychotherapeutic used nonmedically.
Source: SAMHSA, Office of Applied Studies, 2010 National Survey on Drug Use and Health, Detailed Tables, Internet site http://www.samhsa.gov/data/NSDUH/2k10ResultsTables/Web/HTML/TOC.htm

Table 13.12 Marijuana Use by People Aged 12 to 17, 2010

(percent of people aged 12 or older and people aged 12 to 17 who ever used marijuana, who used marijuana in the past year, and who used marijuana in the past month, 2010)

	ever used	used in past year	used in past month
Total people aged 12 or older	**41.9%**	**11.5%**	**6.9%**
Total people aged 12 to 17	**17.0**	**14.0**	**7.4**
Aged 12	1.0	0.9	0.2
Aged 13	4.7	4.0	1.5
Aged 14	10.6	9.1	4.2
Aged 15	20.2	17.0	8.6
Aged 16	27.0	21.8	12.4
Aged 17	36.2	29.2	16.2

Source: SAMHSA, Office of Applied Studies, 2010 National Survey on Drug Use and Health, Detailed Tables, Internet site http://www.samhsa.gov/data/NSDUH/2k10ResultsTables/Web/HTML/TOC.htm

Table 13.13 Marijuana Use by 9th to 12th Graders, 2009

(percent of 9th to 12th graders who have ever used marijuana or who have used marijuana in the past 30 days, by sex, 2009)

	lifetime marijuana use	past month marijuana use
Total high school students	**36.8%**	**20.8%**
Boys	**39.0**	**23.4**
9th grade	26.9	15.5
10th grade	37.7	23.9
11th grade	44.3	26.7
12th grade	50.9	29.9
Girls	**34.3**	**17.9**
9th grade	25.7	15.5
10th grade	33.0	17.9
11th grade	39.5	19.5
12th grade	40.2	19.1

Source: Centers for Disease Control and Prevention, Youth Risk Behavior Surveillance—United States, 2009, Internet site http://www.cdc.gov/HealthyYouth/yrbs/index.htm

Most Children Are Covered by Health Insurance

More than 7 million children do not have health insurance, however.

Among all Americans, 50 million lacked health insurance in 2010—or 16 percent of the population. The figure is a smaller 10 percent among children.

Hispanic children are most likely to be without health insurance. The 16 percent of Hispanic children who are not insured account for 39 percent of all uninsured children—larger than the 38 percent share accounted for by non-Hispanic whites. More than one-third of foreign-born children who are not citizens do not have health insurance.

Nearly 87 percent of children had health expenses in 2009, with a median cost of $548. Private insurance covered 57 percent of the cost, Medicaid (the government health insurance program for the poor) paid another 22 percent of those costs. Most parents are satisfied with the health care their children receive. Seven out of ten parents rated their child's last health care visit a 9 or 10 on a scale of 0 (worst) to 10 (best).

■ Providing health insurance coverage to all children is a thorny policy problem because many without health insurance are children of undocumented immigrants.

Hispanic children are most likely to be without health insurance

(percent of children without health insurance, by race and Hispanic origin, 2010)

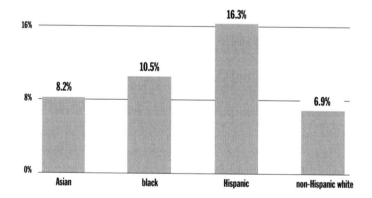

Table 13.14 Health Insurance Coverage of Children, 2010

(number and percent distribution of children under age 18 by age, race, Hispanic origin, and health insurance coverage status, 2010; numbers in thousands)

| | | covered by private or government health insurance | | | | | | | | |
| | | | private insurance | | | government | | | | |
	total	total	total	group health	direct purchase	total	Medicaid	Medicare	Champus	not covered
NUMBER										
Age										
Total children under age 18	74,916	67,609	44,620	41,083	4,291	28,385	26,067	602	2,461	7,307
Under age 3	12,538	11,352	6,553	6,142	560	5,662	5,190	100	507	1,186
Aged 3 to 5	13,017	11,889	7,313	6,809	698	5,525	5,093	133	445	1,128
Aged 6 to 11	24,701	22,400	14,825	13,919	1,377	9,362	8,694	182	715	2,301
Aged 12 to 17	24,660	21,968	15,929	14,212	1,657	7,836	7,090	186	793	2,692
Race and Hispanic origin										
Total children under age 18	74,916	67,609	44,620	41,083	4,291	28,385	26,067	602	2,461	7,307
Asian	4,022	3,690	2,804	2,564	310	1,116	1,007	18	121	332
Black	12,707	11,373	5,313	4,896	514	7,163	6,748	120	491	1,334
Hispanic	17,538	14,676	6,606	6,185	488	9,074	8,671	256	335	2,862
Non-Hispanic white	40,713	37,912	29,778	27,366	2,947	11,169	9,762	218	1,519	2,802
PERCENT DISTRIBUTION										
Age										
Total children under age 18	100.0%	90.2%	59.6%	54.8%	5.7%	37.9%	34.8%	0.8%	3.3%	9.8%
Under age 3	100.0	90.5	52.3	49.0	4.5	45.2	41.4	0.8	4.0	9.5
Aged 3 to 5	100.0	91.3	56.2	52.3	5.4	42.4	39.1	1.0	3.4	8.7
Aged 6 to 11	100.0	90.7	60.0	56.3	5.6	37.9	35.2	0.7	2.9	9.3
Aged 12 to 17	100.0	89.1	64.6	57.6	6.7	31.8	28.8	0.8	3.2	10.9
Race and Hispanic origin										
Total children under age 18	100.0	90.2	59.6	54.8	5.7	37.9	34.8	0.8	3.3	9.8
Asian	100.0	91.7	69.7	63.7	7.7	27.7	25.0	0.4	3.0	8.3
Black	100.0	89.5	41.8	38.5	4.0	56.4	53.1	0.9	3.9	10.5
Hispanic	100.0	83.7	37.7	35.3	2.8	51.7	49.4	1.5	1.9	16.3
Non-Hispanic white	100.0	93.1	73.1	67.2	7.2	27.4	24.0	0.5	3.7	6.9

Note: Asians and blacks are those who identify themselves as being of the race alone and those who identify themselves as being of the race in combination with other races. Hispanics may be of any race. Non-Hispanic whites are only those who identify themselves as being white alone and not Hispanic. Numbers may not add to total because children may be covered by more than one type of health insurance.
Source: Bureau of the Census, Health Insurance, Internet site http://www.census.gov/hhes/www/cpstables/032011/health/toc.htm; calculations by New Strategist

Table 13.15 Children under Age 18 without Health Insurance, 2010

(number and percent distribution of children under age 18 without health insurance by selected characteristics, 2010; numbers in thousands)

	children without health insurance		
	number	percent	percent distribution
Total children under age 18	**7,307**	**9.8%**	**100.0%**
Age			
Under age 3	1,186	9.5	16.2
Aged 3 to 5	1,128	8.7	15.4
Aged 6 to 11	2,301	9.3	31.5
Aged 12 to 17	2,692	10.9	36.8
Race and Hispanic origin			
Asian	332	8.2	4.5
Black	1,334	10.5	18.3
Hispanic	2,862	16.3	39.2
Non-Hispanic white	2,802	6.9	38.3
Region			
Northeast	911	7.4	12.5
Midwest	1,116	7.0	15.3
South	3,320	11.7	45.4
West	1,960	10.7	26.8
Family income			
Under $25,000	2,489	14.7	34.1
$25,000 to $49,999	2,217	13.6	30.3
$50,000 to $74,999	1,192	9.3	16.3
$75,000 or more	1,155	4.2	15.8
Family type			
Married couple	4,186	8.3	57.3
Female householder, no spouse present	2,094	16.7	28.7
Male householder, no spouse present	772	11.3	10.6
Nativity			
Native born	6,556	9.1	89.7
Foreign born	750	29.5	10.3
Naturalized citizen	65	11.9	0.9
Not a citizen	685	34.4	9.4

Note: Asians and blacks are those who identify themselves as being of the race alone and those who identify themselves as being of the race in combination with other races. Hispanics may be of any race. Non-Hispanic whites are those who identify themselves as being white alone and not Hispanic.
Source: Bureau of the Census, Health Insurance, Internet site http://www.census.gov/hhes/www/cpstables/032011/health/toc .htm; calculations by New Strategist

Table 13.16 Spending on Health Care for Children, 2009

(percent of children under age 18 with health care expense, median expense per child, total expenses, and percent distribution of total expenses by source of payment, by age, 2009)

				total expenses	
	total (thousands)	percent with expense	median expense per person	amount (millions)	percent distribution
Total children	**74,836**	**86.5%**	**$548**	**$143,261**	**100.0%**
Under age 6	25,838	88.7	504	62121	43.4
Aged 6 to 11	24,614	86.3	504	36,145	25.2
Aged 12 to 17	24,385	84.3	705	44,995	31.4

	percent distribution by source of payment				
	total	out of pocket	private insurance	Medicaid	other
Total children	**100.0%**	**12.9%**	**57.3%**	**21.7%**	**6.9%**
Under age 6	100.0	5.7	67.9	18.8	7.4
Aged 6 to 11	100.0	14.9	47.0	27.8	6.3
Aged 12 to 17	100.0	21.3	50.9	20.7	6.8

Note: "Other" insurance includes Department of Veterans Affairs (except Tricare), American Indian Health Service, state and local clinics, worker's compensation, homeowner's and automobile insurance, etc.
Source: Agency for Healthcare Research and Quality, Medical Expenditure Panel Survey, 2009, Internet site http://meps.ahrq.gov/mepsweb/survey_comp/household.jsp; calculations by New Strategist

Table 13.17 Parents' Rating of Health Care Received by Children at Doctor's Office or Clinic, 2009

(number of children under age 18 visiting a doctor or health care clinic in past 12 months, and percent distribution by rating given by parents for health care received by children on a scale from 0 (worst) to 10 (best), 2009; children in thousands)

	with health care visit		rating		
	number	percent	9 to 10	7 to 8	0 to 6
Total children	**57,543**	**100.0%**	**70.1%**	**24.8%**	**4.8%**
Under age 6	21,462	100.0	69.2	25.6	5.0
Aged 6 to 11	18,441	100.0	70.3	24.2	5.1
Aged 12 to 17	17,639	100.0	71.0	24.3	4.4

Source: Agency for Healthcare Research and Quality, Medical Expenditure Panel Survey, 2009, Internet site http://meps.ahrq.gov/mepsweb/survey_comp/household.jsp; calculations by New Strategist

Asthma and Allergies Affect Many Children

Boys are more likely than girls to have learning disabilities.

Asthma is a growing problem among children. Fourteen percent of the nation's 75 million children under age 18 have been diagnosed with asthma. Boys are more likely than girls to have been diagnosed with asthma (15.5 versus 11.9 percent), and blacks more likely than other racial or ethnic groups (21 percent versus 12 to 13 percent for Asians, Hispanics, and non-Hispanic whites).

Nearly 5 million children (8 percent) have been diagnosed with a learning disability, and more than 5 million have attention deficit hyperactivity disorder. Boys are far more likely than girls to have these conditions and account for 60 percent of those with learning disabilities and 68 percent of those with attention deficit hyperactivity disorder.

Many children use prescription medications. Ten million children have taken prescription medications regularly for at least three months during the past year. That is a substantial 13.5 percent of the nation's children. Among 12-to-17-year-olds, the figure is an even higher 18 percent.

■ Prescription drug use is becoming common among the nation's children.

Boys are more likely than girls to have attention deficit hyperactivity disorder

(percent of people under age 18 diagnosed with attention deficit hyperactivity disorder, by sex, 2010)

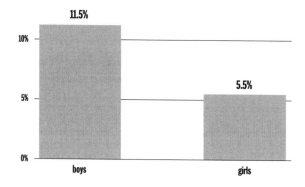

Table 13.18 Health Conditions among Children by Selected Characteristics, 2010

(number of people under age 18 with selected health conditions, by selected characteristics and type of condition, 2010; numbers in thousands)

	total children	diagnosed with asthma	still have asthma	hay fever	respiratory allergies	food allergies	skin allergies	learning disability	attention deficit hyperactivity disorder	prescription medication taken regularly at least 3 months
					experienced in last 12 months			ever told had*		
Total children	74,626	10,133	6,976	7,085	8,581	3,443	9,400	4,838	5,161	10,082
Sex										
Female	36,491	4,307	2,986	3,111	3,812	1,665	4,747	1,921	1,649	4,221
Male	38,135	5,827	3,991	3,973	4,769	1,778	4,653	2,917	3,511	5,861
Age										
Aged 0 to 4	21,414	1,714	1,285	969	1,734	1,092	2,974	267	139	1,526
Aged 5 to 11	28,666	4,200	3,020	2,877	3,653	1,259	3,955	2,291	2,181	4,129
Aged 12 to 17	24,546	4,219	2,672	3,239	3,193	1,092	2,471	2,280	2,840	4,430
Race and Hispanic origin										
Asian	3,354	428	281	293	236	223	336	95	38	206
Black	11,030	2,331	1,742	727	1,167	680	1,853	904	939	1,642
Hispanic	17,167	2,099	1,385	1,168	1,422	491	1,688	895	589	1,483
Non-Hispanic white	40,766	4,936	3,347	4,623	5,375	1,888	5,142	2,765	3,391	6,369
Family structure										
Mother and father	51,329	5,954	4,028	5,077	5,876	2,480	6,240	2,479	2,679	6,319
Mother, no father	18,026	3,367	2,414	1,576	2,177	795	2,629	1,812	1,908	3,061
Father, no mother	2,835	303	191	218	255	104	243	245	284	274
Neither mother nor father	2,436	509	344	213	272	64	288	301	289	428
Parent's education										
Less than high school diploma	9,301	1,207	874	481	642	196	905	697	651	935
High school diploma or GED	14,750	2,267	1,532	1,078	1,482	589	1,661	1,172	1,154	2,008
More than high school	47,913	6,144	4,221	5,304	6,185	2,581	6,540	2,646	3,048	6,691
Household income										
Less than $35,000	24,323	3,910	2,825	1,669	2,483	845	3,117	2,326	2,262	3,624
$35,000 to $49,999	9,438	1,406	998	838	1,213	524	1,170	519	507	1,152
$50,000 to $74,999	12,473	1,542	1,013	1,254	1,562	581	1,657	576	782	1,482
$75,000 to $99,999	8,919	1,192	801	1,056	1,132	507	1,125	458	532	1,201
$100,000 or more	16,241	1,726	1,115	2,101	1,946	851	2,068	795	920	2,349

* Ever told by a school representative or health professional. Data exclude children under age 3.
Note: "Mother and father" includes biological, adoptive, step, in-law, or foster relationships. Legal guardians are classified as "neither mother nor father." "Parent's education" is the education level of the parent with the higher level of education. Race/Hispanic origin, education, and income categories do not sum to total because not all races are shown and those not reporting education or income are not shown.
Source: National Center for Health Statistics, Summary Health Statistics for U.S. Children: National Health Interview Survey, 2010, Series 10, No. 250, 2011, Internet site http://www.cdc.gov/nchs/nhis.htm

Table 13.19 Distribution of Health Conditions among Children by Selected Characteristics, 2010

(percent distribution of people under age 18 with health conditions, by selected characteristics, 2010; numbers in thousands)

	total children	diagnosed with asthma	still have asthma	hay fever	respiratory allergies	food allergies	skin allergies	learning disability	attention deficit hyperactivity disorder	prescription medication taken regularly at least 3 months
				experienced in last 12 months				ever told had*		
Total children	100.0%	100.0%	100.0%	100.0%	100.0%	100.0%	100.0%	100.0%	100.0%	100.0%
Sex										
Female	48.9	42.5	42.8	43.9	44.4	48.4	50.5	39.7	32.0	41.9
Male	51.1	57.5	57.2	56.1	55.6	51.6	49.5	60.3	68.0	58.1
Age										
Aged 0 to 4	28.7	16.9	18.4	13.7	20.2	31.7	31.6	5.5	2.7	15.1
Aged 5 to 11	38.4	41.4	43.3	40.6	42.6	36.6	42.1	47.4	42.3	41.0
Aged 12 to 17	32.9	41.6	38.3	45.7	37.2	31.7	26.3	47.1	55.0	43.9
Race and Hispanic origin										
Asian	4.5	4.2	4.0	4.1	2.8	6.5	3.6	2.0	0.7	2.0
Black	14.8	23.0	25.0	10.3	13.6	19.8	19.7	18.7	18.2	16.3
Hispanic	23.0	20.7	19.9	16.5	16.6	14.3	18.0	18.5	11.4	14.7
Non-Hispanic white	54.6	48.7	48.0	65.3	62.6	54.8	54.7	57.2	65.7	63.2
Family structure										
Mother and father	68.8	58.8	57.7	71.7	68.5	72.0	66.4	51.2	51.9	62.7
Mother, no father	24.2	33.2	34.6	22.2	25.4	23.1	28.0	37.5	37.0	30.4
Father, no mother	3.8	3.0	2.7	3.1	3.0	3.0	2.6	5.1	5.5	2.7
Neither mother nor father	3.3	5.0	4.9	3.0	3.2	1.9	3.1	6.2	5.6	4.2
Parent's education										
Less than high school diploma	12.5	11.9	12.5	6.8	7.5	5.7	9.6	14.4	12.6	9.3
High school diploma or GED	19.8	22.4	22.0	15.2	17.3	17.1	17.7	24.2	22.4	19.9
More than high school	64.2	60.6	60.5	74.9	72.1	75.0	69.6	54.7	59.1	66.4
Household income										
Less than $35,000	32.6	38.6	40.5	23.6	28.9	24.5	33.2	48.1	43.8	35.9
$35,000 to $49,999	12.6	13.9	14.3	11.8	14.1	15.2	12.4	10.7	9.8	11.4
$50,000 to $74,999	16.7	15.2	14.5	17.7	18.2	16.9	17.6	11.9	15.2	14.7
$75,000 to $99,999	12.0	11.8	11.5	14.9	13.2	14.7	12.0	9.5	10.3	11.9
$100,000 or more	21.8	17.0	16.0	29.7	22.7	24.7	22.0	16.4	17.8	23.3

* Ever told by a school representative or health professional. Data exclude children under age 3.
Note: "Mother and father" includes biological, adoptive, step, in-law, or foster relationships. Legal guardians are classified as "neither mother nor father." "Parent's education" is the education level of the parent with the higher level of education. Race/ Hispanic origin, education, and income categories do not sum to total because not all races are shown and those not reporting education or income are not shown.
Source: National Center for Health Statistics, Summary Health Statistics for U.S. Children: National Health Interview Survey, 2010, Series 10, No. 250, 2011, Internet site http://www.cdc.gov/nchs/nhis.htm; calculations by New Strategist

Table 13.20 Percent of Children with Health Conditions by Selected Characteristics, 2010

(percent of people under age 18 with selected health conditions, by type of condition and selected characteristics, 2010)

| | total children | diagnosed with asthma | still have asthma | experienced in last 12 months | | | skin allergies | ever told had* | | prescription medication taken regularly at least 3 months |
				hay fever	respiratory allergies	food allergies		learning disability	attention deficit hyperactivity disorder	
Total children	100.0%	13.6%	9.4%	9.5%	11.5%	4.6%	12.6%	7.9%	8.4%	13.5%
Sex										
Female	100.0	11.9	8.3	8.6	10.6	4.6	13.0	6.4	5.5	11.7
Male	100.0	15.5	10.6	10.6	12.6	4.7	12.2	9.3	11.2	15.5
Age										
Aged 0 to 4	100.0	8.0	6.0	4.5	8.1	5.1	13.9	3.2	1.7	7.1
Aged 5 to 11	100.0	14.7	10.5	10.1	12.8	4.4	13.8	8.0	7.6	14.4
Aged 12 to 17	100.0	17.2	10.9	13.2	13.1	4.5	10.1	9.3	11.6	18.1
Race and Hispanic origin										
Asian	100.0	13.0	8.5	8.8	7.1	6.7	10.0	3.5	1.4	6.2
Black	100.0	21.4	16.0	6.6	10.6	6.1	16.7	10.0	10.5	15.0
Hispanic	100.0	12.7	8.3	7.0	8.5	2.9	9.7	6.7	4.4	8.9
Non-Hispanic white	100.0	12.1	8.2	11.3	13.2	4.6	12.7	8.0	9.8	15.5
Family structure										
Mother and father	100.0	11.9	8.0	10.2	11.7	4.8	12.1	6.0	6.5	12.6
Mother, no father	100.0	18.6	13.4	8.7	12.1	4.4	14.6	11.9	12.5	16.9
Father, no mother	100.0	10.1	6.1	7.7	9.1	4.2	9.3	9.2	10.0	8.6
Neither mother nor father	100.0	20.3	14.0	8.6	11.1	2.7	12.1	14.0	13.0	16.5
Parent's education										
Less than high school diploma	100.0	13.2	9.5	5.4	7.1	2.2	9.5	9.4	8.8	10.3
High school diploma or GED	100.0	15.7	10.6	7.5	10.3	4.0	11.2	10.0	9.8	14.0
More than high school	100.0	12.9	8.9	11.2	13.0	5.4	13.7	6.6	7.7	14.0
Household income										
Less than $35,000	100.0	16.7	12.0	7.2	10.5	3.4	12.6	12.3	12.0	15.6
$35,000 to $49,999	100.0	15.1	10.7	9.1	13.0	5.7	12.4	6.8	6.6	12.4
$50,000 to $74,999	100.0	12.4	8.2	10.1	12.6	4.6	13.3	5.6	7.6	11.9
$75,000 to $99,999	100.0	13.4	9.1	11.9	12.8	5.6	12.7	6.2	7.1	13.5
$100,000 or more	100.0	10.4	6.8	12.6	11.9	5.3	12.9	5.6	6.4	14.1

* Ever told by a school representative or health professional. Data exclude children under age 3.

Note: "Mother and father" includes biological, adoptive, step, in-law, or foster relationships. Legal guardians are classified as "neither mother nor father." "Parent's education" is the education level of the parent with the higher level of education. Race/Hispanic origin, education, and income categories do not sum to total because not all races are shown and those not reporting education or income are not shown.

Source: National Center for Health Statistics, Summary Health Statistics for U.S. Children: National Health Interview Survey, 2010, Series 10, No. 250, 2011, Internet site http://www.cdc.gov/nchs/nhis.htm

Many Children Use Alternative Medicine

Children with the most educated parents are most likely to use alternative medicine.

Among the nation's children under age 18, a substantial 12 percent have used alternative or complementary medicine in the past year, according to a government study. Among children whose parents use alternative medicine, the figure is twice as high at 24 percent.

The most popular types of alternative medicine used by children are nonvitamin, nonmineral natural products (3.9 percent), chiropractic and osteopathic care (2.8 percent), deep breathing exercises (2.2 percent), and yoga (2.1 percent). The children most likely to use alternative medicine are in two-parent families, have the most educated parents, and have multiple health conditions. The more doctor visits a child has had in the past year, the more likely he or she is to use alternative medicine.

■ Many of the children who use alternative medicine have health problems for which their parents are struggling to find a cure.

Children's use of alternative medicine rises with a parent's educational level

(percent of children under age 18 who used alternative medicine in the past year, by parent's education, 2007)

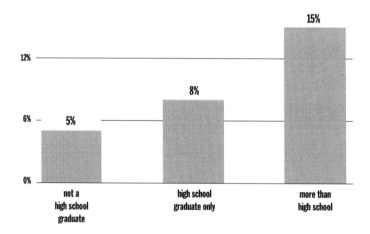

Table 13.21 Use of Alternative and Complementary Medicine by Children, 2007

(number and percent of children under age 18 who used complementary or alternative medicine in the past 12 months, 2007; numbers in thousands)

	children under age 18	
	number	percent
Any use	**8,720**	**11.8%**
Alternative medical systems		
Acupuncture	150	0.2
Homeopathic treatment	907	1.3
Biologically based therapies		
Nonvitamin, nonmineral natural products	2,850	3.9
Diet-based therapies	565	0.8
Vegetarian diet	367	0.5
Atkins diet	88	0.1
South Beach Diet	128	0.2
Manipulative and body-based therapies		
Chiropractic or osteopathic manipulation	2,020	2.8
Massage	743	1.0
Movement therapies	299	0.4
Pilates	245	0.3
Mind-body therapies		
Meditation	725	1.0
Guided imagery	293	0.4
Progressive relaxation	329	0.5
Deep breathing exercises	1,558	2.2
Yoga	1,505	2.1
Tai chi	113	0.2
Energy healing therapy/Reiki	161	0.2

Source: National Center for Health Statistics, Complementary and Alternative Medicine Use Among Adults and Children: United States, 2007, National Health Statistics Report, No. 12, 2008, Internet site http://www.cdc.gov/nchs/products/nhsr.htm

Table 13.22 Characteristics of Children Who Use Complementary and Alternative Medicine, 2007

(percent of people under age 18 who used complementary or alternative medicine (CAM) in the past 12 months, by selected characteristics, 2007)

	any	biologically based therapies	mind-body therapies	alternative medical systems	manipulative and body-based therapies
Total children	**11.8%**	**4.7%**	**4.3%**	**2.6%**	**3.7%**
Children whose parent uses CAM	23.9	10.3	9.8	4.2	7.5
Sex					
Female	12.6	4.6	4.9	2.8	4.2
Male	11.0	4.8	3.8	2.4	3.2
Age					
Aged 0 to 4	7.6	3.2	1.9	2.9	2.1
Aged 5 to 11	10.7	4.3	3.9	2.5	2.8
Aged 12 to 17	16.4	6.3	6.8	2.5	5.9
Race and Hispanic origin					
Black	5.9	1.7	3.0	1.4	0.8
Hispanic	7.9	2.8	2.8	2.5	1.9
White	12.8	5.2	4.4	2.8	4.4
Family structure					
Mother and father	12.7	5.2	4.3	2.7	4.2
Mother, no father	9.6	3.3	4.8	2.2	2.5
Parent's education					
Not a high school graduate	4.8	1.7	1.9	1.5	1.3
High school graduate or GED	8.0	2.8	2.3	1.7	2.5
More than high school	14.7	6.1	5.6	3.2	4.6
Number of health conditions					
No conditions	4.0	1.3	1.1	1.9	1.4
One to two conditions	8.5	2.9	3.2	1.5	2.3
Three to five conditions	14.1	6.0	4.8	2.9	4.2
Six or more conditions	23.8	8.8	10.2	5.6	5.4
Number of visits to doctor in past 12 months					
No visits	7.7	4.9	2.5	2.6	1.9
One visit	7.8	3.6	2.1	1.6	1.9
Two to three visits	11.1	3.4	4.5	2.6	3.1
Four to nine visits	15.0	6.0	5.0	2.5	5.6
10 or more visits	28.4	12.0	12.9	6.3	10.0
Delayed conventional care because of worry about costs					
Yes	16.9	7.3	6.6	5.0	6.2
No	11.6	4.6	4.2	2.6	3.6

Definitions: Biologically based therapies include chelation therapy, nonvitamin, nonmineral, natural products, and diet-based therapies. Mind-body therapies include biofeedback, meditation, guided imagery, progressive relxation, deep breathing exercises, hypnosis, yoga, tai chi, and qi gong. Alternative medical systems include acupuncture, ayurveda, homeopathic treatment, naturopathy, and traditional healers. Manipulative body-based therapies include chiropractic or osteopathic manipulation, massage, and movement therapies.
Note: Asians and blacks are those who identify themselves as being of the race alone. Non-Hispanic whites are those who identify themselves as being white alone and not Hispanic.
Source: National Center for Health Statistics, Complementary and Alternative Medicine Use Among Adults and Children: United States, 2007, National Health Statistics Report, No. 12, 2008, Internet site http://www.cdc.gov/nchs/products/nhsr.htm

Among Children, Accidents Are the Leading Cause of Death

Homicide is an important cause of death as well.

Once past infancy, accidents cause the largest share of deaths among children under age 15—which means a large portion of deaths in the age group are preventable. Among infants, congenital malformations are the leading cause of death.

In the 1-to-4 age group, accidents account for 32 percent of deaths, while congenital malformations rank second. Disturbingly, homicide is the third-leading cause of death in the age group. Among 5-to-14-year-olds, accidents are the leading cause of death followed by cancer, congenital malformations, and suicide. Homicide ranks fifth as a cause of death among 5-to-14-year-olds.

■ As medical science tamed the ailments that once killed many infants and children, accidents have become a more important cause of death.

Accidents are by far the leading cause of death among children aged 1 to 14

(percent of deaths due to the four leading causes of death among children, by age, 2010)

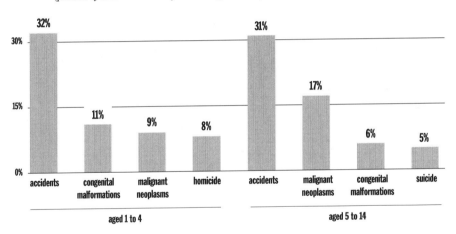

Table 13.23 Leading Causes of Death for Infants, 2010

(number and percent distribution of deaths accounted for by the10 leading causes of death for children under age 1, 2010)

		number	percent distribution
	All causes	**24,548**	**100.0%**
1.	Congenital malformations, deformations, and chromosomal abnormalities	5,077	20.7
2.	Disorders related to short gestation and low birth weight	4,130	16.8
3.	Sudden infant death syndrome	1,890	7.7
4.	Newborn affected by maternal complications of pregnancy	1,555	6.3
5.	Accidents (unintentional injuries)	1,043	4.2
6.	Newborn affected by complications of placenta, cord, and membranes	1,030	4.2
7.	Bacterial sepsis of newborn	569	2.3
8.	Diseases of circulatory system	499	2.0
9.	Respiratory distress of newborn	496	2.0
10.	Necrotizing enterocolitis of newborn	470	1.9
	All other causes	7,789	31.7

Source: National Center for Health Statistics, Deaths: Preliminary Data for 2010, National Vital Statistics Reports, Vol. 60, No. 4, 2012, Internet site http://www.cdc.gov/nchs/deaths.htm; calculations by New Strategist

Table 13.24 Leading Causes of Death for Children Aged 1 to 4, 2010

(number and percent distribution of deaths accounted for by the 10 leading causes of death for children aged 1 to 4, 2010)

| | | | aged 1 to 4 | |
		total	number	percent distribution	share of total
	All causes	**2,465,932**	**4,308**	**100.0%**	**0.2%**
1.	Accidents (unintentional injuries) (5)	118,043	1,367	31.7	1.2
2.	Congenital malformations, deformations	9,587	495	11.5	5.2
3.	Homicide (15)	16,065	367	8.5	2.3
4.	Malignant neoplasms (cancer) (2)	573,855	343	8.0	0.1
5.	Diseases of the heart (1)	595,444	156	3.6	0.0
6.	Influenza and pneumonia (9)	50,003	83	1.9	0.2
7.	Septicemia (11)	34,843	60	1.4	0.2
8.	In situ neoplasms, benign neoplasms	14,892	58	1.3	0.4
9.	Cerebrovascular diseases (4)	129,180	52	1.2	0.0
10.	Certain conditions originating in the perinatal period	12,053	52	1.2	0.4
	All other causes	911,967	1,275	29.6	0.1

Note: Number in parentheses shows cause of death rank for total population if cause is one of top 15.
Source: National Center for Health Statistics, Deaths: Preliminary Data for 2010, National Vital Statistics Reports, Vol. 60, No. 4, 2012, Internet site http://www.cdc.gov/nchs/deaths.htm; calculations by New Strategist

Table 13.25 Leading Causes of Death for Children Aged 5 to 14, 2010

(number and percent distribution of deaths accounted for by the 10 leading causes of death for children aged 5 to 14, 2010)

		total	aged 5 to 14		
			number	percent distribution	share of total
	All causes	**2,465,932**	**5,274**	**100.0%**	**0.2%**
1.	Accidents (unintentional injuries) (5)	118,043	1,626	30.8	1.4
2.	Malignant neoplasms (cancer) (2)	573,855	913	17.3	0.2
3.	Congenital malformations, deformations	9,587	292	5.5	3.0
4.	Suicide (10)	37,793	273	5.2	0.7
5.	Homicide (15)	16,065	254	4.8	1.6
6.	Diseases of the heart (1)	595,444	180	3.4	0.0
7.	Chronic lower respiratory disease (3)	137,789	128	2.4	0.1
8.	Cerebrovascular diseases (4)	129,180	85	1.6	0.1
9.	In situ neoplasms, benign neoplasms	14,892	83	1.6	0.6
10.	Influenza and pneumonia (9)	50,003	69	1.3	0.1
	All other causes	783,281	1,371	26.0	0.2

Note: Number in parentheses shows cause of death rank for total population if cause is one of top 15.
Source: National Center for Health Statistics, Deaths: Preliminary Data for 2010, National Vital Statistics Reports, Vol. 60, No. 4, 2012, Internet site http://www.cdc.gov/nchs/deaths.htm; calculations by New Strategist

14

Housing

■ The homeownership rate of families with children differs by age of child. The rate is lowest among families with preschoolers and no older children. The rate is highest among families with school-aged children and no preschoolers.

■ Children under age 18 have a slightly higher mobility rate than the average person. Between 2010 and 2011, 11.6 percent of Americans aged 1 or older moved from one house to another. Among children under age 18, the mobility rate was 13.4 percent.

■ Among children under age 16 who moved between 2010 and 2011, nearly half (49 percent) moved for housing reasons.

Most Families with Children Are Homeowners

The rate is lowest among families with young children.

The homeownership rate of families with children is almost identical to the overall homeownership rate. But the rate differs by the age of children in the home.

Among all families with own children under age 18, 62.9 percent owned their home, slightly below the 65.4 percent of all households that were homeowners, according to the 2010 American Community Survey. The rate is lowest (52.8 percent) for families with preschoolers and no older children—in other words, the youngest parents. The rate peaks at 68.9 percent among families with school-aged children and no preschoolers—in other words, among older parents.

■ Families with children account for 32 percent of renters and 29 percent of homeowners.

Among households with children, homeownership varies by age of child

(homeownership rate of families with children under age 18, by age of child, 2010)

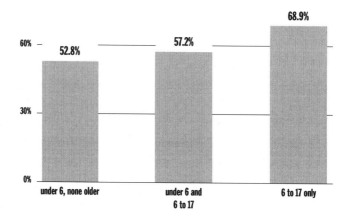

Table 14.1 Homeownership among Families with Children, 2010

(number and percent distribution of households by presence of own children under age 18 and homeownership status, 2010; numbers in thousands)

	total	owners	renters
Total households	**114,567**	**74,873**	**39,694**
With own children under age 18	34,032	21,420	12,611
With children under age 6 only	7,568	3,996	3,572
With children und age 6 and aged 6 to 17	6,925	3,963	2,962
With children aged 6 to 17 only	19,539	13,461	6,078
Without own children under age 18	80,536	53,453	27,083
PERCENT DISTRIBUTION BY TENURE			
Total households	**100.0%**	**65.4%**	**34.6%**
With own children under age 18	100.0	62.9	37.1
With children under age 6 only	100.0	52.8	47.2
With children und age 6 and aged 6 to 17	100.0	57.2	42.8
With children aged 6 to 17 only	100.0	68.9	31.1
Without own children under age 18	100.0	66.4	33.6
PERCENT DISTRIBUTION BY PRESENCE OF CHILDREN			
Total households	**100.0%**	**100.0%**	**100.0%**
With own children under age 18	29.7	28.6	31.8
With children under age 6 only	6.6	5.3	9.0
With children und age 6 and aged 6 to 17	6.0	5.3	7.5
With children aged 6 to 17 only	17.1	18.0	15.3
Without own children under age 18	70.3	71.4	68.2

Source: Bureau of the Census, 2010 American Community Survey, American Factfinder,Internet site http://factfinder2.census .gov/faces/nav/jsf/pages/index.xhtml; calculations by New Strategist

Older Children Are Less Likely to Move

Families try to stay put as children enter middle and high school.

Children under age 18 have a slightly higher mobility rate than the average person. Between 2010 and 2011, 11.6 percent of Americans aged 1 or older moved from one house to another. Among children under age 18, the mobility rate was 13.4 percent. Mobility rates are highest for the youngest children because their parents are searching for bigger and better housing before their children start school. Eighteen percent of children aged 1 to 4 moved between 2010 and 2011. The figure falls as children age, bottoming out at 9 percent among 15-to-17-year-olds. The household mobility statistics confirm this pattern, with the mobility rate highest among families with preschoolers (21 percent) and lowest among families with school-aged children only (10 percent).

Most moves are local, with movers remaining in the same county. Among children under age 16 who moved between 2010 and 2011, nearly half (49 percent) moved for housing reasons. Family reasons ranked second, at 28 percent. Only 17 percent moved because of their parents' employment situation.

■ More than one in 10 children who moved between 2010 and 2011 did so because their parents wanted cheaper housing.

Among children, mobility rates are highest for preschoolers

(percent of people aged 1 to 17 who moved between March 2010 and March 2011, by age)

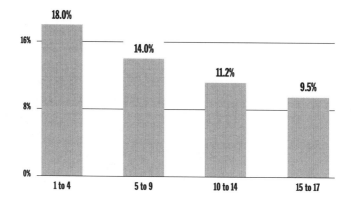

Table 14.2 Geographic Mobility of Children by Age and Type of Move, 2010–11

(total number of people aged 1 or older, and number and percent who moved between March 2010 and March 2011, by age and type of move; numbers in thousands)

	total	total movers	same county	different county, same state	different state total	same region	different region	movers from abroad
Total, aged 1 or older	**302,005**	**35,075**	**23,325**	**5,912**	**4,779**	**2,323**	**2,456**	**1,058**
Under age 18	70,811	9,465	6,591	1,494	1,162	554	608	216
Aged 1 to 4	17,160	3,095	2,099	535	398	202	196	62
Aged 5 to 9	20,870	2,920	2,047	454	336	158	178	84
Aged 10 to 14	20,020	2,244	1,579	332	299	131	168	33
Aged 15 to 17	12,761	1,206	866	173	129	63	66	37
Aged 18 or older	231,194	25,610	16,734	4,418	3,617	1,769	1,848	842

PERCENT DISTRIBUTION BY MOBILITY STATUS

Total, aged 1 or older	**100.0%**	**11.6%**	**7.7%**	**2.0%**	**1.6%**	**0.8%**	**0.8%**	**0.4%**
Under age 18	100.0	13.4	9.3	2.1	1.6	0.8	0.9	0.3
Aged 1 to 4	100.0	18.0	12.2	3.1	2.3	1.2	1.1	0.4
Aged 5 to 9	100.0	14.0	9.8	2.2	1.6	0.8	0.9	0.4
Aged 10 to 14	100.0	11.2	7.9	1.7	1.5	0.7	0.8	0.2
Aged 15 to 17	100.0	9.5	6.8	1.4	1.0	0.5	0.5	0.3
Aged 18 or older	100.0	11.1	7.2	1.9	1.6	0.8	0.8	0.4

PERCENT DISTRIBUTION OF MOVERS BY TYPE OF MOVE

Total, aged 1 or older	–	**100.0%**	**66.5%**	**16.9%**	**13.6%**	**6.6%**	**7.0%**	**3.0%**
Under age 18	–	100.0	69.6	15.8	12.3	5.9	6.4	2.3
Aged 1 to 4	–	100.0	67.8	17.3	12.9	6.5	6.3	2.0
Aged 5 to 9	–	100.0	70.1	15.5	11.5	5.4	6.1	2.9
Aged 10 to 14	–	100.0	70.4	14.8	13.3	5.8	7.5	1.5
Aged 15 to 17	–	100.0	71.8	14.3	10.7	5.2	5.5	3.1
Aged 18 or older	–	100.0	65.3	17.3	14.1	6.9	7.2	3.3

Note: –" means not applicable.
Source: Bureau of the Census, Geographic Mobility: 2010 to 2011, Detailed Tables, Internet site http://www.census.gov/hhes/migration/data/cps/cps2011.html; calculations by New Strategist

Table 14.3 Geographic Mobility of Families with Children, 2010–11

(total number and percent distribution of family householders aged 15 to 54 by mobility status and presence of own children under age 18 at home, March 2010 to March 2011; numbers in thousands)

	total	total movers	same county	different county, same state	different state	movers from abroad
Total family householders	**50,880**	**6,482**	**4,467**	**1,014**	**833**	**169**
No children under 18	17,681	1,904	1,223	311	293	76
With children under 18	33,199	4,577	3,243	703	538	93
Under 6 only	8,391	1,785	1,232	304	218	32
Under 6 and 6 to 17	6,768	977	691	135	133	18
Aged 6 to 17 only	18,040	1,815	1,320	264	187	43
PERCENT DISTRIBUTION BY MOBILITY STATUS						
Total family householders	**100.0%**	**12.7%**	**8.8%**	**2.0%**	**1.6%**	**0.3%**
No children under 18	100.0	10.8	6.9	1.8	1.7	0.4
With children under 18	100.0	13.8	9.8	2.1	1.6	0.3
Under 6 only	100.0	21.3	14.7	3.6	2.6	0.4
Under 6 and 6 to 17	100.0	14.4	10.2	2.0	2.0	0.3
Aged 6 to 17 only	100.0	10.1	7.3	1.5	1.0	0.2
PERCENT DISTRIBUTION OF MOVERS BY TYPE OF MOVE						
Total family householders	–	**100.0%**	**68.9%**	**15.6%**	**12.9%**	**2.6%**
No children under 18	–	100.0	64.2	16.3	15.4	4.0
With children under 18	–	100.0	70.9	15.4	11.8	2.0
Under 6 only	–	100.0	69.0	17.0	12.2	1.8
Under 6 and 6 to 17	–	100.0	70.7	13.8	13.6	1.8
Aged 6 to 17 only	–	100.0	72.7	14.5	10.3	2.4

Note: –" means not applicable.
Source: Bureau of the Census, Geographic Mobility: 2010 to 2011, Detailed Tables, Internet site http://www.census.gov/hhes/migration/data/cps/cps2011.html; calculations by New Strategist

Table 14.4 Reason for Moving among Children under Age 16, 2010–11

(number and percent distribution of movers under age 16 by primary reason household head moved and share of total movers between March 2010 and March 2011; numbers in thousands)

| | total movers | movers under age 16 | | |
		number	percent distribution	share of total
Total movers	35,075	8,612	100.0%	24.6%
Family reasons	9,784	2,449	28.4	25.0
Change in marital status	1,949	411	4.8	21.1
To establish own household	3,334	755	8.8	22.6
Other familiy reasons	4,501	1,283	14.9	28.5
Employment reasons	6,481	1,442	16.7	22.2
New job or job transfer	2,829	631	7.3	22.3
To look for work or lost job	924	237	2.8	25.6
To be closer to work/easier commute	2,081	459	5.3	22.1
Retired	108	3	0.0	2.8
Other job-related reason	539	112	1.3	20.8
Housing reasons	15,736	4,240	49.2	26.9
Wanted own home, not rent	1,530	440	5.1	28.8
Wanted better home/apartment	5,665	1,568	18.2	27.7
Wanted better neighborhood/less crime	1,360	408	4.7	30.0
Wanted cheaper housing	3,684	955	11.1	25.9
Foreclosure/eviction	412	109	1.3	26.5
Other housing reasons	3,085	760	8.8	24.6
Other reasons	3,073	483	5.6	15.7
To attend or leave college	890	61	0.7	6.9
Change of climate	149	23	0.3	15.4
Health reasons	564	59	0.7	10.5
Natural disaster	31	11	0.1	35.5
Other reasons	1,439	329	3.8	22.9

Source: Bureau of the Census, Geographic Mobility: 2010 to 2011, Detailed Tables, Internet site http://www.census.gov/hhes/migration/data/cps/cps2011.html; calculations by New Strategist

15

Income

■ The median income of households with children under age 18 ranged from a low of $24,487 for those in a female-headed family to a high of $77,749 for those in a married-couple family.

■ Regardless of family type, median income is higher for those without preschoolers in the household. Among couples with children aged 6 to 17 and none younger, median income exceeds $83,000.

■ The poverty rate among children under age 18 was a troubling 22.0 percent in 2010. The iGeneration accounts for more than one-third of the nation's poor.

Children in Married-Couple Families Are Better Off

Among families with children, married couples are far more affluent than single parents.

The financial wellbeing of children depends greatly on the type of household in which they live. Those living with married parents are far better off than those living in other types of households.

Among households with children under age 18 at home, the median income of married couples stood at $77,749 in 2010. This compares with a median of $36,290 for male-headed families and just $24,487 for female-headed families.

Married couples with children aged 6 to 17 and none younger have the highest incomes, a median of $83,097 in 2010. Thirty-nine percent have incomes of $100,000 or more. The incomes of male- and female-headed families with school-aged children also surpass the incomes of those with preschoolers. Most householders with school-aged children are in their peak earning years, which accounts for their above-average incomes. Female-headed families with preschoolers have the lowest incomes—a median of just $16,821 in 2010.

■ Regardless of family type, incomes have declined because of the Great Recession.

Single-parent families have the lowest incomes

(median income of families with children under age 18 at home by family type, 2010)

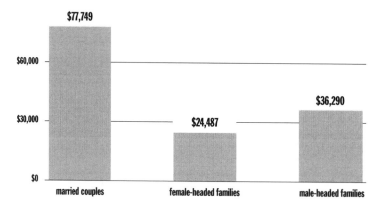

Table 15.1 Income of Households with Children under Age 18 by Household Type, 2010

(number and percent distribution of households with children under age 18 at home, by household income and household type, 2010; households in thousands as of 2011)

	married couples	female-headed families	male-headed families
Total households with children	**25,485**	**10,036**	**2,753**
Under $5,000	266	1,179	160
$5,000 to $9,999	241	1,040	147
$10,000 to $14,999	457	1,014	185
$15,000 to $19,999	610	955	188
$20,000 to $24,999	805	908	245
$25,000 to $29,999	883	777	189
$30,000 to $34,999	857	658	199
$35,000 to $39,999	946	588	198
$40,000 to $44,999	997	461	177
$45,000 to $49,999	954	377	143
$50,000 to $54,999	1,143	319	138
$55,000 to $59,999	975	272	89
$60,000 to $64,999	1,050	235	125
$65,000 to $69,999	968	155	60
$70,000 to $74,999	992	166	79
$75,000 to $79,999	904	151	62
$80,000 to $84,999	992	114	51
$85,000 to $89,999	827	82	41
$90,000 to $94,999	855	80	32
$95,000 to $99,999	681	62	40
$100,000 to $124,999	3,246	223	99
$125,000 to $149,999	1,929	92	40
$150,000 to $174,999	1,299	54	18
$175,000 to $199,999	711	16	12
$200,000 or more	1,893	60	34
Median income	$77,749	$24,487	$36,290

PERCENT DISTRIBUTION

	married couples	female-headed families	male-headed families
Total households with children	**100.0%**	**100.0%**	**100.0%**
Under $25,000	9.3	50.8	33.6
$25,000 to $49,999	18.2	28.5	32.9
$50,000 to $74,999	20.1	11.4	17.8
$75,000 to $99,999	16.7	4.9	8.2
$100,000 or more	35.6	4.4	7.4

Note: The median income of married couples in this table is slightly different from that shown in the household income tables because this figure includes the incomes only of family members and not any unrelated members of the household.
Source: Bureau of the Census, 2011 Current Population Survey, Internet site http://www.census.gov/hhes/www/cpstables/032011/hhinc/toc.htm; calculations by New Strategist

Table 15.2 Married Couples with Children by Family Income and Age of Children, 2010

(number and percent distribution of total married couples and married couples with related children under age 18 by family income and age of related children, 2010; married couples in thousands as of 2011)

	total	one or more children under age 18			
		total	all under 6	some < 6, some 6 to 17	all 6 to 17
Total married couples	**58,047**	**25,485**	**6,334**	**5,519**	**13,632**
Under $5,000	701	266	69	71	126
$5,000 to $9,999	523	241	81	71	89
$10,000 to $14,999	1,157	457	132	126	198
$15,000 to $19,999	1,661	610	192	196	222
$20,000 to $24,999	2,108	805	182	270	353
$25,000 to $29,999	2,432	883	222	262	398
$30,000 to $34,999	2,376	857	217	208	432
$35,000 to $39,999	2,476	946	239	268	438
$40,000 to $44,999	2,510	997	287	244	466
$45,000 to $49,999	2,362	954	224	233	498
$50,000 to $54,999	2,591	1,143	317	276	550
$55,000 to $59,999	2,298	975	240	236	500
$60,000 to $64,999	2,388	1,050	257	224	569
$65,000 to $69,999	2,158	968	209	214	545
$70,000 to $74,999	2,232	992	245	187	560
$75,000 to $79,999	1,988	904	231	157	516
$80,000 to $84,999	2,091	992	269	200	523
$85,000 to $89,999	1,884	827	202	167	459
$90,000 to $94,999	1,747	855	224	162	469
$95,000 to $99,999	1,520	681	143	135	403
$100,000 to $124,999	6,653	3,246	840	620	1,786
$125,000 to $149,999	4,143	1,929	458	341	1,131
$150,000 to $174,999	2,713	1,299	281	193	824
$175,000 to $199,999	1,537	711	175	123	414
$200,000 or more	3,800	1,893	397	333	1,162
Median income	$72,426	$77,749	$75,961	$66,446	$83,097
PERCENT DISTRIBUTION					
Total married couples	**100.0%**	**100.0%**	**100.0%**	**100.0%**	**100.0%**
Under $25,000	10.6	9.3	10.4	13.3	7.2
$25,000 to $49,999	20.9	18.2	18.8	22.0	16.4
$50,000 to $74,999	20.1	20.1	20.0	20.6	20.0
$75,000 to $99,999	15.9	16.7	16.9	14.9	17.4
$100,000 or more	32.5	35.6	34.0	29.2	39.0

Note: The median income of married couples in this table is slightly different from that shown in the household income tables because this figure includes the incomes only of family members and not any unrelated members of the household.
Source: Bureau of the Census, 2011 Current Population Survey, Internet site http://www.census.gov/hhes/www/cpstables/032011/hhinc/toc.htm; calculations by New Strategist

Table 15.3 Female-Headed Families with Children by Family Income and Age of Children, 2010

(number and percent distribution of total female-headed families and female-headed families with related children under age 18 by family income and age of related children, 2010; female-headed families in thousands as of 2011)

		one or more children under age 18			
	total	total	all under 6	some < 6, some 6 to 17	all 6 to 17
Total female-headed families	**15,026**	**10,036**	**2,245**	**1,957**	**5,835**
Under $5,000	1,343	1,179	415	276	488
$5,000 to $9,999	1,235	1,040	331	250	460
$10,000 to $14,999	1,318	1,014	282	213	519
$15,000 to $19,999	1,295	955	217	238	500
$20,000 to $24,999	1,328	908	202	193	513
$25,000 to $29,999	1,154	777	155	163	459
$30,000 to $34,999	1,039	658	137	103	418
$35,000 to $39,999	962	588	84	96	408
$40,000 to $44,999	798	461	74	84	303
$45,000 to $49,999	659	377	60	55	261
$50,000 to $54,999	555	319	32	48	239
$55,000 to $59,999	456	272	36	33	203
$60,000 to $64,999	432	235	33	27	175
$65,000 to $69,999	293	155	30	17	108
$70,000 to $74,999	351	166	23	24	120
$75,000 to $79,999	241	151	20	24	107
$80,000 to $84,999	212	114	20	12	81
$85,000 to $89,999	179	82	11	11	60
$90,000 to $94,999	178	80	7	14	59
$95,000 to $99,999	118	62	7	14	41
$100,000 to $124,999	465	223	28	32	164
$125,000 to $149,999	175	92	23	11	59
$150,000 to $174,999	97	54	5	8	41
$175,000 to $199,999	32	16	4	4	8
$200,000 or more	111	60	10	6	44
Median income	$29,220	$24,487	$16,821	$20,033	$29,728

PERCENT DISTRIBUTION

Total female-headed families	**100.0%**	**100.0%**	**100.0%**	**100.0%**	**100.0%**
Under $25,000	43.4	50.8	64.5	59.8	42.5
$25,000 to $49,999	30.7	28.5	22.7	25.6	31.7
$50,000 to $74,999	13.9	11.4	6.9	7.6	14.5
$75,000 to $99,999	6.2	4.9	2.9	3.8	6.0
$100,000 or more	5.9	4.4	3.1	3.1	5.4

Note: The median income of female-headed families in this table is slightly different from that shown in the household income tables because this figure includes the incomes only of family members and not any unrelated members of the household.
Source: Bureau of the Census, 2011 Current Population Survey, Internet site http://www.census.gov/hhes/www/cpstables/032011/hhinc/toc.htm; calculations by New Strategist

Table 15.4 Male-Headed Families with Children by Family Income and Age of Children, 2010

(number and percent distribution of total male-headed families and male-headed families with related children under age 18 by family income and age of related children, 2010; male-headed families in thousands as of 2011)

	total	one or more children under age 18			
		total	all under 6	some < 6, some 6 to 17	all 6 to 17
Total male-headed families	**5,560**	**2,753**	**863**	**360**	**1,529**
Under $5,000	221	160	42	33	85
$5,000 to $9,999	219	147	56	24	66
$10,000 to $14,999	268	185	58	27	101
$15,000 to $19,999	316	188	79	29	79
$20,000 to $24,999	425	245	101	24	120
$25,000 to $29,999	373	189	92	24	73
$30,000 to $34,999	356	199	52	29	118
$35,000 to $39,999	347	198	69	26	103
$40,000 to $44,999	370	177	53	16	108
$45,000 to $49,999	269	143	48	24	70
$50,000 to $54,999	310	138	32	17	89
$55,000 to $59,999	204	89	15	7	67
$60,000 to $64,999	279	125	24	12	89
$65,000 to $69,999	150	60	15	6	40
$70,000 to $74,999	190	79	23	10	46
$75,000 to $79,999	132	62	10	7	45
$80,000 to $84,999	147	51	16	10	25
$85,000 to $89,999	111	41	5	4	33
$90,000 to $94,999	83	32	8	0	23
$95,000 to $99,999	86	40	12	2	26
$100,000 to $124,999	337	99	26	20	55
$125,000 to $149,999	133	40	9	4	29
$150,000 to $174,999	75	18	5	2	12
$175,000 to $199,999	41	12	5	0	7
$200,000 or more	119	34	10	2	22
Median income	$43,058	$36,290	$30,226	$31,974	$40,678

PERCENT DISTRIBUTION

	total	total	all under 6	some < 6, some 6 to 17	all 6 to 17
Total male-headed families	**100.0%**	**100.0%**	**100.0%**	**100.0%**	**100.0%**
Under $25,000	26.1	33.6	38.9	38.1	29.5
$25,000 to $49,999	30.8	32.9	36.4	33.1	30.9
$50,000 to $74,999	20.4	17.8	12.6	14.4	21.6
$75,000 to $99,999	10.1	8.2	5.9	6.4	9.9
$100,000 or more	12.7	7.4	6.4	7.8	8.2

Note: The median income of male-headed families in this table is slightly different from that shown in the household income tables because this figure includes the incomes only of family members and not any unrelated members of the household.
Source: Bureau of the Census, 2011 Current Population Survey, Internet site http://www.census.gov/hhes/www/ cpstables/032011/hhinc/toc.htm; calculations by New Strategist

Children Have the Highest Poverty Rate

The iGeneration accounts for more than one-third of the nation's poor.

Children and young adults are much more likely to be poor than middle-aged or older adults. While 15.1 percent of all Americans were poor in 2010, the poverty rate among children under age 18 (the iGeneration was under age 17 in 2010) was a larger 22.0 percent. Black and Hispanic members of the iGeneration are much more likely to be poor (38.2 and 35.0 percent, respectively) than non-Hispanic whites or Asians (13.6 and 12.4 percent, respectively). Non-Hispanic whites account for only 30 percent of the iGen poor.

Children under age 18 who live in families headed by married couples are much less likely to be poor than those in single-parent families. Only 8.8 percent of children in married-couple families are poor versus 40.7 percent of those in female-headed families. Among black children living in a married-couple family, the poverty rate is 12.4 percent. Among those living in a female-headed single-parent family, the poverty rate is 47.1 percent.

■ The poverty rate for the iGeneration is well above average because many live in female-headed families—the poorest household type.

In the iGeneration, non-Hispanic whites have the lowest poverty rate

(percent of people under age 18 who live below poverty level, by race and Hispanic origin, 2010)

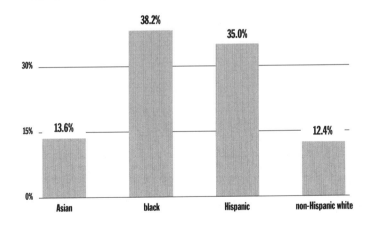

Table 15.5 People under Age 18 below Poverty Level by Race and Hispanic Origin, 2010

(number, percent, and percent distribution of people under age 18 below poverty level by race and Hispanic origin, 2010; people in thousands as of 2011)

	total	Asian	black	Hispanic	non-Hispanic white
NUMBER IN POVERTY					
Total people	**46,180**	**1,859**	**11,361**	**13,243**	**19,599**
Under age 18	16,401	547	4,817	6,110	5,002
Aged 0	1,095	42	350	410	307
Aged 1	1,094	32	351	420	301
Aged 2	1,059	37	301	405	313
Aged 3	1,189	40	376	448	338
Aged 4	1,030	37	311	388	297
Aged 5	1,076	29	312	436	304
Aged 6	910	26	245	392	259
Aged 7	953	39	277	349	285
Aged 8	933	46	237	359	290
Aged 9	856	28	248	307	277
Aged 10	865	21	240	352	266
Aged 11	776	20	207	281	272
Aged 12	808	28	235	293	252
Aged 13	742	22	225	232	260
Aged 14	697	20	222	243	223
Aged 15	713	33	206	249	220
Aged 16	816	12	263	270	275
Aged 17	787	36	211	275	264
PERCENT IN POVERTY					
Total people	**15.1%**	**11.9%**	**27.4%**	**26.6%**	**9.9%**
Under age 18	22.0	13.6	38.2	35.0	12.4
Aged 0	26.8	17.1	49.1	38.5	14.7
Aged 1	26.1	13.3	42.9	38.7	14.4
Aged 2	25.3	14.0	42.7	37.1	14.7
Aged 3	27.2	15.7	46.4	39.5	15.5
Aged 4	24.0	15.6	41.6	34.4	13.5
Aged 5	25.3	11.7	42.0	40.0	13.9
Aged 6	22.4	11.9	39.6	38.2	11.8
Aged 7	22.7	15.4	38.9	35.4	12.6
Aged 8	22.5	17.3	36.2	36.2	13.1
Aged 9	21.0	14.2	36.5	31.5	12.4
Aged 10	21.3	10.3	32.6	38.0	12.1
Aged 11	19.4	9.3	33.7	32.9	11.8
Aged 12	20.6	14.7	35.5	34.3	11.4
Aged 13	18.9	11.2	34.5	29.6	11.4
Aged 14	17.6	9.5	34.3	30.3	9.8
Aged 15	17.7	17.0	31.3	30.2	9.4
Aged 16	18.6	6.8	35.3	29.7	10.8
Aged 17	18.1	17.4	29.8	30.4	10.4

	total	Asian	black	Hispanic	non-Hispanic white
PERCENT DISTRIBUTION OF POOR BY RACE AND HISPANIC ORIGIN					
Total people	**100.0%**	**4.0%**	**24.6%**	**28.7%**	**42.4%**
Under age 18	100.0	3.3	29.4	37.3	30.5
Aged 0	100.0	3.8	32.0	37.4	28.0
Aged 1	100.0	2.9	32.1	38.4	27.5
Aged 2	100.0	3.5	28.4	38.2	29.6
Aged 3	100.0	3.4	31.6	37.7	28.4
Aged 4	100.0	3.6	30.2	37.7	28.8
Aged 5	100.0	2.7	29.0	40.5	28.3
Aged 6	100.0	2.9	26.9	43.1	28.5
Aged 7	100.0	4.1	29.1	36.6	29.9
Aged 8	100.0	4.9	25.4	38.5	31.1
Aged 9	100.0	3.3	29.0	35.9	32.4
Aged 10	100.0	2.4	27.7	40.7	30.8
Aged 11	100.0	2.6	26.7	36.2	35.1
Aged 12	100.0	3.5	29.1	36.3	31.2
Aged 13	100.0	3.0	30.3	31.3	35.0
Aged 14	100.0	2.9	31.9	34.9	32.0
Aged 15	100.0	4.6	28.9	34.9	30.9
Aged 16	100.0	1.5	32.2	33.1	33.7
Aged 17	100.0	4.6	26.8	34.9	33.5

Note: Numbers do not add to total because Asians and blacks are those who identify themselves as being of the race alone and those who identify themselves as being of the race in combination with other races, because Hispanics may be of any race, and because not all races are shown. Non-Hispanic whites are those who identify themselves as being white alone and not Hispanic. Source: Bureau of the Census, 2011 Current Population Survey Annual Social and Economic Supplement, Internet site http:// www.census.gov/hhes/www/cpstables/032011/pov/toc.htm; calculations by New Strategist

Table 15.6 Families with Children in Poverty by Family Type, Race, and Hispanic Origin, 2010

(number and percent of families with children under age 18 in poverty, and percent distribution of families with children in poverty, by type of family and race and Hispanic origin of householder, 2010; families in thousands as of 2011)

	total	Asian	black	Hispanic	non-Hispanic white
NUMBER IN POVERTY					
Total families with children in poverty	**6,997**	**213**	**1,939**	**2,204**	**2,621**
Married couples	2,242	124	264	958	888
Female householders, no spouse present	4,089	80	1,478	1,061	1,476
Male householders, no spouse present	667	10	197	186	256
PERCENT IN POVERTY					
Total families with children	**18.3%**	**10.9%**	**33.7%**	**30.6%**	**11.3%**
Married couples	8.8	7.8	12.4	21.6	5.2
Female householders, no spouse present	40.7	28.7	47.1	50.3	32.7
Male householders, no spouse present	24.2	11.1	40.8	28.3	17.2
PERCENT DISTRIBUTION OF FAMILIES IN POVERTY BY RACE AND HISPANIC ORIGIN					
Total families with children in poverty	**100.0%**	**3.0%**	**27.7%**	**31.5%**	**37.5%**
Married couples	100.0	5.5	11.8	42.7	39.6
Female householders, no spouse present	100.0	2.0	36.1	25.9	36.1
Male householders, no spouse present	100.0	1.5	29.5	27.9	38.4
PERCENT DISTRIBUTION OF FAMILIES IN POVERTY BY FAMILY TYPE					
Total families with children in poverty	**100.0%**	**100.0%**	**100.0%**	**100.0%**	**100.0%**
Married couples	32.0	58.2	13.6	43.5	33.9
Female householders, no spouse present	58.4	37.6	76.2	48.1	56.3
Male householders, no spouse present	9.5	4.7	10.2	8.4	9.8

Note: Numbers do not add to total because Asians and blacks are those who identify themselves as being of the race alone and those who identify themselves as being of the race in combination with other races, because Hispanics may be of any race, and because not all races are shown. Non-Hispanic whites are those who identify themselves as being white alone and not Hispanic. Source: Bureau of the Census, 2011 Current Population Survey Annual Social and Economic Supplement, Internet site http://www.census.gov/hhes/www/cpstables/032011/pov/toc.htm; calculations by New Strategist

16

Labor Force

■ Working parents are the norm for the iGeneration. Among women with children under age 18, fully 71 percent were in the labor force in 2010.

■ In the 58 percent majority of married couples with children under age 18, both husband and wife are employed. In just 30 percent, the father is the only employed parent.

■ Among children under age 3 with working mothers, the largest share is in center-based day care. The second-most-common arrangement is grandparent care.

■ Children from affluent families and with college-educated mothers are more likely than the less affluent and less educated to have nonrelatives care for their children.

Most Children Have Working Parents

For the iGeneration, working mothers are by far the norm.

Among women with children under age 18, fully 71 percent were in the labor force in 2010 (the iGeneration was aged 0 to 16 in that year). Sixty-four percent of women with children under age 18 were employed, most working full-time. Even among women with infants, 57 percent are in the labor force, and most of the workers have full-time jobs.

In 58 percent of married couples with children under age 18, both husband and wife are employed. In just 30 percent, the father is the only employed parent. Children in single-parent families also have parents who work. Sixty-seven percent of women who head single-parent families have jobs, as do 76 percent of their male counterparts.

■ Working parents being the norm, family life is highly scheduled.

For most children in married-couple families, mom and dad are at work

(percent distribution of married couples with children under age 18 by labor force status of parents, 2010)

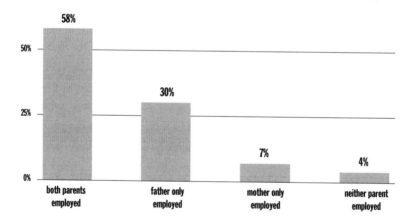

Table 16.1 Labor Force Status of Women by Presence of Children, 2010

(number and percent distribution of women aged 16 or older by labor force status and presence and age of own children under age 18 at home, 2010; numbers in thousands)

		civilian labor force				
	civilian population	total	employed total	full-time	part-time	not in labor force
Total women	**122,656**	**71,904**	**65,705**	**48,214**	**17,491**	**50,752**
No children under age 18	86,631	46,405	42,495	31,108	11,387	40,226
With children under age 18	36,025	25,499	23,210	17,106	6,104	10,526
Children aged 6 to 17, none younger	19,763	15,110	13,939	10,514	3,425	4,653
Children under age 6	16,262	10,388	9,271	6,592	2,679	5,874
Children under age 3	9,503	5,770	5,114	3,570	1,543	3,733
Children under age 1	3,184	1,800	1,590	1,128	462	1,384
Total women	**100.0%**	**58.6%**	**53.6%**	**39.3%**	**14.3%**	**41.4%**
No children under age 18	100.0	53.6	49.1	35.9	13.1	46.4
With children under age 18	100.0	70.8	64.4	47.5	16.9	29.2
Children aged 6 to 17, none younger	100.0	76.5	70.5	53.2	17.3	23.5
Children under age 6	100.0	63.9	57.0	40.5	16.5	36.1
Children under age 3	100.0	60.7	53.8	37.6	16.2	39.3
Children under age 1	100.0	56.5	49.9	35.4	14.5	43.5

Source: Bureau of Labor Statistics, Employment Characteristics of Families, Internet site http://www.bls.gov/news.release/famee.toc.htm; calculations by New Strategist

Table 16.2 Labor Force Status of Families with Children under Age 18, 2010

(number and percent distribution of families by employment status of parent and age of youngest own child under age 18 at home, by family type, 2010; numbers in thousands)

	total	youngest child 6 to 17	youngest child under 6
NUMBER			
Total families with children under age 18	34,513	19,480	15,032
No parent employed	4,359	2,257	2,103
Married couples with children under age 18	23,804	13,203	10,601
One or both parents employed	22,776	12,650	10,125
Mother employed	15,577	9,333	6,244
Both parents employed	13,822	8,256	5,566
Mother employed not father	1,755	1,076	678
Father employed, not mother	7,199	3,318	3,881
Neither parent employed	1,028	553	475
Female-headed families with children under age 18	8,401	1,987	3,414
Mother employed	5,627	3,594	2,033
Mother not employed	2,774	1,393	1,381
Male-headed families with children under age 18	2,308	1,290	1,018
Father employed	1,750	979	771
Father not employed	557	311	247
PERCENT DISTRIBUTION			
Total families with children under age 18	100.0%	100.0%	100.0%
No parent employed	12.6	11.6	14.0
Married couples with children under age 18	100.0	100.0	100.0
One or both parents employed	95.7	95.8	95.5
Mother employed	65.4	70.7	58.9
Both parents employed	58.1	62.5	52.5
Mother employed not father	7.4	8.1	6.4
Father employed, not mother	30.2	25.1	36.6
Neither parent employed	4.3	4.2	4.5
Female-headed families with children under age 18	100.0	100.0	100.0
Mother employed	67.0	180.9	59.5
Mother not employed	33.0	70.1	40.5
Male-headed families with children under age 18	100.0	100.0	100.0
Father employed	75.8	75.9	75.7
Father not employed	24.1	24.1	24.3

Source: Bureau of Labor Statistics, Employment Characteristics of Families, Internet site http://www.bls.gov/news.release/famee.toc.htm; calculations by New Strategist

Many Preschoolers Depend on Grandparent for Day Care

The children of the most-affluent and highly educated mothers are most likely to be in nonrelative care.

Among the nation's preschoolers with working mothers, the largest share (24 percent) are in center-based care during their mother's work hours. The second-most-common care arrangement is grandparent care, with 19 percent under the watchful eye of a grandparent while their mother works. Grandparent care is the second-most-important care arrangement among children aged 5 to 8 as well, but drops to third place below enrichment acvtivities among children aged 9 to 11. Self-care becomes the most important type of day care for children aged 12 to 14 whose mother works.

Many children are cared for by nonrelatives. The proportion ranges from a low of 24 percent among children under age 3 to a high of 46 percent among children aged 3 to 5. The children of mothers with a college degree are more likely than those with less-educated mothers to use nonrelative care. Similarly, children in families with the highest incomes are most likely to be in nonrelative care.

■ Nonrelative day care has become an elite status symbol because of its expense.

College-educated mothers are most likley to have their young children in nonrelative care

(percent of children under age 3 in nonrelative care, by educational attainment of mother, 2009)

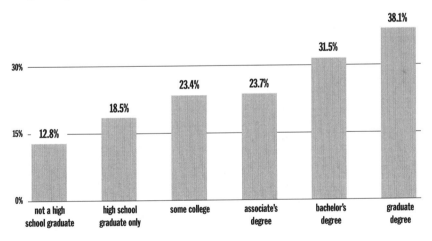

Table 16.3 Primary Child Care Arrangement of Children with Working Mothers, 2010

(percent distribution of children under age 15 with employed mothers by primary type of care arrangement during mother's work hours, by age, 2010)

	0 to 4	5 to 8	9 to 11	12 to 14
Mother care	4.4%	7.3%	6.0%	4.9%
Father care	18.6	29.5	25.1	20.2
Grandparent care	19.4·	21.6	17.9	9.8
Other relative care	5.8	7.8	6.3	4.0
Center-based care	23.7	12.4	3.4	1.4
Enrichment activities	–	14.4	20.9	18.9
Other nonrelative care	13.5	11.0	8.2	4.0
Self-care	–	2.2	10.5	35.7
Other care	14.1	–	–	–

Note: "Other relative" includes siblings; "center-based care" includes day care centers, nursery schools, preschools, and Head Start; "other nonrelative care" includes family day care providers and in-home babysitters; "other care" includes children in kindergarten or with no regular arrangement. Numbers may sum to more than 100 because of multiple arrangements.
Source: Forum on Child and Family Statistics, America's Children: Key National Indicators of Children's Well-Being, 2011, Internet site http://www.childstats.gov/

Table 16.4 Children with Nonrelative Child Care Arrangments, 2009

(percent of children aged 3 to 17 in nonrelative child care and average hours per week spent in nonrelative child care, by selected characteristics of child and parent, 2009)

	percent in nonrelative child care arrangement				average hours per week spent in nonrelative child care			
	under 3	3 to 5	6 to 11	12 to 17	under 3	3 to 5	6 to 11	12 to 17
Total children	**23.7%**	**46.0%**	**41.6%**	**34.3%**	**30.4**	**26.1**	**26.1**	**26.9**
Race/Hispanic origin of child								
Asian	19.8	47.9	38.3	23.3	31.4	25.1	23.8	22.3
Black	25.5	47.4	45.9	40.6	30.4	31.2	29.1	28.4
Hispanic	15.9	36.5	36.2	24.2	31.8	26.6	23.7	24.1
Non-Hispanic white	26.5	49.1	42.2	35.7	29.8	24.5	26.1	27.1
Marital status of parent								
Married	23.0	44.4	39.1	32.7	31.1	25.0	25.3	26.8
Separated, divorced, widowed	29.6	53.9	48.4	35.4	30.6	28.7	28.5	26.9
Never married	23.9	47.0	45.7	42.8	28.6	28.2	26.7	27.7
Educational attainment of parent								
Not a high school graduate	12.8	31.8	29.4	20.8	24.4	22.2	23.0	23.0
High school graduate only	18.5	38.2	37.3	30.5	28.6	25.8	24.8	26.7
Some college	23.4	50.8	44.0	37.9	31.2	27.0	26.7	26.6
Associate's degree	23.7	48.5	45.8	37.8	31.4	28.4	27.9	27.5
Bachelor's degree	31.5	53.4	45.4	39.3	32.2	25.5	25.9	28.3
Graduate degree	38.1	55.2	49.3	40.7	30.9	25.7	27.1	26.9
Employment status of parent								
Worked full-time last month	39.5	54.1	47.9	38.8	33.8	30.1	29.2	29.1
Worked part-time last month	25.6	52.1	42.6	33.9	25.9	22.3	23.3	25.8
Did not work last month	12.0	35.2	34.0	27.5	26.5	22.5	23.1	23.1
Monthly family income								
Under $1,500	18.9	46.0	41.0	32.1	27.3	26.6	25.9	25.8
$1,500 to $2,999	18.2	40.8	37.2	31.4	30.5	26.7	25.2	26.7
$3,000 to $4,499	21.2	43.4	45.7	30.8	27.9	24.6	26.3	24.8
$4,500 to $5,999	24.5	47.9	41.3	31.9	32.7	26.8	26.5	27.6
$6,000 or more	30.8	50.3	43.4	39.1	31.8	25.9	26.6	28.0

Note: Asians and blacks are those who identify themselves as being of the race alone.
Source: Census Bureau, A Child's Day: 2009, Internet site http://www.census.gov/hhes/socdemo/children/data/sipp/well2009/tables.html

17

Living Arrangements

◼ Sixty-nine percent of children under age 18 lived with two parents in 2011—down from 85 percent in 1970.

◼ The proportion of children who live with two parents (married or unmarried) ranges from a low of 39 percent among black children to a high of 85 percent among Asian children.

◼ Non-Hispanic white and Asian children are more likely than black or Hispanic children to participate in sports, clubs, and lessons.

◼ The percentage of tenagers who have dinner with a parent every day ranges from a high of 72 percent for those with the least-educated parents to a low of 49 percent for those with the most-educated parents.

◼ Although most children live in a nice neighborhood, a substantial proportion does not. Twenty percent of children are kept inside the house because of danger.

Most Married Couples Do Not Have Children under Age 18 at Home

Among those who do, few have more than one or two.

Among the nation's 79 million families, only 44 percent include children under age 18. When children of any age are included in the count, the 60 percent majority of families include children. Among married couples, only 41 percent have children under age 18 at home and 53 percent have children of any age living with them. Female-headed families are more likely to have children at home—57 percent include children under age 18 and 85 percent include children of any age. A much smaller 40 percent of male-headed families include children under age 18.

Among married couples with children under age 18, one child is in the home of 39 percent, and another 40 percent have two. Female-headed families are more likely to have only one child under age 18 at home (51 percent), and male-headed families are most likely to have only one (60 percent).

■ The traditional nuclear family—husband, wife, and children under age 18—has been shrinking as the small Generation X replaced Boomers in the married-with-children lifestage.

Only 19 percent of married couples have preschoolers

(percent of married-couple households with children of selected ages in the home, 2011)

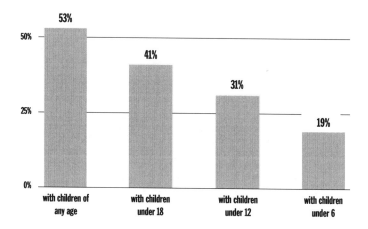

Table 17.1 Total families by Presence and Age of Children, 2011

(number and percent distribution of family households by presence and age of own children under age 18 and type of family, 2011; numbers in thousands)

	total	married couples	female householder, no spouse present	male householder, no spouse present
Total family households	**78,613**	**58,036**	**15,019**	**5,559**
With children of any age	47,150	30,928	12,794	3,428
With children under age 18	34,760	23,938	8,597	2,225
With children under age 12	25,392	17,778	6,005	1,609
With children under age 6	15,314	10,887	3,427	1,000
PERCENT DISTRIBUTION BY PRESENCE AND AGE OF CHILDREN				
Total family households	**100.0%**	**100.0%**	**100.0%**	**100.0%**
With children of any age	60.0	53.3	85.2	61.7
With children under age 18	44.2	41.2	57.2	40.0
With children under age 12	32.3	30.6	40.0	28.9
With children under age 6	19.5	18.8	22.8	18.0
PERCENT DISTRIBUTION BY FAMILY TYPE				
Total family households	**100.0%**	**73.8%**	**19.1%**	**7.1%**
With children of any age	100.0	65.6	27.1	7.3
With children under age 18	100.0	68.9	24.7	6.4
With children under age 12	100.0	70.0	23.6	6.3
With children under age 6	100.0	71.1	22.4	6.5

Source: Bureau of the Census, America's Families and Living Arrangements: 2011, Internet site http://www.census.gov/population/www/socdemo/hh-fam/cps2011.html; calculations by New Strategist

Table 17.2 Families by Number of Children under Age 18, 2011

(number and percent distribution of family households with own children under age 18 by number of children and type of family, 2011; numbers in thousands)

	total	married couples	female householders, no spouse present	male householders, no spouse present
Total families with children under age 18	**34,760**	**23,938**	**8,597**	**2,225**
One child	15,012	9,300	4,375	1,337
Two children	12,835	9,527	2,681	627
Three children	4,917	3,618	1,100	199
Four or more children	1,996	1,493	441	63

PERCENT DISTRIBUTION BY NUMBER OF CHILDREN

Total families with children under age 18	**100.0%**	**100.0%**	**100.0%**	**100.0%**
One child	43.2	38.9	50.9	60.1
Two children	36.9	39.8	31.2	28.2
Three children	14.1	15.1	12.8	8.9
Four or more children	5.7	6.2	5.1	2.8

PERCENT DISTRIBUTION BY FAMILY TYPE

Total families with children under age 18	**100.0%**	**68.9%**	**24.7%**	**6.4%**
One child	100.0	62.0	29.1	8.9
Two children	100.0	74.2	20.9	4.9
Three children	100.0	73.6	22.4	4.0
Four or more children	100.0	74.8	22.1	3.2

Source: Bureau of the Census, America's Families and Living Arrangements: 2011, Internet site http://www.census.gov/ population/www/socdemo/hh-fam/cps2011.html; calculations by New Strategist

Most Children Have Siblings in the Household

The largest share of children has a parent with a bachelor's degree or more education.

Among the nation's 75 million children, about one in five is the only child in the household. Thirty-eight percent are sharing their living quarters with one brother or sister, and a substantial 40 percent have two or more siblings in the home.

More than half of children live in a family with a household income of $50,000 or more. Nearly one in four children—24 percent—live in a family with an annual income of $100,000 or more.

More than one-third of the nation's children under age 18 have a parent with a bachelor's degree or even more education. Another 28 percent have a parent with some college experience or an associate's degree. Combining these two categories reveals that the 63 percent majority of children have parents with college experience.

■ Because so many children have parents with college experience, the pressure on children to attend college themselves is intense.

Many children must share a bathroom with brothers and sisters

(percent distribution of children under age 18 by number of siblings in the home, 2011)

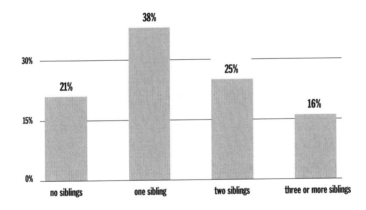

Table 17.3 Children under Age 18 by Family Characteristics, 2011

(number and percent distribution of children under age 18 by child and family characteristics, 2011; numbers in thousands)

	number	percent distribution
TOTAL CHILDREN UNDER AGE 18	**74,630**	**100.0%**
Sex of child		
Female	36,406	48.8
Male	38,224	51.2
Age of child		
Under age 1	4,105	5.5
Aged 1 to 2	8,433	11.3
Aged 3 to 5	13,008	17.4
Aged 6 to 8	12,473	16.7
Aged 9 to 11	12,217	16.4
Aged 12 to 14	11,897	15.9
Aged 15 to 17	12,499	16.7
Number of siblings in household		
None	15,825	21.2
One	28,611	38.3
Two	18,348	24.6
Three or more	11,846	15.9
Family income		
Under $10,000	6,860	9.2
$10,000 to $19,999	6,927	9.3
$20,000 to $29,999	7,906	10.6
$30,000 to $39,999	6,686	9.0
$40,000 to $49,999	5,977	8.0
$50,000 to $74,999	12,779	17.1
$75,000 to $99,999	9,362	12.5
$100,000 or more	18,131	24.3
Education of parent		
Not a high school graduate	7,899	10.6
High school graduate	16,560	22.2
Some college or associate's degree	20,668	27.7
Bachelor's degree	15,283	20.5
Professional or graduate degree	11,310	15.2
No parents present	2,910	3.9
Parents' labor force status		
Two parents, both in labor force	31,164	41.8
Two parents, father only in labor force	16,367	21.9
One parent, mother in labor force	13,016	17.4
One parent, mother not in labor force	4,620	6.2
No parents present	2,910	3.9
One parent, father in labor force	2,257	3.0
Two parents, mother only in labor force	2,326	3.1
Two parents, neither in labor force	1,599	2.1
One parent, father not in labor force	371	0.5

Source: Bureau of the Census, America's Families and Living Arrangements: 2011, Internet site http://www.census.gov/population/www/socdemo/hh-fam/cps2011.html; calculations by New Strategist

Most Moms Are in the Labor Force

Stay-at-home mothers are not the norm, even among couples with preschoolers.

Among married couples with children under age 15, the 69 percent majority has a mom in the labor force. Only 26 percent have a mom who stays home to care for her family. Stay-at-home dads are even less common. Only 1 percent of married couples with children under age 15 have a dad who is not in the labor force because he is caring for the family.

Couples with preschoolers are only slightly more likely than average to have a stay-at-home mother, at 31 percent. They are about equally as likely to have a stay-at-home father, at 1 percent.

■ Perhaps no characteristic distinguishes today's children from those in the past more than working parents. With both mother and father in the labor force, family life has become much more complicated.

One-third of couples with preschoolers have a stay-at-home mom

(percent distribution of married-couple family groups with children under age 6 by labor force status of mother during past year, 2011)

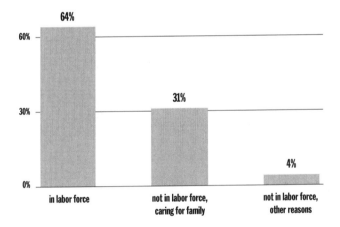

Table 17.4 Stay-at-Home Parents among Married Couples, 2011

(number and percent distribution of married-couple family groups with children under age 15 by stay-at-home status of mother and father and age of child, 2011; numbers in thousands)

	with children under age 15		with children under age 6	
	number	percent distribution	number	percent distribution
TOTAL MARRIED-COUPLE FAMILY GROUPS	**21,689**	**100.0%**	**11,352**	**100.0%**
Mother's labor force status in past year				
In labor force one or more weeks	14,936	68.9	7,310	64.4
Not in labor force, caring for family	5,670	26.1	3,571	31.5
Not in labor force, other reason	1,083	5.0	471	4.1
Father's labor force status in past year				
In labor force one or more weeks	20,203	93.1	10,630	93.6
Not in labor force, caring for family	254	1.2	145	1.3
Not in labor force, other reason	1,232	5.7	577	5.1

Note: Married-couple family groups include married couple householders and married couples living in households headed by others.
Source: Bureau of the Census, America's Families and Living Arrangements: 2011, Internet site http://www.census.gov/ population/www/socdemo/hh-fam/cps2011.html; calculations by New Strategist

Sixty-Nine Percent of Children Live with Two Parents

Fewer than 4 percent live with their father only.

Among the nation's 75 million children under age 18, the 69 percent majority lived with two parents in 2011—down from 85 percent in 1970. The proportion of children who live with two parents (married or unmarried) ranges from a low of 39 percent among black children to a high of 85 percent among Asian children. A smaller share of children lives with their married biological parents, ranging from 29 percent of blacks to 78 percent of Asians.

The proportion of children who live with their mother only ranges from a low of 11 percent among Asians to a high of 50 percent among blacks. Few children live only with their father regardless of race or Hispanic origin.

■ The poverty rate among children is unlikely to decline significantly until fewer children live in single-parent families.

Children's living arrangements vary greatly by race and Hispanic origin

(percent of children living with two married biological parents, by race and Hispanic origin, 2011)

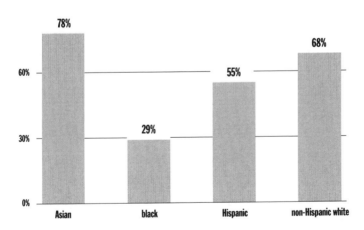

Table 17.5 Living Arrangements of Children, 1970 to 2011

(number and percent distribution of children under age 18 by living arrangement, 1970 to 2011; numbers in thousands)

| Total children | total number | percent | children living with | | | |
			two parents	mother only	father only	neither parent
2011	74,630	100.0%	68.9%	23.6%	3.5%	3.6%
2010	74,718	100.0	69.4	23.1	3.4	3.5
2009	74,230	100.0	69.8	22.8	3.4	3.4
2008	74,104	100.0	69.9	22.8	3.5	3.8
2007	73,746	100.0	70.7	22.6	3.2	3.5
2007	73,746	100.0	67.8	24.2	4.5	3.5
2006	73,664	100.0	67.4	23.3	4.7	4.6
2005	73,523	100.0	67.4	23.4	4.7	4.5
2000	72,012	100.0	69.1	22.4	4.2	4.2
1995	70,254	100.0	68.7	23.5	3.5	4.3
1990	64,137	100.0	72.5	21.6	3.1	2.8
1985	62,475	100.0	73.9	20.9	2.5	2.7
1980	63,427	100.0	76.7	18.0	1.7	3.7
1975	66,087	100.0	80.3	15.5	1.5	2.7
1970	69,162	100.0	85.2	10.8	1.1	2.9

Note: The methodology changed in 2007, allowing two parents to be either married or unmarried and increasing the number of children in two-parent families.
Source: Bureau of the Census, Families and Living Arrangements, Historical Tables—Households, Internet site http://www.census.gov/population/www/socdemo/hh-fam.html; calculations by New Strategist

Table 17.6 Living Arrangements of Children, 2011: Total Children

(number and percent distribution of total children under age 18 by living arrangement, 2011; numbers in thousands)

	number	percent distribution
TOTAL CHILDREN	**74,630**	**100.0%**
Living with two parents	**51,456**	**68.9**
Married parents	48,516	65.0
Unmarried parents	2,940	3.9
Biological mother and father	46,405	62.2
Married parents	43,828	58.7
Biological mother and stepfather	3,075	4.1
Biological father and stepmother	835	1.1
Biological mother and adoptive father	174	0.2
Biological father and adoptive mother	30	0.0
Adoptive mother and father	697	0.9
Other	241	0.3
Living with one parent	**20,264**	**27.2**
Mother only	17,636	23.6
Father only	2,628	3.5
Living with no parents	**2,910**	**3.9**
Grandparents	1,648	2.2
Other	1,262	1.7

Source: Bureau of the Census, America's Families and Living Arrangements: 2011, Internet site http://www.census.gov/ population/www/socdemo/hh-fam/cps2011.html; calculations by New Strategist

Table 17.7 **Living Arrangements of Children, 2011: Asian Children**

(number and percent distribution of Asian children under age 18 by living arrangement, 2011; numbers in thousands)

	number	percent distribution
ASIAN CHILDREN	**4,013**	**100.0%**
Living with two parents	**3,418**	**85.2**
Married parents	3,320	82.7
Unmarried parents	98	2.4
Biological mother and father	3,208	79.9
Married parents	3,116	77.6
Biological mother and stepfather	100	2.5
Biological father and stepmother	25	0.6
Biological mother and adoptive father	2	0.0
Biological father and adoptive mother	1	0.0
Adoptive mother and father	74	1.8
Other	8	0.2
Living with one parent	**494**	**12.3**
Mother only	432	10.8
Father only	61	1.5
Living with no parents	**101**	**2.5**
Grandparents	39	1.0
Other	62	1.5

Note: Asians are those who identify themselves as being of the race alone and those who identify themselves as being of the race in combination with other races.
Source: Bureau of the Census, America's Families and Living Arrangements: 2011, Internet site http://www.census.gov/population/www/socdemo/hh-fam/cps2011.html; calculations by New Strategist

Table 17.8 Living Arrangements of Children, 2011: Black Children

(number and percent distribution of black children under age 18 by living arrangement, 2011; numbers in thousands)

	number	percent distribution
BLACK CHILDREN	**12,645**	**100.0%**
Living with two parents	**4,982**	**39.4**
Married parents	4,311	34.1
Unmarried parents	671	5.3
Biological mother and father	4,246	33.6
Married parents	3,655	28.9
Biological mother and stepfather	461	3.6
Biological father and stepmother	109	0.9
Biological mother and adoptive father	13	0.1
Biological father and adoptive mother	0	0.0
Adoptive mother and father	120	0.9
Other	34	0.3
Living with one parent	**6,736**	**53.3**
Mother only	6,296	49.8
Father only	441	3.5
Living with no parents	**927**	**7.3**
Grandparents	573	4.5
Other	354	2.8

Note: Blacks are those who identify themselves as being of the race alone and those who identify themselves as being of the race in combination with other races.
Source: Bureau of the Census, America's Families and Living Arrangements: 2011, Internet site http://www.census.gov/population/www/socdemo/hh-fam/cps2011.html; calculations by New Strategist

Table 17.9 Living Arrangements of Children, 2011: Hispanic Children

(number and percent distribution of Hispanic children under age 18 by living arrangement, 2011; numbers in thousands)

	number	percent distribution
HISPANIC CHILDREN	**17,418**	**100.0%**
Living with two parents	**11,649**	**66.9**
Married parents	10,484	60.2
Unmarried parents	1,165	6.7
Biological mother and father	10,658	61.2
Married parents	9,595	55.1
Biological mother and stepfather	669	3.8
Biological father and stepmother	136	0.8
Biological mother and adoptive father	16	0.1
Biological father and adoptive mother	12	0.1
Adoptive mother and father	104	0.6
Other	55	0.3
Living with one parent	**5,091**	**29.2**
Mother only	4,613	26.5
Father only	478	2.7
Living with no parents	**677**	**3.9**
Grandparents	343	2.0
Other	334	1.9

Source: Bureau of the Census, America's Families and Living Arrangements: 2011, Internet site http://www.census.gov/population/www/socdemo/hh-fam/cps2011.html; calculations by New Strategist

Table 17.10 Living Arrangements of Children, 2011: Non-Hispanic White Children

(number and percent distribution of non-Hispanic white children under age 18 by living arrangement, 2011; numbers in thousands)

	number	percent distribution
NON-HISPANIC WHITE CHILDREN	**40,616**	**100.0%**
Living with two parents	**31,348**	**77.2**
Married parents	30,311	74.6
Unmarried parents	1,037	2.6
Biological mother and father	28,285	69.6
Married parents	27,424	67.5
Biological mother and stepfather	1,820	4.5
Biological father and stepmother	549	1.4
Biological mother and adoptive father	138	0.3
Biological father and adoptive mother	14	0.0
Adoptive mother and father	398	1.0
Other	144	0.4
Living with one parent	**8,065**	**19.9**
Mother only	6,438	15.9
Father only	1,627	4.0
Living with no parents	**1,203**	**3.0**
Grandparents	699	1.7
Other	504	1.2

Note: Non-Hispanic whites are those who identify themselves as being white alone and not Hispanic.
Source: Bureau of the Census, America's Families and Living Arrangements: 2011, Internet site http://www.census.gov/population/www/socdemo/hh-fam/cps2011.html; calculations by New Strategist

Many Children Do Not Participate in Extracurricular Activities

Asians and non-Hispanic whites are most likely to be involved in sports, clubs, and lessons.

When it's time to fill out college applications, Asian and non-Hispanic white children have a clear advantage. Many have participated in a long list of extracurricular activities that can be used to impress college admissions officers. Asians and non-Hispanic whites are more likely than blacks or Hispanics to participate in sports, clubs, and lessons because their parents have the time and money to shuttle them from one activity to another.

According to a Census Bureau survey of family life, 45 percent of non-Hispanic white teens participated in sports, 38 percent participated in clubs, and 33 percent took lessons in 2009. More than one in 10 took part in all three. Fewer Asian teens participated in sports (37 percent), but more took lessons (41 percent). Blacks are almost as likely as Asians to participate in sports, but blacks and Hispanics are much less likely to participate in clubs or lessons. Similarly, children from the most-affluent families and those with the most-educated parents were much more likely than others to be involved in extracurricular activities.

■ The advantages that accrue to the children of highly educated, affluent parents help them get into college, which helps explains why most college students have college-educated parents.

Blacks and Hispanics are much less likely to participate in sports, clubs, and lessons

(percent of children aged 12 to 17 who participated in extracurricular sports, clubs, and lessons, by race and Hispanic origin, 2009)

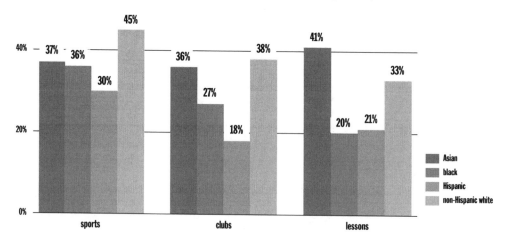

Table 17.11 Extracurricular Activities of Children, 2009

(percent of children aged 6 to 17 who participate in extracurricular sports, clubs, or lessons by characteristics of child and parent, by age of child, 2009)

	sports		clubs		lessons		all three activities	
	6 to 11	12 to 17	6 to 11	12 to 17	6 to 11	12 to 17	6 to 11	12 to 17
TOTAL CHILDREN	**31.7%**	**40.6%**	**29.7%**	**32.3%**	**31.7%**	**28.8%**	**8.5%**	**9.1%**
Race and Hispanic origin of child								
Asian alone	22.5	36.9	32.7	36.4	39.9	40.7	7.3	9.2
Black alone	20.9	35.9	26.3	26.7	24.0	19.5	5.4	5.6
Hispanic	20.7	30.2	18.3	18.1	23.7	20.5	3.9	4.9
Non-Hispanic white	39.3	45.2	35.0	37.9	36.1	32.6	11.1	11.4
Parent's highest level of educational attainment								
Less than high school	15.6	25.6	15.1	15.9	16.2	13.3	2.2	1.7
high school graduate	25.1	33.6	22.2	25.2	21.3	21.7	4.4	5.7
Some college	31.3	42.4	28.5	34.1	30.8	28.8	7.6	7.7
Associate's degree	31.0	40.9	32.5	34.5	32.7	30.9	7.9	9.8
Bachelor's degree	47.0	54.2	41.7	43.8	46.5	40.7	15.3	16.2
Advanced degree	43.0	52.5	41.2	46.4	50.0	44.0	17.6	16.7
Monthly family income								
Under $1,500	18.2	28.6	18.8	22.8	20.2	16.3	4.5	4.3
$1,500 to $2,999	23.9	31.7	24.1	22.2	23.1	20.7	4.4	4.6
$3,000 to $4,499	30.7	36.4	27.9	27.2	26.4	25.7	6.7	7.2
$4,500 to $5,999	32.8	40.2	31.5	33.4	33.4	29.4	7.4	8.7
$6,000 or more	42.8	51.0	38.3	42.1	43.2	38.4	14.0	13.9

Source: Bureau of the Census, A Child's Day: 2009, Internet site http://www.census.gov/hhes/socdemo/children/data/sipp/well2009/tables.html

Most Parents Have Dinner with Their Children Daily

The most-educated and -affluent parents are least likely to have dinner with their children every day.

The percentage of parents who eat breakfast and dinner with their children every day during a typical week falls as children age into their teenage years. The 57 percent majority of preschoolers have breakfast with a parent every day during a typical week. Among 12-to-17-year-olds, the figure is just 25 percent.

The percentage of children who have dinner with a parent every day falls from 81 percent among preschoolers to 58 percent among teenagers. Interestingly, the most affluent and educated parents are least likely to have dinner with their children every day. For teenagers, the figure ranges from a high of 72 percent among those whose parent did not graduate from high school to a low of 49 percent for those whose parent has a graduate-level degree.

■ Educated and affluent parents often have demanding careers that take them away from home.

Most teens with educated parents do not have dinner with them daily

(percent of children aged 12 to 17 who have dinner with a parent every day during a typical week, by educational attainment of parent, 2009)

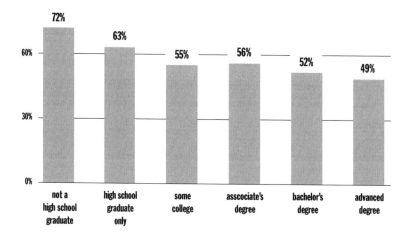

Table 17.12 Meals with Children, 2009

(percent of children under age 18 whose designated parent had selected meals with them every day during a typical week last month by characteristics of child and parent, by age of child, 2009)

	breakfast every day			dinner every day		
	under 6	6 to 11	12 to 17	under 6	6 to 11	12 to 17
TOTAL CHILDREN	**57.2%**	**38.4%**	**24.9%**	**80.6%**	**75.1%**	**58.5%**
Race and Hispanic origin of child						
Asian alone	58.0	48.7	38.6	76.4	81.1	75.1
Black alone	48.2	29.0	20.7	79.1	71.0	62.3
Hispanic	60.7	34.1	28.1	84.3	80.0	69.2
Non-Hispanic white	58.1	42.3	24.8	79.9	74.0	53.8
Parent's highest level of educational attainment						
Less than high school	63.3	35.0	30.8	83.8	79.5	72.0
High school graduate only	59.0	35.5	23.5	82.4	78.8	62.9
Some college	53.5	36.5	20.5	79.8	71.8	55.2
Associate's degree	54.9	37.3	23.1	80.4	74.5	56.3
Bachelor's degree	56.7	42.9	26.8	78.2	73.4	52.2
Advanced degree	55.8	47.8	28.1	78.3	69.0	48.8
Monthly family income						
Under $1,500	57.7	32.4	24.2	84.0	77.7	66.9
$1,500 to $2,999	61.2	36.8	26.3	83.1	79.3	66.0
$3,000 to $4,499	59.5	37.7	24.3	83.0	74.5	62.0
$4,500 to $5,999	56.6	39.4	25.4	82.1	76.4	58.5
$6,000 or more	53.7	42.4	24.2	75.9	71.1	50.3

Source: Bureau of the Census, A Child's Day: 2009, Internet site http://www.census.gov/hhes/socdemo/children/data/sipp/ well2009/tables.html

Most Children Live in Neighborhoods Where People Help Each Other

Nearly half of children live in a neighborhood where there are people who might be a bad influence, however.

In a survey of family life, the Census Bureau queried the parents of children under age 18 about their neighborhood. For the most part, parents report being in the kind of neighborhood where people help one another and children can play safely outside. Seventy-one percent of children live in a neighborhood where people help each other, 73 percent live where people watch one another's children, and 78 percent live where adults nearby would help children outside if necessary. But nearly half (45 percent) of children live in a neighborhood in which there are people who might be a bad influence.

Although most children live in a nice neighborhood, a substantial proportion does not. Twenty percent of children are kept inside the house because of danger. The proportion rises as high as 32 percent among Hispanic children. Among children from the poorest families, 32 percent are kept inside for safety. In the richest families, only 13 percent must stay inside.

■ Although most children live in friendly, safe neighborhoods, a substantial proportion does not.

Hispanic children are most likely to be kept inside for safety

(percentage of children who are kept inside the house because of danger, by race and Hispanic origin, 2009)

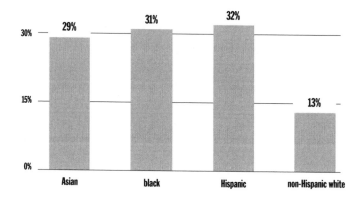

Table 17.13 Neighborhood Characteristics of Children, 2009

(percent of children under age 18 whose parent agrees that the child lives in a neighborhood with the selected characteristics, by characteristics of child and parent, 2009)

	people help each other	people watch each other's children	there are people I can count on	there are people who might be a bad influence	adults nearby would help children outside the house	children are kept inside the house because of danger	there are safe places for children to play
TOTAL CHILDREN	**71.2%**	**73.3%**	**75.6%**	**45.0%**	**77.9%**	**20.3%**	**80.6%**
Race and Hispanic origin of child							
Asian alone	70.1	68.4	68.4	33.5	71.2	28.8	81.5
Black alone	59.9	64.6	64.2	52.2	71.5	31.1	71.2
Hispanic	60.9	67.2	67.8	43.9	68.5	31.8	70.3
Non-Hispanic white	78.3	78.5	82.1	44.0	83.5	12.6	87.0
Parent's highest level of educational attainment							
Less than high school	60.8	68.2	68.8	46.3	71.6	34.5	70.5
high school graduate	66.9	71.1	72.4	47.5	76.2	23.3	76.3
Some college	72.7	74.2	78.0	47.5	79.6	17.1	84.0
Associate's degree	68.9	71.0	72.7	48.0	75.2	18.7	80.5
Bachelor's degree	81.6	79.8	83.4	41.2	84.1	14.7	87.5
Advanced degree	80.2	77.5	81.1	33.4	82.7	11.7	88.2
Monthly family income							
Under $1,500	61.8	67.9	67.1	52.3	72.1	31.8	71.7
$1,500 to $2,999	64.4	68.1	68.8	48.6	72.9	26.7	73.5
$3,000 to $4,499	70.2	71.9	73.5	46.2	75.5	21.7	78.3
$4,500 to $5,999	73.3	75.4	78.9	46.9	79.4	15.4	84.9
$6,000 or more	78.9	78.6	83.0	39.0	83.7	13.2	88.0

Source: Bureau of the Census, A Child's Day: 2009, Internet site http://www.census.gov/hhes/socdemo/children/data/sipp/well2009/tables.html

18

Population

■ The iGeneration numbers 66 million, a figure that includes everyone born in 1995 or later (under age 16 in 2010). The iGeneration accounts for 21 percent of the total population.

■ America's children are much more diverse than middle-aged or older people. While non-Hispanic whites accounted for 64 percent of all Americans in 2010, their share is a smaller 54 percent among the iGeneration.

■ Among school children, most of those who do not speak English at home are able to speak English very well. Only 23 percent of the Spanish speakers aged 5 to 17, for example, cannot speak English very well.

■ Children under age 15 account for 27 percent of the population of Utah. They are only 17 percent of the populations of Florida, Maine, Rhode Island, Vermont, and West Virginia.

■ In many states, the iGeneration is quite diverse. In Mississippi, 44 percent of the iGeneration is black. In California, the 52 percent majority of the iGeneration is Hispanic.

The iGeneration Is Larger than Generation X

More than one in five Americans is in the iGeneration.

The iGeneration numbers 66 million, a figure that includes everyone born in 1995 or later (under age 16 in 2010). The iGeneration accounts for 21 percent of the total population, making it larger than Generation X or the older generations that precede the Baby Boom.

Because births began to decline after peaking in 2007, the end date of the iGeneration may have already occurred (since generations usually are defined by the rise and fall of births). If that is the case, the iGeneration will be smaller than the Millennial generation. Eventually, however, the iGeneration will surpass Boomers in size as the Baby-Boom generation shrinks with age.

■ The iGeneration is the most diverse, making it a difficult market to target.

The iGeneration outnumbers Generation X

(number of people by generation, 2010)

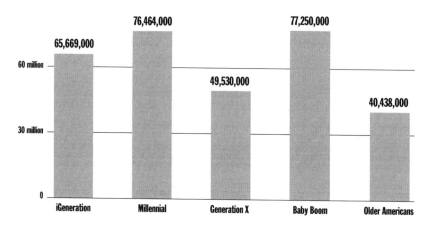

Table 18.1 Population by Age and Generation, 2010

(number and percent distribution of people by age and generation, 2010; numbers in thousands)

	number	percent distribution
Total people	**309,350**	**100.0%**
Under age 15	61,277	19.8
Under age 5	20,201	6.5
Aged 5 to 9	20,382	6.6
Aged 10 to 14	20,694	6.7
Aged 15 to 19	21,959	7.1
Aged 20 to 24	21,668	7.0
Aged 25 to 29	21,153	6.8
Aged 30 to 34	20,094	6.5
Aged 35 to 39	20,082	6.5
Aged 40 to 44	20,899	6.8
Aged 45 to 49	22,648	7.3
Aged 50 to 54	22,365	7.2
Aged 55 to 59	19,779	6.4
Aged 60 to 64	16,987	5.5
Aged 65 to 69	12,515	4.0
Aged 70 to 74	9,326	3.0
Aged 75 to 79	7,313	2.4
Aged 80 to 84	5,750	1.9
Aged 85 or older	5,533	1.8
Total people	**309,350**	**100.0**
iGeneration (under 16)	65,669	21.2
Millennial (16 to 33)	76,464	24.7
Generation X (34 to 45)	49,530	16.0
Baby Boom (46 to 64)	77,250	25.0
Older Americans (65 or older)	40,438	13.1

Source: Bureau of the Census, Population Estimates, Internet site http://www.census.gov/popest/data/intercensal/national/nat2010.html; calculations by New Strategist

Table 18.2 Population by Age and Sex, 2010

(number of people by age and sex, and sex ratio by age, 2010; numbers in thousands)

	total	female	male	sex ratio
Total people	**309,350**	**157,242**	**152,108**	**97**
Under age 15	61,277	29,965	31,312	104
Under age 5	20,201	9,883	10,318	104
Aged 5 to 9	20,382	9,975	10,407	104
Aged 10 to 14	20,694	10,107	10,587	105
Aged 15 to 19	21,959	10,696	11,263	105
Aged 20 to 24	21,668	10,612	11,056	104
Aged 25 to 29	21,153	10,477	10,676	102
Aged 30 to 34	20,094	10,030	10,063	100
Aged 35 to 39	20,082	10,086	9,997	99
Aged 40 to 44	20,899	10,500	10,399	99
Aged 45 to 49	22,648	11,465	11,183	98
Aged 50 to 54	22,365	11,399	10,966	96
Aged 55 to 59	19,779	10,199	9,580	94
Aged 60 to 64	16,987	8,829	8,159	92
Aged 65 to 69	12,515	6,623	5,892	89
Aged 70 to 74	9,326	5,057	4,269	84
Aged 75 to 79	7,313	4,130	3,184	77
Aged 80 to 84	5,750	3,448	2,302	67
Aged 85 or older	5,533	3,726	1,807	49

Note: The sex ratio is the number of males per 100 females.
Source: Bureau of the Census, Population Estimates, Internet site http://www.census.gov/popest/data/intercensal/national/nat2010.html; calculations by New Strategist

Nation's Children Are Diverse

Hispanics outnumber blacks in the iGeneration.

America's children are much more diverse than middle-aged or older people. While non-Hispanic whites accounted for 64 percent of all Americans in 2010, their share is a smaller 54 percent among the iGeneration—children under age 16.

Among the 7 million multiracial U.S. residents counted by the 2010 census, nearly 3 million are children under age 15. Their parents identified them as multiracial on the 2010 census form. When these multiracial children are included in the count of Asians and blacks, those populations expand considerably.

Among the iGeneration, Hispanics account for a larger share of the population than blacks. Twenty-four percent of children under age 15 are Hispanic, 17 percent are black (alone or in combination), and 6 percent are Asian (alone or in combination).

■ Racial and ethnic differences between young and old may divide the nation in the years ahead.

Nearly one in four children is Hispanic

(percent distribution of population under age 15 by race and Hispanic origin, 2010)

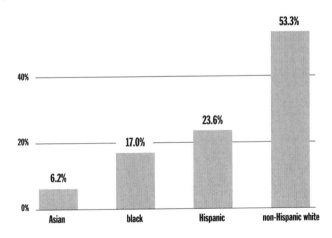

Table 18.3 Number of People by Age, Race Alone, and Hispanic Origin, 2010

(number of people by age, race alone, and Hispanic origin, 2010; numbers in thousands)

	total	Asian	black	Hispanic	non-Hispanic white	two or more races
Total people	**308,746**	**15,160**	**40,251**	**50,478**	**197,319**	**7,026**
Under age 15	61,227	2,842	9,222	14,431	32,642	2,908
Under age 5	20,201	948	3,055	5,114	10,307	1,123
Aged 5 to 9	20,349	972	3,013	4,791	10,885	948
Aged 10 to 14	20,677	922	3,154	4,525	11,449	836
Aged 15 to 19	22,040	999	3,573	4,532	12,387	726
Aged 20 to 24	21,586	1,149	3,240	4,322	12,467	571
Aged 25 to 29	21,102	1,279	2,911	4,310	12,268	491
Aged 30 to 34	19,962	1,284	2,743	4,124	11,534	424
Aged 35 to 39	20,180	1,334	2,706	3,856	12,018	357
Aged 40 to 44	20,891	1,188	2,752	3,442	13,250	315
Aged 45 to 49	22,709	1,105	2,901	3,022	15,387	302
Aged 50 to 54	22,298	1,004	2,753	2,441	15,813	269
Aged 55 to 59	19,665	863	2,246	1,841	14,476	209
Aged 60 to 64	16,818	703	1,715	1,372	12,839	157
Aged 65 to 69	12,435	483	1,181	949	9,693	106
Aged 70 to 74	9,278	361	865	700	7,265	73
Aged 75 to 79	7,318	255	625	511	5,867	51
Aged 80 to 84	5,743	171	430	351	4,751	35
Aged 85 or older	5,493	140	386	271	4,664	30
PERCENT DISTRIBUTION						
Total people	**100.0%**	**4.9%**	**13.0%**	**16.3%**	**63.9%**	**2.3%**
Under age 15	100.0	4.6	15.1	23.6	53.3	4.7
Under age 5	100.0	4.7	15.1	25.3	51.0	5.6
Aged 5 to 9	100.0	4.8	14.8	23.5	53.5	4.7
Aged 10 to 14	100.0	4.5	15.3	21.9	55.4	4.0
Aged 15 to 19	100.0	4.5	16.2	20.6	56.2	3.3
Aged 20 to 24	100.0	5.3	15.0	20.0	57.8	2.6
Aged 25 to 29	100.0	6.1	13.8	20.4	58.1	2.3
Aged 30 to 34	100.0	6.4	13.7	20.7	57.8	2.1
Aged 35 to 39	100.0	6.6	13.4	19.1	59.6	1.8
Aged 40 to 44	100.0	5.7	13.2	16.5	63.4	1.5
Aged 45 to 49	100.0	4.9	12.8	13.3	67.8	1.3
Aged 50 to 54	100.0	4.5	12.3	10.9	70.9	1.2
Aged 55 to 59	100.0	4.4	11.4	9.4	73.6	1.1
Aged 60 to 64	100.0	4.2	10.2	8.2	76.3	0.9
Aged 65 to 69	100.0	3.9	9.5	7.6	78.0	0.9
Aged 70 to 74	100.0	3.9	9.3	7.5	78.3	0.8
Aged 75 to 79	100.0	3.5	8.5	7.0	80.2	0.7
Aged 80 to 84	100.0	3.0	7.5	6.1	82.7	0.6
Aged 85 or older	100.0	2.5	7.0	4.9	84.9	0.6

Note: Asians and blacks are those who identify themselves as being of the race alone. Numbers do not add to total because not all races are shown and Hispanics may be of any race. Non-Hispanic whites are those who identify themselves as being white alone and not Hispanic.
Source: Bureau of the Census, 2010 Census, American Factfinder, Population Estimates, Internet site http:// factfinder2.census.gov/faces/nav/jsf/pages/index.xhtml; calculations by New Strategist

Table 18.4 Number of People by Age, Race Alone or in Combination, and Hispanic Origin, 2010

(number of people by age, race alone or in combination, and Hispanic origin, 2010; numbers in thousands)

	total	Asian	black	Hispanic	non-Hispanic white
Total people	**308,746**	**17,321**	**42,021**	**50,478**	**197,319**
Under age 15	61,227	3,785	10,395	14,431	32,642
Under age 5	20,201	1,317	3,538	5,114	10,307
Aged 5 to 9	20,349	1,285	3,389	4,791	10,885
Aged 10 to 14	20,677	1,184	3,468	4,525	11,449
Aged 15 to 19	22,040	1,229	3,796	4,532	12,387
Aged 20 to 24	21,586	1,333	3,350	4,322	12,467
Aged 25 to 29	21,102	1,433	2,971	4,310	12,268
Aged 30 to 34	19,962	1,412	2,780	4,124	11,534
Aged 35 to 39	20,180	1,445	2,738	3,856	12,018
Aged 40 to 44	20,891	1,279	2,773	3,442	13,250
Aged 45 to 49	22,709	1,188	2,922	3,022	15,387
Aged 50 to 54	22,298	1,076	2,775	2,441	15,813
Aged 55 to 59	19,665	916	2,267	1,841	14,476
Aged 60 to 64	16,818	740	1,732	1,372	12,839
Aged 65 to 69	12,435	508	1,192	949	9,693
Aged 70 to 74	9,278	379	873	700	7,265
Aged 75 to 79	7,318	269	631	511	5,867
Aged 80 to 84	5,743	180	435	351	4,751
Aged 85 or older	5,493	147	392	271	4,664
PERCENT DISTRIBUTION					
Total people	**100.0%**	**5.6%**	**13.6%**	**16.3%**	**63.9%**
Under age 15	100.0	6.2	17.0	23.6	53.3
Under age 5	100.0	6.5	17.5	25.3	51.0
Aged 5 to 9	100.0	6.3	16.7	23.5	53.5
Aged 10 to 14	100.0	5.7	16.8	21.9	55.4
Aged 15 to 19	100.0	5.6	17.2	20.6	56.2
Aged 20 to 24	100.0	6.2	15.5	20.0	57.8
Aged 25 to 29	100.0	6.8	14.1	20.4	58.1
Aged 30 to 34	100.0	7.1	13.9	20.7	57.8
Aged 35 to 39	100.0	7.2	13.6	19.1	59.6
Aged 40 to 44	100.0	6.1	13.3	16.5	63.4
Aged 45 to 49	100.0	5.2	12.9	13.3	67.8
Aged 50 to 54	100.0	4.8	12.4	10.9	70.9
Aged 55 to 59	100.0	4.7	11.5	9.4	73.6
Aged 60 to 64	100.0	4.4	10.3	8.2	76.3
Aged 65 to 69	100.0	4.1	9.6	7.6	78.0
Aged 70 to 74	100.0	4.1	9.4	7.5	78.3
Aged 75 to 79	100.0	3.7	8.6	7.0	80.2
Aged 80 to 84	100.0	3.1	7.6	6.1	82.7
Aged 85 or older	100.0	2.7	7.1	4.9	84.9

Note: Asians and blacks are those who identify themselves as being of the race alone and those who identify themselves as being of the race in combination with other races. Numbers do not add to total because not all races are shown, some mixed-race individuals are counted more than once, and Hispanics may be of any race. Non-Hispanic whites are those who identify themselves as being white alone and not Hispanic.
Source: Bureau of the Census, 2010 Census, American Factfinder, Population Estimates, Internet site http://factfinder2.census.gov/faces/nav/jsf/pages/index.xhtml; calculations by New Strategist

Children Account for Few Immigrants

Young adults are the largest share of immigrants.

In 2011, more than 1 million legal immigrants were admitted to the United States, and only 162,000 of them were under age 15 (the iGeneration was under age 17 in that year). Young adults in their twenties and thirties accounted for a much larger number of 2011 immigrants.

The under-15 age group accounted for 15 percent of total immigrants admitted to the United States in 2011. By five-year age group, 30-to-34-year-olds account for the largest share of immigrants—12 percent in 2011.

■ Immigrants are adding to the diversity of the population.

Many 2011 immigrants were young adults

(percent distribution of 2011 immigrants, by age)

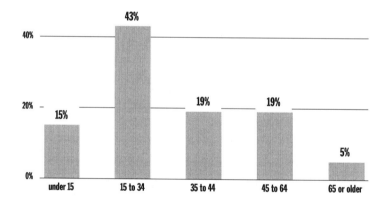

Table 18.5 Immigrants by Age, 2011

(number and percent distribution of immigrants by age, 2011)

	number	percent distribution
Total immigrants	**1,062,040**	**100.0%**
Under age 15	161,501	15.2
Under age 1	4,361	0.4
Aged 1 to 4	34,017	3.2
Aged 5 to 9	52,828	5.0
Aged 10 to 14	70,295	6.6
Aged 15 to 19	88,970	8.4
Aged 20 to 24	110,144	10.4
Aged 25 to 29	122,128	11.5
Aged 30 to 34	130,789	12.3
Aged 35 to 39	112,983	10.6
Aged 40 to 44	84,394	7.9
Aged 45 to 49	68,174	6.4
Aged 50 to 54	52,623	5.0
Aged 55 to 59	42,941	4.0
Aged 60 to 64	34,257	3.2
Aged 65 to 74	39,386	3.7
Aged 75 or older	13,740	1.3

Note: Immigrants are those granted legal permanent residence in the United States. They either arrive in the United States with immigrant visas issued abroad or adjust their status in the United States from temporary to permanent residence. Numbers may not sum to total because "age not stated" is not shown.
Source: Department of Homeland Security, 2011 Yearbook of Immigration Statistics, Internet site http://www.dhs.gov/files/statistics/publications/yearbook.shtm

Many Children Do Not Speak English at Home

Most are Spanish speakers, and most also speak English very well.

Sixty million residents of the United States speak a language other than English at home, according to the Census Bureau's 2010 American Community Survey—21 percent of the population aged 5 or older. Among those who do not speak English at home, 62 percent speak Spanish.

More than one in five children aged 5 to 17 does not speak English at home. Among them, 72 percent are Spanish speakers. Most children who do not speak English at home are also able to speak English very well. Only 23 percent of the Spanish speakers aged 5 to 17, for example, cannot speak English "very well." Among all U.S. residents who speak Spanish at home, a much larger 45 percent cannot speak English very well.

■ The language barrier is a bigger problem for adults than for children.

Few children who speak Spanish at home cannot speak English very well

(percent of people aged 5 or older and aged 5 to 17 who speak Spanish at home and do not speak English "very well," 2010)

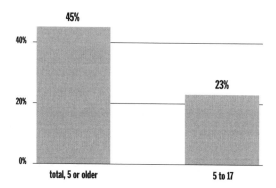

Table 18.6 Language Spoken at Home by People Aged 5 to 17, 2010

(number and percent distribution of people aged 5 or older and aged 5 to 17 who speak a language other than English at home by language spoken at home and ability to speak English very well, 2010; numbers in thousands)

	total		aged 5 to 17	
	number	percent distribution	number	percent distribution
Total, aged 5 or older	**289,216**	**100.0%**	**54,031**	**100.0%**
Speak only English at home	229,673	79.4	42,249	78.2
Speak a language other than English at home	59,542	20.6	11,783	21.8
Speak English less than very well	21,853	7.6	2,704	5.0
Total who speak a language other than English at home	**59,542**	**100.0**	**11,783**	**100.0**
Speak Spanish at home	36,996	62.1	8,457	71.8
Speak other Indo-European language at home	10,666	17.9	1,568	13.3
Speak Asian or Pacific Island language at home	9,340	15.7	1,313	11.1
Speak other language at home	2,540	4.3	445	3.8
Speak Spanish at home	36,996	100.0	8,457	100.0
Speak English less than very well	16,523	44.7	1,982	23.4
Speak other Indo-European language at home	10,666	100.0	1,568	100.0
Speak English less than very well	3,440	32.3	288	18.4
Speak Asian or Pacific Island language at home	9,340	100.0	1,313	100.0
Speak English less than very well	4,471	47.9	341	26.0
Speak other language at home	2,540	100.0	445	100.0
Speak English less than very well	786	30.9	93	20.9

Source: Bureau of the Census, 2010 American Community Survey, Internet site http://factfinder2.census.gov/faces/nav/jsf/pages/index.xhtml; calculations by New Strategist

Largest Share of Children Lives in the South

More than one in four residents of Utah is under age 15.

The South is home to the largest share of the population, and consequently to the largest share of the iGeneration. In 2010, 38 percent of children under age 15 lived in the South (the iGeneration was under age 16 in that year), according to Census Bureau estimates. In the South, they account for 20 percent of the population.

Children under age 15 account for 27 percent of the population of Utah. They are only 17 percent of the populations of Florida, Maine, Rhode Island, Vermont, and West Virginia.

■ The iGeneration will be a growing force in every state and region in the years ahead.

The Northeast is home to just 16 percent of children under age 15

(percent distribution of children under age 15, by region, 2010)

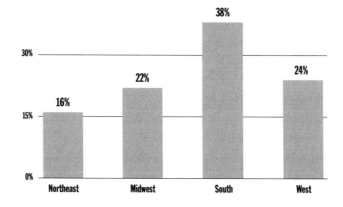

Table 18.7 Population by Age and Region, 2010

(number of people by age and region, 2010; numbers in thousands)

	total	Northeast	Midwest	South	West
Total people	**309,350**	**55,361**	**66,976**	**114,866**	**72,147**
Under age 15	61,277	10,056	13,280	23,082	14,858
Under age 5	20,201	3,219	4,329	7,680	4,973
Aged 5 to 9	20,382	3,339	4,432	7,691	4,921
Aged 10 to 14	20,694	3,498	4,520	7,711	4,965
Aged 15 to 19	21,959	3,873	4,781	8,062	5,243
Aged 20 to 24	21,668	3,830	4,595	8,038	5,205
Aged 25 to 29	21,153	3,623	4,427	7,861	5,243
Aged 30 to 34	20,094	3,433	4,203	7,506	4,952
Aged 35 to 39	20,082	3,487	4,159	7,596	4,840
Aged 40 to 44	20,899	3,888	4,387	7,751	4,872
Aged 45 to 49	22,648	4,261	4,931	8,359	5,096
Aged 50 to 54	22,365	4,225	5,013	8,122	5,005
Aged 55 to 59	19,779	3,691	4,449	7,186	4,453
Aged 60 to 64	16,987	3,165	3,702	6,335	3,785
Aged 65 to 69	12,515	2,298	2,702	4,789	2,726
Aged 70 to 74	9,326	1,718	2,046	3,571	1,992
Aged 75 to 79	7,313	1,416	1,638	2,730	1,530
Aged 80 to 84	5,750	1,191	1,335	2,039	1,184
Aged 85 or older	5,533	1,206	1,328	1,836	1,162

Source: Bureau of the Census, State Population Estimates, Internet site http://www.census.gov/popest/data/intercensal/state/state2010.html; calculations by New Strategist

Table 18.8 Regional Distribution of Population by Age, 2010

(regional distribution of people by age, 2010)

	total	Northeast	Midwest	South	West
Total people	**100.0%**	**17.9%**	**21.7%**	**37.1%**	**23.3%**
Under age 15	100.0	16.4	21.7	37.7	24.2
Under age 5	100.0	15.9	21.4	38.0	24.6
Aged 5 to 9	100.0	16.4	21.7	37.7	24.1
Aged 10 to 14	100.0	16.9	21.8	37.3	24.0
Aged 15 to 19	100.0	17.6	21.8	36.7	23.9
Aged 20 to 24	100.0	17.7	21.2	37.1	24.0
Aged 25 to 29	100.0	17.1	20.9	37.2	24.8
Aged 30 to 34	100.0	17.1	20.9	37.4	24.6
Aged 35 to 39	100.0	17.4	20.7	37.8	24.1
Aged 40 to 44	100.0	18.6	21.0	37.1	23.3
Aged 45 to 49	100.0	18.8	21.8	36.9	22.5
Aged 50 to 54	100.0	18.9	22.4	36.3	22.4
Aged 55 to 59	100.0	18.7	22.5	36.3	22.5
Aged 60 to 64	100.0	18.6	21.8	37.3	22.3
Aged 65 to 69	100.0	18.4	21.6	38.3	21.8
Aged 70 to 74	100.0	18.4	21.9	38.3	21.4
Aged 75 to 79	100.0	19.4	22.4	37.3	20.9
Aged 80 to 84	100.0	20.7	23.2	35.5	20.6
Aged 85 or older	100.0	21.8	24.0	33.2	21.0

Source: Bureau of the Census, State Population Estimates, Internet site http://www.census.gov/popest/data/intercensal/state/state2010.html; calculations by New Strategist

Table 18.9 Age Distribution of Population by Region, 2010

(age distribution of people by region, 2010)

	total	Northeast	Midwest	South	West
Total people	**100.0%**	**100.0%**	**100.0%**	**100.0%**	**100.0%**
Under age 15	19.8	18.2	19.8	20.1	20.6
Under age 5	6.5	5.8	6.5	6.7	6.9
Aged 5 to 9	6.6	6.0	6.6	6.7	6.8
Aged 10 to 14	6.7	6.3	6.7	6.7	6.9
Aged 15 to 19	7.1	7.0	7.1	7.0	7.3
Aged 20 to 24	7.0	6.9	6.9	7.0	7.2
Aged 25 to 29	6.8	6.5	6.6	6.8	7.3
Aged 30 to 34	6.5	6.2	6.3	6.5	6.9
Aged 35 to 39	6.5	6.3	6.2	6.6	6.7
Aged 40 to 44	6.8	7.0	6.6	6.7	6.8
Aged 45 to 49	7.3	7.7	7.4	7.3	7.1
Aged 50 to 54	7.2	7.6	7.5	7.1	6.9
Aged 55 to 59	6.4	6.7	6.6	6.3	6.2
Aged 60 to 64	5.5	5.7	5.5	5.5	5.2
Aged 65 to 69	4.0	4.2	4.0	4.2	3.8
Aged 70 to 74	3.0	3.1	3.1	3.1	2.8
Aged 75 to 79	2.4	2.6	2.4	2.4	2.1
Aged 80 to 84	1.9	2.2	2.0	1.8	1.6
Aged 85 or older	1.8	2.2	2.0	1.6	1.6

Source: Bureau of the Census, State Population Estimates, Internet site http://www.census.gov/popest/data/intercensal/state/state2010.html; calculations by New Strategist

Table 18.10 State Populations by Age, 2010

(total number of people and number under age 15 by state, 2010; numbers in thousands)

	total population	under age 15 total	under age 5	5 to 9	10 to 14
United States	**309,350**	**61,277**	**20,201**	**20,382**	**20,694**
Alabama	4,785	932	305	308	319
Alaska	714	156	54	51	51
Arizona	6,414	1,362	456	456	450
Arkansas	2,922	592	198	197	198
California	37,349	7,644	2,532	2,514	2,598
Colorado	5,049	1,028	345	350	334
Connecticut	3,577	665	202	223	240
Delaware	900	169	56	57	57
District of Columbia	604	84	33	26	25
Florida	18,843	3,287	1,073	1,082	1,131
Georgia	9,713	2,074	688	696	690
Hawaii	1,364	252	87	83	82
Idaho	1,571	360	122	121	117
Illinois	12,843	2,574	835	860	879
Indiana	6,491	1,330	434	445	452
Iowa	3,050	603	202	201	201
Kansas	2,859	607	205	203	199
Kentucky	4,346	849	282	283	284
Louisiana	4,544	928	315	307	307
Maine	1,328	222	69	74	79
Maryland	5,786	1,111	365	367	379
Massachusetts	6,557	1,159	367	386	406
Michigan	9,878	1,905	595	637	674
Minnesota	5,311	1,063	355	356	352
Mississippi	2,970	624	211	206	208
Missouri	5,996	1,177	390	390	397
Montana	991	184	62	61	61
Nebraska	1,830	384	132	129	123
Nevada	2,705	554	187	183	183
New Hampshire	1,317	232	70	78	85
New Jersey	8,802	1,693	540	565	587
New Mexico	2,066	431	145	144	142
New York	19,392	3,529	1,154	1,164	1,210
North Carolina	9,562	1,902	633	637	632
North Dakota	674	125	45	40	40
Ohio	11,536	2,239	719	747	773
Oklahoma	3,762	778	264	260	254
Oregon	3,839	718	237	238	243
Pennsylvania	12,710	2,272	728	753	790
Rhode Island	1,053	182	57	60	64
South Carolina	4,636	896	303	296	297

		under age 15			
	total population	total	under age 5	5 to 9	10 to 14
South Dakota	816	170	60	56	54
Tennessee	6,357	1,239	408	412	419
Texas	25,257	5,761	1,933	1,938	1,890
Utah	2,776	744	264	251	229
Vermont	626	104	32	35	38
Virginia	8,025	1,535	510	513	512
Washington	6,744	1,310	440	431	439
West Virginia	1,854	319	104	106	109
Wisconsin	5,691	1,102	358	369	376
Wyoming	564	114	40	37	36

Source: Bureau of the Census, State Population Estimates, Internet site http://www.census.gov/popest/data/intercensal/state/state2010.html; calculations by New Strategist

Table 18.11 Distribution of State Populations by Age, 2010

(percent distribution of people by state and age, 2010; numbers in thousands)

	total population	under age 15 total	under age 5	5 to 9	10 to 14
United States	**100.0%**	**19.8%**	**6.5%**	**6.6%**	**6.7%**
Alabama	100.0	19.5	6.4	6.4	6.7
Alaska	100.0	21.9	7.6	7.2	7.2
Arizona	100.0	21.2	7.1	7.1	7.0
Arkansas	100.0	20.3	6.8	6.7	6.8
California	100.0	20.5	6.8	6.7	7.0
Colorado	100.0	20.4	6.8	6.9	6.6
Connecticut	100.0	18.6	5.6	6.2	6.7
Delaware	100.0	18.8	6.2	6.3	6.3
District of Columbia	100.0	13.9	5.4	4.4	4.2
Florida	100.0	17.4	5.7	5.7	6.0
Georgia	100.0	21.4	7.1	7.2	7.1
Hawaii	100.0	18.5	6.4	6.1	6.0
Idaho	100.0	22.9	7.7	7.7	7.5
Illinois	100.0	20.0	6.5	6.7	6.8
Indiana	100.0	20.5	6.7	6.9	7.0
Iowa	100.0	19.8	6.6	6.6	6.6
Kansas	100.0	21.2	7.2	7.1	7.0
Kentucky	100.0	19.5	6.5	6.5	6.5
Louisiana	100.0	20.4	6.9	6.7	6.8
Maine	100.0	16.7	5.2	5.6	5.9
Maryland	100.0	19.2	6.3	6.3	6.6
Massachusetts	100.0	17.7	5.6	5.9	6.2
Michigan	100.0	19.3	6.0	6.4	6.8
Minnesota	100.0	20.0	6.7	6.7	6.6
Mississippi	100.0	21.0	7.1	6.9	7.0
Missouri	100.0	19.6	6.5	6.5	6.6
Montana	100.0	18.6	6.3	6.1	6.2
Nebraska	100.0	21.0	7.2	7.1	6.7
Nevada	100.0	20.5	6.9	6.8	6.8
New Hampshire	100.0	17.6	5.3	5.9	6.4
New Jersey	100.0	19.2	6.1	6.4	6.7
New Mexico	100.0	20.9	7.0	7.0	6.9
New York	100.0	18.2	5.9	6.0	6.2
North Carolina	100.0	19.9	6.6	6.7	6.6
North Dakota	100.0	18.5	6.6	6.0	5.9
Ohio	100.0	19.4	6.2	6.5	6.7
Oklahoma	100.0	20.7	7.0	6.9	6.8
Oregon	100.0	18.7	6.2	6.2	6.3
Pennsylvania	100.0	17.9	5.7	5.9	6.2
Rhode Island	100.0	17.3	5.4	5.7	6.1
South Carolina	100.0	19.3	6.5	6.4	6.4

	total population	under age 15			
		total	under age 5	5 to 9	10 to 14
South Dakota	100.0%	20.8%	7.3%	6.8%	6.6%
Tennessee	100.0	19.5	6.4	6.5	6.6
Texas	100.0	22.8	7.7	7.7	7.5
Utah	100.0	26.8	9.5	9.0	8.2
Vermont	100.0	16.7	5.1	5.5	6.0
Virginia	100.0	19.1	6.4	6.4	6.4
Washington	100.0	19.4	6.5	6.4	6.5
West Virginia	100.0	17.2	5.6	5.7	5.9
Wisconsin	100.0	19.4	6.3	6.5	6.6
Wyoming	100.0	20.1	7.1	6.6	6.4

Source: Bureau of the Census, State Population Estimates, Internet site http://www.census.gov/popest/data/intercensal/state/ state2010.html; calculations by New Strategist

19

Spending

■ The spending of married couples with preschoolers fell by a substantial 10 percent between 2006 and 2010, after adjusting for inflation. This household type reined in its spending on most products and services as the cost of health insurance and other necessities climbed.

■ Married couples with school-aged children rank among the nation's biggest spenders, but they cut their spending by 7 percent between 2006 and 2010 after adjusting for inflation. Their spending on food away from home fell 12 percent, and their spending on mortgage interest plunged 16 percent.

■ Single parents with children under age 18 at home spent slightly more in 2010 than in 2000, after adjusting for inflation. This stability is remarkable, considering the dislocations of the Great Recession.

The Spending of Married Couples with Children Is Down

Their spending plunged on many items between 2006 and 2010.

Married couples with children spend much more than the average household because they have the highest incomes and the largest households. In 2010, couples with children of any age at home spent an average of $67,383, much greater than the $48,109 spent by the average household.

Between 2000 and 2006 (the year overall household spending peaked), couples with children boosted their spending by 9 percent, after adjusting for inflation. Between 2006 and 2010, however, couples with children reduced their spending by about the same amount. Overall, this household type spent slightly less in 2010 than in 2000, after adjusting for inflation. Since 2006, couples with children have cut their spending sharply on many discretionary items such as food away from home (down 14 percent), alcoholic beverages (down 22 percent), household furnishings and equipment (down 19 percent), and new vehicles (down 43 percent). They were forced to increase their spending on out-of-pocket health insurance costs (up 19 percent), education (up 10 percent), and property taxes (up 3 percent).

■ The Great Recession has been a setback for families with children because many parents found themselves unemployed.

Married couples with children cut their spending on many items

(percent change in spending by married couples with children of any age at home on selected items, 2006 and 2010; in 2010 dollars)

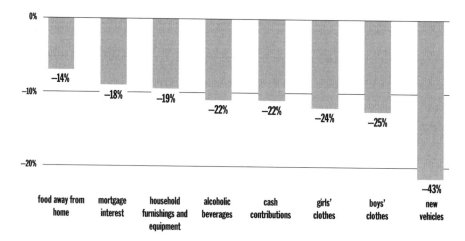

Table 19.1 Average Spending by Married Couples with Children at Home, 2000 to 2010

(average annual spending of consumer units headed by married couples with children at home, 2000 to 2010; percent change for selected years; in 2010 dollars)

	average spending			percent change		
	2010	**2006**	**2000**	**2006–10**	**2000–06**	**2000–10**
Number of consumer units headed by married couples with children at home (in 000s)	28,172	29,381	28,777	–4.1%	2.1%	–2.1%
Average annual spending of consumer units	$67,383	$73,934	$67,856	–8.9	9.0	–0.7
FOOD	8,876	9,588	9,182	–7.4	4.4	–3.3
Food at home	5,314	5,443	5,517	–2.4	–1.4	–3.7
Cereals and bakery products	759	729	861	4.1	–15.3	–11.9
Cereals and cereal products	258	238	304	8.4	–21.7	–15.1
Bakery products	501	491	557	2.0	–11.9	–10.1
Meats, poultry, fish, and eggs	1,119	1,246	1,409	–10.2	–11.6	–20.6
Beef	307	362	424	–15.3	–14.6	–27.6
Pork	204	240	286	–15.0	–16.1	–28.7
Other meats	175	174	187	0.5	–7.1	–6.6
Poultry	206	231	262	–11.0	–11.7	–21.4
Fish and seafood	163	187	194	–12.9	–3.4	–15.9
Eggs	64	52	56	23.3	–6.8	14.9
Dairy products	579	601	609	–3.7	–1.3	–4.9
Fresh milk and cream	222	237	255	–6.3	–6.9	–12.8
Other dairy products	357	365	355	–2.1	2.8	0.7
Fruits and vegetables	978	940	899	4.0	4.5	8.8
Fresh fruits	344	312	274	10.4	13.9	25.8
Fresh vegetables	293	313	267	–6.3	17.0	9.7
Processed fruits	163	172	208	–5.2	–17.2	–21.5
Processed vegetables	179	143	151	25.4	–5.3	18.8
Other food at home	1,879	1,927	1,739	–2.5	10.9	8.1
Sugar and other sweets	197	190	218	3.5	–12.6	–9.6
Fats and oils	143	131	143	9.3	–8.5	–0.1
Miscellaneous foods	1,020	1,033	857	–1.3	20.5	19.0
Nonalcoholic beverages	457	508	451	–10.1	12.8	1.4
Food prepared by consumer unit on trips	61	64	68	–4.4	–6.7	–10.8
Food away from home	3,562	4,144	3,665	–14.0	13.1	–2.8
ALCOHOLIC BEVERAGES	424	541	501	–21.6	7.8	–15.4
HOUSING	22,492	24,339	21,694	–7.6	12.2	3.7
Shelter	13,067	14,015	12,274	–6.8	14.2	6.5
Owned dwellings	9,788	11,097	9,607	–11.8	15.5	1.9
Mortgage interest and charges	5,840	7,104	6,255	–17.8	13.6	–6.6
Property taxes	2,652	2,565	2,049	3.4	25.2	29.4
Maintenance, repair, insurance, other expenses	1,296	1,429	1,303	–9.3	9.7	–0.5
Rented dwellings	2,402	2,097	1,902	14.5	10.3	26.3
Other lodging	877	820	765	7.0	7.2	14.7
Utilities, fuels, and public services	4,709	4,794	4,027	–1.8	19.0	16.9
Natural gas	575	719	501	–20.1	43.4	14.7
Electricity	1,771	1,752	1,470	1.1	19.2	20.5
Fuel oil and other fuels	161	190	152	–15.4	25.3	6.0

	average spending			percent change		
	2010	2006	2000	2006–10	2000–06	2000–10
Telephone	$1,565	$1,555	$1,389	0.6%	12.0%	12.7%
Water and other public services	637	577	513	10.5	12.4	24.2
Household services	**1,799**	**1,939**	**1,546**	**−7.2**	**25.4**	**16.4**
Personal services	951	1,214	950	−21.6	27.8	0.1
Other household services	848	726	596	16.8	21.7	42.2
Housekeeping supplies	**830**	**1,002**	**890**	**−17.1**	**12.5**	**−6.8**
Laundry and cleaning supplies	219	244	257	−10.4	−4.9	−14.8
Other household products	441	552	428	−20.1	28.9	3.0
Postage and stationery	170	206	205	−17.3	0.2	−17.1
Household furnishings and equipment	**2,088**	**2,587**	**2,958**	**−19.3**	**−12.5**	**−29.4**
Household textiles	145	209	205	−30.5	1.8	−29.3
Furniture	501	720	770	−30.5	−6.4	−34.9
Floor coverings	52	75	90	−30.3	−17.0	−42.2
Major appliances	293	386	367	−24.1	5.2	−20.2
Small appliances and miscellaneous housewares	148	146	154	1.4	−5.5	−4.2
Miscellaneous household equipment	949	1,051	1,370	−9.7	−23.3	−30.7
APPAREL AND RELATED SERVICES	**2,438**	**3,034**	**3,481**	**−19.6**	**−12.8**	**−30.0**
Men and boys	**600**	**795**	**865**	**−24.5**	**−8.1**	**−30.6**
Men, aged 16 or older	423	560	591	−24.5	−5.3	−28.5
Boys, aged 2 to 15	177	235	274	−24.6	−14.2	−35.3
Women and girls	**953**	**1,219**	**1,332**	**−21.8**	**−8.5**	**−28.5**
Women, aged 16 or older	708	897	985	−21.0	−9.0	−28.1
Girls, aged 2 to 15	245	322	347	−24.0	−7.1	−29.4
Children under age 2	**186**	**203**	**219**	**−8.5**	**−7.2**	**−15.1**
Footwear	**427**	**481**	**608**	**−11.3**	**−20.8**	**−29.7**
Other apparel products and services	**273**	**335**	**457**	**−18.6**	**−26.7**	**−40.3**
TRANSPORTATION	**10,984**	**13,831**	**14,041**	**−20.6**	**−1.5**	**−21.8**
Vehicle purchases	**3,970**	**6,006**	**6,794**	**−33.9**	**−11.6**	**−41.6**
Cars and trucks, new	1,824	3,221	3,138	−43.4	2.7	−41.9
Cars and trucks, used	2,091	2,695	3,567	−22.4	−24.4	−41.4
Gasoline and motor oil	**3,057**	**3,511**	**2,379**	**−12.9**	**47.6**	**28.5**
Other vehicle expenses	**3,301**	**3,657**	**4,245**	**−9.7**	**−13.8**	**−22.2**
Vehicle finance charges	369	538	676	−31.4	−20.5	−45.4
Maintenance and repairs	1,095	1,036	1,078	5.7	−3.8	1.6
Vehicle insurance	1,242	1,336	1,389	−7.0	−3.8	−10.6
Vehicle rentals, leases, licenses, other charges	595	747	1,103	−20.4	−32.2	−46.1
Public transportation	**655**	**658**	**622**	**−0.4**	**5.8**	**5.3**
HEALTH CARE	**3,742**	**3,389**	**2,920**	**10.4**	**16.0**	**28.1**
Health insurance	2,085	1,755	1,432	18.8	22.6	45.6
Medical services	1,004	942	884	6.6	6.6	13.6
Drugs	494	532	457	−7.2	16.4	8.1
Medical supplies	160	158	147	1.3	7.5	8.9
ENTERTAINMENT	**3,627**	**3,654**	**3,627**	**−0.7**	**0.7**	**0.0**
Fees and admissions	1,089	1,056	1,076	3.2	−1.9	1.2
Audio and visual equipment and services	1,180	1,293	1,081	−8.7	19.5	9.1
Pets, toys, hobbies, and playground equipment	810	620	631	30.7	−1.7	28.4
Other entertainment products and services	549	687	838	−20.1	−18.1	−34.5

	average spending			percent change		
	2010	2006	2000	2006–10	2000–06	2000–10
PERSONAL CARE PRODUCTS AND SERVICES	$794	$879	$974	–9.7%	–9.7%	–18.5%
READING	112	148	223	–24.4	–33.5	–49.7
EDUCATION	2,099	1,913	1,426	9.7	34.2	47.2
TOBACCO PRODUCTS AND SMOKING SUPPLIES	334	336	453	–0.7	–25.8	–26.3
MISCELLANEOUS	996	1,021	1,131	–2.5	–9.7	–11.9
CASH CONTRIBUTIONS	1,763	2,253	1,545	–21.7	45.8	14.1
PERSONAL INSURANCE AND PENSIONS	8,703	9,010	6,657	–3.4	35.3	30.7
Life and other personal insurance	529	542	761	–2.4	–28.8	–30.5
Pensions and Social Security*	8,174	8,468	–	–3.5	–	–
PERSONAL TAXES	2,603	3,555	5,644	–26.8	–37.0	–53.9
Federal income taxes	1,583	2,446	4,390	–35.3	–44.3	–63.9
State and local income taxes	807	859	1,033	–6.0	–16.9	–21.9
Other taxes	212	250	222	–15.2	12.8	–4.3
GIFTS FOR PEOPLE IN OTHER HOUSEHOLDS	1,098	1,391	1,603	–21.1	–13.2	–31.5

Because of changes in methodology, the 2006 and 2010 data on pensions and Social Security are not comparable with earlier years.
Note: The Bureau of Labor Statistics uses consumer unit rather than household as the sampling unit in the Consumer Expenditure Survey. For the definition of consumer unit, see the glossary. Spending on gifts is also included in the preceding product and service categories.
Source: Bureau of Labor Statistics, 2000, 2006, and 2010 Consumer Expenditure Surveys, Internet site http://www.bls.gov/cex/; calculations by New Strategist

Couples with Preschoolers Are Spending Less

The spending of married couples with preschoolers fell between 2006 and 2010.

The spending of married couples with preschoolers fell 10 percent between 2006 (the year overall household spending peaked) and 2010, after adjusting for inflation. This dropwas greater than the 8 percent decline in spending by the average household.

Couples with preschoolers cut their spending on groceries (food at home) by 2 percent between 2006 and 2010, after adjusting for inflation, and they cut their spending on food away from home by a much larger 17 percent during those years. They spent 49 percent less on furniture, 47 percent less on new vehicles, and 8 percent less on entertainment. As the housing market collapsed and some lost their homes, their spending on mortgage interest fell 21 percent while spending on rent increased 30 percent. They spent 38 percent less on women's clothes and 47 percent less on men's clothes. Their spending on clothes for boys and girls also fell. Meanwhile, out-of-pocket spending on health insurance climbed 13 percent.

■ Couples with preschoolers were badly hurt by the Great Recession, and it will take them many years to recover.

Married couples with preschoolers spent less on most things

(percent change in spending by married couples with oldest child under age 6, 2006 to 2010; in 2010 dollars)

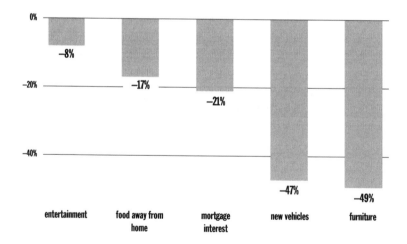

Table 19.2 Average Spending of Married Couples with Preschoolers, 2000 to 2010

(average annual spending of married-couple consumer units with oldest child under age 6, 2000 to 2010; percent change for selected years; in 2010 dollars)

	average spending			percent change		
	2010	2006	2000	2006–10	2000–06	2000–10
Number of consumer units headed by married couples with preschoolers (in 000s)	5,185	5,763	5,291	–10.0%	8.9%	–2.0%
Average annual spending of consumer units	$61,756	$68,592	$64,272	–10.0	6.7	–3.9
FOOD	7,056	7,702	7,366	–8.4	4.6	–4.2
Food at home	4,311	4,384	4,633	–1.7	–5.4	–7.0
Cereals and bakery products	564	551	686	2.4	–19.8	–17.8
Cereals and cereal products	208	181	236	15.2	–23.3	–11.7
Bakery products	356	370	451	–3.8	–17.9	–21.0
Meats, poultry, fish, and eggs	799	852	1,037	–6.3	–17.8	–23.0
Beef	187	265	310	–29.4	–14.6	–39.7
Pork	126	158	191	–20.2	–17.4	–34.1
Other meats	158	109	137	44.6	–20.1	15.5
Poultry	163	167	217	–2.1	–23.1	–24.7
Fish and seafood	116	117	138	–0.7	–15.4	–16.0
Eggs	48	37	42	30.5	–12.0	14.9
Dairy products	486	560	526	–13.3	6.6	–7.5
Fresh milk and cream	200	234	223	–14.4	4.8	–10.3
Other dairy products	285	327	303	–12.8	7.9	–5.8
Fruits and vegetables	839	797	784	5.2	1.7	7.0
Fresh fruits	308	281	238	9.5	18.1	29.4
Fresh vegetables	252	234	233	7.9	0.3	8.2
Processed fruits	146	168	192	–12.9	–12.9	–24.1
Processed vegetables	133	115	119	16.0	–3.7	11.7
Other food at home	1,623	1,622	1,602	0.0	1.3	1.3
Sugar and other sweets	126	142	161	–11.1	–11.9	–21.7
Fats and oils	98	95	94	3.0	1.6	4.6
Miscellaneous foods	1,016	933	928	8.8	0.6	9.5
Nonalcoholic beverages	341	392	362	–12.9	8.1	–5.8
Food prepared by consumer unit on trips	43	59	57	–27.7	4.4	–24.5
Food away from home	2,745	3,318	2,733	–17.3	21.4	0.5
ALCOHOLIC BEVERAGES	440	515	475	–14.5	8.4	–7.3
HOUSING	24,219	26,864	23,682	–9.8	13.4	2.3
Shelter	14,177	15,242	13,167	–7.0	15.8	7.7
Owned dwellings	10,029	11,988	9,958	–16.3	20.4	0.7
Mortgage interest and charges	6,524	8,268	6,946	–21.1	19.0	–6.1
Property taxes	2,206	2,514	1,905	–12.2	32.0	15.8
Maintenance, repair, insurance, other expenses	1,299	1,205	1,107	7.8	8.9	17.4
Rented dwellings	3,478	2,686	2,738	29.5	–1.9	27.0
Other lodging	670	570	471	17.5	21.0	42.2
Utilities, fuels, and public services	3,799	4,036	3,551	–5.9	13.7	7.0
Natural gas	515	655	456	–21.4	43.8	13.0
Electricity	1,382	1,466	1,211	–5.7	21.1	14.2
Fuel oil and other fuels	119	144	144	–17.3	–0.3	–17.6

	average spending			percent change		
	2010	2006	2000	2006–10	2000–06	2000–10
Telephone	$1,267	$1,293	$1,323	−2.0%	−2.3%	−4.3%
Water and other public services	517	478	417	8.1	14.8	24.1
Household services	**3,737**	**3,769**	**3,014**	**−0.9**	**25.1**	**24.0**
Personal services	2,960	3,060	2,520	−3.3	21.4	17.5
Other household services	777	710	494	9.5	43.7	57.3
Housekeeping supplies	**656**	**816**	**783**	**−19.6**	**4.2**	**−16.2**
Laundry and cleaning supplies	159	220	190	−27.6	15.6	−16.3
Other household products	388	410	382	−5.4	7.2	1.5
Postage and stationery	109	186	210	−41.4	−11.5	−48.1
Household furnishings and equipment	**1,851**	**3,002**	**3,168**	**−38.3**	**−5.3**	**−41.6**
Household textiles	107	208	227	−48.5	−8.4	−52.8
Furniture	530	1,043	914	−49.2	14.0	−42.0
Floor coverings	54	74	58	−26.6	26.3	−7.3
Major appliances	302	398	336	−24.1	18.6	−10.0
Small appliances and miscellaneous housewares	139	110	158	26.0	−30.3	−12.2
Miscellaneous household equipment	719	1,170	1,475	−38.6	−20.7	−51.3
APPAREL AND RELATED SERVICES	**2,169**	**2,884**	**3,280**	**−24.8**	**−12.1**	**−33.9**
Men and boys	**357**	**637**	**681**	**−44.0**	**−6.5**	**−47.6**
Men, aged 16 or older	251	472	494	−46.8	−4.5	−49.2
Boys, aged 2 to 15	106	165	187	−35.9	−11.7	−43.4
Women and girls	**678**	**1,012**	**984**	**−33.0**	**2.9**	**−31.1**
Women, aged 16 or older	504	809	789	−37.7	2.6	−36.1
Girls, aged 2 to 15	174	203	195	−14.4	4.3	−10.8
Children under age 2	**613**	**597**	**631**	**2.7**	**−5.3**	**−2.8**
Footwear	**231**	**354**	**569**	**−34.7**	**−37.8**	**−59.4**
Other apparel products and services	**291**	**284**	**415**	**2.3**	**−31.5**	**−29.9**
TRANSPORTATION	**9,357**	**12,101**	**13,606**	**−22.7**	**−11.1**	**−31.2**
Vehicle purchases	**3,761**	**5,636**	**7,084**	**−33.3**	**−20.4**	**−46.9**
Cars and trucks, new	1,764	3,315	3,343	−46.8	−0.8	−47.2
Cars and trucks, used	1,979	2,305	3,566	−14.1	−35.4	−44.5
Gasoline and motor oil	**2,451**	**2,822**	**2,018**	**−13.1**	**39.8**	**21.4**
Other vehicle expenses	**2,639**	**3,146**	**3,989**	**−16.1**	**−21.1**	**−33.8**
Vehicle finance charges	398	561	698	−29.1	−19.5	−43.0
Maintenance and repairs	897	699	902	28.4	−22.5	−0.5
Vehicle insurance	751	1,024	1,212	−26.7	−15.5	−38.0
Vehicle rentals, leases, licenses, other charges	593	862	1,176	−31.2	−26.7	−49.6
Public transportation	**506**	**496**	**515**	**1.9**	**−3.7**	**−1.8**
HEALTH CARE	**3,124**	**2,949**	**2,402**	**6.0**	**22.7**	**30.0**
Health insurance	1,777	1,567	1,298	13.4	20.8	36.9
Medical services	937	925	694	1.3	33.3	35.0
Drugs	303	363	305	−16.6	19.1	−0.7
Medical supplies	108	93	106	16.1	−12.5	1.5
ENTERTAINMENT	**2,869**	**3,114**	**2,774**	**−7.9**	**12.2**	**3.4**
Fees and admissions	541	620	615	−12.7	0.7	−12.1
Audio and visual equipment and services	1,057	1,169	908	−9.6	28.8	16.4
Pets, toys, hobbies, and playground equipment	798	639	609	24.8	5.0	31.0
Other entertainment products and services	472	685	641	−31.1	6.9	−26.3

	average spending			percent change		
	2010	2006	2000	2006–10	2000–06	2000–10
PERSONAL CARE PRODUCTS AND SERVICES	$636	$808	$822	–21.3%	–1.7%	–22.6%
READING	78	114	220	–31.3	–48.5	–64.6
EDUCATION	652	617	532	5.8	15.9	22.6
TOBACCO PRODUCTS AND SMOKING SUPPLIES	245	233	348	5.4	–33.2	–29.6
MISCELLANEOUS	1,132	837	870	35.2	–3.8	30.1
CASH CONTRIBUTIONS	1,214	1,457	1,074	–16.7	35.7	13.1
PERSONAL INSURANCE AND PENSIONS	8,564	8,400	6,823	2.0	23.1	25.5
Life and other personal insurance	468	393	610	19.2	–35.7	–23.3
Pensions and Social Security*	8,096	8,007	–	1.1	–	–
PERSONAL TAXES	2,288	3,812	5,273	–40.0	–27.7	–56.6
Federal income taxes	1,437	2,679	4,128	–46.4	–35.1	–65.2
State and local income taxes	691	924	957	–25.2	–3.5	–27.8
Other taxes	160	210	186	–23.7	12.7	–14.0
GIFTS FOR PEOPLE IN OTHER HOUSEHOLDS	620	978	1,162	–36.6	–15.9	–46.7

* Because of changes in methodology, the 2006 and 2010 data on pensions and Social Security are not comparable with earlier years.
Note: The Bureau of Labor Statistics uses consumer unit rather than household as the sampling unit in the Consumer Expenditure Survey. For the definition of consumer unit, see the glossary. Spending on gifts is also included in the preceding product and service categories.
Source: Bureau of Labor Statistics, 2000, 2006, and 2010 Consumer Expenditure Surveys, Internet site http://www.bls.gov/cex/; calculations by New Strategist

Spending of Couples with School-Aged Children Decreased

They spent less on most categories between 2006 and 2010.

Married couples with school-aged children rank among the most affluent households in the nation, and their spending—averaging $69,536 in 2010—is far above average. Because of the Great Recession, however, these households cut their spending by 7 percent between 2006 and 2010, after adjusting for inflation.

Couples with school-aged children cut their spending on most items between 2006 and 2010. They spent 0.5 percent less on food at home (groceries), after adjusting for inflation. Their spending on food away from home fell by a much larger 12 percent. They spent 23 percent less on alcoholic beverages, and 36 percent less on new cars and trucks. Their spending on mortgage interest, which had increased by 11 percent between 2000 and 2006, fell 16 percent between 2006 and 2010 as some families lost their homes.

Couples with school-aged children spent 18 percent more out-of-pocket on health insurance in 2010 than in 2006, after adjusting for inflation. They spent 15 percent more on education. Despite their reduced overall spending and the increase in their nondiscretionary expenses, couples with school-aged children boosted their spending on entertainment by 3 percent between 2006 and 2010.

■ The spending of married couples with school-aged children will remain muted until these families feel more economically secure.

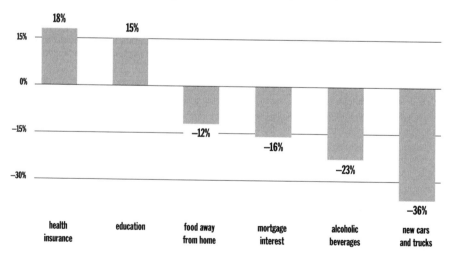

Couples with school-aged children are spending more for health insurance

(percent change in spending by married couples with children aged 6 to 17 on selected items, 2006 to 201

Table 19.3 Average Spending of Married Couples with School-Aged Children, 2000 to 2010

(average annual spending of married-couple consumer units with oldest child aged 6 to 17, 2000 to 2010; percent change for selected years; in 2010 dollars)

	average spending			percent change		
	2010	2006	2000	2006–10	2000–06	2000–10
Number of consumer units headed by married couples with school-aged children (in 000s)	14,242	15,166	15,396	–6.1%	–1.5%	–7.5%
Average annual spending of consumer units	$69,536	$74,802	$68,595	–7.0	9.0	1.4
FOOD	9,386	9,963	9,507	–5.8	4.8	–1.3
Food at home	5,476	5,503	5,645	–0.5	–2.5	–3.0
Cereals and bakery products	811	766	889	5.9	–13.9	–8.8
Cereals and cereal products	278	249	324	11.7	–23.3	–14.2
Bakery products	533	517	564	3.1	–8.2	–5.4
Meats, poultry, fish, and eggs	1,144	1,244	1,463	–8.0	–15.0	–21.8
Beef	305	350	437	–13.0	–19.8	–30.2
Pork	214	237	299	–9.7	–20.7	–28.4
Other meats	175	180	194	–2.5	–7.3	–9.7
Poultry	217	234	266	–7.1	–12.1	–18.4
Fish and seafood	164	190	213	–13.9	–10.5	–22.9
Eggs	69	53	56	30.2	–4.9	23.8
Dairy products	604	620	629	–2.5	–1.5	–4.0
Fresh milk and cream	231	249	265	–7.1	–6.0	–12.7
Other dairy products	373	371	365	0.5	1.7	2.3
Fruits and vegetables	993	939	908	5.8	3.4	9.4
Fresh fruits	357	309	272	15.4	13.6	31.1
Fresh vegetables	293	309	270	–5.3	14.7	8.6
Processed fruits	163	170	214	–4.0	–20.6	–23.8
Processed vegetables	180	150	152	19.7	–1.1	18.5
Other food at home	1,925	1,934	1,758	–0.5	10.0	9.5
Sugar and other sweets	217	195	223	11.5	–12.6	–2.6
Fats and oils	146	129	149	13.4	–13.9	–2.3
Miscellaneous foods	1,031	1,036	859	–0.5	20.7	20.1
Nonalcoholic beverages	462	513	452	–9.9	13.4	2.2
Food prepared by consumer unit on trips	69	63	75	10.0	–16.0	–7.6
Food away from home	3,910	4,460	3,862	–12.3	15.5	1.2
ALCOHOLIC BEVERAGES	421	547	462	–23.1	18.4	–8.9
HOUSING	23,095	24,583	22,075	–6.1	11.4	4.6
Shelter	13,608	14,594	12,707	–6.8	14.9	7.1
Owned dwellings	10,206	11,553	10,051	–11.7	14.9	1.5
Mortgage interest and charges	6,275	7,433	6,686	–15.6	11.2	–6.1
Property taxes	2,725	2,676	2,031	1.8	31.7	34.2
Maintenance, repair, insurance, other expenses	1,205	1,444	1,333	–16.5	8.3	–9.6
Rented dwellings	2,491	2,271	1,954	9.7	16.3	27.5
Other lodging	912	771	704	18.3	9.5	29.5
Utilities, fuels, and public services	4,778	4,854	4,043	–1.6	20.1	18.2
Natural gas	572	729	503	–21.5	45.0	13.8
Electricity	1,819	1,779	1,482	2.2	20.1	22.8
Fuel oil and other fuels	155	207	149	–25.0	38.3	3.7

	average spending			percent change		
	2010	2006	2000	2006–10	2000–06	2000–10
Telephone	$1,567	$1,541	$1,388	1.7%	11.1%	12.9%
Water and other public services	666	598	522	11.3	14.6	27.7
Household services	**1,643**	**1,714**	**1,498**	**–4.2**	**14.4**	**9.7**
Personal services	729	940	837	–22.4	12.3	–12.9
Other household services	914	773	662	18.2	16.8	38.0
Housekeeping supplies	**883**	**1,019**	**917**	**–13.3**	**11.1**	**–3.7**
Laundry and cleaning supplies	243	239	286	1.7	–16.5	–15.1
Other household products	463	578	437	–19.8	32.2	6.0
Postage and stationery	177	202	194	–12.5	4.4	–8.6
Household furnishings and equipment	**2,182**	**2,400**	**2,909**	**–9.1**	**–17.5**	**–25.0**
Household textiles	153	163	199	–6.3	–17.8	–23.0
Furniture	538	680	804	–20.9	–15.4	–33.1
Floor coverings	66	78	76	–15.3	2.5	–13.1
Major appliances	274	337	347	–18.8	–2.7	–21.0
Small appliances and miscellaneous housewares	123	132	152	–6.8	–13.2	–19.1
Miscellaneous household equipment	1,029	1,009	1,332	2.0	–24.2	–22.8
APPAREL AND RELATED SERVICES	**2,672**	**3,085**	**3,594**	**–13.4**	**–14.2**	**–25.6**
Men and boys	**672**	**845**	**908**	**–20.4**	**–7.0**	**–26.0**
Men, aged 16 or older	414	505	533	–18.0	–5.3	–22.3
Boys, aged 2 to 15	258	340	375	–24.0	–9.4	–31.2
Women and girls	**1,109**	**1,244**	**1,385**	**–10.8**	**–10.2**	**–19.9**
Women, aged 16 or older	742	794	880	–6.5	–9.8	–15.7
Girls, aged 2 to 15	367	451	507	–18.6	–11.0	–27.5
Children under age 2	**115**	**132**	**129**	**–12.9**	**2.2**	**–11.0**
Footwear	**502**	**509**	**680**	**–1.5**	**–25.1**	**–26.2**
Other apparel products and services	**274**	**355**	**491**	**–22.8**	**–27.8**	**–44.2**
TRANSPORTATION	**11,184**	**13,811**	**13,478**	**–19.0**	**2.5**	**–17.0**
Vehicle purchases	**4,237**	**6,043**	**6,461**	**–29.9**	**–6.5**	**–34.4**
Cars and trucks, new	2,143	3,329	3,013	–35.6	10.5	–28.9
Cars and trucks, used	2,053	2,611	3,366	–21.4	–22.4	–39.0
Gasoline and motor oil	**3,079**	**3,511**	**2,363**	**–12.3**	**48.6**	**30.3**
Other vehicle expenses	**3,139**	**3,597**	**4,042**	**–12.7**	**–11.0**	**–22.3**
Vehicle finance charges	354	534	655	–33.7	–18.4	–45.9
Maintenance and repairs	1,085	1,076	1,047	0.8	2.8	3.6
Vehicle insurance	1,156	1,230	1,244	–6.0	–1.1	–7.0
Vehicle rentals, leases, licenses, other charges	544	756	1,097	–28.0	–31.1	–50.4
Public transportation	**729**	**660**	**614**	**10.5**	**7.4**	**18.7**
HEALTH CARE	**3,631**	**3,286**	**2,850**	**10.5**	**15.3**	**27.4**
Health insurance	1,999	1,698	1,365	17.7	24.4	46.4
Medical services	1,020	935	926	9.1	1.0	10.2
Drugs	447	485	414	–7.8	17.0	8.0
Medical supplies	164	169	146	–2.8	15.9	12.6
ENTERTAINMENT	**4,175**	**4,043**	**4,115**	**3.3**	**–1.8**	**1.4**
Fees and admissions	1,456	1,329	1,328	9.5	0.1	9.6
Audio and visual equipment and services	1,241	1,342	1,161	–7.5	15.6	6.9
Pets, toys, hobbies, and playground equipment	818	626	693	30.6	–9.6	18.1
Other entertainment products and services	660	745	932	–11.4	–20.0	–29.2

	average spending			percent change		
	2010	2006	2000	2006–10	2000–06	2000–10
PERSONAL CARE PRODUCTS AND SERVICES	$819	$847	$980	–3.3%	–13.6%	–16.4%
READING	117	156	220	–24.9	–29.3	–46.9
EDUCATION	2,030	1,766	1,307	14.9	35.2	55.3
TOBACCO PRODUCTS AND SMOKING SUPPLIES	307	345	425	–11.0	–18.9	–27.8
MISCELLANEOUS	931	1,043	1,216	–10.7	–14.2	–23.4
CASH CONTRIBUTIONS	1,843	2,289	1,608	–19.5	42.3	14.6
PERSONAL INSURANCE AND PENSIONS	8,925	9,038	6,754	–1.3	33.8	32.1
Life and other personal insurance	521	565	747	–7.7	–24.4	–30.3
Pensions and Social Security*	8,404	8,473	–	–0.8	–	–
PERSONAL TAXES	2,659	3,230	5,995	–17.7	–46.1	–55.6
Federal income taxes	1,617	2,203	4,617	–26.6	–52.3	–65.0
State and local income taxes	891	796	1,147	11.9	–30.6	–22.3
Other taxes	151	230	230	–34.5	0.0	–34.5
GIFTS FOR PEOPLE IN OTHER HOUSEHOLDS	1,220	1,555	1,452	–21.6	7.1	–16.0

* Because of changes in methodology, the 2006 and 2010 data on pensions and Social Security are not comparable with earlier years.
Note: The Bureau of Labor Statistics uses consumer unit rather than household as the sampling unit in the Consumer Expenditure Survey. For the definition of consumer unit, see the glossary. Spending on gifts is also included in the preceding product and service categories.
Source: Bureau of Labor Statistics, 2000, 2006, and 2010 Consumer Expenditure Surveys, Internet site http://www.bls.gov/cex/; calculations by New Strategist

Single Parents Increased Their Spending over the Decade

They spent less between 2006 and 2010, however.

Single parents with children under age 18 at home spent an average of $36,933 in 2010—4 percent less than they spent in 2006 but slightly more than they spent in 2000, after adjusting for inflation.

Single-parent families have been cutting expenses in the past few years because the widespread unemployment of the Great Recession reduced their incomes. Between 2006 and 2010, single parents spent 14 percent less on food away from home and 33 percent less on alcoholic beverages, after adjusting for inflation. They cut their spending on entertainment by 15 percent. Mortgage interest payments fell 12 percent as some lost their homes. Spending on rent climbed 4 percent between 2006 and 2010, and out-of-pocket spending on health insurance increased 12 percent. Despite their financial difficulties, single-parent families boosted their spending on women's clothes by 22 percent.

■ The overall spending of single-parent families during the past decade has been remarkably stable despite the dislocations of the Great Recession.

Single parents are cutting corners on many discretionary items

(percent change in spending by single-parent families with children under age 18 at home, 2006 to 2010)

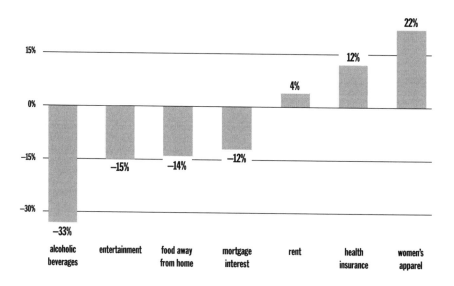

Table 19.4 Average Spending by Single Parents with Children under Age 18 at Home, 2000 to 2010

(average annual spending of consumer units headed by single parents with children under age 18 at home, 2000 to 2010; percent change for selected years; in 2010 dollars)

	average spending			percent change		
	2010	2006	2000	2006–10	2000–06	2000–10
Number of consumer units headed by single parents with children under age 18 at home (in 000s)	7,141	7,225	6,132	–1.2%	17.8%	16.5%
Average annual spending of consumer units	$36,933	$38,388	$36,625	–3.8	4.8	0.8
FOOD	5,227	5,558	5,388	–6.0	3.2	–3.0
Food at home	3,287	3,295	3,352	–0.2	–1.7	–1.9
Cereals and bakery products	451	446	491	1.2	–9.3	–8.2
Cereals and cereal products	148	164	194	–10.0	–15.1	–23.6
Bakery products	303	280	296	8.2	–5.5	2.3
Meats, poultry, fish, and eggs	725	784	955	–7.5	–17.9	–24.1
Beef	186	222	282	–16.1	–21.5	–34.1
Pork	128	154	201	–16.7	–23.7	–36.4
Other meats	110	110	115	–0.3	–4.3	–4.5
Poultry	157	148	194	6.0	–23.5	–19.0
Fish and seafood	101	117	118	–13.5	–0.8	–14.2
Eggs	43	34	42	28.2	–19.8	2.9
Dairy products	318	341	353	–6.7	–3.6	–10.0
Fresh milk and cream	119	146	148	–18.5	–1.4	–19.7
Other dairy products	199	195	205	2.2	–5.1	–3.0
Fruits and vegetables	565	482	517	17.1	–6.6	9.4
Fresh fruits	195	143	144	36.6	–1.1	35.1
Fresh vegetables	139	133	148	4.5	–10.2	–6.2
Processed fruits	114	107	133	6.5	–19.5	–14.3
Processed vegetables	117	100	91	17.6	9.1	28.3
Other food at home	1,230	1,242	1,036	–0.9	19.9	18.7
Sugar and other sweets	113	105	135	7.7	–22.6	–16.6
Fats and oils	91	75	99	21.9	–24.4	–7.9
Miscellaneous foods	680	661	455	2.9	45.4	49.6
Nonalcoholic beverages	323	374	305	–13.7	22.6	5.8
Food prepared by consumer unit on trips	22	27	41	–18.6	–33.3	–45.7
Food away from home	1,939	2,264	2,036	–14.3	11.2	–4.8
ALCOHOLIC BEVERAGES	167	251	237	–33.4	6.0	–29.5
HOUSING	14,224	14,970	13,590	–5.0	10.2	4.7
Shelter	8,263	8,713	8,017	–5.2	8.7	3.1
Owned dwellings	3,638	4,246	3,542	–14.3	19.9	2.7
Mortgage interest and charges	2,304	2,611	2,145	–11.8	21.7	7.4
Property taxes	957	983	818	–2.7	20.2	17.0
Maintenance, repair, insurance, other expenses	378	652	579	–42.0	12.7	–34.7
Rented dwellings	4,422	4,259	4,198	3.8	1.5	5.3
Other lodging	202	206	277	–1.7	–25.9	–27.2
Utilities, fuels, and public services	3,342	3,603	2,957	–7.2	21.9	13.0
Natural gas	381	532	387	–28.4	37.3	–1.7
Electricity	1,360	1,387	1,093	–1.9	26.9	24.4
Fuel oil and other fuels	60	65	54	–7.5	19.2	10.2

	average spending			percent change		
	2010	**2006**	**2000**	**2006–10**	**2000–06**	**2000–10**
Telephone	$1,141	$1,246	$1,131	−8.4%	10.2%	0.9%
Water and other public services	399	373	291	6.9	28.1	37.0
Household services	**1,184**	**1,048**	**995**	**13.0**	**5.3**	**19.0**
Personal services	696	694	742	0.2	−6.4	−6.2
Other household services	489	354	253	38.3	39.7	93.1
Housekeeping supplies	443	458	466	−3.2	−1.8	−4.9
Laundry and cleaning supplies	**157**	**162**	**191**	**−3.2**	**−15.1**	**−17.9**
Other household products	213	191	177	11.3	8.0	20.1
Postage and stationery	73	104	98	−29.7	6.5	−25.1
Household furnishings and equipment	**991**	**1,150**	**1,155**	**−13.8**	**−0.4**	**−14.2**
Household textiles	111	109	76	1.6	43.8	46.1
Furniture	278	330	344	−15.7	−4.2	−19.3
Floor coverings	6	12	28	−49.6	−57.3	−78.5
Major appliances	141	122	132	15.4	−7.2	7.1
Small appliances and miscellaneous housewares	58	75	46	−22.3	63.7	27.2
Miscellaneous household equipment	396	503	528	−21.3	−4.8	−25.0
APPAREL AND RELATED SERVICES	**2,012**	**2,015**	**2,433**	**−0.2**	**−17.2**	**−17.3**
Men and boys	**410**	**356**	**514**	**15.2**	**−30.8**	**−20.3**
Men, aged 16 or older	215	124	187	72.8	−33.6	14.7
Boys, aged 2 to 15	195	231	328	−15.8	−29.4	−40.5
Women and girls	**919**	**878**	**1,028**	**4.6**	**−14.6**	**−10.6**
Women, aged 16 or older	706	577	674	22.5	−14.4	4.8
Girls, aged 2 to 15	212	302	353	−29.7	−14.6	−40.0
Children under age 2	**111**	**119**	**141**	**−6.7**	**−15.4**	**−21.0**
Footwear	**388**	**483**	**520**	**−19.7**	**−7.1**	**−25.4**
Other apparel products and services	**185**	**177**	**228**	**4.3**	**−22.2**	**−18.8**
TRANSPORTATION	**6,428**	**5,953**	**6,353**	**8.0**	**−6.3**	**1.2**
Vehicle purchases	**2,275**	**2,073**	**2,961**	**9.7**	**−30.0**	**−23.2**
Cars and trucks, new	935	598	664	56.3	−9.9	40.9
Cars and trucks, used	1,297	1,463	2,292	−11.4	−36.1	−43.4
Gasoline and motor oil	**1,716**	**1,836**	**1,132**	**−6.5**	**62.1**	**51.6**
Other vehicle expenses	**2,160**	**1,761**	**1,922**	**22.7**	**−8.4**	**12.4**
Vehicle finance charges	223	209	275	6.8	−24.0	−18.8
Maintenance and repairs	594	505	595	17.6	−15.1	−0.2
Vehicle insurance	1,045	720	702	45.1	2.7	49.0
Vehicle rentals, leases, licenses, other charges	297	328	349	−9.4	−6.2	−15.0
Public transportation	**278**	**282**	**338**	**−1.5**	**−16.5**	**−17.8**
HEALTH CARE	**1,513**	**1,413**	**1,284**	**7.1**	**10.0**	**17.8**
Health insurance	783	697	574	12.4	21.4	36.5
Medical services	456	414	460	10.1	−9.9	−0.8
Drugs	216	226	184	−4.5	23.1	17.6
Medical supplies	58	76	68	−23.4	10.7	−15.2
ENTERTAINMENT	**1,709**	**2,011**	**1,815**	**−15.0**	**10.8**	**−5.8**
Fees and admissions	408	435	512	−6.2	−15.0	−20.2
Audio and visual equipment and services	815	886	748	−8.0	18.4	8.9
Pets, toys, hobbies, and playground equipment	331	312	323	6.3	−3.5	2.5
Other entertainment products and services	154	379	230	−59.3	64.3	−33.2

	average spending			percent change		
	2010	**2006**	**2000**	**2006–10**	**2000–06**	**2000–10**
PERSONAL CARE PRODUCTS AND SERVICES	$525	$498	$721	5.5%	−30.9%	−27.1%
READING	42	68	96	−38.4	−29.2	−56.4
EDUCATION	372	816	500	−54.4	63.0	−25.6
TOBACCO PRODUCTS AND SMOKING SUPPLIES	303	280	379	8.2	−26.0	−20.0
MISCELLANEOUS	610	697	993	−12.4	−29.8	−38.6
CASH CONTRIBUTIONS	894	793	515	12.8	53.8	73.5
PERSONAL INSURANCE AND PENSIONS	2,908	3,066	2,322	−5.2	32.0	25.2
Life and other personal insurance	130	162	190	−19.9	−14.6	−31.6
Pensions and Social Security*	2,778	2,905	–	−4.4	–	–
PERSONAL TAXES	−562	238	756	−336.2	−68.5	−174.3
Federal income taxes	−763	−128	447	497.8	−128.6	−270.7
State and local income taxes	141	231	257	−39.1	−10.0	−45.1
Other taxes	60	134	52	−55.3	158.3	15.6
GIFTS FOR PEOPLE IN OTHER HOUSEHOLDS	449	524	865	−14.2	−39.5	−48.1

Because of changes in methodology, the 2006 and 2010 data on pensions and Social Security are not comparable with earlier years.

Note: The Bureau of Labor Statistics uses consumer unit rather than household as the sampling unit in the Consumer Expenditure Survey. For the definition of consumer unit, see the glossary. Spending on gifts is also included in the preceding product and service categories.

Source: Bureau of Labor Statistics, 2000, 2006, and 2010 Consumer Expenditure Surveys, Internet site http://www.bls.gov/cex/; calculations by New Strategist

Married Couples with Children Spend More than Average

Single parents spend much less than average on most products and services.

Because married couples with children under age 18 have higher than average incomes and larger than average households, their spending is also above average. Overall, couples with preschoolers spend 28 percent more than the average household, and couples with school-aged children spend 45 percent more than average. Single-parent families, in contrast, spend 23 percent less than average. Married couples with preschoolers account for 5.5 percent of total household spending, while those with school-aged children account for a much larger 17 percent. Single parents control 4.5 percent of household spending—almost as much as married couples with preschoolers.

Couples with preschoolers spend much more than average on items needed by young children. They spend nearly nine times the average on household personal services (mostly day care) and nearly seven times the average on clothes for infants.

Couples with school-aged children at home spend much more than average on most products and services. Rent, drugs, and tobacco are the only exceptions.

Single parents spend less than average in all but a few categories. They are above average spenders on such items as rent, household personal services (mostly day care), and children's clothes.

■ Many married couples with children under age 18 bought homes during the housing bubble. This explains why their mortgage interest payments are 87 to 95 percent above average.

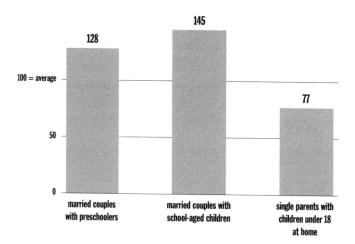

Married couples with school-aged children spend the most

(indexed average annual spending of households with children by type of household, 2010)

Table 19.5 Indexed Spending of Households with Children, 2010

(indexed spending of total consumer units and consumer units with children under age 18 at home, by type of consumer unit, 2010)

	total consumer units	married couples, oldest child under age 6	married couples, oldest child aged 6 to 17	single parents with children under age 18
Number of consumer units (in 000s)	121,107	5,185	14,242	7,141
Indexed average annual spending	100	128	145	77
FOOD	100	115	153	85
Food at home	100	119	151	91
Cereals and bakery products	100	112	162	90
Cereals and cereal products	100	126	168	90
Bakery products	100	106	158	90
Meats, poultry, fish, and eggs	100	102	146	92
Beef	100	86	141	86
Pork	100	85	144	86
Other meats	100	135	150	94
Poultry	100	118	157	114
Fish and seafood	100	99	140	86
Eggs	100	104	150	93
Dairy products	100	128	159	84
Fresh milk and cream	100	142	164	84
Other dairy products	100	119	155	83
Fruits and vegetables	100	124	146	83
Fresh fruits	100	133	154	84
Fresh vegetables	100	120	140	66
Processed fruits	100	129	144	101
Processed vegetables	100	107	145	94
Other food at home	100	127	151	96
Sugar and other sweets	100	95	164	86
Fats and oils	100	95	142	88
Miscellaneous foods	100	152	155	102
Nonalcoholic beverages	100	102	139	97
Food prepared by consumer unit on trips	100	100	160	51
Food away from home	100	110	156	77
ALCOHOLIC BEVERAGES	100	107	102	41
HOUSING	100	146	139	86
Shelter	100	144	139	84
Owned dwellings	100	160	163	58
Mortgage interest and charges	100	195	187	69
Property taxes	100	122	150	53
Maintenance, repair, insurance, other expenses	100	117	108	34
Rented dwellings	100	120	86	152
Other lodging	100	106	144	32
Utilities, fuels, and public services	100	104	131	91
Natural gas	100	117	130	87
Electricity	100	98	129	96
Fuel oil and other fuels	100	85	111	43

	total consumer units	married couples, oldest child under age 6	married couples, oldest child aged 6 to 17	single parents with children under age 18
Telephone	100	108	133	97
Water and other public services	100	106	136	82
Household services	**100**	**371**	**163**	**118**
Personal services	100	871	214	205
Other household services	100	116	137	73
Housekeeping supplies	**100**	**107**	**144**	**72**
Laundry and cleaning supplies	100	106	162	105
Other household products	100	118	141	65
Postage and stationery	100	83	134	55
Household furnishings and equipment	**100**	**126**	**149**	**68**
Household textiles	100	105	150	109
Furniture	100	149	152	78
Floor coverings	100	150	183	17
Major appliances	100	144	131	67
Small appliances and miscellaneous housewares	100	130	115	54
Miscellaneous household equipment	100	109	157	60
APPAREL AND RELATED SERVICES	**100**	**128**	**157**	**118**
Men and boys	**100**	**93**	**176**	**107**
Men, aged 16 or older	100	83	136	71
Boys, aged 2 to 15	100	136	331	250
Women and girls	**100**	**102**	**167**	**139**
Women, aged 16 or older	100	90	132	126
Girls, aged 2 to 15	100	172	363	210
Children under age 2	**100**	**674**	**126**	**122**
Footwear	**100**	**76**	**166**	**128**
Other apparel products and services	**100**	**111**	**105**	**71**
TRANSPORTATION	**100**	**122**	**146**	**84**
Vehicle purchases	**100**	**145**	**164**	**88**
Cars and trucks, new	100	145	176	77
Cars and trucks, used	100	150	156	98
Gasoline and motor oil	**100**	**115**	**144**	**80**
Other vehicle expenses	**100**	**107**	**127**	**88**
Vehicle finance charges	100	164	146	92
Maintenance and repairs	100	114	138	75
Vehicle insurance	100	74	114	103
Vehicle rentals, leases, licenses, other charges	100	140	129	70
Public transportation	**100**	**103**	**148**	**56**
HEALTH CARE	**100**	**99**	**115**	**48**
Health insurance	100	97	109	43
Medical services	100	130	141	63
Drugs	100	62	92	45
Medical supplies	100	91	138	49
ENTERTAINMENT	**100**	**115**	**167**	**68**
Fees and admissions	100	93	251	70
Audio and visual equipment and services	100	111	130	85
Pets, toys, hobbies, and playground equipment	100	132	135	55
Other entertainment products and services	100	130	181	42

	total consumer units	married couples, oldest child under age 6	married couples, oldest child aged 6 to 17	single parents with children under age 18
PERSONAL CARE PRODUCTS AND SERVICES	100	109	141	90
READING	100	78	117	42
EDUCATION	100	61	189	35
TOBACCO PRODUCTS AND SMOKING SUPPLIES	100	68	85	84
MISCELLANEOUS	100	133	110	72
CASH CONTRIBUTIONS	100	74	113	55
PERSONAL INSURANCE AND PENSIONS	100	159	166	54
Life and other personal insurance	100	147	164	41
Pensions and Social Security	100	160	166	55
PERSONAL TAXES	100	129	150	-32
Federal income taxes	100	126	142	-67
State and local income taxes	100	143	185	29
Other taxes	100	106	100	40
GIFTS FOR PEOPLE IN OTHER HOUSEHOLDS	100	60	119	44

Note: The index compares the spending of consumer units with children with the spending of the average consumer unit by dividing the spending of consumer units with children by average spending in each category and multiplying by 100. An index of 100 means the spending of consumer units with children equals average spending. An index of 130 means the spending of consumer units with children is 30 percent above average, while an index of 70 means the spending of consumer units with children is 30 percent below average. The Bureau of Labor Statistics uses consumer unit rather than household as the sampling unit in the Consumer Expenditure Survey. For the definition of consumer unit, see the glossary.
Source: Bureau of Labor Statistics, 2010 Consumer Expenditure Survey, Internet site http://www.bls.gov/cex/; calculations by New Strategist

Table 19.6 Market Share of Spending Controlled by Households with Children, 2010

(percent of total household spending accounted for by consumer units with children under age 18 at home, 2010)

	total consumer units	consumer units with children under age 18	married couples, oldest child under age 6	married couples, oldest child aged 6 to 17	single parents with children under age 18
Number of consumer units (in 000s)	121,107	26,568	5,185	14,242	7,141
Share of consumer units	100.0%	21.9%	4.3%	11.8%	5.9%
Share of total annual spending	100.0	27.0	5.5	17.0	4.5
FOOD	100.0	28.0	4.9	18.0	5.0
Food at home	100.0	28.2	5.1	17.8	5.3
Cereals and bakery products	100.0	29.1	4.8	19.0	5.3
Cereals and cereal products	100.0	30.5	5.4	19.8	5.3
Bakery products	100.0	28.4	4.5	18.6	5.3
Meats, poultry, fish, and eggs	100.0	27.0	4.4	17.2	5.5
Beef	100.0	25.3	3.7	16.5	5.1
Pork	100.0	25.6	3.6	16.9	5.1
Other meats	100.0	28.9	5.8	17.6	5.5
Poultry	100.0	30.3	5.1	18.5	6.7
Fish and seafood	100.0	25.8	4.2	16.5	5.1
Eggs	100.0	27.6	4.5	17.6	5.5
Dairy products	100.0	29.1	5.5	18.7	4.9
Fresh milk and cream	100.0	30.3	6.1	19.3	5.0
Other dairy products	100.0	28.2	5.1	18.3	4.9
Fruits and vegetables	100.0	27.4	5.3	17.2	4.9
Fresh fruits	100.0	28.7	5.7	18.1	5.0
Fresh vegetables	100.0	25.4	5.1	16.4	3.9
Processed fruits	100.0	28.4	5.5	17.0	5.9
Processed vegetables	100.0	27.2	4.6	17.1	5.6
Other food at home	100.0	28.8	5.4	17.7	5.7
Sugar and other sweets	100.0	28.5	4.1	19.3	5.0
Fats and oils	100.0	26.0	4.1	16.7	5.2
Miscellaneous foods	100.0	30.7	6.5	18.2	6.0
Nonalcoholic beverages	100.0	26.4	4.4	16.3	5.7
Food prepared by consumer unit on trips	100.0	26.2	4.3	18.9	3.0
Food away from home	100.0	27.6	4.7	18.4	4.6
ALCOHOLIC BEVERAGES	100.0	19.0	4.6	12.0	2.4
HOUSING	100.0	27.7	6.3	16.4	5.1
Shelter	100.0	27.5	6.2	16.3	5.0
Owned dwellings	100.0	29.4	6.8	19.1	3.4
Mortgage interest and charges	100.0	34.4	8.3	22.0	4.1
Property taxes	100.0	26.0	5.2	17.7	3.1
Maintenance, repair, insurance, other expenses	100.0	19.7	5.0	12.7	2.0
Rented dwellings	100.0	24.2	5.1	10.1	9.0
Other lodging	100.0	23.3	4.5	16.9	1.9
Utilities, fuels, and public services	100.0	25.2	4.4	15.4	5.4
Natural gas	100.0	25.4	5.0	15.3	5.1
Electricity	100.0	25.0	4.2	15.1	5.7
Fuel oil and other fuels	100.0	19.2	3.6	13.0	2.5

	total consumer units	consumer units with children under age 18	married couples, oldest child under age 6	married couples, oldest child aged 6 to 17	single parents with children under age 18
Telephone	100.0%	26.0%	4.6%	15.6%	5.7%
Water and other public services	100.0	25.4	4.5	16.0	4.8
Household services	**100.0**	**42.0**	**15.9**	**19.2**	**6.9**
Personal services	100.0	74.6	37.3	25.2	12.1
Other household services	100.0	25.4	5.0	16.1	4.3
Housekeeping supplies	**100.0**	**25.8**	**4.6**	**17.0**	**4.3**
Laundry and cleaning supplies	100.0	29.8	4.5	19.1	6.2
Other household products	100.0	25.4	5.0	16.5	3.8
Postage and stationery	100.0	22.6	3.5	15.8	3.3
Household furnishings and equipment	**100.0**	**26.9**	**5.4**	**17.5**	**4.0**
Household textiles	100.0	28.5	4.5	17.6	6.4
Furniture	100.0	28.8	6.4	17.8	4.6
Floor coverings	100.0	29.0	6.4	21.6	1.0
Major appliances	100.0	25.6	6.2	15.4	4.0
Small appliances and miscellaneous housewares	100.0	22.3	5.6	13.5	3.2
Miscellaneous household equipment	100.0	26.7	4.7	18.4	3.6
APPAREL AND RELATED SERVICES	**100.0**	**30.9**	**5.5**	**18.5**	**7.0**
Men and boys	**100.0**	**31.0**	**4.0**	**20.7**	**6.3**
Men, aged 16 or older	100.0	23.7	3.5	16.0	4.2
Boys, aged 2 to 15	100.0	59.5	5.8	38.9	14.7
Women and girls	**100.0**	**32.2**	**4.4**	**19.7**	**8.2**
Women, aged 16 or older	100.0	26.8	3.8	15.5	7.4
Girls, aged 2 to 15	100.0	62.5	7.4	42.7	12.4
Children under age 2	**100.0**	**50.9**	**28.8**	**14.9**	**7.2**
Footwear	**100.0**	**30.3**	**3.3**	**19.5**	**7.6**
Other apparel products and services	**100.0**	**21.3**	**4.8**	**12.3**	**4.2**
TRANSPORTATION	**100.0**	**27.3**	**5.2**	**17.1**	**4.9**
Vehicle purchases	**100.0**	**30.7**	**6.2**	**19.3**	**5.2**
Cars and trucks, new	100.0	31.4	6.2	20.7	4.5
Cars and trucks, used	100.0	30.5	6.4	18.3	5.8
Gasoline and motor oil	**100.0**	**26.7**	**4.9**	**17.0**	**4.7**
Other vehicle expenses	**100.0**	**24.7**	**4.6**	**15.0**	**5.2**
Vehicle finance charges	100.0	29.6	7.0	17.1	5.4
Maintenance and repairs	100.0	25.5	4.9	16.2	4.5
Vehicle insurance	100.0	22.7	3.2	13.5	6.1
Vehicle rentals, leases, licenses, other charges	100.0	25.3	6.0	15.1	4.1
Public transportation	**100.0**	**25.1**	**4.4**	**17.4**	**3.3**
HEALTH CARE	**100.0**	**20.6**	**4.2**	**13.5**	**2.8**
Health insurance	100.0	19.5	4.2	12.8	2.5
Medical services	100.0	25.9	5.6	16.6	3.7
Drugs	100.0	16.1	2.7	10.8	2.6
Medical supplies	100.0	23.0	3.9	16.2	2.9
ENTERTAINMENT	**100.0**	**28.5**	**4.9**	**19.6**	**4.0**
Fees and admissions	100.0	37.6	4.0	29.5	4.1
Audio and visual equipment and services	100.0	25.1	4.7	15.3	5.0
Pets, toys, hobbies, and playground equipment	100.0	24.7	5.6	15.9	3.2
Other entertainment products and services	100.0	29.4	5.6	21.3	2.5

	total consumer units	consumer units with children under age 18	married couples, oldest child under age 6	married couples, oldest child aged 6 to 17	single parents with children under age 18
PERSONAL CARE PRODUCTS AND SERVICES	**100.0%**	**26.5%**	**4.7%**	**16.5%**	**5.3%**
READING	**100.0**	**19.6**	**3.3**	**13.8**	**2.5**
EDUCATION	**100.0**	**26.9**	**2.6**	**22.2**	**2.0**
TOBACCO PRODUCTS AND SMOKING SUPPLIES	**100.0**	**17.8**	**2.9**	**10.0**	**4.9**
MISCELLANEOUS	**100.0**	**22.8**	**5.7**	**12.9**	**4.2**
CASH CONTRIBUTIONS	**100.0**	**19.7**	**3.2**	**13.3**	**3.2**
PERSONAL INSURANCE AND PENSIONS	**100.0**	**29.5**	**6.8**	**19.5**	**3.2**
Life and other personal insurance	100.0	28.0	6.3	19.3	2.4
Pensions and Social Security*	100.0	29.7	6.9	19.6	3.2
PERSONAL TAXES	**100.0**	**21.3**	**5.5**	**17.7**	**-1.9**
Federal income taxes	100.0	18.2	5.4	16.7	-4.0
State and local income taxes	100.0	29.6	6.1	21.7	1.7
Other taxes	100.0	18.6	4.5	11.8	2.3
GIFTS FOR PEOPLE IN OTHER HOUSEHOLDS	**100.0**	**19.1**	**2.6**	**13.9**	**2.6**

Note: Market shares are calculated by first multiplying average spending by the total number of households. Using those aggregate figures, the total spending of each segment is divided by the total for all households to determine each segment's share of the total. The Bureau of Labor Statistics uses consumer unit rather than household as the sampling unit in the Consumer Expenditure Survey. For the definition of consumer unit, see the glossary.
Source: Bureau of Labor Statistics, 2010 Consumer Expenditure Survey, Internet site http://www.bls.gov/cex/; calculations by New Strategist

Time Use

■ Most, but not all, of today's young children have working mothers. There are substantial differences in time use depending on a mother's employment status.

■ Employed mothers spend less time caring for children than mothers who are not employed. Fathers spend the same amount of time caring for children, whether or not their wife works.

■ Among dual-income couples with children under age 18, mothers have less leisure time than fathers—2.93 hours per day for mothers and 3.73 hours per day for fathers.

■ Among dual-income couples with children under age 18, wives do 49 percent more childcare than husbands. For their single-earner counterparts, wives do three times more childcare than husbands.

Among Mothers, Time Use Varies Sharply by Employment Status

For fathers, time use varies by their wife's employment status.

Most, but not all, of today's young children have working mothers. Among those mothers, there are substantial differences in time use depending on their employment status. Mothers who are employed full-time spend less time sleeping, doing housework, and shopping than mothers who do not work. Employed mothers also spend less time caring for children than mothers who are not employed, in part because they are more likely to have older children who require less care.

Among dual-income couples with children under age 18, wives do three times more housework than husbands. But among couples with children in which only the husband works, wives do eight times more housework than their husband. Among dual-income couples with children under age 18, wives do 49 percent more childcare than husbands. For their single-earner counterparts, wives do three times more childcare than husbands.

■ Among dual-income couples with children, mothers have less leisure time than fathers.

Working mothers have less leisure time

(average number of hours per day of leisure time for married couples with children under age 18 in which both spouses work full-tme, by sex, 2005–09)

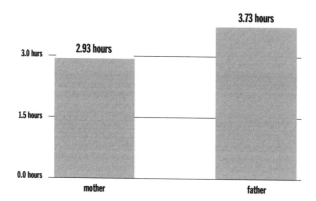

Table 20.1 Time Use of Married Mothers with Children under Age 18 by Employment Status, 2005–09

(average hours per day married mothers with own children under age 18 spend in primary activities, percent participating in primary activities, and index of not-employed mothers to mothers employed full-time, by employment status, 2005–09)

	average hours			percent participating		
	employed full-time	not employed	index, not employed to employed full-time	employed full-time	not employed	index, not employed to employed full-time
MARRIED MOTHERS WITH CHILDREN UNDER AGE 18						
Total, all activities	**24.00**	**24.00**	**100**	**100.0%**	**100.0%**	**100**
Personal care activities	9.04	9.42	104	100.0	100.0	100
Sleeping	8.23	8.79	107	99.9	100.0	100
Household activities	1.98	3.53	178	88.2	95.8	109
Housework	0.85	1.63	192	52.6	74.9	142
Food preparation and cleanup	0.78	1.42	182	73.9	88.1	119
Lawn and garden care	0.08	0.13	163	5.5	9.3	169
Purchasing goods and services	0.56	0.76	136	51.5	56.0	109
Grocery shopping	0.13	0.19	146	17.5	22.2	127
Consumer goods purchases, except grocery shopping	0.34	0.44	129	38.2	40.8	107
Caring for, helping household members	1.24	2.51	202	73.2	86.6	118
Caring for, helping household children	1.22	2.49	204	72.1	86.4	120
Physical care	0.54	1.03	191	53.2	72.8	137
Education-related activities	0.10	0.23	230	11.7	19.9	170
Reading to/with children	0.05	0.09	180	10.3	15.9	154
Playing/doing hobbies with children	0.20	0.56	280	15.1	29.7	197
Working and work-related activities	5.24	0.08	2	69.4	3.3	5
Working	5.21	0.03	1	69.0	1.0	1
Leisure and sports	2.93	4.21	144	92.6	96.4	104
Socializing and communicating	0.61	0.90	148	39.3	46.9	119
Watching television	1.54	2.27	147	73.4	80.9	110
Participating in sports, exercise, and recreation	0.16	0.23	144	13.7	17.3	126
Travel	1.35	1.17	87	94.5	84.4	89
Travel related to caring for and helping household children	0.22	0.31	141	41.0	43.3	106
Other activities	1.66	2.32	140	98.1	98.9	101

Note: Primary activities are those respondents identified as their main activity. Other activities done simultaneously are not included. The index is calculated by dividing time use or participation rate of mothers who are not employed by time use or participation rate of mothers who are employed and multiplying by 100.
Source: Bureau of Labor Statistics, Married Parents' Use of Time, 2005–09 American Time Use Survey, Internet site http://www.bls.gov/tus/; calculations by New Strategist

Table 20.2 Time Use of Married Mothers with Children Aged 6 to 17 by Employment Status, 2005–09

(average hours per day married mothers with youngest own child aged 6 to 17 spend in primary activities, percent participating in primary activities, and index of not-employed mothers to mothers employed full-time, by employment status, 2005–09)

	average hours			percent participating		
	employed full-time	not employed	index, not employed to employed full-time	employed full-time	not employed	index, not employed to employed full-time
MARRIED MOTHERS WITH YOUNGEST CHILD AGED 6 TO 17						
Total, all activities	**24.00**	**24.00**	**100**	**100.0%**	**100.0%**	**100**
Personal care activities	9.04	9.36	104	100.0	100.0	100
Sleeping	8.19	8.63	105	99.9	100.0	100
Household activities	2.08	3.85	185	88.4	95.4	108
Housework	0.89	1.79	201	54.4	75.1	138
Food preparation and cleanup	0.78	1.45	186	73.0	87.7	120
Lawn and garden care	0.09	0.15	167	6.6	11.7	177
Purchasing goods and services	0.56	0.82	146	51.9	60.7	117
Grocery shopping	0.12	0.23	192	17.3	28.2	163
Consumer goods purchases, except grocery shopping	0.35	0.46	131	39.2	42.2	108
Caring for, helping household members	0.71	1.48	208	61.1	76.1	125
Caring for, helping household children	0.70	1.45	207	59.6	75.6	127
Physical care	0.19	0.35	184	33.0	50.7	154
Education-related activities	0.11	0.33	300	13.0	25.9	199
Reading to/with children	0.02	0.04	200	4.3	7.3	170
Playing/doing hobbies with children	0.04	0.10	250	4.1	7.4	180
Working and work-related activities	5.37	0.11	2	70.7	4.6	7
Working	5.34	0.04	1	70.2	1.7	2
Leisure and sports	3.14	4.61	147	94.5	96.9	103
Socializing and communicating	0.61	0.89	146	40.7	47.5	117
Watching television	1.65	2.43	147	75.2	82.4	110
Participating in sports, exercise, and recreation	0.17	0.26	153	14.4	19.4	135
Travel	1.35	1.29	96	94.7	87.5	92
Travel related to caring for and helping household children	0.19	0.34	179	36.4	46.0	126
Other activities	1.74	2.48	143	98.0	98.9	101

Note: Primary activities are those respondents identified as their main activity. Other activities done simultaneously are not included. The index is calculated by dividing time use or participation rate of mothers who are not employed by time use or participation rate of mothers who are employed and multiplying by 100.
Source: Bureau of Labor Statistics, Married Parents' Use of Time, 2005–09 American Time Use Survey, Internet site http://www.bls.gov/tus/; calculations by New Strategist

Table 20.3 Time Use of Married Mothers with Children under Age 6 by Employment Status, 2005–09

(average hours per day married mothers with own children under age 6 spend in primary activities, percent participating in primary activities, and index of not-employed mothers to mothers employed full-time, by employment status, 2005–09)

	average hours			percent participating		
	employed full-time	not employed	index, not employed to employed full-time	employed full-time	not employed	index, not employed to employed full-time
MARRIED MOTHERS WITH YOUNGEST CHILD UNDER AGE 6						
Total, all activities	**24.00**	**24.00**	**100**	**100.0%**	**100.0%**	**100**
Personal care activities	9.03	9.45	105	100.0	100.0	100
Sleeping	8.30	8.90	107	100.0	100.0	100
Household activities	1.84	3.32	180	88.1	96.0	109
Housework	0.79	1.53	194	50.0	74.8	150
Food preparation and cleanup	0.77	1.39	181	75.2	88.3	117
Lawn and garden care	0.06	0.12	200	3.9	7.8	200
Purchasing goods and services	0.57	0.72	126	51.1	52.9	104
Grocery shopping	0.14	0.17	121	17.9	18.3	102
Consumer goods purchases, except grocery shopping	0.33	0.44	133	36.8	39.9	108
Caring for, helping household members	2.00	3.18	159	90.3	93.3	103
Caring for, helping household children	1.98	3.16	160	90.1	93.3	104
Physical care	1.03	1.47	143	82.0	87.0	106
Education-related activities	0.08	0.17	213	10.0	16.0	160
Reading to/with children	0.08	0.12	150	18.8	21.5	114
Playing/doing hobbies with children	0.43	0.86	200	30.9	44.1	143
Working and work-related activities	5.04	0.05	1	67.5	2.5	4
Working	5.02	0.02	0	67.3	0.6	1
Leisure and sports	2.64	3.95	150	89.9	96.2	107
Socializing and communicating	0.61	0.90	148	37.4	46.5	124
Watching television	1.38	2.17	157	70.9	80.0	113
Participating in sports, exercise, and recreation	0.15	0.21	140	12.8	16.0	125
Travel	1.34	1.10	82	94.3	82.4	87
Travel related to caring for and helping household children	0.27	0.28	104	47.5	41.6	88
Other activities	1.55	2.22	143	98.2	98.9	101

Note: Primary activities are those respondents identified as their main activity. Other activities done simultaneously are not included. The index is calculated by dividing time use or participation rate of mothers who are not employed by time use or participation rate of mothers who are employed and multiplying by 100.
Source: Bureau of Labor Statistics, Married Parents' Use of Time, 2005–09 American Time Use Survey, Internet site http://www.bls.gov/tus/; calculations by New Strategist

Table 20.4 Time Use of Dual-Earner and Single-Earner Married Couples with Children under Age 18, 2005–09

(average hours per day married couples with children under age 18 spend in primary activities by employment status, and index of mother's time to father's, 2005–09)

	both spouses work full-time		index of mother's time to father's	mother not employed, father employed full-time		index of mother's time to father's
	mother	father		mother	father	
Total, all activities	**24.00**	**24.00**	**100**	**24.00**	**24.00**	**100**
Personal care activities	9.01	8.62	105	9.39	8.76	107
Sleeping	8.20	8.04	102	8.77	8.15	108
Household activities	2.00	1.35	148	3.58	1.06	338
Housework	0.87	0.27	322	1.67	0.20	835
Food preparation and cleanup	0.78	0.35	223	1.42	0.27	526
Lawn and garden care	0.08	0.23	35	0.13	0.20	65
Purchasing goods and services	0.58	0.37	157	0.75	0.37	203
Grocery shopping	0.13	0.06	217	0.20	0.08	250
Consumer goods purchases, except grocery shopping	0.35	0.24	146	0.44	0.24	183
Caring for, helping household members	1.26	0.86	147	2.62	0.85	308
Caring for, helping household children	1.24	0.83	149	2.60	0.82	317
Physical care	0.54	0.28	193	1.06	0.26	408
Education-related activities	0.10	0.08	125	0.24	0.05	480
Reading to/with children	0.05	0.02	250	0.09	0.03	300
Playing/doing hobbies with children	0.20	0.24	83	0.60	0.33	182
Working and work-related activities	5.20	5.99	87	0.07	6.25	1
Working	5.18	5.95	87	0.01	6.20	0
Leisure and sports	2.93	3.73	79	4.14	3.61	115
Socializing and communicating	0.61	0.54	113	0.90	0.63	143
Watching television	1.52	2.16	70	2.21	1.99	111
Participating in sports, exercise, and recreation	0.17	0.33	52	0.23	0.28	82
Travel	1.36	1.42	96	1.18	1.42	83
Travel related to caring for and helping household children	0.23	0.15	153	0.31	0.07	443
Other activities	1.67	1.66	101	2.28	1.68	136

Note: Primary activities are those respondents identified as their main activity. Other activities done simultaneously are not included. The index is calculated by dividing mother's time by father's time and multiplying by 100.
Source: Bureau of Labor Statistics, Married Parents' Use of Time, 2005–09 American Time Use Survey, Internet site http://www .bls.gov/tus/; calculations by New Strategist

Glossary

adjusted for inflation Income or a change in income that has been adjusted for the rise in the cost of living, or the consumer price index (CPI-U-RS).

age Classification by age is based on the age of the person at his/her last birthday.

American Community Survey The ACS is an ongoing nationwide survey of 250,000 households per month, providing detailed demographic data at the community level. Designed to replace the census long-form questionnaire, the ACS includes more than 60 questions that formerly appeared on the long form, such as language spoken at home, income, and education. ACS data are available for areas as small as census tracts.

American Housing Survey The AHS collects national and metropolitan-level data on the nation's housing, including apartments, single-family homes, and mobile homes. The nationally representative survey, with a sample of 55,000 homes, is conducted by the Census Bureau for the Department of Housing and Urban Development every other year.

American Indians Include Alaska Natives (Eskimos and Aleuts) unless those groups are shown separately.

American Time Use Survey Under contract with the Bureau of Labor Statistics, the Census Bureau collects ATUS information, revealing how people spend their time. The ATUS sample is drawn from U.S. households that have completed their final month of interviews for the Current Population Survey. One individual from each selected household is chosen to participate in the ATUS. Respondents are interviewed by telephone only once about their time use on the previous day.

Asian Includes Native Hawaiians and other Pacific Islanders unless those groups are shown separately.

Baby Boom Americans born between 1946 and 1964.

Baby Bust Americans born between 1965 and 1976, also known as Generation X.

Behavioral Risk Factor Surveillance System The BRFSS is a collaborative project of the Centers for Disease Control and Prevention and U.S. states and territories. It is an ongoing data collection program designed to measure behavioral risk factors in the adult population aged 18 or older. All 50 states, three territories, and the District of Columbia take part in the survey, making the BRFSS the primary source of information on the health-related behaviors of Americans.

black The black racial category includes those who identified themselves as "black" or "African American."

Consumer Expenditure Survey The CEX is an ongoing study of the day-to-day spending of American households administered by the Bureau of Labor Statistics. The CEX includes an interview survey and a diary survey. The average spending figures shown in this book are the integrated data from both the diary and interview components of the survey. Two separate, nationally representative samples are used for the interview and diary surveys. For the interview survey, about 7,500 consumer units are interviewed on a rotating panel basis each quarter for five consecutive quarters. For the diary survey, 7,500 consumer units keep weekly diaries of spending for two consecutive weeks.

consumer unit *(on spending tables only)* For convenience, the term consumer unit and households are used interchangeably in the spending section of this book, although consumer units are somewhat different from the Census Bureau's households. Consumer units are all related members of a household, or financially independent members of a household. A household may include more than one consumer unit.

Current Population Survey The CPS is a nationally representative survey of the civilian noninstitutional population aged 15 or older. It is taken monthly by the Census Bureau for the Bureau of Labor Statistics, collecting information from more than 50,000 households on employment and unemployment. In March of each year, the survey includes the Annual Social and Economic Supplement, which is the source of most national data on the characteristics of Americans, such as educational attainment, living arrangements, and incomes.

disability As defined by the National Health Interview Survey, respondents aged 18 or older are asked whether they have difficulty in physical functioning, probing whether respondents can perform nine activities by themselves without using special equipment. The categories are walking a quarter mile; standing for two hours; sitting for two hours; walking up 10 steps without resting; stooping, bending, kneeling; reaching over one's head; grasping or handling small objects; carrying a 10-pound object; and pushing/pulling a large object. Adults who report that any of these activities is very difficult or they cannot do it at all are defined as having physical difficulties.

dual-earner couple A married couple in which both the householder and the householder's spouse are in the labor force.

earnings A type of income, earnings is the amount of money a person receives from his or her job. *See also* Income.

employed All civilians who did any work as a paid employee or farmer/self-employed worker, or who worked 15 hours or more as an unpaid farm worker or in a family-owned business, during the reference period. All those who have jobs but who are temporarily absent from their jobs due to illness, bad weather, vacation, labor management dispute, or personal reasons are considered employed.

expenditure The transaction cost including excise and sales taxes of goods and services acquired during the survey period. The full cost of each purchase is recorded even though full payment may not have been made at the date of purchase. Average expenditure figures may be artificially low for infrequently purchased items such as cars because figures are calculated using all consumer units within a demographic segment rather than just purchasers. Expenditure estimates include money spent on gifts for others.

family A group of two or more people (one of whom is the householder) related by birth, marriage, or adoption and living in the same household.

family household A household maintained by a householder who lives with one or more people related to him or her by blood, marriage, or adoption.

female/male householder A woman or man who maintains a household without a spouse present. May head family or nonfamily households.

foreign-born population People who are not U.S. citizens at birth.

full-time employment Thirty-five or more hours of work per week during a majority of the weeks worked.

full-time, year-round Fifty or more weeks of full-time employment during the previous calendar year.

Generation X Americans born between 1965 and 1976, also known as the baby-bust generation.

Hispanic Because Hispanic is an ethnic origin rather than a race, Hispanics may be of any race. While most Hispanics are white, there are black, Asian, and American Indian Hispanics.

household All the persons who occupy a housing unit. A household includes the related family members and all the unrelated persons, if any, such as lodgers, foster children, wards, or employees who share the housing unit. A person living alone is counted as a household. A group of unrelated people who share a housing unit as roommates or unmarried partners is also counted as a household. Households do not include group quarters such as college dormitories, prisons, or nursing homes.

household, race/ethnicity of Households are categorized according to the race or ethnicity of the householder only.

householder The person (or one of the persons) in whose name the housing unit is owned or rented or, if there is no such person, any adult member. With married couples, the householder may be either the husband or wife. The householder is the reference person for the household.

householder, age of Used to categorize households into age groups such as those used in this book. Married couples, for example, are classified according to the age of either the husband or wife, depending on which one identified him or herself as the householder.

housing unit A house, an apartment, a group of rooms, or a single room occupied or intended for occupancy as separate living quarters. Separate living quarters are those in which the occupants do not live and eat with any other persons in the structure and that have direct access from the outside of the building or through a common hall that is used or intended for use by the occupants of another unit or by the general public. The occupants may be a single family, one person living alone, two or more families living together, or any other group of related or unrelated persons who share living arrangements.

Housing Vacancy Survey The HVS is a supplement to the Current Population Survey, providing quarterly and annual data on rental and homeowner vacancy rates, characteristics of units available for occupancy, and homeownership rates by age, household type, region, state, and metropolitan area. The Current Population Survey sample includes 72,000 housing units—61,200 occupied and 10,800 vacant.

housing value The respondent's estimate of how much his or her house and lot would sell for if it were for sale.

iGeneration Americans born from 1995 to the present. Also known as the Plurals.

immigration The relatively permanent movement (change of residence) of people into the country of reference.

in-migration The relatively permanent movement (change of residence) of people into a subnational geographic entity, such as a region, division, state, metropolitan area, or county.

income Money received in the preceding calendar year by each person aged 15 or older from each of the following sources: (1) earnings from longest job (or self-employment), (2) earnings from jobs other than longest job, (3) unemployment compensation, (4) workers' compensation, (5) Social Security, (6) Supplemental Security income, (7) public assistance, (8) veterans' payments, (9) survivor benefits, (10) disability benefits, (11) retirement pensions, (12) interest, (13) dividends, (14) rents and royalties or estates and trusts, (15) educational assistance, (16) alimony, (17) child support, (18) financial assistance from outside the household, and other periodic income. Income is reported in several ways in this book. Household income is the combined income of all household members. Income of persons is all income accruing to a person from all sources. Earnings are the money a person receives from his or her job.

industry The industry in which a person worked longest in the preceding calendar year.

job tenure The length of time a person has been employed continuously by the same employer.

labor force The labor force tables in this book show the civilian labor force only. The labor force includes both the employed and the unemployed (people who are looking for work). People are counted as in the labor force if they were working or looking for work during the reference week in which the Census Bureau fields the Current Population Survey.

labor force participation rate The percent of the civilian noninstitutional population that is in the civilian labor force, which includes both the employed and the unemployed.

married couples with or without children under age 18 Refers to married couples with or without own children under age 18 living in the same household. Couples without children under age 18 may be parents of grown children who live elsewhere, or they could be childless couples.

median The amount that divides the population or households into two equal portions: one below and one above the median. Medians can be calculated for income, age, and many other characteristics.

median income The amount that divides the income distribution into two equal groups, half having incomes above the median, half having incomes below the median. The medians for households or families are based on all households or families. The median for persons are based on all persons aged 15 or older with income.

Medical Expenditure Panel Survey MEPS is a nationally representative survey that collects detailed information on the health status, access to care, health care use and expenses and health insurance coverage of the civilian noninstitutionalized population of the U.S. and nursing home residents. MEPS comprises four component surveys: the Household Component, the Medical Provider Component, the Insurance Component, and the Nursing Home Component. The Household Component is the core survey, is conducted each year, and includes 15,000 households and 37,000 people.

metropolitan statistical To be defined as a metropolitan statistical area (or MSA), an area must include a city with 50,000 or more inhabitants, or a Census Bureau-defined urbanized area of at least 50,000 inhabitants and a total metropolitan population of at least 100,000 (75,000 in New England). The county (or counties) that contains the largest city becomes the "central county" (counties), along with any adjacent counties that have at least 50 percent of their population in the urbanized area surrounding the largest city. Additional "outlying counties" are included in the MSA if they meet specified requirements of commuting to the central counties and other selected requirements of metropolitan character (such as population density and percent urban). In New England, MSAs are defined in terms of cities and towns rather than counties. For this reason, the concept of NECMA is used to define metropolitan areas in the New England division.

Millennial generation Americans born between 1977 and 1994.

mobility status People are classified according to their mobility status on the basis of a comparison between their place of residence at the time of the March Current Population Survey and their place of residence in March of the previous year. Nonmovers are people living in the same house at the end of the period as at the beginning of the period. Movers are people living in a different house at the end of the period than at the beginning of the period. Movers from abroad are either citizens or aliens whose place of residence is outside the United States at the beginning of the period, that is, in an outlying area under the jurisdiction of the United States or in a foreign country. The mobility status for children is fully allocated from the mother if she is in the household; otherwise it is allocated from the householder.

National Ambulatory Medical Care Survey The NAMCS is an annual survey of visits to nonfederally employed office-based physicians who are primarily engaged in direct patient care. Data are collected from physicians rather than patients, with each physician assigned a one-week reporting period. During that week, a systematic random sample of visit characteristics are recorded by the physician or office staff.

National Compensation Survey The Bureau of Labor Statistics' NCS examines the incidence and detailed provisions of selected employee benefits in private sector establishments and state and local governments. Each year BLS economists visit a representative sample of establishments across the country, asking questions about the establishment, its employees, and their benefits.

National Health and Nutrition Examination Survey The NHANES is a continuous survey of a representative sample of the U.S. civilian noninstitutionalized population. Respondents are interviewed at home about their health and nutrition, and the interview is followed up by a physical examination that measures such things as height and weight in mobile examination centers.

National Health Interview Survey The NHIS is a continuing nationwide sample survey of the civilian noninstitutional population of the U.S. conducted by the Census Bureau for the National Center for Health Statistics. Each year, data are collected from more than 100,000 people about their illnesses, injuries, impairments, chronic and acute conditions, activity limitations, and the use of health services.

National Hospital Ambulatory Medical Care Survey The NHAMCS, sponsored by the National Center for Health Statistics, is an annual national probability sample survey of visits to emergency departments and outpatient departments at non-Federal, short stay and general hospitals. Data are collected by hospital staff from patient records.

National Household Education Survey The NHES, sponsored by the National Center for Education Statistics, provides descriptive data on the educational activities of the U.S. population, including after-school care and adult education. The NHES is a system of telephone surveys of a representative sample of 45,000 to 60,000 households in the U.S.

National Survey of Family Growth The 2002 NSFG, sponsored by the National Center for Health Statistics, is a nationally representative survey of the civilian noninstitutional population aged 15 to 44. In-person interviews were completed with 12,571 men and women, collecting data on marriage, divorce, contraception, and infertility. The 2002 survey updates previous NSFG surveys taken in 1973, 1976, 1988, and 1995.

National Survey on Drug Use and Health Formerly called the National Household Survey on Drug Abuse, this survey, sponsored by the Substance Abuse and Mental Health Services Administration, has been conducted since 1971. It is the primary source of information on the use of illegal drugs by the U.S. population. Each year, a nationally representative sample of about 70,000 individuals aged 12 or older are surveyed in the 50 states and the District of Columbia.

Native Hawaiian and other Pacific Islander Beginning with the 2000 census, this group was identified as a racial category separate from Asians. In most survey data, however, the population is included with Asians.

net migration Net migration is the result of subtracting out-migration from in-migration for an area. Another way to derive net migration is to subtract natural increase (births minus deaths) from total population change in an area.

net worth The amount of money left over after a household's debts are subtracted from its assets.

nonfamily household A household maintained by a householder who lives alone or who lives with people to whom he or she is not related.

nonfamily householder A householder who lives alone or with nonrelatives.

non-Hispanic People who do not identify themselves as Hispanic are classified as non-Hispanic. Non-Hispanics may be of any race.

non-Hispanic white People who identify their race as white and who do not indicate a Hispanic origin.

nonmetropolitan area Counties that are not classified as metropolitan areas.

occupation Occupational classification is based on the kind of work a person did at his or her job during the previous calendar year. If a person changed jobs during the year, the data refer to the occupation of the job held the longest during that year.

occupied housing units A housing unit is classified as occupied if a person or group of people is living in it or if the occupants are only temporarily absent—on vacation, example. By definition, the count of occupied housing units is the same as the count of households.

outside principal cities The portion of a metropolitan county or counties that falls outside of the principal city or cities; generally regarded as the suburbs.

own children Sons and daughters, including stepchildren and adopted children, of the householder. The totals include never-married children living away from home in college dormitories.

owner occupied A housing unit is "owner occupied" if the owner lives in the unit, even if it is mortgaged or not fully paid for. A cooperative or condominium unit is "owner occupied" only if the owner lives in it. All other occupied units are classified as "renter occupied."

part-time employment Less than 35 hours of work per week in a majority of the weeks worked during the year.

percent change The change (either positive or negative) in a measure that is expressed as a proportion of the starting measure. When median income changes from $20,000 to $25,000, for example, this is a 25 percent increase.

percentage point change The change (either positive or negative) in a value which is already expressed as a percentage. When a labor force participation rate changes from 70 percent of 75 percent, for example, this is a 5 percentage point increase.

poverty level The official income threshold below which families and people are classified as living in poverty. The threshold rises each year with inflation and varies depending on family size and age of householder.

primary activity In the time use tables, primary activities are those respondents identify as their main activity. Other activities done simultaneously are not included.

proportion or share The value of a part expressed as a percentage of the whole. If there are 4 million people aged 25 and 3 million of them are white, then the white proportion is 75 percent.

race Race is self-reported and can be defined in three ways. The "race alone" population comprises people who identify themselves as only one race. The "race in combination" population comprises people who identify themselves as more than one race, such as white and black. The "race, alone or in combination" population includes both those who identify themselves as one race and those who identify themselves as more than one race.

regions The four major regions and nine census divisions of the United States are the state groupings as shown below:

Northeast:
—New England: Connecticut, Maine, Massachusetts, New Hampshire, Rhode Island, and Vermont
—Middle Atlantic: New Jersey, New York, and Pennsylvania

Midwest:
—East North Central: Illinois, Indiana, Michigan, Ohio, and Wisconsin
—West North Central: Iowa, Kansas, Minnesota, Missouri, Nebraska, North Dakota, and South Dakota

South:

—South Atlantic: Delaware, District of Columbia, Florida, Georgia, Maryland, North Carolina, South Carolina, Virginia, and West Virginia
—East South Central: Alabama, Kentucky, Mississippi, and Tennessee
—West South Central: Arkansas, Louisiana, Oklahoma, and Texas

West:

—Mountain: Arizona, Colorado, Idaho, Montana, Nevada, New Mexico, Utah, and Wyoming
—Pacific: Alaska, California, Hawaii, Oregon, and Washington

renter occupied *See* Owner occupied.

Retirement Confidence Survey The RCS, sponsored by the Employee Benefit Research Institute (EBRI), the American Savings Education Council (ASEC), and Mathew Greenwald & Associates (Greenwald), is an annual survey of a nationally representative sample of 1,000 people aged 25 or older. Respondents are asked a core set of questions that have been asked since 1996, measuring attitudes and behavior towards retirement. Additional questions are also asked about current retirement issues.

rounding Percentages are rounded to the nearest tenth of a percent; therefore, the percentages in a distribution do not always add exactly to 100.0 percent. The totals, however, are always shown as 100.0. Moreover, individual figures are rounded to the nearest thousand without being adjusted to group totals, which are independently rounded; percentages are based on the unrounded numbers.

self-employment A person is categorized as self-employed if he or she was self-employed in the job held longest during the reference period. Persons who report self-employment from a second job are excluded, but those who report wage-and-salary income from a second job are included. Unpaid workers in family businesses are excluded. Self-employment statistics include only nonagricultural workers and exclude people who work for themselves in incorporated business.

sex ratio The number of men per 100 women.

suburbs *See* Outside central city.

Survey of Consumer Finances A triennial survey taken by the Federal Reserve Board. It collects data on the assets, debts, and net worth of American households. For the 2007 survey, the Federal Reserve Board interviewed a representative sample of 6,500 households.

unemployed Those who, during the survey period, had no employment but were available and looking for work. Those who were laid off from their jobs and were waiting to be recalled are also classified as unemployed.

white The "white" racial category includes many Hispanics (who may be of any race) unless the term "non-Hispanic white" is used.

Youth Risk Behavior Surveillance System The YRBSS was created by the Centers for Disease Control to monitor health risks being taken by young people at the national, state, and local level. The national survey is taken every two years based on a nationally representative sample of 16,000 students in 9th through 12th grade in public and private schools.

Bibliography

Agency for Healthcare Research and Quality

Internet site http://www.ahrq.gov/

—Medical Expenditure Panel Survey, Internet site http://meps.ahrq.gov/mepsweb/ survey_comp/household.jsp

Bureau of the Census

Internet site http://www.census.gov

—2010 American Community Survey, American FactFinder, Internet site http://factfinder2 .census.gov/faces/nav/jsf/pages/index.xhtml

—2010 Census, American Factfinder, Internet site http://factfinder2.census.gov/faces/nav/ jsf/pages/index.xhtml

—2010 Census, Internet site http://2010.census.gov/2010census/data/

—A Child's Day: 2009, Internet site http://www.census.gov/hhes/socdemo/children/data/ sipp/well2009/tables.html

—American Housing Survey National Tables: 2009, Internet site http://www.census.gov/ housing/ahs/data/ahs2009.html

—Educational Attainment, CPS Historical Time Series Tables, Internet site http://www .census.gov/hhes/socdemo/education/data/cps/historical/index.html

—Educational Attainment, Internet site http://www.census.gov/hhes/socdemo/education/

—Families and Living Arrangements, Internet site http://www.census.gov/population/www/ socdemo/hh-fam.html

—Fertility of American Women: 2010, Detailed Tables, Internet site http://www.census .gov/hhes/fertility/data/cps/2010.html

—Geographical Mobility, Internet site http://www.census.gov/hhes/migration

—Health Insurance, Internet site http://www.census.gov/hhes/www/hlthins/

—Historical Health Insurance Tables, Current Population Survey Annual Social and Economic Supplements, Internet site http://www.census.gov/hhes/www/hlthins/data/ historical/HIB_tables.html

—Historical Income Tables, Internet site http://www.census.gov/hhes/www/income/data/ historical/index.html

—Housing Vacancies and Homeownership Survey, Internet site http://www.census.gov/ hhes/www/housing/hvs/hvs.html

—Income, Current Population Survey, Internet site http://www.census.gov/hhes/www/ income/data/index.html

—Number, Timing, and Duration of Marriages and Divorces: 2009, Current Population Reports P70-125, 2011, Internet site http://www.census.gov/hhes/socdemo/marriage/data/ sipp/index.html

—Population Estimates, Internet site http://www.census.gov/popest/data/index.html

—Poverty, Current Population Survey, Internet site http://www.census.gov/hhes/www/ poverty/index.html

—School Enrollment, Historical Tables, Current Population Survey Annual Social and Economic Supplements, Internet site http://www.census.gov/population/www/socdemo/ school/.html

—School Enrollment, Internet site http://www.census.gov/hhes/school/

Bureau of Labor Statistics

Internet site http://www.bls.gov

—Consumer Expenditure Surveys, various years, Internet site http://www.bls.gov/cex/home .htm

—2010 American Time Use Survey, Internet site http://www.bls.gov/tus/home.htm

—Characteristics of Minimum Wage Workers, 2011, Internet site http://www.bls.gov/cps/ minwage2011tbls.htm

—College Enrollment and Work Activity of 2010 High School Graduates, Internet site http://www.bls.gov/news.release/hsgec.nr0.htm

—Employee Tenure, Internet site http://www.bls.gov/news.release/tenure.toc.htm

—Employment Projections, Internet site http://www.bls.gov/emp/

—Employment and Unemployment among Youth Summary, Internet site http://bls.gov/ news.release/youth.nr0.htm

—Employment Characteristics of Families, Internet site http://www.bls.gov/news.release/ famee.toc.htm

—Labor Force Statistics from the Current Population Survey—Annual Averages, Internet site http://www.bls.gov/cps/tables.htm#empstat

—National Compensation Survey, Internet site http://www.bls.gov/ncs/ebs/home.htm

—Table 15. Employed persons by detailed occupation, sex, and age, Annual Average 2011 (Source: Current Population Survey), unpublished table received from the BLS by special request

Centers for Disease Control and Prevention

Internet site http://www.cdc.gov

—Behavioral Risk Factor Surveillance System, Prevalence Data, Internet site http://apps .nccd.cdc.gov/brfss/

—Cases of HIV/AIDS and AIDS in the United States and Dependent Areas, 2009, Internet site http://www.cdc.gov/hiv/surveillance/resources/reports/2009report/

—Youth Risk Behavior Surveillance–United States, 2009, Internet site http://www.cdc .gov/HealthyYouth/yrbs/index.htm

Employee Benefit Research Institute

Internet site http://www.ebri.org/

—Retirement Confidence Surveys, Internet site http://www.ebri.org/surveys/rcs/

Federal Interagency Forum on Child and Family Statistics

Internet site http://childstats.gov

—America's Children: Key National Indicators of Well-Being, 2011, Internet site http:// www.childstats.gov/

Federal Reserve Board

Internet site http://www.federalreserve.gov/econresdata/scf/scfindex.htm

—*Surveying the Aftermath of the Storm: Changes in Family Finances from 2007 to 2009*, Appendix tables, Internet site http://www.federalreserve.gov/econresdata/scf/scf_2009p.htm

Homeland Security
Internet site http://www.dhs.gov/index.shtm
　　—Yearbook of Immigration Statistics, Internet site http://www.dhs.gov/files/statistics/
publications/yearbook.shtm

National Center for Education Statistics
Internet site http://nces.ed.gov
　　—*The Condition of Education 2011*, Internet site http://nces.ed.gov/programs/coe/
　　—*Digest of Education Statistics: 2011*, Internet site http://nces.ed.gov/programs/digest
　　—National Household Education Survey, Internet site http://nces.ed.gov/nhes/

National Center for Health Statistics
Internet site http://www.cdc.gov/nchs
　　—*Anthropometric Reference Data for Children and Adults: United States, 2003–2006*,
National Health Statistics Reports, Number 10, 2008, Internet site http://www.cdc.gov/nchs/
products/pubs/pubd/nhsr/nhsr.htm
　　—Birth Data, Internet site http://www.cdc.gov/nchs/births.htm
　　—*Complementary and Alternative Medicine Use Among Adults and Children: United States,
2007*, National Health Statistics Report, No. 12, 2008, Internet site http://www.cdc.gov/nchs/
products/nhsr.htm
　　—*Health Characteristics of Adults 55 Years of Age and Over: United States, 2004–2007*,
National Health Statistics Reports, No. 16, 2009, Internet site http://www.cdc.gov/nchs/nhis
.htm
　　—Mortality Data, Internet site http://www.cdc.gov/nchs/deaths.htm
　　—*National Ambulatory Medical Care Survey: 2009 Summary Tables,* Internet site http://
www.cdc.gov/nchs/ahcd/web_tables.htm#2009
　　—*National Hospital Ambulatory Medical Care Survey: 2008 Emergency Department
Summary,* Internet site http://www.cdc.gov/nchs/ahcd/web_tables.htm#2009
　　—*National Hospital Ambulatory Medical Care Survey: 2008 Outpatient Department
Summary,* Internet site http://www.cdc.gov/nchs/ahcd/web_tables.htm#2009
　　—*Health, United States,* various editions, Internet site http://www.cdc.gov/nchs/hus.htm
　　—*Sexual Behavior, Sexual Attraction, and Sexual Identity in the United States: Data
from the 2006–2008 National Survey of Family Growth,* National Health Statistics Reports,
No. 36, 2011, Internet site http://www.cdc.gov/nchs/nsfg/new_nsfg.htm
　　—*Summary Health Statistics for U.S. Adults: National Health Interview Survey, 2010*,
Series 10, No. 252, 2012, Internet site http://www.cdc.gov/nchs/nhis.htm
　　—*Summary Health Statistics for U.S. Children: National Health Interview Survey, 2010*,
Series 10, No. 250, 2011, Internet site http://www.cdc.gov/nchs/nhis.htm
　　—*Summary Health Statistics for the U.S. Population: National Health Interview Survey,
2010*, Series 10, No. 251, 2011, Internet site http://www.cdc.gov/nchs/nhis.htm

National Sporting Goods Association
Internet site http://www.nsga.org
　　—Sports Participation, Internet site http://www.nsga.org

Substance Abuse and Mental Health Services Administration
Internet site http://www.samhsa.gov
   National Survey on Drug Use and Health, 2010, Internet site http://www.samhsa.gov/data/
   NSDUH/2k10ResultsTables/Web/HTML/TOC.htm

University of California, Berkeley, Survey Documentation and Analysis, Computer-assisted Survey Methods Program
Internet site http://sda.berkeley.edu/
   —General Social Surveys 1972-2010 Cumulative Data Files, Internet site http://sda.berkeley
   .edu/cgi-bin/hsda?harcsda+gss10

University of Michigan, Monitoring the Future Study
Internet site http://monitoringthefuture.org
   —Monitoring the Future Study, Data Tables and Figures, Internet site http://
   monitoringthefuture.org/data/data.html

Index

children in extracurricular activities, 374, 453
children in gifted classes, 373
children with disciplinary problems, 373
college enrollment rate, 53
educational attainment, 39–41
employment status, 47, 49, 173, 175
frequency of meals with children, 455
health conditions, 401–403
health insurance status, 397–398
high school dropouts, 45
homeownership, 123
household income, 137
household type, 205, 207, 215
in poverty, 164–165, 426–428
living arrangements of children, 449
marital status, 230
men's income, 151
neighborhood characteristics of children, 457
parental involvement in homework, 377
parental involvement in school activities, 376
parental satisfaction with child's school, 379
population, 241–243, 264–289, 464–465
SAT scores, 51
school enrollment, 368–371
weight, 383
women's income, 157
bonds, 344
bowling, 385
breakfast with children, 455
bronchitis, health condition, 102
business equity, 348

Caesarian section, 87
cancer
    as cause of death, 112–113, 409–410
    health condition, 81–83, 102
Catholic, 21, 369
cash contributions, spending on, 293–316, 481–502
cerebrovascular disease, as cause of death, 112–113,
        409–410
certificates of deposit, 342
child care, 434–435
childbearing. *See* Births.
childbirth, as cause of death, 112
childlessness, 79
children
    average number in household, 211
    ideal number, 16
    number born per woman, 79
    spanking, attitude toward, 16
    standard of living, 14
    time spent caring for, 319–336, 505–508
    time use by age of, 505–508
cigarette smoking, 89, 390. *See also* Tobacco products.
citizenship status, children without health insurance
        by, 398
class membership, 10
climate, as reason for moving, 128–130, 417
clubs, children participating in, 374, 453
college. *See also* Degrees earned, School, and
        School enrollment.

as a reason for moving, 128–130
attendance status of students, 59
employment status of students, 47
enrollment, 58–59
enrollment rate, 53–54
families with children in, 56
type of institution, 58–59
computer, time spent on, 319–336
congenital malformations, as cause of death, 112,
        408–410
conservative political leanings, 27
contraception, 388
coronary, health condition, 102
cost of living. *See* Standard of living.
credit card debt, 352

day care, 434–435
death
    causes of, 112–113, 408–410
    penalty, attitudes toward, 30
debt, household, 350–352
degrees earned, 61–65
Democratic party affiliation, 28
diabetes
    as cause of death, 112–113
    health condition, 102
dieting, 384
dinner with children, 455
disability, learning, 401–403
disciplinary problems in school, 373
divorced, 228–232, 234
doctor visits. *See* Physician visits.
doctoral degree. *See* Degrees earned.
drinking, 91, 392
drugs
    illicit, use of, 93–94, 394–395
    prescription, 401–403
    spending on, 293–316, 481–502
dual-income couples, 178, 432, 442, 508

earnings. *See also* Income.
    by educational attainment, 161–162
    minimum wage, 195
eating with children, 455
education. *See also* College and School.
    debt, 352
    spending on, 293–316, 481–502
    time spent, 319–336, 505–508
educational attainment. *See also* Degrees earned.
    alternative medicine use by parent's, 406
    by generation, 35
    by level of degree, 61–65
    by race and Hispanic origin, 39–41
    by sex, 36–37, 40–41
    children in school by mother's, 363
    earnings by, 161–162
    frequency of meals with children by parent's, 455
    health conditions of children by parent's, 401–403
    neighborhood characteristics of children by
            parent's, 457
    of children's parents, 442